"This text is the perfect complement to a wide-range of courses on media and society. Valdivia has done a grand job in bringing together the influential scholars in media studies offering both a survey of the field and a richness of the voices."

Norma Pecora, Ohio University

"Valdivia has compiled an extraordinarily useful, coherent, and well-articulated book. She provides one of the best overviews of 'media studies' that I have read; presents an especially useful introductory essay that coheres the whole; and has brought together a stellar set of authors writing in terrains that exemplify both current interests and fundamental issues."

Brenda Dervin, Ohio State University

BLACKWELL COMPANIONS IN CULTURAL STUDIES

Advisory editor: David Theo Goldberg, University of California, Irvine

This series aims to provide theoretically ambitious but accessible volumes devoted to the major fields and subfields within cultural studies, whether as single disciplines (film studies) inspired and reconfigured by interventionist cultural studies approaches, or from broad interdisciplinary and multidisciplinary perspectives (gender studies, race and ethnic studies, postcolonial studies). Each volume sets out to ground and orientate the student through a broad range of specially commissioned articles and also to provide the more experienced scholar and teacher with a convenient and comprehensive overview of the latest trends and critical directions. An overarching *Companion to Cultural Studies* will map the territory as a whole.

A Companion to
Media Studies

Edited by
Angharad N. Valdivia

Blackwell
Publishing

BLACKWELL PUBLISHING

350 Main Street, Malden, MA 02148-5020, USA
9600 Garsington Road, Oxford OX4 2DQ, UK
550 Swanston Street, Carlton, Victoria 3053, Australia

First published 2003 by Blackwell Publishing Ltd
First published in paperback 2006 by Blackwell Publishing Ltd

1   2006

Library of Congress Cataloging-in-Publication Data

Valdivia, Angharad N.
  A companion to media studies / Angharad N. Valdivia.
    p. cm. – (Blackwell companions in cultural studies ; 6)
  Includes bibliographical references and index.
  ISBN 0-631-22601-X (hard : alk. paper)
  1. Mass media. I. Title. II. Series.

P91.25.V35 2003
302.23–dc21   2002152791

ISBN-13: 978-0-631-22601-7 (hard : alk. paper)
ISBN-13: 978-1-4051-4174-1 (paper : alk. paper)
ISBN-10: 1-4051-4174-3 (paper : alk. paper)

A catalogue record for this title is available from the British Library.

Set in 11/13pt Ehrhardt
by Graphicraft Ltd, Hong Kong
Printed and bound in the United Kingdom
by TJ International Ltd, Padstow, Cornwall

The publisher's policy is to use permanent paper from mills that operate a sustainable forestry policy,
and which has been manufactured from pulp processed using acid-free and elementary chlorine-free
practices. Furthermore, the publisher ensures that the text paper and cover board used have met
acceptable environmental accreditation standards.

For further information on
Blackwell Publishing, visit our website:
www.blackwellpublishing.com

Contents

Part VI   Futures

Notes on Contributors

Boatema Boateng is Assistant Professor in the Department of Communication, University of California at San Diego. Her research interests include the power dynamics of global cultural flows and the politics of feminist knowledge production.

Sharon L. Bracci is Assistant Professor of Communication Studies at the University of North Carolina, Greensboro. She is the co-editor of *Moral Engagement in Public Life: Theorists for Contemporary Ethics* (with Clifford G. Christians, 2002). She has published in *Philosophy and Rhetoric*, *Journal of Applied Communication Research*, *Argumentation and Advocacy*, and *Qualitative Inquiry* (2002). Her research interests focus on interdisciplinary intersections among communication ethics, public argument, and practical reasoning in contemporary social and healthcare contexts.

Jennings Bryant is Professor of Communication, holder of the Reagan Endowed Chair of Broadcasting, and Director of the Institute for Communication Research at the University of Alabama. He is president of the International Communication Association. Bryant's primary research interests are in entertainment theory, media effects, and uses and effects of new media.

Michael C. Casas is a graduate student in the Department of Communication Studies at the University of Michigan. He is primarily interested in examining the portrayals of people of color in the media and the effects of these portrayals on viewers.

Gail Dines is Professor of Sociology and Women's Studies at Wheelock College in Boston. She is co-editor of the best-selling media text book *Gender, Race and Class in Media* (Sage, 1995, 2003), and co-author of *Pornography: The Production and Consumption of Inequality* (Routledge, 1998). She lectures across the country on pornography and violence against women.

Travis L. Dixon is Assistant Professor of Communication Studies and a Faculty Associate at the Institute for Social Research at the University of Michigan. He is primarily interested in the portrayal of African Americans in the mass media and the effects of these images on audiences.

John D. H. Downing is John T. Jones, Jr. Centennial Professor of Communication in the Radio–Television–Film Department of the University of Texas, Austin. He lived mostly in Britain until 1980 and since then mostly in New York City and Austin. He teaches courses on media theories; political cinema in Africa, Latin America, and the Middle East; racism and communication; alternative media; and Russian media since 1917. His current projects include a co-authored comparative study of racism, ethnicity and media; serving as chief editor of the *Sage International Handbook of Media Studies*; and as editor of the Sage *Encyclopedia of Alternative Media*.

James S. Ettema is Professor and Chair of Communication Studies at Northwestern University. His teaching and research focuses on the social organization and cultural impact of media – especially the news media. His books include *Custodians of Conscience: Investigative Journalism and Public Virtue* (with Theodore Glasser) and *Audiencemaking: How the Media Create the Audience* (with D. Charles Whitney). Professor Ettema earned his Ph.D. from the University of Michigan and formerly taught in the School of Journalism and Mass Communication, University of Minnesota.

Margaret Gallagher is a freelance media researcher and consultant. Her work includes assignments for the United Nations and its agencies, the Council of Europe, the European Commission, the European Audiovisual Observatory and the WACC. Her many publications in the field of gender and media include *An Unfinished Story: Gender Patterns in Media Employment* (Paris: UNESCO, 1995), *From Mexico to Beijing – and Beyond: Covering Women in the World's News* (New York: UNIFEM, 2000), and *Gender Setting: New Agendas for Media Monitoring and Advocacy* (London: Zed Books, 2001).

Joke Hermes teaches television studies at the University of Amsterdam. Her publications include *Reading Women's Magazines* (Polity Press, 1995) and *The Media in Question* (Sage, 1998 edn.). She is editor of the *European Journal of Cultural Studies*.

Robert Huesca is Associate Professor in the Department of Communication at Trinity University in Texas. His areas of study are in mass media and society, democratic media practice, new communication technologies, and international communication. He has published essays in *Communication Theory*, *Journalism & Mass Communication Educator*, *The Journal of International Communication*, *Studies in Latin American Popular Culture*, *Media, Culture and Society*, *Journal of Communication*, and numerous edited books.

Melissa A. Johnson is Associate Professor in the Department of Communication at North Carolina State University. She studies Latino/a ethnic media, general market media issues related to Latinos/as and Latin America, and the role of visual images in media. Her doctorate in mass communication research is from the University of North Carolina at Chapel Hill.

Sonia Livingstone is Professor of Social Psychology and a member of the interdisciplinary teaching and research program, Media@LSE, at the London School of Economics and Political Science. She is author of *Making Sense of Television* (Routledge, 1998) and *Young People and New Media* (Sage, 2002), co-author of *Mass Consumption and Personal Identity* (Open University, 1992) and *Talk on Television* (Routledge, 1994), and co-editor of *Children and Their Changing Media Environment* (Erlbaum, 2001) and *The Handbook of New Media* (Sage, 2002).

Armand Mattelart is Professor of Sciences of Information and Communication at l'Université de Paris VIII. His areas of study include communication theory, media studies, and international communication. He is author of more than 20 books, including *Networking the World, 1794–2000*, *Theories of Communication: A Short Introduction* with Michèle Mattelart, *The Invention of Communication*, and *Mapping World Communication: War, Progress, Culture*.

Sharon R. Mazzarella is Associate Professor and Chair of the Department of Television–Radio at Ithaca College. She is co-editor of *Growing Up Girls: Popular Culture and the Construction of Identity* (Peter Lang, 1999) and of the new journal *Popular Communication* (Lawrence Erlbaum). Her research focuses primarily on media coverage and portrayals of youth.

Matthew P. McAllister is Associate Professor and Director of Graduate Studies in the Department of Communication Studies at Virginia Tech. His research interests include advertising criticism, popular culture, and the political economy of the mass media. He is the author of *The Commercialization of American Culture: New Advertising, Control and Democracy* (Sage, 1996), and the co-editor of *Comics and Ideology* (Peter Lang, 2001). He has also published in *Critical Studies in Mass Communication*, *Journal of Communication*, *Journal of Popular Culture*, *Journal of Popular Film and Television*, and *The Communication Review*.

Cameron McCarthy is University Scholar and Research Professor in the Institute of Communications Research at the University of Illinois at Urbana-Champaign. His books include *Race and Curriculum*, *The Uses of Culture* and *Reading & Teaching the Postcolonial* (with Greg Dimitriadis) as well as several edited collections. He teaches courses in mass communications theory, post-colonialism, and cultural studies.

Denis McQuail is Professor Emeritus attached to the School of Communication Research, University of Amsterdam and Visiting Professor, Department of Sociology, University of Southampton, England. Recent publications include *Mass Communication Theory* (4th edn., 2000) and *Reader in Mass Communication Theory* (2002).

Dorina Miron is a senior research fellow with the Institute for Communication Research at the University of Alabama. She is interested in entertainment and hedonic theory. Her current research focuses on television and video game effects.

Sujata Moorti is Associate Professor at Old Dominion University and is the author of *Color of Rape: Gender, Race, and Television's Public Spheres* (Albany: SUNY Press, 2002) and other articles. Her research and teaching interrogate the representations of gender and race within a global context.

John Nerone is Research Professor of Communications at the University of Illinois at Urbana-Champaign. He has written extensively on the history of the media in the United States, including *Violence against the Press: Policing the Public Sphere in US History* and, most recently, *The Form of News: A History*, co-authored with Kevin G. Barnhurst.

Virginia Nightingale is Associate Professor in the School of Communication, Design and Media at the University of Western Sydney, Australia, where she has taught since 1984. She is co-ordinator of the Affect, Image, Media research group within the MARCS Research Centre at UWS. Her research interests have focused on the theories and practice of audience research. In recent years she has been chief investigator for two studies on children and the media: Children's Views on Media Harm, and Television Advertising and Children's Culture. She is the author of *Studying Audiences: the Shock of the Real* (Routledge, 1996), but has also investigated cross-cultural audience experiences (Australia and Japan), and is currently exploring negative affect in the "horror experience."

Barbara J. O'Keefe is Professor of Communication Studies and Dean of the School of Speech at Northwestern University. Her research areas are inter-personal and organizational communication, with a focus on the role of training and technology in improving the capability of communicators and communities. Her research has been supported by the National Science Foundation, the US Department of Defense, and the National Center for Supercomputing Applications, the Markle Foundation, among others.

Mary Beth Oliver is Associate Professor at Penn State University. Her research pertains to the social and psychological effects of media on viewers, with a focus on issues related to race and gender. Her work has appeared in *Journal of Broadcasting & Electronic Media*, *Journal of Communication*, *Sex Roles*, and *Communication Research*, among others.

Radhika E. Parameswaran is Assistant Professor at the School of Journalism, Indiana University, Bloomington. Her research interests include feminist cultural studies, ethnographic media research, globalization, and postcolonial studies. Her publications have appeared in *Journal of Communication*, *Journalism & Communication Monographs*, *Qualitative Inquiry*, *Journal of Communication Inquiry*, and *Frontiers: A Journal of Women's Studies*.

Elizabeth R. Perea is a doctoral student at the University of Illinois at Urbana-Champaign, Institute of Communications Research. Her research is in cultural studies, popular culture analysis, popular music studies, globalization, and postmodern theory. She is also an instructor in the Media Studies department.

Carrie A. Rentschler teaches in the Department of Communication at the University of Pittsburgh. Her dissertation examines the media activism of the US crime victim movement and the role it plays in news and entertainment crime coverage. Her intellectual interests include the study of media and politics, social movements, and feminism. She has published on the security industry, women's self-defense education, environmental security and sexual violence, and local changes in the media landscape after the September 11 terrorist attacks in the US. She is also a women's and girls' self-defense instructor.

Vickie Rutledge Shields is the Director of the Women's Studies Program and Associate Professor of Telecommunications at Bowling Green State University. Her research has focused on critical/cultural approaches to the study of media and popular culture; gendered images in media; the relationship between media images and women's body discipline; and investigating alternative methodologies for cultural and feminist audience research. She is the author of *Measuring Up: How Advertising Affects Self Image*, from University of Pennsylvania Press. Dr Shields is a Fellow at the Institute for the Study of Culture and Society at Bowling Green State University where she continues her research on the cultural effects of advertising images as experienced by pre- and adolescent girls.

Ronda M. Scantlin has completed postdoctoral research fellowship at the Annenberg Public Policy Center at the University of Pennsylvania and has joined the faculty at the Department of Communication at the University of Dayton. She is a member of the research team examining the impact of V-Chip technology on dynamics within the family and on children's television viewing. Dr Scantlin received her Bachelor of Arts in Psychology from Bethany College, Master of Arts in Human Development from the University of Kansas, and her Ph.D. in Child Development and Family Relationships from the University of Texas at Austin. Her current research interests include exploring the positive and negative implications for interactive technologies to meet the cognitive, social, and health-related needs of children and adolescents.

Dan Schiller is Professor of Library & Information Science, Communications and Media Studies at the University of Illinois at Urbana-Champaign. A communications historian, he has written or edited five books, including *Digital Capitalism: Networking the Global Market System* (MIT Press, 1999) and, with Vincent Mosco, *Continental Order? Integrating North America for Cyber-Capitalism* (Rowman & Littlefield, 2001). Schiller also is a continuing contributor to *Le Monde diplomatique*.

Robert Sloane is a Ph.D. candidate in the Institute of Communications Research at the University of Illinois at Urbana–Champaign. He is writing a dissertation on cultural production and reproduction in an independent record store.

Angharad N. Valdivia is Research Associate Professor at the Institute of Communications Research at the University of Illinois. She is the author of *A Latina in the Land of Hollywood* (Arizona) and editor of *Feminism, Multiculturalism, and the Media* (Sage) and co-editor (with matt garcia and Marie Leger) of the forthcoming *Geographies of Latinidad* (Duke). Her research focuses on transnational multiculturalist feminist issues with a special emphasis on Latinas in popular culture.

Ellen A. Wartella is Dean of the College of Communication, Walter Cronkite Regents Chair in Communication and Mrs Mary Gibbs Jones Centennial Chair in Communication at the University of Texas at Austin. She is co-author or editor of nine books and dozens of book chapters and articles on children and media. She is co-Principal Investigator on a five-year National Science Foundation funded, multi-site research project entitled Children's Research Initiative: Children's Digital Media Centers.

D. Charles Whitney is Professor and graduate adviser in the School of Journalism at the University of Texas at Austin, where he is also Professor of Radio–Television–Film. He was co-editor, with Professor Ettema, of *Audience Making* (Sage, 1994) and *Individuals in Mass Media Organizations* (Sage, 1982) and is co-author or editor of the *Mass Communication Review Yearbook*, 3 vols. (1982) and 4 (1983), and *Individuals in Mass Media Organizations: Creativity and Constraint* (1982). He is the author of more than 75 book chapters, journal articles, reports and papers, and three other books in media studies.

Acknowledgments

This book could not have been put together without the support of numerous individuals and institutions. In addition to the exemplary set of contributors who agreed to submit original manuscripts to this volume, there are others to be thanked. To begin with, the Institute of Communications Research at the University of Illinois remains an extremely generous supporter of all my endeavors. Under the leadership of both Clifford Christians and Paula Treichler, ICR provided the resources necessary to carry out this project. Outstanding assistance from Marie Claire Leger, Robert Sloane, Diem-my Bui, Susan Harewood, and Liz Perea was indispensable. A fellowship from the Illinois Program for Research in the Humanities (IPRH) provided the space and the forum to begin to write the salsa project. The Centre of Latin American Studies at the University of Cambridge, England provided a home during my sabbatical year when I commissioned and put together the bulk of this volume. I am intellectually indebted to Denis McQuail whose introductory volumes to communications theory remain, for me, the most accessible and comprehensive available in our interdiscipline. The breadth and depth of this volume speaks to the wonderful education and collaborations I have had from and with many colleagues in our field. Finally, Cameron McCarthy's continuing advice, help, and encouragement helped make this a better book. If I do not mention my three children, Rhiannon, Tobin, and Ailín, one or all of them would be eternally cross with me. All shortcomings, of course, are purely my own.

Introduction

Angharad N. Valdivia

A Companion to Media Studies intends to provide a broad overview to a generalist academic audience of the dynamic interdiscipline of Media Studies. Widely available as a university major and even included as part of the high school curriculum in some countries, Media Studies is a relatively new interdiscipline, roughly dating back to the 1920s as a set of studies and the fifties as a "formal discipline" (Grossberg, Wartella, and Whitney, 1998). However, early and repeated attempts to demarcate boundaries around this field of study have proven unsustainable. The contemporary situation is such that as an interdisciplinary field, Media Studies has no easy boundaries or parameters. It draws on some of the more established disciplines both in the humanities and the social sciences such as history, political science, sociology, psychology, anthropology, linguistics, and literature. Media Studies also has great overlaps with newer disciplines and interdisciplines such as cultural studies, popular culture studies, film studies, American studies, journalism, communications, speech communication, education, and ethnomusicology, to name a few. While it is a diverse, contested, and growing field of studies which has to be considered in process, there are nonetheless specific concentrations and particular scholars who have come to flesh out the contours of what must by definition be an amorphous and porous field. *A Companion to Media Studies* aims to provide this developing field with an overview of the theories and methodologies which have brought us to the present as well as with current deployments of these. Essays fall into six categories and are written by major scholars of national and international reputation as well as by some of the brightest young scholars in the field. *A Companion to Media Studies* strives for a representative, global, and multicultural approach throughout so that issues of difference will not be bracketed out in separate sections.

Media Studies is a term often used interchangeably with "mass communication" and with "communications." Usage of the term "communication science" has become less common as most scholars acknowledge that one of the central questions posed in the contemporary academy is whether science can continue to be the dominant theoretical discourse. Nonetheless it is important to note

Simpson's history of early communications research where he labels the period and the book *Science of Coercion* (1994) precisely because the "science" of communication was so often put to such crass political uses. However, as with any discipline and period of time, whereas the science approach may have dominated then and to a lesser extent now (certainly even the dwindling availability of US funding still favors scientific approaches), there were then alternative voices though smaller in number and heavily silenced.[1] Moreover, the study of communications was included in humanities based departments such as rhetoric and English, where both journalism and cinema studies, both crucial components of Media Studies, were pursued within humanistic approaches.

Whereas the use of the term media implies some form of mediated communications, usually through the use of mass media technologies, the term "communications" alone can also include the less technological and more personal and individual forms of communication. Although quite often these three terms are used interchangeably, it is more accurate to single out media studies and mass communication as having a major overlap. As well, Media Studies projects can include some measure of interpersonal communications such as the canonical *Personal Influence* (Katz and Lazarsfeld, 1955) which sought to establish a connection or relationship between mass media use and interpersonal communications. Denis McQuail's many editions of his *Mass Communication Theory* build on this fruitful tone set by Katz and develop a study of mass communication that is informed by the individual and psychological all the way to the social and institutional levels of analysis. For the purposes of *A Companion to Media Studies* Media Studies and mass communications will be used interchangeably.

Another major overlap in terms of this interdiscipline is the increasingly common connection between Media Studies and the study of culture. Culture is not synonymous with Cultural Studies though often this is the form that the overlap takes. Journals such as *Media, Culture & Society* include many cultural studies articles but use a more expansive application of the "culture & society" part of the title and thus embody this type of association. Indeed the inclusion of "society" signs in for social science and more traditional US approaches to Media Studies (e.g. Croteau and Hoynes, 1997). Also for example, the enormously successful *Media and Culture: An Introduction to Mass Communication* (Campbell, 2002) brings together mass communication and the study of culture as they overlap with Media Studies but not necessarily in a cultural studies formation. That this volume is already in its best-selling third edition indicates that at least at the US undergraduate teaching level, faculty find it useful to combine these three areas of study into an undifferentiated whole. On the other hand Giles and Middleton's *Studying Culture* (1999) tends to equate the study of culture with cultural studies. While it is a formidable and sophisticated text, *Studying Culture* may well be hampered in the US market because of its firm and inescapable grounding in contemporary British culture. In fact, whereas the influence of French, Italian, and British scholars reached US communications scholarship decades ago, the US mix still includes a healthy, indeed dominant paradigm, dose of social science in general and structural functionalism in particular. Thus it would be very difficult to propose a communication theory reader excluding at least nominal mention of the dominant paradigm in the US whereas the graduate level *The Communication Theory Reader* (Cobley, 1996) and *Media Studies: A Reader* (Marris and Thornham, 2000) present us with good illustrations of the overlap between "cultural studies, communications, and media studies" (Cobley, 1996, p. 1) which nonetheless focuses primarily on influential European structuralist and post-structuralist approaches. Other influential forces in the turn to culture within mass communications and Media Studies is the growing interdiscipline of American Studies wherein the previous hegemony of US literary approaches is being challenged by an ethnically and globally sophisticated consideration of culture at large, much of it greatly overlapping with Media Studies, such as much of the work by George Lipsitz (e.g. 2001).

Thus as we enter the twenty-first century Media Studies remains, and indeed grows in stature, as a central field of academic pursuit influenced by and potentially influencing many other fields (see Downing, this volume). The traditional mass media of newspaper, film, radio, and television have been joined by electronic and digital options which both promise to increase accessibility and democratic potential as well as threaten to intensify economic concentration and knowledge gaps between rich and poor, whether these populations are within the North or between the North and South. Internet deployment; digital cameras, scanners, and video recorders; palm pilots and cellular telephony and internet access; DVD movies; biometric body scanning; and all of the overlapping and synergistic possibilities between these media make the interdiscipline of Media Studies both daunting and exciting. Indeed Turow (1999) repeatedly uses the word "exciting" and titles the first introductory section of his book "An Exciting Time." Even if we consider that electricity remains an issue for a huge proportion of the world's population, the reach of traditional and new media is still nearly complete. Nearly everyone has access to radio technology, for example, and we find digital technology in unexpected places. So coupled with the global reach of these technologies as well as the global mobility of populations, whether it be for voluntary or involuntary reasons, Media Studies stands out as a field that contributes to our understanding of the contemporary context in which communications, the circulation of information, and the representation of identities and issues form and inform our lives.

Given its diverse, and sometimes competing, backgrounds, defining Media Studies remains a project fraught with difficulty (Craig, 1999). Rapid changes in technology as well as increasing paradigm diversity precipitate an extremely dynamic academic formation. Not surprisingly then, there have been many approaches to a description and analysis of this field. One of the formerly most common ways to approach Media Studies was to follow a historical approach, listing each emergent new technology in a linear fashion. Of course every old technology was once a new technology (Marvin, 1988). Given the explosive speed of development of new components to contemporary technology, which render everything that's bought already outdated, and the development of new hardware which not only abets but replaces the old, it is difficult to keep writing books adding yet another chapter on whatever the newest gadget is, but historical patterns of development, deployment, and institutionalization of media are nonetheless discernible. Early technological development, accompanied by utopian and dystopian visions, are usually followed by institutionalization and commercialization in order to distribute uniform interference free content and to derive profits, partly in order to fund the upkeep of technology and production of programming. Thus some attempts to map out the historical map of communications technologies begin as early as oral history whereas others date back to the printing press, or more usually, as is the case with Winston (1998), media technology is traced back to the late nineteenth century and the introduction of the telegraph. By now (2002) most of these historical approaches to media technology end up with an open ended chapter on the internet. Since mass media continues to be technologically intensive and dynamic, we can continue to expect such books to continue being written.

Other approaches to Media Studies explore the tension and possibility derived from the rise of new paradigms. Seldom, however, are new paradigms the exclusive concern as paradigms are themselves components of larger social forces (Craig, 1999). In this vein, on the one hand De Fleur (1999) wistfully asks "where have all the milestones gone?" in an essay that laments the dearth and potential death of large, longitudinal social science projects due both to paradigm shifts and to the decreased funding and increased work load situation under which most of us labor. Whereas De Fleur wishes for a return to the days when the social scientific paradigm reigned supreme, his argument is far more sophisticated than that. He explores the contemporary institutional and social issues why no scholar, not just social scientists, can produce milestones. As such his essay is both a way to police the boundaries around paradigms and the interdiscipline as well as a political intervention in terms of the declining public support for research and education.

Other approaches to Media Studies attempt, without prejudice, to map out the contemporary fault lines and debates of the field. As such succeeding editions of Media Studies "hit" books such as *Questioning the Media* change so substantially that the third edition, as the editors of that project assert, "Betrays little genetic relationship to its ancient great-grandparent" (Downing, Mohammadi, and Sreberny-Mohammadi, 2000, p. 1). Of course, we must notice that time moves rather quickly in the field of Media Studies, as the great-grandparent was published in 1991, barely nine years before the drastically different third edition grandchild! It is important to note, however, that what De Fleur sees as a weakness of our field can also be seen as its strength. Indeed as Downing, Mohammadi, and Sreberny-Mohammadi (2000, p. 2) conclude "Media Studies are therefore in need of constant, vigilant updating, lest the field be isolated not only from the realities of the turbulent changes in the 'real world' but also from the new ideas and perspectives bubbling up in cognate areas." In sum, paradigm revision and shifts are not only desirable but downright necessary.

As a young field, Media Studies has had its share of paradigm shifts. Concerns about children and the body politic in relation to communications and mass media have been with us since the Payne Studies of the 1920s and remain strong in the present scholarship on both children and the media and political communication. Still, despite the persistence of these thematic concerns, the nature and flow of communications has been debated by succeeding generations of scholars. Early unidirectional models of effect and influence, such as what is now known as stimulus-response analysis or the transmission model, have been replaced by increasingly sophisticated quantitative approaches with sociological and psychological roots. However, anthropology and linguistics have also become increasingly influential, especially, but not exclusively, in the rise of Cultural Studies. With this wave of studies we have a turn to include not just technology and content specific traditional pursuits of news, advertising, and television but also overlapping issues of culture and popular culture. James Carey's *Communication as Culture* (1988) signaled a humanistic intervention which foregrounded ritual as an alternative paradigm to transmission. Both *Studying Culture* (Giles and Middleton, 1999) and *Media Making* (Grossberg, Wartella, and Whitney, 1998) either begin from a cultural perspective or attempt to combine traditional Media Studies with cultural approaches. In fact the latter, *Media Making*, is a conscious attempt to bridge the two paradigms as the authors represent prominent figures in both camps: Larry Grossberg, a preeminent US cultural studies scholar and Ellen Wartella and D. Charles Whitney, two major scholars of children and the media and the sociology of news, respectively.

By the 1980s prominent debates in the field had expanded beyond the transmission-ritual binary and into the uneasy tension between Political Economy studies and the then emergent paradigm of Cultural Studies. Journal issues and books attempted to settle this apparent chasm over the unresolved split about the relative merits of social scientific versus more qualitative and interpretive methodological approaches, especially in the US where positivist paradigms remain hegemonic in terms of government and nongovernmental funding. Neither of these fault lines has been resolved. Indeed they remain part of the field and, some would argue, generate vitality and energy. In fact, the blurring of boundaries seems to be one of the ways that we as a field have dealt with these demarcations. Again, whereas some, as Turow above, see this blurring as exciting, enabling, and productive, others (for example, Rosengren, 2000) see it as a sign that we have yet to mature into a formal discipline and that the field remains fragmented. Even here there is diversity for neither the mourners nor the celebrants of the lack of coherence of the field belong to just one camp (Dervin & Chaffee, in press). These two sets of positions illustrate Giles and Middleton's (1999) definition for the different positions on subjectivity. So if we are to think of the field as a subject, we certainly experience subjectivity as both "fragmentization and atomization, and . . . as fluid, flexible and plural" (1999, p. 197).

However, efforts to bring together binary divisions in the field are not so prominent beyond US borders. For example, Latin American scholars not only do not foreground the division but seem to perceive it as inconceivable that one would separate the political–economic from the cultural (for example, Martín Barbero, 1993; Rodríguez, 2001). These two areas are not treated separately. As well, from European perspectives there are other salient approaches. Given the immense structuralist influence upon continental theory, as well as its reach, albeit belatedly, to US shores, there are entire books which approach theory through signification, the sign and post-structuralist approaches to both the sign and the audience (Cobley, 1996). Similarly the work of Armand Mattelart, from the eighties to the present, including his essay in this collection, combines a political–economic analysis with an ever present semiotics of the debate. Whether one looks at his work on Chile, Nicaragua, or the contemporary global situation, Mattelart remains a scholar who demonstrates that political economy and culture can and should be studied together.

Emerging as new sets of research questions in the field, different approaches to difference have generated a growing amount and proportion of Media Studies scholarship (see, for example, the *Howard Journal of Communication* and *Feminist Media Studies*). Perhaps eclipsing both of the already mentioned debates, as we enter the twenty-first century, it is also undeniable that ignoring global realities is untenable in an engaged interdiscipline such as Media Studies. Thus many of the new voices in the third edition of *Questioning the Media* foreground issues of difference. The result is a further deployment of boundary blending. We have gone past the age when we had a side bar or box, a small chapter, or a book focused on, for instance, women and the media. As useful as those pioneer efforts were, they paved the way for yet another level of integration in the field of Media Studies. Indeed this book begins with such an overview by Margaret Gallagher whose *Unequal Opportunities* (1981) paved the way for future scholars of issues of gender, Media Studies, and a global situation. Issues of difference are now approached in a way that combines vectors of gender, race, ethnicity, class, global location, ability, and religion – to name some of the most salient signifiers of difference – into complex and often open-ended analyses (see Valdivia, 1995). Thus we have the best-selling *Gender, Race and Class in Media* (Dines and Humez, 2003 [1995]) in which all essays are diversity intensive. Readers such as *Studying Culture* (Giles and Middleton, 1999) are so thoroughly integrated that by the end of the first chapter students have been introduced not just to a range of abstract definitions of culture but also to grounded discussion points which include post-colonialism, gender, and ethnicity. The new century presents students of Media Studies with an increasingly complex situation as well as with an increasingly sophisticated approach to the study of this situation.

While scholars and textbooks have divided the interdisciplinary field in many ways, *A Companion to Media Studies* goes beyond binary definitions of administrative/critical, scientific/humanistic, quantitative/qualitative, or political economy/cultural studies. The contemporary field is much more complex than that, and methodologies are not necessarily indicative of philosophical, theoretical, or political implications. For example, survey methodology can be used for "administrative" purposes, as in a study of advertising preferences partly funded by an advertising agency, as well as for critical scholarship, such as a study to determine who votes and what degrees of disenfranchisement tell us about the viability of our democratic process. Social scientific methodology applied to the study of the effects of televised violence can be useful in a philosophical, and thoroughly humanistic, discussion about the role and the roots of violence in contemporary culture, such as the essay by Bryant and Miron in this volume. A quantitative body of data about readership can be a springboard for participatory research on adult literacy. *A Companion to Media Studies* builds on the map set out by Denis McQuail in his fourth chapter of *Mass Communication Theory: An Introduction*, in all of its many editions. McQuail suggests four major sub-categories which increasingly overlap with each other as we experience media and as media attempts to reach us. These categories have to be studied separately though we experience them simultaneously. *A Companion to Media Studies* aims to bring both the model and Media Studies into the new century by infusing it with healthy doses of global sensitivity as well as the integral incorporation of issues of difference. At the four levels of production, content, effect, and audience, there is already a strong body of work which is either global and/or inflected by theories of difference. Students and scholars of media studies need to consider the cultural specificity of media messages and processes as well as the tendencies towards homogenization in a global media system that self-consciously fashions itself as crossing borders and erasing differences.

Bookended by "Foundations" and "Futures" (Parts I and VI) *A Companion to Media Studies* is divided into the four areas of studies – production, content, audience, and effects (Parts II–V). As suggested by the boundary crossing characteristic of Media Studies as a whole, many of the essays in these analytically separate sections actually straddle two or more sections. As such they provide a model for scholars who find it necessary to move among and beyond the four areas. The four areas of study are an ideal model to separate what is essentially an integrated reality and experience.

Part I explores some salient themes in Media Studies in an overview manner that provides a foundational, though not necessarily exhaustive, summary of the interdiscipline. Issues of gender, new technologies, international and developmentalist approaches to communications, and the inclusion of popular music and issues of authorship and authenticity give the reader a broad overview of themes in a number of, often interrelated, sub-specialties within Media Studies in all their complexity – that is, including issues of production, content, audience, and effects within a framework sensitive to difference in a global and identity sense. For example, feminist media studies, although quite recent, dating back to Betty Friedan's *The Feminine Mystique* in 1964, signal the pervasiveness of issues of gender in our field. As Gallagher points out, each and every area of Media Studies can be informed by a feminist perspective. Indeed a new collection entitled

Sex & Money (Meehan and Riordan, 2002) makes a forceful argument that political–economic studies can also be infused by a feminist analysis. Gallagher demonstrates that scholars all over the world are engaged in boundary cross-ing studies which foreground gender and Media Studies. In a similarly broad ranging effort, McQuail explores the applicability of "old communication theory" to the new communication technologies and concludes with an impassioned reminder that the uses of and the theories about the new technologies remain in human hands. From the sub-specialty of international and development com-munications, Robert Huesca provides an overview of the theories that have been used in this area of studies. From the early North American theoretical influ-ence, critiques of the dominant modernization paradigm have been followed by different approaches, many of them from Latin America. Huesca privileges participatory communication approaches as embodying a more ethical and demo-cratic philosophy and praxis than the early top-down efforts deployed within the modernization paradigm. Finally, rounding out this foundational section, Sloane proposes a way to cross between production, content, and audience analysis in popular music studies by exploring the agency of an individual communicator or artist such as is the case with Michael Stipes of R.E.M. Sloane explores issues of authenticity and commercialization, so prevalent in cultural and political–economic approaches to the study of music dating back to the work of Theodor Adorno and up to contemporary scholars such as Simon Frith and Larry Grossberg. The essays in this section were chosen to foreground both the diver-sity within the field of Media Studies and the growth in terms of theoretical and methodological sophistication.

   Part II foregrounds the study of production which includes the parameters under which, in contemporary society, we produce mass media products. Within this category we can find the neo-Marxist political economists such as contem-poraries Vinnie Mosco, Robert McChesney, Janet Wasko, Eileen Meehan, and Dan Schiller (for example, see his essay in this volume) as well as the previous, and original, first generation of political economists of communications such as Thomas Guback, Dallas Smythe, and Herbert Schiller, all of whom taught at the Institute of Communications Research at the University of Illinois and left their indelible mark in that doctoral program. Political–economic approaches to the study of media focus on the concentration of ownership and control over the production of media, issues of power, and the justification and challenge of privilege. Given the global reach of US media, beginning with Hollywood film, political–economic research turned our attention to international aspects of Media Studies before the current spate of globalization studies discovered the global situation. As such, Dan Schiller's "Digital Capitalism" in this volume is an excellent example of both the political–economic and its attention to global issues as it maps out the global reach of this economic concentration as it envelops the digital media. Schiller's elegant and exhaustive chapter on digital capitalism outlines some of the contemporary challenges across a broad range of media, countries, legislative, and regulatory bodies.

However, the area of production also includes sociologists of the newsroom, for example people like D. Charles Whitney and James Ettema whose essay in this volume continues to explore the degrees of freedom under which individual, organizational, and institutional communicators operate, especially in a rapidly changing global situation with high speed of technological innovation which presents both an opportunity and a challenge. Issues of history and ethics, both of which implicitly or explicitly pervade much of Media Studies scholarship, are carefully detailed in the essays by Nerone and Bracci in this volume. Approaches to history and to ethics, as one might expect, have changed in the near century of our interdiscipline's existence both in relation to our interdiscipline and to cognate areas.

This second section ends with a transition essay by Gail Dines and Elizabeth Perea comparing the cartoons in *Playboy* to those in the *Hustler* magazine. Underscoring the fact that it is very difficult to keep the analytical components of communication separate, Whitney and Ettema also often spilt over into the area of content as a way to talk about production. Similarly Dines and Perea examine the content of the cartoons through the production of a class-based masculinity and the development of an audience for two versions of mainstream pornography. In both essays production and content issues cannot be separated.

A second area of focus in Media Studies is the analysis of content of media. Here we can draw both on the extensive social scientific work, building on Berelson's famous objective analytical method to more interpretive, usually but not exclusively, semiotic or psychoanalytic approaches. Quantitative methodology forms the backbone of the Berelsonian approach, but it can also be used in conjunction with qualitative analysis. Whereas this may seem the most forward and easiest approach within Media Studies, students should be forewarned that it is neither obvious nor easy. Whether one is accounting for frequency or some numerical or statistical correlation, one still has to define or operationalize, in a mutually exclusive manner, what it is one is trying to measure. In the qualitative tradition, the trend has been to move away from the use of the concept "images" as it implied an untenable mimetic relationship to the use of "representation", as it includes the mediation that is always there in any media content. Representation is a theoretically complex concept about which entire books are written.

The essays in Part III explore a wide variety of content issues. Beginning with Matthew McAllister's essay on *Survivor*, the television show, the section highlights the advantage of using a combination of quantitative and qualitative methodology in one essay. In fact McAllister foregrounds content but against a backdrop of production in general and political economy in particular, a sort of reversal of the Dines and Perea approach. McAllister explores the philosophical and practical ramifications for democracy that the close connection between marketing and news production augurs. Sharon Mazzarella examines the historically rich area of youth. Differing from the audience centered traditions of studying youth, whether these were social scientific or cultural studies inflected, Mazzarella instead focuses on the construction of particular categories of youth within the mass media. Not surprisingly she finds that these categories are much more influenced by social and adult concerns than by youth themselves. As such they tell us much about our larger culture, but little about youth. On a similar vein, but focusing on women and gender and on advertising, Vickie Shields expands her now classic essay on the internally conflictual literature of women's images in advertising (Shields, 1996). Bringing the study of gender and advertising to the contemporary 2002 situation, Shields includes issues of fat pride as well as of eating disorders. She documents some successes and failures in the unhappy marriage between advertising and feminist themes. Melissa Johnson takes the emerging variety of ethnic media, in particular, but not exclusively, Latina women's magazines, and attempts to develop a model which can be tested across the range of available mass media in order to study a continuum of identity. In particular she explores the function of visual media in the dynamic construction of identity. Johnson, while considering a typology of content of Latina or ethnic media, also must consider issues of reception and audience. Wrapping up this section, Sujata Moorti presents us with a feminist, post-colonial analysis of media representational practices that popularize "oriental" symbols and enable them to enter the mainstream vocabulary of the United States. Given that fashion more often than not pertains to women, and that the usage of Indian items and symbols refers to a racialized population within both the United States and Europe, Moorti explores the gender and racial components of the globalization of fashion. Moorti analyzes both advertising and fashion itself as representational of larger geopolitical issues.

Thus the essays in Part III explore a wide breadth of what scholars in Media Studies are currently doing. Whether it be quantitative, qualitative or both; focusing on gender, youth, or ethnic and/or racial populations; and whether it be television news, magazines, advertising, or fashion, all five essays explore the importance of content as it overlaps with major political, social, and economic issues of both media and the wider society, either at a national or a global and transnational level.

Part IV focuses on the study of audiences. Within this deceptively simple rubric, there are at least two major tensions. Audience studies include marketing approaches and attempts to reach a maximum audience as well as efforts to understand interpretive and identificatory positions of individual or group audience members. Within marketing there has been a shift from attempting to reach the largest number possible to contenting oneself with reaching the most desirable demographics that would maximize the likelihood of consumption of a particular product or set of products. Thus we could include both Nielsen studies as well as focus groups within this administrative approach to audiences. However, dating back at least to Janice Radway's *Reading the Romance* in 1984, the study of audiences has also sought to flesh out the agency of individual and group audiences. That is, in particular reacting to the dismissal of female audiences and their feminine genres such as romance novels and other forms of melodrama, Radway proposed the then radical, and now perfectly obvious, notion that we should study the members of those audiences to see what they get out of those particular media and genres. What is their interpretive take on the novel? What does reading mean to them? As opposed to what do we think they ought to be reading. This form of analysis, often using ethnographic or pseudo-ethnographic (Nightingale, 1996) methodology, became increasingly influential as it overlapped with anthropological tendencies brought in with cultural studies. Some manifestations of this type of research celebrate every reading as an emancipatory political act. Resistance lurked around every corner. The essays in this section pull back from that euphoric moment and bring back some of the many contingencies which scholars of issues of power and agency have studied and proposed for the past few centuries. However, audience analysis also continues to be carried out in the more traditional "uses and gratifications" approach (Katz, Blumler, and Gurevitch, 1974) and in survey methodology. As with other sections, audience scholars are trying to understand the uses of new media by a wide range of audiences. The essays in this section provide a globally wide ranging sample of the many contemporary possibilities within audience studies.

Part IV begins with Radhika Parameswaran's essay on post-colonial theory and global audiences, in particular Indian women readers of romantic fiction produced in England. Through her grounded analysis, Parameswaran both deploys and expands the accumulated knowledge of interpretive audience studies. She investigates the complex affiliations that women have to fiction, nation, class, and gender. She demonstrates that easy mappings do nothing but obscure complex and dynamic situations. Switching back to a more traditional approach, Sonia Livingstone deploys her considerable history of audience research to explore the contemporary concerns about the audience in relation to new technology and makes a call to keep the analysis historically grounded. People's continual and intimate engagement with the world through the mass media, especially in industrialized countries, can only be understood by studying previous introductions of "new" media. Virginia Nightingale takes an epistemological and theoretical look at the academic situation that engendered the initial scientific approach to audiences, followed by a cultural turn, and followed, once more, by an attempted combination of the two. She finds that in an age of increasing "manipulation and exploitation of information" it is time to answer the by now old challenge, proposed by Merton (1968/1949) of "middle range theorization" which would force us to consider how information is generated in conjunction with how it is interpreted. Joke Hermes traces the more positive components of audience research in media and cultural studies to feminist roots. Taking the often-ignored feminist legacy seriously means exploring both its useful and restraining aspects, especially the methodological pitfalls. She concludes that "to understand . . . different experiences and to validate serious discussion of all of them is what reception analysis should be about." Building on the broad range of Media Studies audience analysis, Angharad Valdivia proposes that the active audience in fact crosses over into the arena of the production of both identity and of new media situations and products. With increased, voluntary and forced, global mobility, audiences are not what audiences used to be, and the study of audiences needs to consider the hybrid media and situations in which people make sense of themselves, the media, and the world. As with many of the other essays in this book, this chapter begins in audiences and overlaps into production, but not just the production of media but the production of identity, which Hermes and Parameswaran foreground as well.

Part V turns to the still-dominant paradigm within US Media Studies, the study of "effects" and cognition. Given the positivist tone of the US academy, this social-scientific pursuit, based largely on Merton's structural functionalism, remains the dominant paradigm in the US but is usually less central and downright marginal in other countries and continents. To this paradigm we owe the huge literature on children and the media, in particular studies of television and violence, as well as studies of political communications, in terms of voter participation and choice. As well, we have here feminist studies, especially sex role research and the effects of pornography, especially violent pornography, research. In the relatively short history of media studies since the twenties we have already had four distinct eras of dominant theories within the effects tradition. Theories of the strong effects have been overshadowed by focused small effect theory with a swing back to the middle range and a return to strong effects. Not impervious to larger social issues, this area of studies has also incorporated racial and ethnic concerns into its overall attention to issues of violence as well as an attempt to figure out how children are affected by the new media.

Two of the essays in Part V unpack the topic of stereotypes, mostly of African Americans but also of Latinos, and their effects on perceptions of and attitudes about minorities. Mary Beth Oliver suggests that the stereotyping of African Americans as criminals has potentially strong effects in terms of how African Americans are treated and Whites' perceptions and attitudes about African Americans. She also reminds us that effects research seldom relies only on effects research. Instead effects research relies and overlaps with issues of content, production, and audience. The potential of the rather pessimistic literature of the effects of race and crime in the media is that the patterns demonstrated by the scholarship will be highlighted and will therefore encourage a break in the vicious cycle of negative representation followed by negative effect. Oliver's overview of research on crime and the media contextualizes the issue of effects within a foregrounding of both content and audience. Careful to point out some of the logical leap pitfalls that many students and popular press representations of social scientific research engage in – the careful detailing of what a particular data implies and can be misconstrued to imply is something that is sorely needed in an age where there is still much too much distortion of carefully pursued studies.

Michael Casas and Travis Dixon examine the impact of stereotypical and counter-stereotypical representations of Blacks and Latinos in the news media and found that those exposed to stereotypical portrayals of Blacks and Latinos had a greater fear of crime than those exposed to counter-stereotypical portrayals, a combination of portrayals, or those not exposed to news programs. Casas and Dixon insist that televisual content is best for exploring these issues, and suggest that further research might want to differentiate between the race of the perpetrator and the victim.

Commenting on the salience of sex and violence to effects scholars, Jennings Bryant and Dorina Miron argue that issues of sex and violence were on the public agenda before they received extensive attention from "curious scientists." As such, these two concerns should always be considered within the broader social and historical setting which demands we pay attention to them. For example, the Columbine shooting was a wake-up call to anyone who thought the issue of children and media violence was settled. Tracing the connection between pleasure and violence back to Aristotle, Bryant and Miron delve into the contested choice between freedom or censorship in regards to sex and violence in the media. Effects research, they conclude, can guide those responsible with making those choices.

Finally, to round out Part V on effects Ellen Wartella, Barbara O'Keefe, and Ronda Scantlin write on new media, particularly the interactive component and children's cognitive development. Given that children are born into and grow up in media rich homes, with expected differentials according to income, and that mass media is a dominant activity in their childhood, Wartella, O'Keefe, and Scantlin find that there is great potential for the new interactive media. However, that potential needs our parental and social vigilance as well as further research to explore how to maximize the potential benefit of these technologies for children. In sum, scholarship on children and the media in the effects tradition continues to be of great importance in terms of understanding the relationship between media, in its great diversity, and people from an early age.

The book ends with "Futures," which aims to map out some especially promising areas of study as well as ask certain scholars to assess our likelihood of following up on these promising areas. More so than the preceding four parts and paralleling "Foundations," all of these chapters self-consciously or implicitly cross the boundaries between the four areas of Media Studies. Part VI begins with John Downing's call to arms for the field, specially its US variant. He singles out the US because the sheer amount of scholarship produced and published in this country contributes to making it a hegemonic force in the global Media Studies arena. Downing's eight areas for improvement are partially answered in this volume, for example with its global diversity beyond comparing everything with an Anglo-American setting in Gallagher, Hermes, Huesca, Valdivia, Livingstone, and Parameswaran; the move beyond concept fetishism in all essays; and the inclusion and foregrounding of social class in some of the chapters, notably in Dines and Perea. However the volume falls short of two of his suggestions in terms of the importance of religion and human rights both of which are implicitly addressed in Bracci's chapter on ethics and Rentschler's study of activism and the media but are not frontally discussed by any of the other chapters. Were such cross-cutting research potential borne out, Downing suspects that we would experience not only increasing intellectual stimulation but also greater public policy influence and thus an ability to influence the world beyond academic walls.

Downing's chapter is followed by four chapters, each of which extend Media Studies into fruitful areas of study and potential social and policy implications. Cameron McCarthy's essay on the mutually productive relationship between Media Studies and education scholarship takes up the topic of multicultural education, as it is partly struggled over and disseminated through the mass media. He explores the deployment of powerful discourses which potentially inform both educated global citizens and the politics of resentment. The Foucaultian approach is one that increasing numbers of Media Studies scholars are using, and it is beginning to appear even in undergraduate introductory texts such as *Studying Culture* (Giles and Middleton, 1999). Carrie Rentschler explores the ways that different organizations, with different resources and proximity to power, can use the media to get their message out. Rentschler criss-crosses between political economy in terms of production and ownership and control of the media, content, and issues of audiences. Many social movements originally turn to media activism for fund raising reasons, but many find that they also need to reach out to those who need the services they offer. In the process of figuring out how to interact with the media, an organization's way of being may well change. Despite the many potential pitfalls, Rentschler resoundingly holds out great democratic promise for the media overlap with social justice groups.

Stepping back to a global level of analysis, Armand Mattelart discusses the contemporary uses of the term "globalization," which, he admits, signals "a set of new realities destined to deeply change the forms of universal social links" within a historical examination of the uses and geopolitics of the term. Rather than dismiss the global solidarity potential afforded by new communication networks, he urges us not to forget the tensions between the gurus of management and the actors of social change. Boatema Boateng brings us around full circle in her study of issues of intellectual property as they relate to countries of the South, especially Africa, and, in particular, Ghana. Philosophical disagreements over the development and sustainance of intellectual property regimes by the year 2002 have more or less solidified into promoting the needs and interests of transnational corporations as opposed to encouraging and protecting the creativity of individual or group producers. Regulatory frameworks, at the regional, national, and international levels, embody hegemonic approaches to asymmetric relations of power and need to be challenged and changed at all levels. Media Studies research and activism can play a crucial role in this process. Boateng deploys a global analysis of the production of regulation as it influences the production and circulation of cultural products and media.

Thus in six separate but overlapping parts, *A Companion to Media Studies* presents a contemporary overview of the interdiscipline of Media Studies. As readers make their way through the book, they will notice that old themes are hard to abandon, primarily because they remain central themes in the contemporary global setting. The rapid rate of change, innovation, and development in communications technologies and the increasing interoperation of global corporate capital loom as both an opportunity and a challenge for scholarship and for social change. The media have simultaneously imploded and exploded. Thus scholars in all sections of *A Companion to Media Studies* considered the implications of new technologies as well as of the growing synergistic potential of media production through technologies and global markets. The focus on children and youth remains important. Of course, many scholars combine the above two concerns and study new technologies and children and youth. In all the essays, authors acknowledge the great potential of both the technologies and also of the scholarship from the interdiscipline of Media Studies. However, many warn us against historical amnesia given that so many continue to greet each new technology with hallucinogenic celebratory comments that disregard the considerable historical knowledge on which we can draw. Whereas the great potential is there and remains there, it is not necessarily being exploited. Scholars also integrally explore issues of difference from a globally dynamic perspective. Given the broad range of difference, and the relatively small ground we have already covered, this promises to continue to be an area of growth. Contributors to *A Companion to Media Studies* provide us with many venues and tools to extend our interdiscipline. We have been challenged to take Media Studies into the new century – the rest is up to us.

Note

1 I am indebted to Brenda Dervin for her keen reading of this essay in general and of this point in particular.

References

Campbell, R. (2002). *Media and Culture: An introduction to mass communication* (3rd edn.). Boston: Bedford/St. Martin's.

Carey, J. W. (1988). *Communication as Culture*. London: Routledge.

Cobley, P. (ed.) (1996). *The Communication Theory Reader*. New York: Routledge.

Craig, R. T. (1999). Communication theory as a field. *Communication Theory*, 9(2), 119–61.

Croteau, D. and Hoynes, W. (1997). *Media/Society: Industries, images, and audiences*. Thousand Oaks, CA: Pine Forge Press.

Curran, J. and Gurevitch, M. (eds.) (2000). *Mass Media and Society* (3rd edn.). London: Arnold.

DeFleur, M. L. (1999). Where have all the milestones gone? The decline of significant research on the process and effects of mass communication. *Mass Communication and Society*, (1/2), 85–98.

Dervin, B. and Chaffee, S. H. with Foreman-Wernet, L. (eds.) (in press). *Communication: A different kind of horse race: Essays honoring Richard F. Carter*. Cresskill, NJ: Hampton Press.

Dines, G. and Humez, J. M. (eds.) (1995). *Gender, Race and Class in Media: A text-reader*. Thousand Oaks, CA: Sage.

Downing, J., Mohammadi, A., and Sreberny-Mohammadi, A. (eds.) (2000). *Questioning the Media: A critical introduction* (2nd edn.). Thousand Oaks, CA: Sage.

Fleming, D. (ed.) (2000). *Formations: A 21st century media studies textbook*. Manchester, UK: University of Manchester Press.

Gallagher, M. (1981). *Unequal Opportunities: The case of women and the media*. Paris: UNESCO Press.

Giles, J. and Middleton, T. (1999). *Studying Culture: A practical introduction*. Oxford: Blackwell.

Grossberg, L., Wartella, E., and Whitney, D. C. (1998). *Media Making: Mass media and popular culture*. Thousand Oaks, CA: Sage.

Katz, E. and Lazarsfeld, P. F. (1955). *Personal Influence: The part played by people in the flow of mass communication*. New York: The Free Press.

Katz, E., Blumler, J. G., and Gurevitch, M. (1974). Utilization of mass communication by the individual. In J. G. Blumler and E. Katz (eds.), *The Uses of Mass Communications: Current perspectives on gratifications research*. Beverly Hills and London: Sage Publications.

Lipsitz, G. (2001). *American Studies in a Moment of Danger*. Minneapolis: University of Minnesota Press.

Marris, P. and Thornham, S. (eds.) (2000). *Media Studies: A reader* (2nd edn.). New York: New York University Press.

Martín Barbero, J. (1993). *Communication, Culture and Hegemony: From media to mediations*. Newbury Park, CA: Sage.

Marvin, C. (1988). *When Old Technologies Were New: Thinking about electric communication in the late nineteenth century*. New York: Oxford.

Mattelart, A. and Mattelart, M. (1992). *Rethinking Media Theory*, Part 2. Minneapolis: University of Minnesota Press.

McQuail, D. (1994). *Mass Communication Theory: An introduction* (3rd edn.). Thousand Oaks, CA: Sage.

Meehan, E. R. and Riordan, E. (eds.) (2002) *Sex and Money: Feminism and political economy in the media*. Minneapolis: University of Minnesota Press.

Merton, R. K. (1968) [1949]. *Social Theory and Social Structure*. New York: The Free Press; London: Collier-Macmillan.

Nightingale, V. (1996). *Studying Audiences: The shock of the real*. New York: Routledge.

Radway, J. (1984). *Reading the Romance: Women, patriarchy, and popular literature*. Chapel Hill: University of North Carolina Press.

Rodríguez, I. (ed.) (2001). *The Latin American Subaltern Studies Reader*. Durham, NC: Duke.

Rosengren, K. E. (2000). For a lack of models: A field in fragments? In D. Fleming (ed.), *Formations: A 21st century media studies textbook*. Manchester, UK: University of Manchester Press.

Shields, V. R. (1996). Selling the sex that sells: Mapping the evolution of gender advertising research across three decades. In B. Burleson (ed.), *Communication Yearbook 20*. Thousand Oaks, CA: Sage.

Simpson, C. (1994). *Science of Coercion: Communication research and psychological warfare, 1945–1960*. New York: Oxford University Press.

Turow, J. (1999). *Media Today: An introduction to mass communication*. Boston: Houghton Mifflin Company.

Valdivia, A. N. (ed.) (1995). *Feminism, Multiculturalism, and the Media: Global diversities*. Newbury Park, CA: Sage.

Winston, B. (1998). *Media Technology and Society. A history: from the telegraph to the internet*. London: Routledge.

PART ONE

Foundations

CHAPTER ONE

Feminist Media Perspectives

Margaret Gallagher

Feminist media scholarship has emerged as one of the richest and most challenging intellectual projects within the field of media and cultural studies over the past twenty-five years. The range, complexity and transdisciplinarity of feminist media studies today bears little resemblance to the fledgling body of work that began to appear in the 1970s. Nevertheless one common thread underpins feminist media theory and criticism from its origins to the present. The defining characteristic of this body of work is its explicitly political dimension.

> With its substantial project, it is the reciprocal relation between theory, politics and activism, the commitment of feminist academics to have their work contribute to a larger feminist goal (however defined), the blurred line between the feminist as academic and the feminist as activist, that distinguishes feminist perspectives on the media from other possible perspectives. (van Zoonen, 1991, p. 34)

It was indeed a political impetus that first shaped the academic agenda of feminist media analysis. One starting point for Western feminists was Betty Friedan's The Feminine Mystique (1963), with its searing critique of the mass media. At a global level the United Nations International Decade for Women (1975–85) was a catalyst for debate about the many sites of women's subordination, while the media's role as a specific source of oppression was documented in reviews initiated by UNESCO (Ceulemans and Fauconnier, 1979; Gallagher, 1981). These early analyses found the media to be deeply implicated in the patterns of discrimination operating against women in society – patterns which, through the absence, trivialization or condemnation of women in media content amounted to their "symbolic annihilation" (Tuchman, 1978). That general critique quickly came to be positioned around two central axes: an analysis of the structures of power in which women are systematically subordinated; and a focus on the politics of representation and the production of knowledge in which women are objects rather than active subjects. These two concerns were addressed in many studies of the late 1970s and early 1980s as problems of "women in the profession" and "images of women in the media." But they have gradually come together to produce a complex analysis of the structure and process of representation, the cultural and economic formations that support these, the social relations that produce gendered discourse, and the nature of gendered identity.

In many respects the contemporary field of feminist media scholarship looks vastly different from the relatively straightforward terrain occupied by most "women and media" studies of the early 1980s. For instance, initial classifications of feminist media scholarship into categories – socialist, radical, liberal, cultural – designed to highlight its particular theoretical and/or political orientation (Steeves, 1987; van Zoonen, 1991) soon seemed inadequate to depict the "variety and intermingledness of feminist theory" (van Zoonen, 1994, p. 13). In fact, the crossing of intellectual and disciplinary boundaries that characterizes much of today's work can be traced back to some of the most creative points of departure in feminist media studies. For instance, as far back as 1977 Noreene Janus critiqued the theoretical shortcomings of white, middle-class, liberal research into "sex-role stereotypes." Janus advocated more holistic studies of media content, allied with analyses of the economic imperatives of the media industries and with studies of the perceptions of different audience groups, and the linking of media-related questions to other kinds of social analysis. This type of integrated interdisciplinary research agenda will seem familiar territory to many feminist media scholars today. Yet its implementation has demanded the location and articulation of a distinct feminist voice outside the framework of male-defined binary oppositions that characterise Western intellectual work (see Valdivia, 1995). It has required feminist media scholars to "create new spaces of discourse, to rewrite cultural narratives, and to define the terms from another perspective – a view from 'elsewhere'" (de Lauretis, 1987, p. 25).

This has involved a difficult and protracted struggle to achieve intellectual legitimacy within the general field of media and communication studies. An early testimony from the Women's Studies Group at the Centre for Contemporary Cultural Studies (CCCS) at the University of Birmingham in England, speaks to the enormity of the enterprise:

> We found it extremely difficult to participate . . . and felt, without being able to articulate it, that it was a case of the masculine domination of both intellectual work and the environment in which it was being carried out. Intellectually, our questions were still about "absences." (Women's Studies Group, 1978, p. 10)

Twenty five years later, defining and realizing a feminist approach to the study of media remains a sometimes painful venture for those who must "teach against the text" (Rakow, 2001a, p. 383; see also Valdivia, 2001 and Eaton, 2001).

Redefining the Field: Whose Feminism, What Scholarship?

Charlotte Brunsdon, a member of the CCCS Women's Studies Group, later reflected on the intellectual limitations imposed by "the notion of a women's studies group which is 'filling in the gaps' in an already existing analysis, and which has a kind of 'what about women' public presence" (Brunsdon 1976, quoted in 1996, p. 283). Such limitations had a general effect on the initial direction taken by feminist media scholarship, much of which was indeed concerned to "fill in the gaps" in communication studies by identifying areas that had been ignored or rendered invisible by the field's traditional categories of enquiry (see Rakow, 1992). Gradually issues such as the mediation of male violence, sexuality, pornography, language as control, verbal harassment, the body, beauty, consumerism, fashion, and the study of "women's genres" – magazines, soap opera, melodrama and romance – were brought onto the agenda. A more fundamental revisioning, which would have an impact on communication research methods – particularly in terms of the relation of the researcher to the subject of study – also emerged, as new strands of feminism began to modify the original feminist critique of the media.

Early feminist theory had emphasised the commonalities of women's oppression, neglecting profound differences between women in terms of class, age, sexuality, religion, race and nation. As its exclusionary nature became evident, the collective "we" of feminism was called into question. The inadequacies of feminist theorizing that conflated the condition of white, heterosexual, middle-class women with the condition of all women were highlighted in North America by black and Latina feminists (hooks, 1981; Moraga and Anzaldúa, 1981), in Britain by black and Asian feminists (Amos and Parmar, 1984), and by the analyses of lesbian feminists (Lont and Friedley, 1989). Such critiques evoked the concepts of "interlocking identities" and "interlocking oppressions". Black women's experience of sexism, to take one example, could not be conceived as separable from their experience of racism:

> Women of color do not experience sexism in addition to racism, but sexism in the context of racism; thus they cannot be said to bear an additional burden that white women do not bear, but to bear an altogether different burden from that borne by white women. (Houston, 1992, p. 49)

Related and more radical analyses came from feminist scholars in the Third World, where quite different agendas were called for (Bhasin and Khan, 1986). These critiques highlighted the irrelevance of Western feminism's analytical frameworks to the lives of most women around the world, and attempted to reposition feminist debate within broader social, economic and cultural contexts of analysis advocated by scholars such as Janus (1977).

> We are not just concerned with how women are portrayed in the media or how many women work in the media. We are also concerned about what kinds of lives they lead, what status they have, and what kind of society we have. The answers to these questions will determine our future strategies for communication and networking. Communication alternatives therefore need to emerge from our critique of the present world order and our vision of the future. (Bhasin, 1994, p. 4)

Such critiques spoke from a post-colonial position, in which the self-assumed authority of Western feminists to speak about – or indeed for – others was disputed and de-centred. Influential accounts of the tendencies of a masculinist-imperialist ideological formation to construct a "monolithic 'third-world woman'" (Spivak, 1988, p. 296), discursively constituted as the universal victim of Third World patriarchy (Mohanty, 1984), challenged feminists to "unlearn" their privilege and to deconstruct their own authority as intellectuals (Ganguly, 1992). These positions appeared to question the legitimacy of "outside intervention" of any kind, whether intellectual or political.

Although subsequently attenuated by Third World scholars anxious to move beyond standpoints that threatened to mark all feminist politics as either inauthentic or unnecessary (Sunder Rajan, 1993, p. 35), they were enduringly influential in highlighting a fundamental methodological issue in feminist media studies. This issue, which turned on an interrogation of questions of "identity" and "authority" in feminist media criticism, was to affect the ways in which feminist scholars approached and represented their work, particularly in studies of media content and media audiences.

Identity, Position and Authority

> After many years in the academy, I am beginning to feel that I can question some words, such as pleasure and resistance. Why do some scholars talk endlessly about pleasure and the text? I more usually encounter frustration. Why do I read about resistance in every corner when I see more of the same and less of the different? Why do my spectatorship positions continue to be ignored or spoken for without research? (Valdivia, 2000, p. 3)

With this introduction to her volume of critical essays on the location – and locatedness – of Latinas and Latin American women in media culture – Angharad Valdivia speaks from several positions: as a Latina whose experience of popular culture does not easily "fit" within interpretations of audience reception that assume a white, middle-class, Anglo-American subject; as a scholar who brings that experience into play in questioning some of the most influential ideas within the feminist canon; as an individual whose personal story openly and candidly informs her analyses and theoretical starting points. Within the essays themselves, Valdivia sometimes inhabits more specific speaking positions – for example mother, researcher, consumer, citizen. These shifting but inter-related positions, rooted in day-to-day experience, exemplify well the tension and fluctuating nature of identity that has been argued in more abstract terms by feminist theorists such as Rosi Braidotti:

> Speaking "as a feminist woman" does not refer to one dogmatic framework but rather to a knot of interrelated questions that play on different layers, registers, and levels of the self. . . . Feminist theory is a mode of relating thought to life. As such not only does it provide a critical standpoint to deconstruct established forms of knowledge, drawing feminism close to critical theory; it also establishes a new order of values within the thinking process itself, giving to the lived experience priority. (Braidotti, 1989, pp. 94–5)

Speaking "as a feminist woman," or the expression of the "personal voice" in feminist intellectual work, has been partly inspired by a reluctance to speak inappropriately "for" others, or to endorse the grand narratives of communication theory that appeared to permit an impersonal, authoritative objectivity. But the personal voice within feminism is not to be confused with self-centred subjectivity. Historically, it was a route used by feminists to uncover the gendered nature of experience. Charlotte Brunsdon (2000) traces its first politically significant use to the process of "consciousness raising" frequently employed by the women's liberation movement of the 1970s:

> It involved the recounting, usually in closely monitored "turns", by individuals in a group, of chosen experiences . . . This experience telling would provide the data for the group to work collectively to attempt to establish the gender paradigms of the experience. To attempt to see the individual experiences – e.g. of being fed up with always being the one who cleaned the bathroom – as both representative and symptomatic of a gendered rather than simply a personal experience. (p. 88)

If "the personal is the political" was the slogan used to describe this early insistence on the role of experience, contemporary feminist scholarship has gone further, offering accounts that problematize the links between the personal and the wider intellectual context (see Riley, 1992), and eventually using the personal as a means of interrogating theory – articulating a position from which "the personal is the theoretical" (Valdivia, 2000, p. 12).

This emphasis within feminism on a fluctuating, fragmented experience of identity as "position" has had an important impact on understanding, within media scholarship as a whole, of how media processes, texts and audiences should be conceptualized. As Ann Gray (1999) puts it, feminist work has demonstrated "how discourses flow in and out of constructions of identity, self, private and public, national, local and global. Boundaries, thus, are permeable, unstable and uneasy" (p. 31). Similarly, the feminist commitment to rendering visible female experience and agency has quite profound epistemological consequences that prove "troublesome" in a field that remains stubbornly gendered (p. 23). The relationship between the researcher and the subject of research has been a recurrent issue, particularly in feminist ethnographic work on media and culture. The feminist researcher is aware of – indeed may regard as determining – her own position within her field of study. For example, Ann Gray herself, in an early study of the gendered use of home video, speaks plainly about a "class-based" identification with the women in her research:

> I consider this shared position as quite crucial to the quality of the conversations that I had with the women and that the talk that ensued was, in most instances, enriched by that shared knowledge. To put it quite directly, I am a woman in my study. (1992, p. 34)

In fact, as Gray later reflected, "being a woman" in relation to the women in her study was much more ambiguous than she initially suggested. In retrospect, she recounts a complex interplay of gender, class and ethnicity in the production of meanings from her conversations with these women (Gray, 1995). Recognition of the different subject positions between researcher and researched, and the inherent power differential in this relationship, is a theme in much feminist media criticism. The relationship is further complicated by the contradictory positions of the researcher as "one of the group" and as "authority," a tension which is often acknowledged in self-reflexive accounts of the research process. Describing her research with fans of a British crime drama, Lyn Thomas admits being split between a conscious intention to behave as "neutral facilitator" of the discussion and the desire to switch to "fellow fan" mode. As she remarks:

> The combination of being one of the group some of the time and in the powerful position of teacher/researcher the rest means that the cultural agenda which I set is likely to play a significant role in the development of the discussion. (1995, p. 12)

For instance, Thomas recounts how the only man in the group seemed concerned to make an impression on the others and even to obtain a dominant position. She continues: "I certainly saw keeping Jim under control and sabotaging his attempts at dominance as an important part of my role as discussion facilitator" (p. 14). Here Thomas echoes Ellen Seiter's (1990) analysis of how the power differentials between researcher and interviewee may be played out through class differences in the interview, and may then be obscured by the way in which the interview is written up. These and other feminist accounts (for example Walkerdine, 1986; Gillespie, 1995; Seiter, 1999) choose to problematize methodological issues and in particular the role of the researcher. In doing so, they destabilize ideas of objective investigation and authoritative findings. The "voice" that emerges through much contemporary feminist media research is therefore characterized by a high degree of self-reflexivity, which problematizes the relations between researcher and researched. Valerie Walkerdine (1986) has drawn attention to the material significance of these relations, pointing out that the interpretations produced by research are not simply rooted in an abstract struggle over meanings or values. They are, she argues, a "struggle about power with a clear material effectivity. One might therefore ask how far it is possible for the observer to 'speak for' the observed" (p. 191).

Speaking about Women: Approaches to Media Content

The question of how women are "spoken for" or "spoken about" is at the heart of the feminist critique of media content and its implication in the construction of gender. Within feminist scholarship the debate has moved on since the quantitative content analyses of "sex-roles and stereotypes" that typified the mainly North American research of the 1970s. Nevertheless, studies of this kind are still carried out, and they remain important in recording some of the basic elements in a very complex situation.

In an ambitious global monitoring exercise, women from 71 countries studied their news media for one day in January 1995. More than 15,500 stories were analyzed, and the results were dramatic. Only 17 percent of the world's news subjects (news-makers or interviewees in news stories) were women (MediaWatch, 1995). The proportion of female news subjects was lowest in Asia (14 percent) and highest in North America (27 percent). Women were least likely to be news subjects in the fields of politics and government (7 percent of all news subjects in this field) and economy or business (9 percent). They were most likely to make the news in terms of health and social issues (33 percent) or in the field of arts and entertainment (31 percent). The results of a second global monitoring project, carried out in 70 countries in February 2000, suggested that the news world might have been standing still for five years. On that day women accounted for just 18 percent of news subjects (Spears et al., 2000). The degree of concordance between the main results from the two global monitoring projects was remarkable, though hardly surprising. The embedded, gendered nature of news values and news selection processes is such that the overall patterns detected by quantitative monitoring are unlikely to change appreciably even over the medium term.

Yet apart from the statistics, the qualitative analysis in the 2000 global media monitoring project showed a striking absence of female voices in news items that concerned women in very specific ways. For example, stories that covered plans to establish a Family Court in Jamaica, the high abortion rate among teenagers in Scotland, women's rights to seek divorce in Egypt, maternity plans in Northern Ireland, the punishment of women for marital infidelity in Turkey – these were just some of the cases where the exclusion of any women's point of view seemed blatantly negligent. This tendency to ignore women or – at best – to speak about, rather than to or through women, demonstrates a very real and contemporary absence of women's voices in the media, and the profound lack of attention paid by the media to the telling of women's stories generally.

The limitations of such studies have long been clear (see Ang and Hermes, 1991; van Zoonen, 1991). However, particularly at the global level, work in this tradition contributes to the documentation of persistent patterns of exclusion. The data it generates has provided feminists with straightforward arguments with which to challenge media whose mandates include a requirement to pro-mote pluralism and balance (see Gallagher, 2001). While this approach may seem to sit uneasily with that of methodologically sophisticated textual analysis, the two approaches should be considered in terms of the different interpreta-tions and understandings of media content that each aims to produce. For if the broad sweep of media monitoring is directed primarily towards giving women a "voice" in the world of the media, the intense focus of feminist textual analysis has developed at least partly with the intent of giving a "voice" to women within media scholarship itself (see Brunsdon, D'Acci, and Spigel, 1997, pp. 8–10).

The "high culture–mass culture" debate is familiar territory within media studies, where the "mass" is invariably explained as a pejorative referent for (lower) "class" cultural preferences. However, as Huyssen (1986) demonstrates, the high culture–mass culture dichotomy is also permeated by considerations of gender. Europe's late nineteenth-century industrial revolution and cultural modernization, he argues, coincided with the first major women's movement. Huyssen shows how turn-of-the-century political, psychological and aesthetic discourse consistently gendered mass culture and the masses as feminine, and thus inferior. This idea retained a position in much later theories of mass culture – as, for example, when Adorno and Horkheimer conjure up the fairy tale evil queen to claim that "mass culture, in her mirror, is always the most beautiful in the land" (quoted in Huyssen, 1986, p. 192).

The dichotomy that gendered mass culture as feminine and inferior has strongly patterned media criticism and analysis, which disregarded femininity, gender and sexuality in discussions of the "political." Feminist critics rejected the domin-ant, narrow definition of the political in terms of "the market" or "public policy," arguing that it must include a consideration of everyday life, domesticity and consumerism. It was within this context that feminist media scholars set out to "reclaim" the popular media of mass entertainment. As a result, genres such as romance, soap opera, sitcoms, popular drama and rock music became legitimate subjects for critical analysis. The extremely large body of work that developed over the 1980s and 1990s is one in which different critical approaches have become increasingly intertwined (for a comprehensive review, see Brunsdon, D'Acci, and Spigel, 1997). While some scholars have limited their work to textual analysis per se (for example, the close reading of narrative structures, iconography, symbolic codes and themes, and of the solicitation of pleasure, identification and subjectivity within the text), others have increasingly fused textual analysis with other approaches. For instance, studies of the discursive, social and institutional contexts in which the texts themselves are produced have looked at the historical and organizational imperatives and constraints that shape female characters and audience interpretations of them. Studies of the context of reception have focused on how texts are viewed and interpreted in the framework of domestic and familial relations.

Despite these increasingly multi-layered analyses, until the mid-1990s a great deal of feminist criticism continued to focus on "feminine" genres within popular culture. Charlotte Brunsdon's study (2000) of the development of research into television soap opera argues that the feminist approach to "feminine" genres such as soaps and romance not only was innovatory, but had a precise historical specificity. By studying a subaltern field feminist criticism struggled to address the issue of hierarchy within media research in a gendered way. For Brunsdon and the interviewees in her study – all pioneers of television soap research – it was the legitimation of the academic study of popular culture that was, in retrospect, feminism's supreme innovation. Beyond this, however, Brunsdon argues that the feminist study of soaps provided the feminist intellectual with an original – though somewhat ambiguous – "speaking position" within the academy: "it is this, the production of positions, rather than the object of study as such, which was significant in the feminist encounter with soap operas" (p. 217).

Arguing the importance of a feminist move outside expertise in "subaltern" fields, Brunsdon concedes that such a move requires "the difficult production of new speaking positions" (p. 218). And indeed this proved to be a challenge for feminist media scholarship. For instance, the "public knowledge project" – analyses of "the media as an agency of public knowledge and 'definitional' power, with a focus on news and current affairs output and a direct connection with the politics of information and the viewer as citizen" (Corner, 1991, p. 268) – remained a blind spot in feminist media criticism throughout the 1980s and early 1990s. Reflecting on the implications of this, Liesbet van Zoonen (1994) concluded:

> The public knowledge project tends to become a new male preserve, concerned with ostensibly gender-neutral issues such as citizenship, but actually neglecting the problematic relation of non-white, non-male citizens to the public sphere. (p. 125)

The absence of a comprehensive feminist perspective on the full range of media genres and areas of representation – as Christine Geraghty put it, on "blue" as well as "pink" topics (Geraghty, 1996) – was one of two important areas of concern for feminist media scholars as the 1990s progressed. Another was the emphasis on questions of consumption as opposed to "the production of consumption" (McRobbie, 1997, p. 74). These two preoccupations, increasingly voiced in feminist writings in the course of the 1990s, evoked several of the foundational concepts of early feminism – the structural nature of power relations, socioeconomic exclusion, and the representation of gender in public discourse. Certain strands in recent feminist media research witness a re-engagement with those central questions of structure, ideology and agency.

Negotiating the Public–Private Division

Over the past two decades many feminist scholars have focused on gender representation in the news and other forms of journalism (for a useful review see Carter, Branston, and Allan, 1998, pp. 1–8). However until recently the interrelationships between gender, politics and communication have received relatively little attention (Sreberny and van Zoonen, 2000; see also Norris, 1997). The emerging picture is extremely complex. Women entering the political arena provide the news media with a problem. As women they embody a challenge to masculine authority. As active, powerful women they defy easy categorization. Often the media attempt to contain the threats they pose by trying to situate them as "women" rather than as "politicians." Studies show that while the media emphasize the political record and experience of male politicians or political candidates, with women the focus is more on their family situation and their appearance. This pattern is true even in countries with a strong tradition of women in political office such as Finland (Koski, 1994), Norway (Skjeie, 1994) and Sweden (Börjesson, 1995). And while certain types of popular media tend to stress the family relationships of all politicians, men and women are not necessarily presented in the same way in terms of their families. For instance, van Zoonen (2000) found that the Dutch gossip press depicted the families of male politicians as a source of support, while for female politicians the family was portrayed as a source of conflict for women pursuing a political career.

When women disobey the rules of feminine behavior, they may be portrayed as "iron women," aggressive or belligerent. South Africa's Nkosazana Zuma is one example. Said to be the "antithesis of the obedient woman. Her position and her role have brought her into frequent and turbulent contact with the media. Zuma embodies all the qualities that are frequently admired in male politicians" (Media Monitoring Project, 1999, p. 165). Media coverage of such women at times shows clearly how parallel evaluations – of the politician and the woman – run side by side in a way that rarely occurs in the case of men. And while at one level journalists and editors may be aware that these evaluations lead to contradictory conclusions, at another level the framework is hard to resist. In their study of women in South African politics, the Media Monitoring Project illustrated how this dilemma can be simultaneously acknowledged and downplayed by the media. "Zuma has been one of the most effective cabinet ministers in the Mandela government" ran one national newspaper editorial (August 1, 1998). "It is precisely because of her strong character, and the fact that she feels very passionately about her job, that Zuma has attracted the kind of negative publicity that surrounds her." Yet the editorial failed to compare Zuma's treatment with that of male politicians with similar strength of character and passionate commitment. At the same time it distanced the media from the coverage of Zuma by labeling it as "publicity" rather than news reporting (ibid.).

Several studies of media coverage of Hillary Rodham Clinton demonstrate the force of traditional gender interpretations in slanting media coverage. As a "first lady" (wife of the incumbent president), she was constructed as a kind of "gender outlaw" because she stepped outside the conventional dichotomies of citizen and wife, public and private (Brown and Gardetto, 2000, p. 22). As a political candidate in her own right, she was depicted as over-ambitious and power-hungry. Only when portrayed as a victim, in the aftermath of her husband's confession in the Monica Lewinsky case, did Hillary Rodham Clinton attract sustained sympathetic coverage from the media. This leads to a troubling conclusion: "we are to fear women with power, yet admire women with the status of victim" (Parry-Giles, 2000, p. 221). Other studies in the United States have found that the public seems to have a more positive attitude towards political candidates when they act in a way considered gender-appropriate (Chang and Hitchon, 1997) and that female politicians may actually choose to play to gender stereotypes (Kahn and Gordon, 1997). Indeed research in the United Kingdom shows that women in politics are conscious that the images and language used to describe them are different from those used to describe their male colleagues, and that this can have an impact on their ways of dealing with the media (Ross and Sreberny, 2000).

All of this adds up to a complicated scenario. For although it is clear that the image and language of politics as mediated by television, radio and the press "supports the status quo (male as norm) and regards women politicians as novelties" (Ross and Sreberny, 2000, p. 93), it is not at all clear how women can most effectively intervene in and change that system of mediation. Annabelle Sreberny and Liesbet van Zoonen (2000) point to a paradox in feminist attempts to break down the public–private division that characterizes gender definitions and relationships in social and political life.

> [There is] a depressing stability in the articulation of women's politics and communication . . . The underlying frame of reference is that women belong to the family and domestic life and men to the social world of politics and work; that femininity is about care, nurturance and compassion, and that masculinity is about efficiency, rationality and individuality. And whereas women's political activities try to undermine just that gendered distinction between public and private, it seems to remain the inevitable frame of reference to understand it. (p. 17)

The implication is that by accepting the public vs. private divide as the framework through which gender differences are analyzed and interpreted, women help to confirm the very divisions that they seek to undermine. Nevertheless, a good deal of feminist activism in relation to the public sphere is motivated by a belief that women's perspectives and agendas must be given more importance in politics, precisely so that current gender-based divisions in relation to public and private will be eroded (see Gallagher, 2001).

The Socioeconomic Framework, Ideology, and Representation

A broader move towards analyses of the socioeconomic contexts of media struc-tures and processes responds to the concerns of critics who have regarded the post-structuralist feminist concentration on "words, symbols and discourses" as inadequate to an interpolation of the larger social structures of power, and as immobilizing to feminist activist politics (Steeves and Wasko, 2002; also Rakow, 2001b). As these critics point out, media representations and gender discourses take shape within particular, and changing, socioeconomic formations which must themselves be analyzed and understood. For instance, studies of the effects of the German unification process on media structures and content noted a new emphasis on women as mothers and housewives, although in the former German Democratic Republic media portrayals generally depicted women as capable of combining paid employment and family life (Rinke, 1994). Data from Central and Eastern Europe suggest that the transformations of 1989, and the adaptation of the media to market-oriented demands have resulted in previously absent representations of women as sexual objects (Zarkov, 1997; Zabelina, 1996; Azhgikhina, 1995).

As economic ideologies change, so do media discourses and representations. In Asia, for example, the media in many countries have recently seen a spectacular transformation. Dozens of new commercial cable and satellite channels have pro-liferated, and the privatization of old state-run media has led to an explosion of new market-oriented content. Current research from this region highlights the tensions and conflicts that such changes introduce into representations of women. For instance, studies from India and Singapore point to the often contradictory ways in which the media and advertising are accommodating to women's multiple identities in contemporary society. Images of the "new woman" as an independent consumer whose femininity remains intact, or as a hard-headed individualist, whose feminine side must be sacrificed, illustrate changing social and economic demands on women – whose "femaleness" never-theless remains the core issue (Basu, 2001; Malhotra and Rogers, 2000; Munshi, 1998; Bajpai, 1997; Lee, 1998). Economic issues intersect with political analysis in a number of these studies. For instance Mankekar (1993) argues that Indian television of the early 1990s addressed upwardly mobile women as the prime market for consumer goods, while simultaneously trying to engage them in the project of constructing a national culture through television serializations of the great Indian mythological epics – the Ramayana and the Mahabharata – in which women's role in the family, community and nation was depicted as cardinal. So the "liberties" of consumerism were in constant conflict with the duties of nation and family-building as presented in the televized epics.

Going beyond the issue of socioeconomic formations, therefore, some femin-ists have grappled with the wider concept of political ideology, focusing on how women's representation is frequently a site on which wider, public meanings are inscribed. At the simplest level, it is clear that in all parts of the world, at different times in history, representations and images of women have been used as symbols of political aspirations and social change. An obvious example was the widespread use of particular asexual, "emancipated" female images in Soviet culture: the confident, sturdy woman on her tractor, on the farm, or in the factory. As various recent commentators have pointed out, images of this kind never reflected existing reality: "the social realist tradition was intended to create an ideal reality and utilised this model to portray the exemplary woman of the radiant Communist future" (Lipovskaya, 1994, p. 124; see also Voronina, 1994; Azhgikhina, 1995).

In such a situation female imagery becomes a metaphor for a particular political ideology, rather than a representation of women's lives. In her analysis of the powerful media definitions of womanhood in revolutionary China, Elizabeth Croll (1995) argues that "imaging" actually became a substitute for living or experience:

> The eyes of the billboard- or poster-women overlooked the foreground as if it was of no importance, and it frequently was blurred in pictorial representation. . . .
> If we combine this long-sighted distancing revolutionary gaze with its semantic equivalent, that is the language of rhetoric . . . then we have what might be called a "rhetorical gaze". The main characteristic of this rhetorical gaze is that it is separate from the experience of the body and its senses and ultimately denies it. In these circumstances women began to represent their own experience or permit their experience to be represented rhetorically in speech, picture and text as if the rhetoric constituted their experience. (p. 81)

The disjuncture between image and reality becomes profound when governments attempt to mobilize people for certain kinds of social change. In a retrospective analysis, Graham-Brown (1988) gives examples from post-independence Algeria and Nasser's Egypt, where "modernist" and westernized images of women were used as emblems of progress and enlightenment. In contemporary Egypt, according to Lila Abu-Lughod (1993), the ideological message of certain "national interest" television serials conflicts with the experience of life in particular communities. In all these accounts, women emerge as the "sacred markers of culture" (Basu, 2001, p. 184), a point well-illustrated in Dulali Nag's (1991) analysis of contemporary sari advertisements in Bengal. Designed to appeal to the urban, middle-class woman, these ads mingled images of rural utopias, the "high" culture of Bengali poets, and women's domesticity to conjure up a notion of "essential" Bengali tradition. Thus a discourse of modernist consumerism is filtered through the prism of a nostalgic national identity, with women at the center of both.

In his analysis of global shifts in the relations between capital and class, Murdock (2000) points out that emerging narratives of this kind – which reflect and contain several cross-cutting discourses – demonstrate how the meta-ideology of cosmopolitan consumerism and its attendant "new" middle class stratum are both profoundly gendered. The interplay between gender and class in the creation of contemporary consumerist identities – identities that invoke both traditional cultural specificity and a modern, cosmopolitan self – is central to much feminist scholarship (Basu, 2001; Nag, 1991). Indeed this strand of work has lately begun to emerge as one of feminism's significant contributions to the overall field of media and communication studies. For by demonstrating how, in an era of globalizing capitalism, "middle-class women in particular are at the epicentre of the unfolding struggle over the terms of (the) transition" towards consumer modernity, feminist research provides an important entry point for a revitalized and urgently needed class analysis of contemporary change in the organization of communications and culture (Murdock, 2000, p. 24).

Connecting Feminist Theory, Research and Media Practice

The intellectual project that began so hesitantly in the 1970s around "women and media" issues very quickly developed into fully-fledged feminist theorizing. Through the 1980s and 1990s it moved through more complex understandings of power and its manifestations; of gender and identity – its situated, shifting, performative aspects; through ethnographies that brought a shift in the conceptualization of media processes, texts and audiences and the "leaky" boundaries between them; into postmodernism and its concern to throw into question the very notion of "subjecthood"; and on into the realm of cyberfeminism where the concept of the cyborg would transcend all dichotomies – including female/male – promising a genderless utopia. Where does this intellectual journey leave feminist media theory and practice today?

In her review of the contribution of feminist theory to communication studies Andrea Press (2000) distinguishes between the impact of feminism within the academy and in the wider world. On the first point she is optimistic, arguing that the insights of feminism "have made it impossible for us to proceed comfortably with business as usual" (p. 40). Yet it is difficult to find much empirical evidence for this. For instance, as Graham Murdock (2000) points out, despite the wealth of feminist writing on the inter-relationships between gender and class, most class analysts appear to be unable – or unwilling – to assimilate these insights within their existing models and theories (p. 20). Ann Gray (1999) too speaks of the "apparent impermeability of 'male' work to feminist scholarship" (p. 33), particularly in the traditionally gendered field of political economy in media studies. Here Murdock's (2000) integration of feminist perspectives into his "reconstruction" of a class analysis of communication and culture in emerging capital formations is an illuminating exception.

A glance at most current textbooks and curriculae will bear out Ann Gray's assertion that "feminist-inspired work is constantly kept at the margins of media studies" (1999, p. 25). For example, introducing the rationale behind a recently published collection of essays for use in mass communication courses, Elizabeth Toth explains the need that she and her students felt to fill a gap:

> The book took form, in recognition that most standard text-books did not discuss mass communication from the standpoints of gender and diversity. The books we looked at had an air of "objectivity" but no acknowledgement of whose objectivity and experience we were meant to believe. Because we were grappling with material that did not speak to our own gender and diversity, we thought others might have the same problems. (Toth & Aldoory, 2001, pp. viii–ix)

The uncanny resemblance between this contemporary account and that of the Women's Studies Group of the CCCS (quoted at the beginning of this chapter) would seem to indicate that, despite the passage of twenty-five years, "business as usual" remains rather firmly entrenched within academic institutions. In fact, as Charlotte Brunsdon has pointed out, feminist media scholarship has been only semi-institutionalized within the academy. Brunsdon speaks of "academic parallel universes in which a space of difference is cultivated alongside, in opposition to and sometimes in dialogue with, the mainstream" (1997, p. 170). Speaking from this space of difference, feminist criticism thus remains "a subordinate field which although it has had to transform its own foundational category, 'woman,' and has produced a quite substantial literature still seems to have had remarkably little impact on the wider contours of the discipline" (p. 169).

But what of the impact of feminist scholarship in the wider world outside the academy (Press, 2000)? On this point Andrea Press is less positive, believing that the epistemological breakthroughs of feminist theory have yet to be transformed "into ones with actual political effects and impacts" (p. 40). Yet here it seems important, as Liesbet van Zoonen has reminded us, to make a clear distinction between the different struggles in which feminism is involved. It is a "double-edged" social movement: on the one hand, an interest group which lobbies and struggles for social and legal changes beneficial to women; on the other, an intellectual force that aims to challenge cultural "preoccupations and routines" concerning femininity and gender.

> Undeniably, both struggles are political and inform each other, nevertheless, they are of a different kind resulting in different interactions with the media and different requirements of media performance. (1994, p. 152)

These "different interactions" and "different requirements" mean that feminism(s) may engage with media processes and developments in ways that appear to be completely unconnected but can in fact be understood within a shared political framework. Jenny Sundén (2001) gives a useful example of this when she explores how new information and communication technologies are conceptualized – and used – quite differently within two strands of cyberfeminism. One revolves around the sophisticated theoretical debates about identity, most obviously epitomized by Donna Haraway's notion of the gender-less (or gender-free) cyborg. The other is linked to a concrete political movement to construct spaces for women within the structure of the Internet, and to develop women's global networking – thus insisting on the foundational nature of the very category "woman" that cyborg theory strives to abolish. But both approaches arise from a common search for cybersites of "difference" within the patriarchal structures of the Net. Sundén argues that this "doubleness" at the heart of feminism should be seen not as a divisive fault-line but as a dynamic force that can link very different women, in the sense that each "side" will embrace elements from the other. Or, to take van Zoonen's formulation, they will "inform each other" so that the boundaries of each are in constant movement.

This element of push and pull between theorizing, research and activism has been a constant feature of feminist media studies since the earliest days. Over the past twenty years women have not been content merely to denounce biases and inequities in the established media. Women have created and used countless alternative and participatory communication channels to support their struggles, defend their rights, promote reflection, diffuse their own forms of representation. Pilar Riaño (1994) argues that this process has made women the primary subjects of struggle and change in communication systems, by developing oppositional and proactive alternatives that influence language, representations and communication technologies.

Standing outside the mainstream, "women's movement media" have certainly played a crucial role in women's struggle around the world. Part of a global networking, consciousness-raising and knowledge creation project, they have enabled women to communicate through their own words and images. If print and publishing were initially the most widely used formats, in the past two decades other media such as music, radio, video, film and – increasingly – the new communication technologies have also been important. Over the same period, in most regions there has been a steady growth of women's media associations and networks, and an increase in the number of women working in mainstream media (many examples of such developments worldwide can be found in Gallagher and Quindoza-Santiago, 1994, and Allen, Rush, and Kaufman, 1996).

One of the most far-sighted of these initiatives was pioneered by Betty Friedan and the late Nancy Woodhull, when they established the Women, Men and Media project in 1988. Their aim was to carry out regular studies that would track progress, and then release the findings at symposia that would bring together journalists and media executives with activists and academics. Together, these usually separate groups would critically examine the values and priorities that result in the patterns of gender representation we find in the media. The establishment of Women, Men and Media signaled a new development, and a realization that without dialogue – between researchers, activists, advertisers, journalists, radio and television producers – there could be no way out of the impasse in which the debate about gender representation appeared to be locked at that time

(Gibbons, 2000). And indeed, over the past decade, many activist groups around the world – from Cotidiano Mujer in Uruguay, the Centre for Advocacy and Research in India, to Women's Media Watch in Jamaica, to name just a few of them – have opted for a similar strategy (Gallagher, 2001). Central to the recent work of groups like these has been a search for data, concepts and language capable of involving media professionals, and of stimulating them to think about gender as a factor in the choices they make and the representations they produce. In essence, it involves the "translation" of what are often abstract and esoteric academic research findings into terms that strike a chord with media people.

How then can we sum up the role of feminist scholarship and feminist activism in relation to media theory and media practice? Manisha Chaudary uses an apposite analogy: "It's like riding a tiger: once you get on you can't get off. It's a continuous process. You cannot stop it. There is no beginning, there is no end" (quoted in Gallagher, 2001, p. 183). And indeed, the development of the media industries themselves presents constant and ever more complex problems for feminist scholarship. Yet feminist media criticism survives, despite the regular appearance of "post-feminist" arguments and the onslaught of more overt backlash. Stuart Hall, the first director of the Centre for Contemporary Cultural Studies at the University of Birmingham, helps us to understand how and why this happens in his account of what was perceived as the "eruption" of feminism into the work of the Centre in the 1970s. He says, "Many of us in the Centre – mainly, of course, men – thought it was time there was good feminist work in cultural studies. . . . Being good transformed men, we were opening the door to feminist studies. And yet, when it broke in through the window, every single unsuspected resistance rose to the surface – fully installed patriarchal power, which believed it had disavowed itself" (Hall, 1992, p. 282). Indeed, the disruptive challenge of feminism – even when it is considered theoretically and politically desirable – can be very difficult to handle. And perhaps that is how it should be.

Disruption, as Todorov (1977) tells us in his account of the structure of narrative, causes disequilibrium. This is followed by action to re-establish equilibrium. The second equilibrium is similar to the first, but the two are never identical. This is as good a description of the impact of feminism as I can find – disrupting the narrative, which is then restored to equilibrium by other forces, but is never quite the same as before.

References

Abu-Lughod, L. (1993). Finding a place for Islam: Egyptian television serials and the national interest. *Public Culture*, 5(3), 493–513.

Allen, D., Rush, R. R., and Kaufman, S. J. (eds.) (1996). *Women Transforming Communications: Global intersections*. London: Sage.

Amos, V. and Parmar, P. (1984). Challenging feminist imperialism. *Feminist Review*, 17, 3–19.

Ang, I. and Hermes, J. (1991). Gender and/in media consumption. In J. Curran and M. Gurevitch (eds.), *Mass Media and Society*. London: Edward Arnold, pp. 307–28.

Azhgikhina, N. (1995). Back to the kitchen. *Women's Review of Books*, 12(8), 13–14.

Bajpai, S. (1997). Thoroughly modern misses: women on Indian television. *Women: A Cultural Review*, 8(3), 303–10.

Basu, S. (2001). The blunt cutting-edge: the construction of sexuality in the Bengali "feminist" magazine Sananda. *Feminist Media Studies*, 1(2), 179–96.

Bhasin, K. (1994). Women and communication alternatives: Hope for the next century. *Media Development*, 41(2), 4–7.

Bhasin, K. and Khan, N. S. (1986). *Some Questions on Feminism and its Relevance in South Asia*. New Delhi: Kali for Women.

Börjesson, F. (1995). Ladies "excuse me" – gender problems in the written press. *Language and Gender*. Göteborg: University of Göteborg, pp. 113–22.

Braidotti, R. (1989). The politics of ontological difference. In T. Brennan (ed.), *Between Feminism and Psychoanalysis*. London: Routledge, pp. 89–105.

Brown, M. E. and Gardetto, D. C. (2000). Representing Hillary Rodham Clinton: gender, meaning and news media. In A. Sreberny and L. van Zoonen (eds.), *Gender, Politics and Communication*. Cresskill, NJ: Hampton Press, pp. 21–51.

Brunsdon, C. (1996). A thief in the night: stories of feminism in the 1970s at CCCS. In D. Morley and K. Chen (eds.), *Stuart Hall: Critical dialogues in cultural studies*. London: Routledge, pp. 276–86.

Brunsdon, C. (1997). *Screen Tastes: Soap opera to satellite dishes*. London: Routledge.

Brunsdon, C. (2000). *The Feminist, the Housewife, and the Soap Opera*. Oxford: Clarendon Press.

Brunsdon, C., D'Acci, J., and Spigel, L. (eds.) (1997). *Feminist Television Criticism*. Oxford: Clarendon Press.

Carter, C., Branston, G., and Allan, S. (eds.) (1998). *News, Gender and Power*. London: Routledge.

Ceulemans, M. and Fauconnier, G. (1979). *Mass Media: The image, role and social conditions of women*. Paris: UNESCO.

Chang, C. and Hitchon, J. (1997). Mass media impact on voter response to women candidates: theoretical development. *Communication Theory*, 7(1), 29–52.

Chatterji, P. (1989). The Nationalist resolution of the women's question. In K. Sangari and S. Vaid (eds.), *Recasting Women: Essays in colonial history*. New Delhi: Kali for Women, pp. 233–53.

Corner, J. (1991). Meaning, genre and context. In J. Curran and M. Gurevitch (eds.), *Mass Media and Society*. London: Edward Arnold, pp. 267–84.

Croll, E. (1995). *Changing Identities of Chinese Women: Rhetoric, experience and self-perception in twentieth-century China*. London: Zed Books.

de Lauretis, T. (1987). *Technologies of Gender: Essays on theory, film and fiction*. Bloomington: Indiana University Press.

Eaton, C. (2001). The practice of feminist pedagogy. *Feminist Media Studies*, 1(3), 390–1.

Friedan, B. (1963). *The Feminine Mystique*. New York: W.W. Norton.

Gallagher, M. (1981). *Unequal Opportunities: The case of women and the media*. Paris: UNESCO.

Gallagher, M. (2001). *Gender Setting: New agendas for media monitoring and advocacy*. London: Zed Books.

Gallagher, M. and Quindoza-Santiago, L. (eds.) (1994). *Women Empowering Communication: A resource book on women and the globalisation of media*. London/Manila/New York: WACC/Isis International/IWTC.

Ganguly, K. (1992). Accounting for others: feminism and representation. In L. F. Rakow (ed.), *Women Making Meaning: New feminist directions in communication*. New York: Routledge, pp. 60–79.

Geraghty, C. (1996). Feminism and media consumption. In J. Curran, D. Morley, and V. Walkerdine (eds.), *Cultural Studies and Communications*. London: Arnold, pp. 306–22.

Gibbons, S. (2000). Women, men and media. In E. V. Burt (ed.), *Women's Press Organizations 1881–1999*. Westport, CT: Greenwood Press, pp. 256–64.

Gillespie, M. (1995). *Television, Ethnicity and Cultural Change*. London: Routledge.

Graham-Brown, S. (1988). *Images of Women: The portrayal of women in photography of the Middle East 1860–1950*. London: Quartet Books.

Gray, A. (1992). *Video Playtime: The gendering of a leisure technology*. London: Routledge.

Gray, A. (1995). I want to tell you a story: The narratives of Video Playtime. In B. Skeggs (ed.), *Feminist Cultural Theory: Process and production*. Manchester: Manchester University Press, pp. 153–68.

Gray, A. (1999). Audience and reception research in retrospect: the trouble with audiences. In P. Alasuutari (ed.), *Rethinking the Media Audience*. London: Sage, pp. 22–37.

Hall, S. (1992). Cultural studies and its theoretical legacies. In L. Grossberg, C. Nelson, and P. Treichler (eds.), *Cultural Studies*. London: Routledge, pp. 277–94.

Haraway, D. (1991). *Simians, Cyborgs and Women: The reinvention of nature*. New York: Routledge.

hooks, b. (1981). *Ain't I a Woman? Black women and feminism*. Boston: South End Press.

Houston, M. (1992). The politics of difference: race, class, and women's communication. In L. F. Rakow (ed.), *Women Making Meaning: New feminist directions in communication*. New York: Routledge, pp. 45–59.

Huyssen, A. (1986). Mass culture as woman: modernism's other. In T. Modleski (ed.), *Studies in Entertainment*. Bloomington: Indiana University Press, pp. 188–207.

Janus, N. Z. (1977). Research on sex-roles in the mass media: toward a critical approach. *Insurgent Sociologist*, 7(3), 19–30.

Kahn, K. F. and Gordon, A. (1997). How women campaign for the US Senate. In P. Norris (ed.), *Women, Media and Politics*. New York: Oxford University Press, pp. 59–76.

Koski, A. (1994). *Valtiomies: valiomieheyttä ja maskuliinista virtuositeettia. U. Kekkosen ja E. Rehn in valtiotaito kuvasemiootticessa analyysissä* [Statesman: masculine virtuosity. U. Kekkonen and E. Rehn in semiotic analysis]. Helsinki: Finnish Broadcasting Company, Yleisradio report 7/1994.

Lee, C. W. (1998). Feminism in Singapore's advertising: a rising voice. *Media Asia*, 25(4), 193–7.

Lipovskaya, O. (1994). The mythology of womanhood in contemporary "Soviet" culture. In A. Posadskaya (ed.), *Women in Russia: A new era in Russian feminism*. London: Verso, pp. 123–34.

Lont, C. M. and Friedley, S. (eds.) (1989). *Beyond Boundaries: Sex and gender diversity in communication*. Fairfax, VA: George Mason University Press.

Malhotra, S. and Rogers, E. M. (2000). Satellite television and the new Indian woman. *Gazette: The International Journal for Communication Studies*, 62(5), 407–29.

Mankekar, P. (1993). Television tales and a woman's rage: a nationalist recasting of Draupadi's "disrobing." *Public Culture*, 5(3), 469–92.

McRobbie, A. (1997). "Bridging the gap": feminism, fashion and consumption. *Feminist Review*, 55, 73–89.

Media Monitoring Project (1999). Biased? Gender, politics and the media. In *Redefining Politics: South African women and democracy*. Johannesburg: Commission on Gender Equality, pp. 161–7.

MediaWatch (1995). *Women's Participation in the News: Global media monitoring project*. Toronto: MediaWatch.

Mohanty, C. T. (1984). Under Western eyes: feminist scholarship and colonial discourses. *Feminist Review*, 30, 61–88.

Moraga, C. and Anzaldúa, G. (eds.) (1981). *This Bridge Called My Back: Writings by radical women of color*. New York: Kitchen Table Press.

Munshi, S. (1998). Wife/mother/daughter-in-law: multiple avatars of homemaker in 1990s Indian advertising. *Media, Culture and Society*, 20(4), 573–91.

Murdock, G. (2000). Reconstructing the ruined tower: contemporary communications and questions of class. In J. Curran and M. Gurevitch (eds.), *Mass Media and Society*. London: Arnold, pp. 7–26.

Nag, D. (1991). Fashion, gender and the Bengali middle class. *Public Culture*, 3(2), 93–112.

Norris, P. (ed.) (1997). *Women, Media, and Politics*. New York: Oxford University Press.

Parry-Giles, S. J. (2000). Mediating Hillary Rodham Clinton: television news practices and image-making in the postmodern age. *Critical Studies in Media Communication*, 17(2), 205–26.

Press, A. (2000). Recent developments in feminist communication theory: difference, public sphere, body and technology. In J. Curran and M. Gurevitch (eds.), *Mass Media and Society*. London: Arnold, pp. 27–43.

Rakow, L. F. (1992). The field reconsidered. In L. F. Rakow (ed.), *Women Making Meaning: New feminist directions in communication*. New York: Routledge, pp. 3–17.

Rakow, L. F. (2001a). Teaching against the text. *Feminist Media Studies*, 1(3), 381–3.

Rakow, L. F. (2001b). Feminists, media, free speech. *Feminist Media Studies*, 1(1), 41–4.

Riaño, Pilar (ed.) (1994). *Women in Grassroots Communication: Furthering social change*. London: Sage.

Riley, D. (1992). A short history of some preoccupations. In J. Butler and J. Scott (eds.), *Feminists Theorize the Political*. New York: Routledge, pp. 121–9.

Rinke, A. (1994). Wende-Bilder, television images of women in Germany in transition. In E. Boa and J. Wharton (eds.), *Women and the WENDE: Social effects and cultural reflections on the German reunification process*. Amsterdam: Rodopi, BV, pp. 124–38.

Ross, K. and Sreberny, A. (2000). Women in the House: media representation of British politicians. In A. Sreberny and L. van Zoonen (eds.), *Gender, Politics and Communication*. Cresskill, NJ: Hampton Press, pp. 79–99.

Seiter, E. (1990). Making distinctions in TV audience research: case study of a troubling interview. *Cultural Studies*, 4(1), 61–84.

Seiter, E. (1999). *Television and New Media Audiences*. Oxford: Oxford University Press.

Skjeie, H. (1994). Hva kvinnene gjör for politikken [Women in Norwegian politics]. In F. Eeg-Henriksen, B. Fougner, and T. B. Pedersen (eds.), *Backlash i Norge? Rapport fra en Konferanse om Kvinner i 90-åra*. Oslo: Norwegian Research Council, Working Paper 1, pp. 121–31.

Spears, G. and Seydegart, K., with Gallagher, M. (2000). *Who Makes the News? Global media monitoring project 2000*. London: World Association for Christian Communication.

Spivak, G. C. (1988). Can the subaltern speak? In C. Nelson and L. Grossberg (eds.), *Marxism and the Interpretation of Culture*. Chicago: University of Illinois Press, pp. 271–313.

Sreberny, A. and van Zoonen, L. (eds.) (2000). *Gender, Politics and Communication*. Cresskill, NJ: Hampton Press.

Steeves, H. L. (1987). Feminist theories and media studies. *Critical Studies in Mass Communication*, 4(2), 95–135.

Steeves, H. L. and Wasko, J. (2002). Feminist theory and political economy: toward a friendly alliance. In E. Meehan and E. Riordan (eds.), *Sex and Money*. Minneapolis: University of Minnesota Press, pp. 16–29.

Sundén, J. (2001). What happened to difference in cyberspace? The (re)turn of the she-cyborg. *Feminist Media Studies*, 1(2), 215–32.

Sunder Rajan, R. (1993). *Real and Imagined Women: Gender, culture and postcolonialism*. London: Routledge.

Thomas, L. (1995). In love with Inspector Morse: feminist subculture and quality television. *Feminist Review*, 51, 1–25.

Todorov, T. (1977). *The Poetics of Prose*. Ithaca: Cornell University Press.

Toth, E. L. and Aldoory, L. (eds.) (2001). *The Gender Challenge to Media: Diverse voices from the field*. Cresskill, NJ: Hampton Press.

Tuchman, G. (1978). The Symbolic annihilation of women by the mass media. In G. Tuchman, A. C. Daniels, and J. Benét (eds.), *Hearth and Home: Images of women in the media*. New York: Oxford University Press, pp. 3–38.

Valdivia, A. N. (1995). Feminist media studies in a global setting: beyond binary contradictions and into multicultural spectrums. In A. N. Valdivia (ed.), *Feminism, Multiculturalism, and the Media: Global diversities*. Thousand Oaks: Sage, pp. 7–29.

Valdivia, A. N. (2000). Theorizing frustration: media culture and gendered identities. In A. N. Valdivia, *A Latina in the Land of Hollywood and Other Essays on Media Culture*. Tucson: University of Arizona Press, pp. 3–21.

Valdivia, A. N. (2001). Rhythm is gonna get you! Teaching evaluations and the feminist multicultural classroom. *Feminist Media Studies*, 1(3), 387–9.

van Zoonen, L. (1991). Feminist perspectives on the media. In J. Curran and M. Gurevitch (eds.), *Mass Media and Society*. London: Edward Arnold, pp. 33–54.

van Zoonen, L. (1994). *Feminist Media Studies*. London: Sage.

van Zoonen, L. (2000). Broken hearts, broken dreams? Politicians and their families in popular culture. In A. Sreberny and L. van Zoonen (eds.), *Gender, Politics and Communication*. Cresskill, NJ: Hampton Press, pp. 101–19.

Voronina, O. (1994). Virgin Mary or Mary Magdalene? The construction and reconstruction of sex during the perestroika period. In A. Posadskaya (ed.), *Women in Russia: A new era in Russian feminism*. London: Verso, pp. 135–45.

Walkerdine, V. (1986). Video replay: families, films and fantasy. In V. Burgin, J. Donald, and C. Kaplan (eds.), *Formations of Fantasy*. London: Methuen, pp. 167–99.

Women's Studies Group (1978). Trying to do feminist intellectual work. In Women's Studies Group (ed.), *Women Take Issue: Aspects of women's subordination*. London/Birmingham: Hutchinson and the Centre for Contemporary Cultural Studies, University of Birmingham, pp. 7–17.

Zabelina, T. (1996). Sexual violence towards women. In H. Pilkington (ed.), *Gender, Generation and Identity in Contemporary Russia*. London: Routledge, pp. 169–86.

Zarkov, D. (1997). Pictures on the wall of love: Motherhood, womanhood and nationhood in Croatian media. *European Journal of Women's Studies*, 4(3), 305–39.

CHAPTER TWO

New Horizons for Communication Theory in the New Media Age

Denis McQuail

The expression "new horizons" implies either a scanning of the near future or a journey to new places, with discoveries ahead. The metaphor implies that communication theory has a goal of its own or can and should be pursued for its own sake, neither of which is the case. There is no "perfect state" of communication that theory can identify or help come true in human affairs. The role of theory is best conceived of as a navigational tool on journeys to various destinations that we choose for independent reasons, such as the goal of democracy, or freedom, or social harmony as variously defined. Theory in general furnishes ideas and concepts for understanding what is going on and for expressing that understanding. It provides tools of analysis and ways of collecting and integrating the results of observation and experience. It can offer alternative scenarios of what might happen under given conditions, and it continuously guides inquiry. Although there is no single ideal form of communication in society, there are better and worse forms of communicative practice, whether in mass communication, organizational communication or interpersonal communication and consequently no ideal place for a branch of communication theory that is "normative" as well as scientific.

The field of communication science (sometimes under other headings such as "communication and media studies") has prospered in recent years, especially because of its obvious relevance to key social and technological changes taking place in the "information society." Despite its apparent success, it is extremely fragmented and vulnerable for a number of underlying reasons. Reasons for disarray in theory include the following:

- Theoretical paradigms are fractured and disconnected as a result of competition between new and old intellectual traditions, encapsulated by the modernist–postmodernist divide. More fundamental, perhaps, is the divergence of academic approaches ranging from quantitative social science to literary theory. There has always been uncertainty about the core discipline of communication and much dispute about what is the primary object of study as well as about methods and approaches. The enormous diversity of communication phenomena is partly responsible.

- There has been a decline or loss of a clear tradition of critical theory and an apparently diminished social commitment, as well as lack of ethical and moral direction. The postmodernist turn has played some part in this, but it is a consequence of wider changes in the spirit of the times.
- The familiar "marketization" of media on a large and global scale has tended to drive theory and research in the direction of finding commercial opportunities rather than solutions to social, ethical or philosophical problems.
- The appearance of "new media" and new landscapes that theory has not yet been able to incorporate within existing frameworks of thinking about communication and society has added to the current confusion.

It is against this background that I would like to sketch one view of the main options and agenda items facing those who work in this field. If there was an "old communication theory," suitable for older media, especially with reference to political communication and democracy, it was built around an ideal type of *mass communication* to which new media do not conform. This theory emphasized the power of centrally controlled media transmitting uniform views and information to a largely passive mass public, with controlling and unifying effects.

Changes in media and communication have presented a series of challenges to communication systems and at the same time to theory. These can be summarized as follows:

- The increasing proliferation of channels of communication and the abundance of supply of information of all kinds.
- There are many new kinds of communication channels and spaces and a continually changing "map" of uses.
- Communications are being re-institutionalized in new forms of organization.
- The main pattern of communication flow is changing in its balance from the "one to many" form of traditional mass media to consultatory and interactive forms.
- Communication is being delocalized and speeded up.
- New technologies and systems offer both more freedom and more opportunities for surveillance and control.
- Along with innovation comes much flux and uncertainty.

Three main dimensions still structure the field, despite the period of rapid change that we are undergoing. These provide the pillars for theoretical development. One can simply be described (although its content is not simple) as *fundamental theory of communication*. It refers to three main branches of theory:

one dealing with social relations and influence as mediated by communication; another with information processing and analysis; lastly cultural theory, especially relating to the giving and taking of meaning.

A second dimension relates to the carriers or vehicles of communication in their social-technical forms and interactions with the other conditions and circumstances. I will refer to this as *medium theory*, although that is too narrow a term. It mainly originates in a response to the development of successive applications of communication technologies starting with print, rather than in any new idea or any remarkable transformation of content as communicated. It has now been given fresh impetus by the transition of computer mediated communication to the status of mass medium.

The third strand relates to *normative theory* in its widest sense. Arguably, the field has been driven for much of its existence by critical views of society and diverse ethical concerns. The basis for and form of concern has continually changed and the relevant standards as well, but the "normative" imperative remains in place. The remainder of this article is mainly directed at the second and third of the dimensions mentioned, even if the first may still be the most important.

Technology Issues and "Medium Theory"

One does not need to be a technological determinist to believe that the form of technology underlying a medium *can* profoundly influence the content and also the reception of what is communicated and possibly the effects. Communication technology invites new applications and forms of expression and offers new choices to its users.

To go further than this rather vague truism, we need to develop what has been called "medium theory" (e.g. by Meyrowitz, 1993) rather than just theory of the media or of media and society. In this context, what we call a "medium" usually, but not exclusively, has a reference to the specific technology involved. Quite a lot has been done already to rescue the notion of a medium from a purely technological definition, even though it becomes harder, as a result, to arrive at any definition or clear boundaries of what we are talking about. A "medium" is any distinctive social–cultural–technological carrier of meanings and "medium theory" can relate to any kind of influence stemming from the particular communication vehicle in use. However, if the term medium is broadly used as suggested the line of influence back to any particular aspect of the medium, for instance some key technological property, may be very indirect and tenuous.

Characteristic of this type of medium theory is a weak form of determinism, which is hard to escape from without losing the point. The alleged cause or *source* of influence is usually some attribute of the given medium, whether technological or social or cultural, but often a combination of all three. What is influenced can be either the message (meaning) itself as sent or taken, the cultural form in which it is expressed, the receiver, the typical experience of use, or the culture and society in which the communicative transaction takes place. In recent thinking, communication technologies are also themselves regarded as having a range of "meanings" in the sense of perceived identities and qualities that have to be negotiated between producers and users.

Medium theory offers a range of options. One is to follow Innis (1951) and McLuhan (1964) and to differentiate between channels or modalities according to their dominance in a certain historical era (e.g. "the age of print" or "age of television"). This seemed fruitful in writing a retrospective interpretation of print media and for a moment at least promising in relation to radio. In another version of medium theory, appealing to social psychologists, educators, and propagandists, media with different sense-relationships have been compared in terms of their effectiveness for transmitting information with reference to their verbal, visual or aural characteristics. The empirical testing of propositions has produced little on which to base any theory in this vein.

Thirdly, a less technological, more cultural, version of medium theory has proposed that different media have a "bias" for certain kinds of subject matter and for certain kinds of effect (e.g. being more or less emotional than rational/ logical). The "bias" of a medium is an outcome of sense characteristics, audience perceptions and attributed qualities. The selection and presentation of messages follows a certain "logic" which maximizes the supposed potential of the medium, but also selects out certain consequences as more likely than others.

This branch of medium theory has, for instance, emphasized the bias of television towards emotional, personal, intimate and pseudo-interactive relation-ships between presenters/performers and audiences. In so far as the medium of television is defined in this way it affects the way in which would-be commun-icators, for instance journalists or politicians, shape their messages, with possible longer term effects on public ways of knowing, perceiving and relating to society. The notion of "media logic" as a shaper of news and information applies in such situations (Altheide and Snow, 1979).

Nevertheless, existing "medium theory" as applied to mass communication is vitiated by the fact that all technologically-based media are hybrid compositions, in which technological, social, and cultural factors all play a part and cannot be separated out. Media with names such as print, film, radio, or television are arbitrary constructions, often sharing the same features of content or presentation. The correct diagnosis of what is actually the *dominant* feature of any of today's wide range of media also requires a good knowledge of the structures of media systems and organizations, including inter-country and inter-cultural variations.

In practice a *medium* cannot really be defined independently of its many per-ceived attributes or its content. It is inevitably an unstable construction. No generalization about the unique consequences of any one of the familiar public mass media is ever likely to be possible. The same is true of the Internet. The perennial difficulty of distinguishing between consequences of the *medium*, of the *message* carried and of the many relevant conditions of *reception* continues to be an additional reason for caution about predicting the consequences of new information technology. The new forms of communication that are emerging are also likely to prove less new, unique and distinctive once they are integrated into settled patterns of use, along with existing media.

The most recent branch of medium theory focuses on attributes of new electronic communication technology. New technology is thought to have distinctive characteristics which in their turn influence the "content" and the experience of use (see, e.g. Morris and Ogan, 1996; Jones, 1997). The new computer-based digital media are different in four main ways. First, they have enormous capacity for carrying, storing and delivering "information" at great speed. Secondly, the same "channel" can carry all known media forms in combinations and at the same time. Rather than comprising a new medium, they make the old divisions between press, film, radio, television etc. seem obsolete. Thirdly, the new technologies are essentially point-to-point rather than centre-peripheral and can also give rise to many new configurations of group communication. Fourthly, they have a much higher interactive capability, which has the possibility of creating a new kind of social collectivity – the "virtual community" (see Jones, 1997).

The age of "mass media," with their supposed society-wide effects, is often said to be over (this was also said at least 30 years ago). An image of a society in which there is much more intense and diverse *inter*communication begins to emerge. However (leaving aside the evident survival and continued growth of "mass media" and the paradoxical notion that the "new medium" of Internet has become a mass medium), there are a number of alternative and equally plausible options concerning the direction of effects (it appears again) of new media. Interactive technology has a bias towards individuation in media use, implying a break-up of older style mass media audiences based on shared space and social condition. The communicative experience also becomes less "social" in some respects. But, on the other hand, there is also an enhanced possibility for new and closer ties with a wider circle of like-minded individuals, a sense, even if illusory, of intimacy available on-line. This is the "virtual community" mentioned already, although doubts abound about how far it meets the traditional criteria of community.

The possibilities for new media that are now emerging do not only alter the forms of individual expression and representation. They also potentially challenge the dominance of existing social contexts and relationships by their capacity to overcome limits of space and time. They are not tied within the same boundaries and rules of social interaction. The old "rules" governing access to channels of communication are also being broken (or seem to be). The older relationships of power, status, and esteem are also challenged.

Although I am supporting the case for developing new forms of "medium theory" to take seriously the possibility of a "communications revolution" based on digital technology, it is clear from what I have said already that there are severe problems for the would-be "medium theorist." Firstly, it is still unclear and open to definition what counts as a medium. Is it a means or form of encoding? Or a means of transmission or transport? Or is it a social construction of several components? We cannot simply try to sum up diverse characteristics to provide an answer. Secondly, how do we know whether a new element is dominant or essential or significant enough to change the consequences and introduce a new kind of media "bias"? Thirdly, most "new media" seem to be composite or hybrid combinations of a technology, a meaning and a certain type of use.

However we solve these problems, the category "medium theory" is still going to be subordinate to a much larger body of evidence and propositions about human communication processes, as noted above. This relates to the "encoding" of meaning in symbolic forms, the selection and transmission of ideas, information and images, the interaction between participants in communication, the decoding meaning and much more. Any effort to develop medium theory based on properties of the socio-technical vehicles alone, is bound to fail unless it also takes account of this wider body of communication theory. The question is whether the medium change or innovation is sufficient to alter or invalidate existing theory of human communication. There may be some potential for change in the established "laws" of communication theory, but change has to take place at three levels or dimensions at the same time. These are: (i) the level of uses, pragmatics and needs; (ii) the level of the medium; and (iii) the level of institutional and normative frameworks within which communication takes place.

Some lessons do not have to be relearned and there are at least some interesting possibilities for extending and revising medium theory in response, not just to communication technology in the abstract or in isolation, but to its applications in diverse contexts. Even so, the chances of solving the fundamental conundrums of communication are not, in fact, very good. The more theory tries to build on technical and technological features alone, the less progress will be made. The lessons of attempts up to now have really confirmed that what matters much more are: communicative purposes; user motive and motivation; control, access and social power in the communication situation; rights and wrongs of content, behavior and context.

The Normative Dimension of Theory

While it is too early to discern the shape of institutional frameworks in which the new communications technology will be embedded, the public imagination is already being fed with certain images. One is of unbounded freedom and diversity and also of a new beginning, an open frontier, free from old commitments, ties and loyalties. The new technologies and networks are heralded as having no national frontiers and no fixed responsibilities to any government or society, rules or regulation. They are essentially non-institutionalized as well as delocalized. They belong to their participants and have no other purpose than their users choose to give them, no larger purpose in society. The counterpart of this image is one of fear of unlicenced, unwanted and illegal uses of communication that threatens ordered society.

By contrast, the "old media" grew up under the shadow of government and political influence. They were and are subject to the laws of the countries where they are established, and they are run by professionals, whose traditions and training lead them to accept many obligations and limitations, often embodied in codes of ethics and practice and often implemented by national or industry self-regulative agencies. While the new electronic media are not outside the law, it is not always clear which law and whose law they are subject to, and in what jurisdiction they belong. In practice they are not very accountable. It is also intrinsic to the new media that the boundary between what is private and unaccountable in communication and what is public and of wider relevance is often unclear. Most of the body of legal and normative theory applying to "old media" was based on the assumption that all content was public and its producers could therefore be held responsible.

The task ahead is not that of finding ways of controlling the new media but of giving active thought to these questions and finding the appropriate form of accountability for new forms of media, and also identifying appropriate standards for very diverse uses and applications. There are benefits as well as losses in escaping from some of the traditional restrictions and controls. There are also risks in introducing controls before the nature of the new media and their dominant uses is known. It is unlikely that the fundamental issues of performance or the basic contours of the public interest in communication will change dramatically just because there is a new century and new technologies. But there will be a problem of finding new ways for handling these issues. These will certainly involve many issues of structure and control, especially concerning ownership, monopoly and concentration and public rights of access. The normative framing of issues concerning content will express enduring concerns about: morality and decency; vulnerable groups and minorities; violence and crime; national security and order; "hate" communication of all kinds; propaganda, especially for war; personal reputation; privacy; confidentiality; intellectual property. Most relevant will be the expectation of public service in respect of the "public sphere": information, debate, access, diversity and freedom.

More difficult than preventing what "society" believes to be harmful is ensuring the positive informational and cultural benefits which the media have certainly brought to society until now. At first sight, when communication systems become more or less open networks with unlimited access for all, there will be little possibility of influencing what is communicated by any act of public policy. There is also less scope for the exercise of professional responsibility within media, except in very fragmented ways. The solution, if there is one, has to lie in the increased maturity of citizens, the quality of communication itself and in the development of intermediate political, social and cultural organizations which will have more communicative power and more access to public channels. This is essentially a question of re-invigorating the "public sphere" or encouraging it to flourish. The new media forms are intrinsically very promising from this perspective.

The transition from old to new technology may be gradual enough for the invention of new ways of gaining benefits for political and social life. It is quite probable that as the new media develop and become more established, they will also adopt many of the standards and practices which already exist, if only because it is in the interests of both the providers and the users to do so. There will always be a "wild west" fringe, but the need for professionalism and accountability is not likely to disappear. Users of communication services will want sources they can trust, like and respect, and they bring expectations based on past experience to the new services.

A body of media relevant "ethical theory" has to cover a number of disparate perspectives and ideas, but all should have in common some value commitment which takes precedence over description, analysis and explanation. The strong normative bias of the communication field may stem from the origins of much communication research in criticism of the role of mass media in society. The various "theories of the press" which have been debated for half a century (see Siebert et al., 1956; Nerone, 1995; Nordenstreng, 1997) all revolve around issues of freedom, purpose, rights and responsibilities in which one or other "social ethic" or fundamental principle can be identified.

The many choices and decisions of media producers, ranging from journalists to advertisers, are also often subject to ethical criteria formulated from within their own profession or deployed by external critics and watchdogs. At the heart of the matter is the fact that public communication touches on the rights and interests of many others and the media are not exempt from expectations of decency and reason that characterize civilized society. Ethical standards are also continually applied by the general public, by audiences and by special interest groups to the alleged consequences of what the media do or fail to do. The media operate continuously in a climate of potential ethical approval or disapproval, and they are themselves one of the main vehicles for the issuing of judgments on morals and social mores.

Media-ethical theory is necessarily pluralistic in a free society, and there will never be total agreement on what can be permitted, forbidden or encouraged. It will be even more pluralistic in the future. The relation between ethical theory and medium theory will continue to be problematic. Quite often the medium theory, as defined above, has had no place for ethical implications. The consequences of technological progress in human communication may be considered either good or bad, but the drive of technology proceeds regardless of ethical judgments. These depend on how the technology is actually applied and this, in turn, is a matter for users themselves or for later assessment.

Nevertheless, ethical and normative issues cannot be evaded, and they arise as soon as the exploitations and applications of technology begin to emerge. The new interactive and multimedia communication technologies often depend for their promotion on claims to social as well as economic benefits. New identities and definitions are already widely proposed. They are acclaimed for their power to build new communities across old lines of social and cultural division, to make global citizenship a real possibility, to educate and broaden minds at low cost. The same technologies are also suspected of eroding social control and circumventing the many restrictions from society that established mass media have to live with. In any case, it is clear that value-free research into new media is scarcely possible.

In Conclusion: New Communication Developments and Society

The basic dimensions of theory concerning media and society will not be so different from the way they have been in the past, but both the social context and the communication system will be different, so that fundamental rethinking is necessary. I suspect that society will be less firmly under the control of a powerful state or government apparatus, and yet the web of individual surveillance and accountability will be more complex and finer partly as a result of communication technology. The controls will be softer, but just as constraining. Power will be less centralized and visible but still at work and less directly within democratic control, partly as a result of globalization. If these assumptions are correct, the most important concerns for theory (and for action) are likely to be as follows.

First, there is the perennial issue of social cohesion and identity, since the new global communication networks appear to challenge or undermine the identities based on space and guarded frontiers although in a different way than with the old mass media. The main challenge is to rethink the traditional notions of identity in a more global society. We need also to consider the implications of diversity and multiplication of identities opened up rather than focusing on loss of a unity that was more or less involuntary, as in the former local community and in the nation–state. Secondly, given the greater potential for central supervision of communicative transactions, it is more important than ever to consider how to ensure the dispersal of control over and accountancy for communication systems and industries, both hardware and software, even if this goes against the principles of free markets. Under the same heading the real threats of intrusive surveillance and covert registration of all activities have to be exposed.

Thirdly, the old social value of equality gains in salience in a world where access to welfare has to be mediated though complex systems of communication. It is more than ever important for democracy and social justice to ensure not just national opportunities to participate in the new networks but real distribution of informational capacities. Left to itself, under conditions of accelerating informatization, the gaps between the information rich and information poor will only widen. Again, it is clear that this will require new forms of intervention in market mechanisms, although the rationale for doing so and the forms of intervention need to be thought out.

We clearly cannot assume that technology will change everything based on the specifications of those who developed it. Technology only proposes, while society disposes. We should largely discount both the inflated expectations of the promoters of new technology and the fears of the traditionalists. We should apply the lessons of past theory and our knowledge of history to make sensible assessments of the future. We should take seriously the view that the future of communication is something that will not simply "happen," but has to be shaped, directed and guided by collective decisions as well as by the outcome of individual choices in the media market. The future of communication is in human hands rather than at the disposition of technology.

References

Altheide, D. and Snow, R. (1979). *Media Logic*. Beverly Hills, CA: Sage.

Innis, H. (1951). *The Bias of Communication*. Toronto: Toronto University Press.

Jones, S. G. (ed.) (1997). *Virtual Culture*. London: Sage.

McLuhan, M. (1964). *Understanding Media*. Toronto: Toronto University Press.

McQuail, D. (1997). After fire – Television: the past half century in broadcasting, its impact on our civilization. *Studies of Broadcasting*, 33, 7–36.

Meyrowitz, J. (1985). *No Sense of Place*. New York: Oxford University Press.

Meyrowitz, J. (1993). Medium theory. In D. Crowley and D. Mitchell (eds.), *Communication Theory Today*. Cambridge: Polity Press, pp. 50–77.

Morris, M. and Ogan, C. (1996). The internet as mass medium. *Journal of Communication*, 46(1), 39–50.

Nerone, J. C. (ed.) (1995). *Last Rights: Revisiting four theories of the press*. Urbana: Urbana University Press.

Nordenstreng, K. (1997). Beyond four theories of the press. In J. Servaes and L. Rico (eds.), *Media and Politics in Transition*. Leuven: Acco, pp. 97–109.

Siebert, F., Peterson, T., and Schramm, W. (1956). *Four Theories of the Press*. Urbana: University of Illinois Press.

CHAPTER THREE

From Modernization to Participation
The Past and Future of Development Communication in Media Studies

Robert Huesca

The study of development communication – the strategic use of communication to improve human well-being – dates to the 1960s and is marked by significant debates regarding philosophy, theory, methods, and objectives. Early influences on the field came predominantly from North American scholars who left a distinct imprint that not only reflected their particular academic orientations, but also contained Cold War traces associated with the geopolitical struggles of the time. After the first decade of theoretical and applied research, scholars worldwide questioned and criticized the dominant paradigm of development communication, calling for new theories and practices that were more responsive to and compatible with the contexts of developing nations. Over the past 20 years, scholars have debated the direction and forged new paths for the future of development communication. The study of participatory approaches to development communication has emerged as a particularly robust and fruitful direction in this area of inquiry. Many of the issues and debates surrounding the advancement of this field parallel the ideas and controversies emerging from media studies during the same time period. This chapter will trace the history of development communication in terms of the principal concepts and debates that have evolved over the years, paying particular attention to the participatory communication literature, and will suggest the likely direction of this field in the near future.

Dominant Paradigm of Development Communication

Early theories of development communication emerged primarily from North American universities and bore an interdisciplinary imprint from the fields of sociology, political science, and economics. This imprint tended to embrace a quantitative, social scientific orientation and to maintain empiricist assumptions and objectives. Early theorists of development communication sought to isolate variables, identify causal relationships, and construct middle range theories that would explain the complex process of national development and social change.

The role of communication for development was derived from modernization theories of economic and social change. As a description and diagnosis of development and underdevelopment, modernization theories addressed conceptual dimensions ranging from cognition, attitude, and behavior to society, technology, and policy. Shot across these dimensions was a binary schema pitting traditional cultures against modern societies as a way of describing the qualities differentiating underdeveloped and developed nations. The binary categories of traditional and modern provided a convenient, clear, and accessible model for understanding the stark differences that distinguished the affluent, North Atlantic nations from their impoverished, southern neighbors. Traditional societies were described as rural, bound by custom, accepting of fate, family focused, simple, and undifferentiated, in contrast to modern societies, which were viewed as urban, open to innovation, driven by individual achievement, complex, and specialized. Drawing on long-established social and economic theorists such as Ferdinand Tönnies, Max Weber, Adam Smith, and W. W. Rostow provided a substantial cloak of intellectual legitimacy to this description and explanation of comparative wealth and poverty in the world.

Early scholars of development communication adopted this binary schema in its entirety (Lerner, 1958; Rogers, 1962, 1969; Schramm, 1964). Communication questions, therefore, were largely framed in this traditional vs. modern understanding of the roots of global inequities. The clearest example of this wholesale, conceptual adoption was expressed by Rogers (1969) who described 10 qualities constituting the "subculture of the peasantry." Among other attributes, the peasantry suffered from mutual distrust in interpersonal relations, perceived limited good in the world, lack of innovativeness, limited aspirations, lack of deferred gratification, and low empathy, all of which stood as barriers to development. All of the early development communication scholars agreed that internal attributes ranging from individual traits to social structures were the root causes of underdevelopment. Pitting traditional concepts against modern understandings not only provided a description and diagnosis of contrasting societies, it prescribed the necessary steps for intervening in the process of social and economic development.

The prescription of modernization consisted largely of substituting traditional social and cultural attributes with their modern counterparts. It was a strategy that was based implicitly on neo-Darwinian beliefs of social evolution, which conceptualized the affluent North Atlantic societies as more fully evolved than most southern hemisphere nations, hence the terms "developed" and "under-developed." Adopting a social evolution perspective in development effectively naturalized and depoliticized the process of social change, obviating any examination of power or attention to ethics. Rather, development was characterized as a fateful procedure whereby poor nations should imitate the social, political, and economic steps of their wealthier counterparts. This meant cultivating a culture and society that would be prepared to shift from an agrarian, rural base to an industrial, urban core. Investigating the role and function of communication in this shift became the focus of early research in the development communication field.

For the most part, communication was defined as a linear process of information transmission. The most frequent references to communication theory invoked Shannon and Weaver's (1964) mathematical model, Lasswell's (1964) five-point model, or Berlo's (1960) Sender–Message–Channel–Receiver model. On the most basic level, communication was defined as "the process by which messages are transferred from a source to one or more receivers" (Rogers, 1969, p. 7). This early definition was persuasion and effects oriented, with most scholarly attention focused on how transmitted symbols successfully conducted desired meanings and transformed behaviors (Schramm, 1964; Shannon & Weaver, 1964).

On the most brute level, mass media were conceptualized as both an index and agent of modernization. Analyses of statistical abstracts, for example, found that greater accessibility, exposure, and use of mass media correlated positively with literacy, economic well-being, and political participation (Lerner, 1958; Schramm, 1964). Media were considered not only markers of development, but also the "great multipliers" of ideas and information that were necessary to shift beliefs and attitudes from traditional levels to modern plateaus. In response to this kind of theorizing, UNESCO drafted standards for "media sufficiency" that established for every 100 inhabitants, 10 copies of a newspaper, five radios, two cinema seats, and two televisions. Early on, then, mass media occupied unprecedented centrality in the modernization process, and communication scholars began to emerge as experts in modernization.

Despite oversimplifications such as the UNESCO standards noted above, most early development communication scholars did not naively believe that mass media unproblematically functioned as a panacea for social change. Indeed, Schramm (1964) explicitly stated that media were not sufficient to effect change, but they "can create a climate for development" (p. 131). Nevertheless, he and others relied on linear models to explore the complexity of the nexus between communication and development. Working from the communication chain of sender–message–channel–receiver, for example, scholars placed most of their attention on receivers of messages as the key to using media for development.

The receiver characteristic of high "empathy," or the ability to imagine oneself in different situations, roles and times, was a robust concept that made its way into numerous early development studies (Lerner, 1958). According to Lerner, the inability to imagine life in ways that departed from the customary was the principal obstacle facing development efforts. In contrast, high empathy or acute "psychic mobility" was identified as the predominant personality type characterizing modern societies. Mass media were considered to be "mobility multipliers" capable of hastening the cognitive transition necessary to accomplish development goals.

The intense focus on receivers was reflected in the work of numerous development scholars, but none were more influential than Rogers (1962) who fashioned an elaborate research program explained in *Diffusion of Innovations*. In this complex and detailed book, Rogers attempted to explain the process by which new ideas and practices entered, circulated, and ultimately were adopted by cultures. To be sure, the *Diffusion of Innovations* not only attended to receiver qualities, but also discussed the characteristics of innovations themselves, channels of communication, and social structure. Underlying the diffusion model, however, were assumptions and specific details that raised receiver qualities to a prominent level. Through straightforward definitions, such as, "The *adoption process* is the mental process through which an individual passes from first hearing about an innovation to final adoption" (p. 17), Rogers revealed the subtle bias that positioned individual receivers as the locus of scholarly attention. The establishment of detailed categories of receivers, such as opinion leaders, innovators, early adopters, and laggards reinforced this scholarly bias. Though it relied on theories of more complex, two-step models of communication, the *Diffusion of Innovations* ultimately reified existing assumptions of communication as linear transmission to atomized individuals.

Regardless of its conceptual biases, diffusion theory was relatively complex while eminently lucid, a combination that made it the most influential body of work in the early development communication literature. By the end of the mid-1970s, more than 2,600 diffusion research publications had been documented, most of them having been conducted in the 1960s (Rogers, 1976b). Not all of these publications, however, promoted the virtues of this line of research. Beginning in the 1970s, many Third World scholars had been trained in development communication, and they began interrogating the assumptions and biases of the dominant paradigm.

Questioning the Dominant Paradigm

In the 1970s, scholars from developing nations began deconstructing the dominant paradigm of communication for development and pointing to new directions for research. Although flaws in the conceptualization and administration of diffusion of innovations projects, for example, were identified in Africa and Asia

(Röling, Ascroft, & Chege, 1976; Shingi & Mody, 1976), the challenge to the dominant paradigm of development communication emerged most strongly from Latin America. This section briefly summarizes this deconstruction and reconstruction, beginning with an examination of the assertions that development efforts were ideologically and materially related to neocolonialism and the extension of capitalist relations. It continues by introducing key, alternative directions for development efforts, including notions of praxis, dialogue, and communication process.

Communication domination

Prior to the 1970s, almost all of Latin American development communication theory and practice was based on concepts and models imported from the United States and Europe and used in ways that were both incommensurable with and detrimental to the region's social context (Beltrán, 1975). These concepts and models were guided philosophically by a combination of behaviorism and functionalism prevalent in the social sciences and by persuasion definitions of communication dating back to Aristotle in the humanities (Beltrán, 1980). The development programs and research projects falling out of this philosophical frame tended to focus on individual attitudes and effects, while ignoring social, political, and economic structures that frequently stood in contradiction to development goals. Development was often defined in terms of the adoption of new behaviors or technologies, which were rarely, if ever, examined in terms of their social, political, and economic dimensions. Beltrán (1975) concluded, "the classic diffusion model was based on an ideological framework that contradicts the reality of this region" (p. 190). This persuasion-attitude focus of research not only reflected the culture and philosophy of the Western tradition, it resulted in theories that blamed individuals, not systems, for continued underdevelopment.

But more than merely reflecting the intellectual and cultural history of Western research, early development projects were criticized as a form of domination and manipulation. Freire (1973b) analyzed the term, "extension," used in agricultural projects, in terms of its "associative fields" and concluded that they invited "mechanistic," "transmission," and "invasion" models of development communication. The vertical structure of many extension projects paralleled the hierarchical organization of landlord–peasant relations preceding it in Latin American *latifundios*, resulting in an unintended continuity of inegalitarian relations. The sense that development projects frequently perpetuated the interests of dominant elites was echoed by numerous scholars at the "First Latin American Seminar on Participatory Communication" sponsored in 1978 by CIESPAL (Center for Advanced Studies and Research for Latin America). Influenced by dependency theory that was prevalent at the time, scholars there concluded that uses of mass media in development imposed the interests of dominant classes on the majority of marginalized people, resulting in the reinforcement, reproduction, and legitimation of existing, inegalitarian social and material relations of production (O'Sullivan-Ryan & Kaplún, 1978).

The Latin American critique of the dominant paradigm, then, moved from the level of specific and misguided models of communication to the level of historical and global theories of domination and inequity. Early on, Latin American scholars suggested that development communication be interpreted from within a global framework guided by dependency theory (O'Sullivan-Ryan & Kaplún, 1978). Dependency was a school of thought emerging in Latin America in the 1960s that explained underdevelopment as the result or by-product of capitalist expansion, a zero-sum proposition. Furthermore, the development of underdevelopment was interpreted as part of a process of continuous political economic relations occurring globally between the developed north and the impoverished south, or what has been termed "core-periphery" relations (Cardoso & Faletto, 1979; Frank, 1967). Adopting such an interpretive framework suggested that development projects be analyzed as integral elements in a global system that actually maintained asymmetrical relations. Freire (1973a) went as far as to label the various top-down, modernization projects as "assistentialism," or social and financial activities that attack symptoms, not causes, of social ills and function as disguised forms of colonial domination. These early suspicions have been confirmed by a more recent analysis of health and nutrition programs in Latin America, which concluded that development projects operated as an extension of the geopolitical struggle between the capitalist West and the communist East (Escobar, 1995). Moreover, the categories of assistance constructed by donor nations allowed "institutions to distribute socially individuals and populations in ways consistent with the creation and reproduction of modern capitalist relations" (Escobar, 1995, p. 107). The deconstruction of the dominant paradigm of development, then, was a protest against the perpetuation of historical inequities and a call for the invention of humane, egalitarian, and responsive communication theories and practices.

Toward dialogic praxis

Embracing the notion of praxis – self-reflexive, theoretically guided practice – was an immediate and obvious outcome of the Latin American critique of the dominant paradigm. The modernization project and its concomitant theories of development themselves had been shown to illustrate the inextricable connection between theory and practice (Beltrán, 1975, 1980; Escobar, 1995). Through its assumptions regarding the locus of social problems, models of communication as information transfer, methods that placed human objects under the antiseptic gaze of scientists, and findings that confirmed micro explanations of persistent underdevelopment, the modernization approach unconsciously demonstrated the reciprocal and self-confirming relationship between theory and practice. One of the earliest recommendations of the Latin American critics was to acknowledge this relationship consciously, to turn away from scientific positions of objectivity, and to embrace an orientation toward research as praxis.

Much of the inspiration for this shift came from the work of Freire (1970), whose experience in traditional pedagogy was seen as analogous to modernization approaches to development. In traditional pedagogy, teachers typically viewed students as empty – *tabula rasa* – objects characterized by some sort of deficiency and in need of knowledge that could be transferred to them in a linear fashion. Freire denounced this objectivist orientation as sadistic and oppressive, and claimed that humane practitioners could not view themselves as proprietors of knowledge and wisdom. In contrast to this oppressive pedagogy, Freire proposed a liberating approach that centered on praxis. Under this orientation, practitioners attempt to close the distance between teacher and student, development agent and client, researcher and researched in order to enter into a co-learning relationship guided by action and reflection. In a praxis approach to teaching, development, or research, people serve as their own examples in the struggle for and conquest of improved life chances.

The turn toward research praxis was a radical epistemological move that has been adopted and refined by scholars since then (e.g. Fals Borda, 1988). It posits that the combination of critical theory, situation analysis, and action create a fruitful dialectic for the construction of knowledge, which is systematically examined, altered, and expanded in practice. The elimination of the dichotomy between subject and object, combined with an action–reflection orientation toward inquiry resulted in a heightened moral awareness or *conscientização*. This liberating praxis generated "thinking which perceives reality as process, as transformation, rather than as a static entity – thinking which does not separate itself from action, but constantly immerses itself in temporality without fear of the risks involved" (Freire, 1970, p. 81). The turn toward praxis not only rejected dominant approaches to development as oppressive, it argued for integrating scholarship more directly with development practice.

While this turn provided both a philosophical and epistemological framework for scholarship, it also provided a practical, commensurate method in the form of dialogue. Dialogic communication was held in stark contrast to information transmission models predominant in early development research. This required development researchers and practitioners to seek out the experiences, understandings, and aspirations of others to jointly construct reality and formulate actions (Beltrán, 1980). Freire (1970, 1973a) provided concrete exercises for initiating critical dialogues to deconstruct social contexts, separate out their constituent parts, and reconstruct a thematic universe for pursuing social transformation. Such a process resulted in a "cultural synthesis" between development collaborators to arrive at mutually identified problems, needs, and guidelines for action.

Aside from its practical contribution, dialogue was promoted as an ethical communication choice within the development context. Freire (1970) argued that true humanization emerged from one's ability "to name the world" in dialogic encounters. This humanization was not only denied to marginalized or oppressed peoples, but something that leaders and elites were prevented from attaining, as well, in prevailing communication environments. Grounded in Buber's notion of "I–Thou" communication, Freire argued that subject–object distinctions were impossible to maintain in true dialogue because one's sense of self and the world is elicited in interaction with others. The resulting fusion of identities and communal naming of the world did not emerge merely from an exchange of information, however, it required a moral commitment among dialogue partners. "Being dialogic is not invading, not manipulating, not imposing orders. Being dialogic is pledging oneself to the constant transformation of reality" (Freire, 1973b, p. 46). This highly developed sense of dialogue – simultaneously practical and rarefied – pushed scholars to conceptualize the phenomena of their study away from states (attitudes) and entities (media) toward process.

Communication as process

More than any other aspect of the Latin American critique, the observation that communication was frequently conceptualized in static rather than process terms constituted the greatest challenge for development practitioners. Scholars from the north had been struggling with process models of communication since Berlo's (1960) work so convincingly argued in their favor. Yet Berlo's construction of the Sender–Message–Channel–Receiver model of communication demonstrated the tenacity of static, linear models that identified components amenable to survey research and development program design. It also demonstrated the elusiveness of the dynamic, process nature of communication.

Latin American scholars introduced a phenomenological orientation, which radically altered the conceptualization, study, and practice of development communication. Rather than focusing on the constituent parts of communication, Latin American scholars introduced more fluid and elastic concepts that centered on how-meaning-comes-to-be in its definition. Drawing on Continental proponents of phenomenology, Pasquali (1963) argued that knowledge of development needed to be generated phenomenologically, that is, through presuppositionless, intentional action in the world. This position undermined – on the most fundamental level – modernization approaches that assumed a separation between subject and object, researcher and development recipient. This more fluid and meaning-centered conceptualization of communication emphasized co-presence, intersubjectivity, phenomenological "being in the world," and openness of interlocutors. This view introduced a sophisticated epistemology arguing that the understanding of social reality is produced between people, in material contexts, and in communication. Freire (1973b) captured the sense of the phenomenological orientation toward communication writing:

One's consciousness, "intentionality" toward the world, is always consciousness of, and in permanent movement toward reality. . . . This relationship constitutes, with this, a dialectical unity in which knowing-in-solidarity is generated in being and vice versa. For this reason, both objectivist and subjectivist explanations that break this dialectic, dichotomizing that which is not dichotomizable (subject–object), are not capable of understanding reality. (p. 85)

In other words, traditional development approaches of "understanding reality" through the unilateral definition of problems, objectives, and solutions were criticized as violating the very essence of communication.

Pasquali (1963) went as far as stating that the notion of "mass communication" was an oxymoron and that Latin American media constituted an "information oligarchy" that cultivated a social context characterized by "communicational atrophy." Though his analysis was aimed at issues of media and culture broadly, the kinds of development communication projects typical of the period were consistent with his analysis. This fundamental criticism of static models of communication led to calls in development to abandon the "vertical" approaches of information transmission and to adopt "horizontal" projects emphasizing access, dialogue, and participation (Beltrán, 1980). The Latin American critique of the dominant paradigm as an extension of domination and the call for more egalitarian and responsive approaches to development were followed by a robust body of research into "participatory communication," which has emerged as the most influential concept in the subsequent decades.

Alternative Approaches to Development Communication

In the decades following the Latin American critique of the dominant paradigm, scholars produced a wide range of theoretical responses that drew upon the newly introduced notion of "participatory communication." At one end of the participatory spectrum, scholars coming out of the behaviorist, mass media effects tradition acknowledged the critique and have incorporated participatory dimensions – albeit to a limited extent – into their research. On the other end of the spectrum, scholars critical of traditional development communication research embraced participation virtually as an utopian panacea for development. These distinct theoretical positions essentially mark ends on a continuum, where participation is conceptualized as either a means to an end, or as an end in and of itself. These polarized approaches will be described more fully before describing a variety of other themes that reside somewhere between them.

Participation: Technical means or utopian end?

Almost as quickly as Latin American scholars articulated their objections to mainstream approaches to development communication, some of the leading figures of the dominant paradigm acknowledged the criticisms and reformed their projects (Lerner, 1976; Rogers, 1976a; Schramm, 1976). They acknowledged that focusing narrowly on individuals as the locus for change, theorizing in a universal, evolutionary manner, ignoring cultural specificity, and emphasizing mass media had oversimplified their conceptualization of development. But this recognition did not lead to the wholesale rejection of their empiricist approach. In fact, Lerner (1976) defended social science's inviolable methodological assumptions of ontological continuity and social regularity, which were threatened by the Latin American rejection of objectivism and promotion of communication-as-process. Yet, dominant paradigm scholars acknowledged the general value of popular participation in development, recognized new uses of media to "unlock local energies" (Lerner & Schramm, 1976, p. 343), and expanded research to include interpersonal networks in addition to opinion leaders. To an extent, the concept of participation served to reform the dominant paradigm, making it – in the words of its proponents – more expansive, flexible, and humane (Rogers, 1993).

Major institutions such as the World Bank and Mexico's dominant Institutional Revolutionary Party (PRI) use such reformist approaches to participation (White, 1999; Mato, 1999). Their top-down efforts are supported by theoretical arguments that participation be conceptualized in ways that disassociate it from any particular ideology (Chu, 1987; 1994). By ideologically neutralizing it, participation is seen as compatible with social marketing, capitalist expansion, and global trade (Moemeka, 1994). In fact, King and Cushman (1994) have argued that participation be conceptualized on a highly abstract level where a "nation's people and its government" fashion themselves as global competitors participating in the arena of world trade. They discard the value of grass roots participation, local knowledge, and cultural beliefs as "old myths" that are incompatible with the contemporary reality of globalization.

Less dismissive of grassroots participation but still consistent with empiricist, top-down approaches to development is recent research in entertainment-education (Singhal & Rogers, 1988; Storey, 1999). Rather than neutralizing the ideological element of participation, entertainment-education draws on findings emerging from cultural studies to advance predetermined objectives in areas such as "reproductive health." A sophisticated theoretical framework drawing from studies in reception and popular culture has been constructed to conceptualize mediated texts as open systems that are incapable of imposing meaning on active audiences (Storey, 1999, 2000). Coupled with the theoretical contributions of Mikhail Bakhtin, this approach uses the concept of participation both to guide the development of "pro-social content" through audience surveys and focus groups and more importantly to impute wide-ranging and long-term consequences via the "social dialogue" of individuals, institutions, and culture. Within this approach, dialogue is conceptualized not only as concrete, interpersonal practice, but also an abstract, social process that includes interactions between individual, institutional, commercial, and political actors. Rather than using this framework as the basis for promoting grass-roots communication broadly, the notions of "open texts," "active audiences," and "social dialogue" have functioned to justify expert-produced, entertainment-education products, such as soap operas in India, music videos in Mexico, and television dramas in the Philippines that share the theme of family planning. More than any other research genre, entertainment-education has used the concept of participation to bolster the administrative position of the dominant paradigm.

The apparent contradictions of using participatory elements to enhance the status of traditional development practices have received intense attention by communication scholars. A recent, historical analysis focusing on the discourse of development suggests that the Latin American call for participation constituted a counter discourse to the dominant paradigm that was "easily co-opted by the established system and rendered ineffective or counter productive" (Escobar, 1999, p. 326). Indeed, the most pernicious instances of instrumental uses of participation appear to be attached to large agencies connected to the state or to transnational regimes such as the US Agency for International Development (USAID) or the World Bank (Mato, 1999; White, 1999). The role of scholars who have integrated participation into essentially top-down development theories has been interpreted as akin to engaging in a "conspiracy theory" to redeem the dominant paradigm from the interrogation it experienced in the 1970s (Ascroft & Masilela, 1994; Lent, 1987). When put into practice, such uses of participatory communication exemplify, at best, passive collaboration, at worst, manipulative consultation done only to help advance a predetermined objective (Díaz Bordenave, 1994). In fact, one development practitioner argues that any uses of participation will evolve into an "insidious domination tactic" if incorporated into the development discourse due to its historical association with Western political hegemony (White, 1999).

Few scholars would agree with this extreme position, especially those reviewed above who advocate administrative uses of participation. Moreover, a group of scholars conceptualizing participation as an end in and of itself has articulated utopian visions of the role of people in their own development. These visions are premised on a somewhat romantic belief that peasants, indians, and other marginalized persons possess local wisdom and a virtuous cultural ethos, and that participatory processes are inherently humanizing, liberating, and catalyzing (Vargas, 1995; S. White, 1994). Beginning from such premises, scholars have prescribed totalizing processes of participatory communication where all interlocutors experience freedom and equal access to express feelings and experiences and to arrive at collective agendas for action (Díaz Bordenave, 1994; Kaplún, 1985; Nair & White, 1994a). Under these circumstances, all people are said to take ownership of communication and to experience empowering outcomes. These utopian visions of development communication have been called "genuine" and "authentic" participation, as opposed to the manipulative, pseudo-participation reviewed above.

The generalized premises and prescriptions of utopian scholars have been accompanied by equally optimistic renditions of participation by researchers who offer more concrete directions for development practice. For example, various phases in development – identifying problems, setting goals and objectives, planning procedures, assessing actions – have been identified, each one necessitating the full participation of intended beneficiaries (Nair & White, 1994b). This has been accompanied by policy recommendations for the reorganization of major social institutions, such as the media system, in order to bring communication structures in line with participatory communication development approaches (Servaes, 1985). Placed on a continuum, these utopian, normative theories stand as polar opposites to the functional, administrative notions of participation advanced by scholars approaching development from a more conventional perspective.

The evolution of polarized conceptualizations of participatory development communication has been noted in a number of scholarly reviews that have distinguished the two poles in slightly different ways. In fact, early research in this area suggested that participatory communication functions as both a means and an end in development, thus foreshadowing the distinct conceptual paths that would be followed in the decades to come (O'Sullivan-Ryan & Kaplún, 1978). A number of scholars have interpreted this means/end division as a convenient and fruitful way of guiding communication decisions in development projects (Chu, 1994; Kaplún, 1989; Rodríguez, 1994). That is, a limited role for communication – participation-as-means – may be appropriate in projects focused on teaching skills, carrying out prescribed objectives, or producing highly polished media products. Under such circumstances, social impacts are viewed as ephemeral, goals are immediate, and interaction is formal. In contrast, an expansive role for communication – participation-as-end – is appropriate in projects aimed at organizing movements, transforming social relations, and empowering individuals. Under such circumstances, social impacts are perpetual, goals are long-range, and interaction is fluid. Other scholars noting the means–end continuum in the research have been more critical of the distinction, arguing that participation-as-means is nothing more than a thinly veiled reincarnation of the dominant paradigm (Melkote, 1991; Vargas, 1995; S. White, 1994). They argue that this approach invokes participatory communication in an instrumental, manipulative, dominating manner that undercuts its theoretical legitimacy. While they recognize the existence of the gradations in the evolution of the concept of participation, they reject the means-to-an-end perspective as an illegitimate appropriation. Regardless of the subtle distinctions characterizing the ends of this continuum, these scholars have noted that most theory development of participation has not been predominately means or end, teaching or organizing, pseudo or genuine, but some version that resides between the poles. The remainder of this section reviews major concepts and issues that have emerged over the years but that defy convenient location at either end of the conceptual continuum.

Straddling the means/end polarity

The bulk of theoretical research into participatory communication does not claim an exclusive means or ends focus, but does vary in terms of level of abstraction, issue of attention, or topic of interest. The resulting theoretical contributions include both general, abstract scholarship and applied, concrete research. This scholarship touches on general notions of multiplicity, power, and popular mobilization, as well as specific ideas concerning levels of participation, media applications, and concrete methods of inquiry. Sketching out these general patterns and holding them in relief to the origins of interest in participatory communication will form the basis for suggesting future directions of research.

One of the more general and fully articulated concepts to emerge from the participatory communication tradition is the notion of multiplicity in one world (Servaes, 1985, 1989). This approach recommends strong, grassroots participation in development efforts, but explicitly rejects universal approaches to its application (Servaes, 1996). Instead, it emphasizes the terms "diversity" and "pluralism," suggesting that nations and regions cultivate their own, responsive approaches to self-determined development goals that emerge out of participatory processes. The reluctance to advocate universal theorizing stems from the observation that even within fairly homogeneous cultures, competing political, social, and cultural interests and groups will be found (Servaes, 1985). The conflicts inherent in all social systems suggest that "rigid and general strategies for participation are neither possible nor desirable. It is a process that unfolds in each unique situation" (Servaes, 1996, p. 23). Eschewing even "general strategies for participation," however, constitutes a naive faith in the power of communication to negotiate stark political differences and casts multiplicity into a relativistic arena that has difficulty sustaining coherence within the larger discourse of development.

Another area of general, theoretical attention in participatory communication has centered more closely on structural constraints by focusing on the role of power in development. Early advocates of participatory approaches either ignored the issue of power or naively called for its general redistribution within and between nations. More recent research has focused explicitly on power and conceptualized it in a nuanced and problematic way. For the most part, power has been theorized as both multi-centered – not one dimensional – and asymmetrical (Tehranian, 1999). This role acknowledges the force of institutions and structures, but emphasizes the role of human agency in reproducing and transforming them (Tehranian, 1999). Within this generalized framework of power, some scholars view participatory communication as a potential source of social transformation (Nair & White, 1994a; Riaño, 1994). By virtue of the differences – ethnic, gender, sexual, and the like – that multiple social actors bring to development projects, participatory communication reveals how power functions to subordinate certain groups of people (Riaño, 1994). Furthermore, participation functions to cultivate "generative power" where individuals and groups develop the capacity for action, which can be harnessed to reshape and transform conditions of subordination (Nair & White, 1994a). While mindful of the asymmetrical characteristics of power in society, these positions are generally optimistic regarding the prospects of transformation via participatory communication.

Less optimistic are scholars who see participation as either insufficient or problematic in and of itself in terms of altering power relationships in society. For these scholars, participatory communication may be helpful in attaining structural transformations in the land tenure, political, or economic arrangements of society, which are viewed as the root sources of subordination (Hedebro, 1982; Nerfin, 1977). As such, participatory communication is necessary but not sufficient for engaging and altering power relationships. In fact, participatory communication that is not guided toward an a priori structural goal, such as changing the media environment or deconstructing dominating discourses, runs the risk of dissolving into a self-indulgent exercise or being coopted by an established and elitist organization (Escobar, 1999). Worse yet, participatory communication by itself is capable of reproducing inegalitarian power structures, especially in regard to gender relations (Wilkins, 1999, 2000). For these authors, the relationship between participatory communication and dominant power structures is neither transparent nor unproblematic.

An approach to participatory communication that explicitly bridges the divide between the social pluralism evident in the multiplicity concept and the structural limits apparent in power relations is the scholarship that focuses on popular movements. One position in this research argues that popular movements are inherently linked to participatory communication projects because "liberation" is an axiomatic quality of participation (Riaño, 1994). That is, the openness required of participatory communication leads to awareness of differences that reveal inequalities and result in movements to address and transform them. A distinct but related perspective notes that participation emerges from popular movements that engage in structural reforms but rely on continual regeneration through broad social participation (R. White, 1994). Large-scale popular movements, therefore, serve as valuable laboratories for breaking through artificial boundaries that obscure the role of participatory communication in the transformation and reproduction of dominant relations. Some scholars have gone farther and suggested that development research actively align itself with popular movements in order to yield insights that contribute directly to participatory, social change projects (Servaes & Arnst, 1999). This nexus between participation and popular liberation movements constitutes an entry point for negotiating problematic issues of power.

Participatory applications and methods

Research attending to abstract theoretical concerns of multiplicity, power, and mobilization demonstrates the negotiation of the means/end polarity in the participatory communication literature. But a range of scholarship focused on more specific issues and concerns defies simple means/end classification, as well. It examines levels of participation, media applications, and research methods.

A number of researchers have worked to identify differential levels and intensities of participation in development projects. These scholars have identified stages of participation, ranging from initial access to communication resources to active identification of development issues and goals to full authority in project governance (Fraser & Restrepo-Estrada, 1998; Krohling-Peruzzo, 1996; Servaes, 1996). These stages are usually conceptualized as being guided either by contextual qualities of the participants themselves or by organizational constraints of the supporting development institutions. For example, Thapalia (1996) suggested that development practitioners cultivate a stronger, more directive role for themselves – something she labeled "transformational leadership" – aimed at constructing a shared vision and commitment to action in a community. She argues for resurrecting the discredited notion of "leadership" because egalitarian participation is frequently incommensurable with the desires and interests of local people. Like the constraints created by local cultural contexts, organizational characteristics impose limitations on participation as well. Large development agencies most frequently implement participation on a limited level, such as using focus groups in the initial phase of an information campaign, because of organizational goals and limitations on time and resources (Wilkins, 1999). The various levels identified by these researchers are conceptualized in a complex interaction with contextual and structural constraints that move beyond the binary means/end continuum suggested by other scholars. Furthermore, they are acutely concerned with concrete applications of participatory communication in development.

Another area of scholarship that has focused on communication applications concerns participatory uses of media in development. Soon after the Latin American challenge to the dominant paradigm of development, scholars began focusing on participatory applications in media. Fueled by a series of UNESCO meetings that led to the declaration for a New World Information and Communication Order, these scholars identified the concepts of access (to communication resources), participation (in planning, decision-making, and production), and self-management (collective ownership and policy-making) in media development (O'Sullivan-Ryan & Kaplún, 1978; Berrigan, 1981). Within the communication discipline, this turn toward grassroots media development has been criticized as naïve utopianism (Garnham, 1990) and hailed as the best response to media conglomeration (Herman & McChesney, 1997). Regardless of this unresolved debate, systematic attention has been given to various aspects of participatory media, including audience involvement in message creation (Mody, 1991; Nair & White, 1994b), identity construction (Rodríguez, 2001), and institution building (Díaz Bordenave, 1985). In fact, an entire communication subfield of "alternative media" has spun off of the initial criticisms of the dominant paradigm and call for participatory approaches to social change (see Atwood & McAnany, 1986; Huesca & Dervin, 1994; Reyes Matta, 1983; Simpson Grinberg, 1986).

While scholarly attention has been given to many abstract and concrete issues relevant to participatory communication, the area of research methods has been neglected to some extent (Ascroft & Masilela, 1994; Melkote, 1991). Recently this situation has begun to change, however, with scholars emphasizing the importance of advancing research methods that are commensurate with the philosophy and theory that underpins participatory communication for development (Dervin & Huesca, 1999; Jacobson, 1996; Servaes & Arnst, 1999). At the level of methodology, this requires thinking through the ontological and episte-mological assumptions that mandate the dissolution of subject–object relations and lay the groundwork for participatory communication for development (Dervin & Huesca, 1999; Jacobson, 1996). It also requires the establishment of criteria of validity in order to fulfill the self-reflexive, evaluative dimension of research, as well as to advance comparative studies in the field. Such criteria might be imported from parallel communication theories, such as Habermas' ideal speech situation (Jacobson & Kolluri, 1999), or they might emerge from the practical outcomes of the research process itself (Escobar, 1999; Servaes & Arnst, 1999). At the level of method, an orientation toward participatory action research has been suggested as perhaps the most compatible approach to the study of par-ticipatory communication (Einsiedel, 1999; Escobar, 1999). Such methods are explicitly political, calling on researchers to align themselves with specific social actors and to embrace their goals and purposes. The recent attention to method-ology and method may foreshadow renewed interest in conducting empirical research into participatory communication for development. It, combined with the other issues receiveing scholarly attention noted above, points to some fruitful directions for future research.

Looking Backward/Looking Forward

The history of development communication in media studies is marked by con-ceptual struggles and complexities that have advanced both theory and practice while leaving a number of conflicts unresolved. These struggles and complexities are not unique to development communication but parallel similar issues in the larger field of media studies, as well. Early modernization theories followed by the Latin American critique and subsequent rise of participatory communication reflect many of the same concerns that emerged from the effects tradition chal-lenged by critical theorists and leading to both political economic and cultural studies orientations. Issues regarding individual–psychological versus cultural–contextual orientations, quantitative versus qualitative methods, and value-free versus power-laden positions have marked the conceptual advancements of both development communication and media studies. Moreover, criticisms of linear, transmission models of communication have created greater sensitivity to pro-cess, meaning centered conceptualizations of the relationship between media and society. While these struggles and contributions have reshaped communication methods, theories, and practices, the future direction of research continues to be debated.

Despite a lack of consensus regarding the future of development communication, a robust interest has arisen from the notion of participatory communication. Emerging from the Latin American critique of modernization approaches to development, participatory communication has been embraced by scholars of diverse backgrounds and interests. Indeed, participatory communication appears to be an elastic notion amenable to research approaches that embrace contrasting, and even conflicting, ontological, epistemological, and ethical assumptions. Proponents of entertainment education, for example, maintain empiricist and administrative methods and goals while drawing on notions of the active audience and textual openness to guide communication strategies and theoretical interpretations. Critics of this approach rightfully question its conceptual integrity, noting that social marketing approaches to texts and audiences through the use of surveys and focus groups are fundamentally inconsistent with notions of co-presence, dialogue, and process that formed the basis of the critique of the dominant paradigm. Meanwhile, proponents of grassroots communication and alternative media embrace interpretive and cultural methods and goals that invest local participants with understanding and agency in the planning, execution, and evaluation of development projects. Critics of this approach legitimately note its cultural relativism and social and institutional naïveté regarding local distributions of power and global arrangements of media ownership. The challenge facing scholars of development communication is to address the weaknesses and contradictions apparent in the diverse approaches to participatory communication while building on the achievements of research to date.

A major impediment to the advancement of scholarship in this area, however, is the political, economic, and institutional context surrounding development efforts today. Referred to variously by terms such as "neoliberal," "postindustrial," and "globalization," this context is marked by deregulation and privatization accompanied by a retracting role of the state and traditional institutions (Huesca, 2001). This contextual shift has eliminated important forms of structural support on which development efforts have relied and has identified new priorities aimed at bringing individuals and populations into alignment with post-socialist societies and economies. Participatory communication projects often threaten this alignment because they attend explicitly to the distribution of power on the local level and call for its reconfiguration. The institutional reward system surrounding development communication efforts, therefore, will pressure scholars to adopt participatory approaches that tend to exacerbate conceptual inconsistencies that have emerged over the years.

Despite its challenges, the contemporary context of globalization and neoliberalism contains reasons for optimism for the future of participatory communication research, as well. Worldwide structural changes that have shifted authority away from states and traditional institutions have been facilitated by a global rhetoric acknowledging universal human rights, basic environmental protections, and respect for democracy. The rhetorical veneer accompanying the retraction of the authority of states and institutions has enabled an expanding civil society in the form of new social movements that are organized around issues and identities concerned with development problems. Scholarship of participatory communication for development is well positioned to apply its theoretical advancements in ways that take advantage of these emerging movements, which are characterized by decentralized structures and intense local involvement. Years of experience with dialogue, praxis, and communication-as-process in research design and methods have given participatory communication scholars a head start at working with these new movements in ways that are consistent with their characteristics. Furthermore, the moral commitment to strive for social justice explicit in early denunciations of the dominant paradigm, coupled with recent studies advocating action research methods, provide scholars with concrete strategies for responding to some of the weaknesses identified in the participatory communication research to date.

An examination of the history of development communication provides many tools for guiding future research and practice in this area. Early critics of modernization approaches noted the close relationship between development communication research and the global system of post-World War II, capitalist expansion. That relationship is equally apparent today, albeit contemporized for a post-communist world, and it threatens to undercut the advancements of scholars of participatory communication. Future researchers would be well advised to bear in mind the relationship of development communication theory and practice with larger political and economic structures in order to build successfully on the accomplishments of the past 30 years of scholarship.

References

Ascroft, J. and Masilela, S. (1994). Participatory decision making in Third World development. In S. A. White, K. S. Nair, and J. Ascroft (eds.), *Participatory Communication: Working for change and development*. New Delhi: Sage, pp. 259–94.

Atwood, R. and McAnany, E. G. (eds.) (1986). *Communication and Latin American Society*. Madison: University of Wisconsin.

Beltrán, L. R. (1975). Research ideologies in conflict. *Journal of Communication*, 25, 187–93.

Beltrán, L. R. (1980). A farewell to Aristotle: "Horizontal" communication. *Communication*, 5, 5–41.

Berlo, D. (1960). *The Process of Communication: An introduction to theory and practice*. San Francisco: Holt, Rinehart & Winston.

Berrigan, F. J. (1981). *Community Communications: The role of community media in development*. Paris: UNESCO.

Cardoso, F. H. and Faletto, E. (1979). *Dependency and Development in Latin America* (trans. M. Mattingly Urquidi). Berkeley: University of California.

Chu, G. C. (1987). Development communication in the year 2000: Future trends and directions. In N. Jayaweera and S. Amunugama (eds.), *Rethinking Development Communication*. Singapore: Asian Mass Communication Research and Information Centre, pp. 95–107.

Chu, G. C. (1994). Communication and development: Some emerging theoretical perspectives. In A. Moemeka (ed.), *Communicating for Development: A new pan-disciplinary perspective*. Albany: SUNY Press, pp. 34–53.

Dervin, B. and Huesca, R. (1999). The participatory communication for development narrative: An examination of meta-theoretic assumptions and their impacts. In T. L. Jacobson and J. Servaes (eds.), *Theoretical Approaches to Participatory Communication*. Cresskill, NJ: Hampton Press, pp. 169–210.

Díaz Bordenave, J. E. (1985). *Comunicación y sociedad* [Communication and society]. La Paz, Bolivia: CIMCA.

Díaz Bordenave, J. E. (1994). Participative communication as a part of building the participative society. In S. A. White, K. S. Nair, and J. Ascroft (eds.), *Participatory Communication: Working for change and development*. New Delhi: Sage, pp. 35–48.

Einsiedel, E. F. (1999). Action research: Theoretical and methodological considerations for development. In T. L. Jacobson and J. Servaes (eds.), *Theoretical Approaches to Participatory Communication*. Cresskill, NJ: Hampton Press, pp. 359–79.

Escobar, A. (1995). *Encountering Development: The making and unmaking of the Third World*. Princeton: Princeton University Press.

Escobar, A. (1999). Discourse and power in development: Michel Foucault and the relevance of his work to the third world. In T. L. Jacobson and J. Servaes (eds.), *Theoretical Approaches to Participatory Communication*. Cresskill, NJ: Hampton Press, pp. 309–35.

Fals Borda, O. (1988). *Knowledge and People's Power: Lessons with peasants in Nicaragua, Mexico and Colombia*. New Delhi: Indian Social Institute.

Frank, A. G. (1967). *Capitalism and Underdevelopment in Latin America*. New York: Monthly Review Press.

Fraser, C. and Restrepo-Estrada, S. (1998). *Communicating for Development: Human change for survival*. London: I. B. Tauris Publishers.

Freire, P. (1970). *Pedagogy of the Oppressed* (trans. M. Bergman Ramos). New York: Herder & Herder.

Freire, P. (1973a). *Education for Critical Consciousness*. New York: Seabury Press.

Freire, P. (1973b). *¿Extensión o comunicación?* (trans. L. Ronzoni). Buenos Aires: Siglo XXI.

Garnham, N. (1990). The myths of video: A disciplinary reminder. In N. Garnham, *Capitalism and Communication: Global culture and the economics of information*. London: Sage, pp. 64–9.

Hedebro, G. (1982). *Communication and Social Change in Developing Nations*. Ames, IA: Iowa State University Press.

Herman, E. S. and McChesney, R. W. (1997). *The Global Media: The new missionaries of corporate capitalism*. New York: Cassell.

Huesca, R. (2001). Conceptual contributions of new social movements to development communication research. *Communication Theory*, 11, 415–33.

Huesca, R. and Dervin, B. (1994). Theory and practice in Latin American alternative communication research. *Journal of Communication*, 44(4), 53–73.

Jacobson, T. L. (1996). Conclusion: Prospects for theoretical development. In J. Servaes, T. L. Jacobson, and S. A. White (eds.), *Participatory Communication for Social Change*. New Delhi: Sage, pp. 266–77.

Jacobson, T. L. and Kolluri, S. (1999). Participatory communication as communicative action. In T. L. Jacobson and J. Servaes (eds.), *Theoretical Approaches to Participatory Communication*. Cresskill, NJ: Hampton Press, pp. 265–80.

Kaplún, M. (1985). *El comunicador popular* [The popular communicator]. Quito: Ciespal.

Kaplún, M. (1989). Video, comunicación y educación popular: Derroteros para una búsqueda [Video, communication, and popular education: Action plan for a quest]. In P. Valdeavellano (ed.), *El video en la educación popular* [Video in popular education]. Lima: Instituto Para América Latina, pp. 37–58.

King, S. S. and Cushman, D. (1994). Communication in development and social change: Old myths and new realities. In A. Moemeka (ed.), *Communicating for Development: A new pan-disciplinary perspective*. Albany: SUNY Press, pp. 23–33.

Krohling-Peruzzo, C. M. (1996). Participation in community communication. In J. Servaes, T. L. Jacobson, and S. A. White (eds.), *Participatory Communication for Social Change*. New Delhi: Sage, pp. 162–79.

Lasswell, H. D. (1964, c. 1948). The structure and function of communication in society. In L. Bryson (ed.), *The Communication of Ideas*. New York: Cooper Square Publishers, pp. 37–51.

Lent, J. (1987). Devcom: A view from the United States. In N. Jayaweera and S. Amunugama (eds.), *Rethinking Development Communication*. Singapore: Asian Mass Communication Research and Information Centre, pp. 20–41.

Lerner, D. (1958). *The Passing of Traditional Society: Modernizing the Middle East*. New York: The Free Press.

Lerner, D. (1976). Toward a new paradigm. In W. Schramm and D. Lerner (eds.), *Communication and Change: The last ten years – and the next*. Honolulu: East-West Center, pp. 60–3.

Lerner, D. and Schramm, W. (1976). Looking forward. In W. Schramm and D. Lerner (eds.), *Communication and Change: The last ten years – and the next*. Honolulu: East-West Center, pp. 340–4.

Mato, D. (1999). Problems of social participation in "Latin" America in the age of globalization: Theoretical and case-based considerations for practitioners and researchers. In T. L. Jacobson and J. Servaes (eds.), *Theoretical Approaches to Participatory Communication*. Cresskill, NJ: Hampton Press, pp. 51–75.

Melkote, S. R. (1991). *Communication for Development in the Third World*. New Delhi: Sage.

Mody, B. (1991). *Designing Messages for Development Communication: An audience participation-based approach*. New Delhi: Sage.

Moemeka, A. A. (1994). Development communication: A historical and conceptual overview. In A. Moemeka (ed.), *Communicating for Development: A new pan-disciplinary perspective*. Albany: SUNY Press, pp. 3–22.

Nair, K. S. and White, S. A. (1994a). Participatory development communication as cultural renewal. In S. A. White, K. S. Nair, and J. Ascroft (eds.), *Participatory Communication: Working for change and development*. New Delhi: Sage, pp. 138–93.

Nair, K. S. and White, S. A. (1994b). Participatory message development: A conceptual framework. In S. A. White, K. S. Nair, and J. Ascroft (eds.), *Participatory Communication: Working for change and development*. New Delhi: Sage, pp. 345–58.

Nerfin, M. (1977). Introduction. In M. Nerfin (ed.), *Another Development: Approaches and strategies*. Uppsala: Dag Hammarskjöld Foundatio, pp. 9–18.

O'Sullivan-Ryan, J. and Kaplún, M. (1978). *Communication Methods to Promote Grass-roots Participation: A summary of research findings from Latin America, and an annotated bibliography*. Paris: UNESCO.

Pasquali, A. (1963). *Comunicación y cultura de masas*. Caracas: Universidad Central de Venezuela.

Reyes Matta, F. (ed.) (1983). *Comunicación alternativa y búsquedas democráticas* [Alternative communication and democratic quests]. Mexico City: Instituto Latinoamericano de Estudios Transnacionales y Fundación Friedrich Ebert.

Riaño, P. (1994). Women's participation in communication: Elements of a framework. In P. Riaño (ed.), *Women in Grassroots Communication*. Thousand Oaks, CA: Sage, pp. 3–29.

Rodríguez, C. (1994). A process of identity deconstruction: Latin American women producing video stories. In P. Riaño (ed.), *Women in Grassroots Communication*. Thousand Oaks, CA: Sage, pp. 149–60.

Rodríguez, C. (2001). *Fissures in the Mediascape: An international study of citizens' media*. Cresskill, NJ: Hampton Press.

Rogers, E. M. (1962). *Diffusion of Innovations*. New York: The Free Press.

Rogers, E. M. (1969). *Modernization among Peasants: The impact of communication*. New York: Holt, Rinehart & Winston.

Rogers, E. M. (1976a). Communication and development: The passing of the dominant paradigm. *Communication Research*, 3(2), 213–40.

Rogers, E. M. (1976b). Where are we in understanding the diffusion of innovations? In W. Schramm and D. Lerner (eds.), *Communication and Change: The last ten years – and the next*. Honolulu: East-West Center, pp. 204–22.

Rogers, E. M. (1993). Perspectives on development communication. In K. S. Nair and S. A. White (eds.), *Perspectives on Development Communication*. New Deli: Sage, pp. 35–46.

Röling, N. G., Ascroft, J., and Chege, F. W. (1976). The diffusion of innovations and the issue of equity in rural development. In. E. M. Rogers (ed.), *Communication and Development: Critical perspectives*. Beverly Hills: Sage, pp. 63–79.

Schramm, W. (1964). *Mass Media and National Development: The role of information in developing countries*. Stanford, CA: Stanford University Press.

Schramm, W. (1976). End of an old paradigm? In W. Schramm and D. Lerner (eds.), *Communication and Change: The last ten years – and the next*. Honolulu: East-West Center, pp. 45–8.

Servaes, J. (1985). Towards an alternative concept of communication and development. *Media Development*, 4, 2–5.

Servaes, J. (1989). *One World, Multiple Cultures: A new paradigm on communication for development*. Leuven: Acco.

Servaes, J. (1996). Introduction: Participatory communication and research in development settings. In J. Servaes, T. L. Jacobson, and S. A. White (eds.), *Participatory Communication for Social Change*. New Delhi: Sage, pp. 13–25.

Servaes, J. and Arnst, R. (1999). Principles of participatory communication research: Its strengths (!) and weaknesses (?). In T. L. Jacobson and J. Servaes (eds.), *Theoretical Approaches to Participatory Communication*. Cresskill, NJ: Hampton Press, pp. 107–30.

Shannon, C. E. and Weaver, W. (1964). *The Mathematical Theory of Communication*. Urbana: University of Illinois Press.

Shingi, P. M. and Mody, B. (1976). The communication effects gap: A field experiment on television and agricultural ignorance in India. In. E. M. Rogers (ed.), *Communication and Development: Critical perspectives*. Beverly Hills: Sage, pp. 79–98.

Simpson Grinberg, M. (ed.) (1986). *Comunicación alternativa y cambio social* [Alternative communication and social change]. Tlahuapan, Puebla, Mexico: Premiá Editora de Libros.

Singhal, A. and Rogers, E. M. (1988). Television soap operas for development in India. *Gazette*, 41(2), 109–26.

Storey, D. (1999). Popular culture, discourse, and development. In T. L. Jacobson and J. Servaes (eds.), *Theoretical Approaches to Participatory Communication*. Cresskill, NJ: Hampton Press, pp. 337–58.

Storey, D. (2000). A discursive perspective on development theory and practice: Reconceptualizing the role of donor agencies. In K. G. Wilkins (ed.), *Redeveloping Communication for Social Change: Theory, practice, and power*. Lanham, MD: Rowman & Littlefield, pp. 103–17.

Tehranian, M. (1999). *Global Communication and World Politics: Domination, development and discourse*. Boulder, CO: Lynne Rienner.

Thapalia, C. F. (1996). Animation and leadership. In J. Servaes, T. L. Jacobson, and S. A. White (eds.), *Participatory Communication for Social Change*. New Delhi: Sage, pp. 150–61.

Vargas, L. (1995). *Social Uses and Radio Practices: The use of participatory radio by ethnic minorities in Mexico*. Boulder, CO: Westview.

White, K. (1999). The importance of sensitivity to culture in development work. In T. L. Jacobson and J. Servaes (eds.), *Theoretical Approaches to Participatory Communication*. Cresskill, NJ: Hampton Press, pp. 17–49.

White, R. (1994). Participatory development communication as a social-cultural process. In S. A. White, K. S. Nair, and J. Ascroft (eds.), *Participatory Communication: Working for change and development*. New Delhi: Sage, pp. 95–116.

White, S. A. (1994). The concept of participation: Transforming rhetoric to reality. In S. A. White, K. S. Nair, and J. Ascroft (eds.), *Participatory Communication: Working for change and development*. New Delhi: Sage, pp. 15–32.

Wilkins, K. G. (1999). Development discourse on gender and communication in strategies for social change. *Journal of Communication*, 49, 46–68.

Wilkins, K. G. (2000). Accounting for power in development communication. In K. G. Wilkins (ed.), *Redeveloping Communication for Social Change: Theory, practice, and power*. Lanham, MD: Rowman and Littlefield Publishers, pp. 197–210.

CHAPTER FOUR

Tensions between Popular and Alternative Music
R.E.M. as an Artist-Intellectual

Robert Sloane

The subfield of popular music studies occupies an elusive position *vis-à-vis* media studies.[1] Media studies introductory texts (Baran, 2002; Campbell, 2000) acknowledge the importance of recorded music as a communication medium, and there is a body of music research deriving from more traditional social scientific approaches to media (as reviewed by Christenson and Roberts, 1998), but the most visible studies of popular music issue from a wide range of disciplines, including sociology, literary criticism, and musicology, or from interdisciplinary approaches such as cultural studies[2] and ethnomusicology. Of course, media studies itself is an interdisciplinary field, and there have been many studies of popular music that engage with communication issues (e.g. Lull, 1992; Jones, 1992); generally, though, contemporary popular music studies evolved through a trajectory in which "media studies," as a field, was not a major component. This may be, in part, due to the fact that early media studies were focused largely on broadcast media, and thus "radio" became entrenched as a topic of study; Baran (2002) considers radio and sound recording together in one chapter of an overview of media studies. While radio still occupies a site for research in media studies, it would be difficult to argue that it could stand in for the wide-ranging practices and sites surrounding popular music, let alone encapsulate the importance of recorded music in contemporary culture.

This essay, while a study of popular music, is influenced by a set of concerns and approaches that circulate within media and cultural studies; specifically, I look at the ways that different "moments" in the circuit of culture (Johnson, 1996) are articulated in the texts of one musical group, R.E.M. In doing so, I want to show the ways that an artist's music can provide a meaningful discursive intervention into conversations that occupy an important place within popular music: the "authenticity" of artists; the status of the artist–audience relationship; and the potential for an artist to be politically relevant. R.E.M.'s albums constitute such an intervention, as they are full of ruminations, reflections, and assertions about the relationship between mass communicators and their audiences.

The circuit of culture approach described by Johnson (1996) is a useful way to conceptualize the circulation of cultural objects and meanings in certain forms of mass media. The model recurs in various guises within different research trajectories (Weaver, 1949; Hall, 1993). All of these models divide media communication into at least three moments for analysis: the *production* of the text; the *text* itself; and the *reception*, or interpretation and use, of the text. Johnson argues (as does Grossberg, 1996) that the way to do cultural studies is to make sense of these moments not in and of themselves, but in relationship to one another, and as part of the larger social context in which they exist; Kellner (1995, 1997) has also advocated such an approach. In this spirit, and applying this cultural studies model to the subset of media studies, I have tried to choose a topic that lies at the intersection of production, text, and reception. My analysis will proceed methodologically as a content analysis; however, I will attempt to analyze the texts in a way that illuminates their relationship to production (i.e. being on a major or independent label) and reception (i.e. how the audience reacts).[3] Admittedly, this cannot stand in for an analysis in which studies of the three moments would be integrated into a larger statement about the meanings of a cultural object or practice, but it does offer a provocative and economical approach to analyzing the integration of the three moments.

Studies of popular music have also used all three of these moments as a springboard for analysis (in addition to other approaches), but such studies often feel incomplete. Studies of production (Hesmondhalgh, 1998; Chapple & Garofalo, 1977) look at the music industry, and its component parts (record companies, radio, etc.), and tend to focus on economic factors, although Peterson (1976, 1997) has developed a "production of culture" approach that focuses on a set of structural factors that help to determine cultural practices. Textual studies (Middleton, 2000b; Covach & Boone, 1997; Walser, 1993) analyze the structure, composition, and content of music's component parts, both instrumental and lyrical. And studies of reception (Gelder & Thornton, 1997; Thornton, 1996; Willis, 1978), which are perhaps the most common, try to explain the various ways that people use music and/or derive meaning from it. In general, though, these studies only focus on one moment, which is understandable, in the sense that one cannot do everything at once. The model offered here is at least one of many ways that one might begin to think of combining these moments for fruitful analysis.

I have chosen to analyze texts even as I acknowledge the limitations of this approach and the "embattled" status of textual analysis within cultural and media studies in general (see McCarthy, 2001) and within popular music studies in particular (Frith, 1988). Music scholars have shied away from textual analysis for many reasons, but among the most prominent are the difficulty in translating

musicological language to the laity, as well as the excesses to which interpretations of rock lyrics as poetry led in the 1960s and 70s.[4] Still, a recent set of
studies (Middleton, 2000a) attempts to carve out a new space for textual analyses
of popular music, "to locate the texts as species of musically specific human activity, inextricably entangled in the secular life-processes of real people" (p. 16).
Similarly, McCarthy affirms "the vital, transformative potential of texts and
their deep imbrication in the work of the imagination and practical modes of
existence of modern subjects everywhere" (2001, p. 87). I join this affirmation as
I agree that the act of textual interpretation is an important act in itself. Indeed,
the texts that scholars create are vital to developing an understanding of the
world generally, and they can and do inspire new modes of observation and ways
of thinking. Why should we not afford the same potential in artistic, cultural, or
media texts?

That said I want to express my understanding of the limits of content analysis.
The reading included in this essay is my own; I neither claim nor attempt to
provide a "definitive" interpretation. Active readers and different theoretical
approaches produce different readings, and this is a positive thing for the stimulation of new thought. My act of reading here should be understood as one
possible interpretation among many valid ones, but a positive action nonetheless.
Moreover, I understand that my work here is independent of the thoughts and
feelings of other listeners. Many may be completely unaware of any meanings
or ideas in R.E.M.'s music, and may simply enjoy the sound, or the mood;
obviously, this is fine, but I'll leave the consideration of these listeners to those
who deploy, among other methodologies, uses and gratifications of music. Finally,
with music, content analysis becomes more difficult still, because the effect of
music lies in, among other things, its entire sound; songs cannot be reduced to
the interpretation of lyrics, and I have tried, where possible, to describe the total
effect or structure of feeling of this music. However, in every case, I would direct
the reader to the original texts for a fuller understanding of my comments here.

In what follows, I look at the way R.E.M.'s body of work has addressed some
of the anxieties that circulate within the culture of popular music. The band –
comprised of drummer Bill Berry, guitarist Peter Buck, bassist Mike Mills, and
vocalist Michael Stipe – formed in 1980 in Athens, Georgia, and spent most of
the 1980s rising to the top of the US college-rock scene. Through incessant
touring and a string of critically acclaimed recordings for the independent label
I.R.S., the band acquired a loyal and steadily growing audience, and by 1987,
they had a single in *Billboard*'s top ten. When they signed a five-album deal with
the major label Warner Bros. in 1988, there were great expectations for the band.
Supporters hold that they delivered on their promise thus helping to pave the
way for the commercial success of alternative music and in the process becoming
stars in their own right. But the band wrestled with the changes brought by
stardom, and their music reflected this. Here, I will examine the first five albums
that R.E.M. made for Warner Bros. – *Green* (1988), *Out of Time* (1991), *Automatic for the People* (1992), *Monster* (1994), and *New Adventures in Hi-Fi* (1996)

– and explore the trajectory of the band's evolution of thought about the relationship between artist and audience. This body of work can be used as a sort of microcosm for studying the anxieties and concerns associated with modern popular music (punk rock, but also forms of hip hop, jazz, etc.), particularly that part associated with authenticity. My decision to analyze R.E.M. is based in large part on their critical role in the ushering in of a punk-derived college/alternative music (and its attendant ideological positions) to the mainstream, and my consideration of them is one that affords the band the status of an artist-intellectual intervening in salient cultural debates. Frith (1996, chapter 8) argues that artists sometimes use music to pose a rhetorical argument, as in his example of Public Enemy's "Don't Believe the Hype." I, too, see R.E.M.'s communication as meaningful intellectual creation, as an argument of sorts that intervenes into a conversation about the political relevance of recording artists in the aftermath of punk rock.

The I.R.S. Years

Released in 1983, R.E.M.'s first album, *Murmur*, made a moderate splash in the music world. It garnered a wealth of good reviews, and it was even named "Album of the Year" by the music critics of *Rolling Stone*, beating out more highly visible albums such as Michael Jackson's *Thriller*, The Police's *Synchronicity*, and U2's *War*. This is an astounding feat in retrospect, considering the album was a debut album and got virtually no airplay on mainstream (i.e. non-college) radio stations. The album set in motion a career wherein the band built a following slowly and steadily, mostly on US campuses, through continuous touring. Their roots were in the punk movement, but their music did not necessarily sound like the caricature that "punk" has come to signify – that is, an abrasive sound featuring hard, fast guitars, coupled with angry lyrics spewed forth by an angst-ridden singer. Stylistically, they eschewed the sonic barrage of bands like the Sex Pistols or the Ramones and tended toward the more poetic side of punk; Stipe has often affirmed his admiration for Patti Smith. But more importantly, their principles were rooted in the punk ethos. As Hebdige (1979) has written, the punk aesthetic was "formulated in the widening gap between artist and audience," and punk attempted to pull rock 'n' roll back from its bloated largess of the 1970s (p. 63). This included, crucially, a concept known as "do it yourself," or D.I.Y. Punk bands would perform, record, publish, and distribute their music without the help of large companies. No matter what the ideological affiliations of the performers, this was a political act of sorts, and it strove to preserve or reestablish community among performers and audience.

R.E.M. emerged as part of a post-punk scene in the college town of Athens, Georgia, along with bands such as the B-52's, Pylon, and Love Tractor. (The scene is immortalized in Tony Gayton's 1987 documentary *Athens, Ga.: Inside/Out*.) The band released one EP (extended-play single) – *Chronic Town* (1982) –

and five albums – *Murmur* (1983), *Reckoning* (1984), *Fables of the Reconstruction* (1985), *Life's Rich Pageant* (1986), and *Document* (1987) – on I.R.S. Records. Each album sold more copies than the last, and they were, for the most part, critically heralded. In 1987, a *Rolling Stone* cover story declared them "America's Best Rock & Roll Band."

Musically, these albums have a sound that was distinct from both the mainstream pop of the mid-80s and what is traditionally thought of as "punk" (i.e. abrasive guitars and angry lyrics). Often compared to the 1960s folk-rock band The Byrds, R.E.M. created a "jangly" sound – due, in large part, to the playing of guitarist Peter Buck – that somehow captured their "Southern-ness," a characteristic they often stressed (*Murmur*'s cover art features kudzu, the creeping vine found in parts of the South). In addition to this trait, much of the early attention on the band's sound concerned singer Michael Stipe's unintelligible lyrics. It was often claimed that Stipe used his voice as an instrument, attempting to create an overall feeling or tone rather than a specific meaning.

Nevertheless, one could sometimes glean a kernel of understanding. First, it was obvious that Stipe was a gifted wordsmith, with a particular flair for constructing polysemic phrases.[5] For example, the song "Little America," from *Reckoning*, is full of multiple entendres, including the line, "The consul a horse/ Jefferson, I think we're lost." At its root, this appears to be a political critique, as both lines suggest a bankruptcy of political leadership in the United States: the Roman emperor Caligula was thought to be mad when he suggested making a horse a consul, and "Jefferson" is presumably Thomas Jefferson. But the lines also take on a completely different meaning in the context of R.E.M.'s tour bus. While they were making *Reckoning*, the band was touring across the country, and "Little America" is the name of a chain of motels in the West. "Jefferson" referred to Jefferson Holt, the band's manager. This example is meant to show the deft way in which Stipe is able to meld the specific and the broad, the political and the personal – a skill that becomes more and more refined as the singer's career progresses.

Increasingly, R.E.M. became known for its leftist politics, and their music often reflected their concerns. *Life's Rich Pageant*, for example, features songs that address environmental issues (as on "Cuyahoga," about the river that famously caught on fire, or in the lyric "Buy the sky and sell the sky," from "Fall on Me"). The following album, *Document*, is full of political songs rebelling against Reagan's America. "Welcome to the Occupation" addresses the country's involvement in Latin American political struggles, while "Exhuming McCarthy" evokes the repressive atmosphere of the late 1980s. But while these albums were sometimes political in a traditional sense, they were not overly so; and while the band's home on the independent label I.R.S. afforded them an opportunity to voice their concerns, their messages were often conveyed through arty, abstract lyrics, layered over mid- to up-tempo folk-pop songs. R.E.M. was political, but their music wasn't radical, and when they signed a five-album deal with Warner Bros. in the spring of 1988, expectations were high throughout the music world.

R.E.M. has often said that they chose Warner Bros. because of its reputation as an "artist's label," meaning the company respects the creativity of the artist. Although such information is rarely made public, members of the band have stated that they have complete artistic control over their music.

Warner Bros.

Green may be one of the best one-word album titles in music history, for in its mere five letters, R.E.M. was able to sum up its ambivalence about its move to a major label. Released on Election Day, 1988, *Green* suggests at least three meanings: (1) the band's newness and naïveté in the world of major labels; (2) the money they would now receive to make music; and (3) the band's environmental and political concerns. This is a perfect example of the band's penchant for multiple meanings in the symbolic economy of mass communications.

Musically, *Green* is a continuation of the sounds and themes on *Document*. Most of the songs are relatively up-tempo, guitar-based rock numbers; other, more moody tracks, such as "Turn You Inside Out" and "I Remember California," recall *Document*'s "Finest Worksong" and "Oddfellows Local 151," respectively. There are also three songs on *Green* – "You Are the Everything," "The Wrong Child," and "Hairshirt" – that present a new sound for the band; these songs are acoustic ballads that feature a prominent mandolin, and they offer a more contemplative type of music that serves to break up the album's guitar rock. Of course, R.E.M. had done acoustic songs before: "Swan Swan H," a Civil War-themed ballad on *Life's Rich Pageant*, revolved around a hypnotic acoustic guitar, and the band often performed an acoustic version of *Reckoning*'s "So. Central Rain" during concert encores. But the trio on *Green* would come to prefigure the dominant sound on R.E.M.'s next album, *Out of Time*, and set the stage for other future work.

Like *Document*, *Green* includes political material in the typical R.E.M. vein: "Orange Crush" offers a critique of the US military's use of Agent Orange in the Vietnam War, while "I Remember California" sounds like a remembrance of ecological disaster from an imaginary (but potential) future. But perhaps more interestingly, *Green* sounds most like an impassioned call to arms. On this, the band's first major label album, there is no dampening of the political program suggested in their independent efforts; rather, R.E.M. appears to want to grab the listener and show a new reality. The album opens with "Pop Song 89," a swipe at mainstream pop music, in which Stipe asks: "Should we talk about the weather? Should we talk about the government?" Along with its banal verses and chants of "Hi! Hi! Hi!" Stipe suggests that the mainstream music landscape is generally bereft of relevance. Skeptics may say either that this is a way for R.E.M. to save face by launching a pre-emptive strike on the world of major-label music, or that this is merely hypocritical. The point is that it is a calculated move, and one that the band's presence on Warner Bros. does not preclude. This song is followed by "Get Up," which exhorts the listener (and, self-reflexively, the narrator as well) to resist the urge to sleep and/or dream life away. Two songs later, "Get Up" finds a psychic partner in "Stand," an infectious sing-along (complete with carousel calliope sounds) that asks one to "think about the place where you live, [and] wonder why you haven't before." This trio of songs on the first side of the album suggests material, practical concerns, and even as they communicate through melodies that some would dismiss as "pop," they offer a grounded, rational sensibility as an alternative to the hazy ephemera of modern culture.

Other songs, in both their content and their mode of address, appear to stress the importance and potential of the listener himself. On "World Leader Pretend," Stipe's narrator is a flawed but apparently repentant "leader" whose lines are dominated by the first person pronoun ("I have raised the walls, and I will be the one to knock 'em down"). But in the final verse, Stipe turns to the second person, and sings lines that begin with "You . . ." Significantly, "World Leader Pretend" is the first R.E.M. song to have its lyrics printed on the album sleeve, and it is the only song on *Green* to receive this treatment. Thus, whatever its interpretation, the song draws attention to itself as the sole text to be reproduced lyrically. At first glance, Stipe's narrator appears to be a political leader, but the lyrics are written ambiguously enough so that they could refer to an entertainer that fancies himself a "leader." Indeed, I would suggest that, in light of *Green*'s "new beginning," the song is Stipe's statement that he will no longer hide behind the "walls" of artistic obscurity; instead, he will make an active attempt to reach out and truly lead.

Another track, "You Are the Everything," sounds like a conventional love song, although the narrator's admission that he's "very scared for this world" may suggest something larger. But the song takes on added resonance when one considers its reference at the end of R.E.M.'s *Tourfilm*, a long-form video of the *Green* concert tour. The tape's credits end with a dedication and thanks to the fans, from the band, and then the words YOU ARE THE EVERYTHING appear on the screen. Suddenly, the possibility opens up that the song could be a love letter to the fans from Stipe. Indeed, this convergence of love and audience themes is one with which Stipe often experiments after *Green*, most notably, perhaps, on the following album's first single, "Losing My Religion" (discussed below).

As a major-label debut, *Green* is hardly the timid work of a once-political band treading lightly in the land of big money. While it is true that a song like "Stand" – the album's second single – has a distinct "pop" sensibility, and thus may suggest an overt attempt to appease the label executives, the song does not differ much from earlier whimsical singles such as "It's the End of the World as We Know It (And I Feel Fine)" and "Can't Get There From Here." Far from a capitulation, *Green* is the natural outgrowth of their previous work, but still reaches out to a new audience, and as such, it shows the band eagerly embracing the potential of its new position.

After a long tour of arena-sized venues – a first for R.E.M. – filled with these new fans, the band released *Out of Time* in March of 1991, and no one could have predicted this album's sound or the way it would be received. Developing the ideas expressed in *Green*'s acoustic numbers, *Out of Time* is a departure for the band, filled with moody atmosphere and a more contemplative feel than the clarion call of *Green*. While the band claims that it merely ran "out of time" to name the album when it came due to the label, the title also suggests other meanings: (1) an increasingly dire environmental situation (which was a discourse growing in volume at the time of the album's release, as the 1990 return of Earth Day may attest); (2) music out of step with the contemporary scene; and (3) a sort of poetic escape from the constraints of temporality, or a condition of being lost within a moment. Accordingly, *Out of Time* is a turn inward, a meditation, and perhaps a reflection on the aftermath of *Green* and its tour.

Still, there are some elements of the album that make it consistent with others. For example, like *Green*, *Out of Time* begins with a critique of the music industry. "Radio Song" decries the stifling atmosphere of the US radio landscape: "The world is collapsing around our ears," sings Stipe, while rapper KRS-1 (formerly of Boogie Down Productions), providing guest vocals, claims that "now our children grow up prisoners/All their lives radio listeners!" By pulling together various, seemingly incompatible elements – R.E.M. and KRS-1, a loose funk rhythm with strings and a chiming guitar – the track attempts to embody a hybridized alternative to the homogeneity it seems to suggest in its lyrics. (Despite its critical stance, "Radio Song" was released as the third single from *Out of Time*.) "Near Wild Heaven," sung by bassist Mike Mills, recalls earlier R.E.M. songs, but it adds new dimensions in featuring piano, strings, and an overall greater attention to production. Indeed, the whole of *Out of Time* seems occupied with explorations of sound and production techniques, and while this characteristic is common to albums on major labels, such techniques are often used to create glossy, easily-consumed "hits." While R.E.M. "beautifies" its sound with strings and acoustic instruments, it also creates dark, unsettling pieces such as "Low" and "Belong." Here, then, "production" is not necessarily in the service of making hits, although its association with the larger sums of money provided by major labels is enough to link it to "selling out."

So, too, is the overtly cheerful song "Shiny Happy People," which became the second single released from *Out of Time*. Everyone knows that serious, critically-minded musicians should not appear happy; they should appear dour, removed, and perpetually irritated or angry. Stipe claims that he deliberately chose words for "Shiny Happy People" that would force one singing it to smile, and the song is an unabashed love fest. It was also, as Mills has pointed out, an unlikely, or at the very least "weird" radio hit. The song begins with a few measures of a string section playing a completely different tune in waltz time; this portion is then repeated right in the middle of the song. The single was a success, aided by very colorful video that featured mugging band members but also a subtle political statement.[6] Ultimately, though, "Shiny Happy People" sticks out like a sore thumb on the otherwise wistful *Out of Time*. It may have helped to sell many albums, but it is not a representative track in terms of musical mood.

The first single from the album, however, was representative, and the release of "Losing My Religion" propelled R.E.M. into superstardom. Moreover, the song represents a real turning point in the band's career. Propelled by a mandolin melody, the song features an extremely well-crafted lyric that has had people scratching their heads since its release. Stipe has stated many times – most recently, in an episode of *Storytellers* on VH1 – that the song is not about religion, although this did not keep it from getting banned in Ireland, due mostly to religious images used in the stylized video for the song. Rather, "losing my religion" is a Southern phrase for being at the end of one's rope – essentially, one is "losing faith" in something or someone. Stipe usually explains the song's lyric as being about a crush, and the narrator is getting fed up with trying to subtly display his/her feelings, only to be ignored. This interpretation certainly makes sense; however, there are many clues in the song that Stipe is, in fact, addressing this song to the audience. In the wake of the grueling *Green* tour, one imagines an impassioned Stipe singing to his newly enlarged fan base, only to have them generally ignore what he's saying: the lines "the lengths that I will go to/The distance in your eyes," and "I thought that I heard you sing/I think I thought I saw you try," summon up an ambivalent subject of Stipe's admiration, but the verbs "sing" and "try" tend to belie Stipe's explanation that this is an ordinary love song.

Moreover, the line "that's me in the corner/that's me in the spotlight" suggests Stipe's unease with his new public self. By many accounts, it was unusual for the normally reserved and shy Stipe to embrace his position as a public celebrity the way he did with the *Green* album and tour. Significantly, the video for "Losing My Religion" is the first in which Stipe lip-synched his lyrics, as he had always been opposed to the deception involved in the practice. Whereas this decision may appear to some as further proof of "selling out," I think it is significant because I read the song as a plea to the audience to listen to him and see past the artifice. This reading illuminates a line from "Radio Song" – just one track earlier on the album – in which Stipe sings "Look into my eyes/Listen." In another echoing between the songs, Stipe admits, in "Losing My Religion": "Oh, no, I've said too much/I haven't said enough." This directly parallels a statement in "Radio Song": "I've everything to show/I've everything to hide." The upshot is that Stipe appears to want to bare himself, but yet feels awkward, or self-conscious, or ridiculous, thinking that his advances will not be welcomed. It is a testament to his songwriting that he recognizes that this position *vis-à-vis* the audience is reminiscent of a love relationship, and that he can merge the two into one lyric with many possible interpretations.

The frustrating element of this particular reading is that there is no hard evidence that Stipe had any experience that caused him to lose faith in either himself or his audience. Indeed, at the 1991 MTV Music Awards, "Losing My Religion" was nominated for a number of awards, and Stipe wore layers of T-shirts – each with a different political message, and one for each award for which the band was nominated. While they did not win everything they were nominated for, they did win several, including the final award, "Video of the Year." In the band's acceptance speech, Stipe, who had been entertaining the crowd with the T-shirt trick all night, took off the remaining shirts while his band mates talked. Here was Stipe in his newfound stardom, taking his message(s) to the people as a human billboard. And yet the band's next album would delve further into the trappings of celebrity, and continue the ambivalent feelings at the root of "Losing My Religion" and *Out of Time*.

Most ironic, perhaps, is that *Out of Time* became R.E.M.'s biggest selling album, and their first to go to number one on *Billboard*'s album chart. This is significant for the band, of course, in light of what I've been discussing, but it is also significant for the music industry as a whole. While Nirvana is now credited for ushering "alternative" music into the mainstream when its album, *Nevermind*, went to number one in January of 1992, R.E.M.'s rise to the top of the charts paved the way for Nirvana's ascent, or at least presaged it. Particularly with its history in the college music scene of the 1980s, R.E.M.'s feat was the culmination of what was, at the time, called "alternative" music by some, and which was indeed an alternative to most music in the mainstream. Of course, other similar college-music bands, most notably U2, reached this level of success even before R.E.M. did. I think the case can be made, though, that the mainstream *came* to R.E.M. and alternative music, rather than the reverse.

R.E.M. followed up the success of *Out of Time* with 1992's *Automatic for the People*, an album that delved even further into the moody acoustic music the band was now exploring. The album's title comes from a restaurant sign in the band's hometown of Athens, Georgia, but it also sounds a bit ironic, bearing the weight of its own expectations. Now beloved and "mainstream," the band facetiously imagines that it must churn out a carbon copy of the music that made them famous, as is a common occurrence among other popular artists (and a sort of conventional wisdom among certain music executives). Anyone familiar, though, with R.E.M.'s convictions knows that the title is meant to suggest that this is not simply a no-brainer, thrown out to the crowd to cash in on newfound popularity. While *Automatic for the People* explores somewhat similar musical territory as *Out of Time*, it also moves beyond it, and the lyrical content on the album weaves a complex and mournful tone. There isn't anything "automatic" about this album.

However, Stipe's interest in the "people" – i.e. the band's fans – is still present, and colors the album's opening track, "Drive." Evoking David Essex's 1970s hit "Rock On," Stipe sings, "Hey kids, rock 'n' roll, nobody tells you where to go, baby," but it's unclear whether these lines are statements or questions. Later, the line morphs into, "Hey kids, where are you? Nobody tells you what to do, maybe," and with a characteristically simple rearranging of words, Stipe manages to strike a complex chord, at once exhorting youth to assert themselves and their ideas, and yet questioning their ability to do so. This sentiment, and his address of the "kids" more broadly, may derive from the media buzz that surrounded the so-called "generation X" in the early 1990s, referring to the group of teens and "twentysomethings" coming of age at the time that were often stereotyped as apathetic "slackers." With the rise of alternative rock, a much-hyped novel (Douglas Coupland's *Generation X*, 1991), films (including Richard Linklater's *Slacker*, also 1991), and national newsmagazine cover stories (Gross and Scott, 1990; Giles et al., 1994), this youth group was very much in the news in the early part of the 1990s (see Mazzarella, this volume). However, if anything, *Automatic for the People* is about the opposite of youth, or at least its passing. Several of the album's songs have a sort of melancholy about them, and their lyrics frequently reference death ("Try Not to Breathe," "Everybody Hurts," "Sweetness Follows"). By the time the listener gets to the final song, "Find the River," she realizes that Stipe is speaking *to* the "kids," not as one of them. In that song, Stipe's narrator sings of the trials and difficulties of "finding his way" in the world, and he ends the song by directly addressing the listener: "All of this is coming your way." This is the voice of experience, looking back on youth and lost innocence with a sort of longing.

In addition, much was made of Stipe's lyrical references to "dead celebrities" on the album – Montgomery Clift, Andy Kaufman, Elvis Presley – and coupled with the fact that R.E.M. did not tour the United States to support either *Out of Time* or *Automatic for the People*, rumors began to circulate that Stipe was dying of AIDS or cancer. Such conjecture is telling in its own right about the nature of modern media, but this sort of salaciousness obfuscated deeper meanings in Stipe's specific references. Clift and Kaufman are kindred spirits for Stipe, and the singer used them as vehicles for an elaboration of the ideas about the celebrity's relation to audience that he had begun to explore on "Losing My Religion." Clift was a promising actor when he emerged in Hollywood in 1948, but he was uneasy in the spotlight, a reluctant star. He was also, it is speculated, either gay or bisexual, and as such must intrigue Stipe, whose sexuality was often the topic of speculation.[7] In "Monty Got a Raw Deal," Stipe sings, "You don't owe me anything," renouncing the sort of possessive claim that fans often make on stars, particularly in this age wherein the logic of the "market" reigns supreme, and fans may feel they're "owed" because they can take their almighty media attention elsewhere. Stipe's song for Clift presents a sort of understanding sympathy for the troubled star, and as Stipe repeats the line "just let go," the listener feels his desire for absolution and transcendence.

"Man on the Moon" is a thoughtful consideration of the artifice of performance and a tribute to the late comic performer Andy Kaufman. Kaufman's work was known for pushing the boundary between fiction and reality (in the later part of his career he became involved with professional wrestling, faking a feud with wrestler Jerry Lawler), and for pushing the audience as well. He often was intentionally abrasive, obscure, or just irritating, trying to provoke a response from an audience. In this way, his rise to fame in the mid-1970s appropriately parallels the emergence of punk rock, which often attempted to move the audience in a similar way. In a lyric seemingly composed of random pop culture references, Stipe sings, "Let's play Twister, let's play Risk," but the board games to which he refers also suggest the twists and risks that Kaufman made in his groundbreaking performances. He sings to the joy of the put-on: "If you believe there's nothing up his sleeve, then nothing is cool." Stipe wants to retain a sense of play for performance – it is a game, but crucially, it is also not "real." The celebrities we consume are not real, but rather media constructions.

Automatic for the People was another hit, largely due to the singles "Everybody Hurts" and "Man on the Moon." While generally a sort of sad, melancholic affair, the album does feature R.E.M.'s most overt and traditionally political song, "Ignoreland." Distorting his voice by singing through an amplifier, Stipe rants about the debasement of the United States following the so-called "Reagan Revolution." It is clearly meant as an election-year provocation, a call to arms to throw George Bush out of office, but its juxtaposition with the pretty and somber ballads on the album is somewhat jarring. Overall, the album casts quite a different tone than *Green* did just four years before. By *Automatic for the People*, the band and their music had matured, but they had also become more reflective, and Stipe's enthusiasm was getting mired in ruminations on celebrity worship. This theme would hit its fever pitch on the next album.

Monster, released in 1994, was a musical about-face for the group, shunning the acoustic experimentations of the previous two albums for a loud rock album. While some wrote this off as R.E.M.'s "grunge" album, it really had little in common (except loud guitars) with the form of alternative rock performed by bands like those that emerged from Seattle's Sub Pop scene of the early 1990s. However, the ghost of Nirvana's Kurt Cobain (who had committed suicide just months before the album's release) does hang over the album, but he is as much in the lyrics as in the music. *Monster* is, among other things, a biting criticism of the media industry and its celebrity-producing machine.

Broadly, the album concerns distortions, and thus the distorted sounds heard in many of the songs constitute an appropriate aural metaphor, creating layers of separation and "noise" between Stipe and the listener. The guitars make liberal use of feedback, echo, and other guitar effects. Two songs, "Let Me In" and "Circus Envy," feature guitar sounds that are easily among the most abrasive in R.E.M.'s catalog, and far more aggressive than anything the band recorded on I.R.S. Similarly, Stipe's vocals are often muffled or mumbled. On "Star 69," the vocals in each channel are recorded just out of phase, creating a strange echo effect that sounds like the listening equivalent of vertigo. With the exception of a couple of ballads placed in the center of the album, *Monster* is an assault on the ears – that is, compared to R.E.M.'s recorded output to that point. The CD label appropriately shows a graphic similar to the fuzzy static called "snow" or "white noise" that is seen on a television when no frequency is being broadcast.

The noise presented by the musical performance mirrors the sort of noise Stipe describes in his lyrics on the album. Initially, Stipe described the album in press interviews as a record about sex, and there is certainly a sexual element present on *Monster*. But crucially, the album is also about celebrity, and often about where the two intersect (captured perfectly in the title "Star 69"). Some of

Stipe's narrators explore the constructed, malleable nature of sexual identity, as on "Crush with Eyeliner" ("What position should I wear? . . . We all invent ourselves"). At other times, though, this trait merges with the creation involved in making media stars, as when the narrator of "King of Comedy" snarls, "Make it charged with controversy/I'm straight, I'm queer, I'm bi." Clearly, this is a reference to the speculation about Stipe's own sexuality, and *Monster* often plays like Stipe's tell-all in the wake of the rumors surrounding *Automatic for the People*. But if this is so, part of *Monster*'s loud noise is Stipe's anger with the type of media environment that has forced his hand, which makes the sex lives of celebrities a topic for public consumption.

The criticism of media, though, goes deeper than this, transcending Stipe's growing concerns about celebrity and the relation of performer to audience. *Monster* begins with "What's the Frequency Kenneth?" a clever song that uses a phrase from a mysterious street assault on CBS news anchor Dan Rather as a polysemic signifier for the unprecedented proliferation of media.[8] The song's narrator "never understood the frequency," and is seemingly baffled by the endless media environment that surrounds youth. The layers of meaning pile on top of one another: "frequency" connotes both "quantity" and "broadcast medium," while the attack itself happened to a major media figure and was then repeated endlessly through the media echo chamber. Indeed, merely the act of trying to tease out Stipe's intricate lyric evokes the deep web of "cartoons, radio, music, TV, movies, magazines" about which the narrator sings. But the song is also about youth, another reference to "Generation X," and the separation of the narrator from it, as is suggested by lines such as "you wore our expectations like an armored suit," and "you said that irony was the shackles of youth." There's more distance here than was evident on "Drive," the previous album's opening track; Stipe's narrators appear to be getting older and, as he wondered aloud in "Man on the Moon," "losing touch."

Other songs on *Monster* are notable for their critique of the media industry itself. On "King of Comedy," the narrator cynically skewers the business side of media production ("Make your money with a suit and tie"; "Make it easy with product placement"), but finally claims, "I'm not commodity." In an interview with Fricke (1995) Stipe admitted to the narrator's cynical voice, but then commented: "But, of course, I'm a commodity. I know that. And I'm fine with it. Really." The song "I Took Your Name" sounds like a tale of a relationship that's gone bad, but Stipe's narrator uses imagery that evokes the music industry ("master tape," "sales pitch"), suggesting, perhaps, the "marriage" of the band to the media has gone sour. Thus, Stipe's characters lash out in all directions – toward those who produce and consume media – in an attempt to illuminate the twisted world they have wrought.

Stipe's criticism takes on added resonance when one learns of two events that had a large impact on the making of *Monster*, both of which Stipe discussed in interviews. One is the death of Cobain, which came just as he was beginning to forge a friendship with Stipe; the two were discussing a possible musical collaboration. The other was the death of River Phoenix, a close friend of Stipe's, and the person to whom *Monster* is dedicated. Clearly, the untimely deaths of these two very young stars (27 and 23, respectively) is troubling in its own right, but both were known for shunning celebrity, and both were either known or suspected drug users. Stipe's ruminations about the pitfalls of media celebrity – that it can create "monsters" – obviously stem, in part, from the death of his two friends. This is made clear in the song "Let Me In," in which the singer, over an ominous, thunderous guitar, sings, "Yeah, all those stars drip down like butter . . . We hold out our pans, lift our hands to catch them/We eat them up, drink them up, up, up, up." References to "stars" recur in *Monster*, but here, Stipe's sad elegy suggests the result of our rabid desire to consume media celebrities and texts. The song takes on an even greater poignancy when one learns that the guitar played in the song belonged to Cobain, and was given to the band by Cobain's widow, Courtney Love.

Monster was followed by a long world tour which proved to be trying for the band: three of the four members found themselves in the hospital during the tour for unrelated illnesses, including a near-fatal aneurysm in drummer Bill Berry's head. The album spawned a number of singles, and it sold well, but not as well as the previous two. However, its anger and abrasiveness places it light years away from any of the three previous albums the band had completed for Warner Bros. Stipe and co. now seemed fully disillusioned by the media circus in which they lived, and this state of mind set the tone for the next album.

New Adventures in Hi-Fi (1996) is a strange album, recorded in various places during the band's travels during the *Monster* tour. The title is meant to evoke the era of "cocktail music" (1950s and 60s), which was enjoying a resurgence during the mid-1990s, but it is also an ironic reference to the fact that many of the songs were recorded during the sound checks of various tour dates. As the album cover – a black-and-white photo of a desert landscape that Stipe took from the band's tour bus – suggests, this album is about motion, travel, and change. Stylistically, it is a much more diverse album than the band had created in a while, juxtaposing the metallic crunch of *Monster* (as on the songs "The Wake-Up Bomb," "Undertow," and "Leave") with the acoustic feel of *Out of Time* and *Automatic for the People* ("New Test Leper," "E-Bow the Letter," "Electrolite"). It feels very loose and maybe schizophrenic – exactly what one would expect from an album recorded while on tour.

Nevertheless, the lyrics are often troubled, and they produce a general feeling of surrender or withdrawal. Stipe's narrators often voice a sort of despair: "I'm giving up" ("The Wake-Up Bomb"); "I'm drowning" ("Undertow"); "leave it all behind" ("Leave"); "I don't know what I want anymore" ("Bittersweet Me"). And while Stipe's concern with celebrity may not be as prevalent here as it is on *Monster*, it is still very much present. The narrator of "New Test Leper" describes a recent experience as a guest on a tabloid-talk show (e.g. *The Jerry Springer Show*) and speaks of being judged by the audience. On "E-Bow the Letter," Stipe sings, "This fame thing, I don't get it" (replacing the word "fame" with "star" on a later verse) in a haunting sung-spoken lyric. And "The Wake-Up Bomb," a tribute of sorts to the "glam rock" of the early 1970s, features this lyric: "I had to teach the world to sing by the age of 21 . . . I wake up, I threw up when I saw what I'd done." Sonically, this song has a sort of reckless abandon about it, but it is difficult to understand the narrator's motivation. It sounds, though, as if the anger of *Monster* has devolved into self-loathing or regret, and the singer's embrace of glam rock in the song is a cynical championing of a more superficial, less "meaningful" music. Here, and on much of *New Adventures in Hi-Fi*, Stipe sounds as if he's giving up on trying to "make a difference," or to communicate to an audience. Looking back over his career, he appears to feel that his efforts have been for naught.

The sixth song on the album, "Leave," summarizes this confusion and hurt perfectly. The song begins with an acoustic guitar slowly plucking out a melody over a somber-sounding keyboard drone. After about a minute, the song kicks into an urgent siren-like synthesizer riff, and the music gets louder, faster, and darker. The effect is an ominous wail, suggesting a dire emergency at hand. Stipe's vocals sound pained, too, and his narrator admits, "I lost myself in gravity, memory." We're not sure what he wants to leave, but it sounds desperate. Finally, the sentiment is eerily repeated in the final words of "Electrolite" (and thus the album, as it is the last song). As Stipe sings "I'm not scared," the music fades out, and he adds, *a cappella*, "I'm outta here."

New Adventures in Hi-Fi did not sell as well as *Monster*, and R.E.M. continued their slide down from the lofty heights they had enjoyed during *Out of Time* and *Automatic for the People*. Nonetheless, just before its release, Warner Bros. signed R.E.M. for a then unprecedented five-album, $80 million deal, which would begin with the album following *New Adventures in Hi-Fi* (1998's *Up*). Over the course of the band's original five-album contract, it had risen from indie sensation to worldwide stardom, but *New Adventures*, while not an absolute flop (it still sold millions worldwide), suggests that some of the band's luster had faded.

Conclusions

The band's trajectory over the five albums was one that constantly wrestled with ideas that are fundamental to producers and creators of popular music (and indeed of art in general): is being "popular" a good or a bad thing? On *Green*, the band's sound was full of hope and optimism for influencing mainstream audiences in a positive way; on *Out of Time*, they pulled back, exploring quieter moments and reflecting on their new experiences; *Automatic for the People* brought an even greater reflection, and its somber tones were matched with an increased lyrical interest in celebrity; *Monster* took on celebrity and the media head on, creating a loud rage of hurt and disappointment; and finally, on *New Adventures in Hi-Fi*, the band seemed scattered, with vocalist Stipe throwing up his hands and walking away in disgust from the highly-visible status for which he had such high hopes. Uncharacteristically, the band seems to have embraced the idea of becoming mainstream stars, with the idea that their influence would grow similarly. But they soon seemed disappointed with the lack of change and the vapidness of celebrity.

By the time *Up* was released in 1998, R.E.M. and Stipe seemed to be going in yet another direction. Original drummer Bill Berry had quit the band at the beginning of rehearsals for the album, leaving the band a three-piece. (Fiercely loyal, the other members decided not to permanently replace Berry, but rather employ session drummers.) Perhaps because of this departure, *Up* has a sort of down tempo, moody feel, and features a set of chamber-pop songs embellished with various studio effects and tricks. For the most part, Stipe's lyrical content moved on to other topics, but there is a lingering bitterness and perhaps some self-pity. "The Apologist" sounds like a cynical "apology" for ever trying to make a difference ("I wanted to apologize for everything I was"), while "Sad Professor," addressed to "dear readers," is a sad revision of Stipe's lofty intentions ("professors muddle in their intent to try to rope in followers"). Perhaps his most blunt statement comes in the strange opening track "Airportman," on which Stipe literally whispers the lines over a bleeping electronic beat. Ostensibly about a man traversing the "moving sidewalks" of an airport, the song shows Stipe's gift for creating meaning with a limited amount of words. In the beginning of the song, "great opportunity awaits," but then "blinks" in a later formulation of the phrase. The final line of the song, "The people mover, discounted," fits with the sort of futuristic airport environment created on the song, but it also effectively sums up Stipe's feelings about his past aspirations. Those who "move" people are discounted by others; those who are "popular" fall out of favor.

This seems like a fitting way for R.E.M. to start its second long-term contract with Warner Bros., considering the trajectory of the first. This moment is a natural one for reflection, and the "recycled air" Stipe mentions on "Airportman" suggests a hesitation and uneasiness about the band's position and continued relevance. Interestingly, *Up* was the first of the band's albums to include a complete list of printed lyrics in the album liner notes, a practice that was continued on the follow-up, *Reveal* (2001). On that album, Stipe hardly mentions his obsessions with celebrity and popularity. It seems to have played itself out with the slow decline of alternative music and R.E.M.'s status as a leader of that field.

Still, the band's work provides a marvelous entry point for a discussion of concepts central to popular music and other cultural experience: mainstream, popular, independent, celebrity, production, audience. The five albums that comprise R.E.M.'s first contract with Warner Bros. are highly self-reflexive and offer a lucid examination of the types of issues that were central to the post-alternative music "boom" of the 1990s. Methodologically my readings provide a starting point for studies of listener interpretations, or a more in-depth look at the factors (economic, technological, etc.) that helped to produce these albums. These two alternative projects would certainly increase understanding and offer, perhaps, a significantly different evaluation of bands' meanings and people's interpretation of these. But again, it is important and legitimate to stress the actions of the band as those of the artist-intellectual, offering meaningful texts that reflect thoughtfully on the contexts of their production and reception alike. Similarly, I underscore my own act of interpretation as a positive intervention in both the production of the band's artistic value (following social theories of art offered by, among others, Becker, 1982, and Bourdieu, 1993) and as inspiration for further studies of music texts within media studies. Studies of popular music, media, and culture should continue to deploy textual analyses, but these analyses can be formulated in such a way that they provide meaningful information about the various ways that people make, think about, and interact with media in their everyday lives.

Notes

1   I would like to thank Angharad Valdivia, Michael Elavsky, Mark Nimkoff, and Liz Perea for their helpful comments in preparing this essay.
2   I am thinking here of those scholars associated with the International Association for the Study of Popular Music (IASPM), as well as those who publish work in the journals *Popular Music* and the *Journal of Popular Music Studies*.
3   I have also deployed this approach in an analysis of *The Simpsons* (Sloane, 2003).
4   Another very real deterrent to the analysis of lyrics is the increasing crackdown on obtaining the rights to publish lyrics. As such, I have tried to cite lyrics judiciously in this essay, and would direct the reader to compendia of the band's lyrics on the World Wide Web. For a discussion of the legal rights to cite lyrics in academic work, see http://www.iaspm.net/rpm/CopyRi_1.html.
5   While I often refer to Stipe as the author of the lyrics, it should be noted that all of R.E.M.'s original compositions are credited to "Berry/Buck/Mills/Stipe." Thus, the band is the true author of all of its songs, music and lyrics. However, it is common knowledge that Stipe, like many vocalists, writes the majority of the lyrics for the band, and admits as much in interviews and discussions of their recording process.
6   The video for the song, directed by Katherine Dieckmann, depicts a multi-ethnic crowd of people dancing in front of a large banner representing the world, but behind this banner – in a sort of "backstage" area – a man works hard to pedal a bicycle that makes the whole scene out front turn. Thus, even with this "lighthearted" song, the band and Dieckmann are able to make a point about the toil and suffering that often lie beneath "happiness."
7   The singer, who had always given indeterminate answers about his sexuality, described himself as a "queer artist" in a 2001 interview with *Time* magazine.
8   In 1986, Rather was attacked by a man who kept calling him "Kenneth" and asking him, "What's the frequency?" The event received an inordinate amount of press coverage, with many believing that Rather was fabricating the story.

References

Baran, S. J. (2002). *Introduction to Mass Communication: Media literacy and culture* (3rd edn.). Boston: McGraw-Hill.
Becker, H. S. (1982). *Art Worlds*. Berkeley: University of California Press.

Bourdieu, P. (1993). *The Field of Cultural Production: Essays on art and literature* (ed. R. Johnson). New York: Columbia University Press.

Campbell, R. (2000). *Media and Culture: An introduction to mass communication* (2nd edn.). Boston: Bedford/St. Martin's.

Chapple, S. and Garofalo, R. (1977). *Rock 'n' Roll is Here to Pay: The history and politics of the music industry*. Chicago: Nelson-Hall.

Christenson, P. G. and Roberts, D. F. (1998). *It's Not Only Rock & Roll: Popular music in the lives of adolescents*. Cresskill, NJ: Hampton.

Covach, J. and Boone, G. M. (1997). *Understanding Rock: Essays in musical analysis*. New York: Oxford University Press.

Fricke, D. (1995). Monster on the loose. *Rolling Stone*, March 23, 27–32.

Frith, S. (1988). *Music for Pleasure*. New York: Routledge.

Frith, S. (1996). *Performing Rites: On the value of popular music*. Cambridge, MA: Harvard University Press.

Gelder, K. and Thornton, S. (eds.) (1997). *The Subcultures Reader*. London: Routledge.

Giles, J., Quinn, J. B., and Elliott, M. (1994). Generalizations X. *Newsweek*, June 6, 123, 62–72.

Gross, D. M. and Scott, S. (1990). Proceeding with caution. *Time*, July 16, 136, 56–63.

Grossberg, L. (1996). Toward a genealogy of cultural studies: The discipline of communication and the reception of cultural studies in the United States. In C. Nelson and D. P. Gaonkar (eds.), *Disciplinarity and Dissent in Cultural Studies*. New York: Routledge, pp. 131–47.

Hall, S. (1993). Encoding/decoding. In S. During (ed.), *The Cultural Studies Reader* (pp. 90–103). New York: Routledge. (Original work published 1990.)

Hebdige, D. (1979). *Subculture: The meaning of style*. New York: Routledge.

Hesmondhalgh, D. (1998). Post-punk's attempt to democratise the music industry: The success and failure of Rough Trade. *Popular Music*, 16(3), 255–74.

Johnson, R. (1996). What is cultural studies anyway? In J. Storey (ed.), *What is Cultural Studies? A reader*. New York: Arnold, pp. 75–114. (Original work published 1986–7.)

Jones, S. (1992). *Rock Formation: Music, technology, and mass communication*. Newbury Park: Sage.

Kellner, D. (1995). *Media Culture: Cultural studies, identity, and politics between the modern and the postmodern*. New York: Routledge.

Kellner, D. (1997). Critical theory and cultural studies: The missed articulation. In J. McGuigan (ed.), *Cultural Methodologies*. Thousand Oaks, CA: Sage, pp. 12–41.

Lull, J. (ed.) (1992). *Popular Music and Communication* (2nd edn.). Newbury Park: Sage.

McCarthy, C. (2001). Mariners, renegades, and castaways: C. L. R. James and the radical postcolonial imagination. *Cultural Studies ↔ Critical Methodologies*, 1(1), 86–107.

Middleton, R. (2000a). Introduction: Locating the popular music text. In R. Middleton (ed.), *Reading Pop: Approaches to textual analysis in popular music*. Oxford: Oxford University Press, pp. 1–19.

Middleton, R. (ed.) (2000b). *Reading Pop: Approaches to textual analysis in popular music*. Oxford: Oxford University Press.

Peterson, R. A. (1976). The production of culture: A prolegomenon. In R. A. Peterson (ed.), *The Production of Culture*. Beverly Hills: Sage, pp. 7–22.

Peterson, R. A. (1997). *Creating Country Music: Fabricating authenticity*. Chicago: University of Chicago Press.

R.E.M. (1983). *Murmur* [CD]. Universal City, CA: International Record Syndicate.

R.E.M. (1984). *Reckoning* [CD]. Universal City, CA: International Record Syndicate.

R.E.M. (1986). *Life's Rich Pageant* [CD]. Universal City, CA: International Record Syndicate.

R.E.M. (1987). *Document* [CD]. Universal City, CA: International Record Syndicate.

R.E.M. (1988). *Green* [CD]. Burbank, CA: Warner Bros.

R.E.M. (1990). *Tourfilm* [Videotape]. Burbank, CA: Warner Bros.

R.E.M. (1991a). *Out of Time* [CD]. Burbank, CA: Warner Bros.

R.E.M. (1991b). *Shiny Happy People*. [Videotape]. Burbank, CA: Warner Bros.

R.E.M. (1992). *Automatic for the People* [CD]. Burbank, CA: Warner Bros.

R.E.M. (1994). *Monster* [CD]. Burbank, CA: Warner Bros.

R.E.M. (1996). *New Adventures in Hi-fi* [CD]. Burbank, CA: Warner Bros.

R.E.M. (1998). *Up* [CD]. Burbank, CA: Warner Bros.

Sloane, R. (2003). Who wants candy? Disillusionment in *The Simpsons*. In J. Alberti (ed.), *Leaving Springfield*: The Simpsons *and the possibilities of oppositional culture*. Detroit: Wayne State University Press.

Thornton, S. (1996). *Club Cultures: Music, media and subcultural capital*. Hanover, NH: Weslyean University Press of New England.

Walser, R. (1993). *Running with the Devil: Power, gender and madness in heavy metal music*. Hanover, NH: University Press of New England.

Weaver, W. (1949). *The Mathematical Theory of Communication*. Urbana: University of Illinois Press, 3–28.

Willis, P. (1978). *Profane Culture*. Boston: Routledge & Kegan Paul.

Further reading/listening/viewing

DeVito, D., Schamberg, M., and Sher, S. (1999). *Man on the Moon* [film]. Universal City, CA: Universal Pictures.

Editors of *Rolling Stone* (1995). *R.E.M.: The Rolling Stone files*. Hyperion: New York.

Frith, S. and Goodwin, A. (1990). *On record: Rock, pop, and the written word*. London: Routledge.

Platt, J. (ed.) (1998). *The R.E.M. Companion*. New York: Schirmer/Simon & Schuster/Macmillan.

R.E.M. (1985). *Fables of the Reconstruction* [CD]. Universal City, CA: International Record Syndicate.

R.E.M. (1987). *Dead Letter Office/Chronic Town* [CD]. University City, CA: International Record Syndicate.

R.E.M. (2001). *Reveal* [CD]. Burbank, CA: Warner Bros.

Ross, A. and Rose, T. (1994). *Microphone Fiends: Youth music and youth culture*. New York.

PART TWO

Production

CHAPTER FIVE

Approaches to Media History

John Nerone

In his 2000 Presidential Address to the American Historical Association, Robert Darnton, one of the foremost cultural historians and probably the most widely read scholar in the interdiscipline called the history of the book, called for historians to begin working on the history of communication (Darnton, 2000). Depicting it as a neglected dimension of both cultural and political history, Darnton gave a few concrete examples of what such a history would look like in practice. His address was certainly well received by the community of academic historians. Programmatic statements often have negligible impact; we will have to await the "judgment of history" on this one as well.

To the many scholars who have in fact been working to construct a history of communication, Darnton's address gave an eerie sense of having stepped into a time warp. Many lesser voices have called for such a history over the past twenty years, and many think they have answered the call. Nevertheless, Darnton is certainly correct: the community of professional historians has not recognized this work as having its own identity or its own subject matter. At the same time, many cultural or political or social historians would be surprised that their work has been taken up by media scholars as histories of communication. What explains this curious failure to harmonize across disciplinary systems?

The root cause of the failure of professional historians to write a history of communication, or in a narrower register a media history, is the very sense of what it is that separates professional from amateur history on the one hand and speculative or natural history on the other. To explain this statement, I'll need to take a digression through the history of professional history.

History professionalized itself as an academic field in the early nineteenth century, particularly in the German universities, and particularly in the seminars of Leopold von Ranke (Iggers, 1997; Krieger, 1977; Ross, 1990; Novick, 1988). Working off the classical distinction between nomothetic (i.e. theory-positing) and idiographic (describing unique objects) disciplines, Rankean historians developed a series of methods (archival research, philological analysis, the seminar) that would allow historians to claim to set aside both political motivation and philosophical abstraction in order to give accounts of the past as things actually and uniquely happened. In turn, these practices set professional history apart from both the popularizers (including, incidentally, women – Smith, 1998) and from the many other academic ways of representing the past: the evolutionary approaches of biologists and anthropologists, the nomothetic accounts of sociologists, political scientists, and economists, and above all the speculative philosophy of history. Hegel, Marx, Darwin, Spencer, and the other intellectual giants of the nineteenth century all wrote about the past, but in ways that professional historians bracketed off.

The practices that professional historians adopted imposed certain limits on the kinds of narratives they could construct. The reliance on documents and philology meant that historians would focus attention on the kinds of individual and institutional actors that produced documentary records. Professional history emphasized past politics, centering on the nation-state (not coincidentally, the rise of professional history mirrored the rise of the nation-state) and the careers of the great men. The hostility to abstraction and generalities meant that proper professional histories would shun grand narrative, or, to be more precise, would assume their readers shared certain obvious and therefore invisible grand narratives – like the rise of Western civilization and the progress of freedom in the world. And both of these characteristics put together meant that historians as a community would discuss the past by telling progressively more precise and detailed stories. Historical knowledge, it was thought, would advance as historians produced more and more solid little accounts. All of these bricks, as it were, would at some point assemble themselves into a mighty cathedral of knowledge; in the meantime, it only retarded matters for practitioners to assert pretensions as architects. Historians as brickmakers and bricklayers, like journalists as well, viewed with disdain attempts to prematurely assign meaning and significance to historical events and processes. Such idle pursuits populated the leisure of the theory class, they quipped.

This version of the mission of history endured through most of the twentieth century, but not without periodic rebellions. Progressive historians, especially Carl Becker, pointed out the pragmatic work that historians perform as mythmakers (Becker, 1966), celebrating the "relativism" of the craft, and challenging its privileged segregation from the many kinds of remembering that ordinary folk perform. Various movements in social history – the "new history" in the US, the Annales movement in France, and the many forms of marxist historiography – questioned the emphasis on past politics. But all retained a common-sense notion of the distinction between historical work and every other kind of social science.

A tipping point was finally reached in the last quarter of the twentieth century, when theoretical trends in historiography intersected with a crisis in the political economy of the discipline to undermine the brickmaker conception of historical practice. In theory, the structuralist moment called attention to the constructedness of historical narratives, terminally blurring the classic distinction between nomothetic and idiographic disciplines (White, 1973). At the same time, a job crisis hit history, along with the other humanities and social sciences. As a side effect of the scarcity of jobs, the amount of published work required to earn job security multiplied, leading to an out-of-control increase in the amount of reading a competent historian would have to master. Previously, it had been possible for a conscientious historian to read everything scholars published in a fairly large field – early modern Europe, for instance. Subsequently, it became impossible for scholars to simultaneously read up in even a well-focused field and to do the primary research to write one's own contributions.

For both practical and theoretical reasons, then, the brickmaker model has lapsed. One would think that this would result in a tremendous opening up of professional history to new ways of achieving coherence in narratives. To a certain extent, it has, but at the same time scarcities and insecurities have discouraged anything like a new paradigm. Historians exist in the first place because they have created a distinctive set of practices; nothing in the current situation allows them to discard these practices.

The traditional practices of the professional historian make it very difficult to recognize "communication" or "media history," even though professional historians do it all the time. What political history is written without continual if anonymous reference to the processes and effects of political communication? (McGerr, 1986; Remini, 1963; Ward, 1955.) What cultural or intellectual history does not implicity invoke the networks through which notions are diffused and communicated? (Smith, 1950; Slotkin, 1985.) No work has been more influential to media historians than Elizabeth Eisenstein's (1979) *The Printing Press as an Agent of Change*, which was in her mind a work of intellectual history. Because of the practices of historical research and the poetics grounded therein, such work is respected as political or cultural history, and disregarded as media history. This is because to historians the media don't really exist. And they're right, too.

To historians, the proper subjects of historical narratives must always be things in themselves. A good example of a thing-in-itself is, say, George Washington, or the International Monetary Fund, or the Universal Declaration of Human Rights. In addition to their fairly obvious concreteness, each produces a documentary record that allows historians to verify the statements one might make about what each one did. Communication and media, on the other hand, are incoherent assemblages of many different kinds of things – rhetoric, texts, organizations, technologies. To write a history of communication makes about as much sense as writing a history of things that begin with the letter "b."

But the crisis of the profession makes such a comfortable assertion illegitimate. The structuralist moment, the postmodern condition, the humilities of the disciplines make one question the thing-in-itselfness of everything. What is the International Monetary Fund besides a shifting network of alliances between state and financial actors? And wasn't the public George Washington as artificial as Elvis or the Beatles? A sophisticated historical analysis of anything should be a lesson in the constructedness of everything.

Perhaps now, at long last, Darnton and others can call a history of communication into existence, not by inspiring new work but by recasting the many different modalities of writing media history into a recognized field. A quick survey of the kinds of work that media historians constantly invoke will make you dizzy. In addition to all the work by historians, scholars from many other disciplines inhabit our little pantheon of citations – sociologists like the Lynds or Herbert Gans or Anthony Giddens or Pierre Bourdieu, political scientists like Seymour Martin Lipset, scholars of education like Lawrence Cremin, literary scholars like Raymond Williams or Marshall McLuhan, philosophers like Jürgen Habermas or Michel Foucault, economists like Harold Adams Innis or George Rogers Taylor or Alfred Chandler. Candidates for inclusion in a catalog of media historians would include any work in new historicist literary criticism, or the emerging field of the history of the book or of print culture, or the history of literacy, or the history of technology, not to mention the more obvious fields of journalism history and cinema studies and First Amendment law. A big and unruly lineup.

An attention to the poetics of historical scholarship, which I've already invoked, suggests that the best way to map this proposed field would be to focus on the formal elements of narratives – the available plots and characters and so forth. Obviously, the most important poetic choice involves the leading character – the media. The many different ways of defining this term resolve into two basic approaches, which will provide the organizing structure for this essay. Within these two broad characterizations, a series of different plots and frames are deployed by various scholarly communities, and these in turn inhabit different disciplines. Because of their sheer numbers, the treatment of the different disciplinary homes will have to be cursory and selective. In addition to the baseline disciplines, at least two well-defined interdisciplines produce media history – the history of technology and the history of the book. Each has its own scholarly apparatus (the Society for the History of Technology and the Society for the History of Authorship, Reading, and Publishing – SHOT and SHARP). The many varieties of media history give the (valid) impression of a field in search of definition. In recent years, one promising tent with room for most has been the history of civic culture or the public sphere. I'll conclude the essay by discussing the public sphere as an organizing motif.

To begin, the field divides into two families of approaches that are based in two different ways of defining the media.

Two Meanings of Media

Scholars use "media" to mean two different things. One usage refers to the material or technology used to communicate. In this usage, the media are paper, or radio waves, or the spoken word; this reflects the usage of artists, engineers, physicists, and architects, who were using the term "medium" to describe the materials worked with long before anyone ever thought of media as a way of talking about mass communication. In the history of comm scholarship, the most famous users of the term in this sense are Innis, McLuhan, and others of the so-called Canadian School. I'll refer to this usage as media/technology.

The second more familiar usage refers to the organizations that produce media of mass communication. In this usage, the media are broadcast stations and the *New York Times*; this reflects the usage of advertising agencies, who began to describe newspapers, magazines, and radio as media around 1920. Adopted by social scientists in the 1930s, the word "media" suddenly acquired obviousness in the wake of World War II – at this point it came to seem familiar, like it had always been in use, whereas it and the parallel term "mass communication(s)" were really quite novel. I'll refer to this usage as media/institution.

Media/technology

The so-called Canadian school, the most consistent and best known practitioners of this mode of media history, demonstrate both its virtues and problems. Innis (1950, 1951) and McLuhan (1962, 1964) offer a schema of media history that is at once so grand that media/technology are everything and so abstract that media/institution disappear into the background. Although their historical accounts differ in important ways – Innis emphasizing economic mechanisms, and McLuhan psychological ones – both insist that the materialities of communication work as an invisible engine to history.

Much of Innis's and McLuhan's work seems crude, brash, and dated today, and is admired by historians primarily as provocations. Work of such sweep and power inevitably violates the mentality expressed in two of the favorite expressions of historians: "It was more complicated than that," and "Much more work needs to be done. . . ." Innis and McLuhan's media "monocausality" and "technological determinism" violate the historian's conviction that important events always have many causes. More recent scholars working in the same genre, like Walter Ong (1982), James Carey (1988), and Elizabeth Eisenstein (1979), are more careful to qualify and nuance their claims, but still are criticized for being technocentric.

Another defining feature is its insistence on telling really big stories. Innis dealt on the level of Empire; McLuhan on the level of stages of cognitive development. Whether the immediate issue was the transportation of timber in North America or the development of vowels in ancient Greece, the real story, the point of it all, was the world-historical shift in communication systems. In both authors, and in their admirers, the frame of all history is the grand narrative of stages of development from oral to written (alphabetic, printed) to electronic communication. Micronarratives are interesting only because they confirm this grand narrative. This style of history has its predecessor in Enlightenment and positivist histories of cultural development which also tended to pivot on the rise of literacy (Heyer, 1988; Nisbet, 1969) – ironically, the kind of grand narrative or speculative history that historians expelled from the kingdom of professional history during the reign of Ranke.

One can imagine a "denatured" form of this genre, one in which the grand narrative has been sacrificed. Innis and McLuhan suggest that in any age there is a distinct media environment, and this is a useful tool for a kind of media history. This part of their thinking suggests a genre of microhistories that would look like thick descriptions of specific media environments, work on the order of the dense local histories produced by scholars influenced by the French Annales tradition (Le Roy Ladurie, 1978; Davis, 1975. I think here of the "total histories" of the Annales school, as opposed to histories of civilizations.) There is no currently existing genre of such historical work that focuses on the media, though one can point to a few marvelous isolated examples, like William Gilmore's (1990) *Reading Becomes a Necessity of Life*, or David Hall's (1996) essays. The problem here is that in "histoire totale" the function of the media tends to disappear as a foreground category, and gets swallowed almost entire by all the things that the media mediate. This is the flip side of Innis and McLuhan, where media eat everything else.

One way to reclaim the specificity of communication in such total histories is to expand one's definition from the circulation of messages to circulation generally. Armand Mattelart's (1996) *The Invention of Communication* is an interesting case in point. In seeking to free "communication" from its common restriction to "media" and yet to retain some of the concreteness of the more limited term, Mattelart elides the line between communication and transportation. The danger here is that, instead of constructing a suitably large protagonist, one ends up with an unbounded one – a story where anything and everything is communication. After all, what is the difference between the media and the marketplace? Isn't money, for instance, a medium? Mattelart's grand narrative inevitably flattens into something McLuhanesque, though without the media: a history of the linear growth of the uniform space of the nation, one with a patent affinity to other influential French scholarship.

Michel Foucault's (1970, 1977, 1978) historical work, along with that of others influenced by him, including Deleuze and Guattari, shares the poetics of the Canadian school without being aware of the fact. The Foucauldians suggest a media history in which everything is the media, but subsumed under the sign of "discourse" (rather than "technology," as in Innis and McLuhan). In terms of both substance and source material, what results is a totalization of history that is primarily intellectual (just as the Annales school totalized history as economic). In this there is a surprising affinity to the narratives constructed by scholars invoking Weber and finding a progressive "rationalization" and "bureaucratization" in modern Western history. In the grandest version of this history, Beniger (1986) outlines a series of "control revolutions" in which information technologies – from DNA to the computer – emerge as (politically neutral) solutions. He is clearly indebted to the business histories of Alfred Chandler (1977), which also see a stately progression toward efficient organizational forms underlying an apparently messy history. This is Foucault's narrative with exclamation points in place of question marks. Whether it wears the mask of comedy or tragedy, the resulting narrative has a flatness, partly by design but partly by accident. Mattelart, for instance, in deciding that the history of communication is really about the creation of a uniform transparent national space, does not intend his history to turn into a march to the northeast corner, as wags call growth charts that show a continual upward trend. Likewise, Foucault did not intend to have everything pivot simply on the shift from resemblance to representation (in *The Order of Things*) or the shift from punishment to discipline (in *Discipline and Punish*), and doesn't intend to have surveillance march to the northeast corner likewise. But the initial narrative choices prefigure such a plotline.

The unmistakable elegance of this kind of media history comes from the fact that all the important moves have been made before one enters the archives. In writing a Foucauldian history of photography, one will be delighted to discover a connection between the new technology and reforms and shifts in police procedures (Lalvani, 1996) because these confirm the disciplinary vector. But the disciplinary vector will have emerged anyway – the frame demands it. One doesn't do history to find the unexpected – in a Foucauldian genealogy, the unexpected is a given.

The claim that history must emerge from the archives, the rallying cry for the professionalizers since the founding of the discipline, has been called into question many times by scholars who (correctly) note that one cannot enter the archives empty-headed, and that the archives themselves didn't fall from heaven but were placed there by folks with an agenda. Still, historians insist that their discipline requires a fidelity to the past which is disregarded by those who would see it as simply another form of rhetoric in service to present agendas (Morris, 1998). Historians insist on the reality of the past – not a simple, objective reality, but a reality that resists the present in ways that historians are bound to honor. Hence the common (though fading) perception that Foucault and his followers do not honor the past (Poster, 1982) has some credibility. Certainly we don't read Foucault's histories of sexuality to learn how the Greeks screwed; rather, they are exercises in the philosophy of the self, and therefore relatively impervious to falsification from the archives. The same might be said to be true of histories in the mode of media/technology generally, which have a durability that more prosaic histories lack. We will be reading McLuhan, like Foucault, long after diligent scholars have disproven or complexified all of his factual conjectures.

Media/institution

In technological histories, the media seem to continually drift as signifiers. But when the term media was borrowed by social scientists from advertising professionals in the 1930s, its meaning was pretty fixed. To advertising people, the media were anything in which you might place an ad (Agnew, 1932). When scholars began to use it regularly after World War II its meaning was only a little more complex: it referred to what used to be called "the press" plus the film industry, radio, and television – what Malcolm Willey (1933) memorably called instruments of "mass impression."

Postwar communication scholars, especially the institution-builders who founded the earliest doctoral programs in communication, defined the media in such a way as to forward a particular agenda. They wanted to extend the problematics of "press" studies – how did biases, distortions, and stereotypes in the media produce dysfunctions on the individual and societal levels? – but wanted to do so in a way that would liberate them from the confines of "j-schools." They wanted a fully academic field, not one yoked to the requirements of journalism as a profession.

By an accident of history, though, scholars turned to the term media just when a new medium, television, was being introduced. Ironically, then, television has been the archetypal medium for both people and scholars, and most of our ways of thinking about media are bound up in the history of television, just as most of our ways of thinking about "the press" are bound up in the history of the daily newspaper.

This gives media/institution an opposite problem to media/technology when it comes to doing history. For media/technology, all of history becomes media history, so that media institutions disappear. For many versions of media/institution, all of history is prehistory until network television. This tendency is only strengthened by the allergy to the past that infects all media studies: The media belong to OUR generation – the dim past saw ordinary people, imprisoned in boredom, lost to the life of the senses, living little lives in the comforting matrices of "folk" culture. To comb that past for precursors of the media might be amusing, but hardly of any moment. A countervailing disdain comes from "serious" cultural historians, who think that "media historians" have no business in the archives, as there are no media to be found there.

But in fact there was TV before TV. The reason why television was the quintessential medium from late-twentieth-century thinkers was that it allowed for a single text to be put in the eye of virtually everyone – to appear before a mass audience at the same time, to be read in the same flow, and to be received in apparent privacy. Television seemed to represent the culmination of one particular vector of communication history. And we can find earlier such tools in this same vector. That's why most media textbooks begin with printing and feature newspapers (and sometimes books) as mass media.

The typical textbook maneuver is to lay out the different tools in ascending order and call that media history. This history, though, is curiously divorced from concrete history – from the million interwoven stories of everything happening – and confidently triumphalist, marching steadily toward TV heaven. The founding generation of communication scholars produced a history of the media that reads as a history of tools. Wilbur Schramm (1988) offers the paradigm case. This history again was elegant, fitting admirably into strains of comm theory that emphasized a modernization narrative. It also fit the common expectation of non-historians that history be a narrative of individual innovators and specific events with precise names and dates. Samuel F. B. Morse invented the telegraph, Edison the phonograph, Bell the telephone, Daguerre the photograph, Marconi the radio, and so forth. (Odd that there is no inventor for the ultimate medium, television.) But again it explained away all the kinds of history that you would labor in the archives for. The kinds of electric telegraph that preceded Morse's, for instance, are of only antiquarian interest.

Much of the thinking of this genre of media history (we might call it museum history, after Nisbet, 1969) involves meditating on the uses and implications of the various technologies. Sometimes this can be done without a great deal of historical work, just by thinking about the way the telephone allows new forms of presence, for instance. Such work mirrors McLuhan's.

The television vector is especially limiting, however. Earlier tools, like the telegraph, were many things besides precursors to television, and the history of media tools is pleasurably messy. Some of the most influential work in media history is precisely dedicated to finding the anti-modern tendencies in responses to novel communication technologies, to recovering the unexpected noise and struggle that accompanied the construction of any new medium (Cohen, 1990; Czitrom, 1982; Douglas, 1987; Marvin, 1988; Nasaw, 1993; Ohmann, 1996; Spigel, 1992). Czitrom's *Media and the American Mind* stands as the first of these social or cultural histories. It incorporates two recurring tropes that have long histories in other genres of media histories – the inevitability of market forces, and the resulting failure of media to fully achieve their communal and political potential. In Czitrom's account (which is mirrored in the other histories I've cited), each new medium begins with utopian (and complementary dystopian) visions, but then is eventually captured by an emerging corporate order which is essentially conservative.

Czitrom's history shows how paying attention to the construction (rather than the ontology or phenomenology) of media tools has meant also paying attention to markets and industries – the systems of production and exchange that helped define the media. Media/institution histories have usually been pegged to a vague history of capitalism in the same way that media/technology histories are pegged to a vague history of modernism, a connection that is frequently explicit (as in Benedict Anderson's (1991) use of the term "print capitalism" to refer to a particular set of uses of literacy). There are good reasons for this.

The printing press is the first tool of mass production. Long before the invention of standardized parts by Eli Whitney, printers were using moveable type to produce identical copies of finished goods in indefinite numbers. Print workplaces divided and routinized labor long before Ford's assembly line. The newspaper, because it packaged new content under the same nameplate day after day, was the first brand-name good available to ordinary people. So it makes sense that the rise of capitalism is a common frame in media history.

The Capitalism frame dominates much of the media history of the nineteenth century, the century of *The Long Revolution* (Williams, 1961) and *The Making of the English Working Class* (Thompson, 1963), two classic works usually not thought of as media histories. If any media technology is proto–industrial, still the age of industrialization marks the key moment for the formation of the organizations that we now think of as the mass media. One reason is that new sources of mechanical power, and the machines that harnessed them, allowed the media to become much more "mass." The steam press made it possible for newspapers and magazines to print hundreds of thousands of copies in a day, and the railroad made it possible to distribute them across wider regions. Electricity grids tamed unruly urban spaces, and electric lighting allowed reading outside of daylight hours and spaces. Telegraphy annihilated transmission lags for much information. Photography allied with printing allowed visual images with claims to realistic representation to be "broadcast" to distant places. By the mid-nineteenth century, the great illustrated weeklies in western Europe and the US had avowed a mission to provide virtual presence at historic occasions for middle-class readers: Frank Leslie, the great American entrepreneur of illustrated news, set this as his contract with the reader: you couldn't go to Lincoln's inauguration, but if you had, here is the mental image that you would have retained from it.

At the same time, industrialization created the characteristic audiences of the media. Although the media claim to transcend or even erase class boundaries, the fact is that the specific media that advanced mass distribution all began by appealing to the working classes, and by the same token were all opposed by the traditional moral guardians of the middle classes. As a result, the study of media audiences has drawn much attention from historians of working-class culture, many of them deeply influenced by E. P. Thompson (Butsch, 2000; Cohen, 1990; Couvares, 1984; Denning, 1987; Peiss, 1986; Rosenzweig, 1983).

The deep irony in this is that the media simultaneously reflect a class structure and obscure it. The early history of every popular medium involves a frank appeal to the reader as working class – popular print and film are the most familiar examples (Denning, 1987; Jowett, 1976; Lehuu, 2000). But at the same time the media are normatively credited with erasing social distance. And much of the furor that has traditionally greeted new media comes from the class and race mixing that they seem to invite – for instance, the imitation of black culture by middle-class white youth in rock and roll and rap or hip hop.

This irony is written deeply into the first critiques of mass culture. Tocqueville's (1969) *Democracy in America* credits the media with amplifying the "tyranny of the majority," and John Stuart Mill's (1859) *On Liberty* condemns the culture of "mediocrity" that results from improvements in communication, transportation, and mass education. Both authors see the mass public that democracy by its very nature demands and creates as undermining the enlightenment and empowerment that democracy promised. Their critique seems on the surface profoundly elitist. But it need not be read that way. One could read it as a profound populism, blaming not the people but the market and electoral mechanisms that endow numerical majorities with cultural authority. In either case, this original version of the mass culture critique rests on a deep belief in reason and enlightenment, and implies a disappointed vision of the media as a tool of the same.

The mass culture critique is compelling because it displays the conflict between the Capitalism frame of media history and the Democracy frame. If the age of industrial revolution seemed to fix the technological and economic forms of the modern media, it was the age of Revolution, that is, political revolution, that fixed the IDEA of the media, the norms of what it was the media were supposed to do. The mass culture critique has been if nothing else an extended meditation on the conflict between the democratic mission of the media and their mode of production, distribution, and reception.

In Western societies, the modern media have always stood at the intersection between two grand distributive systems, politics and the marketplace. In politics, the logic of the republic – one person one vote – is supposed to guarantee that public reason will produce equitable outcomes. People won't get screwed. In the marketplace, the logic of commerce – one dollar one vote – is supposed to guarantee dynamism and growth. Although somewhat democratic – dollars don't recognize aristocratic privilege – markets are not engines of social equality, thriving as they do on jealousy and emulation, implying that some are rich and others are not. In theory, politics and the marketplace will occupy separate spheres, and mutually police each other, preventing noxious concentrations of power across spheres. The media need to mediate between the two spheres, translating market success into an ability to provide a platform for political deliberation.

This model of liberal democracy drove two early genres of media history: "journalism history" and the history of freedom of the press. Journalism history can be said to have begun, in the US, at least, with Isaiah Thomas's (1970) *History of Printing in America*, published in 1812. Thomas had himself been an important printer, his active career spanning half a century from the 1760s. He intended his *History*, written from the point of view of a craft printer and press entrepreneur, to offer moral exemplars for aspiring printers, on the one hand, and to wrap the history of printing up in the history of the republic. These twin missions – craft memory and the republic – continued to inform journalism history for most of the next century. And there was a lot of it – still is – because pressworkers have and will feel a need to tell their own history. Journalism history started to be an academic enterprise in the twentieth century, with the landmark surveys by Willard Bleyer (1927), Frank Luther Mott (1960), and Edwin Emery (1988), all written from within a "progressive" frame. (Progressive here refers to the movement in historical studies led by Charles Beard, Frederick Jackson Turner, and Carl Becker to refocus attention from the foregrounded political history to the social and economic background, and at the same time to tell history in a politically engaged voice as struggles for power, usually with the "people" as the good guys.)

Journalism history had a natural affinity for progressive themes. Journalism was, after all, the literature of the masses, and the mission of journalism was to afflict the comfortable while comforting the afflicted. This progressive mode of journalism history suited the professionalism project of journalism too. J-history became a natural feature of j-schools generally, and the leading figures in j-education were often the leading historians – Bleyer and Mott in particular. Inevitably, however, the scholarly aims of j-history have come into conflict with its professional ones, leading in the 1970s to a flurry of programmatic statements, seeking to free j-history from bondage to the training of journalists and join it instead in a happy marriage with intellectual history or cultural studies or literary studies or any of a number of other available partners (Carey, 1974; Dicken Garcia, 1980; Hardt, 1995). J-history has not found a suitable mate, and continues to pleasure itself while fantasizing about its prowess.

The second traditional form of "public" media history was the history of freedom of the press. Even more venerable than j-history, the narrative of freedom of the press began at least as early as Milton's (1644) *Aeropagitica*, which projected an opportune history of censorship to buttress its claim that, because the Pope invented censorship, it must be anti-Christian. At various points in English, French, and North American history in the eighteenth century, similar genealogies of state control offered rhetorical support for arguments for liberalization. In the US, these histories achieved scholarly respectability at around the same time as j-history, when a coherent civil liberties community formed around World War I. Zecchariah Chafee's (1941) classic work established a dominant progressive paradigm, which was then complexified by Siebert's (1952) *Freedom of the Press in England* and Leonard Levy's (1960) *Legacy of Suppression*, both of which argued that libertarian practices came about slowly and often unintentionally, rather than being birthed whole by a heroic generation of forward-thinking political activists.

For both j-history and the history of freedom of the press, World War I was a bracketing moment, particularly in the US. An ensemble of factors – the existence of actual censorship and propaganda, the intensifying influence of visual media like film, intellectual currents that emphasized the irrational in human psychology – made both journalists and lawyers more likely to write histories of these sorts. Such scholarship drew strength from a liberal consensus. Journalists and lawyers both considered the big story to be how individuals had been, on the one hand, protected from government encroachments, and on the other hand, informed so as to be able to function as competent citizens.

This narrative depended on an underlying fiction of a public of self-directed rational citizens. It supposed that the media should and could operate as transparent information resources, on the one hand, and as neutral, active champions of the people on the other – a vision of the media that combined an early republican concept with a more recent image of the journalist-as-hero. It also supposed that the marketplace would promote such media. And it projected this image back into the distant past, trying to portray even John Milton as a modern market libertarian.

Although this model of press operation offered real ideological strengths, it also displayed obvious philosophical and historical weaknesses. Shortly after

World War I, Walter Lippmann (1922) gave a convincing anatomy of these weaknesses in his classic work *Public Opinion*. Using Plato's myth of the cave as his text, he preached a damning sermon about the limitations of the ordinary citizen, who can think only in stereotypes and in dramatic story lines, and about the limitations of the mainstream press, which is compelled by the market to cater to the debased thinking of ordinary folk. If public opinion depends on popular intelligence working on information from the press, it will become increasingly stupid, increasingly out of touch with a complicated world. Lippmann's solution involved the creation of "intelligence bureaus," staffed by value-free experts, feeding reliable information to decision-makers. Lippmann himself never thought that the press could work as an intelligence bureau – it was too hampered by the need to make a profit. But the press itself, realizing that its legal protection from supervision needed to rest on something more noble than a simple claim to property rights, began to talk seriously of responsibilities as well as rights – claiming, of course, that its responsibilities were in fact served by its pursuit of profit. This new notion of a professionalized press was ratified in the US by the Hutchins Commission (Commission on Freedom of the Press, 1947; McIntyre, 1987).

The Hutchins Commission is perhaps the most interesting index of common-sense thinking among post-World War II intellectuals about the media. For one thing, it overtly elided the distinction between "the press" and the "media," using the press in its title but taking the subtitle "A General Report on Mass Communication." This move allowed it to use the requirements of a democratic society as a normative frame for thinking about the media. In turn, this yielded a common-sense historical account of media development. In the original moment, when "the media" meant the printing press, access was cheaply available to anyone with any real reason to address the public. The result was an open marketplace of ideas (a phrase of relatively recent coinage that became a default metaphor for the public sphere around the end of World War II).

But economies of scale coming from new technologies turned the media into massive institutions, and new visual technologies accelerated that process. Now the media marketplace no longer provides a marketplace of ideas. So a more enlightened cadre of owners, publishers, artists and journalists must provide it, insuring that all important viewpoints are expressed and all important groups are represented. Providing the proper media environment will produce a progressive society, by which the commission appears to mean that individual citizens, confronting accurate and reliable information and sympathetic portrayals of groups other than their own, will become increasingly tolerant and intelligent, and produce an increasingly fair society. No change in the legal rights of media owners or in the economic structure of the media is needed to effect this change.

This liberal common sense at the same time invokes and ignores its history. On the one hand, it tells a story in which the media operate democratically only when they compete vigorously with each other, and only when they lack the power to define reality – to say unilaterally what "the news of the day" is. This is faithful to Mill's *On Liberty* (1859), which argues that self-government is real only when real individuals do things for themselves. It also expresses the common-sense notion that function follows structure. An accessible media marketplace will produce an accessible marketplace of ideas. But common sense recognizes the inconvenience of these arguments in the modern era. To take these as lessons of history would mean that the media system, to function democratically, would have to be revolutionized from the bottom up. Concentrated ownership needed to be broken up. Journalists needed more autonomy from publishers and readers from journalists. The media world should be turned upside down. How is it that the Hutchins Commission, and by extension liberal thinking about the media, can fail to say that? Only by implicitly appealing to the sovereign reader.

This liberal common sense immediately faced an anti-liberal account. This account begins in the same place, with an imagined past of media competition and active citizen-readers or viewers. But it views the citizen readers as ultimately products of rather than creators of their media environment. Just as a competitive media environment produced active readers, a non-competitive late-industrial media environment produces mass audiences. The most influential formulations of this "culture industry" perspective are Horkheimer and Adorno (1972). In their hyperbolic *Dialectic of Enlightenment*, they present a picture of a media environment dominated not by the *New York Times* but by Hollywood film, an industrial structure which manufactures audiences with characteristic structures of feeling in much the same way as Ford's assembly lines disciplined workers.

Horkheimer and Adorno are so influential because they are so easily caricatured. Critics charge that they see people as cultural "dupes" or "dopes." Instead, critics propose, we should think of modern media culture as the equivalent of folk culture (Levine, 1992). This position combines a real populism – we like people who like media – with the appeal to history from the bottom up, or ethnohistory, that flourished in the historical profession in the 1970s and beyond. The culture industry argument, they explain, mistakes the industrial production of media culture for its meaning. Rather, its meaning is actively produced by its consumers. Taken to its extreme, this position argues that, whatever it is the media make, they do not really act until individual readers or viewers read or view and respond, or that the work of the media exists as the sum total of all the acts of reading by individual audience members.

This project remains I think the dominant vector in the interdiscipline called the History of the Book. A transnational movement with important institutional centers in the US, the UK, France, Italy, and Germany, and an umbrella organization in the Society for the History of Authorship, Reading, and Publishing, the History of the Book is a movement that has reacted to a series of impulses in several different fields. Historians joined up in response to the crisis in the subfield called the History of Ideas, where the crucial absence of empirical support for the influence of canonical ideas was underscored by the appearance of counter-narratives in the 1960s. At this point, formative work in the Annales tradition (Chartier, 1995; Le Roy Ladurie, 1978) inspired more quantitative and business-oriented studies of the diffusion of ideas (Darnton, 1977; Graff, 1995). A similar impulse among literary scholars intensified in response to and in reaction against the post-structuralist and postmodern impulse in literary theory, with some seeing research in the materialities of reading as furthering the work of theorists like Barthes and Derrida, and others seeing the same work as providing refuge from the theorists gone rabid. The major trend in such work is the careful mapping of networks of production, distribution, and consumption of texts. The implicit model is of a bundle of linear transmission circuits, in which ideas are written by an author, then printed and distributed by a publisher, sold by a bookseller, and consumed by a reader. Only when a circuit is completed does any juice – "culture" or "meaning" – flow. That is, only when individual readers consciously encounter and embrace an idea do ideas have historical effect or existence. This model gave historians something concrete to look for, i.e. acts of reading. And it promised that, upon accumulation of enough microhistories of readers reading, we would actually arrive at a coherent composite account of the history of the media.

This position seems hopelessly romantic to media scholars now. A generation of research into reading acts has produced much evidence of contrariness on the part of readers (Radway, 1984; Zboray & Zboray, 1997) but no real coherence across accounts. Instead, the individual reader and the audience seem to exist on different planes. The PUBLIC, a collective body, is not the PEOPLE, all of the individual readers or citizens. Instead, the public exists only through acts of representation, and the media have more power than the people when it comes to representing the public. The history of reading practices remains important as a project in itself. But its status as media history looks more and more like an artifact of a populist version of liberal ideology.

In its place has emerged a history of the spaces of the media. The archetype of this kind of space is the public sphere, the space in which public opinion is said to form. Public sphere histories have been popping up like mold on old bread for more than a decade now, since the translation of Habermas's (1989) *Structural Transformation of the Public Sphere* and the publication of Michael Warner's (1990) *The Letters of the Republic*, and are clearly a counter-trend to the histories of reading in the history of the book.

The allure of Habermas to historians is easy to explain. He provides a way out of key impasses in what used to be called the history of ideas. One is the question of ideology. Historians have one traditional tool for settling disagreements about the shape of prevailing ideologies in the past, and that is a rather crude battle of quotations. You say "liberal" and I say "republican," and so you quote Locke and I quote Macchiavelli, and then you quote everyone quoting Locke and I quote everyone quoting Macchiavelli, and you say my quotations are obscure and unimportant, if numerous, and I say yours are formulaic and superficial, if numerous, and we have a standoff. What Habermas does, as Warner pointed out, is to add a "metadiscursive" dimension to this question of ideologies. Instead of counting words, we can settle our argument by appealing to the shape of the space in which these words worked.

In the process, the public sphere frame turns what had usually been an idealist narrative into a materialist one. Instead of reconstructing the coherence and power of arguments in abstract terms, research into public communication should recover its veiled sociology, displaying the mechanisms by which voices were generated and heard. The approach therefore has the virtue of assigning value to the work to be done in the archives, even while providing an important theoretical framework that combines descriptive and normative dimensions.

Such an approach invites a number of empirical questions from scholars working in the liberal tradition. Who had access to the public sphere – who got to speak, and who tended to listen? How were individual minds made up by public discourse? Did public discourse advance or retard individual rights, including the rights of women and minority group members, or were their interests better served by "civil society?" Not surprisingly, the answers to these questions often challenge a critical account of the public sphere (Baker, 2001; Calhoun, 1992; Landes, 1988; Ryan, 1997).

This "counter-history" of the public has been forcefully synthesized by Michael Schudson (1999). His account challenges a series of attitudes in the Habermasian account of the public sphere: a perceived nostalgia for eighteenth-century rationality in discourse, a notion of an unspoiled Golden Age for the public sphere, a sense of decline attached to first the commercialization and then the industrialization of the media, in terms of both access and content, and the resulting impulse to condemn the contemporary media and especially modern journalism as deviations from a democratic tradition. Schudson argues that early public discourse did NOT involve the bulk of the population, and was closed for the most part to ordinary men, women, and minority group members. Subsequent public discourse invited in a broader spectrum of the people, but more as passive spectators or members of interest groups than as disinterested rational citizens. Disaffected from politics, most individuals have found their interests served more by the marketplace. The people have chosen private life over public life, and the fantasy of deliberative democracy, which has existed at no point in modern history, will and should never exist. This account favors Lippmann over Habermas.

This account seems simply historical. But it shifts its ground in covering US history in disturbing ways. In discussing the Revolutionary generation, much is made of the rhetoric, public and private, of a supposedly homogeneous group of founders, who considered "democratic" to be a bad word. Quite right. No attention, however, is paid to dissident founders (Cornell, 2000), or to movements from the bottom up (Hoerder, 1977; Nash, 1979). Careful attention is paid to the extent of popular participation in terms of voting and reading newspapers and pamphlets, but the level of participation is judged by comparison with later, not earlier standards, in a classic case of anachronism. As a result, it's possible to conclude, with considerable evidence, that the "Revolutionary generation" neither wanted, expected, nor engaged in considerable participatory democracy. Of course, any observer at the time, and, I think, any sympathetic historian, saw the period as convulsed with movements from outside established leadership circles, and as characterized by a continual countermovement to contain an exploding political arena. Sure it's wrong to think Tom Paine stands for the entire "Revolutionary generation," but his success deserves a full explanation.

In moving from the eighteenth century to the nineteenth, though, the account shifts its ground and strategies. The respect paid to the intentions of the founders is absent from discussion of the leaders of the first mass political parties, who are understood purely as opportunists. The children of Tom Paine also disappear from this history, except for the abolitionists. Populism and Socialism don't appear as political movements, and the labor movement gets scant attention too. By ignoring through brute force the flood of scholarship on such matters, one may depict the resulting hegemonic public sphere as both consensual – it's what the people spontaneously chose – and uninteresting – the people didn't seem to care much about it.

This sanitized version of the nineteenth century then foreordains the solution to the problems of the twentieth. How can one help but agree with Walter Lippmann when he proposes to rescue government from the people? They are self-regarding, ill-informed, and easily deluded, and in no way qualified to deal with complexities that are better refereed by experts.

Besides being questionable history, this account also offers a weak reading of the public sphere itself. Again, this is because of its initial choices. As we've already noted, the public is not the people, nor is it any collection of specific people. The public is a particular kind of relationship. Moreover, the public, and hence public opinion, exists only through representation. (Habermas himself misstates this when he declares that a piece of the public is created whenever people gather to discuss issues of common concern.) So it is silly to try to measure the public sphere in terms of raw access, or in crude indexes like voting participation. More important is the observance of "publicity" as a norm; a history not recorded in readership or voting levels, but in the qualitative openness of political discussion. The fact that the major partisan newspapers engaged in protracted discussions of currency policy and tariffs, for instance, demonstrates that "publicity" existed as a norm of discourse. Voting (and its subsequent secularization, polling) are the crudest and perhaps the least reliable measures of publicity. They are, in fact, designed to be private and not public acts. That they demonstrate "the people" to be oriented toward privacy is an artifact of their own design.

There is a more interesting synthesis of the history of the public to be written, one that will be more attentive to space than voting, and one that will be more attentive to the media than news. Solid work has already appeared in this direction, largely concentrating on the history of urban public spaces, and combining a Habermasian approach with the tools of social history (Brooke, 1998; Ethington, 1996; Ryan, 1997).

Moving this work from the local to the national level invokes a media/institution counterpart to media/technology histories of space. Media/technology histories generally work at the nexus of tools and space, whether geographical or social. Media/institution histories of space look at the geographical diffusion of messages through specific networks (Blondheim, 1994; Pred, 1973; Taylor, 1958). Such work naturally merges with and draws upon work done in geography (Glacken, 1967; Harvey, 1989), and promises a point of convergence for media/technology and media/institution histories. Like the virtual space of the public sphere, the actual spaces that communication operates in and constructs can frame a broad history of media.

Conclusion

In the course of this free-ranging survey, I've touched on many different loci of media history – some more appealing than others, but each with its own claim to integrity and legitimacy within its own field. These loci share little beyond their interest to media historians. They do not engage in similar projects and do not consciously address each other. For most, "media history" is a side effect of another agenda. Literary scholars studying the relation of Walt Whitman's poetry to popular culture (Reynolds, 1995) address their work to Whitman scholars, not to, say, journalism historians. Some will react with surprise – even alarm – when learning they've come to the attention of media scholars, or are thought of as contributors to media history.

If media history is at present a secondary orientation for many of its most important exemplars, it is an increasingly important one. Media history organizations have recently formed in the UK and France, and in the US media studies has become a more explicit designation in older academic organizations like the American Studies Association or the Organization of American Historians.

But media history cannot expect to achieve concrete status as a primary scholarly locus until it develops a common vocabulary and set of problems. The very fluidity of the term "media" retards its development as a field, partly by multiplying beyond control the range of ways to problematize aspects of media history. The plenitude of media history, the very thing that makes it most attractive to those of us who do think of ourselves as media historians, is also the thing that makes it unlikely to solidify as a field. It also robs it of its disciplinary force – its ability to set standards for practitioners.

Without a more articulate agenda, media historians will have no clear reason to labor in the archives. As it stands, for most media scholars, historical questions are easily answered without the archives by appealing to a convincing theory-based explanation: one can, for instance, explain the origins of "objectivity" by appealing to the demands of the modern or of late capitalist class relations or of the surveillance imperative, depending on how one understands one's own position.

But the archives is where these different positions must confront one another. Although historians have acknowledged that they do not enter the archives empty-headed, still they insist, rightly, that their discipline obliges them to submit their preconceptions to the rigors of the available documentary record, and therein to the encounter with opposing preconceptions, in a setting where theoretical differences can be, it is hoped, adjusted, rearranged, sharpened, or dismissed.

The beauty of historical scholarship is its ability to queer what seems perfectly clear outside the archives. This delights pros and frustrates amateurs, whose goal in turning to history in the first place is clarity and decisiveness. Amateurs assume that no one can trump the judgment of history. But the pros know that history renders a settled judgment only when no one any longer cares, or, in most cases, when everyone involved is long dead. In the meantime, history produces not clarity but a more intelligent muddle.

This is beauty for the middle-aged and jaded. It is the beauty of nuance, texture, irony, and complexity, the surprise found in the small variations that disturb repetitive processes. It's jazz, not rock. It's baseball. Media studies, which revels in things that rock, may not incline to the leisured attentions of the jazz fan, and sadly, too, because there's no better history to get jazzed on than media history. No other history is obliged to blend more superficially competing voices.

References

Agnew, H. E. (1932). *Advertising Media: How to weigh and measure*. New York: D. Van Nostrand.

Anderson, B. O. (1991). *Imagined Communities: Reflections on the origins and spread of nationalism*. London: Verso.

Baker, H. A. (2001). *Critical Memory: Public spheres, African American writing, and black fathers and sons in America*. Athens: University of Georgia Press.

Becker, C. L. (1966). Everyman his own historian. In C. L. Becker, *Everyman His Own Historian: Essays on history and politics*. Chicago: Quadrangle, pp. 233–55.

Beniger, J. R. (1986). *The Control Revolution: Technological and economic origins of the information society*. Cambridge, MA: Harvard University Press.

Bleyer, W. G. (1927). *Main Currents in the History of American Journalism*. Boston: Houghton Mifflin.

Blondheim, M. (1994). *News Over the Wires: The telegraph and the flow of public information in America, 1844–1897*. Cambridge, MA: Harvard University Press.

Brooke, J. L. (1998). Reason and passion in the public sphere: Habermas and the cultural historians. *Journal of Interdisciplinary History*, 29, 43–67.

Butsch, R. (2000). *The Making of American Audiences: From stage to television, 1750–1990*. New York: Cambridge University Press.

Calhoun, C. (ed.) (1992). *Habermas and the Public Sphere*. Cambridge, MA: MIT Press.

Carey, J. W. (1974). The problem of journalism history. *Journalism History*, 1(3–5), 27.

Carey, J. W. (1988). *Communication as Culture: Essays on media and society*. Boston: Unwin Hyman.

Chafee, Z. (1941). *Free Speech in the United States*. Cambridge, MA: Harvard University Press.

Chandler, A. D. (1977). *The Visible Hand: The managerial revolution in American business*. Cambridge, MA: Harvard University Press.

Chartier, R. (1995). *Forms and Meanings: Texts, performances, and audiences from codex to computer.* Philadelphia: University of Pennsylvania Press.

Cohen L. (1990). *Making a New Deal: Industrial workers in Chicago, 1919–1939.* New York: Cambridge University Press.

Commission on Freedom of the Press (Hutchins Commission) (1947). *A Free and Responsible Press.* Chicago: University of Chicago Press.

Cornell, S. (2000). *The Other Founders: Anti-federalism and the dissenting tradition in America, 1788–1828.* Chapel Hill: University of North Carolina Press.

Couvares, F. G. (1984). *The Remaking of Pittsburgh: Class and culture in an industrializing city, 1877–1919.* Albany: SUNY Press.

Czitrom, D. J. (1982). *Media and the American mind: From Morse to McLuhan.* Chapel Hill: University of North Carolina Press.

Darnton, R. (1977). *The Business of Enlightenment: A publishing history of the Encyclopedia, 1775–1800.* Cambridge, MA: Harvard University Press.

Darnton, R. (2000). An early information society: News and the media in eighteenth-century Paris. *American Historical Review*, 105, 1–29.

Davis, N. Z. (1975). *Society and Culture in Early Modern France: Eight essays.* Stanford, CA: Stanford University Press.

Denning, M. (1987). *Mechanic Accents: Dime novels and working-class culture in America.* New York: Verso.

Dicken Garcia, H. (1980). *Communication History.* Beverly Hills: Sage.

Douglas, S. J. (1987). *Inventing American Broadcasting, 1899–1922.* Baltimore: Johns Hopkins University Press.

Eisenstein, E. L. (1979). *The Printing Press as an Agent of Change: Communications and other culural transformation in early modern Europe.* New York: Cambridge University Press.

Emery, E. and Emery, M. B. (1988). *The Press and America: An interpretive history of the mass media* (7th edn.). Englewood Cliffs, NJ: Prentice-Hall.

Ethington, P. J. (1996). *The Public City: The political construction of urban life in San Francisco, 1850–1900.* Berkeley: University of California Press.

Foucault, M. (1970). *The Order of Things: An archaeology of the human sciences.* New York: Vintage.

Foucault, M. (1977). *Discipline and Punish: The birth of the prison.* New York: Vintage.

Foucault, M. (1978). *The History of Sexuality.* New York: Pantheon.

Gilmore, W. J. (1990). *Reading Becomes a Necessity of Life: Material and cultural life in rural New England, 1780–1835.* Knoxville: University of Tennessee Press.

Glacken, C. J. (1967). *Traces on the Rhodian Shore: Nature and culture in Western thought from ancient times to the end of the eighteenth century.* Berkeley: University of California Press.

Graff, H. J. (1995). *The Labyrinths of Literacy: Reflections on literacy past and present.* Pittsburgh: University of Pittsburgh Press.

Habermas, J. (1989). *Structural Transformation of the Public Sphere: An inquiry into a category of bourgeois society* (trans. Thomas Burger). Cambridge, MA: MIT Press.

Hall, D. D. (1996). *Cultures of Print: Essays in the history of the book.* Amherst: University of Massachusetts Press.

Hardt, H. (1995). Without the rank and file: Journalism history, media workers, and problems of representation. In H. Hardt and B. Brennen (eds.), *Newsworkers: Toward a history of the rank and file.* Minneapolis: University of Minnesota Press, pp. 1–29.

Harvey, D. (1989). *The Condition of Postmodernity: An enquiry into the origins of cultural change.* Oxford: Blackwell.

Heyer, P. (1988). *Communications and History: Theories of media, knowledge, and civilization.* New York: Greenwood Press.

Hoerder, D. (1977). *Crowd Action in Revolutionary Massachusetts, 1765–1780.* New York: Academic Press.

Horkheimer, M. and Adorno, T. (1972). *Dialectic of Enlightenment*. New York: Herder and Herder.

Iggers, G. G. (1997). *Historiography in the Twentieth Century: From scientific objectivity to postmodern challenge*. Hanover, NH: Wesleyan University Press.

Innis, H. A. (1950). *Empire and Communication*. Oxford: Clarendon Press.

Innis, H. A. (1951). *The Bias of Communication*. Toronto: University of Toronto Press.

Jowett, G. (1976). *Film: The democratic art*. New York: Oxford University Press.

Krieger, L. (1977). *Ranke: The meaning of history*. Chicago: University of Chicago Press.

Lalvani, S. (1996). *Photography, Vision, and the Production of Modern Bodies*. Albany: SUNY Press.

Landes, J. B. (1988). *Women and the Public Sphere in the Age of the French Revolution*. Ithaca: Cornell University Press.

Le Roy Ladurie, E. (1978). *Montaillou: Cathars and Catholics in a French village, 1294–1324*. London: Scolar.

Lehuu, I. (2000). *Carnival on the Page: Popular print media in antebellum America*. Chapel Hill: University of North Carolina Press.

Levine, L. W. (1992). The folklore of industrial society: Popular culture and its audiences. *The American Historical Review*, 97, 1369–99.

Levy, L. W. (1960). *Legacy of Suppression*. Cambridge, MA: Harvard University Press.

Lippmann, W. (1922). *Public Opinion*. New York: MacMillan.

Marvin, C. (1988). *When Old Technologies were New: Thinking about electric communication in the late nineteenth century*. New York: Oxford University Press.

Mattelart, A. (1996). *The Invention of Communication*. Minneapolis: University of Minnesota Press.

McGerr, M. E. (1986). *The Decline of Popular Politics: The American north, 1865–1928*. New York: Oxford University Press.

McIntyre, J. S. (1987). Repositioning a landmark: The Hutchins Commission and freedom of the press. *Critical Studies in Mass Communication*, 4, 136–60.

McLuhan, M. (1962). *The Gutenberg Galaxy: The making of typographic man*. New York: New American Library.

McLuhan, M. (1964). *Understanding Media: The extensions of man*. New York: McGraw Hill.

Mill, J. S. (1859). *On Liberty*. London.

Milton, J. (1644). *Areopagitica*. London.

Morris, M. (1998). *Too Soon Too Late: History in popular culture*. Bloomington: Indiana University Press.

Mott, F. L. (1960). *American Journalism* (3rd edn.). New York: MacMillan.

Nasaw, D. (1993). *Going Out: The rise and fall of public amusements*. New York: Basic Books.

Nash, G. B. (1979). *The Urban Crucible: Social change, political consciousness, and the origins of the American revolution*. Cambridge, MA: Harvard University Press.

Nisbet, R. A. (1969). *Social Change and History: Aspects of the western theory of development*. New York: Oxford University Press.

Novick, P. (1988). *That Noble Dream: The objectivity question and the American historical profession*. New York: Cambridge University Press.

Ohmann, R. M. (1996). *Selling Culture: Magazines, markets, and the middle class at the turn of the century*. New York: Verso.

Ong, W. J. (1982). *Orality and Literacy: The technologizing of the word*. London: Methuen.

Peiss, K. L. (1986). *Cheap Amusements: Working women and leisure in New York City, 1880 to 1920*. Philadelphia: Temple University Press.

Poster, M. (1982). Foucault and history. *Social Research*, 49, 20–40.

Pred, A. R. (1973). *Urban Growth and the Circulation of Information: The United States system of cities, 1790–1840*. Cambridge, MA: Harvard University Press.

Radway, J. A. (1984). *Reading the Romance: Women, patriarchy, and popular literature*. Chapel Hill: University of North Carolina Press.

Remini, R. V. (1963). *The Election of Andrew Jackson*. Philadelphia: Lippincott.

Reynolds, D. S. (1995). *Walt Whitman's America: A cultural biography.* New York: Knopf.

Rosenzweig, R. (1983). *Eight Hours for What We Will: Workers and leisure in an industrial city, 1870–1920.* New York: Cambridge University Press.

Ross, D. (1990). *The Origins of American Social Science.* New York: Cambridge University Press.

Ryan, M. P. (1997). *Civic Wars: Democracy and public life in the American city during the nineteenth century.* Berkeley: University of California Press.

Schramm, W. L. (1988). *The Story of Human Communication: Cave painting to microchip.* New York: Harper & Row.

Schudson, M. (1999). *The Good Citizen: A history of American civic life.* Cambridge, MA: Harvard University Press.

Siebert, F. S. (1952). *Freedom of the Press in England, 1476–1776.* Urbana: University of Illinois Press.

Slotkin, R. (1985). *The Fatal Environment: The myth of the frontier in the age of industrialization, 1800–1890.* New York: Atheneum.

Smith, B. G. (1998). *The Gender of History: Men, women, and historical practice.* Cambridge, MA: Harvard University Press.

Smith, H. N. (1950). *Virgin Land.* Cambridge, MA: Harvard University Press.

Spigel, L. (1992). *Make Room for TV: Television and the family ideal in postwar America.* Chicago: University of Chicago Press.

Taylor, G. R. (1958). *The Transportation Revolution, 1815–1860.* New York: Harper & Row.

Thomas, I. (1970). *The History of Printing in America.* New York: Weathervane.

Thompson, E. P. (1963). *The Making of the English Working Class.* New York: Pantheon.

Tocqueville, A. de (1969). *Democracy in America.* New York: Harper & Row.

Ward, J. W. (1955). *Andrew Jackson: Symbol for an age.* New York: Oxford University Press.

Warner, M. (1990). *The Letters of the Republic: Publication and the public sphere in eighteenth-century America.* Cambridge, MA: Harvard University Press.

White, H. V. (1973). *Metahistory: The historical imagination in nineteenth-century Europe.* Baltimore: Johns Hopkins University Press.

Willey, M. M. (1933). *Communication Agencies and Social Life.* New York: Van Nostrand.

Williams, R. (1961). *The Long Revolution.* New York: Columbia University Press.

Zboray, R. J. and Zboray, M. S. (1997). Have you read . . . : Real readers and their responses in antebellum Boston and its region. *Nineteenth-Century Literature, 52,* 139–70.

CHAPTER SIX

Ethical Issues in Media Production

Sharon L. Bracci

Current debates in media ethics address long standing issues within and outside of media structures and practices. Structural issues consider whether organizational patterns intersect media purposes in ways that constrain ethical practices. Contextual concerns take up various economic, political, cultural, and intellectual currents that comprise the larger environment in which media operate. Interest here is on how this broader environment might exacerbate problems and impede solutions to the structural issues. While the scope of issues today echoes historical concerns, efforts to theorize conceptual tools to address media issues reflect both conceptual extensions of and breaks with the past.

Historically, media ethicists in the Western tradition have generally presumed a dual function media system that ideally serves democratic as well as commercial purposes. A second presumption holds that media's broad freedoms of expression entail responsibilities to carry out their democratic function, which is the political rationale for their freedoms. Scrutiny has focused on better and worse ways media pursue their democratic and commercial functions through production efforts that inform, influence, and entertain mass audiences. Ethical considerations today, while wide-ranging and diverse, generally begin from these potentially competing purposes to provide relevant and useful news and information to audiences as citizens and to amuse them as commercial consumers. Ongoing concerns that arise out of this functional perspective center on whether media practices distort, manipulate, or thwart their purposes, and whether media practices harm others, including competitors and audiences.

This attention to how media fulfill their purposes and affect others necessarily engages the technology that makes mass communications possible. Today, ethical debates confront media's rapidly changing and expanding technological shape. These contemporary shifts provide their own momentum for ethical issues to be resolved within "new media" frameworks that blur lines among information, influence, and entertainment values. The possibilities and challenges of technologically driven media are profound. On the one hand, technological innovations can serve media's democratic function by increasing citizen access to and participation in relevant communication practices. These possibilities include the democratizing hopes for the Internet; the enormous speed, volume and diversity of news and information available through broadband channels; and media's powerfully expansive, global connections. On the other hand, many of these innovations are expensive, complex, and highly concentrated, making it very difficult for competing newcomers to form new media channels and for many individuals to participate in the technological bounty. These arrangements raise concerns that innovations create a digital divide that favors antidemocratic market forces. Digitalization also signals content worries over privacy, fairness, and accuracy in high speed, nonstop, and easily anonymous communications. Increasingly, ethical analyses engage power and privilege as key variables of technologically driven media structures.

Innovations in mass communications technology also provide the economic impetus to create media structures that follow business trends toward integrated transnational models. As technological shifts drive media structures, media ethics examines the implications of these global arrangements. Historically, structural tensions have raised ethical interest because media, in democratic societies, are both profit-making private enterprises and institutional mediators of news and information citizens need to become fitted for self-governance. Media organizational patterns place their practices in perpetual ethical tension. While this tug between profit-making and democratic functions is not new, it is particularly salient in the current climate of business consolidation that concentrates global media power into a handful of transnational conglomerates. Concentrated media power increases the potential for conflicts of private versus public interest and rehearses historical concerns that market-driven decisions work against the democratic health that relies on a knowledgeable, engaged citizenry.

A related set of structural issues emerges out of the integral relations between media organizational patterns and advertising supports. As is the case with broader structural conflicts, the relationship between advertising and media functions does not signal unprecedented concerns. Current organizational trends merely heighten interest in the global drive to maximize profits through advertising revenue. Advertizers pay well for exposure in media environments that deliver audiences who are disposed to buying. A commercial media model has powerful economic incentives to use its broad freedoms of expression to deliver programming that keeps audiences in a buying mood and advertisers eager to reach them. Considerable ethical inquiry focuses on the interpenetration of market and production values that serve commercial interests but minimize less profitable pursuits that fulfill media's democratic purposes.

The broader cultural and intellectual context in which media operate also influences the shape and tone of media ethics debates and poses significant challenges for resolving the structural issues. Recurring periods of negative public attitudes toward media, for example, increase perceptions of dysfunctional democratic processes, a situation of civic breakdown in urgent need of repair.

Many analysts argue that, especially in Europe and the US, media confront a current cycle of public cynicism toward media practices. Critics fear that when media news gathering and reporting practices are seen as untrustworthy, self-interested, and biased, citizens become less inclined to seek out the news and information that affect their lives. Negative public attitudes toward media workers and practices, many conclude, correlate to widespread political apathy and disconnection from community life.

Efforts to engage what many characterize as disaffected and sometimes hostile publics bring media ethics debates within the ambit of ethical theory debates. Media ethicists often note a crisis of confidence in the ability of classical moral philosophy to adjudicate differences, guide ethical media practices, and build public trust. Current trends reconceptualize normative models of media structures and practices. These reformulations attempt to serve citizens' interests by bringing media's dual purposes into closer balance. Regulatory proposals include both proactive self-regulation models and hybridized approaches that include legislative reform. Globally, reconceptualizations of speech freedoms are moving toward positive, global human rights and normative models of media ethics seek grounding within a social ethics framework.

In what follows I focus on the technological, structural, and selected contextual dimensions as they contribute to the central ethical issues in media production today. While production issues necessarily overlap related questions regarding potentially harmful content that negatively affects audiences, the focus here is on technologically-driven structural problems and the challenges that outside forces pose to constructive resolutions.

The Digital Revolution

Developments in technology have played a significant role in shifting print and electronic media from local, regional, and national interests to a global reach. In Europe, state owned, public service broadcasting proliferated as "old media," in print and television, emerged while in the US national commercial networks dominated. Increasingly, however, technological innovations significantly affect how media owners shape global organizational infrastructures and media practices.

Media convergence

The contemporary impetus for change is digital convergence. Through digitalization, information is translated into a standardized binary code. As previously distinct communications-related industries (computer, telecommunications, and screen display) converted from analog to digital coding, they reproduced information in a universal computer language that different industries recognized. The resulting convergence of coding, transmission, and retrieval processes for images, text, and sound meant that diverse industries with sufficient interest and resources to convert to digitalization could communicate across national borders. This convergence made possible a global infrastructure that exploited the digital possibilities in radio, cable, fiber optics, and satellite to carry large volumes of information rapidly along a global network.

The volume is possible because digitalization compresses the spectrum space needed to transmit information and images quickly. These changes in communications technology and the Internet not only speed up the global transfer of information, they also signal a potentially democratizing effect, since anyone with the new technology can use it as a forum for global discussion and exchange. Digitalization, as Van Den Bulck (2000) notes, positions the computer screen as a coveted function in this network. It is an increasingly interactive, potentially profitable locus of global news, information and entertainment, where "ever more diverse symbolic data can be stored, transmitted and consulted" simultaneously (p. 217).

New technology

New television and data transmission technology in satellites, fiber optics, and digital compression increases global access to news and information through global broadcasters including CNN, the BBC's WSTV, Reuters, and The News Corp. European countries have added more commercial television to their public broadcasting networks. Current international satellite distribution systems include a consortium of 119 countries and estimates project nearly 800 commercial satellites to serve the Asian Pacific basin. Emerging technology to develop a multi-satellite system that does not rely on ground wires for transmission will enable countries without this infrastructure to gain access to voice and Internet communications (Johnston, 1998, pp. 57–60). Alternatively, innovations in fiber optic technology provide a cost-efficient alternative to satellite costs for video transmission.

It is not only news and information that travel globally to those with broadband or satellite access; commercial information travels as well. As a result, corporations across industries strive to merge strengths in content and delivery in the hopes of gaining profitable access to new technology users. The ability to exploit new markets through Internet distribution becomes more important as phone lines give way to cable, wireless communications expand, and commercial interests place more content on-line. Technological innovations that affect distribution possibilities encourage companies to pursue an advantageous access to consumers and technological efficiencies mean more distribution methods can be used for commercial purposes. A closer look at shifts in media organizational patterns examines how media structures follow technological changes. These shifts also afford a closer look at how media carry out their democratic and entertainment functions within a framework of global possibilities set in motion by digitalization.

Media Ethics: Structural Issues

Democratic underpinnings of mass media

Mass communications technology creates conditions of political possibility, to paraphrase a term from Michel Foucault. Historically, these possibilities served democratic purposes in Europe and the US. The connection between mass mediated messages and political systems took shape with print media's ability, through mass printing technology, to provide a wide forum for public discussion. With the invention of the printing press to transmit ideas, greater numbers of people who could read gained access to and participation in public political debates. Mass communications technology contributed to the rise of democratic societies by disseminating a range of views that enabled public scrutiny of existing political arrangements and their alternatives. Mass mediated messages thus served political purposes by cultivating a public space for debate and action that led to the rise of democratic systems. Within this space, communications served Enlightenment views on human rights, especially rights of access and participation, and became an influential forum for the Jacobins in the French Revolution and the colonists in the American Revolution.

While these emergent democratic structures took diverse institutional forms, they shared some key assumptions about the nature of citizens and governance. These presuppositions regarding the nature of selves in liberal democratic systems undergird media practices and provide fodder for media ethics debates today. A key presumption is that citizens have a need and desire for freedom of thought and expression. In *Aeropagitica*, John Milton pleaded: "Give me liberty to know, to utter, and to argue freely according to conscience, above all liberties." A corollary view is one that Milton shared with the ancient Greeks regarding the natural advantage of truth in democratic settings: Because truth is more powerful than falsity, he believed, it will emerge under conditions of open debate. Even if "all the winds of doctrine were let loose to play upon the earth," Milton concluded, we have little to fear. "Let her and Falsehood grapple; who ever knew Truth put to the worse, in a free and open encounter. Her confuting is the best and surest suppressing" (1940, pp. 56–58). In liberal democracies, this faith in the natural advantage of truth over falsity took shape in the marketplace of ideas metaphor, to symbolize that public space in which the truth on any issue is more likely to emerge in unfettered debate. The marketplace ideal has been articulated in US judicial doctrine as well. In a noteworthy ruling in 1919, Justice O. W. Holmes affirmed that "the best test of truth is the power of thought to get itself accepted in the competition of the market, and that truth is the only ground upon which their wishes safely can be carried out" (*ARAMs v. United States*, 250, US 616).

Not all agree that truth will emerge through open debate. Even so, John Locke argued, this is no reason to foreclose public discussion. Even a tentative, contingent hold on truth should temper intellectual arrogance with tolerance for diversity of expression. Epistemological modesty serves to disabuse citizens of their falsehoods and ill-formed opinions. Locke concluded that, even in the absence of certitude, citizens are better off with political arrangements that favor freedom of expression that can uncover ignorance and error. These Lockian views provide a theoretical foundation for speech freedoms that are codified or constitutionally protected in liberal democratic systems today.

A corollary assumption holds that governmental activities are citizens' business. Access to information about government business is crucial because it enables people to scrutinize government practices and make the important political and social choices citizens are both equipped to make and want to make for themselves. In short, public access to relevant information is also the road to knowledge, understanding, and democratic self government. The Enlightenment view that citizens have dual rights to access and participate in information flow is articulated more recently in the language of the 1948 United Nations Universal Declaration of Human Rights, Article 19, which specifies citizens' rights to search, obtain, and propagate information.

Since citizens need relevant information, both to scrutinize government business and participate in it, mass media in democratic countries have been granted wide and powerful freedoms to provide it. This accent on free expression took shape in the 1789 French Declaration of the Rights of Man, became codified throughout Europe, and laid out in the First Amendment to the US Constitution. These freedoms focus on negative conceptions of liberty in their "no law" language. This includes the right to be left alone to formulate and express one's own beliefs and opinions, and to decide for oneself through the free flow of ideas, free from government intervention or censorship.

During the nineteenth century, press freedoms found articulation as a political surveillance function in terms of a "watchdog" metaphor. The press was to be the faithful eyes and ears of the public, reporting government working to them and raising the alarm when it appeared government representatives were working against public interests. The view emerged that the press was a Fourth Estate that would use its freedom to report on the executive, legislative/parliamentary, and judicial branches of government.

How are we to understand the ethical dimensions of media's twin functions, and their freedoms and responsibilities, in light of current media structural arrangements? Two aspects are relevant. First, the prevailing trend toward media consolidation concentrates global media power into six conglomerates that operate under market rules, which potentially work against democratic goals. Secondly, the integral role of media advertising places additional pressure on media structures to serve commercial interests. Do these factors shrink the marketplace ideal to a venue for special pleading by powerful voices?

Organizational patterns

Technologically driven shifts in the structural organization of media follow broader business trends. As in manufacturing and service sectors, media merger patterns have pursued market penetration and higher profits through economies of scale and functional efficiencies. This trend toward increased size, integrated offerings, and global reach positions media owners to compete profitably for access to potentially large audiences accessible to them through digital technology.

Historically, structural efforts to increase audience size through print media consolidation have been successful. In the early part of the twentieth century, the Northcliffe conglomerate dominated in the UK, and the Hearst empire exerted powerful journalistic influence in the US. Business efforts to dominate and control markets are not new in free market democratic countries, as the experience of the Gilded Age amply demonstrates. Attempts to monopolize steel, railroads, and oil in the last century point to the inherent tendency in markets to gain competitive advantage through consolidated power. This impulse takes its current shape in what can be viewed as an emergent gilded age in media, as the desire for market dominance continues a path of rapid acceleration. A brief summary of recent media mergers and acquisitions makes the point.

During the 1980s, some 50 media organizations dominated US print and electronic forms of news and entertainment. A first round of mergers and acquisitions during this period led companies to increase their presence in their established medium of expertise. A second round favored strategies that would lead to synergistic results through mergers across specific strengths. Acquisitions in this second phase sought integration of different media, such as TV, radio, the Internet, in order to sell diverse products more profitably. Cross-selling, according to this logic, would result in profit levels that would exceed the profits possible by the sum of the individual media for their products. This potential for synergistic profitability led to the acquisitions of the three major US television networks. GE acquired NBC; Disney bought ABC; Viacom absorbed CBS. In addition, Time, Inc. merged with Warner Brothers, and the Time Warner corporation acquired CNN. When the 1996 Telecommunications Act relaxed restrictions on multiple, cross-ownership of media outlets, the corporatization process, already underway, sped up. The 10 largest media entertainment mergers through 1999 demonstrate this concentration (Farhi, 1999) (see table 6.1).

By 2001, six media conglomerates dominated the global market. These six parent firms include General Electric, Viacom, Disney, Bertelsmann, AOL Time Warner, and the News Corporation (Rupert Murdoch). The AOL/Time Warner merger, valued at $166 billion, was the largest merger to date, dwarfing the CBS Viacom merger. The consolidated AOL/Time Warner entity now ranked as the world's largest media corporation.

AOL/Time Warner exemplifies media hopes for synergistic efficiencies in content and distribution, as it expands its audience base and market dominance through the Internet. AOL/Time Warner sees the value of on-line content, and seeks expertise through mergers that will help them transmit content in attractive, compelling ways for consumers (Perrault, 2000). AOL brought to the merger approximately 22 million Internet subscribers and Time Warner provided both distribution power and content via its vast cable technology, movies,

Table 6.1

Date	Buyer	Acquired	Industry	$ Value (billion)
6/98	AT&T Corp	Telecomm. Inc.	Cable TV	69.9
4/99	AT&T Corp	Media One Group Inc.	Cable TV	63.1
9/99	Viacom Inc.	CBS Corp.	Radio, TV, other	40.9
10/99	Clear Channel Comm.	Am/FM Inc.	Radio, TV	21.8
7/95	Walt Disney Co.	Capital Cities/ABC Inc.	TV, other media	18.3
3/89	Time Inc.	Warner Comm.	TV, Movies	15.1
9/95	Time Warner Inc.	Turner Broadcasting	Cable TV, Movies	10.8
2/96	US West Inc.	Continental Cable	Cable TV	10.8
5/98	Seagram Corp.	PolyGram Ent.	Records, Movies	10.6
2/94	Viacom Inc.	Paramount Comm.	Movies, Publishing	10.3

publishing, and cable programming. At the time of the merger, Time Warner was the largest of the entertainment conglomerates. In addition to CNN, it owns the HBO and WB networks, three film studios, three major record companies, and numerous magazines and publishing houses. Time Warner's cable technology enables AOL to transmit this content through its on-line services.

Is big necessarily bad, ethically speaking? As broadband technology replaces low capacity wires, transnational companies like AT&T and AOL/Time Warner will offer communication pipelines that potentially enhance access. They will become enormous channels that deliver a diversity of news and information of unprecedented volume. As audiences both grow and fragment, media organizations justifiably seek to position themselves competitively, to increase their ability to reach diverse groups and regain eroded audience bases. Media mergers, defenders argue, inevitably follow the technological imperative. Consolidation trends are defensive and defensible business moves, hedging bets that future success is through synergistic efficiencies in content and delivery to larger audiences via Internet access.

Currently, some 200 million people worldwide are Internet subscribers, projected to reach about one billion by 2006. All of the national news organizations, and most of the US's 1,500 daily newspapers and 18,000 magazines have launched websites to reach these subscribers. Further, this proliferation and diversity of information sources includes news and discussion outlets such as MSNBC.com, web "zines" such as Slate.com and Salon.com. In traditional media, TV networks have expanded from three (NBC, ABC, CBS) to seven (WB, Fox, PAX, UPN) since the period of media consolidation. In radio, niche programming has grown to include over 500 Spanish-language stations, and a range of Chinese, Japanese and other ethnic formats. Music programming includes increased numbers of jazz, classical, gospel, country, and blues. News and talk radio stations now number close to 2000 (Farhi, 1999). Global news websites, including the

International Herald Tribune, Africa On-line, and the BBC, cover nations across the world.

Larger media corporations also have more financial resources than family-owned community newspapers. Potentially, this means more support for journalistic training, news gathering, and reporting. Financial strength might also support editorial independence. A powerfully rich corporate parent can withstand the negative financial consequences of a subsidiary's news reporting that angers another corporation; an independent owner of a community newspaper is more vulnerable to offended local cronies. With respect to self-coverage, the sheer size of media conglomerates might make routine self-serving news very visible. Favorable media coverage of corporate parents can be transparent to readers and critics alike. Corporate executives argue that the harder task will be to find the confidence to write a legitimately favorable piece about itself in light of current scrutiny (Hickey, 2000).

Despite the democratizing potential of news gathering by integrated transnationals, ethical concerns increase with concentration, as technological developments and corporate infrastructures feed the pressure to increase audiences and profit margins. Critics worry that the shift from family to corporate ownership has significant implications for media's capacity to perform its democratic functions as a corporatized media industry imposes a market model on their respective media subsidiaries.

The corporate model that drove media mergers and acquisitions in the past two decades does not allay concerns over access, because the resultant concentrated media power dwarfs the cumulative power of the niche audience proliferation. The Disney conglomerate provides an example of an integrated global reach. Through merger activities, the Disney movie studio controls the production, storage, distribution, and viewing outlets for all of their affiliated productions. Through movie production in its own studio, Disney also sells video cassettes of its movies and plays them on the Disney cable channel. ABC, a Disney subsidiary, provides a tempting venue to report on and review new Disney productions. This organizational arrangement affords Disney enormous potential power to promulgate a set of values globally to millions of children and their families, with fewer dissonant voices able to break through.

Unfavorable coverage of parent owners or their commercial venture partners is less likely. Self-censorship works to maintain profitability, despite the potential for transparent, truthful coverage in vast corporate settings. Thus, when ABC refused to air a story of Disney hiring practices, Michael Eisner, Disney chairman, explained "I would prefer ABC not cover Disney. I think it's inappropriate for Disney to cover Disney" (Croteau & Hoynes, 2001, p. 177).

The need to justify mergers to individual shareholders and institutional investors with a promise of increased profits creates disincentives to fund news gathering that is expensive, controversial, embarrassing to corporate parents, or potentially litigious. Since the goals of increased market share and profitability are much more difficult to achieve in an atmosphere of social agitation and unrest, media production values strive for the quietude of the status quo. A built-in, structural conservatism, as Leo Bogart notes, follows from media conglomerates who have an economic interest in sustaining the system that allows them to thrive (1995a). Propagandist efforts to direct mass thinking and behavior through carefully crafted messages can easily mask self interest under the guise of public interest. Fear of lawsuits adds to the chilling effect on print and TV investigative journalism's will to pursue issues related to public health and safety. Large monetary awards by juries against media outlets on libel and invasion of privacy judgments – even if the accuracy of the investigation's findings is not at issue – have prompted profit-oriented media conglomerates to avoid controversial and potentially litigious topics (Greenwald & Bernt, 2000). Media interest in providing a forum for open and vigorous democratic debate atrophies, on the belief that the provision of this forum is counterproductive to media's structural goals and market values.

As a consequence, most information accessed by citizens is mediated by a handful of conglomerates whose economic self interest can often work against public interest. Wide exposure to diverse opinions, crucial for the functioning of the marketplace of ideas concept that undergirds media's speech protections, becomes a distant ideal of liberalism. Current media structures, which came to power by exploiting liberalism's ideals, work against the fulfillment of their mediating role in cultivating democratic life.

This mediation, Jürgen Habermas and other critical theorists argue, is more than exploitation; it is a serious flaw in liberal political arrangements, because power thwarts the democratic functioning of the political will. Information, Habermas noted, does not merely pass through to citizens who, through their discursive will formation in the public sphere, enable participatory democracy to thrive. Liberalism's ideal that discussion and debate shape a political will that legitimizes political action remains unfulfilled; instead, opinions are filtered through a media industry with disproportionate power and standing to influence and distort the formation of the political will that is the legitimate basis of liberal state power.

Currently, mass media structural patterns that are also racially stratified weaken the level of communication among multiple publics necessary to build solidarity and political will. Media access requires economic strength, and those with modest financial resources are disadvantaged in their struggle to articulate specific concerns and gain visibility for particular issues. The disproportionate power and privilege of the white mainstream press, for example, provides resources for wide distribution on a daily basis to large audiences. The largest dailies share wire services, maintain comprehensive archives, and run their own polling operations. Results of their frequent polling surveys run regularly as news. Concentrated ownership enables the same syndicated voices to dominate the conversation on major issues, in jointly owned print and television venues.

Conversely, Ronald Jacobs (2000) notes, major African-American newspapers currently experience shrinking circulations and fewer resources. They do not share wire services, complete archives, or a stock of syndicated columnists. Generally, these papers are published on a weekly, not daily basis, which further erodes their ability to participate in national conversations. Finally, the black press is almost invisible to the mainstream media and, consequently, to other publics. So, while the black press has historically reported on the workings of mainstream media for its readership, mainstream media takes little account of the black press. The one-way communication pattern thus reinforces "a sense of white indifference" and "decreases the likelihood of building trust and solidarity across racial lines" (pp. 143–4).

Advertising pressures

Advertising functions to bring buyers and sellers together. As such, it plays a crucial role in markets, helping to move manufactured goods and services from the production through the consumption phases of the business cycle. Capitalism is very good at producing things, as Sut Jhally and others observe, but it needs advertising to convert products into profits through consumer purchases. Advertising also has important work to do in print and electronic media, underwriting much of the production costs of televised commercial programming, newspapers, and magazines not borne by subscribers. Within a free market model, advertisers act rationally when they seek media exposure to prospective buyers, paying what is necessary, but no more, to reach them.

This logic is plausible enough on its face. If options are available, most sellers seek out the most cost-effective medium to reach the greatest number of would-be buyers. From an ethical perspective, the vested interest of a seller to reach prospective buyers is not intrinsically evil or morally reprehensible. What raises ethical concerns is the dominance of the seller's single-minded logic into dual-function media settings. When advertising values become integral to and drive media production decisions, then market logic upsets the balance between media's democratic and commercial functions. The flaw in the market model that advertising operates in is that market logic doesn't account for the democratic function. Advertising reasoning only addresses buyers and sellers and so tends to reduce citizenship to a consumer function. Audiences become commodities themselves, products for sale to advertisers (Albarran, 1996).

From the advertiser's perspective, television programming functions to deliver audiences to their product message. As one Procter & Gamble advertising executive put it: "We're in programming first to assure a good environment for our advertising." Network producers understand the integral relations between programming and commercial messages. An ABC executive agrees, noting that the "network is paying affiliates to carry network commercials, not programs. What we are is a distribution system for Procter & Gamble. Thus, a "program should not move viewers 'too deeply'." To do so competes with the advertiser's message (Bogart, 1995b, pp. 99, 108).

Producers respond to advertisers' perceptions that churning deeply felt emotions will interrupt viewers' receptivity to a commercial message. In this environment, programming should avoid controversy and always strive for the highest ratings. Producers "should never forget that there is safety in numbers" and "always remember that comedy, adventure and escapism provide the best atmosphere for selling." Programming that examines human complexity and social issues that do not yield to easy analysis or simple solutions creates an uncomfortable dissonance with commercials for consumer products that promise those easy answers. The result of this infrastructure is that a "commercially dominated media system is unable to pose hard questions . . . for fear of turning off audiences who are much more used to experiencing pleasant feelings than having to think about hard issues" (Bagdikian, 2000, p. 158). Advertising values push public discussion and debate to the periphery of cultural space, while the dominant cultural conversation is restricted to talk about "desire and fantasy, pleasure and comfort" (Collins & Skover, 1996, pp. 133–4). Market driven media become the "loudest voice" in the cultural landscape, muting other views (Schiller, 1989, p. 4).

Print journalism also grapples with advertising pressures that influence news gathering efforts. Historically, an ideal of independence in news gathering and reporting functions emerged symbolically as a "firewall" of separation between the editorial and business staffs of daily newspapers. The firewall protected editorial decisions about what to print by insulating them from the knowledge of how news reporting affected advertisers and by extension the newspaper's financial status. Historically this ideal has been more or less approximated in the face of policies to provide favorable coverage of prominent local advertisers and self censor unflattering stories that threaten the paper's financial stability. Long-standing arrangements favored some local friends but, since World War I, Bagdikian claims, mainstream American news has reserved its most favored treatment for the corporation (2000, pp. 47–8).

The current structural arrangements of media conglomerates intensifies this preferential treatment by promoting self censorship through institutional practices. This includes the training of journalists and other media workers as well as the system of rewards and penalties for producing content that maximizes profits through advertising revenues. Most often, this "internalization of values," as Schiller puts it (1989, p. 8) is sufficient to ensure structural impulses to continue the status quo. The widespread proliferation of market values, critics argue, positions media as a cultural industry, producing a set of values and aspirations for consumers to absorb. Diversity of opinion becomes increasingly difficult in the media industry since it is cost prohibitive for all but the most financially strong to enter the market. This disproportionate power discredits hopes for a marketplace of ideas, a vibrant public sphere in which open debate helps form the political will and legitimizes the use of liberal state power.

Contextual Challenges

Climate of cynicism

Recurring attention to media ethics has paralleled broader patterns of public cynicism that confound institutional efforts to regulate ethical media practices. An ideal of truthtelling guides media news gathering and reporting practices. Historically this standard took shape in norms of fairness, balance, and compassion. In addition, an ideal of objectivity in the form of "factual" and unbiased truth emerged during the nineteenth century. Prior to that time newspapers were expected to be partisan, and not neutral (Schudson, 1978). During periods of heightened public cynicism, many perceive that these norms are not pursued with much vigor. More recently, objectivity itself has been challenged on grounds that it is neither an attainable nor desirable norm to guide ethical media practices.

Currently, media journalists face a crisis of public confidence in media's will to carry out its watchdog function. Public opinion polls in eight European democratic countries sketch a view of arrogant journalists, whose news coverage is biased and beholden to the commercial interests of media owners and advertisers. These survey results suggest that journalistic priorities contribute to the decline in public confidence by changing production values away from comprehensive news and analysis toward more sensational, hyperactive, tabloid values (Tucher & Bischoff, 1995). In the US, survey results point to similar reactions against media structures that favor amusement and entertainment to recapture fragmented and cynical audiences. Media, as Davis and Owen (1998) emphasize, have the potential to enable citizens to become actors, not mere spectators, in the political process. The question arises whether media's attention to entertainment, confrontation, and sensationalism works against media's democratic function by draining much of the potential political power citizens can wield in these formats.

Additional questions return our attention to technology, to consider the implications of electronic news production. Television, as a series of dynamic and ever changing images, does not require viewers to focus for long periods of time, to think critically, to pause and reflect. Each television image is immediate, temporarily engaging; none is necessarily more important than another or intended to hold the viewer's attention for very long. Electronic production facilitates the convergence of news and entertainment into a "strange equivalence of spectacles," as they compete for diminishing audience numbers (Fallows, 1996, pp. 52–3). As a consequence, production decisions are more cynically oriented toward trivia, scandal, and sex to lure viewers back. At the same time, the investment in time and money to follow ongoing substantive reporting shrinks because it is easier and more profitable to pursue entertainment and minutiae. The pressure to improve profitability each year erodes efforts to reinvest earnings in staff training, investigative journalism, and salaries (Hickey, 2000).

In print journalism, the watchdog function faces related impediments brought on by financial pressures to increase profitability for investors and corporate parents. Efforts to increase profits are frustrated by eroded readership/circulation numbers and competition from electronic media who operate on a 24-hour news cycle. To protect profitability, owners reduce news budgets and call for more cost-efficient stories, including corporate newsfeeds. As a result, newsholes, the newspaper space dedicated to news stories, also shrink, providing less coverage of the investigative reporting that requires time, money, staff, and space to publish its findings. Investigative journalism is at the heart of the watchdog function to be the eyes and ears of government, corporate, or individual wrongdoing that jeopardizes public interests. Despite this centrality, the need to satisfy corporate profitability projections makes the watchdog heritage in the muckraking tradition of Ida Tarbell, Upton Sinclair, Seymour Hersh, Bob Woodward, and Carl Bernstein more difficult to carry out. Readers who invested journalists with the moral authority to determine which news stories are in the public interest now question that reports are truthful, fair, accurate, or in their interest. When news media lose credibility with cynical readers, they also forfeit their cultural voice to lay out specific issues with moral authority (Greenwald & Bernt, 2000, pp. 126–30).

Philosophical challenges

Media's powerful and privileged position to inform, influence, and entertain audiences raises profound questions regarding the ethical boundaries of media responsibility. Historically, intellectual projects in communication ethics to theorize responsible media practices have turned to classical philosophy for intellectual resources. In doing so, communication ethics has generally reflected several key Enlightenment assumptions that undergird liberal democratic and moral philosophy. These include the view that individuals, as autonomous and rational moral agents, can reach consensus on a range of potential issues, and should be allowed to do so without State interference. Further, the Enlightenment legacy insists that rational thinking and self-legislating moral agents separate facts from values and reason from emotion in their deliberations.

In media ethics, these broader philosophical assumptions have supported a libertarian ethic of self reliance, self-regulation, and a near absolutist view of press freedoms among many media practitioners. News journalists within this ethical framework look internally to their own moral gyroscope to guide ethical practice and favor norms of objectivity, fairness, and balance to report factually and truthfully. On this view, to insert a particular set of values into news gathering and reporting is to taint content, which confounds citizens' need to interpret facts and decide issues for themselves. Media ethics tied to the objectivity norm holds that news media should stand somewhat at a distance, so as to report factually, dispassionately, and fairly on what they see. The goal of news gathering to get the story also encourages a somewhat pinched utilitarian calculus in which sensitivity to the feelings of a few must give way to the greater good produced by reporting the story to the many. A libertarian ethic resists efforts to have ethics imposed from the outside and favors self-regulation, personal codes of ethics to determine legitimate means to achieve journalistic ends.

A strong libertarian bias in media systems also derives from the fact that media are privately held businesses. The libertarian view of business within a free market economy is to maximize profits with minimal government interference or regulation. The US economist Milton Friedman exemplifies an extreme of this view with his thesis that the sole social responsibility of business people is to increase their profits, since this is the goal of the shareholders for whom they work. An alternative ethical framework expands the scope of media responsibility beyond shareholders to include media's mass audiences of viewers and readers. In the past, a social responsibility ethic to guide media practices has more frequently found expression in Western social democracies. A business ethic of social responsibility reframes the pursuit of profit as a privilege given by society, a legitimate goal but one that sometimes works against public interests. Efforts to theorize private and public interests within a social responsibility ethic for media practices emphasize media's democratic function to serve the commonweal.

In the US, this alternative view emerged, albeit in small pockets, as early as the nineteenth century when Joseph Pulitzer invoked journalistic moral responsibility to resist business pressures that were "antagonistic to the public welfare" (Day, 1997, p. 36). In 1947, the Hutchins Commission on Freedom of the Press articulated a defense of social responsibility that challenged some rationalist assumptions of the objectivity norm. The Hutchins report argued for a view of social responsibility that included several positive duties, especially to provide contextual, interpretive reporting that clarified societal values even as it served as a public forum for discussion and debate. Efforts by the Commission to balance a free and a responsible press attempted to preserve strong claims for journalistic freedoms and an ideal of self-regulation. Widespread news media resistance to the Commission's proposed values speaks to skepticism that this balance can be easily struck and to fears that antidemocratic regulations will accompany the attempt, however fruitless.

The Way Forward: Current Trends in Media Ethical Analysis

Arguably, the greatest structural challenge for media ethicists working in the Western, liberal tradition is to cultivate the moral imagination to think critically and creatively about the limits of a technologically driven market logic for media systems. The current aggregate of media influences emerging from this logic is cause for concern and calls for a thoughtful response. The salient question for free market democratic supporters is to how to scrutinize and repair the structural flaws without dismantling a market system. If Robert Kuttner (1997) is right to say that markets have virtues, but are insufficient and inappropriate for all media transactions, then reformers face the prospect that some goods in media transactions should not follow pure market principles. The challenge is to create a new synthesis that avoids dismantling democratic principles in every phase of market expansion.

Communication ethicists who theorize philosophical grounds for ethical media practice are similarly challenged to locate conceptual tools to address the structural and contextual dimensions of media ethics. Efforts to shift or expand the theoretical domain need to address broader and persistent contemporary challenges to key Enlightenment assumptions that have penetrated moral reasoning in general and media ethics in particular. If postmodern, feminist, and communitarian critiques of rationality, consensus, and autonomous moral agency can be sustained against modernist ethical theories, then a communication ethics whose normative underpinnings have been historically tied to modernity is similarly vulnerable. The theoretical challenge for communication ethicists is to devise a philosophical infrastructure that leaves behind discredited assumptions and provides normative frameworks that include an account of plurality, diversity, and community useful in media contexts.

Self-regulation

Trends in self-regulatory mechanisms include formalized efforts to exert internal and external moral pressure on media practices. New directions in self-regulation begin from a view that media exert powerful cultural and political influences; that they enjoy legal freedoms and social responsibilities; and that proactive regulation by media and citizens can be effective (Nordenstreng, 2000, p. 80). Claude-Jean Bertrand, arguing from a social responsibility approach, favors "any non-State means" of moral suasion that might make "media responsible to the public" (2000, p. 107). Within his Media Accountability Systems (M*A*S) framework, media owners, media professionals, and media users work to serve their publics through internal and external initiatives. Among these are ethical audits and training in adherence to codes of conduct; local and national press councils comprised of media professionals and citizens; higher education and mentoring for journalists; and media criticism and literacy in the service of citizens. A media survey in 35 European countries reveals all have codes of ethics, whereas fewer than 25 maintain press councils. Obstacles remain, if adhering to codes puts media workers' jobs at risk or if codes are perceived as censorship.

John Merrill (1997) articulates widespread journalistic skepticism toward codes. Merrill characterizes them as merely window-dressing, good faith ideals against which behavior can be judged but not enforced. Since many media workers do not read the codes, and few participate in crafting them, many remain detached from their suasory potential. Unless the provisions of the code conform to values and aspirations internalized by media practitioners already, Merrill argues, they are not likely to direct behavior in meaningful ways. For Merrill, ethics should remain tilted slightly toward its individualistic, personal dimension. "We can have institutionalized laws (which can be enforced), but a journalistic ethics must be personal, and it cannot be enforced" (Gordon & Kittross, 1999, p. 69). Merrill rejects what he views as the extremes of both libertarian and social responsibility standpoints in favor of an "ethical mutualism" that synthesizes the main tenets of individualistic and communal thinking (1997, p. 214). As an alternative, he and Ralph Lowenstein (1990) devised a formula for journalistic ideals to embrace this mutualism through truthful, unbiased, full and fair reportage (acronym: TUFF formula). These four criteria aim at full disclosure that is also sensitive to and tempered by social responsibility.

Hybrid regulation

Other reform proposals expand external approaches beyond self-regulation and market rules. To "keep markets in their place," Bogart calls for a "coherent national policy" that subjects media to "constant public scrutiny and debate" (1995a, p. 3) and Kuttner (1997) proposes a check on market freedoms through extra market institutions that promote extra market human values. Most hybrid proposals emphasize the potential merits of a social responsibility framework to strengthen media's democratic function. Some invoke US schools to add media literacy programs along respected European models. Others urge more private funding for non-profit media. Many focus on structural change through media policy to address the ownership, market logic, and advertising dynamics that drive media attention away from their democratic purposes. While reform proposals vary, many reflect the broad contours laid out by Robert McChesney (1999), who advocates an increase in public funding to establish a viable nonprofit, noncommercial media sector and federal support for public broadcasting through general revenues along British and Japanese models. With others, McChesney also favors legislation that holds commercial media to long-standing public service standards. While the US historically has championed a public service standard, this presumptive ideal has significantly eroded in the past several decades, especially during the 1990s when a climate of deregulation dominated media policymaking. To reinvigorate the public service standard, McChesney calls for a reduction in commercial air time to 18–20 hours per day, and proposes that the rationale of the Clayton and Sherman Acts be extended to media antitrust legislation that would break up conglomerates. Finally, he urges political parties to include media reform in their broader political platforms, following party trends in Canada, Sweden, and New Zealand (pp. 304–14).

Philosophical frameworks

Intellectual trends include a search for new philosophical underpinnings for media ethics. As with trends in regulation, the impulse to find a new paradigm reflects perceptions that the Enlightenment legacy of individualist liberalism as a philosophical basis for media norms of ethical practice has failed to promote the democratic purpose it historically served.

Globally, reconceptualizations of speech freedoms suggest a paradigm shift from the Enlightenment legacy of negative freedom toward a view of positive, global human rights. By bringing the citizen from the margins to the center in conceptualizing freedom of expression, these trends reframe negative rights in "no law" language to positive human rights to communicate. Early articulations of this framework are included in UNESCO's stand on the universal rights of communication access and participation by individuals, groups, and nations. Kaarle Nordenstreng (2000) elaborates several implications of this shift for media. If the dominant frame of reference moves away from media censorship to a human right to information, then media are no longer the vessels of free speech; rather, freedom belongs to citizens whose access and participation vitalizes democratic life. Normative media functions now include the need to organize citizens' use of speech freedoms, which means that responsible media output should be monitored by social norms and self regulation. Open debate, difference, and plurality of views are the goals of freedom of speech, promoted through a more open, transparent wielding of media power. Finally, the public arena for positive rights is local, regional, national, and international, wherein media are charged with promoting plural views at all levels (p. 75).

The public or civic journalism movement seeks media norms within this paradigm shift and bring citizens and media's democratic function to the foreground. Goals strive to invigorate citizen participation in public affairs on issues that matter to them, thereby reversing public cynicism. Within this normative framework, news media bear responsibility to sponsor open forums for community discussion and debate, dedicate editorial space to citizens' viewpoints, interpret and contextualize news to illuminate cultural values and concerns, and substitute substantive analyses for "horserace" coverage of political events. Within this model, publics need more than information, and objectivity is a misguided norm, since understanding follows from placing stories in larger contexts that scrutinize and articulate shared values. Truthfulness, balance, and accuracy remain central in the new paradigm. Justice, in the diligent performance of the watchdog function, free from government and commercial influence, echoes longstanding concerns. Norms of humane stewardship, to manage media power and freedom with regard to the rights of others, to guard speech freedoms that belong to citizens and news media, carry forward the positive rights model and rehabilitate the Hutchins Commission guidelines to give news contextual meaning and increase citizens' access to news (Lambeth, 1992).

Public journalism remains controversial from a libertarian ethic, since it shifts some agenda setting power from media to publics. A libertarian model also strongly resists evaluative language, with fears that a new paradigm to clarify and articulate shared values is a mask for imposing a set of values on citizens. At bottom, however, the public journalism movement rehearses debates early in the twentieth century between Walter Lippmann and John Dewey over the potential capacity of citizens to engage productively in democratic life (Fallows, 1996). Following World War I, Walter Lippmann argued in his influential *Public Opinion* (1922) that wartime propaganda and corporate public relations complicated participatory democracy through successful efforts to manipulate public opinions for political and commercial purposes. To address this ideological threat to democratic interaction, Lippmann proposed a corps of well-trained journalists to counter propaganda and wisely lead public opinion. Against this view John Dewey theorized the journalists' role as one of public education, to cultivate through open debate on relevant issues, citizens' capacity to participate in democratic life. Public journalists align their project with Dewey's pragmatist tradition when they identify journalism's primary social responsibility as the creation and sustenance of a public sphere guided by norms of diversity and debate, and respect for all persons (Iggers, 1999, p. 138).

Finally, a philosophically grounded impetus to rethink a normative framework for media ethics takes up the strands of social responsibility, human rights, and civic participation to address discredited assumptions about ethical reasoning. Normative models of media ethics within a social ethics framework bring community to the foreground because of the formative connection between human selves and community. Social ethics that is community based theorizes a view of dialogical selves, community commitment, civic transformation, and mutuality. The dialogical self, formed in relation to others is a counterpoise to atomistic, unencumbered selves accountable to themselves only. Within this framework, what makes selves human is not freedom, but connection to others. Responsible journalism that is community based provides a framework of meaning, not only to re-engage disconnected publics, but to honor important communal dimensions of the formation of selves. On this view, communication is not the transmission of objective information; it is a range of "value-saturated symbolic systems through which the diverse dimensions of social life are constructed" (Christians, Ferre, & Fackler, 1993, p. xii).

For Clifford Christians, the most promising trend to engage diversity, community, and the nature of selves lies in feminist communitarianism's dual impulse to take account of difference and plurality, even as it seeks communal bonds. An ethical infrastructure for media ethics informed by feminist communitarian insights gives up several modernist assumptions. The search for consensus through agreed upon principles yields to "a complex view" that integrates "facts, principles, and feelings in terms of human wholeness" (Christians, 2000, p. 36).

A feminist communitarian model theorizes that communities of values exist prior to persons. Thus, the nature of selves is constituted and negotiated dialogically, through the social realm. Ethical action therefore intends community, and its fulfillment is achieved through human connection. Emergent feminist models of social ethics provide good reasons to reject the objectivity norm in news media practices, given the shift in journalistic goals. A feminist social ethics

suggests that news is not mere information, but "an agent of community formation" that strives toward civic transformation, a revitalized public sphere of
morally literate citizens (Christians, 2000, p. 39).

These regulatory and philosophical underpinnings suggest that a credible
model for media ethics must take account of the larger context in which media
operate. Surveys that infer attitudes of public cynicism and disengagement inevitably lead to political questions about what might temper these orientations
and nudge public discourse toward as yet unrealized public sphere goals to
cultivate democratic participation. While not all agree on the degree to which
media freedoms should serve their democratic function, there is growing concern that the powerful influence of global media conglomerates works against
any service at all, reducing citizenship to consumerist activities.

The level of media responsibility to attend to their role in democratic life and
the extent of regulations to urge media to accept their role remain controversial
on pragmatic and ethical grounds as well. Libertarian and social responsibility
frameworks differ in fundamental beliefs about which media production values
might best serve this function and how substantive a role citizens should have in
shaping those values.

The largest metaphysical issues that ethical theories grapple with offer perhaps the greatest potential to develop powerful normative models of media
ethics, but face considerable challenges as well. Ethical theories that presume
human deliberations involve isolated moral agents moving rationally toward
consensus on important issues are increasingly hard to sustain as a picture of
diverse and fragmented global publics emerges. Currently, the alternative paths
taken in social ethics and feminism offer promising intellectual vigor and a wide
range of potential policy implications.

References

Albarran, A. (1996). *Media Economics*. Ames, IA: Iowa State University Press.
ARAMS v. United States, 250, US 616, 1919.
Bagdikian, B. H. (2000). *The Media Monopoly* (6th edn.). Boston: Beacon Press.
Bertrand, C. J. (2000). *Media Ethics and Accountability Systems*. New Brunswick and London:
Transaction.
Bogart, L. (1995a). Media and democracy. *Media Studies Journal*, 9, 1–10.
Bogart, L. (1995b). *Commercial Culture: The media system and the public interest*. New York: Oxford
University Press.
Christians, C. G. (2000). An intellectual history of media ethics. In B. Pattyn (ed.), *Media Ethics:
Opening social dialogue*. Leuven, Belgium: Peeters, pp. 15–46.
Christians, C. G., Ferre, J. P., and Fackler, P. M. (1993). *Good News: Social ethics and the press*.
New York: Oxford University Press.
Collins, R. K. L. and Skover, D. M. (1996). *The Death of Discourse*. Boulder, CO: Westview Press.
Croteau, D. and Hoynes W. (2001). *The Business of Media: Corporate media and the public interest*.
Thousand Oaks, CA: Pine Forge Press.
Davis, R. and Owen, D. (1998). *New Media and American Politics*. New York: Oxford University
Press.

Day, L. A. (1997). *Ethics in Media Communications: Cases and controversies* (2nd edn.). Belmont, CA: Wadsworth.

Fallows, J. (1996). *Breaking the News: How the media undermine American democracy.* New York: Pantheon Books.

Farhi, P. (1999, December). How bad is big? *American Journalism Review*, 21, 28–32.

Gordon, A. D. and Kittross, J. M. (eds.) (1999). *Controversies in Media Ethics,* (2nd edn.). New York: Longman.

Greenwald, M. and Bernt, J. (2000). *The Big Chill: Investigative reporting in the current media environment.* Ames, IA: Iowa State University Press.

Hickey, N. (2000). Coping with mega-mergers. *Columbia Journalism Review*, 38, 16–20.

Iggers, J. (1999). *Good News, Bad News: Journalism ethics and the public interest.* Boulder, CO: Westview Press.

Jacobs, R. N. (2000). *Race, Media and the Crisis of Civil Society: From Watts to Rodney King.* Cambridge: Cambridge University Press.

Johnston, C. B. (1998). *Global News Access: The impact of new communication technologies.* Westport, CT: Praeger.

Kuttner, R. (1997). *Everthing for Sale: The virtues and limits of markets.* New York: Alfred A. Knopf.

Lambeth, E. B. (1992). *Committed Journalism: An ethic for the profession* (2nd edn.). Bloomington: Indiana University Press.

Lippmann, Walter (1922). *Public Opinion.* New York: Harcourt Brace.

Lowenstein, R. and Merrill, J. C. (1990). *Macromedia.* White Plains, NY: Longman.

McChesney, R. W. (1999). *Rich Media, Poor Democracy: Communication politics in dubious times.* Urbana and Chicago: University of Illinois Press.

Merrill, J. C. (1997). *Journalism Ethics: Philosophical foundations for news media.* New York: St. Martin's Press.

Milton, J. (1940 [1644]). *Aeropagitica* (ed. R. C. Jebb.) Oxford: Oxford University Press.

Nordenstreng, K. (2000). The structural context of media ethics: How media are regulated in democratic society. In B. Pattyn (ed.), *Media Ethics: Opening social dialogue.* Leuven, Belgium: Peeters, pp. 69–86.

Perrault, L. (2000). The strategic moves of media mergers. *The Quill*, 88, 11–12.

Schiller, H. I. (1989). *Culture, Inc.: The corporate takeover of public expression.* New York: Oxford University Press.

Schudson, M. (1978). *Discovering the News: A social history of American newspapers.* New York: Basic Books.

Tucher, A. and Bischoff, D. (1995). Scorned in an era of triumphant democracy. *Media Studies Journal*, 9, 155–62.

Van Den Bulk, H. (2000). The economic rational behind the mass media. In B. Pattyn (ed.), *Media Ethics: Opening Social Dialogue.* Leuven, Belgium: Peeters, pp. 215–35.

Further reading

Christians, C. G. and Traber, M. (eds.) (1997). *Communication Ethics and Universal Values.* Thousand Oaks, CA: Sage.

Contributors to the volume explore cross-cultural normative models of ethics that can confront the malaise in mass media ethics. Comparative ethical models delineated in the text address conceptual issues, plural cultural norms, and implications for media practice. Contributors sketch an ethical framework for communication ethics based on truthtelling, human dignity, and no harm to the innocent.

Gerbner, G., Mowlana, H., and Schiller, H. I. (1996). *Invisible Crises: What conglomerate control of media means for America and the world.* Boulder, CO: Westview Press.

The collection of essays by prominent critical media scholars explores several pervasive and interrelated crises in media that remain largely hidden to the public. Local and global crises explored include media structural arrangements and global marketing power, as well as gender, race, and class divisions media perpetrate.

Merrill, J. C. and Odem, S. J. (1983). *Philosophy and Journalism*. New York and London: Longman. The authors offer a systematic exploration of the philosophical underpinnings of ethical journalistic practice. Topics range broadly from rationality and semantics to political theory and metaphysics. A summary of classical ethical theories is offered and applied to contemporary issues, such as truthtelling and objectivity norms.

Tester, K. (2001). *Compassion, Morality and the Media*. Buckingham and Philadelphia: Open University Press. Tester takes up the debated phenomenon of "compassion fatigue" in audiences exposed to technologically-driven media portrayals of human suffering to explore the sociological dimensions of ethical journalistic practice. He argues that the relationship between morally compelling journalistic practices and an audience's compassionate response is a complex interplay of journalistic production commitments and the moral horizons audiences bring to portrayals of suffering. Two implications raised by the independent, subjective dimensions of audience responses to suffering include the future authority of objective reporting and media impact on moral ties.

CHAPTER SEVEN

Digital Capitalism
A Status Report on the Corporate Commonwealth of Information

Dan Schiller

Throughout Silicon Valley and other centers of the information industry, "an epidemic of secrecy pacts is spreading through personal relationships, passed between lovers, friends, relatives, roommates, even business partners." Entrepreneurs, managers and scientists are demanding that nondisclosure agreements to protect trade secrets be signed at weddings, private dinner parties, even on dates (Waldman, 1999, p. A1). Personal shredders, meanwhile, have become a standard consumer appliance; in 1999, nearly eight million were sold in the US (Silverstein, 2000). On the other hand, it is becoming harder to *avoid* other information flows, such as the flood of commercial spam that has engulfed e-mail; America Online estimates that no less than one-third of the e-mail messages transiting its network are unwanted, while the number of e-mail ads continues to multiply (Vickers, 2001; Vranica, 2001). How are we to account for the normalization of such pathologies – on one side, intensifying attempts to guard secrets against transgression; on the other, efforts to communicate through channels clogged with garbage?

In fact, the movement toward an informationalized society is not winding down, despite the bursting of the Internet financial bubble. During the present extended transition, indeed, information and communication are being stamped with a radically changed social identity. Three features of this shift stand out: First and foremost, the process of capitalist development is, at last, truly gripping world communications, in their entirety – even as that sector becomes a general platform for subsequent capitalist development (D. Schiller, 1999a). Second, the stewards of this encompassing "digital capitalism" are enfolding national networks into systems that are planned and applied on a transnational basis. Intertwining in a third basic trend, these processes accelerate an existing tendency in the political-economy of informational provision: In different ways, market-deepening initiatives around networks are transforming an array of information-rich activities into commercial commodities. This survey of leading dimensions of the emerging corporate commonwealth of information begins with changes underway in the culture industry.

Global Culture Industry

For years following its introduction during the 1940s, television claimed significant audiences only in wealthy countries; elsewhere it existed as a limited, even an enclave, service. Today, in contrast, vast national audiences have become commonplace worldwide. Just between 1990 and 1996–8, the number of sets per 1,000 people in the world's "low income" countries nearly doubled, increasing from 80 to 145 (United Nations Development Program, 2000). Despite continuing inadequacies in provision – most pronounced throughout sub-Saharan Africa – there can be no doubt that television now operates as a worldwide cultural infrastructure (D. Schiller, 2001a; Schiller and Mosco, 2001).

The center of this system of audiovisual production and distribution remains the United States. But the system's ground rules have been significantly altered. Through the 1970s, television traffic between the US and the rest of the world was justly termed a "one-way street" (Nordenstreng and Varis, 1974). "Throughout the rise of the media business in the twentieth century," as the *Wall Street Journal* sums up the mechanics of this model, "the industry's version of globalization [was] simple: the US creates entertainment, and the rest of the world consumes it" (Orwall, 2001, p. A1). Today, in contrast, cultural commodities originating elsewhere are regularly launched *into* the US market. Following a historical run-up culminating in the hugely successful "Pokemon," low-cost "Japanese-style" cartoons known as *anime* have saturated US children's television at Fox, the WB and the Cartoon Network (Rutenberg, 2001). Aiming at adult viewers are top-rated network TV "reality" programs such as "Who Wants to Be a Millionaire," which originated in England and has been licensed in no less than 80 countries (Schneider, 2000), and "Survivor," another import popular with the young adults advertisers covet (Sutel, 2000). At the movies, the 1998 Italian film, "Life is Beautiful," grossed $58 million in the US, making it the most successful foreign film ever to be screened there until, two years later, "Crouching Tiger, Hidden Dragon," a Taiwanese film distributed by Sony, earned more than $100 million (as of March 2001), garnered 10 Academy-award nominations (including for "Best Picture"), and actually won four awards (Muñoz, 2001).

The pattern of change is actually more general than this. Intertwined shifts in investment, technology, and industrial practice are altering longstanding patterns of cultural-production/distribution and audience-formation. Immigrants to the United States, who today make up a historically high share of the population, thus are targeted with more than 50 non-English-language channels (beginning with Spanish, Italian, Arabic and Greek offerings) by direct-to-home satellite provider EchoStar's Dish Network (Romney, 2001). In the year 2000, more than 350 US cable systems – more than in all of the previous five years – launched international channels (Romney, 2001). News Corporation is sending the signal of its popular Hindi channel, Star Plus, from India to Britain (Flagg, 2000). Another portent: Bill Gates claims that Windows software is "probably paying for [itself]" in "about 45" languages (Gates, 2000), even as Microsoft's Internet service, MSN, maintains Web sites in 33 countries employing 11 different languages (Ellison, 2001). Aware that English is at best a second language for more than half of the world's 370 million Web surfers (as of Fall 2000), Sony too runs Web sites in 14 languages to market its consumer electronics products (Perkin, 2001). Expansion-minded US Web designers are advised to consult "localization providers" and "internationalization providers" because, "if your site is available only in English, you'll be effectively ignoring more than half the market" (Schwartz, 2000, p. 54).

Does all this signify the dawn of a newly diverse cultural economy, as audiovisual works produced in many languages circulate in increasingly omnidirectional patterns? Just such a multicultural renaissance has been celebrated by academic heralds of televisual "contraflow"; more significantly, perhaps, by the late 1990s top US political leaders gave lip-service to the norm of more balanced flows. At a White House Conference on "Culture and Diplomacy," held in late November 2000 (White House, 2000; US Department of State, 2000), then-First Lady Hillary Clinton suggested that, while "fears of a global consumer culture that threatens to homogenize us all are on the rise, we are searching for new ways to share and preserve our unique cultures around the world." Agreeing that cultural exchanges "definitely should be a two-way street," the then-President resolved that "globalization, in the end, will be a force for diversity, not uniformity" (White House Conference on Culture and Diplomacy, 2000).

Even on its face, however, such a pronouncement is too one-sided. Hollywood film, sports programming, video music, news and children's programming continue to push toward common global standards of cultural practice. Now capable of assembling audiences systematically on a supranational basis, the culture industry pumps out mega-events like the 2001 SuperBowl XXXV to hundreds of millions of viewers worldwide (Hebert, 2001). US audiovisual exports continue to grow – the European deficit in audiovisual trade with the US totaled $6.6 billion in 1998 (Commission of the European Communities, 2001) – and, indeed, in some markets the international dominance of US-based audiovisual commodities is actually increasing (Sanchez-Ruiz, 2001; Magder and Burston, 2001). At its leading technological edge, moreover, multiculturalism is an ascending, but still secondary, trend; one survey early in 2001 found that most leading US Web sites (63 percent of the sample) did not provide *any* localized content, design, or translation for foreign users ("Reality Bytes," 2001).

Amid wider social changes in politics, demography, and work organization, however, ever-escalating demand for "content" by proliferating media distribution systems is also injecting a new measure of dynamism and multiformity into global audiovisual production; thankfully, opportunities for creative cross-fertilization and syncretism are also finding somewhat greater legitimacy. But we must not abstract these promising tendencies from the rapidly altering – and still-determining – political-economy of global culture industry.

Genuine cultural diversity would be predicated on a rough measure of equality: comparable opportunities for training, program production and distribution would be equitably available to would-be creators worldwide. Widespread audience access to program offerings hailing from across the globe, and representing diverse idioms and points of view, would be routine. By this standard, current practice continues to fall woefully short, as longtime media analyst Leo Bogart (2000, p. 10) comments: "While non-economic motives are always present in the operation of media . . . these can generally be tolerated only as long as they do not permanently interfere with the main objective – to maximize the return on the owner's investment." To an unprecedented extent, indeed, the walls of the corporate imagination enclose the immensity of global cultural production. Transnational purveyors of the corporate-commercial model have been largely freed to pursue accumulation strategies with local partners as a matter of mutually self-interested private negotiation.

Today's multidirectional and somewhat more multicultural programming streams in turn are symptoms of a dual political-economic shift: that transnational-ized investment, product sourcing, and distribution patterns are being actively and extensively forged; and that culture industry programmers are assembling "most-desired" audiences in new and increasingly comprehensive ways, mainly to suit the needs of global advertisers. The system-in-formation that is today's culture industry includes an unprecedented array of (mainly new) regional and local producers and distributors; and these smaller companies play significant parts in expanding the culture industry's capital-logic toward a global scale (H. Schiller, 1989). The system is dominated, however, by a handful of participants – giant enterprises, whose assets encompass everything from terrestrial broadcast networks, film and television program producers, broadcast station and cable groups, satellite services, print publishers, recorded music companies, and video game packagers, to professional sports teams, theme parks and Web services. These diversified entertainment conglomerates track consumers across media and geographic frontiers, offering advertisers a whole array of synchronized platforms and territories on which to stage the sales effort. On one track, block-buster cultural commodities (with the important though partial exception of news) now emanate from, and ricochet across, a system of transnationalized cultural production and distribution that is no longer simply "American." On a second track, a rich menu of co-production strategies and local investments likewise permits these corporate behemoths to sample the cultural products of numerous local partners and affiliates; those that seem to show a real profit potential may be accorded regional or even global circulation. Through commercial tie-ins of different kinds, the resulting blockbuster products may lay claim to the attention of most of the world.

At this, its dominant level, however, the culture industry has become increasingly multi-polar, as it has been opened to include companies based in several developed market economies: France, Japan, Germany, and Australia, as well as the US. The specific basis of this change has been that large foreign media businesses have been allowed to acquire prime US media assets. To be sure, there remain real limits: foreign investment has flowed into US broadcasting (and, as we will see later, into telecommunications) only on a limited scale. These ownership changes have not transpired, moreover, by way of a wholesale abandonment of national policy restrictions, but rather through a series of carefully calculated and stringently monitored deals. US policy-makers thus adopted a policy of *selectively* authorizing foreign investment in the unmatched domestic market for cultural commodities (US Federal Communications Commission, 1997), in return for a specific quid pro quo: liberalization by trading partners worldwide of corporate investment in, and commercial provision of, communications (Economic Report of the President, 2001).

Even as existing public-service broadcast systems were pillaged and privatized, therefore, restrictions were widely relaxed over corporate–commercial ownership of terrestrial, cable, and satellite broadcasting and over reliance on commercial advertising; and foreign program import policies were often loosened (UK Department of Trade and Industry, 2000). By 1996, of some 250 television channels in the EU, two-thirds were private – a figure that had practically doubled over just six years, and that continued to increase (Commission of the European Communites, 2001). Crucial new media "platforms" (cable, satellite, digital TV, and Internet systems) in turn became free to emerge within the context of a general consolidation of corporate–commercial media dominance.

A business writer aptly glosses the political–economic character of the emerging global culture industry:

> while the US still produces many of the latest models, more and more it serves as a kind of cultural chop shop, retooling offerings from afar. It has a lot to choose from, as there has been an explosion in both the quality and volume of entertainment generated abroad. The privatization of the television business in Asia, Europe and Latin America and the advent of cheap production technology has helped spawn a generation of ambitious young artists and producers who believe they can conquer the world . . .
>
> The big US entertainment conglomerates, and the foreign-owned companies like Sony that run their entertainment operations almost entirely from the US, are embracing this phenomenon. The companies found in recent years that it was getting tougher to just jam American-made product down the world's throat – as when MTV learned that it needed to mix in more local acts on its international channels. So in response, the media giants are increasingly flipping the equation on its head, scouring their overseas operations for talent that can be buffed up for the

big US market. Success in the US, in turn, can open the door to even greater success in the rest of the world. (Orwall, 2001, p. A1)

The emerging system's apparent openness and multicultural diversity thus remain subject to formidable political–economic pressures and constraints. As a result, truly independent, not to speak of oppositional, cultural production may be no less disadvantaged than before. Impressive as they are in their own right, however, these structural changes have to be situated in the context of a concurrent – and hardly trouble-free – transformation in telecommunications.

The New Order in Telecommunications

The dramatically changed political circumstances of the 1990s – in particular, the collapse of Soviet socialism coupled with China's embrace of the capitalist market – created space for a secular increase in overall corporate foreign direct investment. The United Nations Conference on Trade and Development (UNCTAD, 2000, 2001) details the spectacular surge in cross-border corporate mergers and acquisitions that ensued: The value of completed cross-border buyouts rose from less than $100 billion in 1987 to $720 billion in 1999 and well over one trillion dollars in 2000. Underway was a reorganization of ownership, UNCTAD (2000, p. xx) underlines, that functions to remake nationally integrated markets and production systems into "a global market for goods and services and . . . an international production system, complemented by an increasingly global market for firms." This process of political–economic change – the driving force of what is often misleadingly called "globalization" – both rests on and largely motivates the continuing growth of corporate-led network development.

An action plan for accelerated network development initially evolved within the postwar US domestic market: By elevating the precepts of liberalization of commercial market entry, and rapid development of specialized systems and services aimed at privileged user-groups, US policy-makers empowered a few thousand giant corporations and their affiliated managerial and technical strata, as well as a burgeoning group of high-tech network system and service suppliers.

Because large business users of telecommunications were mostly transnational companies, however, by the 1970s the US model duly began to be exported. On one hand, this required that the long-unbalanced pattern of global telecommunications investment be freshly examined, as big business became intent on upgrading the global information infrastructure to sustain its own expanding transnational operations and designs (H. Schiller, 1981). On the other hand, the corresponding policy emphasis on network investment (now heralded not only by US authorities but also by the World Bank as a critical contributor to national economic development), comprised a political response to then-intensifying calls by poor world countries for a new international information order.

This delicate transition was deftly managed. Responding to interventions by organizations of business users were US Federal Communications Commission directives altering key groundrules for the conduct of US international tele-communications (D. Schiller, 1982). Increasingly, as well, the World Bank, the International Monetary Fund, the International Telecommunication Union, and other organizations enrolled in the liberalization effort. As US power groups' confidence increased, bilateral negotiations, US trade law, and an encompassing multilateral initiative all were pursued, interlocking to alter the institutional basis of world telecommunications.

As with the culture industry, the promise of access – in this case access to the gigantic US domestic market for corporate network systems and services – again functioned as a strategic weapon; as one Clinton Administration trade official explained, "we boldly offered to open up our market fully, in return for conces-sions from others" (Esserman, 2000, p. 1). Access to the US market did not, however, come cheap. Throughout such negotiations, the unremitting focus of US agencies was enhanced global market access for transnational corporate carriers, largely on behalf of their own largest corporate customers. Then–Deputy US Trade Representative Richard W. Fisher (2000, p. 3) elaborates: "In the end, the calculus was clear: any broad-based agreement that rapidly opened up global markets to US firms clearly played to our advantages. While we were offering other countries access to a market no other country individually could match, a critical mass of market opening offers would provide opportunities that US firms were uniquely positioned to exploit . . ." Fisher was referring specifically to the World Trade Organization Basic Telecommunications Agreement, forged in 1997. This pact helped harmonize national operating frameworks, subjecting some seventy signatories to binding commitments enforced by a multilateral dispute settlement process, and thereby established more uniformly liberal mar-ket access to network equipment and services – worldwide (Barshefsky, 1999; Blouin, 2000).

There really is no historical precedent for the institutional overhaul of world telecommunications on which the WTO agreement drew – and on which it builds. Between 1984 and July 1999, around $244 billion worth of privatizations of state-owned systems occurred. As a result, of the 189 members of the Inter-national Telecommunication Union, by 1999 almost half (90) had wholly or partially privatized their existing telecommunication operators, 18 completely. Of the remaining non-privatized operators, more than 30 planned to privatize. The process of privatization itself was characteristically structured to ease market entry by transnational carriers. By early 2000, 25 countries had pledged to allow majority foreign-owned carriers seeking to furnish international voice service using their own wholly owned and controlled networks (US Federal Communications Commission, 2000a; Zhao and Schiller, 2001).

Moreover, between 1990 and 2000, the volume of announced mergers and acquisitions in worldwide telecommunications totaled an estimated $1.616 trillion (Blumenstein, 2000); cross-border takeovers constituted a significant share of this total. Domestically integrated networks run by national flag carriers thus began to be superseded in scope and function by transnational systems. The cardinal result of this global shakeup was to grant license to carriers and business users to assimilate networks as desired into a vast and growing range of business processes. In turn, by revolutionizing network systems and services, large corporations acquire new freedom of maneuver in their attempts both to reintegrate the market system on a broadened, supranational basis, and to deepen it by developing information as a commodity.

Huge expenditures were needed to provision digital capitalism with this central production base and control structure: enlarged and upgraded transnationally organized networks, employing a lengthening list of networking technologies including wireless, telephone lines, cable television systems, fiber optics, and satellites. Network-related information technology investment duly functioned as the leading element in the 1990s' economic boom (Oliner and Sichel, 2000; Wellenius, Primo Braga, and Qiang, 2000). In the US, the most highly developed core of the market system, telecommunications accounted for no less than 16 percent of the capital spending of the *Standard & Poor's* 500 in 1999 (Jenkins, 2000). Through the latter half of the 1990s, in particular, the financial markets seemingly answered every call for capital in the networking sector. Joining existing carriers like AT&T, Deutsche Telekom, and British Telecom, a bevy of newer entrants catered to different segments of the market. Withal, system development remained highly uneven. Targeting business users, rival carriers each spent billions of dollars a year to build out proprietary networks with which to link office complexes throughout the world's central cities.

The result was a continuing, spectacular enlargement of information-carrying capacity, though mainly along high-density routes. Two-thirds of the 78 million miles of fiber optic cable laid in the United States over the last two decades of the twentieth century reportedly was installed between 1996 and 2000 (Ramstad and Stringer, 2001). On US trans-Atlantic and trans-Pacific routes, estimated bandwidth in use increased from 2.1 gigabits per second in 1990 to 868.3 gps in 2000 (Galbi, 2001), even as new submarine cable systems were projected to add further huge increments to available capacity (TeleGeography, 2001).

Surging investment also prompted a significant spatial reconfiguration of networks. Into the post-World War II period, effective and inclusive national telecommunications infrastructures were confined mainly to the developed market economies (D. Schiller, 1999b). By 1997–9, in contrast, fully half of global telecommunications investment was being absorbed by so-called "developing and transition" – that is, non-OECD – countries (Wellenius, Primo Braga and Qiang, 2000). To be sure, a fundamental disparity remained, as these poorer countries contained fully four-fifths of global population. Nor was there any guarantee that network buildouts aimed to furnish inclusive access to domestic populations. Still, network expansion was in fact proceeding on an unprecedented scale. A top US trade official enthused about this process: "Peer pressure by liberalizing countries has created a virtuous cycle where countries now compete for global investment by offering more attractive investment opportunities and more effective regulatory regimes" (Fisher, 2000, p. 5).

"Virtuous cycles" of private accumulation, however, may not provide nourishing fare for entire societies. As market entry policies were relaxed, specialized services aimed at corporate users were intensively cultivated, and system-development conformed to transnational corporate preferences rather than needful domestic priorities. Corporate ownership and performance norms were established, and profits made to flow disproportionately to investors rather than to other interests, while the existing – limited – social welfare character of the telecommunications industry was undercut. Often, rates were "rebalanced" to favor business users (above all those making international calls) over low-volume residential callers (Milne, 2000; Commission of the European Communities, 2000). Collective bargaining rights were frequently denied to employees working to build and service newly deregulated network systems; and layoffs became standard practice (Katz, 1997). Quality of service, now more comprehensively tied to the ability to pay, declined for many households (Roycroft and Garcia-Murrilo, 2000; Commission of the European Communities, 2000). Cheats and scams – overbilling of calling card users, illegally transferring long-distance accounts to new carriers, charging telephone users for services they did not order – became regular practices of the now-deregulated industry (Schiesel, 2001). In the US, as national priorities shifted from roads, airports, power plants and bridges to telecommunications networks, existing infrastructures deteriorated (Alonso-Zaldivar, 2001); most ironically, however, the so-called "virtuous" investment cycle turned out to be unhealthy even for the liberalized telecommunications industry itself.

Stoked by investment bankers, and spurred by their own fears of rivals, telecommunications carriers took on mountains of debt to finance network modernization and expansion projects. By one estimate, Europe's telecommunications industry borrowed no less than $300 billion in the form of syndicated loans and bonds, almost entirely between 1997 and 2000, from banks, insurance companies and investment funds (Sesit, 2001). In two years, British Telecom's debt ran up to 50 billion Euros, Deutsche Telekom's to 60 billion Euros, France Telecom's to 64 billion Euros (Cookson, 2001). Across the Atlantic Ocean, newly founded US communications carriers were carrying a total of $74 billion in debt by late 2000, requiring an annual interest expense of about $7 billion (Malik, 2001); and AT&T's debt reached a high of perhaps $62 billion late in 2000 (Rosenbush, 2001). During 2001 alone, over $250 billion of telecommunications industry debt (mostly bonds) needed to be refinanced (Curwen, 2001).

What gave this debt overhang truly ominous implications was the unparalleled network overcapacity that it had financed. Scattered analysts worried that the scale of duplicative system expansion might be outpacing demand throughout the late 1990s (Keefe and Batt, 1997; D. Schiller, 1999a), but Wall Street analysts continued to forecast robust profit growth and capital continued to pour into the industry. During the 1990s in the United States, "private-line" circuit prices (referring to the in-house corporate and organizational telecommunications networks that employ leased circuits and other proprietary facilities on a fulltime basis) dropped sharply, with the prospect of further significant declines (Galbi, 2001); and European bandwidth prices, likewise already decreasing, were projected to decline by 50 percent a year for several years (Logica, 2000; US Department of Commerce, 2000). Prices for circuits on trans-oceanic fiber optic cables experienced analogous – though uneven – declines (TeleGeography, 2001).

During fall 2000, amid the more general rout of technology stocks, industry executives were compelled to reckon with especially violent turbulence. Competitive rate-cutting, investment downgrades, precipitous stock-price drop-offs, financial losses, layoffs, business reorganizations, and bankruptcies were the immediate results. The ultimate costs of the industry's rivalrous network-building binge, however, remained unclear. Telecommunications industry bonds, widely classed as subinvestment grade ("junk") offerings, comprised as much as one-third of the entire junk-bond market by 2001 (Stempel, 2001). Owing to its newfound prominence in the overall system of finance and investment, in turn, the telecommunications sector's precarious state constituted an unknown risk to the health of the larger world economy (Hamilton, 2001).

During periods of economic downturn, however, underlying priorities paradoxically may be clarified and pursued with intensified vigor. And so it is today, as regards networking the global market system. Political circumstances permitting, on one side an epochal new cycle of consolidation among carriers may be expected. On the other side, beyond the unwanted instability that it inspires, the carriers' misfortune does not necessarily come at the expense of transnational business users of network systems and services. Corporate telecommunications users' reintegration of business processes around proprietary networks which, in turn, are increasingly tied together via the Internet, may even be freer to take opportunistic advantage of network overcapacity, thereby deepening their reliance on private line circuits both nationally and transnationally (US Federal Communications Commission, 2000b). To assay the import of the resulting network-enabled services we must engage, finally, with capitalism's new heartland: information.

The Problem of Information

Information constitutes what mainstream economists call a "public good" (Stiglitz, 1999). Because it tends to be cheap to reproduce and hard not to share, their theory holds, corporations cannot automatically hope to recapture the value of the investment that is required to produce it. A corollary of this conception is vital. Historically, a large fraction of society's information resources has been generated and distributed by interlocking government agencies and public-sector institutions: libraries, schools, universities. Taxes rather than corporate outlays paid for a legion of public information programs, which in turn served widely disparate functions and constituencies. Despite their different aims and users, however, these information programs were marked by adherence to a common credo: that needed information would not be produced and made available unless government and public-sector institutions stepped in. Even within a market economy, therefore, the policy of publicly subsidizing a myriad of information resources long commanded adherence.

To this day, some influential voices continue to find virtue in this general arrangement. Economists Stiglitz, Orszag, and Orszag (2000, p. 44) suggest, for example, that the shift "toward an economy in which information is central rather than peripheral" may only confirm the need for "public production" of information. Another prominent economist, Kenneth Arrow (1996, p. 127), likewise forecasts "that we are just beginning to face the contradictions between the systems of private property and of information acquisition and dissemination." And, in a draft report on "public information dissemination," the US National Commission on Libraries and Information Science (2000, p. 2) declares that the federal government should proclaim explicit allegiance to the familiar norm, by "formally recogniz[ing] and affirm[ing] the concept that public information is a strategic national resource."

Through recent decades, however, even as information has become a more visible dimension of the political economy, this longstanding – and still inadequately studied – political economy of quasi-public provision has been progressively destabilized and undercut, and the policy of state subsidy generally reversed. In its place a new and still-just-emerging institutional complex has ascended to power over global information production and distribution.

In 1997, all told, the US information industry generated $623 billion in revenues (US Census Bureau, 1999); it is beyond question that, as one news report put it, "The business of America is . . . information" (Schmid, 1999, p. C3). Subsequent studies and surveys (US Department of Commerce, 2001) have filled out the picture in interesting and important ways, but without altering this fundamental insight: The provision of information in turn actually exhibits not growing *public* control, but *ever-increasing corporate-commercial dominance*. How has this feat been accomplished? Let us turn to inspect the ongoing – and, again, still incomplete – struggle to transform information from a public good to a corporate product.

Corporate Dominance in Information

Corporate control of information, by no means a new trend, nonetheless has been rapidly accelerating in recent years. Corporate initiatives around information are profoundly altering the context for decisions about what information to produce, and on what terms to make it available. Recent hothouse growth of an already-existing, in-house corporate information sphere constitutes the

first massive contributor to this process. The network applications underlying this recent buildup have been undertaken in light of specifically evolving
business needs in such areas as payroll accounting, employment and labor
relations, inventory, sales, marketing, research and development, and so on.
Corporate "knowledge management" practices extend and deepen a century-
long tradition of intervention into the labor process in the name of efficiency.
Augmentation of corporate informational capabilities, it goes without saying,
concurrently enlarges the sphere of what managers regard as proprietary
information.

Consider the case of Wal–Mart, now the largest US-based corporation, owing,
not least, to its legendary network-based capabilities. Wal–Mart's data warehouse
is twice as large as that possessed by any other *Fortune* 500 company, as one
executive relates (Prepared Statement of Wal–Mart, 1999, p. 4): "Previous day's
information, through midnight, on over 10 million customer transactions is
available for every store in every country before 4 a.m. the following day. Today,
over 7,000 suppliers access [this system] and get answers to any question
any time. Wal–Mart current averages 120,000 of these complex trend analyses
questions each week." It would be illuminating to know how this figure compares with the number of inquiries made of leading research libraries. For
public-sector information institutions today not only exhibit less dynamism; they
are also often starved of the resources needed to perform their basic functions. In
turn, the issue raised by the multiplication of corporate information capabilities
is not merely quantitative, but qualitative.

Corporate predominance in the information sector involves more than the
sheer amassment of proprietary information systems and services at the expense
of public information programs. Two other forms of development are typical.
Each of these modes likewise tends to amplify corporate power, even as it also
engages in opposite ways information's propensity to be cheap to copy and hard
not to share. On one hand, underwriting of informational activities – what Oscar
Gandy (1982) calls "information subsidies" – may be transferred to or originated
by corporate sponsors. Corporate commercial advertising (including public relations) furnishes the paramount case.

For many decades, critics have assailed the effects of intensifying commercialism. Their protestations notwithstanding, the sponsor system once more is
enjoying an impressive growth surge. Global advertising spending increased
sevenfold between 1950 and 1996, growing one-third faster than the overall
world economy. In the years since, revenues have only increased (United
Nations Development Programme, 1998; Elliott, 2000; D. Schiller, 2001b). Global
advertising spending (and, as Richard Maxwell [1996] has shown, audience and
market research) also has diffused. Although outlays are still overwhelmingly
concentrated in North America, Europe and Japan, "growth has been faster in
Asia and Latin America, especially since the mid-1980s . . . [Between 1986 and
1996] individual countries in these regions have shown spectacular advertising
growth: for China more than 1,000%, for Indonesia 600%, for Malaysia and

Thailand more than 300% and for India, the Republic of Korea and the Philippines more than 200%" (United Nations Development Programme, 1998, p. 63).

The sponsor system also is annexing whole territories of cultural practice, notably including education. US public schools thus are awash in a commercial curriculum. Specialized TV and web services target children with advertisements in thousands of schools, as chain stores and oil companies furnish videos on everything from local artists to state history. Corporate-sponsored educational materials and teacher training, direct product advertising and sales, and market research are all abundant, particularly at the secondary level (US General Accounting Office, 2000). Public relations programs and direct underwriting of research today are also frequently capable of overwhelming independent academic science (Rampton and Stauber, 2001).

Today's enlargement of the sponsor system stems from two sources. On one side is the current spasm of competition within science-based industry, tending to accelerate the stream of "new and improved" commodities for sale in consumer markets. Between 1995 and 1999, real R&D spending in the US grew at a yearly rate of almost 6 percent, and research spending by corporations actually outpaced this historically high growth rate (Economic Report of the President, 2001). Intensified pressure to advertise is the result of this ensuing flood of new consumer products. On the other side is the development of new media platforms. Yet, there is no iron law that requires that all media accept advertising, and so each new distribution system – cable, satellite, Internet, mobile phones – has spelled a frontier battle-zone for would-be sponsors and sponsorship. Advertisers have gone onto the offensive, to assure themselves of unbroken access to the hearts and minds of consumers no matter where the latter happened to be, and no matter which media platform they engaged. As Mattelart (1991, p. ix) put this more than a decade ago, the advertising industry's governing policy admonition is brutally simple: "No media without advertising."

As corporately subsidized information proliferates, freely proffered information resources typically degrade because the purpose of such subsidies is essentially manipulative or, at least, self-seeking. Consider the 2000 US election, which generated both more paid TV political commercials – a billion dollars' worth (Dreazen, 2001), including perhaps three hundred million dollars just on the presidential contest – than any prior election, and network television news coverage that was widely seen as scandalously inadequate ("Dwindling TV Coverage . . . ," 2000; Dreazen, 2000; Carter 2000; Marks, 2000). Or, consider the consequences of the US drug company practice of making "educational" grants of $50,000–$300,000 each to support Web health sites to showcase their products (Bulkeley, 2000, p. B18): "On a breast-cancer site by HealthTalk Interactive Inc . . . a panel discussion of new therapies features a lengthy section on the drug Hercepton, made by the site's sponsor Genentech Inc." It is hardly reassuring to learn that *The New England Journal of Medicine*, perhaps the world's most renowned medical journal, apologized in 2000 after it came to light that it had published 19 articles that violated its own policy barring drug-assessments written by doctors linked financially with pharmaceutical companies (Bulkeley, 2000). Sponsorship practices likewise have resulted in what a *Business Week* columnist has called "the corruption of TV health news" (Raeburn, 2000). Pharmaceutical advertising of course is only part of the problem. According to one recent US study, no less than one-third of surveyed local TV news directors reported "being pressured to kill negative stories or do positive ones about advertisers" (Hatch, 2000, p. 37).

There is also a third important avenue of corporate control. Information scarcity, rather than information abundance, in many cases best serves the process of profit making. But information scarcity is not a natural condition; it has to be worked at, indeed, *contrived*. And so it is. Restricting access to information requires deployment of legal, technological, and other coercions. By one tally, the single most heavily lobbied set of issues by media industry lobbyists trying to influence the federal government in Washington over the years 1996–2000 pertained to questions of intellectual property (Lewis, 2000). That a dramatic widening and deepening of corporate control over intellectual property rights has been triggered is widely accepted. But we are only beginning to reckon with the fact that the domain of copyright law is itself in the process of being radically extended, so that it no longer merely seeks to regulate multiplication and distribution of works, but rather – through varied pay-per-use systems – the actual practices of media consumption (Litman, 2001). So-called "rights-management" software, declares one recent study, "enables fine-grained control of access, making works as open or as restricted as the rights holder specifies, with considerable ability to fine-tune who has what kind of access" (Committee on Intellectual Property Rights, 2000, p. 7). The recording industry's effort to suppress the free Internet music distribution service Napster (which in two years came to claim 64 million users), and a succession of other free music services, and to supplant them with proprietary online systems, cannot yet claim success – but nonetheless discloses the breathtaking scope of this attempt to control consumption.

Monopolies conferred by intellectual property statutes, meanwhile, also have been enlarged to include new technologies and whole new categories of works, from computer software to genetically modified organisms to business processes (Ryan, 1998). And enforcement too has become newly aggressive. In the run-up to the telecast of SuperBowl 2001, the biggest TV-viewing day on the US calendar, DirecTV "launched an unprecedented electronic attack on an estimated 100,000 consumers who had been bootlegging its satellite TV service," disabling hardware that had enabled viewers (in the US and abroad) to see programs for which they had not paid (Huffstutter and Healey, 2001, p. A19). "[C]ontent owners," one legal scholar sums up, "have successfully promoted their own narrow financial interests over the broader public interest in preserving consumer access to literary, scientific, and other works" (Peter Jaszi in Foster, 2000, p. A44). A *Wall Street Journal* writer is bluntly candid that, as far as intellectual property goes, "monied interests . . . rule" (Murray, 2001, p. A1).

Internationally, policy changes since the 1980s have been congruent. Intellectual property rights, in the words of one authority, have moved "to the forefront of global economic policy-making":

> Indeed, the world is witnessing the greatest expansion ever in the international scope of intellectual property rights. In the 1990s, dozens of countries strengthened their intellectual property laws and regulations (often under pressure from the United States); many others are poised to do likewise. Numerous regional trade and investment agreements, such as the North American Free Trade Agreement (NAFTA) and bilateral accords between the European Union and countries in the Middle East and North Africa, have protection of intellectual property at their core. At the multilateral level, the successful conclusion of the Agreement on Trade-Related Aspects of Intellectual Property Rights (TRIPs) as a founding component of the World Trade Organization (WTO) elevates recognition and enforcement of IPRs to the level of inviolable international commitment. International efforts are also under way to enlarge intellectual property protection for critical new technologies, such as electronic commerce. (Maskus, 2001, p. 1)

It should be stressed that enlarged corporate control over information resources generates something more than a change in the legally enjoined terms of trade with consumers; it is predicated as well on attempts to expropriate *information creators*. In a boon to pharmaceutical companies, for example, so-called "indigenous knowledge" throughout the poor world often has been deemed unworthy of recognition as intellectual property – as it then may be acquired more cheaply (World Bank, 1999). In the US, many publishers have come to demand that freelance writers "sign over the rights to both print and electronic editions of their work" before accepting their texts for publication (Greenberger, 2000, p. B13). Similarly, so-called "work-for-hire" laws are being extended to sound recordings, so that musicians are stripped of their already inadequate rights to their work (Holland, 2000; Harmon, 2000). And, as we saw at the outset, non-disclosure agreements and non-compete clauses are finding increasing use to prevent employees from revealing corporate secrets, most specifically, to rivals (Carley, 1998). The Economic Espionage Age of 1996 indeed turned the theft of trade secrets – an increasingly expansive category, as vigilant managers use it to guard swelling proprietary corporate knowledge stocks – into a federal crime (Armour, 2000).

It is very clear, in consequence, that a resource that many believe brings maximum benefits when free often may be successfully hedged in with barriers to access. Behind this massive enclosure, indeed, great new engines of market development are being built, in agriculture and pharmaceuticals and medicine, in education, and in a variety of business and consumer services. But closely associated social changes may prove far less sanguinary.

"Unarguably," concludes Herbert I. Schiller (1996, p. 20), intensive market development of information "has been of great benefit to affluent users who now have access to kinds and amounts of data that would have been unimaginable not many years ago." The progressive corporate-commercial takeover of information therefore "has been rewarding to private information providers and to their clients. For the rest of the population, the vast majority, the quality and the availability of information leave much to be desired." More generally, the prevailing trend – to spread corporately subsidized commercial information far and wide, while using technological, market and legal means to withhold access to fee-based or simply proprietary corporate information resources and services – promises only to deepen social disparities while undercutting the mechanisms of democratic self-government.

References

Alonso-Zaldivar, R. (2001). Nation's infrastructure crumbling, report says, *Los Angeles Times*, 8 March, A9.

Armour, S. (2000). Does your company own what you know? *USA Today*, 19 January, 1A, 1B.

Arrow, K. J. (1996). The economics of information: an exposition. *Empirica*, 23, 119–28.

Barshefsky, C. (1999). Electronic Commerce: Trade policy in a borderless world. Speech to the Woodrow Wilson Center, Washington, DC, 29 July, 6. Retrieved 23 February 2001 at http://www.ustr.gov.

Blouin, C. (2000). The WTO agreement on basic telecommunications: A reevaluation. *Telecommunications Policy* (24), 135–42.

Blumenstein, R. (2000). Who's on first? *Wall Street Journal*, 18 September, R4.

Bogart, L. (2000). *Commercial Culture: The media system and the public interest*. New Brunswick: Transaction.

Bulkeley, W. L. (2000). New England journal editor blasts some drug industry/academic links. *Wall Street Journal*, 18 May, B18.

Carley, W. M. (1998). Secrets suit: What did he know? *Wall Street Journal*, 19 January, B1, B8.

Carter, B. (2000). Fox decides against debates. *New York Times*, 27 September, B9.

Commission of the European Communities (2000). Communication from the Commission to the Council, The European Parliament, the Economic and Social Committee and the Committee of the Regions, "Sixth Report on the Implementation of the Telecommunications Regulatory Package." Brussels: COM (2000), 814 (7 December).

Commission of the European Communities (2001). Third Report From The Commission To The Council, The European Parliament and the Economic and Social Committee on the application of Directive 89/552/EEC "Television without Frontiers." Brussels: COM (2001), 9 (15 January).

Committee on Intellectual Property Rights and the Emerging Information Infrastructure (2000). Computer Science and Telecommunications Board, National Research Council. *The Digital Dilemma: Intellectual Property in the Information Age*. Washington, DC: National Academy.

Cookson, R. (2001). A $250 billion gamble. *Economist* Survey, 27 January, 10.

Curwen, P. (2001). Buddy, can you spare a billion? *Info*, 3(1), 91–2.

Dreazen, Y. J. (2000). Voter turnout stays low despite barrage of ads, closeness of race. *Wall Street Journal*, 9 November, A16.

Dreazen, Y. J. (2001). Lawmakers aim to put limit on amount broadcasters charge for campaign ads. *Wall Street Journal*, 19 March, A22.

Dwindling TV coverage fell to new low (2000). *USA Today*, 7 November, 8A.

Economic Report of the President (2001). 107th Congress, 1st Session, House Document 107–2. Washington, DC: USGPO.

Elliott, S. (2000). Advertising. *New York Times*, 5 December, C12.

Ellison, S. (2001). MSN service to plan online-ad strategy. *Wall Street Journal*, 5 March, B7.

Esserman, S. G. (2000). (Deputy US Trade Representative) Telecommunications and the International Trade System. Center for Strategic and International Studies, Washington, DC (29 February). Retrieved 23 February 2001 at http://www.ustr.gov.

Fisher, R. W. (2000). Trade in Telecommunications Services. Testimony before the House of Representatives Committee on Commerce, Subcommitee on Telecommunications, Trade and Consumer Protection (7 September). Retrieved 23 February 2001 at http://www.ustr.gov.

Flagg, M. (2000). Broadcaster seeks Arab TV audience beyond the Mideast. *Wall Street Journal*, 27 November, A34.

Foster. A. L. (2000). Scholars decry new copyright rule. *Chronicle of Higher Education*, 10 November, A44.

Galbi, D. A. (2001). Growth in the "new economy": US bandwidth use and pricing across the 1990s. *Telecommunications Policy*, 25, 140–7.

Gandy, Jr., O. H. (1982). *Beyond Agenda Setting: Information subsidies and public policy*. Norwood: Ablex.

Gates, B. (2000). Remarks by Bill Gates. Digital Dividends Conference, Seattle, Washington, 18 October. Retrieved 8 November 2000 at http://www.microsoft/com/billgates/speeches/2000/10-18digitaldividends.htm.

Greenberger, R. S. (2000). Justices to review free-lancers' consent to web. *Wall Street Journal*, 7 November, B13.

Hamilton, W. (2001). Corporate tech spending helped set stage for slump. *Los Angeles Times*, 14 March, A1, A13.

Harmon, A. (2000). Rock musicians enter fray on copyrights. *New York Times*, 13 November, C4.

Hatch, D. (2000). Local news execs feeling ad pressure. *Electronic Media*, 1 December, 37.

Hebert, J. (2001). Brand game. *San Diego Union-Tribune*, 28 January, E1.

Holland, B. (2000). Work-for-hire rollback legislation ready. *Billboard*, 2 September, 5.

Huffstutter, P. J. and Healey, J. (2001). Satellite blows TV pirates right off the tube. *Los Angeles Times*, 27 January, A1, A19.

Jenkins, Jr., H. W. (2000). How a telecom meltdown will cause the next recession. *Wall Street Journal*, 27 September, A27.

Katz, H. C. (1997). *Telecommunications Restructuring and Employment Relations Worldwide*. Ithaca: Cornell.

Keefe, J. H. and Batt, R. (1997). United States. In H. C. Katz (ed.), *Telecommunications Restructuring and Employment Relations Worldwide*. Ithaca: Cornell, pp. 21–62.

Lewis, C. (2000). Media money. *Columbia Journalism Review*, September/October, 21–6.

Litman, J. (2001). *Digital Copyright*. Amherst, NY: Prometheus Books.

Logica Consulting (2000). Assessment of the Leased Line Market in the European Union. A study prepared for the European Commission. Brussels (19 January). Retrieved 20 March 2001 at www.ispo.cec.be/infosoc/telecompolicy.en/Study-en.htm.

Magder, T. and Burston, J. (2001). Whose Hollywood? Changing forms and relations inside the North American entertainment economy. In V. Mosco and D. Schiller (eds.), *Continental Order? Integrating North America for cyber-capitalism*. Lanham: Rowman & Littlefield, pp. 207–34.

Malik, O. (2001). Wrong number. *Red Herring*, 16 January, 66–8.

Marks, P. (2000). Networks cede political coverage to cable. *New York Times*, 7 April, A16.

Maskus, K. E. (2001). *Intellectual Property Rights in the Global Economy*. Washington, DC: Institute for International Economics.

Mattelart, A. (1991). *Advertising International: The privatisation of public space*. London: Comedia.

Maxwell, R. (1996). Out of kindness and into difference: The value of global market research. *Media Culture and Society*, 18, 105–26.

Milne, C. (2000). Affordability of basic telephone service: An income distribution approach. *Telecommunications Policy*, 24, 908–19.

Muñoz, L. (2001). Springing "Crouching Tiger" on U.S. Audiences. *Los Angeles Times*, 26 March, F5.

Murray, A. (2001). Drug makers' battle is one over ideas. *Wall Street Journal*, 19 March, A1.

Nordenstreng, K. and Varis, T. (1974). *Television Traffic – A One-Way Street?* Reports and Papers on Mass Communication, no. 70. Paris: UNESCO.

Oliner, S. D. and Sichel, D. E. (2000). The Resurgence of Growth in the Late 1990s: Is Information Technology the Story? Washington, DC: US Federal Reserve Bank (May). Retrieved 23 February 2001 at http://www.federalreserve.gov/pubs/feds/2000/200020pap.pdf.

Orwall, B. (2001). Colombian pop star taps American taste in repackaged imports. *Wall Street Journal*, 13 February, A1, A6.

Perkin, J. (2001). Multilingual websites widen the way to a new online world. *Financial Times Review of IT*, 7 February, 1.

Prepared Statement of Wal-Mart Stores, Inc. (1999). The Role of Standards in the Growth of Global Electronic Commerce. Testimony before the Subcommittee on Science, Technology and Space of the Committee on Commerce, Science, and Transportation. US Senate, Washington, DC, 28 October.

Raeburn, P. (2000). The corruption of TV health news. *Business Week*, 28 February, 66–8.

Rampton, S. and Stauber, J. (2001). *Trust Us, We're Experts!* New York: Tarcher/Putnam.

Ramstad, E. and Stringer, K. (2001). In race to lay fiber, telecom firms wreak havoc on city streets. *Wall Street Journal*, 27 February, A1.

Reality Bytes (2001). *Wall Street Journal*, 15 January, B10.

Romney, L. (2001). TV talks to immigrant markets. *Los Angeles Times*, 15 January, A1, A12.

Rosenbush, S. (2001). Armstrong's last stand. *Business Week*, 5 February, 88.

Roycroft, T. R. and Garcia-Murrilo, M. (2000). Trouble reports as an indicator of service quality: the influence of competition, technology, and regulation. *Telecommunications Policy*, 24, 945–66.

Rutenberg, J. (2001). A wave of violence engulfs children's cartoon programs. *New York Times*, 28 January, A1, A13.

Ryan, M. P. (1998). *Knowledge Diplomacy: Global competition and the politics of intellectual property*. Washington, DC: Brookings Institution.

Sanchez-Ruiz, E. E. (2001). Globalization, cultural industries, and free trade: the Mexican audio-visual sector in the NAFTA age. In V. Mosco and D. Schiller, (eds.), *Continental Order? Integrating North America for cyber-capitalism*. Lanham: Rowman & Littlefield, pp. 86–119.

Schiesel, S. (2001). For some who use calling cards, the number is 1-800-BEWARE. *New York Times*, 15 February, A1, C4.

Schiller, D. (1982). *Telematics and Government*. Norwood: Ablex.

Schiller, D. (1999a). *Digital Capitalism: Networking the global market system*. Cambridge, MA: MIT.

Schiller, D. (1999b). Deep impact: The web and the changing media economy. *Info*, 1(1), 35–51.

Schiller, D. (2001a). World communications in today's age of capital. *Emergences*, 11(1), 51–68.

Schiller, D. (2001b). Globe with a logo. *Le Monde Diplomatique*, May, 16–17.

Schiller, D. and Mosco, V. (2001). Introduction. In V. Mosco and D. Schiller (eds.), *Continental Order? Integrating North America for cyber-capitalism*. Lanham: Rowman and Littlefield, pp. 1–34.

Schiller, H. I. (1981). *Who Knows: Information in the age of the Fortune 500*. Norwood: Ablex.

Schiller, H. I. (1989). *Culture, Inc.: The corporate takeover of public expression*. New York: Oxford.

Schiller, H. I. (1996). Information deprivation in an information-rich society. In G. Gerbner, H. Mowlana, and H. I. Schiller (eds.), *Invisible Crises: What conglomerate control of media means for America and the world*. Boulder, CO: Westview, pp. 15–26.

Schmid, R. E. (1999). Information a $623-billion industry in '97, U.S. says. *Los Angeles Times*, 25 October, C3.

Schneider, M. (2000). Whiz quiz hits global jackpot. *Variety* (17–23 July), 1, 72.

Schwartz, H. (2000). Going global: Hungry for new markets. *Webtechniques*, 5 (September), 53–6.

Sesit, M. R. (2001). Will Europe's banks founder on the rocks of telecom debt? *Wall Street Journal*, 30 January, A16.

Silverstein, S. (2000). Fear feeds millions of shredders. *Los Angeles Times*, 3 February, A1, A24.

Stempel, J. (2001). Falling telecom issues lead new slump in junk bonds. *Los Angeles Times*, 5 April, C4.

Stiglitz, J. E. (1999). Knowledge as a global public good. In I. Kaul, I. Grunberg, and M. A. Stern (eds.), *Global Public Goods*. New York: Oxford University Press, pp. 308–25.

Stiglitz, J. E., Orszag, P. R., and Orszag, J. M. (2000). The Role of Government in a Digital Age. Washington, DC: Computer & Communications Industry Association (October).

Sutel, S. (2000). U.S. networks mine overseas shows in hopes of finding ratings gold. *San Diego Union-Tribune*, 19 September, E7.

TeleGeography, Inc. (2001). *International Bandwidth 2001*. Washington, DC: TeleGeography, Inc.

UK Department of Trade and Industry (2000). White Paper, "A New Future For Communications." London. Retrieved 30 January 2001 from http://www.dti.gov.uk.

United Nations Conference on Trade and Development (2000). *World Investment Report 2000: Cross-border mergers and acquisitions and development*. New York: United Nations.

United Nations Conference on Trade and Development and United Nations Department of Economic and Social Affairs (2001). *World Economic Situation and Prospects 2001*. New York: United Nations.

United Nations Development Programme (1998). *Human Development Report 1998*. New York: Oxford University Press.

United Nations Development Programme (2000). *Human Development Report 2000*. New York: Oxford University Press.

US Census Bureau (1999). *United States 1997 Economic Census Information Geographic Area Series*. EC97551A-US. Washington, DC (October).

US Department of Commerce (2000). Economics and Statistics Administration, *Digital Economy 2000*. Washington, DC (June).

US Department of Commerce (2001). US Government Working Group on Electronic Commerce, Third Annual Report. "Leadership for the New Millennium: Delivering on Digital Progress and Prosperity." Washington, DC (16 January).

US Department of State (2000). Office of the Spokesman Press Statement, "White House and U.S. Department of State Co-Sponsor The White House Conference on Culture and Diplomacy November 28, 2000." Retrieved 30 January 2001 at http://secretary.state.gov/www/briefings/statements/2000/ps001117b.html.

US Federal Communications Commission (1997). "In the Matter of Rules and Policies on Foreign Participation in the U.S. Telecommunications Market; Market Entry and Regulation of Foreign-Affiliated Entities," IB Dockets No. 97-142 and 95-22, *Report and Order on Reconsideration* (25 November).

US Federal Communications Commission (2000a). International Bureau, "Report on International Telecommunications Markets 1999 Update," Prepared for Senator Ernest F. Hollings, Committee on Commerce, Science and Transportation, US Senate (14 January). Retrieved 23 February 2001 at http://www.fcc.gov.

US Federal Communications Commission (2000b). *International Bureau Report, 1999 Section 43.82 Circuit Status Data* (December 3). Retrieved 23 February 2001 at www.fcc.gov/ib/td/pf/csmanual.html.

US General Accounting Office (2000). Public Education: Commercial Activities in Schools, GAO/HEHS-00-156 (September).

US National Commission on Libraries and Information Science (2000). A Comprehensive Assessment of Public Information Dissemination, *Final Report, Volume 1*. First Draft (27 November). Washington, DC: NCLIS.

Vickers, B. (2001). Europe lags behind U.S. on web privacy. *Wall Street Journal*, 20 February, B11A.

Vranica, S. (2001). Grey direct pushes the e-mail envelope. *Wall Street Journal*, 18 April, B8.

Waldman, P. (1999). Silicon Valley, where the conversation comes with a caveat. *Wall Street Journal*, 3 October, A1.

Wellenius, B., Primo Braga, C. A., and Zhen-Wei Qiang, C. (2000). Investment and growth of the information infrastructure: summary results of a global survey. *Telecommunications Policy*, 24, 635–43.

White House (2000). Office of the Press Secretary, "President Clinton Hosts First White House Conference on Culture and Diplomacy" (November 28). Retrieved 23 February 2001 at http://www.pub.whitehouse.gov/uri-res/12…pdi://oma.eop.gov.us/2000/11/28/5.text.1.

White House Conference on Culture and Diplomacy (2000). 28 November. Retrieved 23 February 2001 at http://www.state.gov/r/whconf/index.html.

World Bank (1999). *World Development Report 1998/99. Knowledge for Development*. New York: Oxford.

Zhao, Y. and Schiller, D. (2001). Dances with wolves? China's integration into digital capitalism. *Info*, 3(2), 137–51.

Further reading

Cohen, J. E. (1999). WIPO copyright treaty implementation in the United States: Will fair use survive? *European Intellectual Property Review*, 21, 236.

Herman, E. S. and McChesney, R. W. (1997). *The Global Media*. London: Cassell.

Mosco, V. (1996). *The Political Economy of Communication: Rethinking and renewal*. London: Sage.

Sidak, J. G. (1997). *Foreign Investment in American Telecommunications*. Chicago: University of Chicago.

Thussu, D. (2000). *International Communication*. London: Arnold.

CHAPTER EIGHT

Media Production
Individuals, Organizations, Institutions

D. Charles Whitney and
James S. Ettema

Aristotle's *Rhetoric*, with its timeless advice about message invention, might be a defensible place to begin a review of "communicator studies." If, however, we take the topic to be "professional mass communicators," then Walter Lippmann's *Public Opinion* (1922), with its wide-ranging analysis of the production and political consequences of the news, might be the place to begin. Or if we insist on a patina of quantitative social science, then Leo Rosten's *The Washington Correspondents* (1937), with its demographic profiles of the press corps, might be the place. Or if we insist that there is more truth in art than science, then we might begin with Evelyn Waugh's novel *Scoop* (1938), a caustic satire of press barons and foreign correspondents that many correspondents themselves still take to be both the first and last word on their craft.

The goal of this chapter, however, is not to exhaustively review the literature on professional mass communicators, but more modestly to outline important recent trends and issues in the research on the individuals and organizations that produce media messages. Thus, we begin with what can be characterized as the rediscovery in the 1970s of mass communicators as an important topic of research within several fields of social inquiry. We then look at levels of analysis and theoretical domains as ways of organizing the research on mass communicators. We focus primarily on the production of news – and that primarily in the US and UK – but we turn briefly to other forms of culture for points of comparison.

The "Rediscovery" of Mass Communicators

In 1972, Herbert Gans wrote an article decrying a "famine" in American mass communication research, especially in what he labeled "institutional studies" – that is, research on professional mass communicators, their organizations and industries. Gans's point was that sociology was ignoring a topic with significance for social theory. Interestingly, that essay mentioned three exemplary articles from the *American Journal of Sociology*. Two of these studies remain particularly noteworthy because they marked entry of two new scholars into the field of communicator studies, both of whom brought new and powerful ideas into the field with them. These articles were Paul Hirsch's (1972) "Processing Fads and Fashions: An Organization-set Analysis of Cultural Industry Systems," an application of the sociology of complex organizations to media industries, and Gaye Tuchman's (1972) "Objectivity as Strategic Ritual: An Examination of Newsmen's Notions of Objectivity," an application of the phenomenological sociology of work life to the newsroom. Both articles now stand as classics of the field.

In 1972, Gans himself was at work on the research that would become *Deciding What's News* (1979). At the same time, Tuchman was extending her work into a book: *Making News* (1978). Meanwhile, an antiwar activist-turned-graduate student, Todd Gitlin, was drawing upon critical-Marxist sociology to understand the oddly symbiotic relationship between the news media and the anti-war movement of the Vietnam era. Soon he published *The Whole World is Watching* (1980). These key moments in the rediscovery of mass communicator studies by US American sociology in the 1970s were largely inspired, as Gans, Tuchman and Gitlin have all acknowledged, by a need to make sense of the way that social institutions shaped the US American experience with Vietnam. Coincidentally, the year in which Gans's essay appeared, 1972, was also the year of an event that helped spur the rediscovery of mass communicator studies by US American political science: the Watergate break-in.

This rediscovery of mass communicators among sociologists and political scientists was a rediscovery of old questions – but new answers. Beginning in the 1970s, "the limited effects model" – the idea that media had little influence on public opinion as articulated in Katz and Lazarsfeld's (1955) *Personal Influence* and Klapper's (1960) *Effects of Mass Communication* – was overturned in favor of models such as agenda-setting that allocated far more sociopolitical power to the mass media. This made the question of how media content is produced more urgent and interesting. In sociology, as noted, this led to work by Hirsch, Gans, Tuchman and Gitlin. In political science, it led to Patterson's *The Mass Media Election* (1980); Paletz and Entman's *Media, Power, Politics* (1981); Lang and Lang's *The Battle for Public Opinion* (1983); Ranney's *Channels of Power* (1983); Robinson and Sheehan's *Over the Wire and on TV* (1983); and Linsky's *Impact: How the Press Affects Federal Policy-Making* (1986), to list only a few. Although not all of these works focused directly on the activities of mass communicators, all discussed the interface between the mass media and the political process.

In the decades since this era of rediscovery, substantial research effort has been devoted to understanding how professional mass communicators, their organizations and industries produce media content and, thereby, produce a sociopolitical impact of some sort. And in those decades, three important trends have emerged:

- The research has tended to move toward higher levels of analysis – that is, from individual roles to organizational processes and from separate organizations to entire industries.
- The research has embraced more diverse theoretical perspectives as it has moved to higher levels of analysis.
- The research has included a wider range of roles, organizations and industries under the rubric of "professional mass communicators."

A review of these trends is a useful way to selectively review the entire body of literature in this area of research.

Levels of Analysis

The production of mass-mediated symbol systems is, at the most basic level of analysis, the work of individuals or small groups. At another level, however, it is the product of complex organizations; and at still another, higher level it reflects the legal, economic and other institutional arrangements of industry systems. Of course, the processes at each of the levels – from the ideas of creators and the decisions of managers to the marketing strategies of firms and the economic bases of entire industries – interpenetrate the processes at all other levels. But while the processes at each level may be difficult to disentangle from the others, the *research* conducted at each level poses distinctive questions about the production of media content and draws upon different theories to help answer those questions. For this reason, as a number of authors have suggested, a literature review can be organized usefully by level analysis. Shoemaker and Reese (1996), for example, identify five levels: individual, media routines, organizational, extramedia and ideological. In this review, we have sorted the research, as parsimoniously as possible, into three levels: individual, organizational and institutional. (The application of this idea can be traced through these additional sources: Dimmick & Coit, 1982; Ettema & Whitney, 1987; McManus, 1995.)

The individual level

At this level the essential research question is the role of individual consciousness in symbol production. In the research on journalists, for example, one such question has concerned the role of individual values – traditionally conceptualized as personal *biases* – in the work of those who serve as gatekeepers for the flow of news. David Manning White's (1950) case study of "Mr. Gates," a wire editor for a daily newspaper, concluded:

> Through studying his overt reasons for rejecting news stories from the press associations, we see how highly subjective, how based on the "gatekeeper's" own set of experiences, attitudes and expectations the communication of "news" really is. (1950, p. 390)

While subsequent interpretations of White's data have undercut this conclusion, the notion that what becomes news is highly dependent upon journalists' biases has been argued frequently by politicians and the public and argued occasionally by academics as well. Lichter and Rothman (1981), for instance, described journalists within "elite" US news organizations (e.g. the *New York Times*) as more liberal politically and socially than a comparison group of major business executives. However, surveys with more representative samples of US journalists showed the tendency toward political and social liberalism to be less pronounced (Associated Press Managing Editors, 1985; Weaver & Wilhoit, 1991).

In response to Lichter and Rothman and other critics (most recently Goldberg, 2002), researchers have long sought, but not found very much evidence that any liberal biases held by reporters actually shape the news (Clancey & Robinson, 1985; Gans, 1985; Robinson, 1983, 1985; Schneider & Lewis, 1985). Robinson's (1983, 1985) content analyses of the 1980 and 1984 presidential elections, for example, indicated biases in the form of heavier coverage of incumbent candidates and lighter coverage of minor party candidates, but no liberal or conservative bias in primary and general election coverage. Similarly, Clarke and Evans's (1983) analysis of congressional campaigns found a pronounced bias in favor of incumbents but no partisan bias. "In short there is no evidence whatsoever of a monolithic liberal bias in the newspaper industry, at least as manifest in presidential campaign coverage," D'Alessio and Allen concluded from their meta-analysis of 59 studies of presidential campaign coverage. "The same can be said of a conservative bias: There is no significant evidence of it" (2000, p. 148).

While Stocking (Stocking & Gross, 1989; Stocking & LaMarca, 1990) used the concept of information processing biases from cognitive psychology to put a new spin on the venerable topic of bias, Michael Schudson's (1995) book, *The Power of News*, eloquently expresses the now widely shared understanding of bias as an organizational and institutional rather than individual phenomenon. The biases of journalism, Schudson argues, arise not from the partisanship of its practitioners but the detachment of its professional culture, a culture with a suspicion of all ideology but a fascination with the mechanics of conflict and the exercise of power.

If the processes of news production (as discussed below) mute partisanship, they also mute the effects of background and environmental factors – such as race and gender – that shape the consciousness of individual journalists. To be sure, some critics argue that the underrepresentation of women and minorities in the newsroom leads to underrepresentation of female and minority perspectives in the selection of stories, in the points of view covered within stories and in the play of stories in the newspaper or newscast (e.g. Gilliam, 1991; Creedon, 1989). On the other hand, there is little research evidence suggesting that women or minorities select and edit news items or write a given news story or editorial in ways distinctly different from majority males employed in similar settings (cf. Bleske, 1997 [1991]). Nonetheless, the demographic composition of the newsroom remains an important topic for research because equitable opportunity for women and minorities in journalism is a value in its own right.

With this in mind it is abundantly clear that racial and ethnic minorities are underrepresented in US newsrooms. A study by the American Society of Newspaper Editors in 2001 found that 2.3 percent of US newspaper journalists were Asian American, 5.23 percent were African American, 3.66 percent Hispanic and 0.44 percent were Native American, percentages that had declined slightly in the past year and show particularly pronounced underrepresentations of African Americans and Hispanic journalists. Women accounted for 37.4 percent of US newspaper journalists and 34 percent of newsroom supervisors in 2001 according to ASNE (see also Weaver and Wilhoit, 1991, 1998). Evidence of inequality extends beyond these basic employment statistics. Dennis (1993) reported that, while women constituted slightly less than 40 percent of US newspaper editorial staffs, a content analysis of ten elite US newspapers found that women wrote slightly less than 30 percent of bylined front-page stories. On these front pages, moreover, men wrote disproportionately more economics, government-and-politics, science-and-technology, war-and-military, and, interestingly, leisure activity stories. Women wrote disproportionately more accident-and-disaster, health-and-medicine and especially education stories.

Turning briefly from the study of individual journalists to the study of the individuals who may be credited with creating entertainment-oriented forms of popular culture finds individual cognitions celebrated as the site of creativity rather than condemned as the source of bias. Many – though certainly not all – of the television producers represented in Cantor's (1987 [1971]) landmark study expressed their belief in the creative possibilities afforded by commercial television and their commitment to the struggle for creative control. They also acknowledged, however, that their personal vision would yield as much as necessary to meet the demands of the ratings-driven television industry. Similarly, the "self-conscious artistic producers" studied by Newcomb and Alley (1982, 1983) all experienced powerful constraints imposed by the commercial demands of their industry, and yet they were able to secure enough creative control within the industry system to provide opportunities for creative self-expression. Countless autobiographies of producers, directors, writers and actors have also developed this theme of a search for meaningful creative opportunity within organizational, industrial and political constraint. (Among the treatments of this topic are

Faulkner, 1971; Cantor, 1980; Gitlin, 1983; Montgomery, 1989; Selnow & Gilbert, 1993; and Tunstall, 1993.)

The organizational level

The rediscovery of communication studies in the 1970s was due, in large part, to interesting new research that shifted the locus of control for media content, especially journalism, from the thinking of individuals such as "Mr Gates" to the work processes of their organizations. Two studies, one by McCombs and Shaw in 1976 and another by Hirsch published in 1977, are illustrative of – and were instrumental in – this theoretical shift. Both studies re-examined White's data and took issue with White's conclusion that gatekeepers' personal biases are a principal determinant of news selection. Both argued, instead, that wire service coverage patterns and priorities, as reflected by the proportion of content in standard news categories (e.g. national politics, natural disasters), are important news determinants – a result later confirmed experimentally by Whitney and Becker (1982). Mr. Gates's decision making, that is to say, was structured, though not fully determined, by the standard operating procedures of news processing.

When viewed from the organizational level of analysis, Mr Gates lost some, though not all, of his autonomy as a decision maker. Such organizational constraints on autonomy render suspect any claims for journalism as one of the professions. (See, for example, Zelizer's 1993 critique of those claims.) Moreover, when viewed from the organizational level of analysis, the features of professionalism that, arguably, can be attributed to journalism – e.g. command of specialized knowledge, commitment to performance standards – are seen to be organizational strategies for accomplishing the tasks at hand. That is, organizations grant workers some autonomy to deal with situations that deviate from the completely routine; and yet, organizations retain substantial control of these workers through the inculcation of professional norms that serve the interests of the organization. As Elliott argued (1977, pp. 149–50):

> Claims to professionalism in journalism are based on such routine competencies as factual accuracy, speed at meeting deadlines, style in presentation and shared sense of news values. The competence involved is that which suits the organizational structure of the medium at a particular time, so professional excellence is valued as much by executives and administrators as by the craft group.

Professionalism, as Soloski (1989a: p. 207) concluded, "is an efficient and economical method by which news organizations control the behavior of reporters and editors," though this does not mean that all journalists hold identical values (Weaver & Wilhoit, 1991) or that they never come into conflict with their organizations. Reporters do sometimes stand up to their editors just as entertainment producers do sometimes resist pressure from the studio brass; but such conflicts are structured by, and resolved within, the system of standardized procedures and internalized norms that help organizations to get the work done. (See also Schlesinger, 1978, for a similar perspective from the UK.)

A central insight to emerge from the communicator studies conducted over the last quarter century is that organizational processes affect not only on the work life of individual mass communicators, but also the form, content and meaning of the work that they produce. In the study of journalists and their organizations, substantial research effort has been directed toward understanding the role of standard operating procedures in determining which occurrences in the world become news and how those occurrences are portrayed. Newsworkers cannot always be certain about the location and timing of newsworthy occurrences, and they cannot process all such occurrences as news. They have, however, devised a variety of procedures that serve, in Tuchman's (1973, 1978) apt phrase, to "routinize the unexpected."

One such procedure, according to Tuchman is the specialized journalistic vocabulary for "typifying" or summarizing expectations about how potential news stories will develop and how they should be covered. Such distinctions as "hard news" versus "soft news" and "spot news" versus "developing news" and "continuing news" help to routinize the processing of events into news by conveying information about scheduling and mode of coverage appropriate to various sorts of occurrences. The term "hard news," for example, identifies occurrences that demand both immediate attention and objective treatment in the process of transforming them into news. Journalists further typify occurrences by major features of the event. For example, Berkowitz (1992) examined the way that television coverage of a major local story – a deadly hotel fire caused by the crash of a military aircraft – was guided by typifying the occurrence not merely as a fire, but as a plane crash. Journalists, particularly editors, may also typify stories in terms of expected audience response. Sumpter (2000) for example found that editors typified some stories as "readers" (stories that the editors themselves seemed eager to read) and some stories as "talkers" (stories that the editors seemed eager to discuss).

Even if the relationship between facts and values is one of "intimate interdependence" (Ettema & Glasser, 1998, p. 131), the norm of journalistic objectivity has guided journalists (in the US at least) to separate facts from values – as best they can. Beginning early in the twentieth century, as Schudson (2001) shows, this norm has united journalists into a professional culture that, among other functions, transmits values and controls subordinates in news organizations. In perhaps the single most influential book about the American news media, *Making News: A Study in the Construction of Reality*, Gaye Tuchman (1978) analyzed how the norm has been put into practice. Objectivity is a set of conventions or rules for reporting and writing the story. These rules, for example, promote the use of quotation marks as a guarantee of the *accuracy* of the account of what a source said – though certainly not as a guarantee of the *honesty* of what was said. These rules demand that "both sides" of controversial issues be covered so long as official spokespersons for both sides can be found. And these rules require that supportive evidence for statements be woven together in a "web of facticity" though that often only means that reporters must interview two official sources rather than one.

Perhaps the single most important implication of journalistic objectivity is that it directs reporters to official sources – typically those in government – whose version of events becomes the stuff of news. "The primary source of reality for news is not what is displayed or what happens in the real world," concluded Ericson, Baranek, and Chan (1989, p. 377). "The reality of news is embedded in the nature and type of social and cultural relations that develop between journalists and their sources, and in the politics of knowledge that emerges on each specific news beat." This politics of knowledge has important implications for sources as well as journalists. "The making of a corporate identity constructed upon the idea of service is a touchstone of the police's current crisis of authority and legitimacy," Schlesinger and Tumber (1994, p. 273) concluded in their study of the police beat in the UK. "In a skeptical world, all police officers have to be media-wise and become exponents of public facework."

On the national and international affairs beat for US journalists, sources in the executive branch of the federal government dominate, as Hallin, Manoff, and Weddle (1993, p. 753) argue, "because they are readily accessible to journalists and because their statements are defined by the political culture as authoritative and newsworthy." A content analysis of seven major newspapers by these authors revealed, for example, that officials in the executive branch of the US government constituted nearly 60 percent of all the sources used in stories about national security issues. Congress accounted for another 15 percent, and foreign officials for about 9 percent. Nongovernmental sources in the United States such as research groups and religious organizations comprised less than 6 percent. These findings echo those from a classic study of 20 years before in which Sigal (1973) found that almost four-fifths of *New York Times* and *Washington Post* national and international news emanated from official sources with about two-thirds of the stories originating in such "pseudo-events" as press conferences and news releases. Soloski (1989b) has shown that local news is produced by much the same newsgathering routines. Thus, the news is not so much an account of what happened as it is a compilation of what officials *say* about what happened. (See among many examples: Hess, 1981, 1996; Brown, Bybee, Wearden, & Straughan, 1987; Whitney et al., 1989; Cook, 1994; Fico & Freedman, 2001.)

Public officials predominate as sources not only because reporters consider them to be knowledgeable but also because reporters accept their administrative procedures as the way the world works. Fishman (1980, 1982) argued that local government and police reporters rely on "bureaucratic phase structures" as a signal that governmental agencies have produced a newsworthy event. A crime, for example, most often becomes a news event at the conclusion of such key phases as arrest, arraignment, discovery, trial, and sentencing. Conversely, the outcomes of nonofficial proceedings and the views of resource-poor organizations are seldom covered unless participants can gain the attention of public officials through, for example, acts of civil disobedience. However, a number of studies across the decades (e.g. Goldenberg, 1975; Gitlin, 1980; Shoemaker, 1984; McLeod and Hertog, 1992) have all demonstrated that when groups do this, they run the risk that their objectives will be seen as radical or, at best, marginal. For example, the editors of the *New York Times* and *Time* magazine, as Entman and Rojecki acerbically concluded, came to the same conclusion about the nuclear freeze movement of the 1980s: "the nuclear weapons policies of the nation should not be dictated by the anxieties of an amorphous movement, one purportedly riven by discord" (1993, p. 170).

Turning briefly, once again, from journalism to other forms of popular culture shows that the reliance on routine production procedures is a fact of life in most other media organizations as well. While film may be a director's medium television remains a producer's medium, as Newcomb and Alley (1982, 1983) argued many television seasons ago, because the producer figures out what networks and audiences will accept and manages the other creative personnel (writers, story editors, directors, etc.). Thus, producers hold creative control both because they are the central decision makers in an organization with a relatively clear division of labor and because they personally deal with many of the uncertainties of satisfying network programmers and, perhaps, the television audience. But even if the producer's role offers the possibility of real creativity, that role calls upon a variety of strategies to cope with uncertainty by routinizing the work.

Turow (1992) distinguished between administrative strategies and content-based strategies for coping with complex creative tasks. The division of labor among personnel, for example, is an administrative coping strategy employed by many organizations. This strategy helps routinize creative tasks by dividing those tasks into more manageable assignments and by allocating assignments to specialists who, presumably, are best able to execute them. At the same time, the division of labor allows for centralized coordination of the overall task. To fill the creative roles generated by this division of labor, producers call upon another administrative coping strategy: the use of "track records" to select creative personnel. Faulkner's (1982) study of track records in the film industry indicated that a majority of producers, directors, screenwriters, and cinematographers worked on only one film during the 15-year period covered by the study while only a tiny fraction worked on more than five or six films. Further, those with few screen credits usually worked with others who had few credits, while those with many credits worked with others of similar accomplishment. The most productive producers tended to hire creative personnel from an "inner circle," Faulkner concluded, to "narrow the complexity of their choices" while "boosting their perceived chances of securing control over a turbulent environment" (1982, p. 95).

Just as there are conventions for the production of news texts so there are conventions for the production of other forms of culture. The formulaic plot lines and stereotypical characters of much popular entertainment are examples of a content-based coping strategy for routinizing symbol production. For example

Turow (1978) found that in the casting of smaller television roles, both the criteria of acceptability (e.g. credibility and visual balance) and the needed "types" (e.g. "real people," "beautiful people") are well-known and widely shared among producers, casting directors and agents. These shared understandings of what must be done – that is, what the producer wants – control work by establishing the *premises* for workers' decision-making. While Sanders (1982) attempted to distinguish *product* conventions such as the basic formula for a particular television series from *production* conventions such as typecasting, Turow (1992) pointed out that product conventions also serve to regulate and coordinate the tasks of production, and so the distinction is not clear. Ryan and Peterson (1982) on the other hand, synthesized the distinction between production and product conventions with the argument that, in country music recording at least, the production process is regulated and coordinated less by well-established conventions or formulas than by "product images" – that is, models or images continually revised by recently successful recordings (see also Peterson, 1994).

In a variety of ways, then, culture-producing organizations struggle to bring their tasks under control through routinization of the production process. And the research at the organizational level of analysis has compellingly demonstrated that these routines are intimately connected to the form, content and meaning of those cultural products. There is, then, an enduring tension in culture-producing industries between what DiMaggio and Hirsch (1976) characterized as "innovation and control" or what Ettema and Whitney (1982) term "creativity and constraint" that results in products that seem to be always new and different, and yet, always much the same.

The institutional level

The processes of cultural production occur within and are shaped by what DiMaggio (1977) called "the cultural economy." While that economy is the subject of other chapters in this volume, it is important to emphasize here that the economic arrangements within media industries have important implications for the work of professional mass communicators and, in turn, for the form, content and meaning of media messages. One important implication concerns the relationship between the degree of competition within a culture industry and the degree of diversity and innovativeness of the products offered by that industry. In highly concentrated industries, a few firms often compete for shares of a single mass market with a few similar products. "The greater the market power a producer has (the greater the opportunity to control risk) the tighter and more standardized will be the formulas," concluded Nord (1980, p. 215). "The business history of book and magazine publishing, filmmaking, song selling, comic stripping and radio and television broadcasting provides evidence in support of this hypothesis."

In more competitive industries, on the other hand, firms may find it more profitable to serve specialized market segments with more unique or specialized products. In this market setting, firms cannot avoid the risks and uncertainties of innovation and may delegate substantial freedom to their creative personnel. For example, Peterson and Berger (1975) found that periods of concentration have been marked by homogeneity in recorded music while times of greater competition have been marked by product innovation and diversity. Rothenbuhler and Dimmick (1982) replicated Peterson and Berger's findings though Lopes's (1992) findings suggested that innovation in popular music is possible under contemporary oligopolistic conditions.

At the same time, however, competition certainly is no guarantee of creativity or quality. Local broadcast journalism provides a case-in-point. McManus (1994) trenchantly argues that the market logic of television news with its drive to minimize costs and maximize profits produces news that is trivial – and often wrong. Pursuing the point, Ehrlich (1995) found that television newsrooms are consumed with the "competitive ethos" in which "not getting beaten" by the competition on breaking stories becomes the basic standard of performance. "The competitive ethos, continually ritualized and enacted via routine newsroom practices, helps give newsworkers a certain degree of control over their work," Ehrlich concludes. And yet:

> [T]he irony of the competitive ethos is that the ferocious social and cultural competition for news and ratings ultimately serves the interests of the corporate oligopoly that controls most of the media industry – an oligopoly that by its very nature discourages competition in the political economic sphere.

The newspaper business provides yet another variation on relationship between economic competition and media content. Kaniss (1991) begins her analysis with the fact that big city newspapers must compete for readers with many smaller community newspapers in suburbs beyond the central city. One content-based marketing strategy for doing so is to cover news of the central city such as large-scale urban development projects that help to promote a positive regional identity. This strategy has implications not only for what events are covered but how they are covered:

> Local news coverage often comes to accord elevated importance to the symbolic aspects of development issues, while de-emphasizing their economic, social, or environmental costs and benefits. The impact of a new project on the image of the city or on the city's ability to compete with other cities in a rivalry not unlike the clash between sports teams often takes precedence in news coverage over considerations of dollars and cents. (1991, p. 5)

Kaniss adds that the skills of individual journalists and the production routines of journalism all converge with corporate strategies to limit news workers' attention to costs and benefits. Most reporters and editors lack the technical expertise to analyze the economic impact of development projects and so they rely on their routine sources in city government – who often are project advocates – for this sort of information. Kaniss, thus, reminds us that each level of analysis provides the context for each of the others. While individual journalists must enact the marketing strategies of their firms, the skills and abilities of individual workers and the work routines that they employ constrain what media firms are able to do. (For more on the economics of news see: Underwood 1993; Cranberg, Bezanson & Soloski, 2001.)

Kaniss's work also reminds us that at the institutional level of analysis, the task of professional mass communicators and their organizations is not so much to produce media content as to produce media audiences. The production of economically meaningful audiences is a process that transcends the boundaries of any particular media organization to encompass the larger media industry system (Ettema & Whitney, 1994). For example, Wildman (1994) showed how "temporal flows" of media content (e.g. films flowing from movie theaters, to video stores and premium cable channels, to network broadcasts, and finally to off-network broadcasts) reflect a strategy of segmenting audiences and employing pricing and distribution strategies that maximize profits from the combination of segments. Also writing on the production of economically-meaningful audiences, Barnes and Thomson (1994) argued that content specialization in magazines and the growth of specialized cable channels in the past two decades became possible because advances in audience measurement technologies (i.e. computerized magazine readership analysis and the "people meter" system for television ratings) facilitated the identification – or more accurately, the creation – of specialized audiences that could be documented and, in turn, sold to advertisers.

As Barnes and Thomson suggested, the old idea of "audience images" held by professional mass communicators takes on new meaning at higher levels of analysis. An enduring truism in media studies is that individual mass communicators "know their audience" in only the most rudimentary and fragmentary ways (e.g. Gans, 1979; Atkin, Burgoon & Burgoon, 1983; Cantor, 1987; Ettema & Whitney, 1994; DeWerth-Pallmeyer, 1997). Nonetheless, industrial and institutional ways of "knowing the audience" profoundly influence media practice and content. For example, Webster and Phalen (1994) argue that in telecommunications policy and regulation, several different models of the audience can be or have been, used to justify different sorts of regulatory decisions. When regulators choose a "marketplace model" that assumes the audience to be rational consumers, then deregulation is a reasonable course of action. But when they choose an "effects model" that assumes the audience is subject to harm from obscenity or violence, then regulation is justified.

Another venerable idea that takes on new meaning at higher levels of analysis is agenda-setting. The notion of agenda-setting began life as an hypothesis concerning the impact of the news media on audiences' perceptions of the importance of various social and political issues. More recently, however, media sociologists have raised the question of how the news media's agenda itself is set; and their answer typically focuses on the complex interaction between the media and policymakers (Reese, 1991; Whitney, 1991; McCombs & Shaw, 1993; Rogers, Dearing, & Bregman, 1993; Cook, 1998). While the media are commonly pre-supposed to be a link between the public and the government, recent agenda-setting research questions this relationship, posing instead a more complex model whereby each institution is viewed as an actor in a "power game," with the media more as a surrogate for a "bystander public" (Ettema, Protess, Leff, Miller, Doppelt, & Cook, 1991). Recognizing this reality, Schudson develops a compelling normative position with regard to the responsibility of the press:

> If the press cannot communicate effectively about government to the people at large, it can nonetheless hold the governors accountable to the relatively small number of other informed and powerful people. The press can serve as a stand-in for the public, holding the governors accountable – not to the public (which is not terribly interested), but to the ideals and rules of the democratic polity itself. (1995, p. 217)

Theoretical Perspectives

A second major development since the rediscovery of professional mass com-municators as a topic of social research is the diversification of the theoretical perspectives that undergird the research. Indeed, it has been this process of diversification that has propelled the study of professional mass communicators from the early gatekeeper studies to higher levels of analysis through the con-tinuous introduction of more macroscopic points of view from disciplines such as economics and anthropology as well as sociology. In a very useful literature review on the production of news, Schudson (1989) outlined three theoretical perspectives that inform much of the research not only on news but on most other forms of media content as well. Reflecting their disciplinary origins, Schudson labeled these perspectives "sociological," "political–economic" and "culturological." While these approaches are not mutually exclusive, each is grounded in a distinct tradition with its own assumptions about the social world and its methods for studying that world. This scheme provides a useful way to survey the increased theoretic diversity of communicator studies in the last several decades.

The sociological perspective

The literature already highlighted in this review provides several important instances of the introduction of theoretical perspectives from sociology that helped to raise the level of analysis in communicator studies. The shift in focus from gatekeepers' decision-making to organizational production routines, for example, was propelled in large part by the application of the idea that the reality portrayed in the news is socially constructed. Berger and Luckmann's *The Social*

Construction of Reality (1967) remains the classic statement of the idea. From this perspective, there is no meaningful social reality independent from humanity's ability to construct and convey meaning. Notions of journalistic bias and objectivity are naive because there is no "really real" to which journalistic accounts can be compared (see, for example, Hackett, 1984; Hackett & Zhao, 1998; Durham, 1998).

Several studies published in the early 1970s by sociologists working within this general theoretical perspective where highly influential in the rediscovery of the importance of professional mass communicators. Articles by Tuchman (1972, 1973) as noted above are now classics of the field, as is an article by Molotch and Lester (1974) that examined the role of news in constructing such fixtures of the social world as accidents and scandals. They argued that "occurrences" – the raw material from which news is made – may be either planned or unplanned. Occurrences, moreover, may be promoted either by the planners or by someone else. Thus, an accident (e.g. an oil spill) is an occurrence that is unplanned and then successfully promoted as news by someone other than the instigators of the occurrence. A scandal, on the other hand is an occurrence that is planned and then promoted by someone other than the planners. Much news, however, is simply routine: planned and then promoted by the planners. Thus a complex sociopolitical process converts occurrences into realities.

An excellent analysis of the role of news media in processing raw occurrences into important social phenomena is Fishman's (1978) study of the social construction of a crime wave against the elderly in New York. Crime waves, Fishman argued, are constructed by the news media from "crime incidents" each of which has been "stripped of the actual context of its occurrence so that it may be relocated in a new, symbolic context: the news theme" (1978: 536). The news media must rely upon police officials to supply crime incidents that can be interpreted or "thematized" as instances of a crime wave, and in this instance, the Senior Citizens Robbery Unit of the NYPD – a unit that let reporters know that it was beleaguered and understaffed – provided what a *Daily News* reporter described as "considerable help" in identifying and reporting appropriate occurrences. The police unit's help to the media in constructing this crime wave is a good example of what Gandy (1982) termed an "information subsidy." (A classic formulation of the argument concerning the social construction of social problems is Blumer, 1970. For more recent theoretical elaborations see Spector & Kitsuse, 1987, and Best, 1995. For additional examples related to crime coverage see, Altheide, 2002, Glassner, 1999, Jenkins, 1994, and Dixon & Linz 2000.)

Fishman's idea of "thematization" would now be recognized as a variation of the idea of a news media "framing." Frames, as Gitlin argued in a highly influential formulation of the idea, are "largely unspoken and unacknowledged" but nonetheless "organize the world both for journalists who report it and, in some important degree, for us who rely on their reports" (1980, p. 19). Thus, for example, Gamson and Modigliani (1989) found that since the beginning of the atomic age, the most common media frame for discussing nuclear power has been that of technological progress and its attendant benefits. With the disasters at Three Mile Island and Chernobyl, however, discussions came more often to be framed in terms of technology as beyond our control and as a bargain with the devil. And in another example of changing media frames, Gamson (1992) demonstrated that celebrity journalism from early in the twentieth century often framed its subjects as those who had naturally risen to the top while such journalism from later in the century more often framed its subjects as the beneficiaries of artificially manufactured celebrity.

In a useful review Scheufele (1999) suggests that "frames" may be understood as either an independent variable (e.g. a causal factor in the public formulation of an issue) or a dependent variable (e.g. the outcome of journalistic practice). In an example of the former, Entman (1991) showed how two similar incidents, the shooting down of a Korean airliner by the Soviet Union and of an Iranian airliner by the United States, were framed quite differently in the US media. The Korean airliner incident was often framed as an "attack" while the Iranian incident was often framed as a "tragedy." This, together with the greater attention to the victims, Entman argued, made the former incident into a "moral outrage" while the later incident was merely a "technical problem." In a dependent-variable media framing study, Durham (2001, p. 131) found that even when "the facts" of a seemingly inexplicable air crash (the still mysterious 1996 crash of TWA Flight 800) suggested no particular frame, journalists turned to "historical pastiche" to frame the episode. But whether cause or effect, as Entman argued in an important formation of the concept, "frames exert their power through the selective description and omission of the features of a situation" (1993, p. 54).

The frames employed by the media to make sense of the world are most often those with "cultural resonance" in Gamson and Modigliani's terms (1989, p. 5). That is, they draw on themes, metaphors, examples and images deeply embedded in the culture's belief systems as, for example, in technological society's simultaneous belief in progress and fear of technology. At this point the sociological literature on the social construction of reality makes contact with research that could just as appropriately be included in the culturological literature. (For another excellent review of framing, see Reese, 2001. For a formulation of the concept in the literature on social movements see, for example, Snow & Benford, 1988, 1992, and Gamson & Meyer, 1996.)

The political–economic perspective

At about the same time that sociological approaches began to dramatically reshape communicator studies, the political–economic perspective grounded in Marxist social criticism also began to influence those studies. Like the scholarship concerned with the social construction of reality, the work within this perspective focused on the ways that powerful institutions shape media content. But unlike the social construction perspective, which began with the premise that there is no socially meaningful reality other than that constituted in social discourse, the political–economic perspective began with the premise that an enduring social reality – especially economic relationships and processes – determines the content of social discourse. If the social constructionist asked how social reality has come to be, the political economist asked how the social reality of inequitably distributed wealth and power has been allowed to remain. For answers, political economists often drew upon Antonio Gramsci's concept of hegemony to examine the ways in which the media construct a coherent but distorted view of the world that serves to maintain institutionalized power and stratified wealth. (For recent application of the concept see Lewis, 1999.)

As Schudson (1989) noted, a strictly political–economic approach relates the economic structure of the media directly to the political content of the news and entertainment without much concern for the individual and organizational processes in between. For example, Dreier (1982) showed the interlocking memberships among the boards of directors of the 25 largest US newspaper-owning firms and the boards of other firms and argued that at this top corporate level, media firms are intimately tied to the US power structure. Dreier suggested that these firms embody a "corporate liberal" perspective more concerned with stability of the entire system than with more conservative or parochial interests often identified with large corporations – a perspective that the news itself embodies as well. (See McChesney, 1999, for an updated version of the approach.)

Beginning in the 1970s with scholars in the UK leading the way, the political–economic critique of the mass media was elaborated into a variety of materialist (e.g. Murdock & Golding, 1977; Murdock, 1982) and cultural (e.g. Hall, 1977, 1980, 1982, 1996) analyses. These authors saw more than a simple deterministic relationship between the economic order and media content. Murdock and Golding maintained that while Marx "saw the basic economic relations of capitalism as structuring the overall framework and 'general process' of intellectual life, within these general limits he allowed a good deal of room for intellectual autonomy and innovation" (1977, p. 16). Authors in this critical tradition usually argued that the relationship between capitalist ownership of the means of mass communication and the content of the news is mediated by the professional culture and practices of journalism. (For the history of this culture and what Carey, 1969, called "the purely commercial motives behind it, see Roshco, 1975; Schudson, 1978; Schiller, 1981.)

This culture of objectivity allows – indeed, it prizes – autonomy, as evidenced by occasional clashes with corporate and governmental authorities; but it also demands fairness and balance within the limits of the "consensus" (Schlesinger, 1978) or the "enduring values" (Gans 1979) or the "common sense" (Hartley, 1982) of liberal capitalism. The partisanship of an earlier era is reduced considerably, but this culture is subject to biases of its own – biases not so much *in* the news as biases *of* the news (as we have previously argued). Gitlin (1980), for example, argued that journalistic devotion to hard facts and editorial balance led to coverage of the Vietnam-era antiwar movement that emphasized confrontation with authorities rather than analysis of issues and that portrayed the movement as operating beyond the bounds of reasonable dissent. Thus, as Bennett concluded, the news media "achieve their ideological effectivity precisely through their observation of the statutory requirements of balance and impartiality" (1982, p. 306).

If journalism is a tool of social control – and one need not be a Marxist to argue that it is – the tool is used with subtlety in liberal democracies. While a few authors such as Herman and Chomsky (1988) suggested that the mainstream news media work to stifle dissent entirely, most have argued that the media primarily direct and shape political dialogue or limit the diversity of opinion and information that is expressed. Hallin (1994) argued that the press, at least occasionally, is the site of serious debate on policy – even ideology – because the press must attend to its own legitimacy as the presumed "honest broker" of information and opinion. Hallin also argued, however, that such debates are most likely to occur when policy elites are themselves seriously divided on policy as was the situation in the later years of the wars in Vietnam and in Central America. In this same vein, Bennett (1990) argues that the range or diversity of voices heard in press coverage of events is "indexed" less to the range of public opinion than to the range of governmental debate (see also Entman & Page, 1994). In the absence of intra-elite conflict, the news offers up routinely uncritical treatment of corporate and governmental power sources (e.g. Bennett, 2001) and may even undertake some "repair work" on behalf of corporate and governmental sources whose credibility has been damaged (Bennett, Gressett, & Haltom, 1985).

Maintenance and repair of journalism's own credibility and authority has become a theme of communicator studies that draws on political–economic concerns. For example, the scandal that forced the Washington Post to return a Pulitzer Prize after the disclosure that its reporter, Janet Cooke, had fictionalized portions of the award-winning story led many journalists, according to Eason (1986), to conclude that attempts to overcome the limitations of traditional journalistic objectivity had gone too far threatening the authority not only of journalism but of the truth itself. Moreover, two books on the process of "social memory" (Zelizer, 1992, writing on the assassination of John F. Kennedy and Schudson, 1992, writing on Watergate) suggested that journalistic authority is negotiated between the elite news media and other power-and-authority centers, especially government. Both books note, however, that journalistic authority never reaches closure, for within the nation's cultural-value system are countervailing forces that render any attempt at closure only partial.

The culturological perspective

Culture might be taken as the highest possible level of analysis at which communicator studies – or any human studies – can be conducted. Culture, understood to be a symbolic system constituted primarily in language, is the context in which individuals, organizations, industries, and institutions function. Thus the culturological approach to the study of mass communicators focuses on the "cultural givens" as Schudson called the widely shared assumptions about the world and the widely used strategies for making sense of it. Beyond this very general prospectus, however, the culturological approach is difficult to characterize because, as Schudson pointed out, it has not been "codified nor established as any sort of 'school'" (1989, p. 275).

Much of the work collected under the rubric of "cultural studies" in communication draws on the British tradition of research on working-class life (e.g. Hoggart, 1957; Williams, 1958, 1961) to focus on ethnographic accounts of audience responses to television news and entertainment, recorded music and other forms of popular culture. (Morley, 1980; Radway, 1984; Fiske, 1987; and Jenkins, 1992, provide widely cited examples.) An attempt to identify "culturological" research that focuses on professional mass communicators, however, might begin with those studies that have tried to learn about culture producers (professional mass communicators in this case) by carefully analyzing their cultural products.

Communicator studies recently have begun to call upon the vast critical scholarship on the content of film, television, literature and other cultural forms for fresh perspectives from which to examine the work of professional mass communicators. Perhaps the most important of these perspectives is that of narrative theory, which has been applied not only to the study of explicitly fictional media content but also to the study of putatively factual content as well. That news stories are just that – stories – was the point of a charming and insightful memoir by Robert Darnton (1975), a noted historian who was once a reporter. Recalling his summer as a novice on the police beat, Darnton remembered that one day, with nothing better to do, he reviewed a police report about a boy whose bicycle had been stolen. He wrote a few paragraphs as practice. During a lull in the pressroom poker game, one of Darnton's veteran colleagues looked over the paragraphs and, apparently with some pity, typed out a different version of the story. With the new version in hand, the young journalist phoned the boy's father with a few pertinent questions; for now he realized he had not merely a crime to report but a story to tell. "Soon I had enough details to fit the new pattern of the story," he recalled. "I rewrote it in the new style, and it appeared the next day in a special box, above the fold, on the front page" (1975, p. 190). It was his first byline. On reflection Darnton realized that facts and stories are mutually constituted: a story requires facts for its existence but the facts require a story for theirs. That is, a news story is, indeed, assembled from available and relevant facts, but those facts become available only if journalists know how to locate them. And they are relevant only if journalists know what to make of them. It is a story selected from among the cultural-given repertoire of stories that guides journalists in the gathering and the evaluation of the facts even though, as Ettema and Glasser concluded, "the story lines that help to constitute the facts remain submerged in the unexamined common sense of the culture" (1998, p. 152).

The news is not, then, a mere collection of facts. It is an attempt to bring sense to the world through the imposition of narrative structures on the raw occurrences of the world. These structures, as Schudson eloquently argued, have implications for the meaning of the news:

> [T]he power of the media lies not only (and not even primarily) in its power to declare things to be true, but in its power to provide the forms in which the declarations appear. News in a newspaper or on television has a relationship to the "real world" not only in content but in form; that is, in the way the world is incorporated into unquestioned and unnoticed conventions of narration, and then transfigured, no longer a subject for discussion but a premise of any conversation at all. (1995, p. 54)

An example of how narrative form becomes "a premise of any conversation at all" comes from Ettema and Glasser's (1998) study of investigative reporting. The task of investigative journalists is to tell stories that elicit public indignation at the breakdown of some social system, such as government wrongdoing or the malfeasance of those in charge. To accomplish this task, reporters employ all the devices of dramatic storytelling, particularly irony, to portray those caught in the middle of the breakdown (e.g. prisoners who have been sexually assaulted in jail) as innocent victims and to portray those in charge of the system (e.g. administrators of the jail) as guilty of immoral, if not always illegal, behavior. The authors argued that the content of such stories demands that the public confront very real and terrible injustice, but that the simplistic, though highly dramatic, *form* of the stories shapes and narrows that confrontation, just as Schudson would suggest. The individual experiences of the innocent and the guilty are emphasized in these stories while the larger social and cultural issues are marginalized. "Although specific instances of civic vice and a corresponding affirmation of virtue vividly emerge from these stories, the social and political – not to mention moral – complexities all submerge into them," the authors argue. "These story are, then, testament to both the powers and the limits of the moral force within narrative form" (1998, pp. 128–9).

Another example of the rapidly growing body of literature that seeks to understand how journalism makes sense of particular kinds of occurrences by invoking particular kinds of stories is Vincent, Crow, and Davis's (1989) analysis of the standardized story line in the network television news coverage of major airliner crashes. Journalists take such crashes to be "the archetypal disaster of the technological age," and they invoke stories with the theme of technology defeated by fate. There may be technical answers as to what happened, of course, but there will always be an eternal mystery. "The ever-present *black box* of airline stories is the perfect visual condensation of the fate versus technology conflict," the authors argued (1989, p. 16). "But the whole concept of a 'black box' is invested with mystery and godlike omniscience, and the black box often refuses to tell what it knows." Whatever technical answers the authorities may eventually offer can never really resolve the eternal question: "why?" We can only listen in reverence and terror as the most ancient of stories must be told once again as here in the form of an NBC report of air crash in New Orleans:

> Arthur Cunnings of Howell, Michigan, was in San Diego for the funeral of his son who was killed in a motorcycle accident there. His two daughters and three grandchildren were driving to that funeral from Florida when their car broke down Friday. So they got on an airplane in New Orleans: Pan Am Flight 759. In a week, Mr Cunnings lost three children and three grandchildren. He was able to say today, "I cannot describe the sorrow." (Vincent, Crow, & Davis, 1989, p. 16)

(For other recent treatments of news myth see: Bird & Dardenne, 1988; Cornfield, 1988; Lule, 1995 and 2001. For treatments of news as ritual, in addition to James Carey's, 1989, celebrated statement of the idea, see: Cazeneuve, 1974; Elliott, 1982; Ettema, 1990, Katz & Dayan, 1992; Rothenbuhler, 1998; Kitch, 2000.)

Studies of news-as-narrative offer insight not only into the eternal question of life, they offer insight into the eternal question of journalism: what is news? The list of attributes or "news values" that journalists supposedly consider when judging newsworthiness typically includes the presence of conflictual or un-expected events, the prominence of those involved in the events, and the degree of impact on readers and viewers. In addition, the proximity of the events to the audience and the timeliness of the report are considerations in a story's news-worthiness. (Shoemaker, Danielian, & Brendlinger, 1991, and Wu, 2000, provide examples of relative success in specifying the attributes of newsworthiness.) It's clear, however, that any textbook list of story attributes just can't explain the diverse array of topics that constitute the news. What, then, does the press cover? Romano's tongue-in-cheek answer was: "box scores, beauty pageants, press conferences, Richard Nixon and so on" (1986, p. 42). Though Romano was teasing us, he went on to make a point that serves as a useful point of departure for any attempt to understand how journalists decide what's news. "The prin-ciples that govern those decisions while rational aren't scientific or logically compelling," he argued. "No one need accept them the way one must accept the rules of gravity." News stories, in other words, do not correspond to the reality of human affairs in the way that theories of physics, presumably, correspond to the reality of quarks and quasars. We shouldn't expect elegant and timeless theories that can predict the sorts of occurrences that will become news. We shouldn't even expect unambiguous criteria for recognizing news when we see it. Knowing what's news is partly just a matter of knowing what's always been news – politics, disasters and so on – and, as Darnton wryly showed, it is partly a matter of knowing a good story when one hears it.

In sum, the culturological approach to the study of professional communicators shows how communicators draw upon their culture to recognize and to tell their stories. Paradoxically, the study of communicators at the highest level of analysis, the cultural, returns us to the most basic level, the individual, and offers insight into that most elusive of processes: creativity. Communicators, whether working on stories to be sold as fact or as fiction, draw upon cultural traditions as creative resources and, in turn, become the interpreters of those traditions thereby renewing the ability of the traditions to make sense of the world. Those who create for the mass media, as Newcomb and Hirsch argued of television producers, are "seeking and creating new meaning in the combination of cultural elements with embedded significance" (1984, p. 60). Thus to understand the nature of mass mediated creativity would be to understand both widely shared narrative forms and ritual processes of the culture as well as uniquely personal inspirations and insights of the individual communicator.

Range of Communicators

While research on professional mass communicators has always privileged the public affairs journalist as the object of study, this research has never been limited to that role. Powdermaker's sociological analysis of Hollywood filmmakers appeared in 1950, for example, the same year as White's study of "Mr. Gates." Still, much of what we think we know about mass communicators is based on the analysis of a few work roles (e.g. political and general assignment reporters, television producers) in a few types of media organizations (e.g. daily newspapers, television studios). Studies concerned with other roles and organizations do, however, regularly appear and are expanding our conceptions of news-making and other media processes.

Other roles

Beginning in the 1980s research on specialized journalistic beats such as health and science revealed some interesting variations on the basic problems of news production. For example, the event-centered focus of journalism along with the scientific illiteracy of many journalists leads to highly dramatic coverage of individual technological disasters but little coverage of entire technical systems (e.g. transportation, energy). As Singer and Endreny (1993) pointed out, the news media report immediate harms but neither long-term risks nor benefits in such technical domains as nuclear energy and hazardous materials. The effect of this sort of coverage, as Wilkins and Patterson (1987) argued, is that the technological sky always seems to be falling (see also: Greenberg, Sachsman, Sandman, & Salomone, 1989; Singer, 1990; Coleman, 1995). The news media's failings in this regard, however, are probably exacerbated by many scientists' reluctance to serve as sources (Dunwoody & Ryan, 1985; 1987).

Research on health and science journalism also offers insight into the processes of coverage prioritization (i.e. agenda-setting) and source–reporter relations.

Research on the coverage of AIDS, for example, has shown the answer to the question of who sets the agenda for the press can be more complex than merely "the government." Rogers, Dearing, and Chang (1991) demonstrated that the AIDS "issue" remained high on the media's agenda because it was, in fact, several issues or themes (e.g. basic science, human toll, policy response) each with its own issue entrepreneurs to promote coverage (e.g. medical researchers, gay activists, policy elites). Altogether, the waxing and waning of these subissues kept the overall issue of AIDS high on the coverage agenda.

An interesting analog to health and science news is provided by Turow's (1989) study of "health entertainment" – i.e. television medical dramas. It can be no surprise that these shows, much like technological disaster news, have always embraced drama while ignoring socioeconomic context. That is, they have emphasized the dedication of healers and the miracles of technology but have de-emphasized the cost of it all. And perhaps it is also no surprise that Turow found the medical establishment to play an important role in producing programs with this message.

Finally, research on news production outside the mainstream press has warned against easy generalizations about "the media." Eliasoph (1988), for example, argued that the news production routines that much of the literature holds responsible for journalistic adherence to the status quo, do not in themselves explain such adherence. The author found, in an examination of the newsroom in a counter-culture radio station, that the news workers there also had routines to facilitate news coverage although those routines focused on sources and issues left uncovered by the "mainstream" press. At the same time, however, Seeger (1987) argued from participant observations of the *Berkeley Barb* that the oppositional press is clearly not free from its own ideological blinders, while Meyers (1992) argued from observations of a major Midwestern newspaper that the mainstream press may publish oppositional news when individual reporters pursue it. (See also Stark, 1964, and Reese, 1990.)

Other organizations and industries

Advertising and public relations both have ancient and intimate connections to news and entertainment. Indeed, the distinctions between these sorts of media content are not now clear, nor have they ever been clear (Schudson, 1978; Turow, 1985). And yet, the practitioners and the organizations in the advertising and public relations industries are rarely studied under the rubric of professional mass communicators. There is, of course, substantial literature aimed at practitioners that purports to enhance creativity or overall effectiveness but there is much less analysis of how advertising and public relations campaigns are, in fact, created. (See, however, Hirschman's 1989 analysis of work roles in the creation of televised advertising.) And while news, entertainment, advertising and public relations have already converged into "the media," other forms of communication are now converging with the traditional vehicles of mass communication. We may not yet think of video game designers under the rubric of professional mass communicators; but at least scholars have begun to study the individuals, organizations and institutions credited with the invention of computing and telecommunications systems, including the Internet, as part of the history of communication (e.g. Beniger, 1986; Winston, 1998; Abbate, 1999). Scholars have also begun to study the nature of, and prospects for less celebrated but essential "information work" such as telephone and data entry workers (Martin, 1991), and to study journalists within the context of labor history (Hardt & Brennen, 1995).

Thus, while more research attention is being paid to communicators other than mainstream journalists, the rapid rate of change in communications technologies and businesses looms as both an opportunity and a challenge for scholarship. The media have simultaneously imploded and exploded. Previously distinct technologies have converged into integrated systems and previously distinction businesses have consolidated into industry leviathans. And yet far more information and communication products and services are available now than ever before. This changing media environment can outrun efforts to answer – or even formulate – important questions about the social, political and cultural role of professional mass communicators. For example, did the pseudo-documentary, "The Real West Wing," arranged by the White House in January 2002 immediately before the fictional program, "West Wing," signal an important new "disintermediated" (Rosenstiel, 1993) communication tactic that will force both researchers and media professionals to rethink the political role of traditional journalism? At the same time, this new media environment can make old questions new again. For example, gatekeeping has reemerged as concern of both researchers and practitioners in the "mixed media culture" (Kovach & Rosenstiel, (1999) created by cable news and the Internet. Thus Williams and Delli Carpini concluded from their study of "the collapse of gatekeeping" in the Clinton-Lewinsky scandal that "any approach to political communication based upon clear cut distinctions between fact and opinion or public affairs and entertainment cannot hope to understand the mediated politics at the end of the twentieth century" (2000, p. 78). And, we might add, well into the twenty-first.

Media convergence raises anew such traditional research questions as the implications for content diversity when the technology is ever more unified and the ownership of firms is ever more concentrated. At the same time, convergence raises the question of media professionals' ability to creatively respond to the new possibilities presented by the new media. And it raises the question of whether the audience, who, after all, is promised not only more content but also greater control of content, can respond both creatively and rationally to those possibilities. Altogether, these changes in communication technologies and industries suggest that, while professional mass communicators are very unlikely ever to become obsolete, they are likely to become more difficult to define.

References

Abbate, J. (1999). *Inventing the Internet*. Cambridge, MA: MIT Press.

Altheide, D. (2002). *Creating Fear: News and the construction of crisis*. New York: Aldine de Gruyter.

Associated Press Managing Editors (1985). *Journalists and Readers: Bridging the credibility gap*. San Francisco: APME Credibility Committee.

Atkin, C., Burgoon, J., and Burgoon, M. (1983). How journalists perceive the reading audience. *Newspaper Research Journal*, 4(2), 51–63.

Barnes, E. and Thomson, L. M. (1994). Power to the people (meter): Audience measurement technology and specialization. In J. S. Ettema and D. C. Whitney (eds.), *AudienceMaking*. Newbury Park, CA: Sage, pp. 75–94.

Beniger, J. R. (1986). *The Control Revolution: Technological and economic origins of the information society*. Cambridge, MA: Harvard University Press.

Bennett, T. (1982). Media, reality, signification. In M. Gurevitch, T. Bennett, J. Curran, and J. Woollacott (eds.), *Culture, Society and the Media*. London: Methuen, pp. 287–308.

Bennett, W. L. (1990). Toward a theory of press–state relations in the United States. *Journal of Communication*, 40(2), 103–25.

Bennett, W. L. (2001). *News: The politics of illusion* (4th edn.). New York: Longman.

Bennett, W. L., Gressett, L. A., and Haltom, W. (1985). Repairing the news: A case study of the news paradigm. *Journal of Communication*, 35(2), 50–68.

Berger, P. L. and Luckmann, T. (1967). *The Social Construction of Reality: A treatise in the sociology of knowledge*. New York: Anchor.

Berkowitz, D. (1992). Non-routine news and newswork: Exploring a what-a-story. *Journal of Communication*, 42(1), 82–94

Best, J. (ed.) (1995). *Images of Issues: Typifying contemporary social problems*. New York: Aldine DeGruyter.

Bird, E. and Dardenne, R. (1988). Myth, chronicle and story: exploring the narrative qualities of news. In J. W. Carey, (ed.), *Media, Myths and Narratives*. Newbury Park, CA: Sage, pp. 67–86.

Bleske, G. (1997). Ms. Gates takes over. In D. Berkowitz (ed.), *Social Meanings of News*. Thousand Oaks, CA: Sage, pp. 72–80. Reprinted from *Newspaper Research Journal*, 12, 88–97 (1991).

Blumer, H. (1970). Social problems as collective behavior. *Social Problems*, 18(2), 298–306.

Brown, J. D., Bybee, C. R., Wearden, S. T., and Straughan, D. M. (1987). Invisible power: Newspaper news sources and the limits of diversity. *Journalism Quarterly*, 64(1), 45–54.

Cantor, M. G. (1987 [1971]). *The Hollywood Television Producer*. New Brunswick, NJ: Transaction Books.

Cantor, M. G. (1980). *Prime-Time Television: Content and control*. Newbury Park, CA: Sage.

Carey, J. W. (1969). The communications revolution and the professional communicator. In P. Halmos (ed.), *The Sociology of Mass Media Communicators*, (Sociological Review Monograph no. 13), pp. 23–38.

Carey, J. W. (1989). *Communication as Culture*. Boston: Unwin Hyman.

Cazeneuve, J. (1974). Television as a functional alternative to traditional sources of need satisfaction. In J. G. Blumler and E. Katz (eds.), *The Uses of Mass Communication*. Beverly Hills: Sage, pp. 223–31.

Clancey, M. and Robinson, J. J. (1985). The media in Campaign '84: General election coverage. *Public Opinion*, December/January, 49–54, 59.

Clarke, P. and Evans, S. H. (1983). *Covering Campaigns*. Stanford, CA: Stanford University Press.

Coleman, C. (1995). Science, technology and risk coverage of a community conflict. *Media, Culture and Society*, 17, 65–79.

Cook, T. E. (1994). Domesticating a crisis: Washington news beats and network news after the Iraq invasion of Kuwait. In W. L. Bennett and D. L. Paletz (eds.), *Taken by Storm: Media, public opinion, and US foreign policy in the Gulf War*. Chicago: University of Chicago Press, pp. 105–30.

Cook, T. E. (1998). *Governing with the News: The news media as a political institution*. Chicago: University of Chicago Press.

Cornfield, M. (1988). The Watergate audience: Parsing the powers of the press. In J. Carey (ed.), *Media, Myths and Narratives*. Newbury Park, CA: Sage, pp. 180–204.

Cranberg, G., Bezanson, R., and Soloski, J. (2001). *Taking Stock: Journalism and the publicly traded newspaper company*. Ames: Iowa State University Press.

Creedon, P. (ed.) (1989). *Women in Mass Communications: Challenging gender values*. Newbury Park, CA: Sage.

D'Alessio, D. and Allen, M. (2000). Media bias in presidential elections: A meta-analysis. *Journal of Communication*, 50(4), 133–56.

Darnton, R. (1975). Writing news and telling stories. *Daedalus*, 104, 175–94.

Dennis, E. (1993). Who's covering what in the Year of the Woman? *Media Studies Journal*, 7(1–2), 134–9.

DeWerth-Pallmeyer, D. (1997). *The Audience in the News*. Mahwah, NJ: Erlbaum.

DiMaggio, P. (1977). Market structure, the creative process and popular culture: Toward an organizational reinterpretation of mass culture theory. *Journal of Popular Culture*, 11, 436–52.

DiMaggio, P. and Hirsch, P. (1976). Production organizations in the arts. *American Behavioral Scientist*, 19, 735–49.

Dimmick, J. and Coit, P. (1982). Levels of analysis in mass media decision making. *Communication Research*, 9(1), 3–32.

Dixon, T. and Linz, D. (2000). Race and the misrepresentation of victimization on local television news. *Communication Research*, 27(5), 547–73.

Dreier, P. (1982). The position of the press in the US power structure. *Social Problems*, 29, 298–310.

Dunwoody, S. and Ryan, M. (1985). Scientific barriers to the popularization of science in the mass media. *Journal of Communication*, 35(1), 26–42.

Dunwoody, S. and Ryan, M. (1987). The credible scientific source. *Journalism Quarterly*, 64(1), 21–7.

Durham, F. D. (2001). Breaching powerful boundaries: a postmodern critique of framing. In S. D. Reese, O. Gandy, and A. Grant (eds.), *Framing Public Life*. Mahwah, NJ: Erlbaum, pp. 123–36.

Durham, M. G. (1998). On the relevance of standpoint epistemology to the practice of journalism: The case for "strong objectivity." *Communication Theory*, 8(2), 117–40.

Eason, D. L. (1986). On journalistic authority: The Janet Cooke scandal. *Critical Studies in Mass Communication*, 3, 429–47.

Ehrlich, M. (1995). The competitive ethos in television newswork. *Critical Studies in Mass Communication*, 12(2), 196–212.

Eliasoph, N. (1988). Routines and the making of oppositional news. *Critical Studies in Mass Communication*, 5(4), 313–34.

Elliott, P. (1977). Media organizations and occupations: An overview. In J. Curran, M. Gurevitch, and J. Woollacott (eds.), *Mass Communication and Society*. London: Edward Arnold, pp. 142–73.

Elliott, P. (1982). Press performance as political ritual. In D. C. Whitney, E. Wartella, and S. Windahl (eds.), *Mass Communication Review Yearbook*, vol. 3. Beverly Hills, CA: Sage, pp. 583–619.

Entman, R. M. (1991). Framing US coverage of international news: Contrasts in narratives of the KAL and Iran Air incidents. *Journal of Communication*, 41(4), 6–27.

Entman, R. M. (1993) Framing: Toward clarification of fractured paradigm. *Journal of Communication*, 43(4), 51–68.

Entman, R. M. and Page, B. I. (1994). The news before the storm: The Iraq War debate and the limits of media independence. In W. L. Bennett and D. L. Paletz (eds.), *Taken by Storm: Media, public opinion, and US foreign policy in the Gulf War*. Chicago: University of Chicago Press, pp. 82–101.

Entman, R. M. and Rojecki, A. (1993). Freezing out the public: Elite and media framing of the US anti-nuclear movement. *Political Communication*, 10, 155–73.

Ericson, R. V., Baranek, P. M., and Chan, J. B. (1989). *Negotiating Control: A study of news sources*. Toronto: University of Toronto Press.

Ettema, J. S. (1990). Press rites and race relations: A study of mass-mediated ritual. *Critical Studies in Mass Communication*, 7(4), 309–31.

Ettema, J. S. and Glasser, T. L. (1998). *Custodians of Conscience: Investigative journalism and public virtue*. New York: Columbia University Press.

Ettema, J. S., Protess, D., Leff, D., Miller, P., Doppelt, J., and Cook, F. L. (1991). Agenda-setting as politics: A case study of the press-public-policy connection. *Communication*, 12(2), 75–98.

Ettema, J. S., and Whitney, D. C. (eds.) (1982). Individuals in mass media organizations: Creativity and constraint. *Sage Annual Reviews of Communication Research*, vol. 10. Beverly Hills, CA: Sage Publications.

Ettema, J. S. and Whitney, D. C., with Wackman, D. B. (1987). Professional mass communicators. In C. R. Berger and S. H. Chaffee (eds.), *Handbook of Communication Science*. Newbury Park, CA: Sage, pp. 747–80.

Ettema, J. S. and Whitney, D. C. (1994). The money arrow: An introduction to audiencemaking. In J. S. Ettema and D. C. Whitney (eds.), *Audiencemaking*. Newbury Park, CA: Sage pp. 1–18.

Faulkner, R. R. (1971). *Hollywood Studio Musicians*. Chicago: Aldine.

Faulkner, R. R. (1982). Improvising on a triad. In J. Van Maanen, J. M. Dabs, Jr., and R. R. Faulkner (eds.), *Varieties of Qualitative Research*. Newbury Park, CA: Sage.

Fico, F. and Freedman, E. (2001). Setting the news story agenda: Candidates and commentators in news coverage of a governor's race. *Journalism and Mass Communication Quarterly*, 78(3), 437–49.

Fishman, M. (1978). Crime waves as ideology. *Social Problems*, 25, 531–43.

Fishman, M. (1980). *Manufacturing the News*. Austin: University of Texas Press.

Fishman, M. (1982). News and nonevents: Making the invisible visible. In J. S. Ettema and D. C. Whitney (eds.), *Individuals in Mass Media Organizations: Creativity and constraint*. Beverly Hills, CA: Sage, pp. 219–40.

Fiske, J. (1987). *Television Culture*. London: Methuen.

Gamson, J. (1992). The assembly line of greatness: Celebrity in twentieth century America. *Critical Studies in Mass Communication*, 9(1), 1–24.

Gamson, W. and Meyer, D. (1996) Framing political opportunity. In D. McAdam, J. McCarthy, and M. Zald (eds.), *Comparative Perspectives on Social Movements: Political opportunities, mobilizing structures, and cultural framings*. Cambridge: Cambridge University Press.

Gamson, W. and Modigliani, A. (1989). Media discourse and public opinion on nuclear power: A constructionist approach. *American Journal of Sociology*, 95(1), 1–37.

Gandy, O. (1982). *Beyond Agenda Setting: Information subsidies and public policy*. Norwood, NJ: Ablex.

Gans, H. J. (1972). The famine in American mass communications research. *American Journal of Sociology*, 77(4), 697–705.

Gans, H. J. (1979). *Deciding What's News*. New York: Pantheon.

Gans, H. J. (1985). Are US journalists dangerously liberal? *Columbia Journalism Review*, November/December, 29–33.

Gilliam, D. (1991). Media diversity: Harnessing the assets of a multicultural future. *Media Studies Journal*, 5(4), 127–36.

Gitlin, T. (1980). *The Whole World is Watching: The role of the news media in the making and unmaking of the New Left*. Berkeley: University of California Press.

Gitlin, T. (1983). *Inside Prime Time*. New York: Pantheon.

Glassner, B. (1999). *The Culture of Fear: Why Americans are afraid of the wrong things*. New York: Basic Books.

Goldberg, B. (2002). *Bias: A CBS insider exposes how the media distort the news*. Washington, DC: Regnery Publishing.

Goldenberg, E. (1975). *Making the Papers*. Lexington, MA: D. C. Heath.

Greenberg, M. R., Sachsman, D. B., Sandman, P. M., and Salomone, K. L. (1989). Risk, drama and geography in coverage of environmental risk by network TV. *Journalism Quarterly*, 66(2), 267–76.

Hackett, R. A. (1984). Decline of a paradigm? Bias and objectivity in news media studies. *Critical Studies in Mass Communication*, 1(2), 29–259.

Hackett, R. A. and Zhao, Y. (1998). *Sustaining Democracy?: Journalism and the politics of objectivity*. Toronto: Garamond Press.

Hall, S. (1977). Culture, the media and the "ideological" effect. In J. Curran, M. Gurevitch, and J. Woollacott (eds.), *Mass Communication and Society*. London: Edward Arnold, pp. 315–48.

Hall, S. (1980). Encoding and decoding in television discourse. In S. Hall, D. Hobson, A. Lowe, and P. Willis (eds.), *Culture, Media, Language*. London: Hutchinson, pp. 128–38.

Hall, S. (1982). The rediscovery of "ideology": Return of the repressed in media studies. In M. Gurevitch, T. Bennett, J. Curran, and J. Woollacott (eds.), *Culture, Society and the Media*. London: Methuen, pp. 56–90.

Hall, S. (1996). The problem of ideology: Marxism without guarantees. In D. Morley and K.-H. Chen (eds.), *Stuart Hall: Critical developments in cultural studies*. London: Routledge, pp. 25–46.

Hallin, D. C. (1994). *We Keep America on Top of the World: Television journalism and the public sphere*. London: Routledge.

Hallin, D. C., Manoff, R. K., and Weddle, J. K. (1993). Sourcing patterns of national security reporters. *Journalism Quarterly*, 70(4), 753–66.

Hardt, H. and Brennen, B. (1995). *Newsworkers: Toward a history of the rank and file*. Minneapolis: University of Minnesota Press.

Hartley, J. (1982). *Understanding News*. London: Methuen.

Herman, E. S. and Chomsky, N. (1988). *Manufacturing Consent: The political economy of the mass media*. New York: Pantheon.

Hess, S. (1981). *The Washington Reporters*. Washington, DC: The Brookings Institution.

Hess, S. (1996). *International News and Foreign Correspondents*. Washington, DC: The Brookings Institution.

Hirsch, P. M. (1972). Processing fads and fashions: An organization-set analysis of cultural industry systems. *American Journal of Sociology*, 77, 639–59.

Hirsch, P. M. (1977). Occupational, organizational and institutional models in mass media research: Toward an integrated framework. In P. M. Hirsch, P. V. Miller, and F. G. Kline (eds.), *Strategies for Communication Research*. Beverly Hills, CA: Sage, pp. 13–42.

Hirschman, E. C. (1989). Role-based models of advertising creation and production. *Journal of Advertising*, 18(4), 42–53.

Hoggart, R. (1957). *The Uses of Literacy*. London: Chatto and Windus.

Jenkins, H. (1992). *Textual Poachers: Television fans and participatory culture*. New York: Routledge.

Jenkins, P. (1994). *Using Murder: The social construction of serial homicide*. New York: Aldine DeGruyter.

Kaniss, P. (1991). *Making Local News*. Chicago: University of Chicago Press.

Katz, E. and Dayan, D. (1992). *Media Events: The live broadcasting of history*. Cambridge, MA: Harvard University Press.

Katz, E. and Lazarsfeld, P. F. (1955). *Personal Influence*. New York: Free Press.

Kitch, C. (2000). "A news of feeling as well as fact": Mourning and memorial in American newsmagazines. *Journalism Theory, Practice and Criticism*, 1(2), 171–95.

Klapper, J. (1960). *The Effects of Mass Communication*. New York: Free Press.

Kovach, B. and Rosenstiel, T. (1999). *Warp Speed: American in the age of mixed media*. New York: The Century Foundation Press.

Lang, G. E. and Lang, K. (1983). *The Battle for Public Opinion*. New York: Columbia University.

Lewis, J. (1999). Reproducing political hegemony in the United States. *Critical Studies in Mass Communication*, 16(3), 251–67.

Lichter, S. R. and Rothman, S. (1981). Media and business elites. *Public Opinion*, October–November, 42–6, 59–60.

Linsky, M. (1986). *Impact: How the press affects federal policy-making*. New York: W. W. Norton.

Lippmann, W. (1922). *Public Opinion*. New York: Macmillan.

Lopes, P. D. (1992). Innovation and diversity in the popular music industry, 1969–1990. *American Sociological Review*, 57, 56–71.

Lule, J. (1995). The rape of Mike Tyson: race, the press, and symbolic types. *Critical Studies in Mass Communication*, 12, 176–95.

Lule, J. (2001). *Daily News, Eternal Stories: The mythological role of journalism*. New York: Guilford.

Martin, M. (1991). *"Hello, Central?": Technology, culture and gender in the development of telephone systems, 1878–1920*. Montreal: McGill-Queen's University Press.

McChesney, R. (1999). *Rich Media, Poor Democracy: Communication politics in dubious times*. Urbana: University of Illinois Press.

McCombs, M. E. and Shaw, D. L. (1976). Structuring the "unseen environment." *Journal of Communication*, 26(2), 18–22.

McCombs, M. E. and Shaw, D. L. (1993). The evolution of agenda-setting research: Twenty-five years in the marketplace. *Journal of Communication*, 43(2), 58–67.

McLeod, D. M. and Hertog, J. K. (1992). The manufacture of "public opinion" by reporters: Informal cues for public perceptions of protest groups. *Discourse and Society*, 3(3), 259–75.

McManus, J. (1994). *Market-Driven Journalism: Let the citizen beware?* Newbury Park, CA: Sage.

McManus, J. (1995). A market-based model of news production. *Communication Theory*, 5(4), 301–38.

Meyers, M. (1992). Reporters and beats: the making of oppositional news. *Critical Studies in Mass Communication*, 9(1), 75–90.

Molotch, H. and Lester, M. (1974). News as purposive behavior: On the strategic use of routine events, accidents and scandals. *American Sociological Review*, 39, 101–12.

Montgomery, K. (1989). *Target: Prime-Time: Advocacy groups and the struggle over entertainment television*. New York: Oxford University Press.

Morley, D. (1980). *The "Nationwide" Audience*. London: British Film Institute.

Murdock, G. (1982). Large corporations and the control of communications industries. In M. Gurevitch, T. Bennett, J. Curran, and J. Woollacott (eds.), *Culture, Society and the Media*. London: Methuen, pp. 118–50.

Murdock, G. and Golding, P. (1977). Capitalism, communication and class relations. In J. Curran, M. Gurevitch, and J. Woollacott (eds.), *Mass Communication and Society*. London: Edward Arnold, pp. 12–43.

Newcomb, H. M. and Alley, R. S. (1982). The producer as artist: commerical television. In J. S. Ettema and D. C. Whitney (eds.), *Individuals in Mass Media Organizations: Creativity and constraint*. Beverly Hills, CA: Sage, pp. 69–90.

Newcomb, H. M. and Alley, R. S. (1983). *The Producer's Medium*. New York: Oxford University Press.

Newcomb, H. M. and Hirsch, P. M. (1984). Television as a cultural forum: implications for research. In W. Rowland and B. Watkins (eds.), *Interpreting Television: Recent research perspectives*. Newbury Park, CA: Sage, pp. 58–73.

Nord, D. P. (1980). An economic perspective on formula in popular culture. *Journal of American Culture*, 3, 17–31.

Paletz, D. and Entman, R. M. (1981). *Media, Power, Politics.* New York: Free Press.

Patterson, T. (1980). *The Mass Media Election.* New York: Praeger.

Peterson, R. A. (1994). Culture studies through the production perspective: Progress and prospects. In D. Crane (ed.), *Emerging Theoretical Perspectives in the Sociology of Culture.* Oxford: Blackwell, pp. 162–89.

Peterson, R. A. and Berger, D. G. (1975). Cycles in symbol production: the case of popular music. *American Sociological Review*, 40, 158–73.

Powdermaker, H. (1950). *Hollywood: The dream factory.* Boston: Little, Brown.

Radway, J. A. (1984). *Reading the Romance: Women, patriarchy, and popular literature.* Chapel Hill: University of North Carolina Press.

Ranney, A. (1983). *Channels of Power.* Washington, DC: American Enterprise Institute.

Reese, S. D. (1990). The news paradigm and the ideology of objectivity: A socialist at the Wall Street Journal. *Critical Studies in Mass Communication*, 7(4), 390–409.

Reese, S. D. (1991). Setting the media's agenda: A power balance perspective. In J. Anderson (ed.), *Communication Yearbook*, vol. 14. Newbury Park, CA: Sage, pp. 309–40.

Reese, S. D. (2001). Prologue – framing public life: A bridging model for media research. In S. D. Reese, O. Gandy Jr., and A. Grant (eds.), *Framing Public Life.* Mahwah, NJ: Lawrence Erlbaum.

Robinson, M. J. (1983). Just how liberal is the news? 1980 revisited. *Public Opinion*, February/March, 55–60.

Robinson, M. J. (1985). The media in Campaign '84, part II: wingless, toothless and hopeless. *Public Opinion*, February/March, 43–8.

Robinson, M. J. and Sheehan, M. (1983). *Over the Wire and on TV.* New York: Russell Sage.

Rogers, E., Dearing, J., and Bregman, D. (1993). The anatomy of agenda-setting research. *Journal of Communication*, 42(2), 68–84.

Rogers, E., Dearing, J., and Chang, S. (1991). AIDS in the 1980s: The agenda setting process for a public issue. *Journalism Monographs*, no. 126.

Romano, C. (1986). What? The grisly truth about bare facts. In R. K. Manoff and M. Schudson (eds.), *Reading the News.* New York: Pantheon, pp. 38–78.

Rosenstiel, T. (1993). Potus and the posties. *Los Angeles Times Magazine*, May 16, 20–1, 24–5, 36.

Roshco, B. (1975). *Newsmaking.* Chicago: University of Chicago Press.

Rosten, L. (1937). *The Washington Correspondents.* New York: Harcourt Brace Jovanovich.

Rothenbuhler, E. (1998). *Ritual Communication: From everyday conversation to mediated ceremony.* Thousand Oaks, CA: Sage.

Rothenbuhler, E. and Dimmick, J. W. (1982). Popular music: Concentration and diversity in the industry. *Journal of Communication*, 32(1), 143–9.

Ryan, J. and Peterson, R. A. (1982). The product image: The fate of creativity in country music songwriting. In J. S. Ettema and D. C. Whitney (eds.), *Individuals in Mass Media Organizations: Creativity and constraint.* Beverly Hills, CA: Sage, pp. 11–32.

Sanders, C. R. (1982). Structural and interactional features of popular culture production: An introduction to the production of culture perspective. *Journal of Popular Culture*, 16, 66–74.

Scheufele, D. A. (1999). Framing as a theory of media effects. *Journal of Communication*, 49(1), 103–22.

Schiller, D. (1981). *Objectivity and the News.* Philadelphia: University of Pennsylvania Press.

Schlesinger, P. (1978). *Putting "Reality" Together: BBC News.* London: Constable.

Schlesinger, P. and Tumber, H. (1994). *Reporting Crime: The media politics of criminal justice.* Oxford: Clarendon Press.

Schneider, W. and Lewis, I. A. (1985). Views on the news. *Public Opinion*, August/September, 6–11, 58–9.

Schudson, M. (1978). *Discovering the News.* New York: Basic Books.

Schudson, M. (1989). The sociology of news production. *Media, Culture and Society*, 11, 263–82.

Schudson, M. (1992). *Watergate in American Memory.* New York: Basic Books.

Schudson, M. (1995). *The Power of News*. Cambridge, MA: Harvard University Press.

Schudson, M. (2001). The objectivity norm in American journalism. *Journalism Theory, Practice and Criticism*, 2(2), 149–70.

Seeger, A. (1987). An unreported class war: Ideology and self-censorship on the Berkeley Barb. *Communication*, 10(1), 31–50.

Selnow, G. W. and Gilbert, R. R. (1993). *Society's Impact on Television: How the viewing public shapes television programming*. Westport, CT: Praeger.

Shoemaker, P. (1984). Media treatment of deviant political groups. *Journalism Quarterly*, 61(1), 66–75, 82.

Shoemaker, P., Danielian, L., and Brendlinger, N. (1991). Deviant acts, risky business and US interests: The newsworthiness of world events. *Journalism Quarterly*, 68(4), 781–95.

Shoemaker, P. and Reese, S. D. (1996). *Mediating the Message* (2nd edn.). White Plains, NY: Longman.

Sigal, L. V. (1973). *Reporters and Officials*. Lexington, MA: D. C. Heath.

Singer, E. (1990). A question of accuracy: How journalists and scientists report research on hazards. *Journal of Communication*, 40(4), 102–16.

Singer, E. and Endreny, P. M. (1993). *Reporting on Risk: How the mass media portray accidents, diseases, disasters, and other hazards*. New York: Russell Sage.

Snow, D. and Benford, R. (1988). Ideology, frame resonance, and participant mobilization. *International Social Movement Research*, 1, 197–217.

Snow, D. and Benford, R. (1992). Master frames and cycles of protest. In A. Morris and C. Mueller (eds.), *Frontiers in Social Movement Theory*. New Haven: Yale University Press, pp. 133–55.

Soloski, J. (1989a). News reporting and professionalism: Some constraints on the reporting of the news. *Media, Culture and Society*, 11, 207–28.

Soloski, J. (1989b). Sources and channels of local news. *Journalism Quarterly*, 66(4), 864–70.

Spector, M. and Kitsuse, J. I. (1987). *Constructing Social Problems*. New York: Aldine DeGruyter.

Stark, R. (1964). Policy and the pros. *Berkeley Journal of Sociology*, 7, 11–31.

Stocking, H. and Gross, P. (1989). *How Do Journalists Think?* Bloomington, IN: ERIC Clearinghouse on Reading and Communication.

Stocking, H. and LaMarca, N. (1990). How journalists describe their stories: Hypotheses and assumptions in newsmaking. *Journalism Quarterly*, 67(2), 295–301.

Sumpter, R. (2000). Daily newspaper editors' audience construction routines: A case study. *Critical Studies in Media Communication*, 17(3), 334–46.

Tuchman, G. (1972). Objectivity as strategic ritual: An examination of newsmen's notions of objectivity. *American Journal of Sociology*, 77(4), 660–79.

Tuchman, G. (1973). Making news by doing work: Routinizing the unexpected. *American Journal of Sociology*, 79, 110–31.

Tuchman, G. (1978). *Making News: A study in the construction of reality*. New York: Free Press.

Tunstall, J. (1993). *Television Producers*. London: Routledge.

Turow, J. (1978). Casting for television: The anatomy of social typing. *Journal of Communication*, 28(4), 18–24.

Turow, J. (1985). Cultural argumentation through the mass media: A framework for organizational research. *Communication*, 8, 139–64.

Turow, J. (1989). *Playing Doctor: Television, storytelling and medical power*. New York: Oxford University Press.

Turow, J. (1992). *Media Systems in Society*. New York: Longman.

Underwood, D. (1993). *When MBAs Rule the Newsroom*. New York: Columbia University Press.

Vincent, R. C., Crow, B. K., and Davis, D. K. (1989). When technology fails: The drama of airline crashes in network television news. *Journalism Monographs*, no. 117.

Waugh, E. (1938). *Scoop*. Boston: Little, Brown.

Weaver, D. H. and Wilhoit, G. C. (1991). *The American Journalist: A portrait of US news people and their work* (2nd edn.). Bloomington: Indiana University Press.

Weaver, D. H., and Wilhoit, G. C. (1998). Journalists in the United States. In D. H. Weaver (ed.), *The Global Journalist: News people around the world.* Creskill, NJ: Hampton Press, pp. 395–414.

Webster, J. G. and Phalen, P. F. (1994). Victim, consumer or commodity: Audience models in communication policy. In J. S. Ettema and D. C. Whitney (eds.), *Audiencemaking*. Newbury Park, CA: Sage, pp. 19–37.

White, D. M. (1950). The gate keeper: A case study in the selection of news. *Journalism Quarterly*, 27, 383–96.

Whitney, D. C. (1991). Agenda-setting: power and contingency. In J. Anderson (ed.), *Communication Yearbook*, vol. 14. Newbury Park, CA: Sage, pp. 347–56.

Whitney, D. C. and Becker, L. B. (1982). "Keeping the gates" for gatekeepers: The effects of wire news. *Journalism Quarterly*, 59, 60–5.

Whitney, D. C., Fritzler, M., Jones, S., Mazzarella, S., and Rakow, L. (1989). Geographic and source biases in network television news 1982–1984. *Journal of Broadcasting and Electronic Media*, 33(2), 159–74.

Wildman, S. S. (1994). One-way flows and the economics of audiencemaking. In In J. S. Ettema and D. C. Whitney (eds.), *Audiencemaking*. Newbury Park, CA: Sage, pp. 115–41.

Wilkins, L. and Patterson, P. (1987). Risk analysis and the construction of news. *Journal of Communication*, 37(3), 80–92.

Williams, B. and Delli Carpini, M. (2000). Unchained reaction: The collapse of media gatekeeping and the Clinton–Lewinsky scandal. *Journalism Theory, Practice and Criticism*, 1(1), 61–85.

Williams, R. (1958). *Culture and Society: 1780–1950*. New York: Harper & Row.

Williams, R. (1961). *The Long Revolution*. New York: Columbia University Press.

Winston, B. (1998). *Media, Technology and Society*. New York: Routledge.

Wu, D. (2000). Systemic determinants of international news coverage: A comparison of 38 countries. *Journal of Communication*, 50(2), 110–30.

Zelizer, B. (1992). *Covering the Body: The Kennedy assassination, the media, and the shaping of collective Memory*. Chicago: University of Chicago Press.

Zelizer, B. (1993). Journalists as interpretive communities. *Critical Studies in Mass Communication*, 10(3), 219–37.

CHAPTER NINE

From the *Playboy* to the *Hustler*
Class, Race, and the Marketing of Masculinity

Gail Dines and Elizabeth R. Perea

While there have been numerous books and articles on pornography (see, for example, Carol, 1994; Cole, 1952; Drakeford & Hamm, 1973; Dworkin, 1974; Faust, 1980; Gibson & Gibson, 1993; Ginzburg, 1958; Hazen, 1983; Hebditch & Anning, 1988; Huer, 1987; Strossen, 1995; Weitzer, 2000), little has been written on how the pornography industry functions within the wider capitalist economy. One of the reasons for this effacement of the material realities of cultural production is the tendency in the literature to focus solely on the text, often decontextualized from the economic, social, and historical conditions within which it is constructed, distributed, circulated and consumed. One possible reason for this is that it has offered academics a way out of dealing with the more messy questions regarding the nature of production and political economy in late industrial capitalism. According to McChesney (2000), scholarship on pornography was not the only area to opt for this position, since media studies in general has moved away from "important epistemological, theoretical and political debates" (p. 109).

It is apparent that there is a wealth of unexplored territory regarding how the pornography industry functions within capitalism and how this impacts the form and content of the textual material (Dines, Jensen, & Russo, 1998). One place to begin to explore this relationship between the symbolic and economic dimensions of media is to further examine the two primary ways in which magazines finance production – advertising and subscription (Mackay, 1997). While these two financial resources may often be utilized in conjunction with one another, within a particular magazine, one will often dominate as a source of revenue. Of particular interest to this project is the unique position held by *Hustler* as a high circulation publication that successfully relies solely on subscription revenue. Focusing on the content of cartoons, the aim of this discussion is to examine the relationships between marketing strategies designed to produce revenue and the content of the two largest circulation pornographic magazines, *Playboy* and *Hustler*. Foregrounded within these relationships are the construction of masculinity and ideologies of race and class.

While *Playboy* (with monthly sales of 3.4 million) and *Hustler* (with monthly sales of 1.4 million), are often lumped together under the heading of pornography (Norton, 1999), they occupy very different locations in the mass-distributed print-pornography industry. In terms of the continuum from soft-core to hard-core – the latter being distinguished by the presence of internal female genitalia (called "pink" in the magazines), semi-erect to erect penises and sexual activity between women and men and women and women – *Playboy* is the premier publication of the soft-core end of the market and *Hustler* of the hard-core. This is a major difference, not simply in terms of textual construction but also economics; to be defined as hard-core is to be denied access to advertising revenue since most corporations do not want their products to be associated with explicit imagery. Thus, while *Hustler* only carries poorly produced advertisements for phone sex or penis enlargers, *Playboy* regularly carries full page, color advertisements from Revlon, Philip Morris, Fruit of the Loom, Reebok, and Seagrams. The significance of these economic distinctions can be seen in the relationships between marketing strategies, magazine content and the construction of the reader. Thus it would seem reasonable to expect pornography magazines such as *Playboy*, which rely on corporate advertising, to differ from those such as *Hustler*, which are subscription driven. This essay discusses the critical position and ideological function of the cartoon in pornographic literature, the marketing and ideological positioning of *Playboy* and *Hustler* and the contemporary constructions of masculinity fashioned within the frames of comic relief.

While there has been little systematic analysis of the differences between the content of *Playboy* and *Hustler*, some feminist writers (Dines et al., 1998; Easton, 1994; Shortes, 1998) have attempted to compare and contrast soft-core and hard-core pictorials. However, unlike film and video pornography, mass-distributed pornography magazines such as *Playboy* and *Hustler* are not simply made up of representations of female (and sometimes male) bodies designed to arouse the male spectator to masturbation and orgasm. Rather, these magazines also include readers' letters, advice columns, reviews of movies, news clips, articles on current affairs, interviews, and cartoons, some of which are designed to arouse, some to amuse, and some to provide markers of respectability. While the different types of content of these magazines are all important for the overall construction of reality presented (Berger, 1972; McCracken, 1993), there is some research to suggest that the pictorials and the cartoons are the two most widely read sections and, indeed, the most expensive parts to produce (Brady, 1974; Stauffer and Frost, 1976; Urry, 1990).

That the pictorials as a constructed text have attracted much interest from scholars in fields as varied as art history, psychology, and film theory is understandable, given their promotional role in the marketing of the magazines. The limited attention that cartoons have received seems surprising, however, in light of the research on the role of the cartoons in newspapers and current affairs magazines. Seymour-Ure (1975), in his study of the history of the cartoon, has suggested that the cartoon is a central feature of any publication since it helps to increase sales, provides light relief from the serious business of reading, and is used by the publishers/editors to key the reader into the ideologies of the editorial staff. The cartoon, because of its comedic license, is often used to interrogate issues or take positions which would be considered unacceptable in written editorials (Emerson, 1969; Harrison, 1981; Wilson; 1979). Although there are cases of cartoonists holding different political views from the publishers/editors of the host newspaper/magazine, according to Seymour-Ure (1975), this is unusual and is only granted to well-known cartoonists. For example, Gary Trudeau's *Doonesbury* was often accompanied by a disclaimer. Indeed, most studies have found that the political positions of the newspaper and the cartoonists generally coincide and if there is disagreement, it is the cartoonist that is forced to change his/her political position, is fired, or is dropped from syndication (Harrison, 1981; Hess and Kaplan, 1975; Streicher, 1967; Urry, 1990).

Furthermore, the cartoon in most mainstream pornography magazines is the one place where representations of men consistently appear and where "dramatic scriptings" (Goffman, 1975, p. 53) of interactions between women and men are the actual theme. In *Playboy*, there are almost no pictorials which include men, and while *Penthouse* and *Hustler* do tend to have the occasional male–female pictorial, these are greatly outnumbered by pictorials comprised only of women. The cartoon is thus the only place where the magazine regularly presents the reader with an image of men, of masculinity, of home life, of relationships, and of sexual activity between women and men which are a "mock-up of everyday life, a put-together script of unscripted social doings" (Goffman, 1975, p. 53). Decoding the "mock-up of everyday life" provides one way of examining the potentially different worlds that pornographic magazines present to their readers and how the cartoons and the pictorials "combine to build a master tale that aims to win readers to [their] consensual view about reality" (McCracken, 1993, p. 299).

Differentiation and Segmentation: Constructing the *Playboy* and the *Hustler*

In place of the poor quality, under-the-counter pin-up magazines which dominated the print pornography industry of the post-World War II years, Hugh Hefner, founder and publisher of *Playboy*, wanted to create what he called a "quality lifestyle magazine" (Miller, 1984, p. 23), which would appeal to the upwardly mobile professional man. This quality magazine would have at its center the airbrushed, soft-focus pin-up-style pictorials of women but it would be packaged in the trappings of upper-middle-class life. Hefner's belief was that the only way he was going to get mass distribution and advertising for his magazine was to cloak it in an aura of upper-middle-class respectability, which would, according to John Mastro, former product manager of *Playboy* "take some of the shock off nudity" (quoted in Weyr, 1978, p. 33).

Toward this end, all the products offered by the magazine were to be of the highest quality: the short stories, the interviews with famous people, the cars, the alcohol, the clothes, the food, the advice about consumer items to buy, and, of course, the women. From the very start Hefner was clear about whom he wanted as readers. He wrote in the first issue of *Playboy* published in October 1953:

> If you are a man between 18 and 80, *Playboy* is meant for you . . . We want to make it clear from the start, we aren't a "family" magazine . . . Within the pages of *Playboy* you will find articles, fiction, pictures, stories, cartoons, humor and special features . . . to form a pleasure-primer styled to the masculine taste.

Hefner, in the *Playboy* of the 1950s was not so much appealing to an audience as constructing one. Lipsitz (1990), in his analysis of the formation of the consumer ideology of the 1950s, argues that the major role of the media in post-World War II America was to transform the population from ethnic and class-identified citizens to homogenized consumers, which required providing "legitimation for transformations in values initiated by the new economic imperatives of postwar America" (p. 44). Because the Depression years had seriously undermined the legitimacy of capitalism and the attendant values of individualism, installment buying and excessive materialism, the advertising industries, together with the media, embarked on a massive campaign to "educate" the public into being good consumers by demonstrating "that the hedonistic approach to life is a moral one, not an immoral one" (Dichter, quoted in Lipsitz, 1990, p. 47; see also Ewen, 1976). This ideological shift required the adoption of a societal perception of economic feasability. In other words, people had to believe that they could consume and with this perception came the birth of what Vermehren (1997) refers to as the myth of the middle class. Hefner became a major player in this campaign, providing an image to men of what constitutes a *Playboy* life-style. In the April 1956 issue, Hefner wrote:

> What is a playboy? He can be a sharp-minded young business executive, a worker in the arts, a university professor, an architect or an engineer. He can be many things, provided he possesses a certain kind of view. [H]e must be an alert man, a man of taste, a man sensitive to pleasure, a man who – can live life to the hilt. This is the sort of man we mean when we use the word playboy.

A close reading of the early issues of *Playboy* reveals the degree to which "living life to the hilt" was really about consuming. Articles abound on what to buy for the office, what to wear, where to eat, what gadgets to play with, and how to decorate an apartment (the "service" side of the magazine). As with all advertising, the actual product on offer was not the commodity being advertised but rather the fantasy of transformation that this product promised to bring to the consumer's life. Within *Playboy*, the high-quality products would transform the reader into a "playboy" who could then have the real prize: all the high-quality women he wanted – just like the ones who populated the magazine.

Hefner, by sexualizing consumption, provided an extremely hospitable environment for advertisers looking to expand markets in the post-war boom. By the end of 1955, advertisers had overcome their initial fear of advertising in a "men's entertainment" magazine and were, according to Weyr, "clamoring to buy" (1978, p. 32). During the 1950s and 1960s, *Playboy* continued to increase its readership and its advertising revenue and by the late 1960s the circulation figures reached an all time high of 4.5 million.

By the time Larry Flynt produced the first issue of *Hustler* in 1974, *Playboy* and *Penthouse* had been involved in a five-year battle to see who could produce the most explicit pictorials. The battle ended with Hugh Hefner sending a memo to the editorial staff, which called for a return to the more soft-core imagery. Hefner wrote: "our standards will be our own and will not be dictated by competitive pressure" (Miller, 1984, p. 205). Nonetheless, one of the results of what Miller calls the "pubic wars" (p. 182) between *Playboy* and *Penthouse* was a growing acceptance in the mainstream soft-core market of more explicit imagery, thus opening the way for mass distribution of the more hard-core materials. Without a doubt, Flynt has had to fight many legal battles (he wrote the editorial for the ten-year anniversary issue from his prison cell), but the groundwork laid by *Playboy* and *Penthouse* facilitated Flynt's aim of being the "first nationally distributed magazine to show pink" (Flynt, 1984, p. 7).

Understanding the pivotal role that product differentiation plays in capitalism, Flynt wrote in the first issue of *Hustler*, "Anyone can be a playboy and have a penthouse, but it takes a man to be a Hustler" (Flynt, 1974, p. 4). Flynt repeatedly writes in *Hustler* that his target audience is "the average American" (Flynt, 1984, p. 7), whose income makes it impossible to identify with the high level consumption and life-style associated with *Playboy* and *Penthouse*. Taking shots at *Playboy* and *Penthouse* for being too up market, for taking themselves too seriously, and for masquerading the "pornography as art by wrapping it in articles purporting to have socially redeeming values" (Flynt, 1983c, p. 5), *Hustler* has carved out a role for itself in a glutted market as a no-holds-barred magazine which tells it like it is, "unaffected by sacred cows of advertising. . . ." (Flynt, 1988, p. 5). Over the years Flynt has carefully crafted an image of *Hustler* magazine as one which is targeted at the working-class white guy who likes "no-frills" pornography.

Through its economic success *Hustler* demonstrates that "sexuality and desire cannot function as universal categories" (Valdivia, 2000) for they are implicated within the sociocultural experiences of race, class and ethnicity. In her analysis of the gendered class representations within two lingerie mail-order catalogs – *Victoria's Secret* and *Frederick's of Hollywood*, Valdivia illustrates that similar to *Hustler's* marketing of a working-class aesthetic, the imagery within the pages of *Fredericks of Hollywood* promotes a "no frills" consumption of sexuality and desire through its construction of a class-consciousness void of upper-class pretense (*Victoria's Secret* thus paralleling the leisure world of *Playboy*). This marketing strategy has been quite successful for *Fredericks of Hollywood*, as have Flynt's economic choices.

The decision to sacrifice advertising revenue and instead rely on subscription-financed revenue appears to have paid off since *Hustler* is the most successful hard-core magazine in the history of the pornography industry, and Flynt is a multimillionaire today. Moreover, given the type of magazine Flynt wanted to produce, he had no choice; it seems unlikely that even the most daring of advertisers would place their advertisements next to a cartoon whose theme was child molestation or next to the "Asshole of the Month" section which features a photograph of a male bending over, testicles in full view and the picture of a politician or celebrity pasted onto the anal opening.

Given the different images that *Playboy* and *Hustler* have cultivated, it is not surprising that their cartoons differ, since both Flynt and Hefner see the cartoons as embodying the philosophy of the magazine. Hefner, in an interview, stated that he sees the cartoons as the visual and humorous vehicle for transmitting the key element of the magazine which is the "combination of sex with status" (Brady, 1974, p. 95). Hefner, himself an aspiring cartoonist, ran the cartoon department for over twenty years until he promoted his assistant, Michelle Urry, to cartoon editor. In an interview, Urry (1990) discussed the procedure the editors use for choosing the twenty or so cartoons a month from among the thousands that are submitted by amateur and professional cartoonists. She highlights the importance that "the cartoons speak in the same voice as the rest of the magazine . . ." and that this requires above all "an ambiance of good taste." This ambiance is created by locating the characters in high-status surroundings, which signal a lifestyle that "*Playboy* readers can identify with if not actually live" (Urry, 1990). Thus, the cartoon offers to the viewer an image of what his life could be like if he consumed products to the same degree as his cartoon counterpart, the very same products that are advertised in the surrounding pages of the magazine.

In contrast *Hustler*, unconstrained by the need to present an ambiance consistent with consumption, has used the cartoons to promote the image of *Hustler* as "outrageous" and "provocative." The cartoons play a key role in marketing *Hustler* since the form and comedic license allows them to depict "outrageous" scenarios such as torture, murder, and child molestation which may, in a less humorous form such as pictorials, deny the magazine access to the mass distribution channels. Flynt, recognizing that "we can't just rely on top-notch erotic photography to sell the magazine" (Flynt, 1984, p. 7), has marketed Dwaine Tinsley, the cartoon editor of *Hustler*, as the most daring cartoonist of his time. He is described as creating "some of the most controversial and thought-provoking humor to appear in any magazine" (Flynt, 1983a, p. 7). One of the marketing tactics is to suggest that Tinsley is so "outrageous" that he is in fact out of step with the magazine's editors because some of his cartoons have been "so tasteless that even Larry Flynt has had to think twice before running them" (Flynt, 1983b, p. 65). We are, however, reassured by *Hustler* that the "tastelessness" will continue since "Larry is determined not to sell out and censor his creative artists" (Flynt, 1983b, p. 65).

Thus from their inception, both *Playboy* and *Hustler* cartoons have played a major role in promoting the image of their respective magazines. Over the years specific social contexts have influenced the creation of particular images within this medium, yet the ideological function of the construction of a gendered, racial, and socially classed subject has remained consistent. These cartoons are thus as integral as the pictorials to the overall construction of reality promoted by the magazines and, because they provide "readers with a glimpse of drawn action that is unambiguous and constructed in such a way as to allow the reader access to everything that is relevant" (Dines-Levy & Smith, 1988, p. 244), they deserve serious analysis.

Any analysis that attempts to compare *Playboy* and *Hustler* cartoon characters must explore the ways in which class is coded in these two magazines since the former depicts an upper-middle-class White world and the latter a working-class White world. One of the key techniques used by these magazines to signify the class location of their cartoon characters is the absence or presence of Blacks. *Playboy* depicts a world so affluent that Blacks are excluded by invisible market forces. Indeed, even the White working class is invisible in the *Playboy* world of expensive clothes, gourmet restaurants and well appointed homes. In *Hustler*, however, Black cartoon characters do make regular appearances, intruding on the world of the poor whites in ways that suggest that poor Blacks and Whites are locked in a struggle for diminishing resources, in this case, sexually available attractive White women. The working-class world of *Hustler* is depicted as a world of seething racial tensions brought about, not only by the Black man's insatiable appetite for White women, but also by his ultimate victory over the White man by gaining access to White women. As will be argued in the following pages, the role of the caricatured Black male in *Hustler* is to make the *Hustler* reader feel superior to the White working-class male depicted in the magazine who can neither sustain an erection nor a job. Thus while marketing itself to the working-class White male, and depicting caricatures of the working-class White male, *Hustler* ideologically functions within the myth of the middle class. While the *Hustler* reader may identify as an "average Joe," his subjectivity lies above the poor slobs he slums with in the comic frames of Hustler. He is free to live in the middle ground of the average American male.

The Social Construction of (Racialized) Masculinity: From *Playboy* to *Hustler*

The successful production of *Playboy*, similar to any other advertising-driven magazine, requires that the readers identify with the world created in the text. Through identification, the reader hopes to gain access to this world through buying the magazine and the products advertised within. Nowhere is this world more carefully constructed than in the cartoons. The cartoon world of *Playboy* is an idealized, upper-middle-class one, populated by rich, White playboys who epitomize the success story of the "American Dream." They live in expensive, large homes, drive upscale cars and eat in fancy restaurants with crystal wine-glasses and matching dinnerware on the table and wine or champagne chilling in ice buckets. One cartoon for example, has a well dressed couple sitting in a French restaurant with silver candle sticks on the table and fabric covered menus in their hands (*Playboy*, May 1989, p. 112). Hotels are sometimes used for extra-marital sexual encounters and they resemble elite establishments and/or exotic travel destinations. For example, a cartoon of a couple on their honeymoon includes an expensive looking hotel room furnished with a bedside table covered with tropical fruit and wine chilling in an ice bucket. A balcony overlooks a white sandy beach. The setting implies a May Caribbean getaway (*Playboy*, January 1989, p. 227).

The world of *Hustler* cartoons, on the other hand, is one populated by white working class hustlers and losers. In place of luxury homes, *Hustler*'s white cartoon characters dwell in trailer parks, tract houses and small apartments. Their homes are decorated with cheap furniture, brightly colored carpet, and Formica countertops. The food consumed tends to be hamburgers and hot dogs, and in place of wine chilling in a bucket is the ever-present beer can in the hand of the male cartoon character. Out-of-the-home sex tends to take place in cheap motels rather than in hotels (above the bed is often the sign "Motel Rules") or on the street. The cartoon characters are rarely shown vacationing or spending leisure time outside of the house, and when they do eat out, it is generally in cheap diners with seats at the counter.

As expected, the images of the men and women, which populate the two cartoon worlds, are very different. *Playboy* men and women cartoon characters are overwhelmingly attractive, well dressed and always White. The women in the *Playboy* cartoons tend to be young, voluptuous, blonde, lacking body hair, and dressed in tight and revealing clothing. The form and conventions of cartooning allow for the women to be drawn with extra large breasts, overly curvaceous bottoms and tiny waists; bodily proportions, which although caricatured, are nonetheless traditionally seen as the epitome of female sexual attractiveness. In fact as Valdivia (2000) has demonstrated this image of ideal thinness and beauty carries with it clear distinctions of the privileged upper-middle class. In *Hustler*, the females are also caricatured but in ways which make them appear, within the conventions of pornography, sexually unattractive in the extreme. They are overwhelmingly White, middle-aged and fat with huge stomachs, thighs and legs. Their vaginas are depicted as extra large with unusually large amounts of hair. They often have one or more of the following: rotten teeth, big noses, spotty skin, unkempt hair and stubble on their legs and thighs. Their clothes are ill fitting and look cheaply made. If lingerie is worn, it is drawn in a way to suggest humor since their unkempt large bodies render these women as anything but sexually attractive. The men do not fare much better since they tend to be fat with huge beer guts, several days' stubble on their faces and a receding hairline. These images once again conform to a notion of class distinction foregrounded by Valdivia (2000) in which fat is a component of a working-class representation concomitant with poor nutrition, diet, and self-care. Thus sexuality and desire are problematized within the greater cultural relationships of race and class.

The nature of the sex also differs markedly in the two magazines. In *Playboy* cartoons it is almost always depicted as consensual and in the missionary position, the implication being that the level of consumption enjoyed by the White male cartoon character provides him access to a whole range of willing and beautiful young women. The choice of sexual position further substantiates the submissiveness and passivity of Playboy women. Because women are always sexually available in the *Playboy* world, there is little need for rape, harassment, manipulation or coercion of any sort. It is a world of male fantasy where any man, irrespective of age, physical appearance and marital status, can have his pick of young, big-breasted, sexually available women who lack agency, will or needs.

In comparison to the White successful playboy, *Hustler*'s white male cartoon characters are depicted as pathetic losers who fail to attract real women. Indeed, many cartoons have as their theme an unshaven, unkempt, desperate man looking for female substitutes which may include blow-up dolls, animals, children, plastic vaginas, pornography magazines and bowling balls. The *Hustler* cartoon white male is often desperate because his partner refuses to have sex with him. The *Hustler* female cartoon character, unlike her *Playboy* sister, does have agency, will, and needs. The cartoons are filled with women who refuse their partners because they prefer to read a book, watch television or masturbate. He is often shown with a large erection and swollen testicles, pleading to have sex. One cartoon, which epitomizes the way wives are depicted, shows a middle-aged male blowing up a sex doll. However, this doll is called "Wife Doll" and on the package is written "The talking inflatable wife doll, She's overweight, She's mean, She has no pussy." As he blows her up she says "Forget it! Roll Over, and go to Sleep" (*Hustler*, August 1991, p. 51). Another way that Hustler women are depicted as having agency is in their demand for non-missionary sex which requires more skill than the male partner possesses. One cartoon, for example, has a couple trying to untangle their bodies while the woman derides her husband for not knowing how to do the "69" (*Hustler*, April 1989, p. 32).

Probably one of the most desperate *Hustler* male cartoon characters has been "Chester the Molester," who appeared regularly in the 1970s and 1980s. Chester, a White, overweight, middle-aged pedophile, was created by Dwaine Tinsley,[1] the cartoon editor of *Hustler*. Every month Chester would appear in a full-page, color cartoon, scheming and plotting how to capture female children. In one cartoon, a little girl is attracted by a big sign, which says, "candy for free." Behind the sign Chester hides with a baseball bat raised, ready to hit the girl as she approaches (*Hustler*, July 1984, p. 93). Another cartoon (*Hustler*, September 1977, p. 63) has Chester wearing a swastika, waving a five-dollar bill in an attempt to attract a young Jewish girl (the signifiers of which are a long nose, a Star of David around her neck, a father with a Jewish Yarmulke and a mother with a padlocked purse). Chester was never actually shown having sex with children, but his penis was regularly drawn as erect and he was panting with sexual desire for the children. On those rare occasions when Chester was shown courting adult women, he was depicted as a social and sexual incompetent who could not control his defecations or ejaculations.

Chester, however, is the not the only *Hustler* cartoon male to have sexual problems. Indeed, the magazine cartoons are populated with men who prematurely ejaculate, defecate instead of ejaculate and vomit because of the smell of their partner's vagina. Without doubt, however, one of the major causes of sexual dysfunction is, in White men, a small penis, which fails to excite the female partner. The female is portrayed as sarcastic, lacking empathy and ridiculing. One cartoon, for example, has a man and woman in bed; the woman, searching for his small penis, triumphantly tells him, "Ooh! I found it" (*Hustler Humor*, May 1992, p. 10). The man is clearly embarrassed and covering up his penis. Other cartoons show the White man endlessly searching pornography shops for penis enlargers (presumably the same enlargers which can be mail ordered from the ads in the back of *Hustler*).

The size of the White male's penis in *Hustler* is further ridiculed by the caricatured image of the Black male's enormous penis. Whether erect or limp, the penis visually dominates the cartoon and is the focus of humor; a form of representation that has historical currency in mainstream media's depictions of Black masculinity (see Snead, 1994; Cowan & Campbell, 1994). This huge penis is depicted as a source of great pride and as a feature that distinguishes Black men from White men. For example, in one cartoon, a Black man and a White man are walking next to a fence. The White man makes a noise by dragging a stick along the fence, while the Black man is doing the same using his large penis, which is much bigger than the stick. The Black man, who is walking behind the White man, is snickering at the White man's stick (*Hustler*, February 1989, p. 95).

The Black men's obsession with the size of their penises is one example of how the dominant regime of racist representation constructs Blacks as "having bodies but not minds" (Mercer, 1994, p. 138). In one cartoon, a large Black male with an undersized head is looking at his newborn son and screaming at the White nurse "Never mind how much he weighs, bitch! How long's my boy's dick?" (*Hustler*, December 1988, p. 32). Not only is the Black male depicted as verbally abusive but also as lacking care and interest in his son's health and well-being. This image fits in with the dominant representation of Black men as either abusive or absent fathers who take advantage of the welfare system developed by misguided liberals.

While the White man in *Hustler* is sexually inept and desperate for a woman, the black male has no problem finding attractive white women. However, the cartoons showing White women with Black men often have as their theme the sexual abuse of women. The image of the Black male as sexually aggressive began appearing in the late 1970s and by the mid-1980s, *Hustler* was running an average of two to three such cartoons an issue. One common theme of the joke is the severely traumatized vagina of the white sexual partner. In one cartoon, a naked White woman is sitting on a bed, legs open, revealing her vagina encircled by red stars, suggesting pain. Sitting on the end of the bed is a naked, very dark, ape-like male, his huge, erect penis dominating the image. He is on the phone asking room service to send in a shoehorn. The White woman looks terrified (*Hustler*, November 1988, p. 100). In another cartoon, a similar-looking couple is walking down the street. The Black male has his arm around the White female and on his shirt is written "Fucker," on hers is "Fuckee" (*Hustler*, May 1987, p. 79). Although the male is clothed, the outline of his huge penis can be seen. The woman's vagina on the other hand is clearly visible since it is hanging below her knees and is again red and sore, a marker of what black men can and will do to White women if not stopped by the White male protector of White woman-hood. This scenario functions as part of the production and reproduction of race relations in American culture. As McCarthy (1998) illustrates, it is manifested in the need to "hold the line against the threat of invasion by the morally cor-rupt other, the socially different, the culturally deviant and deprived . . . It is a game of exclusions intended to preserve the safety of the suburban domestic space" (p. 87). McCarthy (1998) identities this as Nietzsche's (1967) discourse of resentment.

As a component of a frustrated resentment, the white male in *Hustler* cartoons is constructed as anything but the protector of White womanhood. Indeed, he cannot even prevent attractive White women from freely choosing to be with Black men. The white sexual partners of Black men tend to be thin, attractive and lacking body hair. This is a very unusual female image in *Hustler* cartoons and suggests that the black male is siphoning off the few sexually available, attractive women, leaving the White man with rejects. In another example the message that White women prefer Black men is the theme of a spoof on Barbie, a doll that represents the all-American female with her blonde hair, tiny waist and silicone-like breasts. The image has Barbie dressed in black underwear, with ejaculate around her mouth, kneeling next to a standing black male doll pulling a very large penis out of her mouth. The caption reads "in an attempt to capture the market the manufacturer has been testing some new designs. . . . We're not sure, but perhaps this Slut Barbie, (with her hard nipples, a permanently wet, open pussy and sperm dripping from her mouth) goes a bit too far" (*Hustler*,

July 1984, p. 23). The obvious choice for Barbie's sex partner would have been Ken, her long-term boyfriend, but the suggestion here is that Ken, with his White penis, would not have been enticing enough for this all–American girl to give up her virginal status.

Because of the lack of willing sex partners, the White man is often reduced to paying for sex. However, once again, Black men have the upper hand since almost all the pimps in *Hustler* cartoons are Black. While this was a familiar image of 1970s Black film genre (i.e. *The Mack, Superfly*), in the world of *Hustler* the pimp has remained a key figure to this day. These Black men have, in contrast to the well-endowed characters of *Hustler*, traded in their large penises for big Cadillacs, heavy gold jewelry and fur coats, riches no doubt obtained from white johns. The prostitutes are both Black and White but the johns are almost always depicted as white. Many of the cartoons have as their theme the White man trying to barter down the Black pimp, with the Black pimp refusing to change the price. The power of the Black man is now absolute – not only can he get his pick of attractive White women, he also controls White prostitutes, leaving the White man having to negotiate to buy what he once got for free.

Not only is the Black man draining the White man's access to women, he is also draining his pocket in the form of welfare. The Black male is shown as deserting his family and numerous unkempt, diseased children, leaving the welfare system to pick up the tab. One cartoon features a Black woman surrounded by children saying to a White interviewer, "Yes, we does (sic) believe in Welfare" (*Hustler*, December 1992, p. 47). Another example is a cartoon advertising different dolls. The first doll is called "Beach Darbie" which is a Barbie look-alike in a bathing costume. The second doll, also Barbie, is dressed in a white jacket and is called "Ski Darbie". The third doll is an overweight White female with bedroom slippers and a cigarette hanging out of her mouth, she is called "Knocked-Up Inner-City Welfare Darbie." In each hand she has a Black baby (*Hustler*, December 1992, p. 107).

Thus, in *Hustler* cartoons black men have precisely the two status symbols that White men lack, big penises and money. The White man's poor sexual performance is matched by his poor economic performance. Reduced to living in trailer homes, poorly furnished apartments or tract houses, the *Hustler* White male cartoon character is clearly depicted as lower-working class. His beer gut, stubble, bad teeth and working man's clothes signify his economic status and stand in sharp contrast to the signifiers of power attached to the image of the Black male.

Porno-User or Sophisticate: Decoding the Reader Implied in the Text

As McCracken (1993) has argued, one of the major marketing strategies adopted by magazines is to create an "idealized image . . . for potential readers to desire, identify with, and expect to attain through consuming the magazine" (p. 15). It is clear, from the above discussion, that *Playboy* and *Hustler* create two very different worlds for the reader to identify with. For the *Playboy* reader, embracing the image of the reader implied in the text is pleasurable since he is a sophistic-ated, upper middle-class man who wines and dines on the best and consumes only up-market products (actual *Playboy* figures show that the median income for readers is $24,786, a figure which barely places the reader in the middle class and certainly not in the upper-middle class lifestyle suggested by the magazine). He reads *Playboy* for the fine articles, high-quality reviews and in-depth inter-views and not for the centerfolds. He is not a porn-user but rather a man who appreciates the finer things in life.

The *Hustler* reader would seem to have a more problematic image to embrace since the magazine unashamedly positions itself as a magazine for the lower-working-class White male ("trailer trash" in *Hustler* terms), who buys the maga-zine for the "pink" and for the "tasteless" humor. Moreover, he is a White man who cannot compete in the sexual or financial arena with Black men. This is about as low as any White man can get in a racist world. Thus, the obvious question is why do White men buy *Hustler*? The answer to this is complex since it requires an understanding of how race functions within White supremacy, particularly in relation to class identity for Whites.

Within North American White racist discourse, the term working class is interchangeable with Blacks. In her discussion of "the assumption of the uni-versality of middle-class aesthetics" (p. 66), Valdivia notes that "in the United States, one of the most powerful myths is that of the middle class" (Vermehren 1997). That is, people believe that they belong to this mythical middle class regardless of their income, education, or standard of living. Although the pro-fessional, managerial middle class amounts to "no more than 20 percent of the US population," the industrial working class, those working for wages rather than salaries, amounts to nearly 70 percent of the population (Ehrenreich 1990, p. 46); (Valdivia, 2000, pp. 69, 70). In a society where most Whites see them-selves as middle class, and where "class differences become racial differences" (Jhally and Lewis, 1992, p. 83), *Hustler* promotes an image of itself as targeting a specific audience that few see themselves as belonging to. Herein lies the brilliant marketing strategy of *Hustler* since no one is meant to see themselves as the "implied reader." This allows the White male reader, be he working class, middle class or upper class, to buy *Hustler* while also distancing himself from a magazine, filled with images of semen, feces, child molesters, and women with leaking vaginas. For the duration of the reading and masturbation, he is slumming in the world of the "white trash," an observer to the workings of a social class that is clearly not his.

While *Hustler*'s preoccupation with body fluids, oversized bad-smelling genitals and defecation is well documented in the academic discussion on porno-graphy, few have linked *Hustler*'s attempt to "gross its readers out" (a regular promise in *Hustler* editorials) to its marketing strategy. In her attempt to explore how *Hustler* markets itself, Kipnis (1992) suggests that the cartoons specializing in "gaseous, fluid–emitting, embarrassing bodies . . ." (p. 375) that threaten to erupt at any moment are potentially "counter hegemonic in [their] refusal of bourgeois proprieties" (p. 388). She further argues that these images should thus be read as texts that, at times and with limits, "powerfully articulate class resent-ment . . ." (p. 389). This articulation of working-class resentment is, according to Kipnis, one way that *Hustler* hails the working–class reader since "professional classes – doctors, optometrists, dentists – are favored targets" (p. 378). While it is indeed correct that there are cartoons which target the professional classes, Kipnis overrepresents their status as the "favored targets." While members of the professional class are ridiculed in an occasional cartoon (usually one every couple of months), they are completely outnumbered by the cartoons which depict the working-class male as financially incompetent, sexually inept and socially retarded.

Thus *Hustler*, rather than articulating working-class resentment at being excluded from the fruits of capitalism and the White middle class, actually trades in the most crude and oppressive stereotypes of the working class in order to draw in readers who can feel morally superior to the "disgusting" bodies which populate the pages. This is the most profitable and hegemonic utilization of the discourse of resentment. Indeed, recognizing that the reader wants to distance himself from the reader implied in the text, *Hustler* editors write in their intro-duction to a review of Tinsley's cartoons, "Dwaine Tinsley is not a black, a Jew, a wino, a child molester, or a bigot. But the characters in his cartoons are. They are everything you have nightmares about, everything you despise . . ." (*Hustler*, November, 1983, p. 65). Aside from the incredible racism and anti-Semitism of this statement, the actual intention is to let the reader know what he is not, he is not a member of the lower class (Black, wino, bigot and child molester) and he is not a member of the elite (Jew). He is rather just an "average white American guy" who, for $4.95 a month, can get a glimpse of "trailer trash" life. Thus, in coded terms *Hustler* provides distance between the reader and the cartoon characters by leaving open the "middle class," the category where most white Americans situate themselves (Jhally and Lewis, 1992) and developing identity through negation of the other.

Conclusion

The aim of this discussion was to explore how the inter-relationships between the marketing strategies and the content, particularly the cartoons of two major pornography magazines. *Playboy*, by relying on advertising revenue, has created a world of upper-middle-class life in which advertisers find comfort and that readers identify with, even if they don't actually experience it in their everyday lives. *Hustler* on the other hand has constructed a world that few readers would want to identify with, even if it is closer to their real class position than the

Playboy lifestyle. In *Playboy*, white masculinity is presented in idealized forms while in *Hustler* it is ridiculed, mocked and derided. However, when class is factored into the analysis, it becomes apparent that it is not White men as a group who are being ridiculed. The debasement of White masculinity in *Hustler* cartoons is played out on the caricatured flabby, unkempt body of the lower-working-class White male, a class that few whites see themselves as belonging to, irrespective of their income. Thus, in between the hyper-masculinity of the Black male (Jones, 1993), and the under-masculinized White lower-working-class male, is the reader inscribed in the text, who can feel superior to both types of "deviants." The reader is being invited to identify with what is absent in the cartoons, a "real man" (*Hustler*'s first issue ran an editorial which introduced the magazine as one for "real men"), who turns to *Hustler* because it is, according to its editors, "truly the only magazine that deals with the concerns and interests of the average American" (*Hustler*, 1984, p. 5).

The two very different marketing strategies have had consequences for the way the pictorials are promoted by the magazine. Hefner, from the very first edition of *Playboy* has, in public, minimized the role the pictorials play, arguing that the readers buy the magazine for its literature, interviews and sophisticated cartoon humor. Indeed, in their promotional material aimed at potential advertisers, *Playboy* describes its magazine as being about "The way men live in the nineties . . .[2] Entertainment, fashion, cars, sports, the issues, the scene, the people who make waves, the women men idealize" (*Playboy* Advertising Rate Card # 44). In private meetings, however, Hefner has been very clear about the importance of the "women men idealize." During an editorial meeting where some of the literary editors were arguing for more space, Hefner claimed that:

> We could have all the Nabokovs in the world and the best articles on correct attire without attracting readers. They bought the magazine for the girls (sic). We couldn't take the sex out. The magazine would die like a dog. (Weyr, 1978, p. 35)

Flynt, unlike Hefner, acknowledges in the magazine just how important the "girls" are to the readers and regularly promises explicitness that does "it better than any of our so-called competitors" (*Hustler*, November, 1983, p. 5). Indeed, *Hustler* has no desire to compete with *Playboy* on *Playboy*'s terms and thus does not make any pretense about what's on offer. The centerfold is the commodity and masturbation is the end product. In *Hustler*, there are no articles to hide behind or interviews with ex-presidents to talk about because the magazine is not selling an idealized image of the reader, rather the pleasure in the case of *Hustler* comes from feeling superior to the reader implied in the text.

This type of analysis makes it clear that to simply focus on pornography as a monolithic text is to miss the complex ways in which the products of the industry differ in production, content and consumption. Exploring the relationship between the pornography text(s) and conditions of production requires that we examine the way that the pornography industry is located within a wider capitalist society where product differentiation is the key to economic survival. In this way, the focus of attention will shift from the preoccupation with the text, decontextualized from its conditions of production and consumption, to a more nuanced approach which examines how pornography works as both an industry and a mode of representation.

Notes

1   In the spring of 1989, Dwaine Tinsley was arrested and found guilty of sexually molesting a teenage girl (Valley Times, May 20, 1989). While serving time in prison, his wife, Susan Tinsley, took over his position as cartoon editor for a brief period. Tinsley has since returned to *Hustler*.
2   Though as we've seen this is an ideology originating in post-World War II America that has been continued to function quite successfully for Hefner.

References

Berger, J. (1972). *Ways of Seeing*. London: Penguin Books.

Brady, F. (1974). *Hefner*. New York: Macmillan.

Carol, A. (1994). *Nudes, Prudes and Attitudes: Pornography and censorship*. London: New Clarion Press.

Cole, S. G. (1952). *Pornography and the Sex Crisis*. Toronto: Amanita Enterprises.

Cowan, G. and Campbell, R. (1994). Racism and sexism in interracial pornography: A content analysis. *Psychology of Women Quarterly*, 18, 323–38.

Dines, G., Jensen, B., and Russo, A. (1998). *Pornography: The production and consumption of inequality*. New York: Routledge.

Dines-Levy, G. and Smith, G. W. H. (1988). Representations of women and men in Playboy sex cartoons. In C. Powell and G. Paton (eds.), *Humor in Society: Resistance and control*. London: Macmillan.

Drakeford, J. W. and Hamm, J. (1973). *Pornography: The sexual mirage*. Nashville: T. Nelson Publishing.

Dworkin, A. (1974). *Woman Hating*. New York: Dutton Publishing.

Easton, S. (1994). *The Problem of Pornography: Regulation and the right to free speech*. London: Routledge.

Ehrenreich, B. (1990). The silenced majority: Why the average working person had disappeared from American media and culture. *Utne Reader*, January/February, 46–7.

Emerson, J. (1969). Negotiating the serious import of humor. *Sociometry*, 33, 169–81.

Ewen, S. (1976). *Captains of Consciousness: Advertising and the social roots of the consumer culture*. New York: McGraw-Hill.

Faust, B. (1980). *Women, Sex, and Pornography: A controversial and unique study*. New York: Macmillan Publishing.

Flynt, L. (ed.) (1974). *Hustler*, vol. 1, July (4).

Flynt, L. (ed.) (1983a). Show and tell. *Hustler*, vol. 10, November (7).

Flynt, L. (ed.) (1983b). Review. *Hustler*, vol. 10, November (65).

Flynt, L. (ed.) (1983c). Politics of porn. *Hustler*, vol. 10, November (5).

Flynt, L. (ed.) (1984). Ten great years. *Hustler*, vol. 11, July (7).

Flynt, L. (ed.) (1988). *Hustler*, vol. 15, July (5).

Gibson, P. and Gibson R. (1993). *Dirty Looks: Women, pornography, power*. London: British Film Institute.

Ginzburg, R. (1958). *An Unhurried View of Erotica*. New York: Ace Publishing.

Goffman, E. (1975). *Frame Analysis: An essay on the organization of experience*. Harmondsworth: Penguin.

Harrison, R. (1981). *The Cartoon: Communication to the quick*. Thousand Oaks, CA: Sage.

Hazen, H. (1983). *Endless Rapture: Rape, romance, and the female imagination*. New York: Scribner.

Hebditch, D. and Anning, N. (1988). *Porn Gold: Inside the pornography business*. London: Faber Publishing.

Hefner, H. (ed.) (1953). *Playboy*, October.

Hefner, H. (ed.) (1956). *Playboy*, April.

Hess, S. and Kaplan M. (1975). *The Ungentlemanly Art: A history of American political cartoons*. New York: Macmillan.

Huer, J. (1987). *Art, Beauty, and Pornography: A journey through American culture*. Buffalo, NY: Prometheus Press.

Jhally, S. and Lewis J. (1992). *Enlightened Racism: The Cosby Show, audiences, and the myth of the American dream*. Boulder, CO: Westview Press.

Jones, J. (1993). The construction of black sexuality: Towards normalizing the black cinematic experience. In M. Diawara (ed.), *Black American Cinema*. New York: Routledge.

Kipnis, L. (1992). (Male) desire and (female) disgust: Reading *Hustler*. In L. Grossberg, C. Nelson, and P. Treichler (eds.), *Cultural Studies*. New York: Routledge.

Lipsitz, G. (1990). *Time Passages: Collective memory and American popular culture*. Minneapolis: University of Minnesota Press.

Mackay, H. (ed.) (1997). *Consumption and Everyday Life*. London: Sage.

McCarthy, C. (1998). *The Uses of Culture: Education and the limits of ethnic affiliation*. New York: Routledge.

McChesney, R. (2000). The political economy of communications and the future of the field. *Media, Culture and Society*, 22, 109–16.

McCracken, E. (1993). *Decoding Women's Magazines: From Mademoiselle to Ms*. New York: St. Martin's Press.

Mercer, K. (1994). *Welcome to the Jungle: New positions in black Cultural Studies*. New York: Routledge.

Miller, R. (1984). *Bunny: The real story of Playboy*. London: Michael Joseph.

Nietzsche, F. (1967). *On the Genealogy of Morals* (trans. W. Kaufman). New York: Vintage.

Norton, J. (1999). Invisible man: A queer critique of feminist anti-pornography theory. In B. Dank and R. Refinetti (eds.), *Sex Work and Sex Workers*. Sage: London.

Seymour-Ure, C. (1975). How special are cartoonists? In Anon., *Getting Them in Line*. University of Kent at Canterbury: Center for the study of cartoons and caricature.

Shortes, C. (1998). The containment of S/M pornography. *Journal of Popular Film and Television*, 23, 72–9.

Snead, J. (1994). *White Screen, Black Images: Hollywood from the dark side*. New York: Routledge.

Stauffer, J. and Frost, R. (1976). Male and female interest in sexually orientated magazines. *Journal of Communication*, 26, 25–30.

Streicher, L. (1967). On a theory of political caricature. *Comparative Studies in Society and History*, 9, 429–45.

Strossen, N. (1995). *Defending Pornography: Free speech, sex, and the fight for women's rights*. New York: Scribner.

Urry, M. (1990). Interview by author. New York, 23 April.

Valdivia, A. N. (2000). Visions of desire: Class and femininity in lingerie ads. In A. N. Valdivia, *A Latina in the Land of Hollywood and Other Essays on Media Culture*. Tucson: University of Arizona Press, pp. 65–177.

Vermehren, C. (1997). Cultural capital: The cultural economy of US advertising. In K. T. Frith (ed.), *Undressing the Ad: Reading culture in advertising*. New York: Peter Lang.

Weitzer, R. (2000). *Sex for Sale: Prostitution, pornography and the sex industry*. New York: Routledge.

Weyr, T. (1978). *Reaching for Paradise: The Playboy vision of America*. New York: Times Books.

Wilson, C. (1979). *Jokes: Form, content, use and function*. London: Academic Press.

PART THREE

Media Content

CHAPTER TEN

Selling *Survivor*
The Use of TV News to Promote Commercial Entertainment

Matthew P. McAllister

As most Americans who were not stranded on a tropical island knew, the hot television program of both summer 2000 and winter–spring 2001 was CBS's *Survivor*. The program about contestants stranded on, and then ceremoniously voted off, exotic and isolated locations was a television phenomenon. *Survivor* involves physical endurance, group dynamics, Machiavellian strategy, and most importantly for CBS, large commercial revenue. Ratings, advertiser visibility, and network promotion were sky-high for the program.

During the April 26, 2001 episode of *Survivor: Australian Outback*, an announcer told US viewers at the beginning of the broadcast that the program was "sponsored by the 2001 Aztek from Pontiac." The announcer was not kidding. Less than a minute later, a paid commercial spot for the Aztek aired, touting the vehicle's ability to be used as a camping tent. About nine minutes later, the four remaining contestants of the reality-based game show met host Jeff Probst who informed them of a "reward challenge." The prize to be rewarded, as described by Probst, was "a Pontiac Aztek; this is a car that converts into a tent. . . . it's pretty cool." Later in the program, in what was termed by Bill Carter of *The New York Times* as "perhaps the longest in-program commercial in television history" (Carter, 2001, p. A1), the winner of the challenge, Colby, is given his prize. As Colby (and the camera) look over the car, he says,

> Look at that thing. She looks good. How wild is this thing? God, look at the interior. Now this is a trip. It's awesome. I mean, the car is way cooler than I thought it was going to be. . . . And it's got some of the neatest amenities a vehicle has ever had. You've got a stereo in the back of it, not to mention a huge tent.

Colby spends the night in the car, using its tent feature. As Colby falls asleep in his new Aztek, the program fades into a commercial break, with the first ad being, of course, for the Pontiac Aztek.

Such blatant blurring of commercial and program raises concerns about the control over programming decisions that may be relinquished to marketers and promoters. But, ultimately, *Survivor* is designed to be entertainment, and makes few claims otherwise. Perhaps such blurring is not particularly egregious in the fluff-oriented universe of prime-time commercial television programming. However, the mixing of the commercial and the promotional with news programming is more problematic and has been an enduring concern in the field of media studies. During the following morning, CBS's *The Early Show*, the journalistic program produced by CBS News, aired a "Round Table" discussion of the previous night's episode. During this discussion, panelists (consisting of a humor columnist from Newsweek.com, a model, and a former *Survivor* participant) were asked their opinions of the previous night's *Survivor*. Lasting over six minutes (an eternity for the precious commodity of network airtime), this "forum" was a regular feature on Friday installments of *The Early Show* since the first episode of the first *Survivor* in June 2000. Anchor Bryant Gumbel asked the three discussants, "What did you think of Colby's reward for last night?" Humorist Andy Borowitz responded with

> Well, it was kind of big. You know, a Pontiac Aztek, you know, it sets up all kinds of unfair expectations, because now that doctor down in the South Pole wants one. He thinks he should get one, too, so it's really unfair. But, you know, it had that – an enormous tent and everything, but it really changed his life. You know, you get an Aztek and girls start giving you flowers; relatives start appearing out of nowhere.

As Borowitz describes – admittedly tongue-in-cheek – the enormity of the reward, Aztek-dominated video excerpts from the previous night's *Survivor* were replayed. During the discussion, viewers were urged to visit the CBS-*Survivor* website, where more promotion of the program, and more advertising for the Aztek, could be found. And the panel discussion was not the only *Survivor* story on that day's program; in fact, it was relatively modest. Over 15 minutes of CBS's morning news was devoted to interviewing Elisabeth Filarski, the latest person to be voted off the Outback.

The *Survivor* Aztek example represents many disturbing trends in modern commercial and promotional culture: the power of commercial sponsorship to influence content; the invasion of entertainment texts by product placement; the increased media life of promotional messages through the Internet and, most significantly for this essay, the use of news to promote corporate holdings. A major assumption of many of the critics of commercial and promotional culture is that modern democracies require vibrant and diverse media systems to provide the kind of information and perspectives for informed decisions and true public participation. As an important component of media studies, analyses of news content track the democratic potential and embodiment of media technologies and genres. Critics wonder if the growth of commercial influences – giving such a loud and self-interested voice to the selling function at the expense of other information and perspectives – subverts the democratic potential of information and entertainment systems.

This essay discusses the temptation the media feel in promoting both their own holdings as well as the products of advertisers, using as a case study the promotion of *Survivor* and *Survivor* advertisers on CBS' *The Early Show*. Ultimately CBS's use of news to publicize *Survivor* sets the promotional bar higher than it had been before for television news and paints one particularly disturbing picture of the role of news in commercial culture. Although this role may be beneficial to corporate owners and advertisers, it also undermines the needs of a democratic society.

News, Democracy, and Commercialism

News, as a supplier of information and social analysis, is viewed by governments, scholars and journalists as a special genre of media. Although certainly entertainment media – with its ability to educate and enflame the passions – may do more than merely entertain, journalism, in its ideal Western form, is *designed* to pillar democracy. We may think of the news as giving us "just the facts," but in a modern society, the role of news is more complex. In a democracy, diversity of information – necessary for a full consideration of social ideas – is key. No one sector or partisan force should dominate the news, but rather the media "should be organized in a way that enables diverse social groups and organizations to express alternative viewpoints" (Curran, 1991, p. 103). Sometimes this means giving us unpopular views, including ideas that we may not want to be exposed to, but that we need for a healthy democracy. Similarly, news should be relevant, offering us information and perspectives that are central in making important social and political decisions. Democratically relevant news should ideally facilitate social and political participation; encourage citizenship, active engagement with the social activism and organizing; and "create the conditions in which alternative viewpoints and perspectives are brought into play" (Curran, 1991, p. 102).

To approach these goals, journalism must avoid any one voice dominating its discourse. Although the typical first amendment approach may see government as a dangerous influence on news, commercial interests loom at least as large as the state as a danger to democratically vibrant news. "Commercial interests" here refer both to the more general sense of the term (the profit motive overwhelming content decisions) and the more specific sense of the term (commercial advertisers overwhelming content decisions). In the ideal world of journalism, then, there should be a barrier separating the business side from the editorial side to protect the institution's democratic function. As Ben Bagdikian argues,

"Within journalism, the ideal policy has always been proudly referred to as 'The Wall of Separation Between Church and State.' The newsroom was the Church, and the business side of the news company, the secular State" (2000, p. xxv).

McChesney writes that it is naïve to think that modern journalism ever had such pure separation. Professionalism in news, including the norm of objectivity, was created in large part as a way to effectively deliver audiences to advertisers, for instance (McChesney, 1999, p. 49). Historians and critics have highlighted the earlier tendencies of advertising to "camouflage" themselves as news articles (Lawson, 1988; Baker, 1994) and the power of major advertisers, like tobacco companies, to influence media content throughout this century (Bagdikian, 2000; Baker, 1994). Focusing on television, the role of commercial interests, including the advertising industry, in shaping the very foundational structure and assumptions of US broadcasting systems is a major theme in the research of scholars like Barnouw (1978) and McChesney (1993, 1999).

Critics have also argued that the danger of the commercial voice overwhelming news – especially television news – is even more of a reality in the post-1990s than before this time. Television news has found itself in a highly competitive environment for ratings because of the increased competition generally in television (via such delivery systems as cable and satellites) and the creation of additional news outlets like Fox News. Personal Video Recorders (also known as Digital Video Recorders) like TiVO make the recording of programming – and the avoiding of commercials – even easier than VCRs and have encouraged advertisers to demand more promotion than the typical (and easily avoidable) spot advertisement (Bernstein, 2001). The increased expenses for "star anchor" salaries and high-tech news and weather equipment and changes in news organization ownership may stress the economic bottom line for news divisions (for reviews of these factors, see Alger, 1998; Bagdikian, 2000; Cohen, 1997; Croteau & Hoynes, 2001; Hickey, 1998; McAllister, 2002; McChesney, 1999). These factors alter news in several ways, including a stress on "ratings friendly" news (fast-paced news about celebrities and scandal) and a pressure to avoid criticism of advertisers and other business partners. This context also influences journalism toward more coverage of commercial activities and to serve as promotional outlets for advertisers and corporate owners. Such pressures are profoundly anti-democratic and encourage passivity. As Richard Cohen, a former CBS news producer, summarizes, "TV cannot sell successfully to an audience that is more provoked than pleased, more challenged than cheered" (Cohen, 1997, p. 33).

If news about media and celebrities may attract viewers, then news about innovative, giant and/or shocking advertising campaigns also serve this function, and at the same time flatter advertisers. We see this trend in coverage of Super Bowl advertising. Newspaper coverage of Super Bowl commercials increased significantly from the mid-1980s to the late-1990s (McAllister, 1999). The day after the Super Bowl, it is typical for the morning news programs of ABC, CBS, CNN and NBC to review the best and worst Super Bowl commercials in lengthy segments. The week before the 2001 Super Bowl, CNN interviewed Barbara

Lippert from the trade journal *Adweek* about the upcoming ads, CBS's *The Early Show* interviewed the actors on the Budweiser "Whassup?" commercials, and ABC's *20/20* aired a profile of TV commercial director Joe Pytka. Many commercials receive free airtime when they are excerpted during these stories, and such coverage treats advertising more as entertainment discourse rather than product-information discourse. Similarly, the news loves to cover especially shocking or provocative campaigns, such as the controversial advertising of Benetton (Falk, 1997; Tinic, 1997) and Calvin Klein (Tucker, 1998), often showing the ads during these news reports.

Perhaps more influential are the promotional pressures from corporate ties that weigh upon news organizations. In the US, the elimination in 1995 of the Financial Interest and Syndication Rules encouraged the purchasing of television networks by movie studios (Walker & Ferguson, 1998), further advancing a trend in media concentration that had been evident at least since the 1980s. With such corporate ownership, pressure may also be placed on news divisions to fit in with the larger entertainment imperative of media corporations. Journalists in such organizations are concerned about news divisions being subordinate to the larger entertainment enterprise when mergers occur between news organizations and entertainment corporations (Turow, 1994). Indeed, the changing corporate name of what was once the Time empire illustrates this potential subordination. The early name, Time, Inc., symbolized the primacy of the news function; the corporation shared the same name with the flagship division, the journalistic *Time* magazine. After the 1989 merger with Warner Communications Inc., however, *Time* had to share the corporate name with its larger entertainment sibling when Time Warner, Inc. was formed. News was symbolically devalued even more in 2001 when the corporation once again changed its name to AOL-Time Warner, Inc., as the corporation added a huge Internet component. The place of news in the organization, like the placement of *Time* in the name, has slipped in stature in the organization, going from the primary function to just being one more cog in a larger entertainment machine. Few would argue now that *Time* magazine is the most visible or powerful division in AOL-Time Warner.

Concerns about the subordination of news in entertainment-driven media corporations are reasonable given the use of news outlets to promote corporate product. "Plugola" on television news, where news stories become publicity-based coverage of corporate holdings, are routinely found on certain news outlets, especially morning news programs, local news and prime-time news. Given the added pressure to create ratings friendly journalism – which includes coverage of entertainment products – the synergistic pressure to promote is difficult to resist. The last episode of *Seinfeld* in 1998, for example, was not only heavily publicized in fawning coverage by NBC and NBC owned and operated stations, but also by news organizations that benefited from *Seinfeld*'s syndication deals, such as CNN and CBS (McAllister, 2002). Such heavy coverage pushes other, more newsworthy topics, off the news agenda. In addition, often the promotional function of such stories is hidden from viewers. Many of these outlets do not have policies about disclosing the corporate ties of news topics for "plugola" stories (Seitz, 2000).

Such is the modern journalistic context in which *Survivor* maneuvered. But *Survivor* also found itself in a genre – reality-based programming – that was especially product friendly and at a network – CBS – that was in need of both advertiser-friendly demographics and a higher rated morning news program. The next section explores these factors.

Reality-based Programming and Commercial Influence

Reality-based programs such as *Survivor* and *Temptation Island* are attractive to the broadcast networks for several reasons. Such programming, for example, is often cheap to produce, or at least cheaper to produce when compared to star-oriented sitcoms and evening melodramas (Flint, 2001). In addition, such programs stand out as appearing more spontaneous and unplanned than other highly scripted prime-time fare. Of course, the "spontaneity" of reality based programs (much like the spontaneity of news programming) is to a large extent manufactured with careful planning in pre-production (through the hand-picked selection of telegenic participants), production (through the artificial premise of the programs and built-in plot complications like *Survivor*'s Immunity Challenges) and post-production (through heavy editing). Nevertheless, the "reality" part of reality-based creates an image of an "anything can happen" environment. And much of the "anything" often involves the attention-grabbing power of sexual innuendo (such as in Fox's hyper-hormoned *Temptation Island*) and over-the-top gross outs (like NBC's *Fear Factor*) which are particularly enticing to young, advertising-friendly audiences. *Survivor*, with its flirtatious, barely clothed attractive castaways and bug/rat-eating challenges, provides both.

Reality-based programs offer advertising and promotional advantages as well. The genre is receptive to product placement, a topic much discussed in the critical scholarly literature (Andersen, 1995; Fuller, 1997; Miller, 1990; Wasko, 1994). Product placement may not only add to the financial bottom line of a movie or television program, but may also enhance the promotional punch of the movie/show when product placers create their own advertisements touting the connection (Avery & Ferraro, 2000; McAllister, 2000). Although certainly not unheard of on television in the 1980s and 1990s, product placement was normally a domain of film more than television because of regulatory rules with broadcasting and the pressures of juggling the demands of competing brands (Andersen, 1995, p. 45).

One study found that there was a higher proportion of product placement in genres like documentaries and prime-time news magazines than there were in highly scripted genres like sitcoms (Avery & Ferraro, 2000). As *Advertising Age* columnist Bob Garfield pointed out in an April 3, 2001 appearance on ABC's

Good Morning America, programs with a strong promise of becoming syndicated are not attractive for product placement since the in-program advertisement may alienate future advertisers. Because reality-based shows do not usually have much of a future in syndication as repeat airings blunt their image of spontaneity, product placement is more likely in the genre. Also, since the creation of a more "real" atmosphere is often used as a justification for product placement (Miller, 1990), program executives may feel audiences will accept embedded products in reality-based programs more than in other types of programs. The 2001–2002 television season saw other product-friendly programs besides *Survivor*. Other tie-ins include Taco Bell in the Fox program *Murder in Small Town X* and Ford in the WB's *No Boundaries* (the title itself is a Ford slogan). In fact, the producer of *No Boundaries* has implied that the WB was lukewarm about picking up the program until a product placement deal was secured with Ford (Poniewozik, 2001).

There is one last promotional advantage to reality-based programs. Given the heightened image of realism and spontaneity, it may be easier to justify using news programs to promote such shows than to justify the promotion of sit-coms. After all, since the programs are "real," the events that take place in the program may be reported as news – at least marginally more than plot complications such as Rachel's pregnancy on *Friends*. It is with these promotional pressures in mind that we move to the next section: looking at the extensive coverage of *Survivor* on CBS's *The Early Show*.

Survivor as News Plugola

Morning network news shows in the US have always been a mix of news and entertainment. One *Today Show* broadcast in the 1950s featured both mathematician Norbert Wiener and ballplayer Mickey Mantle, and the national morning news format itself was only truly established as a popular one with the regular appearance of a chimpanzee, J. Fred Muggs, on NBC's program (Metz, 1977). However, all three major morning TV news programs are produced by the networks' news divisions, not the entertainment divisions. Traditionally, CBS's morning news was the most news oriented of the three. It comes out of the news division with the most storied history, and was the first all-news morning program (Gates, 1978, p. 104). One illustrative incident involving the clash of news values and entertainment pressures occurred when the executive producer of the program in the early 1980s, George Merlis, butted heads with other network personnel over his decision to not extensively cover the final episode of M*A*S*H on the then titled *CBS Morning News* (Boyer, 1988, p. 216).

Things have changed since then. As will be seen, *The Early Show* reached an absurdist level in its very heavy coverage of its sibling program *Survivor*. What has facilitated this change? Besides the general pressures on news to entertain and promote that were discussed in the previous section, CBS had additional contextual factors which may have encouraged the television network to plug hard the reality-based show. *Survivor*, for example, debuted in the summer of 2000. This timing is significant. Throughout the 1990s, summer was a time when the erosion of the ratings of the US broadcast networks accelerated because of new programming shown by cable networks and the reruns aired by the broadcast networks (Kim, 1999). The successful airing of original programming by the broadcast networks was seen as a way to slow down or even reverse the losses to their cable competitors. In addition, CBS's ratings traditionally have been skewed toward older groups than is ideally desired by advertisers. The network saw the reality program as a way to attract younger viewers before the fall TV season (Schneider & Adalian, 2000). The cultivation of *Survivor* and other reality based programming – less scripted and acted than other typical prime-time entertainment – was also beneficial to CBS as insurance in case of a writers' and actors' strike in Hollywood in Summer 2001 (Adalian & Schneider, 2001). Finally, the "reality-based" element of *Survivor* did give it a bit more rationale to be covered more like a sports story than a highly scripted weekly sitcom or drama would reasonably allow, at least at that time. Other factors had less to do with the importance of the prime time schedule, and more to do with the situation involving CBS's morning news program, *The Early Show*. Revamped in 1999 at a cost of $30 million with a new name and new hosts – including highly paid Bryant Gumbel, the former NBC *Today Show* host known for tough interviewing – *The Early Show* was at first a ratings disappointment. Viewership was so poor that some local affiliates were considering preempting at least part of the network program for local news (Trigoboff, 2000).

These factors combined to turn *The Early Show* into a promotional flack for *Survivor*. Table 10.1 compares the coverage of the first US version of *Survivor* by the news divisions of ABC, CBS and NBC. One could argue that the premise and popularity of *Survivor* had some legitimate news value. In fact, *Survivor I* was covered fairly extensively by the two major broadcast news competitors of CBS. As table 10.1 shows, ABC devoted 21 news stories to *Survivor*, while NBC aired 15. The program was also covered by major news outlets like the *New York Times* and *Time* magazine. A key issue, though, is the boundary between adequate coverage and overkill/public relations flack coverage. Table 10.1 illustrates that the boundary may have been crossed, as CBS devoted five times as many stories to the program as the next nearest competitor, ABC.

CBS's coverage of *Survivor* began over four-and-a-half-months before the first episode of *Survivor* even aired, with *The Early Show* co-host Jane Clayson's interview of Executive Producer Mark Burnett on January 10, 2000. Five stories on CBS were about *Survivor* – all on the morning news – before the program even debuted. Four of these stories were broadcast the week before the first episode on May 31, including one that morning. And as the time toward the debut approached, the hyperbole of the news stories increased. The first story on January 10 was introduced with a simple description as Clayson noted, in an allusion to ABC's then-hot *Who Wants to be a Millionaire?*, "Being stranded on a

Table 10.1 Number of news stories devoted to *Survivor* on US national broadcast TV networks, January 1, 2000 to August 24, 2000

Network	Morning		Evening News		Prime Time		Totals
	Pre	Post	Pre	Post	Pre	Post	
ABC	16	4	1	0	0	0	21
NBC	10	3	1	0	1	0	15
CBS	94	11	1	1	1	0	108

Note: Stories were collected from the database Lexis/Nexis. A story was only counted once in a newscast, even if it might have been repeated later in that same newscast. If the same story appeared in a different newscast on the same station later that day, however, it was counted again. "Co-op" stories during the morning news programs that are made available to local affiliates if that affiliate shows no local news break, a rarity in most markets, were also excluded. Although brief "teaser" segments that preview upcoming news stories (themselves a kind of plugola) are listed by Lexis/Nexis, these segments were not included in the count unless the anchors/reporters commented at length on the forthcoming story. Late night news was also excluded. "Pre" is the number of news stories aired previous to the August 23, 2000 final episode; "Post" is the number of news stories aired on August 24, 2000, after the episode aired.

desert island would have been the only way you could have missed the network game show craze sweeping the nation. Of course, that would also make you the perfect contestant on the newest show to enter the fray." On May 27, Saturday host Russ Mitchell begins a story on the show by citing another source with "The *New York Daily News* calls it the wildest TV show in history." On May 30, Clayson labels the program as "eagerly anticipated" and on May 31 begins the story with "Tonight, the long-awaited *Survivor* series kicks off here on CBS, giving us all a front-row seat to a unique television event . . ."

At this point, CBS is using *The Early Show* to plug *Survivor*. However, after the show debuts and becomes a ratings hit, the relationship between the two programs begin to benefit the morning news show more than the other way around, with *Survivor* being used as a ratings hook for *The Early Show*. Bryant Gumbel, the co-host with the more "hard news" journalistic reputation, becomes more actively involved with *Survivor* stories on June 7. Contestants kicked off the island were interviewed in multiple segments the following morning. The ubiquitous "round table" discussions are introduced the morning after the first episode, with minor celebrities and authors with their own books to tout appearing on the program to dissect the previous night's episode. Tie-in stories focused on such topics as a Big Apple *Survivor* contest, the benefits of such *Survivor* activities as using mud as a skin moisturizer and eating insects for protein, and an interview with an astrologer who tries to predict future developments based upon the contestants' star signs.

CBS News went on to promote the second *Survivor* series even more heavily than the first installment. Now *Survivor* was a proven ratings winner and

Table 10.2 Number of news stories devoted to *Survivor II: Australian Outback* on US national broadcast TV networks, January 1, 2001 to May 4, 2001

Network	Morning		Evening News		Prime Time		Totals
	Pre	Post	Pre	Post	Pre	Post	
ABC	7	0	1	0	0	0	8
NBC	12	4	0	0	0	0	16
CBS	157	12	0	0	0	0	169

Note: Stories were collected from the database Lexis/Nexis. A story was only counted once in a newscast, even if it might have been repeated later in that same newscast. If the same story appeared in a different newscast on the same station later that day, however, it was counted again. "Co-op" stories during the morning news programs that are made available to local affiliates if that affiliate shows no local news break, a rarity in most markets, were also excluded. Although brief "teaser" segments that preview upcoming news stories (themselves a kind of plugola) are listed by Lexis/Nexis, these segments were not included in the count unless the anchors/reporters commented at length on the forthcoming story. Late night news was also excluded. "Pre" is the number of news stories aired previous to the May 3, 2001 final episode; "Post" is the number of news stories aired on May 4, 2001, after the episode aired.

advertisers were spending three times as much to sponsor this version as the previous – as much as $12.5 million to be a sponsor compared to the earlier $4 million (Flint, 2001). Table 10.2 shows increased coverage by CBS for the second *Survivor* compared to the first during a shorter time frame (four months compared to *Survivor I*'s eight months). As this table shows, CBS devoted a whopping 169 news stories to *Survivor*, all airing on *The Early Show*.[1] This is over ten times the amount of coverage that the closest competitor, NBC, devoted to it. While CBS aired 61 more *Survivor* stories for the Australian series versus the Borneo series, ABC decreased its coverage by 13 stories (NBC stayed about the same).[2] As with the first installment, coverage became heavier as the season finale approached. Of the 23 days that *The Early Show* broadcast in April 2001 (minus Sundays), for example, viewers saw *Survivor* stories on 20 of these days. As with the Borneo version, *The Early Show* devoted virtually all of its two hours – 12 segments – to the finale and to the post-*Survivor* prime time special that was hosted by, appropriately enough, Bryant Gumbel.

From a more qualitative point of view, *The Early Show* did more than just plug *Survivor*; it was overwhelmed by *Survivor*. The reality-based show symbolically co-opted *The Early Show* and any journalistic credibility that the show may have had in both the 2000 and early 2001 versions. The program gave itself up without a touch of irony, turning a program produced by the News Division of CBS into a virtual two-hour promotional spot in many cases. This promotional ethos is illustrated in many ways.

The graphics and audio of *The Early Show* would often feature *Survivor* iconography. Wednesdays became labeled by the co-hosts as "*Survivor* Wednesdays," featuring previews of that night's episode. The following post-episode installment was "*Survivor* Thursdays," with the panels and interviews. The graphics and music of *Survivor* were integrated into the graphics and music of *The Early Show*, often signaling when a *Survivor*-oriented segment was about to air.

Nor were the *Survivor*-segments relegated to "soft-news" times, such as during the second hour or only after all hard news had been exhausted. On "*Survivor* Thursdays," in the opening recap of major stories, the latest *Survivor* happenings would be equated with world events. A typical teaser segment from March 9, 2001 begins with co-hosts Gumbel and Clayson summarizing the major news items of the day:

> *Gumbel*:   Memorials are planned for the weekend for the victims of the Santana school shooting.
> *Clayson*:   The House gives President Bush his first legislative victory, approving the heart of his tax cut.
> *Clayson*:   And *Survivor*'s new Barramundi tribe claims its first victim.

In this opening, then, reality-based game show contestants become "victims" who are linguistically equated with murdered school children. For 16 weeks in 2000 and 2001, *Survivor* was always the second or third most important news story on Thursday mornings for CBS.

Immediately after these opening teasers, but before going to the news updates, the two co-hosts, whose reporting credentials are stressed on the CBS News website, would chat about the latest episode in the sign-on and sign-off segments. Such chats, in what could be termed "fan talk," often would discuss developments on the show with the gravity of political coups. One example, which aired August 3, 2000 from two locations (the Republican National Convention in Philadelphia and their studios in New York), mixed *Survivor* and politics:

> *Gumbel*:   And good morning. Welcome to *The Early Show* on this Thursday morning. It may be a split program, but it's still *Survivor* Thursday here in New York. Jane Clayson's in Philly. Were you as shocked as I was that Gervase is out?
> *Clayson*:   I was – I was completely shocked, Bryant.
> *Gumbel*:   I was stunned.
> *Clayson*:   The moment that Richard got immunity, we were having a little party in my room, the room exploded because everybody knew, and then when Gervase got voted out, they almost voted us out of the hotel, we were so loud.
> *Gumbel*:   You know, he was – he was below the radar screen with me. I thought for sure that it was Sean's turn or maybe Susan or Kelly, depending on which way it broke. That Gervase wound up getting four, maybe five votes – we don't know – shocked me.
> *Clayson*:   Well, so many people thought that Gervase would take it all, and the fact that he was voted out last night, it – people here can't believe it. Unbelievable.
> *Gumbel*:   A stunner, a stunner.

Clayson: Yeah. It really is.

Gumbel: We're going to be talking with Gervase in our second hour, Jane, as you know.

Clayson: At 8:15, right, Bry?

Gumbel: Yeah.

Clayson: It also turns out this morning that one of the biggest *Survivor* fans at the convention is a member of the Bush family. Marvin Bush, George W.'s brother, will join us in just a few moments.

"What about Gervase?" Jane Clayson later asked Mr. Bush in the above-mentioned interview.

A new wrinkle was added in the plugola for *Survivor II*: the use of former *Survivor* contestants as commentators, guest co-hosts, and even reporters for *The Early Show*. It may be natural that ex-*Survivors* would appear on the Thursday Round Table discussions. But when acting as reporters, these faux-journalists would report on non-*Survivor* stories. For example, on the day after the 2001 Super Bowl, CBS aired a graphic-labeled "HealthWatch" story, meant to explain a recent medical development or healthful practice. Clayson introduces the story with

> Six percent of American workers are expected to call in sick today, a day in which sales of antacids are expected to be 26 percent above normal. If you think all that has anything to do with all the partying that people did on Super Bowl Sunday, you would be right. Here in Tampa the parties were going all weekend and our special *Survivor* correspondent Jenna Lewis was among the revelers.

Lewis then appears in the video package where she hops from party to party. Such is the nature of "Health Reports" in the post-*Survivor* era: a report on Super Bowl parties using the reporting skills of a former game show contestant. Additional stories in this category include an earlier Lewis piece about the People's Choice awards where she again reported on the party scene and designer dresses (January 8), Gervase Peterson reporting on Media Day at the Super Bowl (January 26), and Jeff Varner at the National Cheer and Dance Championships (April 12). Other *Survivor* celebrities were used as authoritative sources on non-*Survivor* stories, such as host Jeff Probst being interviewed about the Puppy Chow mobile dog clinic (April 17) and Alicia Calaway, described as "the buffest babe in the Outback" by Clayson, who talked about personal training (April 19) and plugged her then-upcoming stories in the magazines *Muscle and Fitness* and *Sports Illustrated for Women*. And on May 2 – in a move that symbolized the subordination of journalism to promotion – Richard Hatch, the winner of *Survivor I*, sat at the anchor desk and co-hosted *The Early Show*, replacing Bryant Gumbel who was preparing for the prime-time special.

As implied above, like *Survivor* itself, *Survivor* news stories are very commodity friendly. Serving as "multi-leveled commercials" that tout two products in one promotional space (McAllister, 1996, p. 158), *Survivor* stories would not only plug the prime-time program, but often would also plug other products or media outlets. It was mentioned earlier that panelists on the Friday morning Round Tables would often have something to promote themselves, such as books or websites that would be illustrated with a graphic while they were introduced. In an especially commodified installment on January 29, 2001 that illustrates the commercial essence of these segments, one of the panelists was Fred Thomas, described as "one of the 'Whassup?'" guys from the much-aired Budweiser commercials. Similarly, one brief story (May 1) discussed *Survivor* finalists appearing on milk-mustache ads.

Often multi-leveled promotional stories about *Survivor* would mention or show the sponsors of that program, as in the Aztek example discussed at the beginning of this essay. When asked if she wore her own designs during the contest, *Survivor*-participant and shoe-designer Elisabeth Filarski observed that "I did not wear my own design in the outback. We wore Reeboks in the outback. Very cool and very functional." During the coverage of *Survivor II*, Doritos was mentioned in at least six different segments (on February 15, February 16 (three stories), March 15 and May 4), and a clip of the *Survivor* participants celebrating over a Doritos offering was shown at least twice. An especially Doritos-friendly exchange took place on February 16, when former contestant Mitchell Olson was interviewed by Jane Clayson and substitute co-anchor John Roberts:

Olson: At that point, I was so hungry and so tired, really, the million dollars didn't mean anything to me. I'm not kidding.
Roberts: You would have – you would have taken it and blown it all on a bag of Doritos, right?
Olson: Right. Exactly.
Clayson: It was a bag of Doritos, right? B – Doritos and Coke?
Olson: Doritos and Coke right away, and I remember saying to the [CBS-hired] psychiatrist, I was like, "This means more to me than being out there." That's the first thing I said to her, and it really did.
Roberts: Interesting.
Clayson: About five minutes after you made those final comments – Right? – you were chowing down.
Olson: Right. A – absolutely.
Roberts: I wonder where in the DSM4 scale that one lies? "The most important thing in my life right now is this bag of Doritos."

For the sponsors of *Survivor*, this becomes a "value-added" benefit of the sponsorship. Not only do they receive heavy commercial time during *Survivor*, sponsorship tags during the program ("Brought to you by . . ."), and product placement in *Survivor*, but, with *The Early Show*'s heavy coverage, they also often receive product placement in the news.

Some stories could be described as touting products that were part of the growing "*Survivor* Industry." Looking at *Survivor II*, stories were aired promoting *Survivor*-oriented websites (January 26, featuring an interview with a college student who "dropped out of college to run a site called SurvivorFire.com"), *Survivor*-themed vacations (March 29) and training programs for potential *Survivor* contestants (April 26). One story not only promoted *Survivor* but also plugged into CBS's synergistic corporate environment. The music group Destiny's Child was interviewed on May 1 (the week of the *Survivor II* finale) by weather anchor Mark McEwen. The topic of the interview was their new single and music video, entitled "Survivor." McEwen begins the interview by showing the group's CD and saying "Hot little record. Title track is already the number one song on the radio. The video, if you haven't seen it, you haven't been watching. It's every-where as well." By "everywhere," McEwen meant MTV and VH-1, two sibling organizations of Viacom, the company that also owns CBS. He also meant CBS, because scenes of the music video were integrated into CBS promotions for *Survivor* aired during that week.

Discussion and Conclusion

Survivor III: Africa debuted on October 11, 2001, exactly one month after the events of September 11 in New York, Washington, DC and Pennsylvania. Of course this event dominated US and world news and reappropriated, for a time at least, the cultural connotations of the word "survivor." Logical questions to ask are, did September 11 and the subsequent US invasion of Afghanistan recontextualize the program and the reality-based genre for viewers, and did these events in turn recontextualize journalists' roles – specifically, CBS News – in a complicated world?

Some commentators wondered if Americans could no longer stomach reality-based programs given the intensity of September 11 and the accompanying video footage (Chunovic, 2001). However, although other reality-based programs failed to perform, in terms of the popularity of *Survivor III*, the ratings did indeed decrease from the previous two versions, but the program was still considered a solid performer with future versions planned (Friedman, 2001).

Similarly, CBS's *The Early Show* still promoted *Survivor III*, but not to nearly the extent of the Borneo and Australia installments. Coverage took on a more somber tone, especially at first, but nevertheless maintained its promo-tional ethos. In a preview airing September 24, weather anchor Mark McEwen introduced the feature with "While the show has certainly taken on a very different tone in the scheme of things, millions are sure not only to appreciate the entertainment, but the distraction as well." Gone were the panel Round Tables, most of the ancillary tie-in stories and the "fan talk," but multiple interviews with the cast-off participants remained. The January 11 news program – exactly four months after September 11 and the day after the final episode of *Survivor III* – was, like the old days, dominated by stories and interviews about the last remaining *Survivor*. Given the current state of corporate media and their willingness to use the news (as well as other genres of programming) to promote themselves and their advertisers, it is not much of a stretch to argue that the media will have a short memory about the sober restraint placed on promotional efforts encouraged by September 11.

The events in Afghanistan can help us to understand the implications of *Survivor* in other ways. It was earlier argued that two ideal functions of journalism in a democracy are to create access to diverse and relevant news. What are the implications of *Survivor* coverage for these criteria? Clearly, *Survivor* was a dominant news topic on CBS during the run of the first two versions; perhaps, in fact, it was *the* dominant news topic for the network during *Survivor II*'s run. Lexis/Nexis, the main database used for this essay to calculate the number of *Survivor* stories on *The Early Show*, does not indicate the time length of stories. However, based upon selected taped episodes and the transcripts of all stories, one may conservatively estimate that, for *Survivor II*, CBS News devoted over six-and-a-half *hours* to covering that one television series.

Perhaps, though, such promotional activity is harmless. Why should we care that a morning news program is used as a flack for an entertainment show? One reason we should care is that other possible stories may not be covered – or at least not covered as extensively as they should be – because of the attention devoted to *Survivor*. Thus, the large amount of coverage about this TV show should be placed into the context of other, non-self-interested and more politically or socially significant stories. How does *Survivor* compare to coverage of other important events, say events in pre-September 11 Afghanistan? Taking the same four-month period as *Survivor II* (January 1, 2001 to May 4, 2001), and counting all stories on the Evening News, *The Early Show*, and prime-time news magazines, CBS News aired a total of 12 stories about Afghanistan.[3] These stories were a combined 7 minutes, 40 seconds of airtime, or half the time that was devoted to interviewing one contestant on the one April 27 installment of *The Early Show* discussed at the beginning of this essay. Ten of these Afghanistan stories were 30 seconds or less. Critics have argued that over the last decades the television networks have seriously decreased the amount of international news coverage and have increased coverage of entertainment and celebrity (Alger, 1998; Cohen, 1997; McChesney, 1999). In the *Survivor*-versus-Afghanistan comparison, there may be dire consequences. Without reasonable coverage of Afghanistan and the immediate surrounding regions, US citizens may not have had the proper historical, social and cultural context to understand the events of September 11 and US action subsequent to these events.

Besides covering many different important topics, news also must be relevant, encouraging democratic participation and active engagement in social decisions. News should facilitate how to become involved in our communities and how to maximize our voices to make progressive social change. But stories about TV programs such as *Survivor* do not encourage such participation. Rather, the only things they encourage are the watching of television and the purchasing of sponsors' products. With their promotion and celebration of a popular television program, these stories are anti-democratic, encouraging viewers to speculate more on who is going to be voted off the island next, rather than how to become involved in local politics or civic organizations.

Fortunately, a few critics in the popular, trade and political media have not let the negative implications of CBS's *Survivor* plugola go unnoticed (Miller, 2002; Rosenberg, 2001), including the former president of NBC news asking in a column for the *Columbia Journalism Review*, "Can CBS News Survive *Survivor*?" (Grossman, 2000). Other works, focusing on changing the corporate and promotional status quo – including revitalizing the public service mission of journalism – are essentially primers designed to help citizens as well as media activists resist and critique the power of large corporate media and intrusive advertising (Coco, 1996; Jacobson & Mazur, 1995; Klein, 1999; Lasn, 1999; McChesney & Nichols, 2002). By developing alternative media outlets, highlighting resistant practices of the consumer/citizen and recognizing the influential force that grassroots organizing and lobbying may have, such engaged scholarship argues that it is imperative and possible to become agents of change for – and not just survivors of – commercial culture.

Notes

1 Thirty-three of CBS's stories were "*Survivor* Marketwatch" stories, about a financial investment contest using a *Survivor* label. Many of these stories mentioned *Survivor* and/or showed clips from *Survivor*. Even if these stories were removed, however, coverage still significantly increased in the Australian version compared to the Borneo version.
2 NBC's coverage of *Survivor II* also was connected to plugola. *Survivor II* was scheduled against NBC powerhouse *Friends*, and NBC's *The Today Show* exploited this fact by discussing *Friends* in six of its 16 *Survivor* stories. Tellingly, one *Survivor* story that both NBC and ABC covered but that CBS did not cover (despite the latter's 169 *Survivor*-oriented segments) was a story critical of the program: a lawsuit filed by former contestant Stacey Stillman arguing that contestants' voting was influenced by the producer of the program.
3 Ten of the 12 CBS news stories about Afghanistan focused on the destruction of the giant Buddha statues by the Taliban in March, a story that had a strong visual component. Only one of these stories was longer than one minute.

References

Adalian, J. and Schneider, M. (2001). "Survivor" deal has eye toward strike. *Variety*, January 15, 42.

Alger, D. (1998). *Megamedia: How giant corporations dominate mass media, distort competition, and endanger democracy*. Lanham, MD: Rowman & Littlefield.

Andersen, R. (1995). *Consumer Culture and TV Programming*. Boulder, CO: Westview Press.

Avery, R. J. and Ferraro, R. (2000). Verisimilitude or advertising?: Brand appearances on prime-time television. *Journal of Consumer Affairs*, 34(2), 217–44.

Bagdikian, B. (2000). *The Media Monopoly* (6th edn.). Boston: Beacon Press.

Baker, C. E. (1994). *Advertising and a Democratic Press*. Princeton, NJ: Princeton University Press.

Barnouw, E. (1978). *The Sponsor: Notes on a modern potentate*. New York: Oxford University Press.

Bernstein, P. (2001). Sponsor's message is medium. *Variety*, April 2, 13.

Boyer, P. J. (1988). *Who Killed CBS?: The undoing of America's number one news network*. New York: Random House.

Carter, B. (2001). New reality show planning to put ads between the ads. *The New York Times*, April 30, A1–17.

Chunovic, L. (2001). Attack on US may soften TV. *Electronic Media*, September 24, 7.

Coco, L. (ed.) (1996). *Children First!: A parent's guide to fighting corporate predators*. Washington, DC: Corporate Accountability Research Group.

Cohen, R. M. (1997). The corporate takeover of news: Blunting the sword. In E. Barnouw, P. Aufderheide, R. M. Cohen, T. Frank, T. Gitlin, D. Lieberman, M. C. Miller, G. Roberts, and T. Schatz, *Conglomerates and the Media*. New York; The New Press, pp. 31–60.

Croteau, D. and Hoynes, W. (2001). *The Business of Media: Corporate media and the public interest*. Thousand Oaks, CA: Pine Forge Press.

Curran, J. (1991). Mass media and democracy: A reappraisal. In J. Curran and M. Gurevitch (eds.), *Mass Media in Society*. New York: Routledge, pp. 82–117.

Falk, P. (1997). The Benetton-Toscani effect: Testing the limits of conventional advertising. In M. Nava, A. Blake, I. MacRury, and B. Richards (eds.), *Buy this Book: Studies in advertising and consumption*. New York: Routledge, pp. 64–86.

Flint, J. (2001). Sponsors get a role in CBS reality show. *The Wall Street Journal*, January 13, B16.

Friedman, W. (2001). Few "Survivors" as reality bites. *Advertising Age*, October 22, 61.

Fuller, L. K. (1997). We can't duck the issue: Imbedded advertising in motion pictures. In K. T. Frith (ed.), *Undressing the Ad: Reading culture in advertising*. New York: Peter Lang, pp. 109–29.

Gates, G. P. (1978). *Air Time: The inside story of CBS News*. New York: Harper & Row.

Grossman, L. (2000). Shilling for prime time: Can CBS News survive *Survivor? Columbia Journalism Review*, September, 70.

Hickey, M. (1998). Money lust: How pressure for profit is perverting journalism. *Columbia Journalism Review*, July/August, 28–36.

Jacobson, N. F. and Mazur, L. A. (1995). *Marketing Madness: A survival guide for a consumer society*. Boulder, CO: Westview Press.

Kim, H. (1999). Ratings show cable's hot summer. *Multichannel News*, September 6, 3.

Klein, N. (1999). *No Logo: Taking aim at the brand bullies*. New York: Picador.

Lasn, K. (1999). *Culture Jam: The uncooling of America*. New York: Eagle Brook.

Lawson, L. (1988). Advertisements masquerading as news in turn-of-the-century American periodicals. *American Journalism*, 5(2), 81–96.

McAllister, M. P. (1996). *The Commercialization of American Culture: New advertising, control and democracy*. Thousand Oaks, CA: Sage.

McAllister, M. P. (1999). Super Bowl advertising as commercial celebration. *The Communication Review*, 3(4), 403–28.

McAllister, M. P. (2000). From flick to flack: The increased emphasis on marketing by media entertainment corporations. In R. Anderson and L. A. Strate (eds.), *Critical Studies in Media Commercialism*. New York: Oxford University Press, pp. 101–22.

McAllister, M. P. (2002). Television news plugola and the last episode of *Seinfeld*. *Journal of Communication*, 42(3), 383–401.

McChesney, R. W. (1993). *Telecommunications, Mass Media, and Democracy*. New York: Oxford University Press.

McChesney, R. W. (1999). *Rich Media, Poor Democracy: Communication politics in dubious times*. Urbana: University of Illinois Press.

McChesney, R. W. and Nichols, J. (2002). The making of a movement: Getting serious about media reform. *The Nation*, January 7/14, pp. 11, 13, 16, 17.

Metz, R. (1977). *The Today Show*. Chicago: Playboy Press.

Miller, M. C. (1990). End of story. In M. C. Miller (ed.), *Seeing Through Movies*. New York: Pantheon, pp. 186–246.

Miller, M. C. (2002). What's wrong with this picture? *The Nation*, January 7/14, pp. 18–20, 22.

Poniewozik, J. (2001). This plug's for you. *Time*, June 18, 76.

Rosenberg, H. (2001). CBS only has eyes for "Survivor." *The Los Angeles Times*, February 12, F1.

Schneider, M. and Adalian, J. (2000). "Survivor" changes webs' reality. *Variety*, June 12, 9.

Seitz, M. Z. (2000). Strange bedfellows: Journalism in the shadow of synergy. *The Newark Star-Ledger*, November 12, A1.

Tinic, S. A. (1997). United Colors and untied meanings: Benetton and the commodification of social issues. *Journal of Communication*, 47(3), 3–25.

Trigoboff, D. (2000). Affils mull a.m. switch. *Broadcasting and Cable*, April 10, 6.

Tucker, L. R. (1998). The framing of Calvin Klein: A frame analysis of media discourse about the August 1995 Calvin Klein jeans advertising controversy. *Critical Studies in Mass Communication*, 15(2), 141–57.

Turow, J. (1994). Hidden conflicts and journalistic norms: The case of self-coverage. *Journal of Communication*, 44(2), 29–46.

Walker, J. and Ferguson, D. (1998). *The Broadcast Television Industry*. Boston: Allen & Bacon.

Wasko, J. (1994). *Hollywood in the Information Age: Beyond the silver screen*. Austin: University of Texas Press.

CHAPTER ELEVEN

Constructing Youth
Media, Youth, and the Politics of Representation

Sharon R. Mazzarella

> Youth have once again become the object of public analysis. Headlines proliferate like dispatches from a combat zone, frequently coupling youth and violence in the interests of promoting a new kind of commonsense relationship.
>
> Henry Giroux (1996, p. 27)

Historically within the field of media studies there have been two primary and often contradictory strains of scholarship on youth. The first, quantitative studies of the effects of media on youth have been the standard in the United States since the middle of the twentieth century. Grounded in the theories and methods of social psychology, and growing out of public concern about media, such studies have sought to understand the influence the media have on young people. In contrast, youth scholarship in the cultural studies tradition, as defined first by the work of scholars at the Centre for Contemporary Cultural Studies in Great Britain and later in the United States, has sought primarily to understand the ways in which youth incorporate mass culture into their lives and the ways in which they create their own culture. Although often contradictory, both of these traditions are audience-centered – i.e. asking questions either about how the audience is affected by media or what the audience does with media. In contrast, a more recent and growing strain of inquiry within media studies is to examine media constructions and representations of youth. It is this focus on "representational politics" (Giroux, 1998, p. 28) as exemplified in the work of such scholars as Henry Jenkins, Henry Giroux, Mike Males, Larry Grossberg, Donna Gaines, and others with which this essay, and my own scholarship, is concerned. This essay examines the way in which "youth" is constructed in our culture, focusing specifically on the media's role in this process. Following Joe Austin and Michael Nevin Willard's (1998) lead, "youth" in this essay refers to young people roughly between the ages of twelve to twenty-four. Although I predominantly focus on this age group, often I will discuss children of a younger age. This is not to imply that children and "youth" are one and the same, but rather is an acknowledgment that, at times, the issues related to their mediated representations do overlap.

Youth as a Construct

> Youth cannot be represented, for it is an identity largely defined by and for the adults who, in a variety of ways, invest in it and use it to locate themselves.
>
> Larry Grossberg (1994, p. 26)

In 1985 Ellen Wartella and Byron Reeves conducted an exhaustive literature review of the research done on children and media during the first half of the twentieth century. They found that the introduction into US American society of each of the major electronic technologies of film, radio, and television was accompanied by considerable public discussion and debate over their perceived impact on audiences, in particular youth. Springhall (1998) has shown this to have been the case in Great Britain as well. These debates, according to Wartella and Reeves, subsequently influenced the research agenda, thereby defining the dominant paradigm of studies of youth and media in the US as "effects" studies. The arguments and debates identified by Wartella and Reeves recurred throughout the twentieth century, and indeed, continue today. The same concerns we hear now about gangsta rap (see, for example, Lipsitz, 1998), Goth, the Internet and videogame violence (see, for example Jenkins, 1999) were expressed in the 1920s about movies, in the 1930s about radio, in the 1940s and 1950s about comic books, in the 1950s about rock 'n' roll and television, and so on. The recurrence of these debates is directly linked with the way in which society at a given time defines youth and constitutes what James Gilbert calls an "episodic notion" (1986, p. 4). For example, Wartella and Mazzarella (1990) point out that many of the concerns expressed about children and television during the late twentieth century were reminiscent of concerns expressed in the 1920s about college students – the first youth culture. Drawing on the work of Paula Fass (1977), Wartella and Mazzarella (1990, pp. 178–9) report that:

> The moral panic [in the 1920s] arose out of the fact that adolescents were developing an autonomous peer-oriented leisure-time culture, a culture independent of adults, outside the home, unsupervised, and increasingly commercialized. Indeed, the late 1920s established a pattern of public concern about all children's use of media for leisure time that would continue in succeeding decades.

While not addressed in either the Wartella and Reeves or Wartella and Mazzarella studies, the press historically has played a significant role in both constructing youth and in fueling moral panics over youth. As defined by

Springhall, a moral panic occurs "when the official or press reaction to a deviant social or cultural phenomenon is 'out of all proportion' to the actual threat offered" (1998, pp. 4–5). While I disagree with Springhall's use of the word "deviant," preferring instead less judgmental words as "different," "new," or "unfamiliar," his point that adults' reaction is out of proportion is the key. In order to understand the press's role in perpetuating moral panics about youth, we first must understand the changing construction of childhood and adolescence that occurred during the late nineteenth and early twentieth centuries (see, for example Aries, 1962; Hawes & Hiner, 1985), a change that created a climate in which adults could easily lapse into moral panic about youth culture.

Quite simply, childhood and adolescence are socially constructed phenomena. The child, according to Lynn Spigel (1993, p. 259) is a "cultural construct, a pleasing image that adults need in order to sustain their own identities. Childhood is the difference against which adults define themselves" (p. 259). Giroux (1996, p. 10) advances this argument by noting that today "youth as a self and social construction has become indeterminant, alien, and sometimes hazardous to the public eye." How did we get to this point?

Prior to the late nineteenth and early twentieth centuries, children were not necessarily considered as a distinct social group, but rather as miniature adults who, in all but upper-class families, played specific and vital economic roles within the family structure. In most rural families, for example, boys learned their fathers' trades at a young age, and girls learned domesticity from their mothers. As a result, with the exception of bourgeois children, most children did not attend school beyond just a few years. With industrialization and urbanization, the structure of families began to change. They were no longer self-sufficient, and children ceased to fill the same economic role within families, leaving them with more time on their hands.

Deriving from these changes in the construction of childhood was a belief in the innocence and naivete of children. According to Spigel, since the beginning "of industrialization, children have been conceptualized as blank slates upon whom parents 'write' their culture" (1993, p. 261). As a result of this belief, the early years of the twentieth century witnessed the designation of children as a group meriting the attention and intervention of reformers and activists (Wartella & Mazzarella, 1990). Specifically, it was at this time that public education was institutionalized. In fact, gradually across the decades of the twentieth century, an increasing percentage of youth stayed in schools for longer and longer periods of time, a phenomenon that immersed them in a world dominated by peers and kept them further out of their parents' control. Moreover, children and adolescents (by this time also defined as a distinct group) became the focus of scientific study and inquiry. It was around this time that G. Stanley Hall (1904) founded the discipline of adolescent psychology, advancing his now-discredited belief that all adolescents go through a period of "storm and stress." Accompanying this inquiry were assorted pieces of federal legislation (e.g. child labor laws, mandatory schooling laws) designed to "protect" innocent children. Henry Giroux argues that this "myth of childhood innocence" (2000, p. 5) continues to this day to be at the heart of adult concerns about youth and mass culture.

A primary contributor to these moral panics over youth and youth culture was a shift over the course of the twentieth century in the leisure behaviors of society at large (Wartella & Mazzarella, 1990). Many of the early critiques of the new leisure centered on youth, and many of these focused on media such as motion pictures of which "children were early and heavy users" (Wartella & Mazzarella, 1990, p. 175). As Wartella and Mazzarella point out:

> during the twentieth century, independent, autonomous youth cultures developed around leisure activities, and . . . the mass media became the social catalysts promoting, sustaining, and commercializing the leisure of each succeeding youth culture. (p. 173)

Several major studies and reports (see, for example, Hurt, 1924; Walter, 1927) were issued in the mid-twentieth century, documenting that youth were spending their newfound leisure time in questionable and "unworthy" pursuits (i.e. hanging out with friends, movies, etc.). These reports called for the need to institutionalize leisure through such adult-sanctioned and supervised activities as scouting. Reminiscent of the mass culture debates of the mid-1800s, these studies, according to Wartella and Mazzarella (1990):

> articulate the Progressive era's concern about adolescent youth's leisure time. In general, young people of fourteen to eighteen were seen as having too much time simply to hang around with their peers, unsupervised, or to spend in commercial activities, like the movies, that were thought to have questionable moral standards. Child savers were concerned that such ill-spent leisure would lead to moral degeneration, particularly in the absence of control by family, church, and school. The reformers argued that unless young people occupied their leisure more constructively, leisure could become a hazard, breeding delinquency and crime outside the home. (p. 177)

In the midst of this leisure revolution and its attendant public outcry, a new youth culture was born. "By the 1940s, high school students as a group were labeled, identified, and the subject of popular attention and concern" (Wartella & Mazzarella, 1990, p. 181). The label "teenager" first appeared in a 1941 issue of the magazine *Popular Science* (Hine, 1999), and *Seventeen* magazine was founded in 1944 as one of many attempts to exploit and capitalize on the newly-emergent, postwar, middle-class youth culture and their vast disposable income (Palladino, 1996). According to Larry Grossberg (1994, p. 26) "the very existence of youth, at least in the twentieth century, is intimately tied to the media and vice versa: we might say that, perhaps more than any other social identity, youth always exists, as a style, with and within the media." This media-centered youth culture came to full fruition during the 1950s as did the contradictory belief in the "innocence" of children and of the necessity for parents to "mold" their children (Spigel, 1993). The clash between these two phenomena led adults who witnessed youth's new look, slang, and leisure to label such behaviors as delinquent, with the result that the decade produced a massive moral panic over juvenile delinquency and mass culture's alleged contribution (see, for example, Gilbert, 1986; Springhall, 1998).

Given this belief in the "innocence" of children and of the role of parents in "molding" the values of their children as well as "shielding" them from harmful messages, it is no wonder that mass culture historically has been fodder for moral panics. In the case of child and youth culture, moral panic has resided along generational fault lines. For example, in the 1950s, according to Spigel: "The anxieties about television's effects on youth were connected to more general fears about its disruption of generational roles, particularly with regard to power struggles over what constituted proper children's entertainment" (1993, p. 268). Spigel argues that the primary concern in this struggle was that the innocence of children was at stake. "At the heart of the advice on children and television was a marked desire to keep childhood as a period distinct from adulthood. Critics of the medium feared that television might abolish such distinctions by making children privy to adult secrets" (1993, p. 271).

While Spigel is specifically referring to the early panic over children and television, James Gilbert (1986) addresses the simultaneous panic over youth and comic books. In the latter instance, psychiatrist Fredric Wertham, along with a host of adults and media pundits, argued that comic books were a key cause of the perceived rash of juvenile delinquency, a claim that culminated in a hearing before a Senate subcommittee investigating juvenile delinquency. Gilbert describes the 1950s debate over youth culture as "a struggle in which the participants were arguing over power – over who had the right and responsibility to shape American culture" (p. 7).

Constructing Youth Today

> Youth become an easy target for a public discourse in which the dual strategies of scapegoating and commodifying take on the proportions of a national policy and minor revolution in the media.
>
> Henry Giroux (1998, p. 34)

Some 50 years later, the arguments remain the same. For example, both Henry Giroux and Henry Jenkins discuss the moral panics that occurred in the aftermath of the 1999 Columbine High School shootings in which two male students killed 13 others at the school before taking their own lives. Hundreds of articles were published addressing the "causes" of this tragedy, a significant proportion of which singled out media and popular culture. Giroux and Jenkins argue that adults were so concerned with protecting children from what they perceived to be the harmful outside influences of mass culture (e.g. videogames, Goth music, the Internet) that they failed to understand what "our children are doing with media" (Jenkins, 1999, p. 2). More specifically, Jenkins attributes three factors with being behind such negative media coverage of youth in general and this most recent of moral panics in particular: 1) adults fear adolescents, 2) they also fear new technologies, in part because they lack the knowledge and expertise to incorporate these technologies into their own lives, and 3) youth culture has grown increasingly visible, making it harder than ever to ignore. "We are afraid of our children. We are afraid of their reactions to digital media. And we suddenly can't avoid either" (Jenkins, 1999, p. 9).

Scholars including Giroux, Jenkins, Mike Males, John Hartley and others have turned their attention to press coverage of youth and its role in perpetuating what Giroux calls "an essentialist representation of youth" (1996, p. 36). Giroux describes recent press coverage of youth as characterized by a "mean spirited discourse" (1996, p. 30) which has resulted in "crisis in representation" (1998, p. 30). Further, within this crisis, however, scholars have identified a puzzling contradiction (see, for example, Giroux, 1998; Hartley, 1998; Tucker, 1998). While, on the one hand, the press and popular culture construct youth as a problem, at the same time, they also construct youth as a commodity and/or a target market either to sell "youth" to an aging adult population eager to recapture their own lost youth, or to sell products to young people themselves. Each of these phenomena will be discussed in the sections that follow.

Youth as a problem

> Atrocity tales appearing in newspaper headlines, on magazine covers, and during television newscasts ask us, with alarming regularity, to see young people as animalistic, alien Others.... We are left to wonder whether the new 'Evil Empire' will be located in our schools, streets, and homes, among our friends, siblings, neighbors, and children: "youth."
>
> Joe Austin and Michael Nevin Willard (1998, p. 1)

According to sociologist Donna Gaines (1994) popular media "misrepresentation(s)" of youth often include "images of kids as 'thugs,' 'animals,' drive-by shoot-outs, gangsters and teenage crack moms rocking in the free world, jock gang rapists, parricide perps, low math and science scorers, zombies without morals" (p. 231). Such misrepresentations, Gaines argues, are so powerful, that she includes them as part of her "laundry list" of the problems confronting present-day youth. Gaines is not alone in exposing the media's war on kids. (See, for example, a theme issue of the magazine *Extra!* Titled "Media Take Aim at Youth" [1994].) For example, in his studies of the press's construction of young girls in Australia, John Hartley (1998) identifies a phenomenon he labels "juvenation" (p. 51) – an intense, contradictory press focus on youth in which youthful visual images are celebrated in order to draw in adult readers, while news stories of youth's shortcomings, troubles, and transgressions stigmatize these same youth. As a result of this phenomenon, Hartley argues that "children have become so caught up in the rhetoric of foe-creation in the hard-news media that they now occupy the structural position of 'theydom'" (p. 52). In other words, they have become the "other," a group to be protected, saved and/or feared. Hartley's research has led him to assert that "media campaigns against young people are a staple genre, whether they're about sex, drugs, rock 'n' roll or violence, they are always available to serve for the time being as the immediate signifier of the general need for governability" (p. 48). Such articles, argues Hartley, are written not for youth, but for adult readers – the "we" in the "we"/"they" dichotomy.

In his aptly titled book, *Framing Youth*, Mike Males deconstructs the press coverage of teenagers in the United States. While Giroux (1996) argues that when the press covers youth it does so incompletely, without all the facts, Males takes this one step further. Focusing primarily on coverage of youth violence, Males compellingly shows how the press consciously and systematically distorts the facts about youth, whom he calls "the officially designated scapegoat of the 90s" (p. 288), so as to "frame" them. In one study of the *Los Angeles Times*, Males found that "media reporting on youth murder and violence as a policy issue was *triple* what youths' contribution to violence arrest would warrant, *five times* more than youths' contribution to the volume of homicide merited, and *nine times* more than adult violence as an issue" (1999, p. 281). This phenomenon is even more pronounced when covering youth of color. In a study of local (California) television news coverage of juvenile crime, Travis L. Dixon, Daniel Linz, and Cristina Azocar (2000) found that African-American and Latino youth were "significantly more likely than White juveniles to be portrayed as law-breakers" (2000, p. 2).

Giroux (2000) has argued that when the notion of childhood innocence comes into play in media coverage of youth, it is generally applied only to White, middle-class youth. Some of the most compelling examples of this can be found in news coverage of the Columbine High School shootings, which were accompanied by headlines announcing: "If It Could Happen Here, Many Say, It Could Happen Anywhere" or questioning "How Could This Happen?" The implication being how could this happen *here* (i.e. in White, middle-class suburbia)? Moreover, other articles quoted sources exclaiming, "They were good" (i.e. White, middle-class suburban) "kids." Implicit in such statements is the belief that this kind of behavior is to be expected of urban, poor, and/or African-American and Latino youth, but that these kinds of things just don't happen in White suburbia. Henry Giroux exposes this bias in his book *Stealing Innocence* (2000) in which he argues that "white middle-class children often are protected by the myth of innocence and are considered incapable of exhibiting at-risk behavior" (p. 8). When they do exhibit such behavior, as in the case of Columbine, it is accompanied both by a wave of "soul searching" (p. 8) and the need to identify outside causes (e.g. popular culture) "well removed from the spaces of 'whiteness' and affluence" (p. 8). He argues that the media, and indeed the White power elite, perceive poor children and children of color "to be beyond the boundaries of both childhood and innocence" as "they have been associated with the cultures of crime, rampant sexuality, and drug use. In fact, they are quite often perceived as a threat to the innocence of White middle-class kids who inhabit increasingly fortress-like suburbs, shielded from the immorality, violence, and other 'dangers' lurking within the ever-expanding multiethnic cities" (p. 9).

Amy Binder (1993) offers compelling evidence of this in her comparative analysis of "mainstream" (a.k.a. White) news coverage of the controversies over heavy metal music in the mid-1980s versus the coverage of rap a few year later. Informed by frame theory (see, for example, Gamson, 1989), Binder documents that when covering the panic over heavy metal, a musical genre associated primarily with White youth, the mainstream press consistently employed what she termed the "corruption" frame – asking how this harmful, outside force was going to corrupt "our" (a.k.a. White) children – and the "protection" frame – asking how "we" were going to protect "our" kids from this outside influence. On the other hand, just a few short years later when covering the panic over rap, a musical genre associated primarily with urban, African-American youth, the mainstream press abandoned the corruption and protection frames and opted instead for the "danger to society" frame – expressing concern about how listeners of this music (a.k.a. urban, African-American youth) posed a danger to society as a result of engaging in criminal behavior related to listening to this music. There was no concern that the music might corrupt African-American youth, prompting Binder to assert: "Clearly, the listener's welfare was no longer the focus of concern" (1993, p. 762).

While there are differences in press coverage of youth of color versus White youth, there also are gender differences. Despite a small flurry of articles warning of "girl gangs" and the like, when the press covers girls, they are often portrayed as victims and in need of intervention rather than as violent and/or criminals. Informed by frame theory, Norma Pecora and I (Mazzarella & Pecora, 2002) have analyzed how the lives of adolescent girls were covered in US newspapers between 1993 and 1999. These articles overwhelmingly present a portrait of a generation of girls in crisis, notably in terms of such issues as self-esteem, body image and eating disorders. One does not even need to go beyond the headlines themselves to get the picture. These headlines warn us of the "Perils of Puberty: Girls 'Crash and Burn' in Adolescence"; that "Girls Face Greater Hurdles Today"; that "Body Size is an Obsession for Adolescents with Eating Disorders"; that "Crossing [the] 'Confidence Gap' Poses High Hurdle for Girls"; and that girls today are "Suffering in Silence," "Desperately Seeking Perfection," and "Starving for Self Esteem." In addition, they warn that adolescence is: "A Perilous Age for Girls," a time when "Young Girls Face [a] Tough Time Living Up to Expectations," and when "Teen Girls No Longer Enjoy an Age of Innocence." They inform us about "Adolescent Girls and the Self-Esteem Gap," and about "The Rocky Road to a Girl's Adolescence." They warn that "Growing Up is Risky Business for Girls," that "Sexual Abuse [is] Tied to 1 in 4 Girls in Teens," and that "Emotional Ills [are] Tied to Stunted Growth in Girls." Such headlines, we conclude "herald a growing crisis" (p. 17), or more accurately, a *perceived* crisis. Rarely, if ever are contradictory viewpoints expressed as there are few articles that celebrate adolescent girls or present solely positive pictures of their lives.

While not blaming or scapegoating girls for broader social problems, these articles construct girls themselves as a social problem. Such representations are disturbing in that they present youth, in this case adolescent girls, as weak and vulnerable, thereby denying them any form of agency. According to Giroux, "Current representations of youth – which range from depicting kids as a threat to society or as defenseless against the corrupting influence of the all-powerful popular culture – often work to undermine any productive sense of agency among young people, offering few possibilities for analyzing how children actually experience and mediate relationships with each other or with adults" (2000, p. 20).

Indeed, these articles present to the reader a world in which adults need to step in and save this lost generation of girls. Over half of the articles focus on intervention and prevention – how can *adults* and *adult-sanctioned* programs "save" this generation in crisis. Moreover, these articles are more likely to quote from adult experts than from girls themselves. Less than 20 percent of articles analyzed included quotes from girls, preferring instead to quote from various "experts" – social workers, psychologists, academics, politicians, and so on. Girls are rarely given the opportunity to speak for themselves. They are denied both agency and a voice.

Similarly, in her analysis of the furor over a series of 1995 ads for Calvin Klein jeans, which were labeled by the media and many in the adult society as "kiddie porn," Lauren Tucker (1998) found that youth themselves were rarely used as sources in articles about the controversy. Instead, articles relied heavily on various "official" sources both inside and outside of the advertising industry. In another analysis of press coverage of teen pregnancy, Janine Jackson found that "only a handful" (p. 14) of articles quoted teen mothers. The sources most often quoted in these stories were conservatives who blamed girls and advocated denial of social services to teen mothers. This phenomenon, what Jackson (1994, p. 14) calls "constricted sources," is typical of press coverage of youth.

These phenomena are not limited to news coverage of teenagers. The advocacy organization Children Now recently sponsored a study of local television news coverage of children, concluding that children receive "scant attention" (2001, p. 3) in such stories, that when they are covered, it is most likely to be in a story about crime, and that children are most likely to be presented as victims. In addition, the study found that children themselves were quoted in less than 20 percent of stories about them, while nearly half of such stories featured adult sources – doctors, parents, law enforcement, and others. Certainly, interviewing children about such topics as crime poses a unique set of problems for journalists. However, it does presage the press's tendency to deny even older youth a voice in stories about themselves.

Both Hartley (1998) and Giroux (1998) have argued that youth (including children) are not afforded a voice when covered in the press. According to Hartley, they:

are "powerless" over their own image, presumed incapable of self-representation, not imagined to have a collective interest which needs to be defended in the news, and represented in ways which are comparable to a colonised people; perhaps the West's last colony, in discursive terms. (1998, p. 52)

Larry Grossberg (1994, p. 25) describes youth as "the most silenced population in society."

When adult experts are quoted, it is rarely those who speak in favor of children, youth and/or popular culture. Jenkins offers compelling evidence of this when reflecting on his experience testifying about popular culture before a Senate committee in the aftermath of the Columbine shootings – an experience he likens to a "national witch hunt" (1999, p. 1). Both the Senators and the press covering the hearing clearly had their minds made up in advance, and he, as the only scholar speaking from outside of the media effects tradition, was attacked and dismissed. "The press," Jenkins reports, "swarmed around the anti-violence speakers but didn't seem to want to talk to me" (1999, p. 6).

Clearly, the government and the press in this example had an agenda to deliver to the US public a particular message and a predesignated enemy – to blame popular culture. Jenkins' views simply did not support the plan, so he was silenced. Reliance on a "constricted" set of experts in news stories is not limited to coverage of children and youth. Numerous scholars have documented a "source bias" (see, for example, Whitney, Fritzler, Jones, Mazzarella, & Rakow, 1989) in news coverage in general, whereby certain official, institutional, government, and business "experts" are more likely to be quoted than are other sources. This tendency is so well-ingrained in corporate journalistic practice, that Noam Chomsky and Edward S. Herman (1988) include it as a primary component of their "propaganda model" of news.

While being denied a voice, youth are also subjected to the media's (read adult's) attempts to categorize them. In particular, my own research has examined the trend of generational labeling – the need to create labels to identify and define post-baby boom youth, and to enable adults to employ such labels as explanations for a variety of social, cultural and economic phenomena. For example, in 1991 the phrase Generation X became firmly entrenched in the public's consciousness as the name given to the generation of young adults born in the United States since 1965. Previously referred to as the "Baby Bust" generation – in reference to the declining birthrates in the United States following the 1964 end of the "baby boom" – the so-called Generation X has generated extensive media coverage and attention.

Since its widespread introduction, the phrase has proven to be more than a convenient, innocuous label. As Ray Gozzi has observed: "The *Generation X* metaphor is explicitly vague. It allows us to project our own experiences with young people into it, and then classify them as confirming the existence of a *Generation X*" (1995, p. 332). More often than not, the Generation X label/metaphor evokes a wealth of negative connotations and stereotypes. The alternative press publication *Utne Reader* (1992, p. 117) asserts that major sources of such stereotyping are the mainstream media which have a tendency to describe "Xers" as:

> politically apathetic, materialistic, ill-informed, MTV-obsessed, lazy louts who are content to spend at least five years after college sleeping in the twin beds of their youths while sucking food and money off good old mom and dad.

Such stereotyping is not lost on "members" of the so-called Generation X. One of my studies (Pecora & Mazzarella, 1995) found that college students surveyed felt that the media tend to portray their generation in a negative and unflattering light – as apathetic, bored, and self-centered slackers. Similarly, these students strongly rejected the application of these negative stereotypes to either themselves or to their generation as a whole (although they did admit that *some* members of their generation do fit these descriptons.) Remember, however, that youth themselves are not often allowed to speak in articles about them.

While the negative descriptors typically attributed to Generation X by the press have raised concern, so has the use of the label to lump all young people in this age group together thereby ignoring their differences. Such an essentialist reduction is problematic. According to Michael Hoechsmann (1996, p. 91): "the term 'generation' is imprecise at the best of times. Issues of difference, whether in terms of class, race, gender or sexuality, are systematically excluded by this generalizing term which puts everybody in the same boat."

One example of the negative construction of youth can be found in press coverage of the April 8, 1994 suicide of grunge rocker Kurt Cobain – coverage that persisted in linking Cobain to Generation X (Mazzarella, 1995). Across the numerous newspaper and magazine articles on Cobain's suicide, the press applied one or more of four representational strategies in order to structure the story. Specifically, press coverage: (1) identified similarities between Cobain's death and the deaths of earlier rock 'n' roll icons; (2) focused attention on "grieving" Gen X fans in an attempt to understand what Cobain meant to them; (3) asked why Cobain killed himself, a question they then went on to answer by focusing on problems allegedly endemic to Generation X as a whole; and (4) used Cobain's suicide to construct suicide as a Generation X "plague." Each of these representational strategies allowed the press "to neatly package and commodify Kurt Cobain, and to directly and indirectly link him, his music, and his death to Generation X" (pp. 50–1). In their coverage of Cobain's suicide it was almost as if the baby boomer-led media were attempting to make sense of an entire generation instead of the suicide of a rock star. This study presents evidence that the press machine constructed and labeled an entire generation, and then went on to position Kurt Cobain as the voice of that generation.

The ramifications of such generational labeling and stereotyping is underscored by research on youth subcultures. In his now classic analysis of youth subcultures in Great Britain, Dick Hebdige (1979) found that there are two means by which the dominant culture weakens a seemingly threatening sub-culture. The first is to commodify the signs (i.e. fashion, music, language) of the subculture. The second is the "'labeling' and re-definition" (1979, p. 94) of that subculture. The latter, what Hebdige calls the "ideological form" (1979, p. 94), results in dismissing the importance of the subculture. While not a true sub-culture, Generation X, on the surface, appears to have garnered the kind of media coverage typically reserved for more traditionally-defined, spectacular youth subcultures (e.g. punk). Further, the label Generation X itself can be seen to serve the same ideological function as subcultural labels, enabling adults to dismiss the generation. For example, Tucker (1998) argues that this labeling and stereotyping of Generation X by the baby boomer-led media legitimizes "the Generational Equity discourse (which) specifies the need to cut social and educational programs that primarily benefit young adults, teens and children to provide middle-class tax 'relief'" (p. 197). In other words, why should anything be done to help young people when they are perceived as unwilling to help themselves? As Grossberg asserts, "there are real material stakes in the struggle to construct youth in particular ways" (1994, p. 34).

Ryan Moore (1998) argues that the best way to understand the Generation X stereotype is in the context of the downward mobility of the middle class in the age of late capitalism. At the height of the Generation X phenomenon, the press often told us that this was the first generation in the history of the United States that was expected *not* to do better economically than their parents' generation. In fact, early articles on the Baby Bust generation were often positive, extolling the vast educational and employment opportunities that awaited this new, smaller generation of youth. As time went on, paralleling a downturn in the economy and an ever-dwindling job market for young college grads, the label Generation X and its attendant negative descriptors became more prevalent, replacing the positive framing employed in earlier articles on the Baby Bust. According to Moore, such negative stereotypes of Generation X as the slacker and under-achiever "should be seen partially as the projected anxieties of a class whose parents fear that their children are not succeeding or will not succeed in an increasingly competitive environment because they lack the proper motivation and self-discipline" (p. 265). Quite simply, it enables adults and their institutions to blame youth for broader problems, in this case economic downturn.

In fact, a diverse group of scholars have begun to argue that negative media representations of youth enable adults and adult institutions to blame youth for a variety of problems created by those very same adults and adult institutions. George Lipsitz (1998) compellingly demonstrates that the moral panic over hip hop in general and gangsta rap in particular have served to blame the music for problems (crime and violence, for example) that are more appropriately attributed to "deindustrialization, economic restructuring, and neoconservative politics" (p. 395). Similarly, Giroux (2000) argues that the panic over popular culture as it is linked to the myth of childhood innocence takes attention away from the real problems confronting youth in our society – notably the dramatic decline in government funding of education, the reduction in social services for children, the disappearances of public spaces for children, and the increasing commercial and sexual exploitation of children, not to mention the epidemic of adult-perpetrated violence against children, a crisis that is powerfully, statistically documented by Males (1999).

Youth as a Commodity and/or a Market

For no matter what we profess to believe about teenagers and their vital importance to the future, we tend to value them most as consumers.

Grace Palladino (1996, p. xi)

I am not a target market.

Douglas Coupland (1991, p. 17)

While at the same time as they are being constructed as a problem, youth, even Generation X, have been constructed as a commodity and/or a target market, a phenomenon that is far from new. The founding of *Seventeen* magazine in 1944 has often been considered to be evidence of the media's response to the needs of the burgeoning postwar, teenage youth culture. Closer analysis, however, reveals that *Seventeen* did more than respond to the needs of the teenage subculture, but rather actively constructed and defined teenage *girls* as a target market, creating needs along the way, reminiscent of the way in which adult women's magazines of the time defined and addressed women as consumers (Friedan, 1963). As a result of editor Helen Valentine's active lobbying of advertisers, *Seventeen* played a major role in creating the teenage girl consumer. Initially, advertisers were resistant to the idea that teen girls might be a viable market. Through tireless campaigning, research, and product tie-ins, however, Valentine eventually convinced advertisers that targeting teen girls as a market made sound financial sense and further served to indoctrinate girls into their future roles as adult women consumers (Palladino, 1996).

Nearly 50 years later, one woman shook up the advertising industry again by convincing her colleagues that they would be wise to target their campaigns and products to yet another generation of young Americans – Generation X. In an October 4, 1992 speech to the Magazine Publishers' Association, Karen Ritchie, an advertising executive with McCann-Erickson Worldwide, wowed the audience by announcing: "Face it. Boomers are getting old" (Ritchie, 1992, p. 21). She went on to urge her fellow advertising executives to stop targeting their campaigns to aging baby boomers, and instead to target what she called "the purple-haired people" (p. 21) – i.e. Generation X.

At the close of her 1992 speech, Karen Ritchie predicted: "Five short years from now, it will not only be leading edge marketers, but mainstream advertisers, too, who will want and need to talk to Generation X" (p. 21). In the years following her speech, Ritchie wrote a book titled *Marketing to Generation X* (1995), and her colleagues heeded her advice. Within weeks of her speech, articles about marketing to Generation X began appearing in *Advertising Age*, including the text of her October 1992 speech (Ritchie, 1992). Articles on advertising and marketing to Generation X have appeared in hundreds of business and trade magazines, including such well-known periodicals as *Advertising Age*, *Business Week*, *American Demographics*, and *Brandweek*. Yet even smaller, more narrow trade periodicals such as *Bank Marketing*, *Restaurant Business*, and *Progressive Grocer* have featured articles on this generation. Featuring headlines such as "Understanding Generation X," "Talkin' 'bout My Generation," and "Generation X a Double-Edged Sword," such articles have sought to advise marketers on how to reach this generation. Interestingly, article after article stresses the same two key points: (1) the difficulty of reaching this target market through the same media channels as advertisers had reached baby boomers; and (2) the dangers of using generational stereotypes to structure ad campaigns since this generation is particularly media savvy as well as sensitive to the stereotyping of their generation.

More importantly, these articles point out how "media savvy" Xers are, and that they are extremely sensitive to hype, especially when it involves them. This is a generation that grew up surrounded by media, in particular, advertising. As a result, while they do not hate advertising, they are very cynical of it. Again, Ritchie (1995, pp. 114, 116) led the way:

> How did Generation X get so smart about media? It started, of course, when they were children. . . . Generation X learned to handle television like a team of lawyers handle a hostile witness – we did not raise a stupid generation here. The ground rules were established early: Generation X would take from the media what they needed and what they found entertaining, but they would never accept information from the media at face value. They would learn to be critical. They would learn to recognize hype, "weasel words," and exaggeration. . . . Just as earlier generations took cars and trucks apart to dissect their engines and learn their secrets, Generation X examines commercials, cartoons, and prime-time movies.

As a result, articles warn of the dangers of using stereotypes or of co-opting elements of youth culture to reach this generation. As Richard Thau, executive director of Third Millennium (a New York-based Gen X advocacy organization) declared in a speech to the 1996 Conference on Generation X:

> It comes back to that hatred of condescension. If an ad is read as a genuine window into their lives, Gen Xers come running. But if they catch the slightest hint of pretense, the slightest inclination that they're simply being exploited, well, their condemnation is swift and terrible. (p. 667)

Thau and others cite as examples failed television campaigns for Budweiser featuring a group of male Xers playing pool while comparing female characters from classic television programs such as Gilligan's Island, as well as a campaign for Subaru featuring a Christian Slater-like slacker figure. Interestingly, the campaign that has received the most praise for successfully targeting Generation X is the original Neon "Hi" campaign. Xers and marketers alike agree the campaign was successful because it avoided generational stereotypes, and spoke to Xers as practical, economical, and savvy individuals. Despite the wealth of advice not to employ generational stereotypes in advertising to Generation X, ads often did, and Xers rebelled, refusing to be stereotyped, looked down upon, and marketed to. Yet their moment as the ideal target market faded fast, as the media quickly constructed another, more willing target, Generation Y – youth born since 1979.

While offering an overwhelmingly negative portrait of the generation it labeled X, the media have done the opposite with the generation it has now labeled Y. While doing research on newspaper coverage of Generation X, I came across an article in the June 7, 1994 *St. Petersburg Times* which declared: "Forget Generation X. They're history. What about Generation Y? Who are they and, more important, what are they wearing?" This, the first article on Generation Y to appear in a US newspaper in the Lexis-Nexis Academic Universe database, exemplifies two of the predominant representational strategies employed by US newspapers in constructing this generation – to identify them as the next big thing and as consumers – a target market. Informed by frame theory, I identified four primary frames employed in newspaper coverage of this generation (Mazzarella, 2002).

The first is what I have called the "size matters" frame, defined as an overwhelming emphasis on the fact that this generation is the largest in history. Common across most of the articles is an acknowledgment that this generation represents, according to the *Denver Post* "the largest demographic cohort in history – larger even than the baby boom." Such articles typically report dramatic statistics documenting the size of this generation, generally in comparison to the baby boom, and then use that size to set up other frames, notably frames related to power.

The second frame, and one that derives directly from the first is what, borrowing a phrase from the *Arizona Republic*, I call the "youthquake" frame. Because of the vast size of Generation Y, these articles feel compelled to warn us of the impending "youthquake" or "tidal wave" expected in their wake. The language of natural disasters is surprising since, as I will discuss later, most of these articles employ primarily positive frames when covering this generation. Although not framing Generation Y in a negative way, articles often advise us of their impending arrival, an arrival that promises to shake things up a bit. While the early articles about this generation occasionally featured warnings, including "Caution: Teenagers on the way," most articles are more likely to be advisories featuring headlines such as: "Here Come the Kids of 2000; Indulged by their baby boomer parents, the millennials may be the generation that saves the world"; "Generation Y The young and the boundless are taking over pop culture"; "Millennials; Kids under 18 represent force of future"; and "Generation Y: Next population bulge shows its might". The pronounced application of power terms – "saves," "taking over," "force," "might" – is a predominant characteristic of the youthquake frame. According to these articles, Generation Y's primary power is to bring about change – change in our culture, values, lifestyles, and so on. They are described as: "financial and cultural powerhouse generation," a "cultural force" that "will shape our world" and, indeed is "already turning our world upside down." According to the *Wall Street Journal*, "the tastes, habits and beliefs of this group . . . will reverberate through American culture well into the next century."

Yet this power is expected to come at the expense of previous generations, a sentiment found in articles employing the "passing the torch" frame. Often these articles go even further in heralding the arrival of this new generation by specifically warning the previous generations to get out of the way. This frame can be seen in headlines such as: "The Wonder Year$ Boomers & Gen-Xers? Forget 'em. Teens are what every marketer wants a piece of"; "Move Over X, Make Way for Y – Generation Y, that is"; "X-ed Out: Gen Y takes over; A new group is setting the cultural standard"; "Gen X, Move Over for the Millennials"; "Boomers, Move Over: It's Time for the Millennials"; "Move Over, Baby Boomers". Interestingly, many of the articles choose to overlook Generation X and tell the Boomers that they need to move over. Unlike their older brothers and sisters labeled Generation X, Generation Y is constructed in a much more positive fashion. While articles on Generation X typically frame them in negative ways – slackers, lazy, apathetic – articles on Generation Y have only good things to say related to the latter's optimism, morals, commitment, and social conscience.

In fact, of the articles analyzed, only a handful offered any negatives about this generation. What is interesting is that these are the same young people (primarily adolescents) who have been the focus of intense negative coverage related to Columbine and other issues. In fact, of the thousands of articles appearing in the Lexis-Nexis Academic Universe database about the Columbine shootings, only six include the phrase Generation Y, and none of these makes a link between the generation and the shootings – i.e. constructing violence as endemic to Generation Y. While suicide was defined as the plague that haunted Generation X (Mazzarella, 1995), violence *is not* defined as the plague that haunts Generation Y, at least not when the Generation Y label is used. Indeed, the difference between the hundreds of articles on Generation Y and the articles discussed by Giroux, Jenkins and others, for example, *is* one of labels, clearly evidencing the press's role in constructing youth. When the label Generation Y is used, the coverage is overwhelmingly positive, optimistic, and upbeat. On the other hand, when it is teens or teenagers (i.e. teen pregnancy, teen violence) who are covered, pessimism predominates. Clearly this exemplifies the point discussed earlier that when youth are covered by the press, it often is in contradictory terms – on the one hand scapegoated and demonized, as in the case when "teens" are covered, and on the other hand commodified, as in the case when "Generation Y" is covered.

Moreover, this is a far cry from the predominantly negative framing of Generation X just a few short years ago. In fact, when Generation X is mentioned in articles about Generation Y, the negative representation of the former is glaring. One explanation for this phenomenon is found in the fourth of the major frames identified in this study, the "marketing motherload" (to borrow a phrase from *Women's Wear Daily*.) The Baby Boomers and Generation X are no longer perceived as desirable target markets by advertisers. Generation Y, on the other hand, is. Articles describe them as "the most sought-after consumers," "the greatest force in consumerism since their baby-boomer parents," "the most significant consumer group in America," "in short, a marketing motherload." Referring back to Moore's argument about the role of the Gen X label in late capitalism, there is a clear link here as well. The Gen X label and stereotype were prevalent during an economic downturn while the Gen Y label flourished during an economic boom in the US. However, the recent shaky state of the US economy may soon change that. In fact, recent newspaper articles warn that "College Seniors Face Particularly Tough Job Market" and "US Graduates Facing Miserable Job Market."

It is clear that the media have learned from the mistakes made in their construction of Generation X. By framing that generation in negative terms, they alienated them, driving them away from products employing the Generation X stereotype in their advertising. On the other hand, by framing and representing Generation Y in a positive light, the media have created a generation ripe for the selling. Overall, the differences between the media's construction of Generations X and Y is dramatic, with the end result being a more positive, optimistic construction of Generation Y. They, as were their baby boomer parents when they were younger, are being celebrated and courted by the media, and their potential to change the world is being highly anticipated and welcomed. Unlike the Xers, whom the media reviled and dismissed, Generation Y is being framed as the greatest thing since sliced bread, or at least since the Baby Boom. One of my students summed up the representational politics behind the media's framing of Generation Y as constructing "a marketing friendly pseudo-generation."

Conclusion

> It would be a mistake to think that there is some fixed or natural definition of youth, however convenient it might be to have one.
>
> Deena Weinstein (1994, p. 67)

As this essay and others have shown, youth is a construct. From the beginning, whether defined as innocent, a problem, a commodity, a target market, or the future, youth has been defined by adults – parents, politicians, psychologists, journalists, filmmakers, advertisers, marketers, even academics. While this essay has focused primarily on the role of the press in this construction, they are not alone. It takes politicians eager to make a name for themselves and attempting to shift attention from more difficult social, cultural, and economic problems to hold high-profile Capitol Hill hearings on juvenile delinquency, music lyrics, movies, the Internet and so on. Again, I highly recommend reading Henry Jenkins' (1999) enlightening description of his Senate testimony after Columbine. It takes, at times, filmmakers coming to terms with their own troubled childhoods to make films that stereotype or demonize youth. Henry Giroux's deconstruction of the films of Larry Clark (e.g. *Kids*) is quite compelling in this regard (1997, 1998). It takes multinational conglomerates such as those who own MTV, record companies, TV networks, teen magazines and film studios focusing only on the bottom line to continue to recycle the same old tired clichéd and stereotyped portrayals of youth. Mostly, however, what it takes is an adult culture that does not give youth a chance to speak for themselves, or does not listen when they do. It is clear that when adults construct youth they invest it with properties and characteristics that they (adults) need for whatever reason at that particular time – the need to sell products, the need to justify cutbacks in government funding for youth programs, the need to make excuses for the downward mobility of the middle class, the need to look for simple solutions to complex problems, the need to feel good about themselves as they age. Whatever the reason, it is clear that the *mainstream* (for we cannot deny that youth do construct their own identities "on the margins of society" (Giroux, 1998, p. 24)) construction of youth is done by adults, for adults.

References

Aries, P. (1962). *Centuries of Childhood: A social history of family life* (trans. R. Baldick). New York: Vintage Books.

Austin, J. and Willard, M. N. (eds.) (1998). Introduction: Angels of history, demons of culture. In J. Austin and M. N. Willard (eds.), *Generations of Youth: Youth cultures and history in twentieth-century America*. New York: New York University Press, pp. 1–20.

Binder, A. (1993). Constructing racial rhetoric: Media depictions of harm in heavy metal and rap music. *American Sociological Review*, 58, 753–67.

Children Now (2001). The local television news media's picture of children. Available: http://www.childrennow.org/media/local-news-study/local-news-01.pdf.

Chomsky, N. and Herman, E. S. (1988). *Manufacturing Consent: The political economy of the mass media*. New York: Pantheon.

Coupland, D. (1991). *Generation X: Tales for an accelerated culture*. New York: St. Martin's Press.

Dixon, T. L., Linz, D., and Azocar, C. (2000). Overrepresentation and underrepresentation of African American and Latino juvenile lawbreakers on local television news. Paper presented at the meeting of the International Communication Association, Acapulco, Mexico, June.

Fass, P. (1977). *The Damned and the Beautiful: American youth in the 1920s*. New York: Oxford University Press.

Friedan, B. (1963). *The Feminine Mystique*. New York: Norton.

Gaines, D. (1994). Border crossing in the U.S.A. In A. Ross and T. Rose (eds.), *Microphone Fiends: Youth music and youth culture*. New York: Routledge, pp. 227–34.

Gamson, W. A. (1989). News as framing: Comments on Graber. *American Behavioral Scientist*, 33(2), 157–61.

Gilbert, J. (1986). *A Cycle of Outrage: America's reaction to the juvenile delinquent in the 1950s.* New York: Oxford University Press.

Giles, J. (1994). Generalizations X. *Newsweek*, June 6, 62–6.

Giroux, H. A. (1996). *Fugitive Cultures: Race, violence, and youth.* New York: Routledge.

Giroux, H. A. (1997). *Channel Surfing: Racism, the media, and the deconstruction of today's youth.* New York: St. Martin's Griffin.

Giroux, H. A. (1998). Teenage sexuality, body politics, and the pedagogy of display. In J. S. Epstein (ed.), *Youth Culture: Identity in a postmodern world.* Malden, MA: Blackwell, pp. 24–55.

Giroux, H. A. (2000). *Stealing Innocence: Corporate culture's war on children.* New York: Palgrave.

Gozzi, R., Jr. (1995). The generation X and boomers metaphors. *Et cetera*, 52(3), 331–35.

Grossberg, L. (1994). The political status of youth and youth culture. In J. S. Epstein (ed.), *Adolescents and their Music: If it's too loud, you're too old.* New York: Garland, pp. 25–46.

Hall, G. S. (1904). *Adolescence: Its psychology and its relation to psychology, anthropology, sociology, sex, crime, religion, and education.* Englewood Cliffs, NJ: Erlbaum.

Hartley, J. (1998). Juvenation: News, girls and power. In C. Carter, G. Branston, and S. Allan (eds.), *News, Gender and Power.* New York: Routledge, pp. 47–70.

Hawes, J. M. and Hiner, N. R. (eds.) (1985). *American Childhood: A research guide and historical handbook.* Westport, CT: Greenwood Press.

Hebdige, D. (1979). *Subculture: The meaning of style.* New York: Methuen.

Hine, T. (1999) The rise and decline of the teenager. *American Heritage*, September, 71–82.

Hoechsmann, M. (1996). I am white, male and middle-class in a global era: Marketing (to) Generation X. In. M. Pomerance and J. Sakeris (eds.), *Pictures of a Generation on Hold: Selected papers.* Toronto: Media Studies Working Group, pp. 85–95.

Hurt, H. W. (1924). *Boy Facts: A study from existing sources.* New York: Boy Scouts of America.

Jackson, J. (1994). The "crisis" of teen pregnancy: Girls pay the price for media distortion. *Extra!*, 7(2), 13–14.

Jenkins, H. (1999). Professor Jenkins goes to Washington. Available: http://web.mit.edu/21fms/www/faculty/henry3/profjenkins.html.

Lipsitz, G. (1998). The hip hop hearings: Censorship, social memory, and intergenerational tensions among African Americans. In J. Austin and M. N. Willard (eds.), *Generations of Youth: Youth cultures and history in twentieth-century America.* New York: New York University Press, pp. 395–411.

Males, M. (1999). *Framing Youth: 10 myths about the next generation.* Monroe, ME: Common Courage Books.

Mazzarella, S. R. (1995). "The voice of a generation"? Media coverage of the suicide of Kurt Cobain. *Popular Music and Society*, 19(2), 49–68.

Mazzarella, S. R. (2002). The Impending "Youthquake": Newspaper framing of Generation Y. Manuscript in preparation.

Mazzarella, S. R. and Pecora, N. (2002). Girls in Crisis: Newspaper framing of adolescent girls. Paper presented at the Annual Meeting of the National Communication Association, New Orleans, LA.

Media Take Aim At Youth (1994). *Extra!*, 7(2), March/April.

Moore, R. (1998). "And tomorrow is just another crazy scam": Postmodernity, youth, and the downward mobility of the middle class. In J. Austin and M. N. Willard (eds.), *Generations of Youth: Youth cultures and history in twentieth-century America.* New York: New York University Press, pp. 253–71.

Palladino, G. (1996). *Teenagers: An American history.* New York: Basic Books.

Pecora, N. and Mazzarella, S. R. (1995). Kurt Cobain, Generation X, and the press: College students respond. *Popular Music and Society*, 19(2), 3–22.

Ritchie, K. (1992). Get ready for "Generation X." *Advertising Age*, November 9, 21.

Ritchie, K. (1995). *Marketing to Generation X.* New York: Lexington Books.

Spigel, L. (1993). Seducing the innocent: Childhood and television in postwar America. In W. S. Solomon (ed.), *Ruthless Criticism: New perspectives in U.S. communication history*. Minneapolis: University of Minnesota Press, pp. 259–90.

Springhall, J. (1998). *Youth, Popular Culture and Moral Panics: Penny gaffs to gangsta rap, 1830–1996*. New York: St. Martin's Press.

Thau, R. (1996). So-called Generation X: How do you target a market that wants to be left alone? *Vital Speeches of the Day*, 62(21), 664–7.

Tucker, L. (1998). The framing of Calvin Klein: A frame analysis of media discourse about the August 1995 Calvin Klein jeans advertising campaign. *Critical Studies in Mass Communication*, 15(2), 141–57.

Utne Reader (1992) July/August, 117.

Walter, H. R. (1927). *Girl Life in America*. New York: National Committee for the Study of Juvenile Reading.

Wartella, E. and Mazzarella, S. (1990). A historical comparison of children's use of leisure time. In R. Butsch (ed.), *For Fun and Profit: The transformation of leisure into consumption*. Philadelphia: Temple University Press, pp. 173–94.

Wartella, E. and Reeves, B. (1985). Historical trends in research on children and the media, 1900–1960. *Journal of Communication*, 35(2), 118–33.

Weinstein, D. (1994). Expandable youth: The rise and fall of youth culture. In J. S. Epstein (ed.), *Adolescents and Their Music: If it's too loud, you're too old*. New York: Garland, pp. 67–85.

Whitney, D. C., Fritzler, M., Jones, S., Mazzarella, S., and Rakow, L. (1989). Geographic and source bias in network television news 1982–1984. *Journal of Broadcasting and Electronic Media*, 33(2), 159–74.

CHAPTER TWELVE

The Less Space We Take, the More Powerful We'll Be

How Advertising Uses Gender to Invert Signs of Empowerment and Social Equality

Vickie Rutledge Shields

How do advertisements show us and tell us how to "gender" ourselves through the images and messages in their content? Within the field of media studies, questions of content, gender, and advertising have a long and fruitful albeit internally tense history. Researchers in the fields of communication, marketing, sociology and philosophy, to name a few, have been actively addressing this question for about 30 years (see Shields, 1996). Scholars began to approach the issue through empirical analyses. Early research implying mimetic effects evolved to more sophisticated quantitative and qualitative research. By the turn of the century, scholars, activists, and industry all draw from this long tradition to come out with research, strategies, and ads that both exploit the findings and attempt to create more gender sensitive ads. However, given that ads are a crucial component of the circulation of goods in a capitalist system, all of this research, activism, and ad production occur in a setting where commodification parameters themselves are seldom challenged.

The 1970s US was infused with second-wave feminist politics, increasing support for an Equal Rights Amendment, and the increase of female researchers in higher education. In this climate feminist scholars raced to produce empirical analyses of sex-role stereotyping found in print and television. This type of research originating then and, to a lesser extent continuing on today, is commonly referred to as *sex-roles research*. Through the use of content analysis these studies investigated questions pertaining to gender difference and inequality within the *content* of ads. Specifically, early sex-roles research revealed that women in advertising were portrayed by restrictive categories, such as housewife or sex-object, and that advertising reflected a false picture of women's real lives (see Courtney & Whipple, 1974). This type of research fit in nicely with the research methods already established in communication studies while serving a political imperative, the improvement of the representation of women in the media (Rakow, 1986).

Early researchers in the area of sex-role stereotyping in the mass media examined large numbers of ads at a time in order to classify and count particular types of representations. For example, a typical content analysis might examine 500–1,000 ads in popular fashion magazines. These ads would be examined for categories such as: how many times males appeared in business roles, how many times females appeared in bathrooms, how many times females were posed as sex-objects, and so on. The aim of this research was to demonstrate how prevalent sex-role stereotypes were in advertising.

By shining a light on the gender inequities in advertising through empirical analysis, these researchers hoped to show where the most harmful and most frequent stereotyping occurs. The expectations were that the results of this type of research would have two types of effects. First, the research would reveal to the producers of ads where and how they could improve their campaigns to more adequately reflect "real" gender relations in society. Second, the research was intended to reveal to all audiences of advertising how the images viewed each day, and generally taken for granted, were really showing us a warped, sexually inequitable vision of our society.

The rush to research the image of gender portrayal across the mass media in the 1970s could be attributed to at least two major factors. The first was the re-emergence of feminist writing in the academy spurred on by Betty Friedan's (1963) *The Feminine Mystique*. Second, advertising and print journalism received special attention because women were dominating, more than ever, many of the consumer groups targeted by advertisers and common sense dictated that the ways in which women viewed themselves in ads might greatly impact the effectiveness of commercial marketing campaigns (Lundstrom & Sciglimpaglia, 1977; Morrison & Sherman, 1972; Wise, King, & Merenski, 1974; Wortzel & Frisbie, 1974). This research was concerned with advertising "effectiveness," examining whether, and under what conditions, more progressive, less stereotyped portrayals may be preferred to traditional ones. Of foremost concern was the measurement of causal relationships between women's heightened attitudes about "Women's Liberation," role portrayal, and product desirability. Several studies, for instance, hypothesized that women would view products more positively if the role portrayal were that of women in jobs or careers (Wortzel & Frisbie, 1974).

Alice Courtney and Sarah Lockeretz's (1971) content analysis of the portrayal of men and women in print advertising was one of the first and also one of the most widely cited and replicated research studies on the subject. These authors concluded that four general stereotypes of women existed across advertisements in eight major general-interest magazines in the years 1958, 1968, and 1978: 1) a woman's place is in the home; 2) women do not make important decisions or do important things; 3) women are dependent and need men's protection; and 4) men regard women primarily as sex objects (Courtney, 1983, p. 7).

Issues and findings from content analyses of television advertisements showed very similar results. Television studies showed that: 1) prevalent female roles were – maternal, housekeeping, and aesthetic; 2) women and girls were seen less frequently than men; 3) women were shown to have different characteristics than males (less authoritative, decisive, powerful, rational); 4) women were housewives or in subservient, low-status occupations; and 5) women were depicted as less intelligent than men (Ferrante, Haynes, & Kingsley, 1988; Kimball, 1986; Lazier & Kendrick, 1993). It is important to note that the findings in the print advertising research and the television advertising research revealed similar results. Because we as audience members do not generally experience only one mass medium in any given day or week, but are instead positioned within a web of media viewing, the greater the consistency of messages, such as gender stereotypes, across the media the more powerful their potential effect is on how audiences transfer that knowledge to their social relationships.

Studies charting progress in these images in the next few years also charted new problems. Louis Wagner and Janis Banos (1973) found that the percentage of women in working roles had increased, but in non-working roles women were being seen less in family settings and more in decorative capacities. Further, women were seldom depicted interacting with one another or making major purchases without a male also in the picture. These authors concluded that stereotypes pre-dating the women's movement remained and advertising was not keeping up with the times in failing to portray realistically the diversity of women's roles (see also Belkaoui & Belkaoui, 1976).

Little attention was paid to male sex-role portrayal in print ads at this time, with the exception of one major study replicating Courtney and Lockeretz's sample from a male standpoint (Wohleter & Lammers, 1980) and one minor study (Skelly & Lundstrom, 1981). These studies found that men were more likely to be shown working outside the home and to be involved in the major purchases of expensive goods. All of these studies concluded that roles of men and women in print advertisements had changed little over twenty years (Busby, 1975; Dominick & Rauch, 1972; Fejes, 1992). Men were depicted in mainstream advertising as autonomous; pictured outdoors or in business settings; and are less likely to be at home than women and they are more likely to advertise alcohol, vehicles, and business products (Downs, 1981; Fejes, 1992; Fowles, 1996).

In the 1980s and early 1990s there has been a decrease in the number of sex-roles studies conducted than was the case in the 1970s. Furthermore, recent empirical studies investigate highly specialized areas such as "women's adoption of the business uniform" (Saunders & Stearn, 1986), sex-role stereotyping of children on TV (Furnham, Abramsky, & Gunter, 1997; Peirce, 1989), women in advertisements in medical journals (Hawkins & Aber, 1993), perception studies (Rossi & Rossi, 1985), achievement studies (Geis et al., 1984), and self-consciousness variables studies (Gould, 1987). Additional recent studies have examined cross-cultural or international perspectives on gender representation in advertising (Furnham, 1989; Gilly, 1988; Griffin, Viswanath, & Schwartz, 1992; Mazzella et al., 1992; Neto & Pinto, 1998).

Most recent sex-roles research, however, have used the vast data collected over the last 20 to 30 years to: 1) either advance theory on sex-role representation and possible debilitating "effects" stereotypical images can have for society or 2) revisit this early research, replicating studies to see whether advertising images have progressed in the past 20 years (Whipple & Courtney, 1985). According to Linda Lazier and Alice Kendrick (1993), stereotyping of portrayals of women was still important to study because the portrayals were not only debilitating and demeaning, but they continue to be "inaccurate." Advertisements "do not reflect the significant strides (both socially and statistically) made by women in the past two decades into the work force" (p. 201). Further, women were still not seen as decision makers for major purchases (although women actually make more family financial decisions than do men) and finally, "by using outdated stereotypes, ads are simplistically ignoring the complexities of modern women's lives" (p. 201).

Lynn Lovdal (1989), in a study of 354 TV commercials, found that men's voices were still dominant in voice-overs and that men were portrayed in three times the variety of occupational roles as were women. Other recent research has found that men were more likely to be portrayed in independent roles in relation to women who were portrayed in a variety of stereotyped roles such as wife, mother, bride, waitress, actress, dancer (Bretl & Cantor, 1988; Gilly, 1988; Lazier & Kendrick, 1993). Even the feminist publication, *Ms.*, whose editorial policy states that it will not run advertising harmful to women, did not fare well under the scrutiny of content analysis. A 1990 study by Jill Ferguson, Peggy Kreshel, and Spencer Tinkham found that a substantial proportion of advertising promoted products considered harmful, such as cigarettes and alcohol. Further, although images of women in subordinate and decorative capacities had decreased overall in the ads in *Ms.*, the amount of ads depicting women as alluring sex-objects increased. The editors of *Ms.* found that pleasing advertisers and offering serious feminist-oriented articles were often in conflict. In 1990 *Ms.* adopted a no-ads policy much as a result of Gloria Steinem's own critical proclamation in the pages of *Ms.* as its founding editor that "what became more and more clear is how few media are able to give consumers facts that may displease their advertisers" (p. 17). Although *Ms.* magazine is now more expensive to purchase, the no-ads policy has allowed *Ms.* to "present a renewed vision of feminism" (McKinnon, 1995).

In 1989 Linda Lazier-Smith conducted research replicating the three major studies of Suzanne Pingree, Robert Hawkins, Matilda Butler and William Paisley (1976), Erving Goffman (1976), and Jeane Kilbourne (1987). In her research the author replicated the method, categories and procedures of Pingree and Hawkins'

"Consciousness Scale of Sexism" and reapplied it along with Goffman's and Kilbourne's sexism in representation categories to one full year of advertisements in *Ms.*, *Playboy*, *Time* and *Newsweek*. Lazier-Smith found no significant change between the 1970s analyses and the 1988 representations. The authors reported that preliminary results showed a decrease in (sex object/decoration/bimbo) portrayals, however, the categories applying to women's subordination to men were still as prevalent.

Sex-roles research, in particular, has played an important part in diffusing the concept of the "sexual stereotype" throughout the language of this culture. A review of Alice Courtney and Thomas Whipple's (1974) four categories of sexual stereotyping in advertising are instructive here: (1) a woman's place is in the home; (2) women do not make important decisions or do important things; (3) women are dependent and need men's protection; and (4) men regard women primarily as sex objects. Although the variety of roles of women represented in ads has increased, current feminist literature on gender and advertising argues that these content categories have changed very little. These roles are masked by the appearance of variety. Stereotypical representations seem less harmful when served up smorgasbord style.

Advertising Content: A Different View

When exploring how people discuss the content of ads, we are really asking how advertising images that we see over and over again affect our thoughts, emotions and behaviors. Cultural studies scholar and Media Education Foundation video entrepreneur, Sut Jhally, levels an important critique at sex-roles research in *Codes of Advertisements* (1987). According to Jhally, content analysis research of gender stereotyping in advertising places its emphasis on the truth or falsity of representation, when in fact "advertisement images are neither false nor true reflections of social reality because they are in fact *part* of social reality" (p. 135). As such, advertising needs to be studied as a constituent part of our social reality, not as a distorted reflection of it. Therefore, emphasis must shift from questions of trueness or falseness to processes of "signification," or the ability of advertisements to "communicate" to social actors. This change marks a theoretical and methodological shift in advertising research focused on gender from analyses of manifest content to analyses of the "symbolic potential" of that content.

The work of Erving Goffman provides one of the first significant examples in this shift in emphasis from the examination of manifest content to the symbolic potential of ads. In the midst of the flurry of content analysis research, Goffman (1976) published his own empirical manifesto on the nature of advertising portrayals in *Gender Advertisements*. However, Goffman asked very different questions of his data than sex-roles researchers and also employed a very different method for analyzing his results. Guided by the tenets of symbolic interactionism and sociology, Goffman suggested that the most relevant questions we can ask of advertising are: of what aspects of real life do advertisements provide us a fair picture, and what social effects do the advertisements have upon the lives purportedly pictured in them?

Goffman's *Gender Advertisements* was one of the first and is to this day one of the most influential textual analyses of the symbolic potential of advertising images. Central to his view of how gender operates in advertising is his notion of "gender display": "[I]f gender be defined as the culturally established correlates of sex (whether in consequence of biology or learning), then gender display refers to conventionalized portrayals of these correlates" (p. 1). The key, then, to understanding how gender is communicated through advertisements is to understand the notion that advertisements present to us familiar ritual-like displays. However, gender displays in advertising are *polysemic* (containing myriad possible meanings). More than one piece of cultural information may be encoded into them. Further, once a display becomes well-established and stylized the stylization itself becomes the object of attention. Standardization, exaggeration and simplification are found to an extended degree in advertising. Gender displays in advertising are familiar because they show us ritual – that is, bits of behaviors in which we engage in real life.

Goffman's research was unique at the time for employing a method now being labeled "semiotic content analysis." His analysis focused on message structures across the entire discourse of print advertisements containing gender components. Goffman revealed patterns in messages about gender that when repeated constantly and consistently provide a picture of reality that seems natural and real, but is in fact over stylized and conventionalized, or what Goffman called *hyper-ritualized*. Five prominent hyper-ritualizations, or for coding purposes, categories emerged from Goffman's empirical analysis: (1) Relative Size – women in ads are shown as smaller or lower relative to men. (2) Feminine Touch – women are constantly touching themselves, others or objects in ads. (3) Function Ranking – male occupations rank higher in ads than female occupations, consistently. (4) Ritualization of Subordination – women and children are often lower in the frame of the ad, lying on floors or beds or canting the body in ways that convey submission. (5) Licensed Withdrawal – women are never quite part of the scene in a meaningful way.

Goffman's analysis forced the reader to reconsider the relationship between advertising and reality. "He also uncovers the assumptions underlying the interpretive codes buried in advertisements and the way advertising acts as an accomplice in perpetuating regressive forms of social relations" (Leiss, Kline, & Jhally, 1986, p. 169). In all its familiarity, advertising does not merely reflect reality. Although it draws its materials from everyday life, from real gender displays for instance, the bits of everyday life used are selected carefully and much is habitually omitted. By selecting some things to integrate continuously into the message system of advertising (a good example is the ideal female body image), and continuously omitting others (say, the "fleshy" female body), ads create new meanings that are not found elsewhere necessarily.

Cultural critics of communication have attempted to build upon, as well as push beyond, Goffman's ideas of gender display. Taken in historical context, these new directions in theorizing are beginning to address more adequately how gender relations can be reproduced when viewed across time and symbolic conventions (Coward, 1982; Hay, 1989; Kilbourne, 1999, 1987; Masse & Rosenblum, 1988; Millium, 1975; Myers, 1982, 1986; Williamson, 1986; Winship, 1981, 1985). Prominent themes have emerged in this body of work that are of particular relevance here.

The first of these themes involves the "photographic cropping" (Millium, 1975) of female body parts to substitute for the entire body in advertising representations. Women in advertising are very often signified in a fragmented way, by their lips, legs, hair, eyes or hands. The "bit" (lips, legs, breasts, etc.) represents the whole: the sexualized woman (Winship, 1981, p. 25). Men, on the other hand, are less likely to be "dismembered" in this way in advertisements. Jeane Kilbourne (1999, 1987), in particular, describes the cropping of photographs of women in advertising as one of the major elements that present the female as dehumanized and as an object, which is the first step toward the legitimation of committing violence toward that person. This, she argues, contributes to a general climate of violence against women. Kilbourne identifies at least two other hyper-ritualizations in gender advertisements: (1) Innocence is Sexy – ads tend to sexualize female youth and (2) Food and Sex – in recent advertisements food and eating are portrayed as modern woman's sin, replacing sex.

In her analysis of the relationship between the positioning of hands and sexuality in advertising, Janice Winship (1981) brings together the theme of photographic cropping with a second theme, "the public male and the domestic female." Male and female hands are a part of an entire message system of social representation signifying appropriate gender behavior. In her analysis, Winship juxtaposes an ad of a man's hand holding an open pack of Rothman's cigarettes, the "World Leader," and a woman's hand pouring a pitcher of Bird's custard over a dessert, the caption reading, "home-made goodness." A switching of the hands would disrupt the meanings with which each gender imbues the ad:

> A woman's hand does not signify "world leader"; a man's hand does not signify "home-made." But as it is, the appropriately gendered hand allows us to key into familiar ideologies of masculinity and femininity. Those ideologies see "naturally" masculine or feminine, and the represented hand is "naturally" a man's or a woman's. (p. 30)

In 1997 Mee-Eun Kang published a "conceptual replication" of Goffman's *Gender Advertisements*. He sampled over 500 advertisements in all picturing human subjects. One half of the sample was drawn from 1979 magazines and the other half was drawn from the 1991 counterparts to those magazines. Kang added the categories of (1) Body Display – females in ads are often scantily clad or nude and (2) Independence and Self-Assertiveness – how self reliant and independent does the woman appear in the ad?, to Goffman's original five categories. Kang found that few changes had occurred in the representation of women in magazine ads since 1979 (three years after Goffman's findings were published). Although "Function Ranking" and "Relative Size" featured less prominently in 1991 than in 1979, in the two categories of "Licensed Withdrawal" and "Body Display" the 1991 ads showed more stereotyping of women than in 1979.

Race and Gender Display

In media theory, the serious under-representation of a particular group has been coined "symbolic annihilation" (Gerbner & Gross, 1976; Tuchman, Daniels & Benet, 1978). Symbolic annihilation refers to the most profound inequities in "the spectrum of mediated representations of social groups" (see Kielwasser & Wolf, 1992, p. 351). Those consistently annihilated from visual representation in mainstream ads include: Native Americans, Latinos, Asians, gays, lesbians, fat people and little people, to name a few. Blacks, on the other hand, have appeared in advertising almost from its beginning. However, the nature of those representations until very recently has been dubious at best. In her study of the "raceing" of advertising featuring women between 1876 and 1900, Marilyn Maness Mehaffy (1997) charts how negative depictions of Black women were instrumental to the construction of the ideal White female consumer. In image after image the "visual narrative of ideal (White) consuming domesticity takes shape through her juxtaposition with a mirroring Black female figure, typically associated, in contrast, with pre-industrial technologies and economies of home production" (p. 135). The Black woman was the "domestic" to ideal domesticity occupied by the White woman (consumer).

> In today's putatively race- and gender-blind era, the raced-gender allocations of late nineteenth-century advertising cards haunt the rhetorics of contemporary media, and, in the perennial, dually raced invocations of "welfare queens" and sanctified white motherhood, they haunt contemporary politics and government as well. (p. 172)

Since World War II until very recently, women of color were required to be light-skinned fine-featured, resembling the European ideal of beauty, in order to be represented as anything other than a Mammy-figure in print or television advertising. Feminist scholars such as Roach and Felix (1989) suggest that we live in a culture where the dominant gaze is not only male, but white. Up until the last decade or so, representations of African Americans were mostly excluded, but when included highly stereotyped and ghettoized, placed outside "natural" and "beautiful" representation in advertising and positioned as "other." However, unlike the "exotic other" of the Hawaiian or Philippino "girls" in suntan advertisements (see Williamson, 1986), African Americans are society's mundane other, (Cui, 2000; Fredrickson, 1988; McLaughlin & Goulet, 1999; Miles, 1989; Omi & Winant, 1986).

Scott Coltrane and Melinda Messineo (2000) content analyzed 1,699 television commercials that aired on programs with high ratings from 1992 to 1994 in order to study the interrelationship between race and gender in advertising. The authors suggest that

> television commercials do more than offer people images of selves defined through the consumption of products. In addition, they shape images of others and sustain group boundaries that come to be taken for granted. Feelings of entitlement, subtle forms of prejudice, and institutional racism are thus reproduced in and through commercial television imagery. (p. 385)

Coltrane and Messineo found that although African-American images were more plentiful than in previous decades, the ways they are represented still reinforce established prejudices. Characters in television commercials still "enjoy more prominence and exercise more authority" if they are White or men. Women and Whites occupy most family-oriented commercial imagery. "In general, 1990s television commercials tend to portray White men as powerful, White women as sex objects, African-American men as aggressive, and African-American women as inconsequential" (p. 363).

The Semiotics of Gender in Advertising

Many of the most illuminating studies of advertising images have employed some variation of semiology (see Barthes, 1977, 1988; Leiss, Kline, & Jhally, 1986; Nichols, 1981; Williamson, 1978, 1986). By treating the advertising image as a "text," semiotic analyses concentrate on the relationships between the ads' internal meaning structures as they relate to the larger cultural codes shared by viewers. Semiology's relationship to advertising is explained succinctly by Sut Jhally (1987):

> Semiology is the study of signs, or more specifically the *system of signs*. A sign is something that has significance within a system of meaning and is constituted of two key elements: the signifier (the material vehicle) and the signified (the mental construct, the idea). The two elements are equally necessary and can be separated only analytically . . . This is the difference between the signifier and the sign. A diamond as signifier is *empty* of meaning. The diamond as sign is *full* of meaning. . . . production produces commodities as signifiers while advertising produces them as signs. (p. 130)

Advertising operates in the realm of symbols, drawing from those already familiar, and inventing new signs where none existed before. The symbol is a sign that has been arbitrarily imbued with meaning, either through culture, habit, or through the intentional strategy of marketing. For example, the signifier of a rose is literally the plant (its petals, stem, leaves, thorns, pigment). However, in this culture the most prevalent signifieds of rose are "love," "affection," and "beauty." These meanings are arbitrary in that there is nothing in the plant itself that either resembles or points to these things. However, culture has "naturalized" these connotations for us. Marketing campaigns achieve this. For example when the early 1990s marketing campaign for Guess? jeans repeatedly used the photographic image of super model Claudia Schiffer in their ads, the image of Claudia Schiffer became a symbol of Guess? jeans, or, more accurately, a symbol of the Guess? style and "look." This pairing of Schiffer and Guess? jeans was arbitrary.

The meaning of any given sign is culturally defined and culturally specific. When advertising and marketing campaigns attempt to sell commodities (signifiers) to the public, they either work with the cultural connotations with which the commodity is already imbued, or, in the case of a new product (a generic commodity), the significance of the commodity is invented entirely in the process of advertising. For example, the long-running "Diamonds are Forever" ad campaign draws on cultural meanings of a diamond familiar to consumers, but then imbues particular types of diamond rings (signifiers) with very particular signifieds. The eternity diamond ring, for example, through the magic of this advertising campaign now signifies to us, "marriage anniversary," or "milestones within marriage" such as the birth of a child. The ad campaign draws heavily on the persuasive appeal of "guilt" to convey especially to the male consumer that if he lets these milestones go by without rewarding "her" with an eternity diamond ring, he is some kind of clod. So, in this regard, the "Diamonds are Forever" campaign signifies as much about what it means if one has reached these marital milestones and does *not* own an eternity ring, as it signifies about what it means *to* own and wear a diamond eternity ring. The campaign presents us with the diamond eternity ring as a full sign, both in its presence and in its absence (Shields, 2002).

Pioneering scholars in the area of semiotics and advertising such as Judith Williamson (1978), Bill Nichols (1981) and Sut Jhally (1987) were concerned with how individual advertisements are interdependent on one another for meaning – as a *code*. "Signs do not occur singly; they occur in groups . . . placing signs into appropriate groupings stresses that meaning arises not solely, not even primarily, from the relationship of signifier to signified but relations between signs" (Leeds-Hurwitz, 1993, p. 51). A code is not a mere grouping of signs, however. A code is a system of associations governed by rules agreed upon (explicitly or implicitly) between members of a culture. The code unifies the different elements of the process of meaning construction. In advertising, a code is the store of experience upon which both the advertiser and audience draw in their participation in the construction of "commodity meaning" (Jhally, 1987, p. 140).

As cultural codes shift within dominant ideologies some signs acquire different signifieds, sometimes in direct opposition to the previous signifieds – such is the case with the sign of the cigarette. In the 1950s celebrities with squeaky clean images, like Donna Reed, advertised for Chesterfields, while major league baseball players endorsed Camels, and Lucky Strikes used images of teenage cheerleaders. In the 1950s the cigarette was a somewhat empty signifier and the challenge for advertisers was differentiating between brands of a fairly generic product. Today the cigarette itself is a "full sign" of negative connotations *before* advertisers try to invest it with a particular image. The challenge for advertisers today is to deal with the fullness of the sign in the first place, and then attach some kind of positive signification to it (Shields, 2002). Camel has done it with a cartoon character; Malboro is still using the image of the rugged outdoorsman; and Virginia Slims has attempted to incorporate advances from the women's movement into their campaigns. Many cigarette ads marketed to women still implicitly push them as an appetite suppressant and aid in weight-loss.

Advertising insists that we differentiate what kind of person we "are" in relation to a specific product. Differentiation cannot be interpreted as a wholly overt and cognitively conscious process, however. Differentiation is often emotional and sensual. Many fashion advertisements, for example, operate at a level of social significance that is once-removed from the utility of the product being advertised (Shields, 1990). The sensuality of the image does not define the commodity, so much as it differentiates the sensuousness of one commodity from the sensuousness of another.

The transfer of codes of sexuality to commodities in this culture is widely accessible to both males and females because the transfer has become "naturalized" in our popular iconography. More specifically, the transfer of codes of ideal female beauty or attractiveness to commodities has become common sense, even though the relationship between, say, a woman in a swimsuit and a can of beer is in itself arbitrary. However, the sign of the ideal female body, in this culturally naturalized state takes on an exchange-value all its own. It is an ambiguous discourse that can be visually attached to virtually any commodity in order to lend the commodity value. Therefore, when the woman in the swimsuit appears in an advertisement for beer, the relationship between the sexuality of the female body and the commodity (beer) does not appear to be arbitrary. The sexuality of the female body has a general exchange-value lent in this case to the value of beer, but could just as easily be lent to the value of an automobile or cigarettes (Shields, 1996).

Ideologies of the Body in Ads

The "general exchange-value" of the ideal female body reaches far beyond advertising in this culture. This exchange-value is what John Berger (1972) coined, a cultural way of seeing. Ways of seeing the female body are culturally imbued codes which are consistent across not only advertising images but other visual images as well such as film, television programs, music videos, soft-porn and even portraiture. This consistency in representation helps define what is "natural" to be seen and enjoyed – what is ideal. A photograph or an advertising image is a selective view of reality. In this culture, advertising images of females frequently contain an invisible yet implicit man who approves of and defines the feminine ideal. Thus, the "point-of-view" in advertisements featuring the perfect female body is most always that of an implied male spectator. This implied approval by an often invisible male spectator is referred to by feminist scholars as the "male gaze." Seen through the lens of the "male gaze" females are the objects of the gaze as opposed to the subjects of the gaze.

The male gaze connotes significantly more than mere voyeurism. It is a controlling gaze. "To possess the image of a woman's sexuality is, however massproduced the image, also in some way to possess, to maintain a degree of control over the woman in general (Kuhn, 1985, p. 11)." Laura Mulvey (1975) further explains the concept of the gendered gaze:

> In a world ordered by sexual imbalance, pleasure in looking has been split between active/male and passive/female. The determining male gaze projects its fantasy onto the female figure, which is styled accordingly. In their traditional exhibitionist role women are simultaneously looked at and displayed, with their appearance coded for strong visual and erotic impact so that they can be said to connote *to-be-looked-at-ness*. (p. 366)

For Rosalind Coward (1985), the male gaze encoded in photographic images is an extension of how men view women in the streets. The naturalness of this way of seeing the female body follows from its pervasiveness in all arenas of female representation as well as experience. In this schema, the female looking at an image is always a "split-subject." Women in patriarchal cultures are placed in a position of always being the embodiment of the object of the sight for someone else's pleasure and simultaneously being aware that she is this object of the sight. It also allows for a way of seeing that seems natural in appeal to both male and female spectators. If aesthetic appeal of the female body is naturalized for both males and females, it also seems natural that the female body is represented as sexualized more often than the male body.

Patricia Mellencamp (1995) explains the phenomena in this way:

> It is precisely this misrecognition [the split between a woman's self-image and her mirror image], a real alienation effect – woman divided against her inadequate self, body versus mind, mother versus daughter or son, woman versus woman – that must be overcome. After all, the body is an image and a sack of flesh; it is a historical, personal fiction or style as much as a reality. Certainly, the body is neither self nor identity nor value; we are much more, much greater, than our bodies. Sex and the body don't grant identity, as Michel Foucault said over a decade ago, yet we keep looking there for answers. (p. 3)

Weight and Discipline

Just as the female body is the site of idealization and spectacle for the male gaze, it is also the site of anxiety and insecurity for women, who, constrained by the gaze, feel less embodied than objectified and reach out for ways to transform the body into the ideal, or as close as possible. The symbolic annihilation of body fat within the realm of the media means that we rarely ever see role models of heavy women looking attractive, receiving love or attention, particularly from handsome men. Moreover, when images of heavier women are shown, they tend to be negative images – jealous, angry villains like Ursula of Disney's *The Little Mermaid*, Sally Struthers in *South Park*, Mimi of *The Drew Carey Show*, or child-like pathetic creatures (the suicidal girl of *Heathers*, the mother of *What's Eating Gilbert Grape*).

As a culture, then we conceive of fat as being something outside the norm or linked to socially unacceptable behavior. When the vast percentage of media stars, actresses, and models we see are extraordinarily thin, many women and girls in particular begin to lose perspective on what really is the average weight of most women, and get a sense of the "norm" as being accurately represented in print, on TV and in film. In fact the "normal" weight of actresses and models is far below what is actually the average weight of everyday women, generally by up to 23 percent less (Women's Action Coalition, 1993).

In *Unbearable Weight* (1993), Susan Bordo convincingly shows how narcissism, the self-directed gaze, is a logical extension of a long tradition of Western thought: the epistemological and philosophical obsession with dualism. Dualism is the splitting of the head (the self, the "me," the part that thinks and reasons, the spiritual self) from the body. Bordo observes that the "self" in dualist thought is identified as that which has control, while the body has historically been conceived of as the enemy. The body is subject to disease and distracts the mind from thinking or spiritual activity because of its need for food, warmth, rest and other bodily functions. Importantly, women, as "irrational" and representative of nature, have been depicted as being closer to the body, while men, who have been depicted as the rational architects of society, are seen to be closer to "the mind" (Shields, 2002).

Bordo shows how contemporary views on the virtues of slenderness simply reiterate the way that the "self" is expected to control and discipline the body. Just as today we make assumptions about an individual's worth, self-liking, or laziness based on their weight, in the past the ascetic values of fasting monks and saints were represented by their wasted flesh. The saints' ability to fast, to deny the needs of their body, was a way of demonstrating their control, and thus the superiority of their mind and spirit, over the unholy body. The spirit was seen as separated from the body. In other words, one measure of our mental and spiritual control, indeed, our morality, is through how well we control our bodies. Slenderness thus becomes not only a sign of our mental health, but represents our status as a good person.

As Bordo reveals, this theme reappears today as thin people are likewise popularly represented as having mental control (will power and self-discipline). In contrast, fat is associated with the lack of will – the inability to control the needs and processes of one's body and hunger. Fat is seen as a demonstration of the person's lack of control over their demanding body. So, in addition to being symbolically annihilated, when they *do* appear in the media or in literature, heavy people are characterized as out of control, greedy, childish, or even mentally unwell. Carole Spitzack (1990) has likewise observed that fat people are often portrayed as disliking themselves.

As Susie Orbach (1978) has noted, fat is a particularly sensitive issue for women not only because of the historical association between women and the body, but because of women's position in the cultural pecking order and access to resources. Cultural and feminist scholars like Orbach, Bordo, Spitzack, and Naomi Wolf (1991) have all examined the ways that female consumption – of food and other resources – for both nourishment and pleasure has been suppressed throughout history. Consequently, female hunger for food, like female desire for sex or knowledge, has been derided and suppressed.

Following Michel Foucault (1977), Rowe, like Bordo (1993) and Spitzack (1990), describes how social groups maintain control over their members by setting standards of "normalcy." In a famous example, Foucault describes the idea of the panopticon in which prisoners are so used to being observed by the prison guards that they begin to police their own behavior to conform to the set standards of the prison (or society). The body that refuses to follow the aesthetic standards of its culture whether in bodily beauty or behavior can thus "communicate resistance to social discipline" (Rowe, 1995, p. 65). Therefore, women whose bodies show their willingness to eat, to have sex, or who break the rules of femininity in other ways are perceived as transgressing against the social bounds of propriety. At some level they are refusing to limit themselves, refusing to pretend that their hunger and desires do not exist – and thereby posing an unspoken threat to patriarchy. Thus, Rowe argues that female fat is hated in part because "it signifies a disturbing unresponsiveness to social control" (Rowe, 1995, p. 61). In today's culture, body fat may be read, albeit unconsciously, as a sign of women rebelling against the male gaze by refusing to conform to standards of beauty. Female fat also signifies a woman's ability and desire to consume for herself as subject – rather than to merely exist as object and for the pleasures of others.

In *Confessing Excess* (1990), Carole Spitzack suggests that this arrangement is aided by an ideology of women's health that condones policing the body in order to reap the reward of "freedom" or "release" from the unhealthy fat body. In order to maintain the healthy liberated body, one must continuously discipline it, police its cravings and excesses, and reprimand the self when discipline falters. Advertisements for diet products, fitness gyms, clothing and cosmetics tap into this ideology of the female body. These advertisements offer "solutions" to the disjuncture between the image of fashion models' bodies and real women's bodies by disciplining the body in the name of fitness – the triumph of culture over nature. The 1980s ushered in a new female physique complementary to aerobic exercise and activity. This curvaceous, muscular look, which is now most closely associated in its ideal form with supermodel Heidi Klum, is the combination of cultural antitheses: thin and muscular, hard and curvaceous, it suggests power and yet a slender boyishness; furthermore those very muscles which empower are also the material of feminine curves (Shields, 2002).

Achieving this combination of attributes is difficult, involving an investment of large amounts of time, money and effort on "body work." As Susan Bordo (1993) has observed, the ultra-thin look of the 1960s and 1970s could be achieved through starvation diets alone, but today, thinness without muscle tone falls short of the ideal feminine physique. The ideal must be achieved through a regimen of diet plus exercise.

As Spitzack argues, "Women are socialized to view the ongoing surveillance of their bodies as a form of empowerment that arises from self-love. The newly slender woman purchases a new wardrobe, presumably, because she likes herself now that she is thin: when fat, she did not like herself and consequently did not give adequate attention to appearance" (p. 35). These competing discourses surrounding body reduction help to position the discourse of thinness with "health," thereby placing weightiness or fatness in binary opposition with "health," as "disease." These discourses work with numerous other institutions and practices to encourage self-correction and, therefore, "liberation" from the disease of fat, especially for women. Thus, women, whose bodies are made to put on weight, find their natural bodies represented as diseased and abnormal. The possession of fat itself – of femaleness itself – is a sign of disease.

Selling Women Their "New Freedom"

In the past 10 years or so marketers have made a concerted effort to develop ad campaigns that seem to speak directly to female experience. Advertisers have tried also to capitalize on the fact that women are more conscious than ever before; that blindly striving toward the idealized body in ads, film and on MTV shouldn't be their raison d'être; and that the rewards are hollow and the time and effort lost could be put to more meaningful and sustaining use (Shields, 2002). Advertisers have also picked up on the fact that women are tired of the size four body being presented as "everywoman." However, most of these ad campaigns offer "a wink" toward women and not a viable alternative to traditional sex-sells campaigns. Advertising scholar Daniel Nicholson (1997) describes the wink – or self-referentiality within an ad: when advertisers want the reader to recognize that "we know you know what we're trying to do, but because we're letting you know we know, it makes it okay – because we're so hip to your hipness. Get it?" (182–3). Just as Sprite was marketed to teens as the only soft drink that respects its consumer's media savvy, brands such as Special K, Levi's, Chic and Virginia Slims have tried to "anti-market" to women.

Take recent advertisements for Special K cereal. A television ad campaign for Special K in the mid-1990s suggested that women shouldn't be taken in by the prescriptions they see in the media, they should accept themselves. This particular campaign doesn't linger visually on any female body, but features a woman, probably in her forties, moving to light music as if in a yoga class. She is shot in soft-focus and no full body shots are revealed and no body fetishes are lingered over. This campaign showed that Special K could provide an intervention if they really tried; however can we as consumers above the age of 35 really forget that it was Special K commercials that got the whole nation obsessing in the 1970s about whether we could "pinch an inch"? Yet, this quickly became another measure of whether one was too fat in the 1970s. Pinching an inch of flesh was shameful and meant one needed to get right to work on the body. Their campaign tapped completely and directly into a culture of thin-obsessed girls and women who were willing to take advice from almost anywhere, even a cereal commercial, to achieve that "goal" of ultra-thinness (Shields, 2002).

The marketers of Special K seemed to suffer from a type of schizophrenia in the 1990s. Around the same time they were suggesting that women just relax and accept their bodies and themselves, a print ad in women's magazines featured a small floral bikini simply lying against a white background. The caption reads "it's not doing any good in your drawer." Again, Special K couldn't resist tapping into one of women's phobias – being seen in a bathing suit. A recent ad for Special K seems to be one of the biggest winks toward women yet. The television ad features supermodel Cindy Crawford first making fun of her/our participation in fashion trends and then suggesting it is just as silly to participate in eating fads, finally suggesting that Special K always has been and remains a sensible diet food; positioned somehow outside of diet trends. A very natural looking and un-glamorous Crawford is metaphorically winking at us saying, "I know that you know I've probably done as much as anybody to make you feel paranoid about your body, but when we are all in our jeans and t-shirts we are just the same – responsible grown-ups who can live both in and outside of diet trends and fads – Right?"

More than a Wink: Intervening in the Imagery Landscape

Stuart Hall and Sut Jhally in their writings, but more explicitly in their respective Media Education Foundation videos, "Media and Representation" (1996) and "Dreamworlds II" (1995), theorize that the changes in media representation that will radically improve the image landscape for those currently or traditionally symbolically annihilated needs to come from within the oppressive media forms themselves. Alternative media has its important place in activism and disruption to traditional media systems in the form of exposing viewers to alternatives. However, the leftist agenda of concentrating its creative energies primarily on alternative interventions has left the stifling codes and conventions of white, male, heterosexist media to flourish in the twentieth century and into the new millennium.

There are current media images of women that are attempting to implode cultural expectations for women's beauty, bodies and lives from *within* the aesthetics and conventions of well-established and popular media forms such as the women's magazine and the 60-second commercial radio and TV ad. Several magazines now exist which are geared towards larger women – both in content and in ads. Of these magazines, *Mode* (in circulation from 1977 to 2001) has perhaps received the most publicity for its stated intent to provide attractive images of women that reflect the diversity of women, both size-wise and racially. In fact, unlike *Big, Bold and Beautiful*, a magazine that caters to larger women, *Mode's* stated goal is to promote positive self-image of women of all sizes. It presents itself as not only anti-fat oppression, but anti-sizeism.

For example, in the February 2000 issue under the regular feature "Mode Matters" a story titled, "Can't Lick It!" addresses how sizeism affects all women, thick or thin:

> Size discrimination in Hollywood has taken a new turn. Lara Flynn Boyle, Jennifer Aniston, Calista Flockhart, and others are being referred to as "The Lollipop Girls" (big heads, stick bodies). After our initial snicker, we realized that it's still size discrimination. We believe no one should look to anyone for validation. Give your body what it needs to live a happy life. Oh, and of course, read *Mode* for real inspiration. (Day, 2000, p. 32)

Reflecting the unwillingness to label by size, until January, 2000 the cover of *Mode* used to read "*Mode: 12, 14, 16 . . .*" Now it simply reads "*Mode: The new shape in fashion.*"

The slightly knowing, "in with the joke" tone in the last sentence of "Lollipop Girls" cues us into another quality of *Mode*. It presumes and plays upon a high level of media literacy and the fact that its readers are cognizant of the pressures found in mainstream advertising. In other words, its readers are already presumed to be negotiating or resistant readers. This is clearly evidenced in the letters to the editor section, which offer much more interesting and often critical responses to the content of *Mode* than are found in other magazines. For example, in the February, 2000 edition, MH writes:

> Regarding your recent query about *Mode* men, please don't go there!!! Virtually every other women's magazine on the market has scores of articles on men, sex, dating, etc. The very thing that keeps me hooked on *Mode* is that it helps me (at size 14–16) look the best *I* can. I don't need any more advice on relationships or men or anything else. Please keep your wonderful magazine in its original, fresh, relevant, and helpful state. (21)

Unlike *Ms.*, *Mode* does not take a "feminist" perspective per se and is not presented as an "alternative" magazine. *Mode's* glossy paper is like that of any mainstream fashion magazine. The advertisements reflect both "traditional" advertising aesthetics, but also offer more images of "normal" sized women. Indeed, the content, format and style of *Mode* is much like any other fashion magazine. The articles deal with dating tips, new seasonal styles, a health and fitness section, and make-up tips and bridal pages. The products offered inside its covers are primarily clothing and make-up, with an occasional car ad or other product featured. *Mode* stresses the fact that all women want to be and can be stylish. The similarity of *Mode* to other fashion magazines means that women can read *Mode* as a familiar genre without feeling ostracized from other women. The magazine is not positioned as alternative or "other," but as addressing the same concerns other women's magazines have, except for allowing greater diversity of size.

However, while the rhetoric of anti-sizeism is clear and there is a repeated editorial insistence on the dangers of labeling, *Mode* actually does quite a bit of size labeling. Many letters to the editor feature profiles on notable women, and blurbs on the magazine models feature some kind of reference to their size, framed usually within a clothing size (14–16 or 22). While on one hand this reinforces the idea of size as a label, it also projects and speaks what is usually unspoken for women of normal and heavier weights and/or sizes. By speaking and naming the size as 22 or 18, those sizes seem more acceptable. Yet this also reinforces the idea of women fitting into pre-categorized shapes.

Just My Size Pantyhose has created a series of ads that are quite successful in this tactic, titled "Just My Opinion," that consistently run in *Mode* magazine. In one ad the left-hand bottom shows a color picture of an African-American woman partially reclining against some pillows with one leg stretched in the air and her hand caressing her leg. She wears a black bra, white pearls, a wedding band on her finger, and a pair of pantyhose. She is smiling and looking out at the spectator. While part of her stomach is hidden by her arm and leg, we can see the fleshy creases around her lower belly, and her legs and partially-exposed bottom appear thick. Her skin has rich brown sheen. Her eyes sparkle. She looks like she is glowing. Partially printed across this image are the words "I am the product of a lifetime of learning." The image works against the grain of the anti-age aesthetic by stressing the "lifetime of learning"; weight is somehow being associated with knowledge and experience. That experience, as suggested by the wedding ring, includes a man. Her pearls signify economic stability.

The woman in this ad is clearly posed in a way that is sexual. Half dressed, she reclines on what appears to be a couch, but there is a blanket that is half pulled off. The fact that it is clearly daytime, the couch, her state of undress, and her provocative pose suggests that she has recently had or is about to have a noon-time sexual rendezvous. Obviously the sight of a large-sized woman being shown in dishabille and posed sexually is new, even for the pages of *Mode*. The idea of "looseness" that the ad urges goes against most traditional ideas of advertising. Most ads urge for control over "loose" bodies that threaten to go out of control. This *Just My Size* ad clearly equates a large, lived-in body with sexuality, a romantic life and comfort.

The power of this image, particularly for those who have not seen their images represented as attractive or sexual, cannot be overlooked. The psycho-sexual rejection of many fat women, the exclusion from "normalcy," is powerful in its negativity. Exclusion means that not only is one different – but in an odd way one is almost inhuman. A fat woman loses her right to sexuality – the very thing that defines her as a woman (supposedly). If she cannot appeal sexually she loses the right to not only representation, but to things like sex, men, a home and family. The image of a thicker woman in this ad is revolutionary in that not only does it (partly) reveal a heavy body, but suggests the sexuality of that body. Moreover, unlike most ads, it does not associate fat bodies with negativity or low self-esteem, but high self-esteem.

There appears to be a contradiction here. Feminist scholars generally argue against the objectification of woman. Why then might it be desirable to objectify large women anymore than thin women? The difference is in the right to be seen as a sexual object. Ads gain their meaning from context – from their relationship to other ads as well as their relationship to the larger world. As Sut Jhally (1990) has observed, there is nothing inherently bad about visual objectification. It is part of human nature to objectify and to want to be objectified at times. The evaluation of that objectification as positive or negative comes from the image's relationship to other images in a system. In a sign system in which female sexuality and objectification is a sign of female success, the absence of objectified heavy women as sexual means that they are symbolically annihilated from being seen as sexual beings. And, in not being shown as sexual objects, fat women lose the right to be seen as laying claim to the privileges of that objectification – love, marriage, children and other aspects of "feminine" success.

The *Just My Size* campaign offers its audience images of women that directly confront ideas of women as lacking subjectivity. They feature an attitude that heavily promotes ideas of individualism, physical freedom and choice. This is not itself an unusual tactic; most ads do this. However, in contrast to many ads discussed earlier, the *Just My Size* campaign places notions of individuality in a slightly different context, suggesting that the women are already there. These ads feature images of happy women who are happy because they already possess the right attitude. Her subjectivity will not be created by the use of a new product. Her subjectivity will occur when she recognizes she already has it. Obviously in a culture and an advertising standard that continually urges women to take up less space and control their desires, these *Just My Size* ads are radical in that they present an idea of the woman as being already refined.

Resistant Encoding: NARAL Ads

At least one series of ads work, not by distancing themselves from the concepts of individuality utilized by most advertisers, but, curiously, by co-opting them; reframing messages of individuality, placing them in a new context in a way that does work for feminist goals. These advertising campaigns may be read as interventions in that they consciously deal with the female body as a contested terrain over which political and ideological battles are fought.

In the mainstream media, we often see the female body being depicted as a sexualized object. As an object, of course, female bodies lose subjectivity and individuality. The attitude that fosters this dehumanization of the female body is accompanied by and linked to attitudes in which the female becomes separated from her body. Depicting women as dehumanized objects removes their subjectivity, their capacity to be seen as individuals and to make individual choices. If the female body is an object to be enjoyed and controlled by others, then the female herself has no right to her body. No right to control her body against the advances of others, no right to sexual pleasure in her own body, and particularly lacking in the ability to control her reproductive choices.

The NARAL (National Abortion and Reproductive Rights Action League) "Choice for America" advertising campaign co-opts the rhetoric and discourses of right-wing politics and pro-life factions. These ads frame reproductive rights as being intrinsically linked to "American" values of individuality and freedom – the foundation of subjectivity. They also co-opt the language of faith and responsibility frequently used in pro-life rhetoric. By using these tactics, NARAL promotes female subjectivity at the same time the body is presented for examination, asking us to reconsider meanings of that bodily representation.

NARAL ads play with themes of individuality and concepts of individual freedom as an essential "American" quality. They also explicitly reference the battles that Americans have fought, equating the pro-choice position with protection against the "invasion" of foreign forces. This is a typical right-wing rhetoric used against the perceived threat of forces that would "invade" and take over the "American" way of life – such as Islamic extremists. The ad appeals to the history of the American military by evoking images of battle and bravery and America as a nation of fighters.

The use of the word "blessed" is telling. It presents freedom as a "natural" gift and also suggests that NARAL is articulating a religious view. In contrast to those who would argue that abortion is a godless act, the ad suggests that not only does God exist, but that God sanctions a woman's right to choose. The appeal to the pro-life ideal of protecting life is twisted as the ad references social responsibility as including concern for the well-being of woman and child.

In NARAL ads, a woman's body becomes linked to a sense of eternity, infinity and the always-existing value of "freedom." By doing so, the body becomes imbued with an over-determination of meaning connected to individuality. In this way the NARAL campaign has moved from the body as object, to one in which the body becomes a sign of individuality, of movement and identity bursting beyond restraint. This visual technique echoes other new media forms which are representing the female body in new and different ways, such as the female action hero in such television shows as *Buffy the Vampire Slayer*, *La Femme Nikita* and *Xena: Warrior Princess* (Heinecken, 1999).

Conclusion

The analysis of the content of gender advertisements has been studied from a variety of methodological, theoretical and epistemological perspectives since the rash of sex-roles research and Goffman's semiotic content analysis in the 1970s. Scholars replicating the early content analyses of pioneers such as Courtney and Whipple and those testing the longevity of Goffman's categories reported little difference in the representation of women from the 1970s to the 1990s.

Feminist scholars, in particular, have been instrumental in focusing their analyses of gender and advertising in the larger theoretical and epistemological debates bubbling up in feminist scholarship, the social sciences and humanities in order to better understand the consistent ideology of the body portrayed in ads. For example, scholars such as Judith Williamson and Ros Coward employed advances in film theory, psychoanalysis and structuralism to analyze how our gender subjectivities are positioned through advertising. The psychoanalytic perspective can be credited with giving scholars of gender advertising the theoretical tools to analyze the concept of the "male gaze" encoded in most mass media in this society. Further, feminist scholars of gender advertising have relied heavily on the construct of the "split-consciousness" of the female subject to theorize how advertising works to encourage women to continuously view themselves as objects to be improved upon for the male other, rather than to view themselves as subjects of their own femaleness.

Obviously advertising is not produced or consumed in a vacuum; to a great extent, the liberatory potential of any image is reliant upon the social structures that surround it. To that extent, changing imagery is not enough. The culture itself must change, from being one in which girls and women are devalued to one in which they are cherished. Yet positive imagery must also play a role. Pipher (1994) argues that "Adolescent girls need a more public place in our culture, not as sex objects, but as interesting and complicated human beings" (p. 289). Similarly, more positive images of women may be central in influencing females' self-perception. More positive reporting on female public figures like politicians, athletes and women in entertainment are necessary. Women's magazines and their advertisements play a central role.

In recent years, advertisers seem to have recognized that women are tired of being presented with uniform, unrealistic visions of the "ideal" woman. As a result, they have created campaigns that on one hand seem to address women's concerns, while on the other hand offer only "a wink" toward women. The wink is a way of addressing the audience, suggesting that social equality for women has already been achieved. However, closer examination reveals that the wink is one way that traditionally conservative ideals are recycled into a more palatable "feminist" or progressive framework, while in fact achieving no real significant change in how women are represented.

Nonetheless, there are an increasing number of media forms that seem to be seriously trying to present more positive images of women. *Mode* magazine presents itself as an "anti-sizeist" fashion magazine. While *Mode* often fails to present truly progressive images, it has been somewhat successful in normalizing some images, like those of large-size women, that have previously been outside the dominant frame. The success of such ads can at least partly be measured by letters to *Mode*'s editor that consistently express the joy readers feel at finally recognizing themselves in ads. However, one possible reason for the success of *Mode*'s ads is that there is really very little difference between them and mainstream ads. The different sizes and shapes of *Mode*'s models, no matter how revolutionary, remain contextualized within a traditional discourse of individuality and consumer choice.

Such rhetoric has also been co-opted by at least one ad campaign that is truly revolutionary and progressive, consciously dealing with the female body as a site where political and ideological battles are fought. NARAL's recent campaign reinforces notions of individuality. Recalling the way that men's bodies have been glorified in western and action films, the women of the NARAL ads always seem to be *more* than their bodies, imbued with an over-determination of meaning connected to individuality. In this way NARAL ads move from presenting the female body as object, to one in which the body becomes a sign of subjectivity. Unlike Special K's mythology of the individual women's new-found body acceptance as a means to sell cereal, NARAL ads tie their imagery to a truly feminist goal.

References

Barthes, R. (1977). *Image Music Text*. New York: The Noonday Press.

Barthes, R. (1988). *The Semiotic Challenge* (trans. R. Howard). New York: Hill and Wang.

Belkaoui, A. and Belkaoui, J. M. (1976). A comparative study of the roles portrayed by women in print advertisements: 1958, 1969, 1972. *Journal of Marketing Research*, 13, 168–72.

Berger, J. (1972). *Ways of Seeing*. London: British Film Institute.

Bordo, S. (1993). *Unbearable Weight*. Los Angeles: University of California Press.

Bretl, D. J. and Cantor, J. (1988). The portrayal of men and women in U.S. television commercials: A recent content analysis and trends over 15 years. *Sex Roles*, 18(9/10), 595–609.

Busby, L. J. (1975). Sex-role research on the mass media. *Journal of Communication*, 25(4), 107–31.

Coltrane, S. and Messineo, M. (2000). The perpetuation of subtle prejudice: Race and gender imagery in 1990s television advertising. *Sex Roles*, 42(5–6), 363–89.

Courtney, A. E. (1983). *Sex Stereotyping in Advertising*. Lexington, MA: Lexington Books.

Courtney, A. E. and Lockeretz, S. W. (1971). A woman's place: An analysis of the roles portrayed by women in magazine advertisements. *Journal of Marketing Research*, 8(1), 92–5.

Courtney, A. E. and Whipple, T. W. (1974). Women in TV commercials. *Journal of Communication*, 24(2), 110–18.

Coward, R. (1982). Sexual violence and sexuality. *Feminist Review*, 1(11), 9–22.

Coward, R. (1985). *Female Desires: How they are sought, bought and packaged*. New York: Grove Press.

Cui, G. (2000). Advertising of alcoholic beverages in African-American and women's magazines: Implications for health communication. *Howard Journal of Communication*, 11, 279–93.

Day, H. (2000). Can't lick it. *Mode Magazine*, February, 32.

Dominick, J. R. and Rauch, G. E. (1972). The image of women in network TV commercials. *Journal of Broadcasting*, 16(3), 259–65.

Downs, A. C. (1981). Sex-role stereotyping on prime-time television. *The Journal of Genetic Psychology*, 138, 253–8.

Fejes, F. (1992). Masculinity as fact: A review of empirical mass communication research on masculinity. In S. Craig (ed.), *Men, Masculinity, and the Media*. Newbury Park, CA: Sage, pp. 219–22.

Ferguson, J. H., Kreshel, P. J., and Tinkham, S. F. (1990). In the pages of *Ms.*: Sex role portrayals of women in advertising. *Journal of Advertising*, 19(1), 40–51.

Ferrante, C. L., Haynes, A. M., and Kingsley, S. M. (1988). Image of women in television advertising. *Journal of Broadcasting and Electronic Media*, 32(2), 231–7.

Foucault, M. (1977). *Discipline and Punish: The birth of the prison* (trans. A. Sheridan). London: Penguin Press.

Fowles, J. (1996). *Advertising and Popular Culture*. Thousand Oaks, CA: Sage.

Fredrickson, G. M. (1988). *The Arrogance of Race: Historical perspectives on slavery, racism, and social inequality*. Middleton, CT: Wesleyan University Press.

Friedan, B. (1963). *The Feminine Mystique*. New York: Dell.

Furnham, A. (1989). Gender stereotypes in Italian television advertisements. *Journal of Broadcasting and Electronic Media*, 33(2), 175–85.

Furnham, A., Abramsky, S., and Gunter, B. (1997). A cross-cultural content analysis of children's television advertisements. *Sex Roles*, 37(1–2), 91–9.

Geis, F. L., Brown, V., Jennings, J., and Porter, N. (1984). TV commercials as achievement scripts for women. *Sex Roles*, 10(7/8), 513–25.

Gerbner, G. and Gross, L. (1976). Living with television: The violence profile. *Journal of Communication*, 26(2), 172–99.

Gilly, M. C. (1988). Sex roles in advertising: A comparison of television advertisements in Australia, Mexico, and the United States. *Journal of Marketing*, 52, 75–85.

Goffman, E. (1976). *Gender Advertisements*. New York: Harper and Row.

Gould, S. J. (1987). Gender differences in advertising response and self-consciousness variables. *Sex Roles*, 16(5/6), 215–25.

Griffin, M., Viswanath, K., and Schwartz, D. (1992). *Gender Advertising in the U.S. and India: Exporting cultural stereotypes*. Minneapolis: University of Minnesota School of Journalism and Mass Communication.

Hall, S. (1996). *Representation and the Media*. Video. Amherst, MA: Media Education Foundation.

Hawkins, J. W. and Aber, C. S. (1993). Women in advertisements in medical journals. *Sex Roles*, 28(3/4), 233–42.

Hay, J. (1989). Advertising as a cultural text (rethinking message analysis in a recombinant culture). In B. Dervin, L. Grossberg, B. J. O'Keefe and E. Wartella (eds.), *Rethinking Communication*. Newbury Park, CA: Sage, pp. 129–51.

Heinecken, D. (1999). The Warrior Women of TV: A feminist cultural analysis of the new female body in popular culture. Doctoral dissertation. Bowling Green State University, Bowling Green, OH.

Jhally, S. (1987). *Codes of Advertising*. London: Frances Pinter.

Jhally, S. (1990). *Dreamworlds*. Video. Amherst, MA: Media Education Foundation.

Jhally, S. (1995). *Dreamworlds II: Desire, sex and power in music videos*. Video. Amherst, MA: Media Education Foundation.

Kang, M. (1997). The portrayal of women's images in magazine advertisements: Goffman's gender analysis revisited. *Sex Roles*, 37(11–12), 979–97.

Kielwasser, A. P. and Wolf, M. A. (1992). Mainstream television, adolescent homosexuality, and significant silence. *Critical Studies in Mass Communication*, 9(4), 350–73.

Kilbourne, J. (1987). *Still Killing Us Softly: Advertising images of women*. Film. Cambridge.

Kilbourne, J. (1999). *Deadly Persuasion: Why women and girls must fight the addictive power of advertising*. New York: The Free Press.

Kimball, M. M. (1986). Television and sex-role attitudes. In T. M. Williams (ed.), *The Impact of Television: A natural experiment in three communities*. New York: Academic Press, pp. 265–84.

Kuhn, A. (1985). *The Power of the Image*. Boston: Routledge & Kegan Paul.

Lazier, L. and Kendrick, A. G. (1993). Women in advertisements: Sizing up the images, roles, and functions. In P. J. Creedon (ed.), *Women in Mass Communication* (2nd edn.). Newbury Park, CA: Sage, pp. 199–219.

Lazier-Smith, L. (1989). A new "generation" of images to women. In P. J. Creedon (ed.), *Women in Mass Communication: Challenging gender values*. Newbury Park, CA: Sage.

Leeds-Hurwitz (1993). *Semiotics and Communication: Signs, codes, cultures*. Hillsdale, NJ: Lawrence Erlbaum.

Leiss, W., Kline, S., and Jhally, S. (1986). *Social Communication in Advertising: Persons, products, and images of well being*. London: Methuen.

Lovdal, L. T. (1989). Sex role messages in television commercials: An update. *Sex Roles*, 21(11/12), 715–24.

Lundstrom, W. J. and Sciglimpaglia, D. (1977). Sex role portrayals in advertising. *Journal of Marketing*, 72–9.

Masse, M. A. and Rosenblum, K. (1988). Male and female created they them: The depiction of gender in the advertising of traditional women's and men's magazines. *Women's Studies International Forum*, 11(2), 127–44.

Mazzella, C., Durkin, K., Cerini, E., and Buralli, P. (1992). Sex role stereotyping in Australian television advertisements. *Sex Roles*, 26(7/8), 243–59.

McKinnon, L. M. (1995). *Ms*.ing the free press: The advertising and editorial content of Ms. magazine, 1972–1992. In D. Abrahamson (ed.), *The American Magazine: Research perspectives and prospects*. Aimes, IA: Iowa State University Press, pp. 98–107.

McLaughlin, T. L. and Goulet, N. (1999). Gender advertisements in magazines aimed at African Americans: A comparison to their occurrence in magazines aimed at Caucasians. *Sex Roles*, 40(1–2), 61–71.

Mehaffy, M. M. (1997). Advertising race/raceing advertising: The feminine consumer(-nation), 1876–1900. *Signs*, 23(1), 131–74.

Mellencamp, P. (1995). *A Fine Romance: Five ages of film feminism*. Philadelphia: Temple University Press.

Miles, R. (1989). *Racism*. London: Routledge.

Millium, T. (1975). *Images of Women: Advertising in women's magazines*. London: Chatto and Windus.

Mode Magazine (2000). February.

Morrison, B. J. and Sherman. (1972). Who responds to sex in advertising? *Journal of Advertising Research*, 12(2), 15–19.

Mulvey, L. (1975). Visual pleasure and narrative cinema. *Screen*, 16(3), 6–18.

Myers, K. (1982). Fashion 'n' passion. *Screen*, 23(2–3), 89–97.

Myers, K. (1986). *Understains: The sense and seduction of advertising*. London: Comedia.

Neto, F. and Pinto, I. (1998). Gender stereotypes in Portuguese television advertisements. *Sex Roles*, 39(1–2), 153–64.

Nichols, B. (1981). *Ideology and the Image*. Bloomington: University of Indiana Press.

Nicholson, D. (1997). The Diesal jeans and workwear advertising campaign and the commodification of resistance. In K. Frith (ed.), *Undressing the Ad: Reading culture in advertising*. New York: Peter Lang, pp. 175–96.

Omi, M. and Winant, H. (1986). *Racial Formation in the United States from the 1960s to the 1980s*. London: Routledge.

Orbach, S. (1978). *Fat is a Feminist Issue*. London: Hamlyn.

Peirce, K. (1989). Sex-role stereotyping of children on television: A content analysis of the roles and attributes of child characters. *Sociological Spectrum*, 9, 321–8.

Pingree, S., Hawkins, R. P., Butler, M., and Paisley, W. (1976). Equality in advertising/A scale for sexism. *Journal of Communication*, 26(2), 193–200.

Pipher, M. (1994). *Reviving Ophelia: Saving the selves of adolescent girls*. New York: Ballantine.

Press, A. (1996). Toward a qualitative methodology of audience study: Using ethnography to study. In J. Hay, L. Grossberg, and E. Wartella (eds.), *The Audience and its Landscape*. Boulder, CO: Westview, pp. 113–30.

Rakow, L. (1986). Rethinking gender in communication. *Journal of Communication*, 36(4), 11–26.

Roach, J. and Felix, P. (1989). Black looks. In L. Gamman and M. Marshment (eds.), *The Female Gaze: Women as viewers of popular culture*. Seattle: The Real Comet Press, pp. 130–42.

Rossi, S. R. and Rossi, J. S. (1985). Gender differences in the perception of women in magazine advertising. *Sex Roles*, 12(9/10), 1033–9.

Rowe, K. (1995). *The Unruly Woman*. Austin: The University of Texas Press.

Saunders, C. S. and Stearn, B. A. (1986). Women's adoption of a business uniform: A content analysis of magazine advertisements. *Sex Roles*, 15(3/4), 197–205.

Shields, V. R. (1990). Advertising visual images: Gendered ways of seeing and looking. *Journal of Communication Inquiry*, 14(2), 25–39.

Shields, V. R. (1996). Selling the sex that sells: Mapping the evolution of gender advertising research across three decades. In B. Burleson (ed.), *Communication Yearbook 20*. Thousand Oaks, CA: Sage, pp. 71–109.

Shields, V. R. (2002). *Measuring Up: How advertising affects self image*. Philadelphia: University of Pennsylvania Press.

Skelly, G. U. and Lundstrom, W. J. (1981). Male sex roles in magazine advertising, 1959–1979. *Journal of Communication*, Autumn, 52–7.

Spitzack, C. (1990). *Confessing Excess: Women and the politics of body reduction*. Albany: State University of New York Press.

Steinem, G. (1990). Sex, lies, and advertising. *Ms.*, 1(1), 1–20.

Tuchman, G., Daniels, A. K., and Benet, J. (eds.) (1978). *Hearth and Home: Images of women in the mass media*. New York: Oxford University Press.

Wagner, L. C. and Banos, J. B. (1973). A woman's place: A follow-up analysis of the roles portrayed by women in magazine advertisements. *Journal of Marketing Research*, 10, 213–14.

Whipple, T. W. and Courtney, A. E. (1985). Female role portrayals in advertising and communication effectiveness: A review. *Journal of Advertising*, 14(3), 4–8.

Williamson, J. (1978). *Decoding Advertisements*. London: Methuen.

Williamson, J. (1986). Woman is an island: Femininity and colonization. In T. Modleski (ed.), *Studies in Entertainment: Critical approaches to mass culture*. Bloomington and Indianapolis: Indiana University Press, pp. 99–118.

Winship, J. (1981). Handling sex. *Media, Culture and Society*, 3(3), 25–41.

Winship, J. (1985). "A girl needs to get street-wise": Magazines of the 1980s. *Feminist Review*, 21, 25–46.

Wise, G. L., King, A. L., and Merenski, J. P. (1974). Reactions to sexy ads vary with age. *Journal of Advertising Research*, 14(4), 11–16.

Wohleter, M. and Lammers, B. H. (1980). An analysis of male roles in print advertisements over a 20-year span: 1958–1978. In J. C. Olson (ed.), *Advances in Consumer Research*, vol. 7. Ann Arbor: Association for Consumer Research, pp. 138–50.

Wolf, N. (1991). *The Beauty Myth: How images of beauty are used against women*. New York: Anchor Books.

Women's Action Coalition (1993). *The Facts about Women*. New York: The New Press.

Wortzel, L. and Frisbie, J. M. (1974). Women's role portrayal preferences in advertisements. *Journal of Marketing*, 38, 41–6.

CHAPTER THIRTEEN

Constructing a New Model of Ethnic Media
Image-Saturated Latina Magazines as Touchstones

Melissa A. Johnson

With sporadic exceptions in the twentieth century, US Americans with brown or black skin have been the subjects of negative stereotypes. Ethnic media have claimed to be havens from these negative stereotypes, although not all studies of content have supported this claim. Most of the research on US Latino media, as of general media, describes the content, audience uses and gratifications, and effects of usage of Spanish-language broadcasting and publications. Models of ethnic media functions from the late 1970s through the 1990s focused on content devoted to pluralistic concerns and content that helps ethnic group members to assimilate to the majority society. Other scholarship on ethnic media has investigated political, economic, and institutional power issues. More recently, a growing body of literature on ethnic identity has expanded notions of ethnic affiliation. Scholars have considered multidimensional concepts of ethnic identity that extend beyond the linear continuum of pluralism (identity with one's ethnic group) to assimilation (identity with a majority group). This paper proposes an expanded ethnic media model that can be tested in broadcast, print, and digital media contexts. The model's purpose is threefold: to shift ethnic media models away from a linear assimilation continuum to two dimensions of identity continua; to incorporate the concept of cultural projection into the ethnic media model; and to incorporate the role of visual communication into the research on ethnic media functions.

To illustrate how the various sections of the model intersect, this essay begins with the literature on ethnic media, ethnic identity, and hybridity and describes how it contributes to the different dimensions of identity delineated in the model. Second, the essay explores the role of ethnic media in projecting cultural identity into the society. Third, the chapter emphasizes visual communication's importance in ethnic media and shows how visual communication relates to the model elements. Finally, limitations and the implications of the model for future ethnic media studies will be discussed. This configuration of the model is discussed within the US Latino/a magazine context. This particular medium was chosen due to the limited descriptive power of other ethnic media models. As discussed in the last section of this paper, testing from scholars of additional ethnic media will help determine how generalizable this model is.

Latino/a magazines are defined as publications whose producers claim are targeted to Latinos/as in the United States, although they may have cross-border distributions (like the Spanish-language magazines published by Editorial Televisa) and cross-cultural appeal. For the purposes of this paper Latinos/Latinas are defined as individuals who trace their ancestry to Latin America or Spain and who self-identify with Ibero-Latin American countries, including those in the Caribbean. The terms pan-Raza and pan-Hispanic refer to unity across a number of different Latino cultures, such as Mexican American, Puerto Rican, or Peruvian. Pan-ethnic refers to unity across groups linked by cultural heritage or race since Latina/os come in all races and ethnicities. For example, not only are Latina/os pan-Hispanic – Mexican Americans, Colombian Americans, and Venezuelan Americans – but they are also pan-ethnic – black, White, Asian, Native American, etc. This paper uses Latino/a examples; one possible counterpart in a Black pan-Afro-American could be individuals with Cape Verdean, Nigerian, or Bahamian cultural backgrounds.

Ethnic Media and Identity

This paper makes several assumptions about identity. First, identity is self-defined, not placed on someone by another person, organization, or society. That is why some Latinas prefer to self-identify with a subgroup (e.g. Dominican), or as a Latina, rather than identify themselves as Hispanic. Construction of that identity may include counteracting negative stereotypes others place on your group (Collier, 1998). Some would add that cultural identity is not only self-identification, but recognition and acceptance of that self-identification by other members of the group (Tanno & González, 1998).

Second, identity moves from the local to the transnational. Newly arrived Puerto Rican immigrants might see themselves as Puerto Rican and then might make a move to a Latina/o identity. Numerous examples of this identity transformation exist in relation to US Latina/os (e.g. Bailey, 2001; Cortes-Rodriguez, 1990; Melville, 1998; Omi and Winant, 1986). As an Afro-American example, Halter's (1993) history of Cape Verdeans describes how the concept of identity moves from the very local to a broader self-notion. Halter found that first-generation Cape Verdean immigrants in Southeastern New England identified themselves as natives of the specific island of origin (e.g. Brava or Fogo). However, as ensuing generations of these immigrants remained in Massachusetts and Rhode Island, they tended to identify as Cape Verdeans, or depending on the individual, the historical period, or the situation, as Portuguese-Americans (White) or Black Americans.

Third, identity is situational (Rodriguez, 2000; Subervi-Vélez, 1994). Like Rodriguez (2000), I assert that individuals have a core self-identity, but one's ethnic identity shifts depending on the situation and the relationships with others within that context. For instance, one may identify as White in an office where the majority of workers are Anglo-Americans, as Puerto Rican at home with one's family, and as Latina at a political rally for a Mexican-American candidate. Some group members have the option of expressing their own identity or not (because others find it harder to "label" them), and some never have that option (Collier, 1998). Many Latinos have such options. Women also may be more comfortable with identity fluctuation because of the constant role switching that occurs in many women's lives (e.g. work, home manager, spouse, mother, daughter roles).

Role of Media in Creating and Maintaining Identity

Communication researchers have analyzed the media's role in identity creation (Gergen, 1991; Merelman, 1995; Turow, 1997), in particular, the way female readers use magazines to construct self-identity and socialize to societal norms (Brown, White, & Nikopoulou, 1993; Currie, 1999; Ferguson, 1983; McCracken, 1993; Simonds, 1996; Valdivia, 2000). For instance, Currie (1999) investigated magazine readers and found that they accepted magazine images as "valid messages about femininity" even though they also were sources of anxiety and unmet standards (Currie, 1999). Magazine images may also serve as "valid messages about ethnicity." While academic research addressing ethnic media has concentrated on assimilation and pluralism concerns, current research on hybridity opens up a space for a more complex continuum.

Ethnic media functions

Ethnic media is defined in this study as broadcast, print, and digital channels that serve a particular racial or cultural group. Traditionally, ethnic media has been defined according to the language of origin of the target population. Scholars have identified a number of pluralistic functions of ethnic media: to preserve and transmit native culture and identity by maintaining the language and promoting ethnic pride; to establish a minority news agenda; to announce community events and cover minority social activities; to promote the group's political/social interests and motivate them to be socially and politically active;

to serve as collective expressions of anger at injustices; and to provide comfort and respite from negative images in general market media (Constantakis-Valdés, 1992; Downing, 1992; Fox, 1996; Gutiérrez, 1977; Huntzicker, 1995; Riggins, 1992; Subervi-Vélez, 1994). For example, readers may shift between use of ethnic media for ethnic maintenance and reliance on ethnic media as road maps for the larger society. Ríos's fieldwork with Latinas found that women used media for cultural "self-preservation" as well as for acculturation to the English language or other US values (Ríos, 2000). Another function that has been clustered with the pluralistic orientation is symbolic empowerment (Riggins, 1992), although I will also discuss it within the context of cultural projection later in this paper.

Scholars also have discussed assimilation functions of ethnic media, including: serving as instruments of social control; maintaining the dominant languages of the host society; maintaining the dominant ideology; borrowing general market media genres; and socializing to "the modern" (Anselmi & Gouliarmos, 1998; Constantakis-Valdés, 1992; Gutiérrez, 1977; Riggins, 1992). Anselmi and Gouliarmos argue that ethnic media's transmission of dominant cultural norms distracts ethnic groups from more important concerns of political and economic ethnic class subordination.

Rather than be assimilative or pluralistic, content can serve mixed functions. Delgado found a tension in *Low Rider Magazine* letter writers between maintaining cultural group boundaries (e.g. Mexican-Americans differing from Puerto Ricans), and "uniting under one umbrella term" (1998, p. 430). He surmised that models of assimilation or acculturation "beginning at Mexican and ending at American" are simplistic. "Assimilation models based on linguistic, cultural, or national identities do not account for political or even geographic modifiers (such as Tejano or Californio) that uncomfortably fit into a national/cultural continuum" (1998, p. 429). Johnson (2000) noted a similar tension in studies of bilingual and English-language Latina magazine content.

Recently researchers have moved from the pluralism-assimilation dichotomy to other models. Mayer (2001) identified four types of relationships between Latino media producers and their "imagined audiences" in San Antonio, Texas: segmentation, massification, pan-ethnicization, and fragmentation. She discussed how Mexican-Americans, Anglo-Americans, and Mexican nationals collaborated to mobilize a mass Mexican-American audience to deliver to advertisers during the early days of Latino broadcast media. She explained how panethnic media, unlike local San Antonio media that were specifically targeted to the community, homogenized an imagined audience into Spanish–speaking consumers, without regards for their national origin or immigration history. "Mexican-Americans in San Antonio thus became part of a complex web of multi-ethnic and multi-national players in a global media market" (Mayer, 2001, p. 296). The fragmentation stage in San Antonio featured niche segments of Latino consumers like hip hop fans, Tejano fans, lowriders, and gay Latinos/as.

Consumption, not assimilation

Like Mayer, a number of scholars have said that ethnic media's major function is to deliver an audience to advertisers rather than primarily serve its readers (Johnson, 2000; Rodriguez, 1999). A national look at this pan-Latino commodification process by Dávila (2000; 2001) confirms this tendency to market to Latina/os both in Spanish and in a homogeneous manner in an internally contradictory effort to segment yet discipline ethnic populations. Halter (2000) also documents how this segmentation of ethnicity for the purposes of shopping for identity has spread to virtually all people in the US, whether it be new immigrants or older roots oriented segments of the population. In advertising trade publications, Latino readers/viewers/listeners are commonly referred to as the "Hispanic market." In a media system like the United States that relies on advertising support, much of the editorial content is aimed – just like advertising – at persuading readers or viewers to consume.

As media content pulls away from cultural messages it often heads toward consumption messages, although these must also be seen as two poles in a continuum. In Western ethnic media, consumption content is the editorial content[1] that subtly or overtly promotes purchases. Examples in Latina magazine, as well as in most women's magazines, content are the fashion, beauty, home, and travel sections. Class cannot be divorced from consumption messages because the implication is that product or service consumption can symbolically move you into an aspired class. Spanish-language women's magazines (e.g. the Editorial Televisa publications like *Vanidades, Cristina, Glamour en Español*) that are sold in the United States and throughout Latin America are examples of media with content that assimilates readers to a Westernized consumption culture, rather than to a particular nation-state's ideology although these publications also have culture-oriented content.

The other end of the spectrum is culture. Examples are a news article on Mexican-American Heritage Week or a feature on a Latino organization. Visual examples on the culture continuum are people who represent a diversity of subgroups in the cultural group, icons, and symbols. An intermediate culture-consumption example is the discussion of books, art, and music by and/or about Latinas as these encourage ethnic pride, history, and culture as well as the purchasing of items. Dominant visual examples on the consumption end of the continuum are items to be purchased such as make-up, clothing, and perfume.

Media and Pan-Latino Identity

Another function of ethnic media is the unification of subgroups (Dávila, 2001; Flores, 1997; Fox, 1996; Husband, 1994; Rodriguez, 1997). Through the "virtual" unification of subgroups such as Dominican, Cuban, or Mexican-American, media owners can deliver a bigger audience to advertisers than they could by focusing on any one subgroup. According to Appadurai, a central feature of modern merchandising is the ability to create nostalgia because media create experiences of duration that "rewrite the lived histories of individuals, families, ethnic groups . . ." (1996, p. 77). Magazines like *Latina* and *Latina Style* create an imagined nostalgia for the subgroup (e.g. reference to one's family being from Chile) while catapulting the reader toward the pan–Latina contemporary group identity. English-language and bilingual Latina magazines, in particular, appear to do this effectively by referring often to the place or subgroup from which a person descended in the past tense, but characterizing their present-tense identity as "Latina" (Johnson, 2000). These text identity markers switch back and forth like the narrow gauge train to Machu Picchu, reaching back to the local past to gain steam for rushing toward the panethnic. Consequently, the other identity dimension is the continuum from ethnic subgroup to pan-ethnic – "Latino/a" in this case. Subgroups often embody a local context, because as one moves away from neighborhoods or communities of Latino subgroups one is more likely to find oneself in a larger Latino/a context (see Massey, 1987, or other migration studies). In the center, however, where the subcultural identity continuum meets the cultural identity continuum, is a hybrid zone of combination and tension which scholars ranging from Homi Bhabba, Gloria Anzaldúa to Mary Louise Pratt have called a third space, *nepantla*, or zone of conflict.

Hybridity

According to Rodriguez (1999) the core of the bilingual Latino media audience is the hybridity of US Latinos, who maintain a Latin American heritage – at least symbolically – but also wish to retain their US American standing. Previous studies of Latina magazines suggest that they create a vehicle for hybrid identities (Delgado, 1998). Rather than a fixed state – like the way acculturation levels of immigrants at particular times as measured by empirical scholars – hybridity is a continuous process of "borrowing and lending" between cultures so that one is never in a fixed "zone of purity" (García Canclini, 1995). Although his unit of analysis is nation-states, García Canclini describes the shifts between tradition and modernity as creating hybrid identities. Indeed, such shifting tensions characterize the postmodern condition. Collier (1998) suggests that hybridity challenges traditional authority by the continual and mutual development of independent cultural traditions, and the interweaving of new cultural forms and practices with the maintenance of established cultural forms. Studies of Latina magazines suggest that images are powerful manifestations of hybridity. Hybrid identities may have the opportunity to transcend time, since subgroup identities are sometimes treated as "old" identities, and pan-ethnic identities are positioned as "new" identities.

Conceptually hybridity has precursors in the Latin American context. For example, *mestizaje* is an older Latin American concept that aligns well with current notions of hybridity. *Mestizaje* does not equal homogeneity. It is a principle

Figure 13.1 Ethnic media identity portrayals

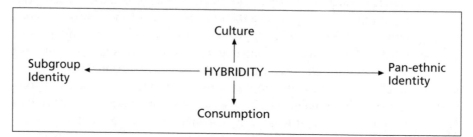

of union, or of mixing, without implying a homogenization that obliterates contributions made by different ethnic and racial elements. Mestizaje preserves differences, but it does not suggest assimilation (García, 2000). However, since hybridity also encompasses a sense of tension and an unfixed state, and therefore incorporates issues of power into the previously racial category, I use it in this model.

In summary, ethnic media functions include complex portrayals of cultural identity. Identity encompasses one's identity in the larger society (especially as it relates to ethnicity, class, and consumption-orientations) and one's identity in the ethnic group. Ethnic group members can manifest different combinations of these states depending on the situation or the group context. Hybridity describes the zone where different aspects of these identities meet; creating a state of internal tension but also allowing for interesting combinations that can benefit individuals. The following description outlines how these forms of identity and tensions can be illustrated in an ethnic media model. The first section of the model is pictured in figure 13.1.

Model Section One: Ethnic Media and Identity

The model conceptualizes identity falling along two continua (see figure 13.1). The vertical axis of the model is the Cultural Identity dimension. Polar positions are "consumption" and "culture." This continuum describes identity relative to the larger society. The horizontal axis, which is labeled Subcultural Identity in the model, has "subgroup" and "pan–ethnic" polar positions. This continuum describes identity internal to the ethnic group.

We can locate elements of media content along the continua. For instance, reports of community news such as a Mexican–American Foundation scholarship dinner, or a Cuban American political event, would cluster near the subgroup/ local end of the horizontal continuum. A feature article about Hispanic heritage month would be positioned nearer the panethnic end of the horizontal continuum. The Latina herself moves back and forth on this continuum; her identity may be very situational. It will shift depending on whether she is with others of her subgroup (e.g. with other Venezuelans) or with a more diverse group (e.g.

Figure 13.2 Ethnic media cultural projection

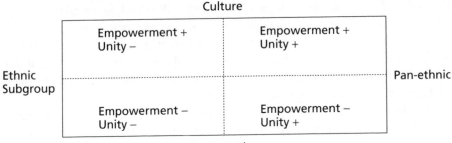

Latinos/as). Both of these examples also would fall in the top half of the Cultural Identity continuum (vertical axis), since the content is more culture-oriented than consumption-oriented.

The vertical axis is also where we can locate the traditional pluralism to assimilation functions of traditional ethnic media models. In my 2000 study, I found ethnic media content that promoted ethnic pride, preserved ethnic culture, and transmitted ethnic culture. Ethnic media content like this would cluster near the top of the vertical continuum. Purchase messages (in editorial content, not necessarily in advertising) would fall at the bottom of the continuum. For example, a study in progress of 2001 editions of *Latina* and *Latina Style* found that out of the 239 women's images analyzed so far, 25 percent were product- or service-related. The hybridity zone would be an area characterized by the tension created when ranges of identities, culture messages, and consumption messages are juxtaposed in media content or where media content and audience identities are negotiated.

In short, ethnic media functions encompass complex portrayals of cultural identity. Figure 13.1 illustrates the two-dimensional continua of identity that can be investigated with ethnic media content analyses. The second level of the model deals with ethnic media's functions beyond its own ethnic audience (see figure 13.2).

Cultural projection

As noted in the discussion of pluralistic media functions, Riggins (1992) stated that just having one's own media was a source of symbolic empowerment for ethnic groups. In other words, walking into Barnes and Noble and seeing a cluster of Latino/a publications on the rack symbolically represents both difference and visible status among other legitimatized media niches. Merelman develops this general concept further and calls it cultural projection. The second layer of this model focuses on ethnic media's role in cultural projection. "Cultural projection is the conscious or unconscious effort by a social group and its allies to place new images of itself before other social groups, and before the general public" (Merelman, 1995, p. 3). Merelman adds that a culturally subordinated group engages in cultural projection when it or others presents new representations of itself that counteract negative stereotypes. Although he focuses on image, Merelman doesn't limit the definition to visual images (for instance, he documents the rise of Black culture-related grants by private foundations). Among other factors, the growth in media industries and the increased value of cultural capital in the United States allow us to experience, or, indeed, makes it inevitable that we see, more manifestations of cultural forms.

Merelman outlines four types of cultural projection: syncretism, hegemony, polarization, and counter-hegemony. Syncretism is mixing different cultures to create a new body – mutual cultural projection to create a "melting pot" of something different. Others might term this acculturation, if one conceptualizes acculturation as two-way change where the minority group's culture diffuses and changes the majority group culture (e.g. Guatemalan textile designs in home furnishings, use of salsa on hamburgers) and vice versa (e.g. Guatemalans shop at Ikea, and hamburger replaces some more cultural specific foods). Hegemony is subordination of the subordinate to the dominant group, which ethnic media scholars would term assimilation. This is what ethnic media supposedly resist by their mere existence. Polarization is where media images of subordinate and dominant cultural groups remain isolated or alienated from each other, creating conflicting images. And counter hegemony exists when subordinate culture members persuade dominant culture members to accept their values or worldviews.

Merelman recommended that Black cultural projection focus on themes of interdependence between cultural groups – so that by emphasizing mutual dependence and mutual support syncretic US culture would be possible. Similarly, Entman and Rojecki advocate racial comity – where Blacks and Whites would "cooperate in good faith to achieve mutually beneficial objectives" (2000, p. 12). While these authors deal with Black Americans, the ethnic media model proposed in this essay incorporates the concept of cultural projection in a model to be used with Latino/a media as well as other ethnic media. In doing so, I expand Riggins' (1992) statement that just having one's own media outlets is symbolic empowerment.

Cultural projection can be conceptualized as a form of empowerment, albeit symbolic or limited empowerment. Merelman, for instance, notes that while US Black cultural projection is vigorous, the US government remains an institution where White power is exerted. Images and representations, on their own, cannot do all the cultural work of transformation. While Merelman applies this concept by investigating subordinate group cultural projection into the larger society, he notes that ethnic group members also use media images to discover their own identities (1995, p. 35). I hypothesize that the availability of non-language bound ethnic media – particularly in the colorful, glossy forms of Latina magazines – not only helps a widely diverse group discover what it means to be a Latino/a in the United States, but it projects to other groups what it means to be a Latina. Thus I apply Merelman's concept in both instances. US Latinos/as historically have been less able to unify, especially politically (see DeSipio & de la Garza, forthcoming). So Latino/a media projection to the group is as important as to the larger culture. Latino/a media have the opportunity (which they don't always employ) to project back into the group the positive core values and aspects of identity that the subgroups share.

Empowerment is a crucial issue for Latina media because readers suffer from the doubly unempowered position of being female and ethnic. One downside is that as Latinas become more culturally projected and therefore more public, their self-image standards may grow to be less cultural specific and maybe more symbolic along with becoming more consumption-oriented, though nonetheless rooted in a pan-Latina cultural specificity. These potentials and possible internal contradictions are discussed below.

Model Section Two: Ethnic Media Cultural Projection

The model's second layer (see figure 13.2) imagines the possible outcomes of cultural projection via ethnic media, with effects on ethnic unity and empowerment in the four quadrants depending on where the content falls on the subcultural identity and cultural identity dimensions. In each corner are hypothesized impacts on symbolic ethnic group unity and empowerment when various identity foci are projected into the dominant culture. In the upper left quadrant, where media content features subgroup specifics and focuses on culture more often than consumption, the effect could be greater empowerment, but lower pan-Latina cultural unity. When a medium focuses on linking subgroups with dominant panethnic content, and focuses on culture more than consumption and class, the outcome could be greater empowerment and unity (upper right quadrant). Ethnic media with subgroup-specific content but who are highly commercial could create less empowered, less unified projections (lower left quadrant). And commercially based media that concentrate on panethnic content could project highly unified stances, but not empowered content (lower right quadrant).

Identity becomes less specific and more symbolic as it moves in the panethnic direction. In addition, it can become less place-based and more transnational if it focuses on pan-ethnic portrayals. Consequently, as it moves toward the pan-ethnic and the transnational, ethnic media content may rely more on visual image-based ethnicity and less on language, especially since the Spanish language, in the case of Latinas, differs from country to country and region to region.

Transcending language: image-based identity

Most ethnic media studies have investigated written content or audience uses and interpretations of text. For a number of reasons, ethnic media scholars also should study visual content. First, it can replace language as the defining characteristic of what it means to be "ethnic" when the medium no longer relies on the culture's language. Second, because visual image is a critical component of cultural projection, we can't study the projection functions without looking at visuals. Media visuals are the lubricants that make cultural projection possible, especially when language is a cultural barrier (e.g. Spanish-language women's magazines). Third, physical identity is integral to ethnic identity, especially for women, who are judged more on appearance than men, at least in Western and Latin American cultures. Fourth, media body images – especially skin color – are laden with cultural symbolism and reflective of social power relations. Analyzing them allows us to look at these phenomena. The following further describes why visual communication needs to be considered in ethnic media models.

Although new immigrants use language criteria to self-identify and to identify with others in a group, as third- and fourth-generation-Latinos self-identify, their criteria may shift (e.g. most Irish Americans don't speak Gaelic but may describe themselves as Irish). Latino/a magazines are examples of media that have shifted away from a reliance on language to define themselves as ethnic. In Latina magazines the role of visual images helps fill the gap left by the absence of a language identity marker. According to Banks and Murphy, visual systems "can create emotional states and feelings of identity and separation" (1997, p. 23). This affords the opportunity to engage the reader or viewer in identity exploration and to present new images of ethnic group members.

A question this creates is whether visual images are interpreted similarly by readers/viewers, especially non-group members. Whereas some scholars assert that visuals, like language, are culturally bound (e.g. the classic Segall, Campbell, & Herskovits, 1966), Messaris argues against cultural relativism and posits that there are cross-cultural commonalities to understanding visual images – "visual syntax" (1994, p. 173). This bolsters the argument that Latina magazines can communicate Latina identity(ies) to non-Latinas. But the meaning of some culture-specific images (e.g. Quetzcoatal) would not be familiar to non-Latinas, nor to non-Mexicans, for that matter, even if the syntax were common between a magazine like *Latina* and other general market women's magazines. Supporting this interpretation are cross-cultural audience studies of television programs like *Dallas* (Katz & Liebes, 1990) or magazines (e.g. Duke, 2000) that found differences in how various cultural or national groups interpreted media content. A postmodern critique would assert that the meaning of the visual is constructed by the individual media communicator and the viewer, both of whom carry their social positions to the social construction of its meaning (e.g. Harper, 1998). This means that the reader comes to the image with all of her own cultural values, societal rules, and visual memory for interpreting it, which suggests no universal meaning.

Transcending language: the body and identity

In addition to being a way for media to carve out ethnic niches when not relying on the group's language, visual communication is a vital part of the audience member's identity construction. Identity is an important element of ethnic media, and as has been discussed in this essay, physical portrayals in media also are important because of the way individuals use media in the construction of self-identity. Therefore analyzing physical portrayals within ethnic media is critical to the study of ethnic construction.

Rentaría discusses the "language of bodies, particularly women's bodies, to symbolize cultural differences." (1998, p. 78). Although she uses examples from murals, theatre, and other non-mass media genres, she explores the intersection of culture and visual communication through her analysis of bodies. She finds multi-leveled codes embedded in body images and argues that one level relates to "appearance and attraction, what one should look like and what kind of bodies one should desire. At another level they are about competing cultures . . . different ways of constructing social reality" (1998, p. 79). The body is perceived as a site of contestation of one's perceived social reality.

The thin, blonde, light-skinned ideal

Bodies in ethnic media content move along the ethnic subgroup-panethnic continuum and along the culture-to-consumption continuum as they are pictured in cultural settings or with cultural icons, or photographed with products to be consumed. However one cannot investigate portrayals of bodies in media without considering the thin, light, ideal in Eurocentric culture.

Communication research has supported the effects of media on women's body image perceptions (Botta, 1999; David & Johnson, 1998; Harrison & Cantor, 1997; Myers & Biocca, 1992; Shields, 2002). Women of color were excluded from most body image studies until the last decade; Latinas (and Native Americans) remain less studied than African Americans and Asian Americans. A study of 1,749 non-advertising images in 13 different Latina magazines showed Latina magazines were no haven from unrealistically thin images of women in general market media (Johnson, David, & Huey, in press, a). In another study, ideal traits listed by US Latinas were large breasts, long hair, tallness, and thinness (Altabe, 1998). This similarity to the Western thin ideal is found in both general market and ethnic media. Along with Anglo-Americans, Latinas in the Altabe study reported the most body image disturbance (perception of ideal physique versus perception of one's own body). If we can build on the research already conducted on white, middle class girls and women, the mental and physical health consequences for Latinas who have high degrees of dissatisfaction with their bodies include eating disorders to suicide attempts. Foregrounding the power of visual body portrayals, some psychologists use photos in clinical practice to change a client's self-image by using them to provide feedback and to confront distorted self-images (Cronin, 1998).

While the shape of one's body is one identity consideration, color can be even more problematic. According to Rodriguez (2000), some Latin Americans are born brown but become white with upward mobility, underscoring the fact that color can be correlated with class distinctions and power differentials. "Passing" is the term used by those who choose to perform a more powerful, and therefore less or discriminated race (Haney Lopez, 1996; Piper, 1998) whether for class aspirations or to avoid discrimination. Women in particular may choose hair color, clothing styles, or even colored contact lenses that allow them to non-verbally code-switch from Anglo to Latina or to some ambiguously hybrid identity depending on the situation.

Magazine portrayals suggest that Eurocentric images cut across mainstream and ethnic media. A study of skin color in 1,579 non-advertising images in Latino magazines found that women in the magazines were overwhelmingly light-skinned, despite the publishers' statements about representing diversity among Latinos/as (Johnson, David, & Huey, in press, b). The exclusion of dark-skinned Latinas and attempts to align their images with lighter, upper-class portrayals suggests that ethnic media are not beyond Eurocentric beauty ideals and that therefore ideologies of race continue to privilege whiteness in Latina as in mainstream Anglo magazines.

Lightness and whiteness are associated with political and socioeconomic power in Latin America and in the United States (Entman & Book, 2000; Robinson & Ward, 1995). However, Martinez (1998) documents US legal precedents that defined Mexican-Americans as White but did not grant the status or protection from discrimination that normally comes with being White. According to Rentaría, the Mexican tendency to base status and beauty on hierarchy of physiognomy is rooted in the colonial history of Latin America and Spain (1998). "Advertising billboards in Mexico regularly depict upper-class looking, blue-eyed blondes curled around various products . . . symbolically linking the consuming of certain goods with social mobility, status, and European and/or 'Anglo' looking women" (Rentaría, 1998, p. 81). This finding is consistent with previous research in Latin America. As a response and reaction, the US Chicano movement in the 1960s and 1970s elevated the Aztecs and Mayans – browner peoples – to the status of noble ancestors. This gave status to non-European images at the same time the "Black is Beautiful" movement demonstrated parallel goals. Contemporary metaphors of "the browning of America" bear out the influence of this resignification of roots of origin.

However, the immense diversity among Latina/os means that there are white, brown, and black people within this ethnic umbrella. Color markers thus continue to refer to class and power. The term "blanco" or "blanquito" is increasingly used to refer to powerful, or upper-class people, regardless of their actual skin color (C. Rodriguez, 2000). However an additional component of this multiplicitous definition of color is the cultural specific association between some colors and perceived temperatures. For example, the association between aloofness and White is interesting. White may be desired and powerful, but it also carries with it a connotation of coldness whereas, relationally, Brown is warmer. While in many settings[2] brown-skinned images may be symbolic of less power, they may lend themselves better to creation of parasocial relationships between

Figure 13.3 Ethnic media and cultural identity

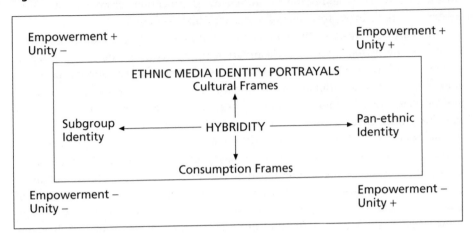

audiences and media personalities. (For instance, although most observers might point to a talk show host's intelligence, communication skills, or personality as factors in her media success, one could speculate that beautiful brown skin also creates an on-screen warmth that penetrates the iciness of the television medium.) Traditional or digital media producers interested in creating virtual communities may value relationship-building aspects of their images more than traditional media that positioned themselves as aloof, objective, experts. Following this reasoning, brownness may be more important in media that depend on viewer/reader involvement.

In summary, ethnic identity and cultural projection research will benefit from analyses of visual content, analyses of audience interpretations of visual content, and effects of visual content on audiences. Body image is of particular interest because of its relationship to ethnic identity, its impact on individual cultural group members' mental and physical health; and its role in cultural projection. Figure 13.3 presents the full model, with the ethnic identity continua in the inner box and the cultural projection aspects in the outer box.

Discussion

Although this model was developed using Latino/a magazines as a touchstone, it should be tested with other ethnic media that are visually laden – especially television and digital media. The model is intended to be a template that can be empirically and quantitatively tested but can also be explored qualitatively. It is aimed at improving our understanding of ethnic media content, and the interaction between audiences and content. Analyzing content with a broader approach to identity may provide a fuller understanding than possible with searches for assimilation/pluralism content. The continuum approach opens to researchers broader possibilities about media audiences' gratifications from use of ethnic media, and their interpretations of visual and text content.

There are a number of limitations to the model. First, it doesn't adequately address some of the traditional assimilation functions of ethnic media, such as serving as instruments of social control beyond consumption–orientation functions. Second, like traditional assimilation–pluralism models, it doesn't adequately address class considerations, although it begins to address class both by recognizing the prominence of consumption messages and the complexity of meaning in the concept of "color." Third, although less linear than its predecessors, it doesn't demonstrate participative or symmetric media-audience relations – important considerations of interactive media. Fourth, this model may not apply to ethnic community newspapers and radio stations. Local ethnic media will more likely continue to be language-based and place-based than national and transnational ethnic media. Because of their community affiliations, their primary audience will often be subgroups – like Mexican-Americans in San Diego or Cuban Americans in South Florida. However this may cease to be the case as the homogeneity of regional Latina/o populations begins to disappear (Davis, 2000). Fifth, just as traditional assimilation–pluralism models did not accommodate all content, some news topics and visual images might not fit into this model. Whereas future studies will extend dimensions of this model, this configuration is intended to build on current assimilation models with an initial focus on identity and cultural projection. Sixth, not all cultural projection "works," especially when it faces language and institutional challenges or visual mismatches. Valdivia and Curry (1998) note that some of the reasons the successful Latin American star Xuxa did not succeed in US children's programming included US parental perceptions of language problems and dissonance in both parents' and broadcasters' perceptions of the way Xuxa should look. The thin, blue-eyed, blonde ideal deemed suitable in programming targeted to adult men does not embody the trust factors women and US broadcasters may want in role models for their children. Another aspect of Xuxa's programs that didn't transfer well cross-culturally was the rapid pace of the children's show, with her activity described by some as frenetic (Valdivia & Curry, 1998). Perhaps the thin, light-skinned, blonde ideal should also include the word passive. Thus investigations of cultural projection can unearth many more concerns than cultural empowerment and unity. Analysis of sound, pacing, and other editing issues in moving image media like television or digital communication should be added to visual analysis.

Although this model certainly will be refined with more study and testing, it is an improvement over traditional pluralism–assimilation structures. First, traditional assimilation–pluralism models leave out class considerations. Class is not fully explicated in this model but is linked to consumption and color. Ethnic media function models also give short shrift to the commercial functions of media, which become increasingly important as ethnic media shift from targeting first- or second-generation immigrants to multi-generations of ethnic groups and the entire population. A second weakness of the pluralism–assimilation approaches is that they tended to focus on the individual *vis-à-vis* society. They did not allow for psychological or psychosocial media functions, which are an aspect of identity maintenance and also affect physical and mental health outcomes. Third, pan-ethnic functions of media (Fox, 1996), symbolic empowerment (Riggins, 1992), and cultural transmission (Park, 1922) did not fit well into the assimilation–pluralism continuum. In another piece on Latina media (Johnson, 2000) these concepts were tacked onto the pluralism function. In this ethnic media model, the more fully explicated concept of cultural projection encompasses and replaces symbolic empowerment and cultural transmission. The cultural identity continuum stretches from the cultural subgroup to the panethnic.

Although the editorial staff controls much of media content – for instance, fashion layouts and beauty tips – ethnic groups must gain control of their own images and representations whenever they can. One way to accomplish this is through more purposeful media relations efforts by ethnic organizations to suggest interviewees and news/feature topics that allow for hybrid identities in media stories and media images. Another strategy is by serving as watchdogs for ethnic media, as well as general market media. Ethnic media are often excused from debates about cultural stereotypes because the assumption is that they are paradigms of diversity. Public praise and strongly worded critiques may attempt to keep ethnic media focused on their traditional key functions, though changing conditions, such as the ascendance of a culture of consumption and branded identities may challenge the very definition and functions of ethnic media. Finally, cultural organizations must consider visual impact of cultural events (like festivals), and how they will be covered in ethnic as well as general market media (see Halter, 2000).

A pan-ethnic, culture-oriented identity may serve as the most unified, and therefore symbolically powerful cultural projection into mainstream US culture, especially in regards to Latina/os in the US given their growing heterogeneity. Moreover a panethnic, consumption-oriented identity is the least conflictive both internally and externally *vis-à-vis* a hyper-capitalist, consumer-oriented economy. However, identities based on hybridity may present the most opportunity for realistic, ethical projection and normative ideals for ethnic media's mission and its changing role in a changing society.

Notes

1 Advertising is excluded from this discussion, but obviously, it is present, too.
2 For example, brown skin is a status symbol during winter in the North, suggesting that those who have brown skin have the resources to tan in warmer climes as opposed to the rest of the population who have no access to the sun, so to speak.

References

Altabe, M. (1998). Ethnicity and body image: Quantitative and qualitative analysis. *International Journal of Eating Disorders*, 23(2), 153–59.

Anselmi, W. and Gouliarmos, K. (1998). *Elusive Margins: Consuming media, ethnicity, and culture.* Toronto: Guernica.

Appadurai, A. (1996). *Modernity at Large: Cultural dimensions of globalization.* Minneapolis: University of Minnesota.

Bailey, B. (2001). Dominican-American ethnic/racial identities and United States social categories. *International Migration Review*, 3, 677–708.

Banks, M. and Murphy, H. (1997). *Rethinking Visual Anthropology.* New Haven, CT: Yale.

Botta, R. A. (1999). Television images and adolescent girls' body image disturbance. *Journal of Communication*, 49(2), 22–41.

Brown, J., White, A. B., and Nikopoulou, L. (1993). Disinterest, intrigue, resistance: Early adolescent girls' use of sexual media content. In B. S. Greenberg, J. D. Brown, and N. Buerkell-Rothfuss (eds.), *Media, Sex, and the Adolescent.* Cresskill, NJ: Hampton Press, pp. 177–95.

Collier, M. J. (1998). Researching cultural identity: Reconciling interpretive and postcolonial perspectives. In D. V. Tanno and A. Gonzalez (eds.), *Communication Identity Across Cultures: International and intercultural communication annual*, vol. 21. Thousand Oaks, CA: Sage, pp. 122–47.

Constantakis-Valdés, P. (1992). Toward a theory of "immigrant" and "ethnic" media: The case of Spanish-language television. Paper presented at the annual convention of the International Communication Association, Miami, FL.

Cortes-Rodriguez, C. (1990). Social practices of ethnic identity: A Puerto Rican psycho cultural event. *Hispanic Journal of Behavioral Sciences*, 12, 380–95.

Cronin, O. (1998). Psychology and photographic theory. In J. Prosser (ed.), *Image-Based Research: A sourcebook for qualitative researchers.* London: Taylor & Francis, pp. 69–83.

Currie, D. H. (1999). *Girl Talk: Adolescent magazines and their readers.* Toronto: University of Toronto.

David, P. and Johnson, M. A. (1998). The role of self in third-person effects about body image. *Journal of Communication*, 48(4), 37–58.

Dávila, A. (2000). Mapping Latinidad: Language and culture in the Spanish TV battlefront. *Television and New Media*, 1(1), 75–94.

Dávila, A. (2001). *Latinos Inc.: The marketing and making of a people.* Berkeley: University of California Press.

Davis, M. (2000). *Magical Urbanism: Latinos reinvent the US city.* London: Verso.

Delgado, F. (1998). When the silenced speak: The textualization and complications of Latina/o identity. *Western Journal of Communication*, 62(4), 420–38.

DeSipio, L. and de la Garza, R. O. (forthcoming). Beyond Civil Rights Immigration and The Shifting Foundation of Latino Politics. In m. garcia, M. Leger, and A. Valdivia (eds.), *Geographies of Latinidad: Latina/o studies into the twenty first century.* Durham, NC: Duke University Press.

Downing, J. D. H. (1992). Spanish-language media in the greater New York region during the 1980s. In S. H. Riggins (ed.), *Ethnic Minority Media: An international perspective.* Newbury Park, CA: Sage, pp. 256–75.

Duke, L. (2000). Black in a blonde world: race and girls' interpretations of the feminine ideal in teen magazines. *Journalism and Mass Communication Quarterly*, 77(2), 367–92.

Entman, R. M. and Book, C. L. (2000). Light makes right: Skin color and racial hierarchy in television advertising. In R. Anderson and L. Strate (eds.), *Critical Studies in Media Commercialism.* New York: Oxford.

Entman, R. M. and Rojecki, A. (2000). *The Black Image in the White Mind: Media and race in America.* Chicago: University of Illinois.

Ferguson, M. (1983). *Forever Feminine: Women's magazines and the cult of femininity*. London: Heinemann.

Flores, J. (1997). The Latino imaginary: Dimensions of community and identity. In F. R. Aparicio and S. Chávez-Silverman (eds.), *Tropicalizations: Transcultural representations of Latinidad*. Hanover, NH: University Press of New England, pp. 183–93.

Fox, G. (1996). *Hispanic Nation: Culture, politics, and the constructing of identity*. Secaucus, NJ: Birch Lane Press.

García, J. J. (2000). *Hispanic/Latino Identity: A philosophical perspective*. Malden, MA: Blackwell.

García Canclini, N. (1995). *Hybrid Cultures: Strategies for entering and leaving modernity* (trans. L. Chiaparri and S. L. Lopez). Minneapolis: University of Minnesota.

Gergen, K. J. (1991). *The Saturated Self: Dilemmas of identity in contemporary life*. New York: Basic Books.

Gowan, L. K., Hayward, C., Killen, J. D., Robinson, T. N., and Taylor, C. B. (1999). Acculturation and eating disorder symptoms in adolescent girls. *Journal of Research on Adolescence*, 9(1), 67–83.

Gutiérrez, F. (1977). Spanish-language media in America: Background, resources, history. *Journalism History*, 4(2), 34–41.

Halter, M. (1993). *Between Race and Ethnicity: Cape Verdean American immigrants, 1860–1965*. Urbana: University of Illinois.

Halter, M. (2000). *Shopping for Identity: The marketing of ethnicity*. New York: Schocken Books.

Haney Lopez, I. (1996). *White by Law: The legal construction of race*. New York: New York University Press.

Haney Lopez, I. (1998). Change, context, and choice in the social construction of race. In R. Delgado and J. Stefancic (eds.), *The Latino/a Condition: A critical reader*. New York: New York University, pp. 9–16.

Harper, D. (1998). An argument for visual sociology. In J. Prosser (ed.), *Image-Based Research: A sourcebook for qualitative researchers*. London: Taylor & Francis, pp. 24–41.

Harrison, K. and Cantor, J. (1997). The relationship between media consumption and eating disorders. *Journal of Communication*, 47(1), 40–67.

Huntzicker, W. E. (1995). Chinese-American newspapers. In F. Hutton and B. S. Reed (eds.), *Outsiders in 19th-Century Press History: Multicultural perspectives*. Bowling Green, OH: Bowling Green State University Popular Press, pp. 71–92.

Husband, C. (1994). General introduction: Ethnicity and media democratization within the nation-state. In C. Husband (ed.), *A Richer Vision: The development of ethnic minority media in Western democracies*. Paris: UNESCO, pp. 1–19.

Johnson, M. A. (2000). How ethnic are U.S. ethnic media: The case of Latina magazines. *Mass Communication and Society*, 3(2/3), 229–48.

Johnson, M. A., David, P., and Huey, D. (in press, a). Looks like me? Body image in Hispanic women's magazines. In A. Tait and G. Meiss (eds.), *AHANA (African American, Hispanic, Asian and Native American) and Media* book series. Westport, CT: Greenwood.

Johnson, M. A., David, P., and Huey, D. (in press, b). Beauty in brown: Skin color in Latina magazines. In D. L. Rios and A. N. Mohamed (eds.), *Communication in Brown and Black: Latino and African American conflict and convergence in mass media and cross-cultural contexts*. Westport, CT: Greenwood.

Katz, E. and Liebes, T. (1990). Interacting with "Dallas": Cross cultural readings of American TV. *Canadian Journal of Communication*, 15(1), 45–66.

Martinez, G. A. (1998). Mexican Americans and whiteness. In R. Delgado and J. Stefancic (eds.), *The Latino/a Condition: A critical reader*. New York: New York University Press, pp. 175–9.

Massey, D. S. (1987). *Return to Aztlan: The social process of international migration from western Mexico*. Berkeley: University of California.

Mayer, V. (2001). From segmented to fragmented: Latino media in San Antonio, Texas. *Journalism and Mass Communication Quarterly*, 78(2), 291–306.

McCracken, E. (1993). *Decoding Women's Magazines: From* Mademoiselle *to* Ms. New York: St. Martin's Press.

Melville, M. (1998). Hispanics: Race, class or ethnicity. *The Journal of Ethnic Studies*, 16, 67–84.

Merelman, R. M. (1995). *Representing Black Culture: Racial conflict and cultural politics in the United States*. New York: Routledge.

Messaris, P. (1994). *Visual Literacy: Image, mind, and reality*. Boulder, CO: Westview.

Myers, P. N., Jr. and Biocca, F. (1992). The elastic body image: The effect of television advertising and programming on body image distortions in young women. *Journal of Communication*, 42(3), 108–33.

Omi, M. and Winant, H. (1986). *Racial Formation in the United States: From the 1960s to the 1980s*. San Francisco: Routledge.

Park, R. E. (1922). *The Immigrant Press and Its Control*. Westport, CT: Greenwood Press. (Reprinted, 1970.)

Piper, A. (1998). Passing for white, passing for white. In E. Shohat (ed.), *Talking Visions: Multicultural feminism in a transnational age*. New York: New Museum of Contemporary Art/The MIT Press.

Rentaría, T. H. (1998). *Chicano Professionals: Culture, conflict, and identity*. New York: Garland.

Riggins, S. H. (1992). The promise and limits of ethnic minority media. In S. H. Riggins (ed.), *Ethnic Minority Media: An international perspective*. Newbury Park, CA: Sage, pp. 276–88.

Ríos, D. I. (2000). Latino/a experiences with mediated communication. In A. González, M. Houston, and V. Chen (eds.), *Our Voices: Essays culture, ethnicity, and communication* (3rd edn.). Los Angeles: Roxbury, pp. 105–12.

Robinson, T. L. and Ward, J. V. (1995). African-American adolescents and skin color. *Journal of Black Psychology*, 21(3), 256–74.

Rodriguez, A. (1997). Cultural agendas: The case of Latino-oriented U.S. media. In M. McCombs, D. L. Shaw, and D. Weaver (eds.), *Communication and Democracy: Exploring the intellectual frontiers in agenda-setting theory*. Mahwah, NJ: Lawrence Erlbaum, pp. 183–94.

Rodriguez, A. (1999). *Making Latino News: Race, language, class*. Thousand Oaks, CA: Sage.

Rodriguez, C. (2000). *Changing Race: Latinos, the census, and the history of ethnicity in the United States*. New York: New York University.

Segall, M. H., Campbell, D. T., and Herskovits, M. J. (1966). *The Influence of Culture in Visual Perception*. Indianapolis: Bobbs-Merrill.

Shields, V. with Heinecken, D. (2002). *Measuring Up: How advertising affects self-image*. Philadelphia: University of Pennsylvania.

Simonds, W. (1996). All consuming selves: Self-help literature and women's identities. In D. Grodin and T. R. Lindlof (eds.), *Constructing the Self in a Mediated World*. Thousand Oaks, CA: Sage, pp. 15–29.

Subervi-Vélez, F. A. (1994). Mass communication and Hispanics. In N. Kanellos, C. Esteva-Fabregat, F. M. Padilla, N. Kanellos, and C. Esteva (eds.), *Handbook of Hispanic Cultures in the United States: Sociology*. Houston, TX: Arte Publico Press, pp. 304–57.

Tanno, D. V. and González, A. (eds.) (1998). *Communication and Identity Across Cultures: International and intercultural communication annual*, vol. 21. Thousand Oaks, CA: Sage.

Turow, J. (1997). *Breaking up America: Advertisers and the new media world*. Chicago: University of Chicago.

Valdivia, A. N. (2000). *A Latina in the Land of Hollywood and Other Essays on Media Culture*. Temple: University of Arizona Press.

Further reading

Ballon, M. (1997). Start-up mambos to beat of booming market. *Inc*, September, 19, 23.

Beam, C. (1996). The Latina link in two languages. *Folio: The Magazine for Magazine Management*, 25, 23–4, September 1.

Bowen, L. and Schmid, J. (1997). Minority presence and portrayal in mainstream magazine advertising: An update. *Journalism and Mass Communication Quarterly*, 74(1), 134–46.

Caitlin, K. (1997). A Spanish "sleeping giant" looks northward. *Folio: The Magazine for Magazine Management*, 26(15), 14–15, November 15.

Chabram-Dernersesian, A. (1997). On the social construction of whiteness within selected Chicana/o discourses. In R. Frankenberg (ed.), *Displacing Whiteness: Essays in social and cultural criticism*. Durham, NC: Duke University Press, pp. 107–64.

Dixon, T. L. and Linz, D. (2000). Overrepresentation and underrepresentation of African Americans and Latinos as lawbreakers on television news. *Journal of Communication*, 50(2), 131–54.

Fest, G. (1997). Speaking the language. *Adweek*, 38, 25–30, October 27.

Gremillion, J. (1996). Young, gifted, and "Latina." *Mediaweek*, 6, 34, June 10.

Jeffres, L. W. and Hur, K. K. (1981). Communication channels within ethnic groups. *International Journal of Intercultural Relations*, 5(2), 115–32.

Johnson, M. A. (1996). Latinas and television in the United States: Relationships among genre identification, acculturation, and acculturation stress. *Howard Journal of Communications*, 7(4), 289–313.

Keenan, K. L. (1996). Skin tones and physical features of Blacks in magazine advertisements. *Journalism and Mass Communication Quarterly*, 73(4), 905–12.

Keith, V. M. and Herring, C. (1991). Skin tone and stratification in the Black community. *American Journal of Sociology*, 97, 760–78.

Kim, Y. Y. (2001). *Becoming Intercultural: An integrative theory of communication and cross-cultural adaptation*. Thousand Oaks, CA: Sage.

Korzenny, F., Neuendorf, K., Burgoon, M., Burgoon, J. K., and Greenberg, B. S. (1983). Cultural identification as a predictor of content preferences of Hispanics. *Journalism Quarterly*, 60(2), 329–33.

Leslie, M. (1995). Slow fade to?: Advertising in Ebony magazine, 1957–1989. *Journalism and Mass Communication Quarterly*, 72, 426–35.

Lutz, C. and Collins, J. (1994). The photograph as an intersection of gazes: The example of National Geographic. In L. Taylor (ed.), *Visualizing Theory: Selected essays from V.A. R. 1990–1994*. New York: Routledge.

Nuiry, O. E. (1997). Cashing in on Latinas. *Latina Style*, 3(4), 23–33.

Oboler, S. (1995). *Ethnic Labels, Latino Lives: Identity and the politics of (re)presentation in the United States*. Minneapolis: University of Minnesota.

Oboler, S. (1998). Hispanics? That's what they call us. In R. Delgado and J. Stefancic (eds.), *The Latino/a Condition: A critical reader*. New York: New York University Press, pp. 3–5.

Padilla, F. M. (1985). *Latino Ethnic Consciousness: The case of Mexican Americans and Puerto Ricans in Chicago*. Notre Dame, IN: University of Notre Dame Press.

Ríos, D. I. and Gaines, S. O., Jr. (1998). Latino media use for cultural maintenance. *Journalism and Mass Communication Quarterly*, 75(4), 746–61.

Rodriguez, C. (1998). *Latin Looks: Images of Latinas and Latinos in the US media*. Boulder, CO: Westview.

Seltzer, R. and Smith, R. C. (1991). Color differences in the Afro-American community and the differences they make. *Journal of Black Studies*, 21(3), 279–86.

Shoemaker, P. J., Reese, S. D., and Danielson, W. A. (1985). Spanish language print media use as an indicator of acculturation. *Journalism Quarterly*, 62(4), 734–40.

Shoemaker, P. J., Reese, S. D., Danielson, W. A., and Hsu, K. (1987). Ethnic concentration as a predictor of media use. *Journalism Quarterly*, 64(3), 593–7.

Supriya, K. E. (1999). White difference: Cultural constructions of white identity. In T. K. Nakayama and J. N. Martin (eds.), *Whiteness: The communication of social identity*. Thousand Oaks, CA: Sage, pp. 129–48.

Tanno, D. (2000). Names, narratives, and the evolution of ethnic identity. In A. Gonzalez, M. Houston, and V. Chen (eds.), *Our Voices: Essays in culture, ethnicity, and communication* (3rd edn.). Los Angeles: Roxbury, pp. 25–8.

Taylor, C. R. and Bang, H. (1997). Portrayals of Latinos in magazine advertising. *Journalism and Mass Communication Quarterly*, 74(2), 285–303.

Valdivia, Angharad and Curry, Ramona (1998). Xuxa at the borders of global television. *Camera Obscura*, 38.

Wolf, N. (1991). *The Beauty Myth*. New York: Anchor Books.

Zmud, J. P. (1992). Ethnic Identity, Language, and Mass Communication: An empirical investigation of assimilation among US Hispanics. Doctoral dissertation, University of Southern California, Los Angeles.

CHAPTER FOURTEEN

Out of India
Fashion Culture and the Marketing of Ethnic Style

Sujata Moorti

Recently, I walked into the New York Public Library and the woman at the circulation desk who assisted me was sporting a bindi, a vermilion marking on the forehead, and a nose ring, both characteristic of Indian women's self-adornment practices.[1] In the school I teach in southern United States, several students regularly wear bindis and nose rings. Similarly, one can find henna painting kits from up-scale cosmetic companies in exclusive department stores, in toy stores, as well as in mainstream beauty outlets. This body painting style and design associated with women's beauty rituals in the South Asian subcontinent, the Persian Gulf countries, and North Africa has since the mid-nineties found its way to various parts of the United States where henna painting stalls are commonplace in community gatherings, festivals, and celebrations. A number of popular books have also been published constructing a genealogy for this cosmetic art. These books are both how-to manuals and perform the function of bringing Asian art to Western audiences. The spread of these trends in both metropolitan and non-metropolitan areas is at first sight unnerving and discombobulating to a South Asian immigrant but also signals the complex and contradictory ways in which contemporary US culture interacts with cultures from around the world. In some instances, the exotic becomes American and in others banal. This essay explores the manner in which media representational practices popularize "oriental" symbols and enable them to enter the mainstream vocabulary of the United States. It also underscores the consequences of this process. Since this appropriation of "foreign" sartorial habits is associated almost exclusively with women, through an examination of the use of "Indian" markers in contemporary media culture the essay unpacks as well the racialized and gendered national identities that are constituted within transnational commodity culture. The media images that I analyze in this essay are no doubt impelled by interactions with immigrant populations but they are also indicative of the ways in which US culture negotiates with conditions of globality. They enable an interrogation of the modalities through which the global enters the field of the local to create a transnational arena of consumption.

Before I examine media images, a clarification of some key terms I use is imperative. In the essay I characterize as "Indian" some self-adornment practices that were once specific to the South Asian subcontinent. I am not suggesting that Indians, because of their historical ties with these practices, have exclusive rights to them. Indeed, no one can enjoy a proprietary relationship to any specific aspect of culture. Since culture is always dynamic, shifting, contested, and negotiated, rather than argue that US media falsely represent Indian practices I want to draw attention to the cultural work performed by these exotic symbols.

I have limited this analysis to media representations of Indian beauty rituals not only because this is a part of the world I am intimately familiar with, but also because India has a unique salience in US popular culture. As I explain later in the essay, the allure of things Indian can partly be accounted for by the romance of the Raj and partly by the exotic cultural capital that has been associated with Indian philosophy and religions. (While the term Raj in Hindi signifies rule, in popular usage it has come to be associated exclusively with the period of British colonization. In the Western popular imaginary this time frame is associated with glamorous and alluring images of romance, danger, and exoticism rather than with oppressive practices.) The trends that I identify in the uses of "Indian" markers are similar to the modalities through which other Asian cultures and those that are marked as Other enter media space.

Most discussions of globalization and culture examine the impact of the United States and the West on the Third World, the ways in which "native" culture is transformed through practices of globalization. Through the use of a powerful set of statistics and quantitative information Barber (1996), for instance, has documented the dominance of US American popular culture around the world. Appadurai (1996), on the other hand, elucidates the diverse ways in which peoples of the Third World appropriate and recodify US American popular cultural products. Through a focus on the devalued and denigrated field of media fashion culture in this essay I examine the obverse process: how "local" US culture is informed by the global and how US American popular culture mediates the social and cultural transformations that accompany processes of globalization. As several scholars have noted, the performance of contemporary capitalism is made visible at the level of the local. The circulation of "global" products in the US media, a terrain where local concerns are articulated, creates a space that forces us to re-view questions of consumption, desire, and national identity.

The paper evolves from and is located within the body of scholarship on media content and representations. The earliest studies in this brand of media theory sought to quantitatively elucidate positive and negative content in media materials. Later studies focused on the latent content of media practices to tease out the embedded ideological messages. The body of work emanating from a cultural studies perspective has, through textual analysis and audience reception studies, underscored the significance of the dominant messages encoded in representational practices, foregrounded those that have been marginalized, and highlighted the significance of these practices. This essay is shaped particularly by cultural studies scholarship since it situates media content and representations within a broad social, historical, and cultural context.

Drawing on arguments from multiple disciplines I examine fashion spreads and fashion advertisements to unravel the discourses of nation, identity, and sexuality that come into play within the field of global flows. I observed women's magazines such as *Elle*, *Glamour*, *Cosmopolitan*, and *Ladies' Home Journal* and catalogs from specialty stores such as *Anthropologie* and *Pottery Barn* and clothing retailers such as *La Redoute* and *Tweeds* between 1995 and 2000. I have specifically not included elite fashion magazines such as *Vogue* and *W*, which focus on haute couture and attempt to solicit an upper-class fashion-conscious audience. Instead through a focus on mainstream publications, female magazines and lifestyle catalogs, I outline the definitions of ideal female beauty and femininity that are promoted through the use of "Indian" symbols.

Informed by scholarship within the fields of cultural studies, feminism, and postcolonial studies this essay on media representational practices develops a two-pronged argument that constantly oscillates between global and local loci. First, I demonstrate that media images of fashion culture replicate the broad contours of hegemonic beauty conventions, albeit with a touch of India, to produce a US American exotica. Secondly, since the fashion spreads and advertisements self-consciously reference India I use these images to isolate the cultural and sexual modes of differentiation that emerge to mark the problematic and generative interplay between the US and the non-Western world, center and periphery. I will show that the figure of woman in these images functions as a threshold figure, a boundary marker between home and the world, the native and the alien.

Above all, a central point I will repeatedly emphasize is that media images of fashion culture are neither innocent nor are they frivolous. Rather, they conduct important cultural work that both enables and explains transnational economic flows. At the global level, the use of Indian symbols by Western women allows them to claim a unique brand of cosmopolitanism, one where the world serves as a glossy prop for US Americans. Such a display of the global as an exotic panorama for US activities helps allay anxieties about the complex processes of globalization. At the local level, in a counter-intuitive move, the proliferation of "Indian" exotic symbols reinscribes the centrality of White womanhood to US American identity. What appears at first glance as an exemplary celebration of multiculturalism on closer analysis proves the contrary. Rather than provide a better understanding of other cultures, media images appropriate and manage difference, a move I characterize as symbolic cannibalism. The use of "Indian" markers in mainstream fashion culture domesticates and naturalizes the exotic to produce a unique brand of (White) US American beauty. A central point in this essay is that media practices and practitioners do not deliberately and consciously construct images to produce negative or positive images of India, rather they encode dominant ideas already present in society.

As Kumar (1997) has argued the presence of crude caricatures under the influence of Orientalism – the essentialized and stereotypical modes of representing colonized peoples – requires postcolonial scholars to translate what seems natural and commonsensical into that which is political. This task also entails providing alternative histories, new readings, and a context for the consumption of cultural texts. The intent of this essay is not to seize a predetermined, correct representation, rather it seeks to intervene and transform the encoded effects and apparatus of representation. Consequently, this analysis does not engage with issues of authenticity, whether media representations are faithful to the real India or not. I do not focus on the reductive stereotypes that underlie this visual grammar, instead I examine the representations to tease out the politics and ideologies that are promoted and whose interests are served.

The essay makes an intervention into the broader arenas of commodity culture and transnational studies and urges scholars to pay more attention to media practices because seemingly innocent images perform the important function of reproducing and naturalizing key structures of global flows. As numerous scholars have noted popular culture, although often devalued, is one of the primary sites where struggles over who belongs occur and questions of national identity are worked out. Lowe (1996) has pointed out that it is through culture that the subject becomes, acts, and speaks itself as "American." I use popular culture in this spirit to unravel the specific ways in which hegemonic ideas about the globe and US are reasserted. Media representational practices thus serve as an important site where ideas about globalization processes are ritually enacted. They help us make sense of complex political and economic structures and permit an understanding of the modalities through which visual culture participates in constructing dominant ideas about "aliens" and alien cultures.

In what follows I outline first the historical role advertisements have played in promoting values of capitalism and consumerism. This brief exegesis into British advertising practices during high colonialism (the mid-to-late nineteenth century) lays the ground for the significance of my findings. A comparison with nineteenth-century advertising practices illustrates how contemporary advertising has encoded concerns central to and arising from the emergence of transnational capitalism. After a brief outline of the vast scholarship conducted in the fields of advertising and fashion studies the essay provides a series of fashion vignettes illustrating the visual and rhetorical tropes that go into the uses of "Indian" markers.

A brief detour explaining the terms globalization and cosmopolitanism though is necessary. Globalization is a portmanteau concept that covers a vast array of economic, human, and cultural activities that cross national boundaries. While it is used most often to signify high velocity transnational financial activities and the unification of capital markets, globalization encompasses as well the disparate flows of people, products, labor, and culture. Globalization as a phenomenon threatens to dissipate the category of the nation state. While the rhetoric surrounding these processes tends to present globalization as a fairly stable and uniform phenomenon it has proved to be highly uneven. Globalization affects first and third world countries and their peoples in radically different ways.

Although the term cosmopolitanism has lengthy antecedents in the fields of philosophy and political science (beginning with Kant) it has gained new salience in contemporary society, where, like globalization, it registers a stance against nationalism. Modern usage of the term cosmopolitanism attempts to capture how conditions of globality have altered people's sense of home and belonging and thus the politics they practice. In common parlance, cosmopolitanism signifies an apolitical stance and a sense of feeling at home in the world, where one is not bounded by national borders. Hence, a cosmopolitan subject is a citizen of the world and the antithesis of the nationalist. In fashion culture and in advertising such a structure of feeling is iconically reproduced by presenting an international arena in the background. Glossy depictions of the non-western world, in particular, come to stand in for a cosmopolitan sensibility.

Global Panoramas

If the Victorian Era marked the rise of a particular kind of commodity culture, one that was facilitated by colonialism and a newly emerging capitalist mode of relations, the contemporary era of global capitalism inscribes a new set of imperial relations that are indicative of a new brand of unequal transnational relations. Contemporary processes of globalization mark radical changes in transnational relations, and we can see traces of these structural shifts in media images of fashion culture.

McClintock (1995) and Richards (1990) in their perceptive studies of nineteenth-century British advertisements have pointed out that during the moment of high imperialism commodity culture was a primary vehicle through which colonial culture and its underpinning racial ideologies were materialized. They argue that images of Africa, and the empire in general, were mobilized to not just sell products but also to justify imperial domination. During the late-nineteenth century, advertisements facilitated images of empire to infiltrate every aspect of the domestic realm and naturalized racial difference. In contemporary global commodity culture there exists an analogous structure of feeling, but with crucial inversions. In the nineteenth century, images of empire came home through advertisements. For instance, advertisements for soaps used African children with whitened bodies to highlight their cleaning capacity. In contemporary images, as the following analysis reveals, the West ventures out into the world. Specifically, US American bodies inhabit the globe and accommodate the world out there within the local. Today, the spoils of the new globalized empire are brought home by US Americans, not by the exotic Other. The globe appears as a spectacle or the backdrop against which US American consumerism is mobilized and legitimized.

The role of the female figure too is significantly altered. During the nineteenth century, although products were clearly aimed at women, advertisements that represented the world out there did not include the female body. In the global commodity culture of transnational capitalism, it is the figure of the female that becomes central. She is the vehicle through which transactions of global products are domesticated and US hegemony is normalized. In images set against a foreign background the Western woman appears always as stylish, attractive, glamorous, and comfortable, striding confidently through the world. Both globalization and cosmopolitanism appear as lifestyle choices, which can be effected through the purchase of commodities. Rarely are men deployed similarly in media images: as unthreatening, cosmopolitan, glossy figures who inhabit the world at ease through the use of fashion accessories. Men appear in media images depicting a global landscape primarily in two arenas: sports and war.

Allure of the exotic

In this analysis I rely on two very broad areas of scholarship, that of advertising and of fashion. The studies I enumerate are specific to the arguments I make and vastly condense the sophisticated and nuanced arguments that have been developed in these fields. There exists a vast array of scholarship on advertising, its representational practices, and its relation to society. Most of these studies either elucidate or disprove advertising's status as a weapon of persuasion. Schudson (1984) for instance has discounted the power of advertising while Williamson (1978) and other feminist scholars have underlined its ability to reinforce patriarchal ideologies. Highlighting the dominant ideologies of capitalism and consumerism advertising promotes, Goldman (1992) and Jhally (1990) conceptualize advertisements as a discourse through and about objects. Advertisements offer a unique window for observing how commodity interests conceptualize social relations and facilitate the production and reproduction of ideology. They are "an apparatus for *reframing meanings* in order to add value to products. Ads arrange, organize and steer *meanings* into *signs* that can be inscribed on products" (Goldman, 1992, p. 5). In this paper I do not engage in the debate over the power of advertisements, rather I examine the social relations that are structured into their signifying practices. Through advertisements one can observe also the manner in which the logic of commodity form expresses itself culturally and socially. Although in what follows I do characterize the use of "Indian" markers in fashion culture as appropriation my purpose here is to call attention to the cultural work conducted by such imagery.

Fashion is a slippery phenomenon. It is filled with ambivalences, polyvalence, and excess; it could be conceived of as a masquerade that signals place and identity. I deploy a very broad definition of fashion in this paper, as "styles of dressing that come to be accepted as desirable in a particular period. Defined thus, fashion embodies change, it is itself only by being forever transient. It is often understood to be a mark of the ideologically modern" (Nag, 1991, p. 93). Most contemporary theorists of fashion concur that the phenomenon is not unique to the culture of capitalism; it exists and existed in non-metropolitan centers as well. Nevertheless the structure of fashion systems coincides with the interests of a capitalist system: fashion has a built-in mechanism of obsolescence; it pivots around nowness and newness and repeatedly constructs desire for new products. The analysis in this paper is influenced also by Bourdieu's (1986) notion that fashion and clothing are performative phenomena that help establish social distinction.

Scholarship on fashion and the garment industry has emerged in recent years as a locus of cross–disciplinary studies. It has become as well a primary site from which to examine the transnational flows of labor, products, and economies. Within the realm of art history, scholarship such as that of Hollander (1978) has centered on haute couture to enumerate the aesthetic qualities of the system. Sociologists have underscored the ideological structures and class relations that are sustained by fashion culture. Crane (2000), for instance, deploys clothing as a strategic site for studying changes in the meanings of cultural goods in relation to changes in social structures, in the character of cultural organization, and in the forms of culture. Clothes and fashionable clothing styles are "carriers" of a wide range of ideological meanings or social agendas, she contends. While these studies lay to rest the cavil that fashion is a frivolous field, scholarship from a cultural studies perspective has been the most effective in transforming some basic assumptions about the field. Paying attention to audience reception these scholars have recast fashion from being considered a passive act into an active process, one where individuals resist and negotiate their own meanings (Craik, 1998).

Shifting attention from the form and content of fashion and focusing on the political economy, scholars such as Ross (1997) have underscored the labor and material conditions of production. In particular, they have pointed out that the transnational dispersal of the garment industry makes it difficult to separate the sweat from the glamour (Skoggard, 1998). While alert to the vicissitudes of fashion trends few though have examined the specific ways in which Western fashion appropriates from "foreign" cultures and the ideologies that are promoted by this construction of a transnational chic. This essay clears the space for such an intervention.

As a field and practice that centers on women feminist scholarship has repeatedly engaged with the topic of fashion but the responses have been largely ambivalent. Nevertheless, there have been significant shifts in perspectives. The early seventies movement dismissed fashion as yet another instrument of women's subordination. More recently, feminists have started to leaven this criticism by foregrounding the pleasure fashion can provoke in individual women (Wilson, 1992). Increasingly, even as scholars have started to examine the complex manner in which individuals derive pleasure from fashion, the focus has also shifted from haute couture to everyday practices, or what Craik (1998) has termed the "technology of civility," the sanctioned codes of conduct in the practices of self-formation and self-presentation.

Reflecting the growing interest in globalization, feminist scholars too are beginning to address how processes of globalization have placed bodily adornment and fashion in the global–local nexus. For instance, Li (1998) believes that contemporary investigations in this context have to examine the conjunction between fashion, global capitalism, and modernity. They cannot avoid "questions of imperialism and colonialism, nor can they be detached from analyses of the dynamics of globalization and localization" (p. 74). Similarly, in her subtle and powerful analysis of the "Japanese invasion" of the Western fashion world, Kondo (1997) underscores the constitutive contradictions of the industry: it is transnational in its dispersal and reach yet rife with essentializing gestures that reiterate national boundaries. My analysis is informed by these studies particularly those that call attention to fashion as a productive site on an individual level but at the global level as a site where hegemonic discourses are reiterated. The essay also underscores the modalities through which certain aspects of globalization processes are naturalized through fashion practices.

Like other scholars of fashion, such as Ash and Wilson (1992), my analysis assumes that clothing and its trends invoke rather accurately wider crises. Dressing negotiates between the intensely personal and the prescribed and constructed layers of the social; it also concerns ideology, seduction, and North–South relations. Thus through bodily adornment one can acquire symbolic and economic capital.

In both fields of advertising and fashion the allure of the exotic has been a recurring motif and a strategy to construct desire. In the realm of advertising, as Schudson (1984, p. 162) has pointed out, mid-nineteenth-century patent medicines were the first products in the United States to turn to the exotic. To establish identification with their product, advertisers came up with names that seemed remote, ancient, and mystical. Consequently products with names such as Hayne's Arabian Balsam, Hoofland's Greek Oil, Osgood's Indian Cholagogue, Jayne's Spanish Alterative were commonplace. In the United Kingdom, Richards (1990) and McClintock (1995) have persuasively demonstrated the ways in which soap advertisements in particular deployed empire and the exotic. They suggest that the use of such imagery naturalized imperial ideology. Shifting the focus to contemporary advertising where the rise of ethnic-based niche marketing has made the exotic a "hot" commodity (Halter, 2000; Dávila, 2001), this essay facilitates a similar unraveling of the ideologies promoted by the use of exotic markers.

Within the realm of fashion, Craik (1998) and Steele (1996) have suggested that the use of exotic motifs is commonplace because these symbols are seen as transgressive. Since all fashion relies on the tension between the familiar and the foreign these systems tend to rely on discourses of exoticism, the primitive, orientalism, and authenticity. Craik clarifies that in Western fashion the term exotic is used to refer to elements of new fashion codes or "new looks" codified as profoundly different from previous or contemporary fashion techniques. The ethnocentric underpinnings of Western fashion (European or European derived) ensure that difference between codes of exoticism and mundanity are played up. By narrowing the focus to the appropriation of "Indian" symbols within fashion, my analysis underscores how such representational practices mobilize new structures of desire, identification, and relations of looking.

While the use of the exotic in fashion and in advertisements is not novel, I contend that within the context of globalization they provide an important aperture from which to understand the specific ways in which the logic of commodity form expresses itself culturally and socially. I read fashion advertisements as producing what Schudson (1984) has termed capitalist realism, "a set of aesthetic conventions" that celebrate and promote the values of the transnational political economy.

In the analysis that follows I examine media representations from within the contours of commodity cosmopolitanism and femininity. In these representations ideas of femininity and globalism converge in a spectacle of the commodity. They envisage globalization as coming into being through the figure of woman, in effect through the domestic realm. Within a cosmopolitanism that is configured through woman, her body becomes the space for the display of global spectacle. In what follows I describe the particular ways in which so-called Indian markers are deployed by fashion advertisements to register multiple meanings of transgression and the allure of the different.

Fabricating Karma

"Indian" motifs and fabrics have long been used in haute couture and high fashion culture. However, the appearance of this form of poaching in everyday fashion advertisements signals a proletarianization of this practice. According to Craik (1998), haute couture has institutionalized plagiarism, borrowing elements from different style systems and underscoring the foreign origins of their designs. She describes designers as "birds of prey" who "rob the nests of other fashion systems in their quest for new ideas. Stylistic motifs are reconstituted in a process of bricolage – the creation of new patterns and modes from the kaleidoscopic bits and pieces of cultural debris" (p. ix). Haute couture deliberately inscribes its exotic origins, highlighting difference. The deployment of "Indian" markers in everyday advertisements is remarkably different. The exotic and the Other may be integral to depict a glossy cosmopolitan style but they are stripped of their foreign origins and are presented as ordinary symbols Western women can meld with comfortably. India and Asia in general contribute to the glamour these advertisements strive to achieve. India becomes an affect; it represents difference.

There are two dominant forms in which India and the Orient appear in images of everyday fashion culture: either as a backdrop against which Western fashions are displayed or as symbols that have been integrated in everyday fashion so thoroughly as to appear mundane and ordinary. In media images the use of India and Indian symbols becomes a shorthand term for presenting a glamorous and exoticized persona. One could read this pervasive use of India and Indian symbols as another example of neo-imperialism, the global is deployed exploitatively to serve the interests of the First World. Advertisements and the global commodity culture underpinning this system of signs, though, call for a more nuanced and complex understanding, one that underscores issues of interdependency and exploitation.

It is difficult to identify an originary moment for India-exotica chic since a counter-culture India style consisting primarily of the use of incense, cotton skirts, and yoga has existed at least since the sixties. As Islam (1994) points out nostalgia for the glamour of the Raj has always kept India, the jewel in the British Crown, visible in the West. The contemporary structure of feeling is different though. Media images have transformed what had been isolated to alternative stores into mainstream practices, similar to those that I have alluded to in the beginning of the essay. I characterize the nineties popularization of Indian symbols as the proletarianization of India chic. It includes a full-fledged domestication of the "Indian" exotic and is marked by the commoditization of all aspects of Indian culture as ethno-exotic chic.

For instance, the lead singer of the pop group No Doubt, Gwen Stefani, has for long worn a bindi, the marking on her forehead, both in her everyday appearances and in her albums. Popular magazines now refer to it as her "trademark" bindi. Similarly, Madonna and Janet Jackson have deployed bindis, sari fabrics, nose rings, and henna decorations in their music videos and in their everyday appearances. Since then the presence of bindis, nose rings, and henna decorations have become commonplace, especially in fashion spreads oriented to youth culture. It is easy to dismiss the pointed use of these body markings as another effort made by celebrities to mark out their brand and by youth to carve out a new identity, as integral to the presentation of the self as "different." Nevertheless, these practices conceal important cultural processes. Markers of "Indian" female beauty rituals function as props for the display of hegemonic (white) femininity. Following Frankenberg (1993) I use the terms white and West here to signify not so much a skin color or a geographic space as to refer to a position of privilege and power. By repeatedly erasing the cultural specificity of "Indian" symbols, these representational practices transform the meanings associated with them, metamorphosing them into an integral aspect of a brand of American fashion.

Under Western eyes, differences among Asian women and Asian countries are flattened; motifs from Southeast Asia are blended with those from South Asia as though they were the same cultures. Fashion spreads use bindis, bangles, and sarongs within the same spread; or use Indonesian batiks against a Chinese landscape. This selective and decontextualized use of foreign traditions permits Americans to feel they are partaking a cosmopolitan ethno-exotica culture. Shed of all referents to the cultures from which the trends originate cultural difference is reduced to curry, something that can be easily consumed by the dominant culture. Cultural critic hooks (1992) has characterized such commodification processes as consumer cannibalism. The difference the other inhabits is eradicated and all other cultural specificity is erased. In fashion spreads we see a similar form of cannibalism enacted except that in this case it is made possible symbolically.

The presentation of India as integral to fashion is not limited to these symbols but encompasses a broader range of accoutrements. Designer lines such as Liz Claiborne advertise their collections through the use of Indian fabrics and emphasize the practice of poaching by providing close ups of body art associated with some Indian traditions that mark the model's legs. Similarly, cosmetic spreads from powerhouses Revlon and Maybelline try to capture the general aura of India and the East by juxtaposing disparate symbols to produce the affect of an alluring and exotic Orient. India is made present through stereotypes that emerged in high colonialism. Elements such as hookah (the smoking pipe), silhouettes of buildings that resemble the Taj Mahal, and elephants that represent India in the collective imaginary are highlighted to signify an India-inspired fashion. These objects form the frame through which India and Indian culture are filtered into fashion consciousness. Many of these spreads share a representational grammar; their visual codes never explicitly spell out the Indian roots of the exotic aura they seek to cultivate. By presenting the aura of a majestic, mysterious, alluring, and primitively glamorous land these advertisements recreate a nostalgic, romantic, and imaginary India. These images emerge from and continue to reproduce key features of Orientalist discourses.

The appropriation and cannibalization of "Indian" symbols culminate in the complete domestication of the product/symbol. The everyday use of the pashmina shawl or the use of paisley designs exemplify this process whereby the products shed all reference to their cultures of origin and are instead seen as Western or as British as is the case with paisley (Askari & Arthur, 1999; Lévi–Strauss, 1987). An examination of the pashmina shawl's integration within the fashion vocabulary in the West is instructive here. What once started with references to the exotic, with slogans lyrically referring to the origins of the wool in Nepal and the Himalayan mountains, has now lost all linkages with the Indian subcontinent. It has instead been thoroughly incorporated as US chic.

Commodity multiculturalism

The production and circulation of these images of Indian artifacts and symbols in such a broad arena is significant. It reflects the increased presence of middle-class South Asians in US society; everyday Americans come into contact with South Asians in numerous contexts. Singer Gwen Stefani has noted that one of her boyfriends was of Indian origin, and this association may have contributed to her use of the bindi. The use of these markers may reflect as well a liberal response to a marginalized, oppressed group. In the eighties, Indian women in New Jersey who wore bindis faced violence from groups of White US Americans who proclaimed themselves dot-busters. Today, we find the meaning associated with the bindi has been radically transformed by its location. The use of the bindi permits Western women to perform an enlightened, multicultural appreciation of other cultures, but when used by Indian women, it continues to point to the residues of a primordial, primitive culture.

Notwithstanding the obduracy of the stereotypes associated with Indian women, among diasporic populations the proletarianization of India chic has resulted in an appreciation of "home" culture and traditions. Durham (2001) and Maira (2000), among other scholars, have enumerated the effects of this appropriation of "Indian" symbols on immigrant populations. I have also explored elsewhere how these trends in US media images have transformed responses to traditional practices within the subcontinent itself. Indeed, the symbolic capital associated with these images lends credibility and cultural capital to particularized "native" uses of such invented traditions. Indian fashion magazines mimic Western practices and ironically participate in a process of self-Orientalizing, or what Savigliano (1995) has termed autoexoticizing.

The proletarianization of India chic in the US is a unique phenomenon. As I have indicated already, haute couture designers market their wares by deliberately poaching from other cultures and have underscored their appropriation of exotic motifs from foreign lands. The use of the exotic provides symbolic and cultural capital both to the designer and those who wear the clothes. The exotic functions not only to mark difference but also to signify a cosmopolitan aura. In the proletarianization of this practice we find that the exotic roots of the motifs are erased or referenced obliquely. India appears as affect, an indirect reference to the exotic, whereas in high fashion the appropriation of Indian motifs are not only celebrated but explicitly referenced to bestow the aura of romance, danger, and the exotic to everyday fashion. Negative stereotypes associated with India are held in abeyance by locating the symbols on Western women's bodies. In fashion culture, the use of Indian markers enhances the desirability of Western woman but does little to alter the existing Orientalist discourses.

US fashion culture taps into Asian culture and the Orient with a voracious appetite. When India is deployed as background, every aspect of the image is saturated with markers of the Orient. The entire continent of Asia is collapsed into a site where the Western woman could enhance her desirability through the use of a fantastic exoticism. Against an Asian panorama, Western women's self is recentered; the globe is transformed as a stage for the construction of a desiring (White) female subject. Indeed, Western woman emerges as the "master" subject in the transnational arena of consumption. She is the consummate consumer subject. Such representations libidinize the global arena as an erotic zone.

Further, the images of Western women cast against a foreign/global backdrop help associate the home with the world, and the world with the home, thereby domesticating the global arena. These representations tap into dominant understandings that associate woman with the domestic arena, the private space, to allay anxieties associated with globalization processes.

Simultaneously, even as she stakes her claim to a cosmopolitan identity the figure of woman continues to function as a metonym for nation. The figure of woman stitches together the fragments of a gendered transnational political economy. In this visual grammar, national and cultural identities are resurrected as glossy commodities in the transnational libidinization of the market. They produce a space where Jameson (1991) suggests commodity and ideology become indistinguishable. Yet, because of their reliance on only Western woman as "carriers" of the exotic, these representations produce a desired and desirable femininity that domesticates and naturalizes the exotic. In the following section I elaborate on this aspect.

Racial hierarchies

In addition to the appropriation of "Indian" markers, media images are also characterized by a near-complete absence of Brown women. (I use the awkward phrasing Brown women to reference Indian women and those from the sub-continent; as Kondo (1997) and other scholars have noted haute couture often uses Black women to add exotic color when they use foreign motifs.) At the very moment that aspects of Indian society are positioned at the center, Brown women themselves are banished to the invisible regions of the periphery. For the most part, Asian women disappear from the use of Orientalist imagery; the East and India are deployed to add an exotic dimension to dominant beauty standards. The erasure of Indian/Asian women from these representations allows consumer culture to present a decontextualized international ethno-exotica.

When Brown women appear in media representations, as in the advertisement for the Swissair commercial, they resemble White women in brown face. The so-called Indian women are identical in features to the White woman, the only distinguishing features are the color of their skin. Thereby even though these representations may escape the charge of monochromatism they continue to reiterate dominant beauty standards.

These advertisements are often slyly reflexive, commenting on their practices of poaching. They acknowledge with a nod and a wink the conditions of their own production. "I wonder what makes a tradition become a trend?" the Swissair advertisement queries. The smaller text indicates that trends are rooted in traditions. These ideas are used in a playful manner to promote a new consumption. Like Madonna or Gwen Stefani this image transforms a tradition into a trend to market its iconicity. In these instances, the Orient serves to demarcate and confine cultural boundaries.

There is an aspect of this postmodern pastiche that is very playful and appealing. "Pastiche designates a cultural form built on copying, scavenging and recombining particles of cultural texts regardless of context. Pastiche is the visual representation composed of decontextualized and fetishized signifiers" (Goldman,

1992, p. 214). It is also considered a central mode through which postmodern concerns are articulated. As I have already elucidated, in media representations cultural markers from disparate cultures are juxtaposed to produce a seemingly apolitical product.

On the surface, these representations seem to belie Kipling's oft-repeated statement, "Oh East is East and West is West and never the twain shall meet." On the bodies of (White) Western women the two seem to meet. However, on closer examination these glamorous images can be seen to reify the differences between East and West. The presence of brown-skinned women or even the use of "Indian" symbols may appear at first glance to be a celebration of multi-culturalism and the diversity of cultures that coexist in the US. Nevertheless, the decontextualized manner in which the exotic is mobilized fractures any sense of heritage. In the final analysis, these images are about the cultural representation of the West to itself by way of a detour through the Other.

These images in everyday fashion are propelled by the climate of multi-culturalism prevalent in the larger society. Yet, the manner in which India and other cultures are represented reinscribes the normative power of the center; the Other is apprehended only in terms defined by the dominant culture not on their own terms. The ethnic spectacle of these fashion spreads demonstrates how a certain kind of "Indian" identity is created, gains currency, and is promoted through the body of the non-brown woman. India is contained within a cultural garden of bindis, nose rings, henna, and sari fabric. Indianness is repackaged as a newly improved product and sold as Oriental fantasy of female identity and desire.

There is a surplus value to these images. They recuperate a particular US nationalism, one where it remains central to the operations of global flows. It also constitutes a female subject who is desirable and exotic by using "Indian" symbols; thereby the presence of the Western woman allows for a partial new understanding of some key facets of Orientalist discourse. If these symbols were placed on Indian women the messages conveyed about globalization would tap into a series of stereotypes about the hypersexualized, dangerous, and exotic Oriental female, which would hardly serve to quell anxieties that have been prevalent since colonial times.

In media representations of "Indian" symbols all culture is turned into com-modity. These images celebrate difference and yet manage and regulate diver-sity. These images facilitate a sense of home as no place, or, at the very least, home as a composite of different parts of the world. They produce India as commodity sign; instead of a Third World country, they present an exotic and romantic view of India that is a legacy of Orientalism and a hangover of the fascination with the Raj. India becomes not only portable commodity but an integral element in the discourse of style. As Appadurai (1996) has hypothesized under conditions of global flows pastiche and nostalgia are the dominant modes of image production and reception. We see both these aspects, particularly a nostalgia for a mythical India, repeatedly inscribed in these representations.

The images I have examined in the essay exemplify the West's fascination with the Other, the desire to know the Other so it can become less potent, and the repeated efforts to position the Other within a discourse of being always-already different, condemning the Other in perpetuity to the land of difference. Despite the use of "Indian" markers, the performance of race and identity (of whiteness) in these representational practices is predicated on an opposition to being not-Indian. This visual grammar gains salience only in the context of the transnational circuits of capital and culture. The tensions and ambivalences that structure these representations are specific to contemporary conditions of globality; they exemplify how the West looks at the globe and also how the West positions itself within it. The world and all cultures are only apprehended through consumable goods. Further the global arena is presented as a feminine, domestic space which naturalizes US hegemony in processes of globalization.

Above all, India becomes a site for the articulation of a capitalist nostalgia. The consumer can experience the world without jeopardizing the comforts of advanced capitalism. Tropes of Orientalism continue to circulate in the fashion world and gain new visibility. Indeed, as I have illustrated in this essay, in the battleground of style, Orientalist tropes are transposed, recuperated, and recodified. Media images, including those that are rarely considered significant, such as advertisements and fashion spreads, perform the important cultural work of helping us understand and re-produce a specific brand of globalization. The analysis of media content and representational practices, as this essay has indicated, provides an important vantage into complex economic and political practices.

Note

1   I would like to thank the anonymous reviewers for comments that have strengthened the essay and above all to Angharad Valdivia for her encouragement and patience.

References

Appadurai, A. (1996). *Modernity at Large: Cultural dimensions of globalization*. Minneapolis: University of Minnesota Press.

Ash, J. and Wilson, E. (eds.) (1992). *Chic Thrills: A fashion reader*. London: Pandora.

Askari, N. and Arthur, L. (1999). *Uncut Cloth: Saris, shawls and sashes*. London: Merrell Holberton.

Barber, B. (1996). *Jihad vs. McWorld: How globalism and tribalism are reshaping the world*. New York: Ballantine.

Bourdieu, P. (1986). *Distinction: A social critique of the judgment of taste*. London: Routledge.

Craik, J. (1998). *The Face of Fashion: Cultural studies in fashion*. New York: Routledge.

Crane, D. (2000). *Fashion and Its Social Agendas: Class, gender and identity in clothing*. Chicago: University of Chicago Press.

Dávila, A. M. (2001). *Latinos, Inc.: The marketing and making of a people*. Berkeley: University of California Press.

Durham, M. G. (2001). Displaced persons: symbols of South Asian femininity and the returned gaze in US media culture. *Communication Theory*, 11, 201–18.

Frankenberg, R. (1993). *White Woman, Race Matters: The social construction of whiteness*. New York: Routledge.

Goldman, R. (1992). *Reading Ads Socially*. New York: Routledge.

Halter, M. (2000). *Shopping For Identity: The marketing of ethnicity*. New York: Schocken Books.

Hollander, A. (1978). *Seeing Through Clothes*. New York: Viking.

hooks, b. (1992). *Black Looks: Race and representation*. Boston: South End Press.

Islam, N. (1994). Signs of belonging. In S. Maira and R. Srikanth (eds.), *Contours of the Heart: South Asians map North America*. New York: Asian American Writer's Workshop, pp. 132–45.

Jameson, F. (1991). *Postmodernism; Or, the cultural logic of late capitalism*. Durham, NC: Duke University Press.

Jhally, S. (1990). *The Codes of Advertising: Fetishism and the political economy of meaning in the consumer society*. New York: Routledge.

Kondo, D. (1997). *About Face: Performing race in fashion and theater*. New York: Routledge.

Kumar, A. (1997). Translating resistance. In A. Cvetkovich and D. Kellner (eds.), *Articulating the Global and the Local: Globalization and cultural studies*. Boulder, CO: Westview, pp. 207–25.

Lévi-Strauss, M. (1987). *The Cashmere Shawl*. London: Dryad Press.

Li, X. (1998). Fashioning the body in post-Mao China. In A. Brydon and S. Niessen (eds.), *Consuming Fashion: Adorning the transnational body*. New York: Berg, pp. 71–89.

Lowe, L. (1996). *Immigrant Acts: On Asian American cultural politics*. Durham, NC: Duke University Press.

Maira, S. (2000). Henna and hip hop: the politics of cultural production and the work of cultural studies. *Journal of Asian American Studies*, 3, 324–64.

McClintock, A. (1995). *Imperial Leather: Race, gender and sexuality in the colonial contest*. New York: Routledge.

Nag, D. (1991). Fashion, gender, and the Bengali middle class. *Public Culture*, 3, 93–112.

Richards, T. (1990). *The Commodity Culture of Victorian England: Advertising and spectacle, 1851–1914*. Stanford, CA: Stanford University Press.

Ross, A. (ed.) (1997). *No Sweat: Fashion, free trade, and the rights of garment workers*. New York: Verso.

Savigliano, M. (1995). *Tango: The political economy of desire*. New Brunswick: Rutgers University Press.

Schudson, M. (1984). *Advertising, the Uneasy Persuasion: Its dubious impact on American society*. New York: Basic Books.

Skoggard, I. (1998). Transnational commodity flows and the global phenomenon of the brand. In A. Brydon and S. Niessen (eds.), *Consuming Fashion: Adorning the transnational body*. New York: Berg, pp. 57–70.

Steele, V. (1996). *Fetish: Fashion, sex, and power*. New York: Oxford University Press.

Williamson, J. (1978). *Decoding Advertisements: Ideology and meaning in advertising*. London: Boyars.

Wilson, E. (1992). Fashion and the postmodern body. In J. Ash and E. Wilson (eds.), *Chic Thrills: A fashion reader*. London: Pandora, pp. 1–16.

PART FOUR

Media Audiences

CHAPTER FIFTEEN

Resuscitating Feminist Audience Studies
Revisiting the Politics of Representation and Resistance

Radhika E. Parameswaran

Questions of what constitutes the most appropriate object of study and related debates over the academy's potential to challenge structures of domination have come to occupy a central position in recent speculations on the future of critical media studies. One crucial strand linking these critiques of media research in the cultural studies tradition is a growing dissatisfaction with the celebratory tenor of ethnographic projects, which have claimed that readers'/viewers' interpretive creativity offers evidence of subversive political resistance in audiences' everyday lives. In arguing for a reinvigorated approach to media audiences, one that insists on recentering issues of ideology and power, this chapter builds on and responds to those critiques of populist audience ethnographies that have attempted to recuperate critical media studies' originary allegiances to a progressive global politics of race, class, and gender. I articulate my engagement with the politics of knowledge production and audience representation through the lens of my specific location within a newly emerging body of work in postcolonial feminist media studies.

This chapter's discussion comprises four parts. The first section contends that in battling tendencies toward audience populism and media polysemy, First World media scholars, who urge the abandonment of audience ethnography and a nostalgic return to media texts and political economy, fail to recognize the racial privilege and ethnocentrism that lurks beneath the surface of their prescriptive arguments. I suggest that instead of ignoring the audience (women or men), what we need at this specific juncture, when corporate globalization is eager to conquer new territories *and* religious fundamentalism endeavors to capture the imagination of local and transnational diasporic communities, is a renewed commitment to discovering global media's role in constraining *and* enabling progressive social-democratic practices. In the second and third parts, I address critiques of the problematic ways in which some strains of ethnographic audience research have theorized the import and implications of audiences' interpretive skills. In these two sections where I draw on my research among young middle- and upper-class women in India, I show that historically inflected and locally contextualized feminist audience studies can avoid the pitfalls of resurrecting the autonomous, rational, identifiable, and predictable subject of Enlightenment and capitalist discourses.

The Limits of Multiculturalism/Internationalism in Media Studies: Challenging Western Ethnocentrism

Following the boom in media reception studies during the eighties, a slowly brewing backlash against empirical audience research has been steadily gaining momentum. Within the field of feminist media and cultural studies, for instance, Radway's ethnographic research on romance reading in the United States was first hailed as a pioneering effort to rectify the self-indulgent tendencies of textual analyses and the elitist economic determinism of the Frankfurt School and allied political economy approaches (Allor, 1988; Markert, 1985; Newman, 1988; Schudson, 1987; Schwichtenberg, 1989). Gradually, however, Radway's research on romance readers was criticized for its exclusive focus on middle-class readers and for her failure to theorize the impact of readers' class positions on their interpretations of popular literature (Press, 1986). Another critical response to Radway's work has suggested that in her over-reliance on individual readers' statements, Radway (1984) did not adequately account for the larger social/material context of women's lives, and for the possibility that interviewees, in their extreme anxiousness to please the feminist ethnographer, could have been less than forthcoming about the realities of their lives (McRobbie, 1990). Focusing attention on the material and discursive forces that influence the process of media reception, recent critics of populist audience studies have also argued that ethnographies, which celebrate audiences' consumption practices as effective forms of resistance, ultimately disavow the unequal distribution of economic resources and cultural capital in society (Angus et al., 1989; Budd, Entman, & Steinman, 1990; Carragee, 1990; Clarke, 1990).

While the above critiques directed against Radway's work were articulated in the spirit of advancing the feminist project of audience ethnography, textual critic Modleski went one step further when she attacked Radway (and feminist ethnographers in general) for embracing the ideology of mass culture. Modleski (1986) argued that the danger of ethnography lies in the fact that "critics immersed in their [the audience's] culture, half in love with their subject are incapable of achieving a critical distance from it" (p. xii). Targeting feminist ethnographic research on women audiences in particular, Modleski charged that in mindlessly celebrating the critical "micro-resistant" viewing/reading practices of female soap opera fans and romance novel readers, feminist scholars have naïvely colluded with capitalist entities. When confronted with charges of cultural colonization and manipulation, corporations also claim that savvy consumers, who possess keen skills of discrimination, have the power to accept or reject commercial culture in a "free marketplace." Similarly, other critics advocating political economy approaches have alleged that audience ethnographies (painting them with a broad stroke) have led critical media studies away from its original intent of intervening into and challenging the power of dominant social and economic institutions (Garnham, 1995; Kellner, 1995; Murdock, 1989).

In some cases, despair over ethnographic audience studies' repeated production of the resistive consumer, a subject who is excised from her ideologically infused economic context, has led critics to renounce any progressive possibilities for empirical audience research. In a leading undergraduate text on race, gender, and class in the media, the introductory chapter outlines and reviews production, textual, and audience approaches to media research (Dines & Humez, 1995). In the section on audience studies, after citing problems with populist ethnographies of media reception (avoidance of class and lack of attention to media ownership and marketing), the author concludes that one solution to ending the celebration of the active audience at the expense of mapping out the social structures of late capitalism is to avoid the human audience altogether: "A new way, in fact, to study media effects is to use computer databases that collect references to media texts (such as Dialog or Nexis–Lexis) and to trace the effects of media artifacts through analysis of references to them in the news media" (Kellner, 1995, p. 14). Although it is crucial to examine the ways in which diverse media texts creatively harness audiences as consumers or as citizens, analysis of the imagined audience alone cannot speak for the myriad complexities of everyday social experience.

A vital, ongoing critique of research practices is essential for promoting self-reflexivity in critical media studies, an enterprise that strives to be vigilant of the ways in which modes of knowledge production can silently reproduce power asymmetries. However, the recent questioning of and backlash against empirical audience research at recent conferences and other academic settings is more reminiscent of regressive turf policing rather than thoughtful wrestling with theories or tools of interpretation. One "trendy" mode of demonstrating a sympathetic alignment with grassroots activism, socialist political practice, and ideological critique is to distance oneself from the field of audience studies and the research practice of ethnography. Assumptions guiding critiques that frame the return to textual analyses/political economy as an antidote to problems with audience research include the notion that audience studies cannot release itself from the trap of regurgitating Fiske's early emphasis on subversion/polysemy and the belief that the field has produced all that we need to know about audience activity.

As feminist scholars and activists working within the academy, it is critical that we interrogate trends in academic research before we participate in or endorse research agendas that gain currency as the latest "fashion." In fact, many of the problems with ethnographic audience research in the United States including the facile insistence on polysemy and preoccupation with viewers'/readers' individualized voices and interpretations, can themselves be traced to the appetite for "cutting edge" theories and the impulse to promote a culture of academic stardom and celebrity (Moran, 1998). The temptation to earn cultural capital by blindly emulating the latest academic celebrity's theories can lead to the unreflexive recycling of reified concepts or the combative impulse to trumpet the contributions of new research by dismissing wholesale the tentative observations of pioneers in the field. Postcolonial feminist Ganguly (1992, p. 69) questions the politics of feminist audience researchers who "take up the latest critical practice as they do clothing fashions," but she also argues against the disciplinary divisions created by those who posit the only analytical possibility for audience research as located in the banal reaffirmation of the active consumer. Guided by Ganguly's felicitous move to recuperate a politics of accountability for audience studies, I argue that in deliberately turning away from the audience as an object of study, media studies could be throwing the "baby out with the bathwater."

Rather than advocating a wholesale renunciation of the audience, media scholars can begin to seek out refinements in interpretive theories and innovative modes of analyses that are better equipped to transcribe the wide spectrum of everyday relations between structures of power and audiences' media practices. Undertaking precisely such an ambitious project to redirect the future of audience studies, Nightingale (1996) points to the need for a more enlightened and interdisciplinary orientation to media reception research. Nightingale argues that although audience studies has undoubtedly demonstrated the merits of fieldwork engagement with communities of readers and viewers, media researchers have yet to pursue the provocative methodological implications of anthropology's radical critiques of ethnography (pp. 114–17). She suggests that the term "ethnographic," in its superficial context in media and cultural studies, has come to be associated with a set of qualitative research terms like "empirical," "cultural," or "depth interviews," but debates on ethnography in anthropology have become entangled with far transformative epistemological questions of colonial histories, ethics of research practices, and the politics of representation.

Taking seriously Nightingale's imperative to chart new horizons for audience research, I contend that exhortations to bury the project of audience ethnography so we can move on to new pastures overlook the historical marginalization of race and ethnicity in the academy. It is dangerous to pretend that the body of work on White metropolitan audiences in critical media research can masquerade with its "unnamed, universalizing normativity as knowledge of audiences everywhere" (Juluri, 1998, p. 85). Examining the corpus of writings in feminist media studies, for instance, it becomes apparent that until very recently, ethnographic research on audience activity was mostly confined to the experiences of

White women audiences in the First World. Numerous studies produced in the eighties and early nineties have analyzed white women's interactions with popular culture (Ang, 1985; Brown, 1994; Brundson, 1981; McRobbie, 1990; Press, 1991; Radway, 1984; Thurston, 1988), but the publication of audience research on women of color and non-Western women is still a fairly recent phenomenon (Bobo, 1995; Gillespie, 1995; Duke, 2000; Durham, 1999; Parameswaran, 1999; Valdivia, 2000). Disturbed by the elision of race and ethnicity in studies of film and television spectatorship, Valdivia (2000) enjoins feminists to forge a multicultural vision that rejects the hegemonic allure of racial binaries (White and Black women only) to make visible a range of diverse immigrant women's popular culture experiences.

To date, despite the popular and widely-cited text *Cultural Studies*' (Grossberg, Nelson, & Treichler, 1992) claim that the field was witnessing an international boom (the text included few studies outside the US, UK and Australia), we have only initiated the process of describing and analyzing media structures, texts, and audience reception in Latin America, Asia and Africa. Commenting on the powerful discourses of nostalgia and closure in the First World, which promote audience research as an enterprise of the past that has outlived its potential, Juluri (1998) writes, "As someone entering the field in the mid-1990s, I wonder what it means that the high moment of audience studies seems to have passed, perhaps to travel, like old American sitcoms, to the rest of the world" (p. 86). Deconstructing the politics of race, class, and location that invisibly structures the games of publication, canonization, and contestation in the academy, Juluri urges critics in metropolitan Western academies where "the world is written into knowledge" to be aware of discourses and practices that render research on the Third World as a cross-culturalist footnote or appendix (p. 85).

For postcolonial feminist ethnographers in audience studies, it seems ironic that just as they have launched efforts to record non-Western women audiences' responses to popular culture, media studies is eager to "pack up" and herald the demise of the audience as an object of study. The capricious politics of temporality and canonicity, which produces the dilemma of "catching up" (Juluri, 1998, p. 87) for postcolonial audience researchers is in one sense similar to the discomfort that women's studies scholars and critical race theorists expressed when radical postmodernism began heralding the death of space, subjectivity, history, and resistance. While evaluating the strengths of postmodernism, Kumar (1994) adopts a cautious approach to arguments that advocate a return to pure discourse and genealogy because she finds it important to "retain the subject for, let us say, political reasons, being unable to live up to the epistemological task of giving up subjectivity on having been denied it for so long and just discovering it" (p. 8). Similarly, Braidotti (1987) notes skeptically the coterminous rise of postmodernism and the increasing numbers of immigrants and women of color within the humanities and social sciences, "in order to announce the death of the subject, one must have first gained the right to speak as one" (p. 80). For postcolonial media ethnographers, empirical audience research offers an opportunity to generate alternative knowledges of the non-West, knowledges that revise, revisit, and complicate the narratives that have been fashioned by European/colonial anthropologists and administrators. Proposing a sense of audience representation as deeply linked to intellectual practice, Juluri (1998) argues, "I am particularly invoking those of us who share the burden and privilege of certain kinds of colonialized and racialized subjectivities that allow us to speak as both insiders and outsiders, as transnational intellectuals and as representatives of specific national and or/local constituencies. I am concerned with the possibilities that are enabled in audience research for a politics of representation involving third world/diasporic scholars of media as well as Third World audiences" (86).

In searching for alternatives to the political paralysis implicated in certain strains of postmodernism, feminist audience researchers cannot fall into the trap of authentic essentialism or nostalgia for originary and utopian moments of pre-modern/pre-colonial belonging. Orchestrating a polycentric vision of multicultural feminism, Shohat (1998) writes that we are "obliged to . . . work through a politics whereby the de-centering of identities" does not prevent us from examining the power asymmetries that privilege a few and disenfranchise many others (p. 6). Multicultural feminism, as Shohat envisions, transcends national and disciplinary borders to not only emphasize a range of distinct cultural subjectivities, but to also engage the fissures and dialogical relations *within* and between ethnicities, classes, and nations. Inspired by Shohat's efforts to seek a balance between resisting analytical binarisms and negotiating the straitjacket of identity politics, our attention to audiences in the rest of the world must offer more than a vacuous, corporate vision of multiculturalism or a frenzied inclusive empiricism. As Shohat argues, simplistic models of global diversity based in the "flavor of the month" paradigm reduce feminists of color into native informants who collect new and exotic forms of Third World subalternity for regular consumption in the First World (p. 16).

Our investment in progressive racial politics and goals of achieving a radically global perspective need not lead to the mere addition of African, Indian, or Malaysian women to the smorgasbord of existing audiences in the canon. Firstly, rather than being a "guilty" afterthought, ethnographic audience studies in Asia or Africa can engage with questions that are germane to a new politics of audience research that interrogates the modes and practices of global capitalism *and* avoids essentialized models of the viewing/reading process. For instance, Valdivia (2000) questions models of feminist media reception that assume viewer/reader identification to be a linear, one-way process of horizontal gender correspondence where men relate to men and women to women (p. 155). Hence, research on Third World women's consumption of Western media, which predominantly represent the lives of White characters, would demand an analysis of media consumption that accounts for audiences' contradictory experiences of affiliation and alienation. Secondly, audience research must stress the relational web of porous social formations within which the media constitute viewers' identities. Therefore, when we study communities of color as spectators of mainstream popular culture, we are not only studying race as "blackness" or "brownness," but also as the circulation of whiteness and vice versa. Foregrounding race in examining a group of White middle-class American girls' playful consumption of Hispanic dolls can tell us volumes about the ways in which powerful discourses on immigration and citizenship percolate the quotidian practices of everyday life (Acosta-Alzuru & Kreshel, 2000). Finally, in negotiating the fine balance between power/ideology and agency/resistance in audience research, feminists can adopt a modified Foucauldian approach that views women as historical subjects who are molded by authoritative (and persuasive) media discourses, but are not "passive recipients" of dominant messages (Kumar, 1994, p. 21).

Gender, Resistance, and Colonial History

In my project on young urban middle- and upper-class Indian women's leisure reading practices, I analyze the cultural space occupied by the practice of popular romance fiction reading in women's everyday lives. I conducted ethnographic research for five months in Hyderabad, a city in South India and the capital of the state of Andhra Pradesh, among women between the ages of 17 and 21 years old. As part of my fieldwork, I moderated discussions about romance novels among seven groups of women; women in each group were friends before my arrival, and some women had known each other since their childhood. I conducted two- to three-hour-long interviews with 30 regular romance readers and read over a hundred novels they recommended. To gain insight into the discourses about romance reading that young women encountered, I interviewed parents, teachers, library owners, publishers, and used-book vendors. My involvement in readers' everyday routines included "hanging out" with them at their colleges; joining their visits to lending libraries, restaurants, and movie theaters; accompanying them on shopping trips and picnics; and eating meals with women in their homes.

Typically, women from urban English-speaking middle- and upper-class communities read imported Western romance novels in India. Historically, middle-class urban Indian communities gained power and status through their access to economic and cultural capital – private school instruction, university education, and professional employment – during the colonial period. As members of the expanding Indian middle- and upper-classes, the women readers who shared their time with me belonged to a socioeconomic bloc whose purchasing power and desire to consume fueled the processes of economic liberalization and globalization (Varma, 1998, pp. 170–1). In the media's hegemonic visions of upward mobility for Indian citizens, the fantasy lifestyle of the urban Indian middle classes is widely promoted as a symbol of postcolonial modernity. Hyper-visible images of middle- and upper-class urban Indian women circulate in the imaginary economies of consumerism and state discourse. These "modern" women who represent the ideal subjects of success in models of national development shape the aspirations of poor, working-class, and rural women.

Media critics sympathetic to the project of refining ethnographic audience studies have argued for radically historicized and socially contextualized analyses of the processes that shape readers' identities (Ang, 1996). Commenting that audiences, not just media products created for consumption, are socially constructed and influenced by economic and social changes, Schudson (1987) urges researchers to unravel the historical constitution of audiences because "audiences are not born but made" (p. 63). In his thoughtful essay on ethnography and media reception research, Gibson (2000) proposes a model of audience studies that would allow researchers to avoid the trap of becoming ensnared in the semiotic worlds of popular culture's fans and devotees (p. 253). Arguing for deep contextualization of audience activity while drawing from the writings of Morley (1986) and Hall (1980), Gibson proposes a three-pronged approach to understanding how readers' interpretations are located within and against shifting fields of alliances, articulations, and historically-produced structures:

> three important sites of analysis that must be explored if the context of audience meaning-making is to be reconstructed. These three sites include (1) the media text and its discursive structures, (2) the overdetermined social positions occupied by readers of texts, and (3) the social context of use and interpretation. (p. 261)

As Gibson notes, when considered together these three sites underscore the profound importance of context because "the context of a practice or discourse is not the background necessary for analysis, it is the product or goal of analysis . . . analyses of the audience, then should rebuild the historical and social context – in essence the context of prior articulations – which structures a particular text/audience relationship" (p. 261). While Gibson's model subtly over-emphasizes the need to analyze the ways in which historically determined structures *constrain* the production of meaning, that is, induce audience *passivity*, what would an ethnography that historicized *resistance* against domination reveal? How can our knowledge of the historical formation of reading publics code particular leisure practices as "resistance" far before feminist ethnographers arrive in the field eager to discover women's everyday acts of resistance? What new light can the history of colonial modernities in the Third World shed on our understanding of global women audiences' consumption of Western media? In the case of romance reading in India, my project's ethnographic exploration of Indian women's interpretive agency was enriched by accounting for the impact of colonial reading histories on postcolonial leisure practices.

Although, on the surface, the circulation of romance novels in India offers evidence of global/Western media's economic power to become *present* in non-Western settings, in a historical sense, women's consumption of "trashy romances" in postcolonial India can be traced to the resistance the Indian reading public expressed against nineteenth-century British colonial elites' project of civilization for the colonies. The sheer volume of print culture's material artifacts in urban spaces – hardcover fiction displayed in the windows of plush chain bookstores, magazines hung outside small bookstores in busy strip shopping areas, brightly-colored comics laid out on vendors' carts at train stations, and faded, damaged paperbacks spread out on pavements by used booksellers – offers a glimpse of the vibrancy and range of leisure reading practices in postcolonial India. Urban Indian women's contemporary English-language romance reading, coexisting alongside other reading practices, is historically linked to the arrival of print technology, the establishment of colonial educational institutions, the introduction and dissemination of the English language, and the importing of British novels into eighteenth- and nineteenth-century colonial India. Together, these political and economic events marked the ushering in of colonial modernity, the triggering of new forms of national consciousness, and the creation of reading publics in British India (Dharwadker, 1997; Joshi, 1998; Paddikal, 1993; Viswanathan, 1989).

Historicizing questions of Western domination that have preoccupied media scholars' writings on cultural imperialism in the post-World War II era, Joshi (1998) excavates data on urban Indians' reading preferences in the mid-to-late nineteenth century to "uncover the complicated processes at work in the transmission of culture between Britain and India" (p. 198). Questioning the politics of colonial histories that yield bland narratives of "imperial zealots" and "compliant natives," Joshi argues that an excessive emphasis on British imperial policies and pronouncements has concealed a more complex portrait of cross-cultural exchange that was taking place on the ground in colonial India. Combining the methodological insights of the history of the book and the sociology of reading, she attempts to document urban Indians' selective appropriation and consumption of British literature during colonialism, a process that challenges unidimensional propositions about Western cultural conquest in nineteenth-century India.

Following the establishment of the English Education Act of 1835 by Baron Macaulay, who proposed that English language and literature would be instrumental in creating a "class of persons Indian in blood and colour, but English in taste, in opinions, in morals, and in intellect," British book imports to India gradually increased, and between 1850 and 1900, printed matter from Britain constituted almost 95 percent of all book imports into India (Joshi, 1998, p. 207). Initially, the colonial government encouraged publishers and booksellers in Britain to produce and export paperback editions to India by offering financial incentives. Gradually, as English-language literacy spread throughout urban Indian centers of commerce and politics, the growing numbers of readers in India became a highly lucrative market for British publishers. Colonial policies that elevated the English language over vernacular languages and the subsequent steady flow of printed material from Britain into India point to the potentially powerful effects of cultural and economic imperialism. However, Joshi argues that archival records of import statistics maintained during colonialism document the conditions of the colonial market, not the precise content of this market or the "archaeology of consumption" that emerged due to the creative agency expressed by Indian readers.

Turning to reading data contained within book advertisements and book reviews published in Indian newspapers between 1861 and 1881, Joshi demonstrates that contrary to the elitist/ethnocentric model of citizenship propagated in colonial education policies, urban Indians did not seek out those novels the colonial administration listed as ideal instruments to inculcate the best "English" values among the natives:

> For one, the "good" English novels that were part of the colonial curriculum and were entrusted with creating an Indian who was English in "taste, in opinions, in morals, and in intellect" were in practice not the novels sought out by Indian readers for leisure reading. The canon of popular literature and the books most avidly and spontaneously consumed by Indian readers were increasingly disjunct from those prescribed by the Department of Public Instruction. (p. 204)

Throughout the colonial period, Indian readers avidly sought out sensational, gothic, and melodramatic serial novels – middle-brow and pulp fiction – rather than novels authored by Dickens, Austen, Eliot, Thackeray, Meredith, and the Brontes, which the colonial elites held in high esteem. Rejecting the confining codes of high realism in "good" English novels, Indian readers enthusiastically consumed anti-realist literary forms because these fictional genres shared a symbolic and structural affinity with older Indian literary forms, and as such "paradoxically bridged the gulf between the premodern world and modernity" (p. 213). These anti-realist tales that were reminiscent of pre-modern Indian tales, myths, and epics permitted Indian readers entry into their fantasy worlds with few cross-cultural restrictions. Furthermore, numerous books of such minor authors as G. W. M. Reynolds, Marion Crawford, Marie Corelli, and G. P. R. James were translated into Marathi, Hindi, Urdu, Bengali, Tamil, Kannada, and Telugu, thus reaching a much wider audience of Indian readers than the populace that could read in English. Joshi argues that ultimately, on probing the interstices between colonial policies and native readers' responses, scholars will have to acknowledge that the success of the novel and the emergence of the leisure reading public in India are rooted in the "failure of British high culture to penetrate fully the Indian marketplace of ideas" (p. 216). In Joshi's historical analysis of colonial interventions into India's reading culture, Indian readers' subtle yet significant practices of counterproduction became evident in their selective appropriation of specific forms of colonial modernity that could be easily assimilated into pre-existing indigenous imaginary landscapes.

What if my project's analysis of leisure reading moved from one historical site, which precipitated cross-cultural negotiations between West and non-West, to another historical moment in India's reading culture, one that points to the contentious debates that took place over gender, class, and women's consumption of pulp fiction *within* Indian communities? As Priya Joshi's work demonstrates, the Indian reading public's tastes for fiction subtly subverted the priorities of colonial imperatives to a certain degree. However, as fiction reading spread rapidly in the early part of the twentieth century, urban Indian readers' voracious appetite for pulp novels did not go unnoticed by elite Indian male intellectuals, who were at the vanguard of creating a nationalist, anti-colonial culture for the Indian middle classes. In the southern state of Tamilnadu, a flood of novels, including adaptations and translations of popular British detective, romance, and melodrama series fiction, deluged Tamil society in the mid-1910s. Analyzing editorials, essays, and advertisements pertaining to fiction reading in Tamil periodicals between 1910 and 1930, Venkatachalapathy (1997) documents the reception accorded to vernacular fiction that closely imitated the styles of Western fiction among Tamil community leaders, writers, poets, and politicians.

Venkatachalapathy notes that Indian male public intellectuals expressed alarm and deep concern for the damaging effects that fiction reading would have on the average "gullible" reader, who supposedly lacked the critical skills to distinguish between fantasy and reality. Arguing that serial fiction would destroy Indian culture, these intellectuals argued that newly available popular pulp novels would only encourage unbridled Western materialism, corrupt spirituality, promote the use of poor language, and eventually limit the range of vocabulary used in Indian prose and poetry. One leading Tamil writer, who had no reservations about the impact of cheap novels on Tamil literary production, wrote unequivocally: "Contemporary novels spread the habits, customs, and attitudes of foreign countries and send the Tamil people tumbling into the abyss of immorality. The Tamil people who know not the true novel are gobbling up this trash like fowls eating termites" (quoted in Venkatachalapathy, 1997, p. 59).

Drawing attention to the gendered discourse that characterized intellectuals' strident criticism of fiction reading, Venkatachalapathy writes that the most scathing comments in Tamil periodicals were reserved for the devastating impact sensational escapist narratives would have on *Indian women*, and hence the very moral fabric of a newly emerging national Hindu culture. As novels were published in increasing numbers and women flocked to read them, discourse in Tamil periodicals on women's fiction reading became deeply implicated within Indian elite males' fears over the unshackling of Indian women's sexuality by colonial modernity, a contaminating force that had the potential to fracture the essence of Hindu identity. In one text on Tamil womanhood, a prominent Tamil writer went so far as to entreat women not to physically "touch" these tales of titillation: "Young women should not be permitted to hear titillating stories, pseudo-novels, and other such stuff; nor should they even touch these books. Parents should take special care in this regard . . ." (quoted in Venkatachalapathy, 1997, p. 62). Furthermore, Tamil authors who reproduced the styles of Western pulp fiction in vernacular novels, defended their work by strategically deploying women's sexual subjectivity as the litmus test for claiming respectability:

"Dear readers, like my other novels this one too does not contain any repulsive aspects or words that are not fit to be read by chaste women" (quoted in Venkatachalapathy, 1997, p. 64). Following the agenda outlined by community leaders, elders in families, pandits, and officials in educational institutions began to forbid young women from reading fiction, and strove to prevent women's access to novels.

On shifting from one cross-cultural historical experience, which engendered the formation of an Indian reading public under conditions of Western domination, to another "internal" historical articulation, we see that Indian women readers struggled with the ideological authority of patriarchal discourses; ideas of besieged female sexuality and endangered Hindu morality became vehicles to convey male elites' passion for preserving the authenticity of indigenous culture. Middle-class Indian women's early leisure reading experiences thus represented a gendered form of resistance against structures of domination on two levels – against high culture Western modernity and against the Indian patriarchal power structure that sought to control "native" women. Together, these two contexts point to the intricate associational network of historical events and discourses that organize the trajectories of contemporary cultural phenomena.

On returning to my project's goal – investigating Indian women's pleasure in consuming imported English-language romance fiction in postcolonial India – we can infer from the above discussion that audience ethnographies cannot be coded as naive voyages of discovery or recovery that hinge only upon the empiricist desire to reveal "real" (and contemporary) women informants' oppositional forms of resistance. A thick ethnographic reconstruction of contemporary reading practices in India would have to acknowledge, at the outset, that fiction reading is embedded within and shaped by the historical constitution of the Western text/non-Western audience relationship in colonial India. Regardless of the kinds of empirical data I hoped to gather in the field, data that would be eventually analyzed as evidence of resistance, submission, or coping mechanisms, my discussion of the subject positions occupied by Indian women romance readers had to engage with prior historical articulations against Western imperialism and local patriarchy.

While an extended discussion of young Indian women's interpretations of Western romance fiction is not possible here, a few examples will suffice to illustrate how strategies of resistance or compliance in women's contemporary leisure practices are suffused with the legacies of historical articulations. Many young Indian women who participated in my ethnographic study argued that they resented their parents' and English teachers' repeated admonishments that they should read English-language high culture – Shakespeare, Wordsworth, and Jane Austen – to improve their reading comprehension and language skills. In discussions that were held away from the presence of teachers and parents, Indian women's "hidden transcripts" of resistance located romance reading within socially legitimate practices of literacy (Scott, 1990). Calculatedly invoking utilitarian, middle-class discourses of productive labor, some women insisted that authority figures in their lives were ignorant of the redemptive and didactic qualities of formula fiction. Claiming instructional value in romance reading, these women suggested that new and difficult words, descriptions of far away lands, and details of material life in Western romance novels trained them for careers, marriage, and cosmopolitan life in a rapidly modernizing India. Furthermore, in defense of their romance reading as a culturally permissible ritual, some women claimed a seamless affinity between Western narratives of romance and the elaborate traditions of erotic love and courtship in Indian (Hindu and Islamic) poetry and mythology.

Speaking to the gendered aspects of women's fiction reading, many concerned parents, elders, and teachers cast young women's romance reading as a transgressive practice that flouted codes of middle-class feminine respectability. Negotiating parental expectations of appropriate behavior at home, a few young women revealed that they covered romance fiction with newspaper, read in the privacy of their rooms at night, and ensured that their novels were never casually exposed in living and dining room areas. For some Indian women, much like the midwestern sixth grade girls in Finders' compelling study of underground literacies, these elaborate ruses to hide their novels from teachers and parents became the basis for intense allegiance with other women in their groups (Finders, 1997). Finders' ethnography of girls' covert and extracurricular literacy practices shows that complicated expressions of agency and intricate power plays related to reading and writing characterize the subculture of feminine adolescence. Documenting girls' "literate underlife," multiple practices of literacy that disrupted sanctioned literacies recognized by authorities, Finders argues that reading and displaying specific magazines and books, writing notes, and preferences for sharing or not sharing written assignments were a crucial means for traversing boundaries between rebellion and conformity. Engaging the histories of Indian women's postcolonial practices of "literate underlife" deepened my empirical observations of the ambivalent ways in which they maneuvered romance reading to ally with and oppose discourses of authority.

Othering the West: Sexuality, Gender, and Agency

How can ethnographic audience studies in non-Western locations affirm the promise of robust interdisciplinarity? How can feminist audience research on non-Western women's consumption of Western popular culture enrich and modify existing paradigms of First World–Third World relations? How can historicized research on women's encounters with discourses of tradition and modernity challenge the bifurcated ways in which scholars have approached resistance and compliance? Revealing the cross-cutting and overlapping texture of multiple social identities, women audiences' discourses of resistance can sometimes become complicit with the very ideologies that sanction control over female sexuality. As the ensuing discussion of my research illustrates, non-Western women audiences' resistance against Western media narratives can simultaneously announce allegiance to another power structure – the troubling resurgence of patriarchal nationalisms based in religious fundamentalism. Identifying one of the greatest paradoxes of the current epoch, Castells (1997, pp. 27–32) observes that the age of globalization, standardization, and universalism is also the age of fragmented and heterogeneous cultural and ethnic nationalisms. By accounting for questions of cross–cultural reception to Western media images in the midst of nationalist discourses, feminist audience studies has much to contribute to ongoing interdisciplinary concerns with Orientalism and Occidentalism, and hence to our knowledge of the discursive relations between East and West.

Edward Said's controversial *Orientalism*, a pioneering literary contribution to postcolonial theory, sought to map out Europe's discursive construction of the Middle East (and the non-West) during Western colonial expansion. Deeply influenced by Foucault's arguments about the inextricable links among representation, ideology, and cultural/economic practices, Said explicitly approached his work as a political intervention into the relations of domination and hierarchy between East and West. Describing Orientalism as a discursive body of knowledge that facilitated Europe's colonization of Asia, Africa, and the Middle East, Said (1978) defines Orientalism, a regime of hierarchical representations that originated during colonial expansion, as a "Western style for dominating, restructuring, and having authority over the Orient" (p. 7). Since the publication of *Orientalism* in the late seventies, numerous scholars in anthropology, history, comparative literature, film studies, and Women's Studies have drawn inspiration from Said's theoretical insights to deconstruct Othered/Orientalist representations of the non-West in a wide range of Western cultural texts.

Gradually, some postcolonial critics also began to modify, challenge, and revamp Said's paradigm of discursive domination because it subtly reproduced the epistemology of colonial discourse. As these critics argued, Orientalism was a binary, bifurcated mapping of the world into the stable oppositional categories of East–West, representer–represented, and powerful–powerless. Literary critic Porter (1994) writes that in his eagerness to confront Western hegemonic discourses, Said asserted the unified character of diverse European texts and experiences at the expense of counterhegemonic European voices that lingered at the periphery of the colonial empire. Porter suggests that Said's diagnosis of Orientalism was predicated on the very same problematic representational techniques he identified in Western images of the Middle East; over-generalization of diverse experiences, lack of attention to contradictions within European texts, and homogenization of texts across time and space. Locating the traffic in theory within the currency of academic capital, Aijaz (1994) proposes that Third World intellectuals seeking to position themselves within "hip" First World discourses on marginality (the race–gender matrix) have promoted Orientalism/colonialism as their legitimate badges of oppression. The warm reception accorded to Orientalism and related postcolonial scholarship, according to such critics, has more to do with the petty struggles for legitimacy within the academy rather than a radical politics that is genuinely interested in dismantling the West's cultural and economic domination of the world.

Notwithstanding such cynical musings about the institutionalization of post-colonial studies in the Western academy, other scholars have pointed out that Said's textual analysis of Orientalism in literature and art elides crucial questions of the colonized subject's agency. Examining discourses and practices of Othering *within* metropolitan China that were targeted at the Miao, a rural ethnic minority community living on the periphery of China's economy, Schein (2000) writes, "Pitting East and West as opposites in a dyadic, but unequal relation stopped short at the conclusion that the East is muted and therefore, by extension, rendered incapable of othering" (p. 103). Schein suggests that in accepting Said's formulation of Orientalism, scholars may unwittingly reproduce the East as a mute, passive participant in history, one that is incapable of producing or negotiating its own discourses of power and hierarchy. In her analysis of Japanese imperialism, Robertson (1995) points out that such critiques as Orientalism "privilege Euro-American intellectual and theoretical trends as universal and obfuscate and neutralize the histories and legacies of non-Western imperialisms and associated 'othering' practices" (p. 973). Furthermore, as Schein (2000) and Nader (1989) argue, Said's analysis of Orientalism fails to explore how gender – the trope of the feminine – becomes a compelling cultural hinge of Otherness in Western views of the Eastern world and vice versa.

Underscoring the disturbing tendency in social science media research to ignore the analytical insights of the humanities, Said's work has been rarely, if ever, discussed in empirical studies of non-Western audiences or in international communication debates that consider the impact of Western media on the Third World. For example, Said's analysis of the imperial West's proliferating images and products, discursive representations that predated the global ubiquity of contemporary Western consumer culture is conspicuously missing in John Tomlinson's critique of "hypodermic needle" models of cross-cultural reading and viewing practices. Although Tomlinson (1992) examines the implications of nationalism for media reception in the Third World, he does not raise the possibility that cultural imperialism can be cross-cut and mediated by Occidentalism, an obvious by-product of the non-Western world's steady exposure to Western media.

Defining Occidentalism as ideologically related to Orientalism, Chen (1995) writes, "Orientalism has been accompanied by instances of what might be termed Occidentalism, a discursive practice that, by constructing its Western Other, has allowed the Orient to participate actively and with indigenous creativity in the process of self appropriation, even after being appropriated and constructed by Western Others" (pp. 4–5). Chen notes that the seemingly unified discursive practice of Occidentalism exists in a paradoxical relationship to the discursive practices of Orientalism, and in fact, shares with it many ideological techniques and strategies. Urging scholars to examine the mobile meanings and strategic uses of Occidentalism in specific locations, Chen argues that non-Western discourses on the Western world can become a means to enable liberation or oppression depending on the context within which it is articulated. Distancing himself from postcolonial paradigms that promote Orientalism and cultural imperialism as unified discourses of uninterrupted and homogenous power, Chen writes that Occidentalism, in some cases, can even become a metaphor for liberation from indigenous forms of oppression.

Pointing to the little knowledge we have of how the East constructs the West, Nader (1989) comments that the West has been accessible to non-Western peoples through a wide variety of global media forms, but the contours of Occidentalist discourse still remain a mystery. Lamenting the neglect of ethno-Occidentalism, that is, essentialist renderings of the West by members of the "primitive" non-Western societies that anthropologists have studied, Carrier (1992) argues that although fieldworkers have informally recorded constructions of the West among "natives," such data has rarely entered the world of published scholarly work. Carrier writes that non-Western informants' impressions of Western culture have remained scribbles in researchers' fieldnotes because this data was deemed to be marginal to the larger enterprise of producing knowledge on Western modernity's impact on Third World societies. Building on recent interdisciplinary responses to Said's arguments, feminist media ethnographies, which explore the ways in which non-Western audiences read and (mis)read representations of the West, can offer significant contributions to questions of cultural imperialism, gender, and audiences' agency.

My reception research suggests that the mechanisms underlying the production of Orientalist discourse – homogenizing, distancing, and exoticizing the racial object of desire – were also deeply implicated within non-Western women's descriptions of Western culture. Young women readers' interpretations of Western romances certainly showed some evidence of Western media's hegemonic authority; however, Indian women's Occidentalist descriptions of Western culture also drew on Hindu nationalist ideologies to construct the West as immoral, inferior, and homogenous. My discussion of Indian women's views of the West and white women, intertextual interpretations that oscillated between the "fantasy" of romance fiction and the "reality" of the Western world, does not intend to resurrect dyadic, binary ideas of East versus West. Rather, I want to demonstrate the self-conscious, historically specific and contingent ways in which Indian women readers deployed a specific form of Occidentalism – a pre-colonial legacy of Othering the West in India – to explain their tremendously productive responses to Western popular culture.

Middle-class urban Indian women's fascination for modernity disguised as Western material culture became apparent in their strong dislike for and rejection of mythological/historical romance novels. Most readers expressed their categorical preferences for romance fiction that described contemporary culture in the United States, the United Kingdom, and other metropolitan tourist locations. As Mallika explained, she found the contextual details in historical romance novels "boring, bland, and distracting" and besides, as other readers claimed, in their rapidly modernizing urban milieu in India, they were better off learning about the codes, practices, and symbols of Western cosmopolitan life. In a style reminiscent of consumer advertising (beauty products, food, and tourism), the "favorite" novels that many readers recommended to me were filled with details of gourmet food, designer clothing, bathing rituals, cruises and vacations, landscaped gardens, and expensive homes. Young women strongly identified with the consumerist middle-class white heroine whose material and romantic fantasies were realized as she is gradually incorporated into the upper-class world of the affluent hero. Speaking in sharply gender-inflected narratives, some women informants argued that Western-style consumerism mapped onto the bodies of white heroines in romance fiction allowed them to pursue individualistic "selfish" pleasure and thus gain temporary respite from the selflessness their families and communities expected from them as dutiful, honorable daughters.

Although Indian women expressed unqualified admiration for Western consumerism, their interpretations of the West shifted when they began sharing their opinions on courtship and sexuality in Western romance fiction. Explaining their reasons for turning to these novels for relaxation and entertainment, some women insisted that these "simple" stories allowed them escape from the restrictive norms of middle-class Hindu femininity that constrained the possibilities of romance in their own lives. I soon learned that Indian women readers' identification of romance fiction as "simple" was an insider classification that had little to do with my own judgment of these books as enacting a relatively simple and standard formula. Gently pointing out my mistake, several readers patiently clarified that the stories in Western romance fiction were simple because of the marked absence of secondary characters – parents, community members, family, and clergy – who exerted pressure on the heroes and heroines to conform to traditions or social conventions. Contrasting the unbounded quality of white heroines' pursuit of romance with the complexities and tensions of accommodating religious, class, and ethnic boundaries in their own lives, some women insisted that courtship in Western culture was a matter of free choice. Individuals in Western culture, some women claimed, had no obligations to family or kin, and did not have to fear isolation, exile or loss of family support because the penalties for disregarding tradition were non-existent or minimal. Seamlessly conflating fiction with reality, Indian women readers produced Occidentalism here through their construction of romance novels as transparent representations that reflected the West as a homogenous cultural space where social differences and hierarchies were invisible and easily surmounted.

If the fiction of romance in the West as a practice that transcended socioeconomic hierarchies proved to be convincing to women, interestingly, they scornfully dismissed other ingredients of fictive representations in the very same popular novels as unrealistic fantasy. Women's skeptic evaluations of Western romance fiction as perpetuating "false" and inaccurate images, which distorted the disturbing truths they knew about the West, revolved around white heroines' virginal persona and the requisite happy endings that promised to last forever. Challenging the veracity of fictional descriptions of white heroines' sexual innocence, several women were surprised to hear that romance fiction was popular among women in many Western countries – this particular piece of fiction, according to them, bore little resemblance to their knowledge of "real" white women's sexuality. Several young women argued that, contrary to the representations of virginal white heroines in romance fiction, "real" white women were immoral and sexually promiscuous. In women's ideological distilling of Occidentalist difference, white women, in their essentialized and intractable Otherness, became problematic symbols of unregulated Western modernity.

Similarly, the happy endings in romance fiction became another site of Othering where women intertextually referred to "credible" sources of reality (the news, relatives living in the West, and travelers' stories) to foreground their concerns about the lack of morality in Western culture. Some readers argued that the "objective" news information they had about AIDS, divorces, teenage pregnancies, and child abuse in many Western nations exposed the happy ending in romance fiction as pure farce, a mere figment of authors' imagination. Women's discussions about moral chaos in Western culture were frequently accompanied by contrasting statements about the superior stability of Indian culture – Indian marriages lasted forever and Indian families were close, supportive, and united. Previous research shows that such constructions of the West as culturally/ morally inferior exist across regional, ethnic, and class boundaries in India. In her ethnography of Indian viewers' responses to television, feminist anthropologist Mankekar (1999) recounts that working-class and lower-middle-class viewers who lived in and around New Delhi in North India passionately defended India's greatest strengths as located in the loving and enduring Indian family and the loyal Indian wife and mother. Mankekar's informants asserted their national identity by comparing the superior quality of moral life in India to the immoral and decadent West.

My informants' Occidentalist discourse, perceptually filtered through their immersion in Western popular literature, offers a counterpoint to Said's discussion of Orientalism. As critics of Orientalism have suggested, we have to account for the possibility that the West may become the Othered object of its own Others. What are the implications of Indian romance readers' Othering of the West for debates over cultural imperialism? Demonstrating the importance of approaching cultural imperialism as multi-layered and multi-dimensional, Indian women's responses demonstrated the power of Western culture at the level of fantasies related to transnational consumerism, but on another level, in the realm of the private sphere – family, kinship, and moral character – the West became an object of contempt and scorn. However, before feminist ethnographers prematurely celebrate non-Western women audiences' critical observations about Western culture as resistance against cultural imperialism, they would have to "radically contextualize" the oppositional content of such Occidentalist responses (Ang, 1996, p. 70).

Advocating for deep contextualization in ethnography, Carrier (1992) writes that if scholars want to avoid essentializing concepts such as Occidentalism, what we discover in fieldwork must be situated against the backdrop of local structures and processes: "Attention to relationships will help sensitize researchers to just how a particular society is linked to the larger world. Just as important, it will help motivate researchers to recognize the incongruities in what they observe" (p. 206). On applying Carrier's advice about deep contextualization to Indian women's statements about the West, we can begin to understand the contradictory impulses in audiences' resistance to structures of power. When situated against the social fabric of elders', parents', and teachers' discourses of disapproval, my informants' Occidentalist responses can be interpreted as a strategic form of emotional justification. While they readily agreed to interviews, some women were eager to reassure me (and other authority figures) that their absorption and pleasure in reading romance fiction would not transform them into sexually active "white women." Many women spoke about the subversive tactics – hiding romance novels in textbooks, reading books when parents were away at work, and combining visits to lending libraries with other womanly/domestic chores – they had devised so they could avoid constant surveillance. Reading romance fiction thus allowed these Indian women to partially resist norms of chaste Hindu middle-class femininity, yet in order to minimize and distance their feelings of guilt they turned to Occidentalism. Transposing promiscuous sexuality onto white women's bodies becomes a strategic defense to repress feelings of guilt, experience moral superiority, and respond to charges that these sexually explicit narratives could corrupt their minds.

Going beyond the immediate milieu of their experiences within families and communities, women's Occidentalism is also related to the ideological context of middle-class Hindu nationalism. Over the past decade, the exclusionary myths of religious Hindu fundamentalism have gained a remarkable foothold among the Hindu middle classes. Tensions around religion, communalism, and culture have become highly public issues in India, especially since the early nineties with the outbreak of violence and rioting between Hindus and Muslims during the Babri Masjid incident (Appadurai & Breckenridge, 1995; Basu et al., 1993; Basu, 1996; Nandy et al., 1995; Rajagopal, 1996; Setalwad, 1996). The Babri Masjid or Ramajanmaboomi incident took place on December 6, 1992, when a mob of Hindus belonging to various political and religious groups destroyed a mosque in the city of Ayodhya in Uttar Pradesh. Religious leaders, who coordinated the destructive campaign, claimed that the mosque had been built by Muslim invaders on a sacred site that was the original birthplace of the Hindu god Ram (Basu et al., 1993, p. viii). Since the Babri Masjid incident, the Bharatiya Janata Party (the Hindu nationalist party), and other associated Hindu revivalist organizations have been gaining political power and popularity among Hindu communities. Promoting Occidentalist views of the West, Hindu fundamentalist politicians and clergy have celebrated the enduring chastity and fidelity of the loyal Indian wife and mother, whose virtue, they have argued, distinguishes India from the West.

Analyzing contemporary Hindu nationalism in India and its continuities with nineteenth- and twentieth-century anti-colonial struggles, feminist scholars have critiqued the patriarchal representation of Indian womanhood that male social reformers strategically constructed to counter colonialism (Kandiyoti, 1991; Katrak, 1989; Mazumdar, 1994). Eager to challenge British colonizers' Orientalist descriptions of Indian culture as barbaric and heathen, upper-caste Indian male reformers began to fashion a rhetoric of defense that emphasized cultural traditions, gender relations, and family values. As carriers of tradition and symbols of India's resilient national spirit in the face of numerous invasions, middle-class Indian women were glorified as devoted mothers and wives. Chatterjee (1990) locates the idealization of middle-class Hindu women as pure/virtuous within the ideology of Hindu nationalism, which proposed a powerful distinction between "inner/outer worlds," and correspondingly between "home, private/ material world, public." Seen as part of home, the private world, Indian women became symbols of this unpolluted inner life, and hence the ground for establishing difference from Western society. Even more importantly, as Chatterjee notes, the desexualization of the bourgeois Hindu woman in post-independent India was achieved by displacing active female sexuality onto European and local racially and economically marginalized Others. The purity of the upper-caste Hindu woman was pitted against two opposing images – the vulgar and sexually accessible low-caste, poor Indian woman (Rege, 1995) and the immoral and sexually licentious Western woman (Chatterjee, 1990). Middle-class Indian women readers' Occidentalist mapping of promiscuous sexuality on white women's bodies is thus a pernicious legacy of nationalist ideology that continues to inflect numerous vernacular popular culture accounts of wholesome Indian romances, families, and communities.

Indian women's reliance on Occidentalist discourses to defuse criticism of their romance reading and declare their loyal alliance to their own culture reveals the contradictory qualities of audiences' resistance. From a feminist standpoint, Indian women's contrastive strategy of Othering the West is fraught with contradictions; seeking distance from the "promiscuity" of white women reiterates the very forms of control over their sexuality that they seek to disturb and rupture. Occidentalism and Orientalism are thus discourses of power that ultimately serve as mechanisms of control over women in the *West and the East*; both these discourses of domination use the comparative method of describing women's inferior status in the East or West to convince "native" women that they should be content with the status quo because they are "better off" or superior to "those" women. Discussing the ways in which covert and overt nationalisms deploy cultural comparison (Orientalist and Occidentalist) to control women, Nader (1989) writes, "Misleading cultural comparisons support contentions of positional superiority, which divert attention from the processes, which are controlling women in both worlds" (p. 323). To date, Occidentalism may not have the global economic power of Orientalism; however, it does have power within specific national contexts where dominant religious groups gain power by promoting a return to the glorious days of tradition, a period when the nation in the guise of the "native" woman was unpolluted by imperialism.

The Politics of Representation and Resistance

How can concerned critics advance the field of media studies in a manner that does not silently reiterate racial/neocolonial power and privilege? To what extent does the promotion or marginalization of specific research agendas, at the expense of paying attention to the locations and ideological positions from which we speak, legitimize the hegemony of the West? These questions demand a candid assessment of academic fashion's significant impact on emergent intellectual developments and debates. The interrelated ingredients that drive academic fashion in the First World – the economy of celebrity stardom and fan clubs, a market-driven university system, a promotional ethos of worship and attack, and the hierarchical circulation of cultural capital – can often militate against cultural and media studies' fundamental interests in encouraging scholarship that is sensitive to global geopolitics (Moran, 1998). Citing acute self-reflexivity in knowledge production as one of the driving forces in a postcolonial approach to communication and rhetoric, Shome (1996) urges scholars to continuously situate academic discourses within the larger political and economic practices of nations:

> What is the ideology that operates in us that makes research agenda A seem more significant than research agenda B? How are we always already "interpellated" into examining A but not B? What does that interpellation say about our role in reproducing and participating in the hegemonic global domination of the rest by the West? (p. 46)

Examining the challenges that globalization poses for research practices and theorization in feminist communication scholarship, Hegde (1998) writes, "Research is an expression of our location in a world connected by lines of power and cultural asymmetry" (p. 285). Taken together, Shome and Hegde point to the political critique of knowledge as the foundation for creating an academic space where scholars interrogate the modes through which we establish disciplinary authority. By unpacking the assumptions that invisibly guide the trajectories of our research practices and rejecting monologic models of writing and speaking, media scholars can lay "the epistemic basis for a genuine multiculturalism" (Hegde, 1998, p. 275) that facilitates the democratization of knowledge production.

This essay is one effort towards "decentering" and foregrounding global and racial hegemony in recent efforts to shape agendas for future critical media studies research. Predicting the premature death of audience studies because we believe the field has produced "enough" knowledge of media reception or because we cannot imagine better ways of conducting empirical research only reiterates a limited vision of multiculturalism that does not question power differentials. Recognizing the urgency of "outing" the silent ways in which racial privilege permeates popular media, Shome (2000) calls upon communication scholars to deconstruct the ways in which "whiteness remains the organizing principle of the social fabric and yet remains masked because of the normativity that this principle acquires in the social imaginary" (p. 367). Destabilizing the invisible authority of whiteness, as Shome argues, can perhaps propel whites to begin acknowledging their privileges as members of a globally dominant group, even if they accrue these privileges unintentionally.

Similarly, I suggest that feminist media critics in the First World (regardless of racial/gender affiliations) must be aware of which specific audiences' voices and experiences we have recorded before we begin to sing requiems for the audience or recommend a shift to other "more important" objects of study. Research in audience studies has barely scratched the surface of the exploding mediascape in numerous non-Western locations where "global audiencehood" (Juluri, 1998) is implicated simultaneously within a range of Western media *and* local, vernacular cultural productions. Highlighting the widespread global media presence of Western nations, a phenomenon that we have only begun to investigate, Said (1993) comments, "Rarely before in human history has there been so massive an intervention of force and ideas from one culture to another as there is today from America to the rest of the world" (p. 319). Recuperating the insights of postmodernism and postcolonialism for a more nuanced feminist analysis of women's lived experiences in the era of globalization, Hegde (1998) writes, "The commitment to globalize the theoretical scope in communication needs an engagement with the meaning of experience" (p. 287).

Rather than stretching, adding, or extending the canon whereby the problematic contours of the canon itself remain unchanged, how can audience studies in non-Western locations resuscitate the practice of feminist media ethnography? Drawing from constructive critiques of audience research, feminist ethnographers can avoid the uncritical reproduction of well-rehearsed, banal mantras of resistance, agency, and the active audience. A feminist rethinking of audience research in postcolonial contexts would emphasize the vital importance of engaging local historical discourses as a constitutive element of women's national/gender identities. Historicizing middle-class Indian women's romance reading shows us that contemporary cultural practices in urban India are shaped by and articulated within the ideological contexts of colonialism and nationalism. On the one hand, despite the obvious evidence of cultural imperialism that could be inferred from the ubiquitous material presence of global Western media, Indian women readers' consumption of imported serial romance fiction belongs to a history of Indians' subtle resistance against the civilizing mission of colonial high culture. On the other hand, unlike Indian men, the reading of pulp fiction for Indian women, who are interpellated as symbols of purity in nationalist ideology, invoked resistance against two structures of power – against colonialism and religious patriarchy. The feminist critical enterprise in the non-Western world, as Chow (1993) points out, has to contend with more than the legacies of colonialism alone, "While for the non-Western world that something is imperialism, for the feminist it is also patriarchy" (p. 59).

Moreover, a critical feminist ethnography of media reception must acknowledge that the "process of weaving in and out of gendered systems of meaning is punctuated with contestation and resistance, as well as acquiescence" (Hegde, 1998, p. 288). Outlining an anti-essentialist approach to studying women's experiences, Hegde writes, "It is important when portraying the material conditions of cultural others that we do not impose a false unity by essentializing a cultural core and thereby produce lives as artifacts or, for example, romanticize the woman as victim (Hegde, 1998, p. 289). Along with exploring women's resistance to global commodity culture, feminist media ethnographies should also document the constraints on women's agency, that is, our analyses must interrogate how equally important and sometimes dominant class/religious/national identities are woven together in the subjective space that constitutes "woman." In India, as well as in other postcolonial locations, religious nationalism, which draws from the gender ideologies of nineteenth-century nationalism, is masquerading as a grassroots response against Western imperialism and globalization. In Indian women's active engagement with virginal white heroines as false reflections of real white women's promiscuous sexuality, romance reading becomes a site of mis-identification and Othering; these popular culture texts provoked readers to resurrect the binary configurations of East and West, which are embedded in Occidentalist *and* Orientalist ideologies. Although middle-class Indian women's efforts to read romance novels signified resistance against norms that attempted to control women's sexual pleasure and agency, articulating their resistance through an emphasis on the immorality of "foreign/Western women" simultaneously endorsed Occidentalist Hindu nationalism.

For postcolonial feminist ethnographers, scholarship in a multicultural context thus cannot be limited to the deconstruction of Western imperialism alone if the goal of our audience research in the non-West is to engage politically with difference – across nations, but also within the hegemonic context of the nation itself. Navigating the complex relationality between local culture and global media flows, postcolonial feminism's deconstruction of Eurocentrism and the emancipatory patina of globalization must include a vigorous critique of nationalism's limited promises of salvation (Shohat, 1998, p. 52). Theories of the "Big, Bad West" cannot explain why Indian women, who repeatedly expressed a desire for freedom and escape from the demands of family and community, should resort to nationalism's Occidentalist renderings of the West. Distinguishing themselves from "real" white women while identifying with white heroines, these readers insisted that romance reading was theoretical knowledge in the service of future matrimony (*not* for pre-marital sex). Radical contextualization of audience ethnographies in postcolonial locations thus involves probing the problematic ideologies of colonial regimes, neo-colonial economies, *and* local nationalisms. Challenging nationalism along with imperialism becomes a crucial task for postcolonial feminist media ethnographers because "native chauvinism" (Dirlik, 1990, p. 401) with its regressive models of "native" women's identities and reversed binaries of "us" versus "them" only reproduces the epistemological legacies of colonial modernity.

References

Acosta-Alzuru, C. and Kreshel, P. J. (2000). I'm an American girl . . . whatever that means: Girls consuming Pleasant Company's American girl identity. Paper presented at the annual meeting of the International Communication Association. Acapulco, Mexico, August.

Aijaz, A. (1994). Orientalism and after. In P. Williams and L. Chrisman (eds.), *Colonial Discourse and Postcolonial Theory*. New York: Columbia University Press, pp. 162–71.

Allor, M. (1988). Relocating the site of the audience. *Critical Studies in Mass Communication*, 5(3), 217–33.

Ang, I. (1985). *Watching Dallas*. London: Methuen.

Ang, I. (1996). *Living Room Wars: Rethinking media audiences for a postmodern world*. London: Routledge.

Angus, I., Jhally, S., Lewis, J., and Schwichtenberg, C. (1989). Commentary: On pluralist apology. *Critical Studies in Mass Communcation*, 6(4), 441–9.

Appadurai, A. and Breckenridge, C. (1995). Public modernity in India. In C. Breckenridge (ed.), *Consuming Modernity: Public culture in a South Asian world*. Minneapolis: University of Minnesota Press, pp. 1–20.

Basu, A. (1996). Caste and class: The rise of Hindu nationalism in India. *Harvard International Review*, 18(3), 28–31.

Basu, T., Datta, P., Sarkar, S., Sarkar, T., and Sen, S. (1993). *Khaki Shorts, Saffron Flags: Tracts for the times*. New Delhi: Orient Longman Ltd.

Bobo, J. (1995). *Black Women as Cultural Readers*. New York: Columbia University Press.

Braidotti, R. (1987). Envy: Or with your brain and my looks. In A. Jardine and P. Smith (eds.), *Men in Feminism*. New York: Methuen, pp. 231–41.

Brown, M. E. (1994). *Soap Opera and Women's Talk: The pleasure of resistance*. Thousand Oaks, CA: Sage.

Brundson, C. (1981). Crossroads: Notes on soap opera. *Screen*, 22(4), 32–7.

Budd, M., Entman, R., and Steinman, C. (1990). The affirmative character of American cultural studies. *Critical Studies in Mass Communication*, 7(2), 169–84.

Carragee, K. (1990). Interpretive media study and interpretive social science. *Critical Studies in Mass Communication*, 7(2), 81–96.

Carrier, J. (1992). Occidentalism: The world turned upside down. *American Ethnologist*, 19(2), 195–212.

Castells, M. (1997). *The Power of Identity*. Oxford: Blackwell.

Chatterjee, P. (1990). Recasting women: Essays in Indian colonial history. In K. Sangari and S. Vaid (eds.), *The Nationalist Resolution of the Women's Question*. New Jersey: Rutgers University Press, pp. 233–53.

Chen, X. (1995). *Occidentalism: A theory of counter-discourse in Post-Mao China*. Oxford: Oxford University Press.

Chow, R. (1993). *Writing Diaspora: Tactics of intervention in contemporary cultural studies*. Bloomington: Indiana University Press.

Clarke, J. (1990). Pessimism versus populism. In R. Butsch (ed.), *For Fun and Profit: The transformation of leisure into consumption*. Philadelphia, PA: Temple University Press, pp. 28–42.

Dharwadker, V. (1997). Print culture and literary markets in colonial India. In J. Masten, P. Stallybrass, and N. Wickers (eds.), *Language Machines*. New York: Routledge, pp. 108–33.

Dines, G. and Humez, J. (eds.) (1995). *Gender, Race, and Class in Media*. Thousand Oaks, CA: Sage.

Dirlik, A. (1990). Culturalism as hegemonic ideology and liberating practice. In A. JanMohamed and D. Lloyd (eds.), *The Nature and Practice of Minority Discourse*. New York: Oxford University Press, pp. 394–431.

Duke, L. (2000). Black in a blonde world: Race and girls' interpretations of the feminine ideal in teen magazines. *Journalism and Mass Communication Quarterly*, 77(2), 367–92.

Durham, M. G. (1999). Girls, media, and the negotiation of sexuality: A study of race, class, and gender in adolescent peer groups. *Journalism and Mass Communication Quarterly*, 76(2), 193–216.

Finders, M. (1997). *Just Girls: Hidden literacies and life in junior high*. New York: Teacher's College Press.

Ganguly, K. (1992). Accounting for others: Feminism and representation. In L. Rakow (ed.), *Women Making Meaning*. New York: Routledge, pp. 60–82.

Garnham, N. (1995). Political economy and cultural studies: Reconciliation or divorce? *Critical Studies in Mass Communication*, 12(1), 62–71.

Gibson, T. (2000). Beyond cultural populism: Notes toward the critical ethnography of media audiences. *Journal of Communication Inquiry*, 24(3), 253–73.

Gillespie, M. (1995). *Television, Ethnicity, and Cultural Change*. London: Routledge.

Grossberg, L., Nelson, C., and Treichler, P. (1992). *Cultural Studies*. New York: Routledge.

Hall, S. (1980). Encoding/decoding. In S. Hall, D. Hobson, A. Lowe, and P. Willis (eds.), *Culture, Media, and Language*. London: Hutchinson, pp. 128–38.

Hegde, R. (1998). A view from elsewhere: Locating difference and the politics of representation from a transnational feminist perspective. *Communication Theory*, 8(3), 271–97.

Joshi, P. (1998). Culture and consumption: Fiction, the reading public, and the British novel in colonial India. In E. Greenspan and J. Rose (eds.), *Book History 1*. University Park, PA: The Pennsylvania State University Press, pp. 196–220.

Juluri, V. (1998). Globalizing audience studies: The audience and its landscape and living room wars. *Critical Studies in Mass Communication*, 15(1), 85–90.

Kandiyoti, D. (1991). Identity and its discontents: Women and the nation. *Millennium: Journal of international studies*, 20(3), 429–43.

Katrak, K. (1989). Decolonizing culture: Toward a theory for postcolonial women's texts. *Modern Fiction Studies*, 35(1), 157–79.

Kellner, D. (1995). Cultural studies, multiculturalism, and media culture. In G. Dines and J. Humez (eds.), *Gender, Race, and Class in Media*. Thousand Oaks, CA: Sage, pp. 5–17.

Kumar, N. (ed.) (1994). Introduction. In N. Kumar (ed.), *Women as Subjects: South Asian histories*. Charlottesville, VA: University of Virginia Press.

Mankekar, P. (1999). *Screening Culture, Viewing Politics: An ethnography of television, womanhood, and nation*. Durham, NC: Duke University Press.

Markert, J. (1985). Love's labors. *Contemporary sociology*, 14(6), 682–4.

Mazumdar, S. (1994). Moving away from a secular vision? Women, nation, and the cultural construction of Hindu India. In V. Moghadam (ed.), *Identity Politics and Women: Cultural reassertions and feminisms in international perspective*. Boulder, CO: Westview, pp. 243–72.

McRobbie, A. (1990). *Feminism and Youth Culture*. Boston: Unwin Hyman.

Modleski, T. (1986). *Studies in Entertainment: Critical approaches to mass culture*. Bloomington: Indiana University Press.

Moran, J. (1998). Cultural studies and academic stardom. *International Journal of Cultural Studies*, 1(1), 67–82.

Morley, D. (1986). *Family Television: Cultural power and domestic leisure*. London: Comedia.

Murdock, G. (1989). Cultural studies: Missing links. *Critical Studies in Mass Communication*, 6(4), 436–40.

Nader, L. (1989). Orientalism, occidentalism, and women's lives. *Cultural Dynamics*, 11(3), 323–55.

Nandy, A., Trivedy, S., Mayaram, S., and Yagnik, A. (1995). *Creating a Nationality: The Rama-janmabhumi movement and fear of the self*. New Delhi: Oxford University Press.

Newman, K. (1988). On openings and closings. *Critical Studies in Mass Communication*, 5(4), 243–6.

Nightingale, V. (1996). *Studying Audiences: The shock of the real*. New York: Routledge.

Paddikal, S. (1993). Inventing modernity: The emergence of the novel in India. In T. Niranjana, P. Sudhir, and V. Dhareshwar (eds.), *Interrogating Modernity: Culture and colonialism in India*. Calcutta: Seagull Books, pp. 220–41.

Parameswaran, R. (1999). Western romance fiction as English-language media in postcolonial India. *Journal of Communication*, 49(2), 84–105.

Porter, D. (1994). Orientalism and its problems. In P. Williams and L. Chrisman (eds.), *Colonial Discourse and Postcolonial Theory*. New York: Columbia University Press, pp. 150–61.

Press, A. (1986). New views in the mass production of women's culture. *Communication Research*, 13(1), 139–49.

Press, A. (1991). *Women Watching Television: Gender, class, and generation in the American televisual experience*. Philadelphia: University of Pennsylvania Press.

Radway, J. (1984). *Reading the Romance: Women, patriarchy, and popular literature*. Chapel Hill: University of North Carolina Press.

Rajagopal, A. (1996). Mediating modernity: Theorizing reception in a non-Western society. *The Communication Review*, 1(4), 441–70.

Rege, S. (1995). The hegemonic appropriation of sexuality: The case of the lavani performers of Maharashtra. *Contributions to Indian Sociology*, 29(1 and 2), 23–38.

Robertson, J. (1995). Mon Japon: The revue theater as a technology of Japanese imperialism. *American Ethnologist*, 22(4), 970–96.

Said, E. (1978). *Orientalism*. New York: Vintage Books.

Said, E. (1993). *Culture and Imperialism*. New York: Knopf.

Schein, L. (1997). Gender and internal Orientalism in China. *Modern China*, 23(1), 69–99.

Schein, L. (2000). *Minority Rules: The Miao and the feminine in China's cultural politics*. Durham, NC: Duke University Press.

Schudson, M. (1987). The new validation of popular culture: Sense and sentimentality in academia. *Critical Studies in Mass Communication*, 4(1), 51–68.

Schwichtenberg, C. (1989). Feminist cultural studies. *Critical Studies in Mass Communication*, 6(2), 202–7.

Scott, J. (1990). *Domination and the Arts of Resistance: Hidden transcripts*. New Haven, CT: Yale University Press.

Setalwad, T. (1996). The politics of the Sangh Parivar: Playing the Hindutva card. *Voices: A Journal on Communication for Development*, 4(3), 23–5.

Shohat, E. (1998). *Talking Visions: Multicultural feminism in a transnational age*. Cambridge, MA: MIT Press.

Shome, R. (1996). Postcolonial interventions in the rhetorical canon: An "other" view. *Communication Theory*, 6(1), 40–59.

Shome, R. (2000). Outing whiteness. *Critical Studies in Mass Communication*, 17(3), 365–71.

Thurston, C. (1988). *The Romance Revolution: Erotic novels for women and the quest for a new sexual identity*. Illinois: University of Illinois Press.

Tomlinson, J. (1992). *Cultural Imperialism*. Baltimore, MD: Johns Hopkins University Press.

Valdivia, A. N. (2000). *A Latina in the Land of Hollywood and Other Essays on Media Culture*. Tucson: University of Arizona Press.

Varma, P. (1998). *The Great Indian Middle-Class*. New Delhi, India: Viking Penguin India.

Venkatachalapathy, A. R. (1997). Domesticating the novel: Society and culture in inter-war Tamil Nadu. *The Indian Economic and Social History Review*, 34(1), 53–67.

Viswanathan, G. (1989). *Masks of Conquest: Literary study and British rule in India*. New York: Columbia University Press.

CHAPTER SIXTEEN

The Changing Nature of Audiences
From the Mass Audience to the Interactive Media User

Sonia Livingstone

Changing Media, Changing Audiences

Modern media and communication technologies possess a hitherto unprecedented power to encode and circulate symbolic representations. Throughout much of the world, though especially in industrialized countries, people routinely spend a considerable proportion of their leisure hours with the mass media, often more than they spend at work or school or in face-to-face communication. Moreover, leisure is increasingly focused on the media-rich home, a significant shift in a matter of a single generation. Despite the popular anxieties that flare up sporadically over media content and regulation, it is easy to take the media for granted precisely because of their ubiquity as background features of everyday life. Yet it is through this continual engagement with the media that people are positioned in relation to a flood of images and information both about worlds distant in space or time and about the world close to home, and this has implications for our domestic practices, our social relationships, and our very identity. This chapter overviews current debates within audience research, arguing that although developments in technology may threaten to overtake these debates, audience research will be better prepared to understand the changing media environment by adopting a historical framework, looking back the better to look forward. But let us begin with a scenario from the future:

> You'll go to the electronics store and buy a "home gateway" box the size of today's VCR for maybe $300. You'll hook it to a broadband cable, then connect it to your wired or wireless home network. You'll call the cable provider and sign up for its custom-TV digital recording service for maybe $50 a month. You'll hang a flat plasma display . . . on the living-room wall and connect it to a wall socket that also

taps into the home grid. You'll put modest displays in other rooms, too. As you leave the bedroom you'll say "off" to its screen, and as you enter the kitchen you'll say, "Screen, show me my stock numbers." During a commercial you'll use a little wireless remote to instruct the hidden gateway box to find, download and play an original *Star Trek* episode. When the episode ends you'll grab the game controller off the coffee table, become Captain Kirk on the plasma screen and engage in a live, on-line dogfight in the Neutral Zone with an opponent from Tokyo. (Fischetti, 2001: 40)

Notwithstanding the hazards of attempting to predict the future, it is notable that such futuristic – or realistic – scenarios are becoming commonplace. Moreover, in certain respects, this quotation neatly illustrates what is, perhaps, happening to "the audience," at least in industrialized countries, my focus here. It reflects an already-present pressure to develop and market intelligent, personalized, flexible information and communication technologies that increasingly bring the outside world into the domestic space. These technologies converge on the electronic screen, while screens are themselves increasingly dispersed throughout the home. We are promised the satisfaction of our egocentric desires to have our individualistic tastes or fandom precisely catered for, whether on television, computer games, etc., thereby permitting us the satisfying shift from passive observer to active participant in a virtual world.

Contextualizing technological change in everyday life

There is a tension, however, between such visions of radical technological change and our knowledge of the slow-to-change conditions that underpin identity, sociality and community. Hence it is imperative to put media, especially new media, into context, so as to locate them within the social landscape, to map the changing media environment in relation to the prior communicative practices which, in turn, shape that environment. The very multiplicity of contextualizing processes undermines the simple account of the impacts of technology on society which circulate in popular discourses. The practices of our everyday lives, both material and symbolic, are dependent on structures of work, family, economy, nation, and cannot be so quickly overturned by technological change. For example, changes in disposable leisure time, in working practices or in the gendered division of domestic labor profoundly shape the ways in which new information and communication technologies diffuse through society and find a place in our daily lives.

Furthermore, given what we already know from today's technology, the above scenario leaves open some crucial questions. Where is everyone else in this scenario – the people we live with, the people who want to watch something other than *Star Trek*, who laugh us out of our pretence at being Captain Kirk or who, irritatingly, have lost the wireless remote? The history of researching mass communication is a history of how the mass mediated world relates to the social world of the viewer and, even in the short history of the Internet, research has already moved beyond characterizing the supposedly autonomous on-line world towards exploring its complex connections with the off-line world (Slater, 2002). Surely, the social consequences of new technologies will be mediated through existing patterns of social interaction. Further, how does our protagonist know in this scenario that he or she likes *Star Trek*? We know we like it because that was what everyone watched on Wednesday evenings for years, so that it became embedded in our daily lives as we compared the different series with friends, laughed at the clothes, and followed the lives of the stars on the talk shows. For the generations with a common culture already established, this individually tailored future may be enticing. But how will the new generation establish content preferences in the first place, faced with an overwhelming range of unfamiliar choices? And once they've made their choice, how will they share the experience with others, drawing media into the common discourses of playground and office?

This is not to say that the media have no influence on society, but rather that such processes of influence are far more indirect and complex than popularly thought. Central to recent work on media audiences is an analysis of the ways in which people can be said to be active in shaping their media culture, contributing to the process of shaping or co-constructing their material and symbolic environments. Today, such research has two main foci, one centered on the contexts of media *use*, the other on the *interpretation* of media content. Though one or other of these foci tends to dominate the agenda at any point, it is assumed in this chapter that both are integral to an adequate theory of audiences. In adding a reflexive spin on the consequences of both social and technological change, Pertti Alasuutari (1999: 6) argues that "the audience" as a social phenomenon "out there" must be replaced by the recognition that the audience is "a discursive construct produced by a particular analytic gaze." Hence the analysis of audiences must also include the very discourses which construct people as audiences (or publics or markets, etc.), including "the audience's notions of themselves as the 'audience'" (p. 7).

History does not stand still

While in the main, media research restricts itself to the contemporary, it is clear that researchers are studying a moving target: what were once "new" media become familiar while yet newer media emerge. Changing social and cultural contexts also shape audience practices. Consider the shift from the physically contiguous mass spectatorship of the eighteenth-century theater or show to the spatially separated "virtual" mass of press and broadcasting audiences in the nineteenth and twentieth century. Even the half century of national television – which in the USA, Europe, and many other countries spans the period from the 1940s to the 1990s – has witnessed major social transformations, including world war, postwar austerity and then consumer boom, the unsettling conflicts of the sixties, the rise of free-market ideology and, now, *fin-de-siècle* uncertainty, these affecting all aspects of society from economic globalization to the patterns of family life.

Yet, too often media researchers talk of "television" – and, by implication, "the television audience" – as if it were unchanging over its own history. Thus throughout the many decades of audience research, researchers have asked important questions about the uses of media, and about the effects of the media (McQuail, 1997). Yet audience research has shown too little inclination to seek a historical explanation for research findings, though this may help to explain the often unwelcome variation in findings. Only since the 1990s – or a little earlier in some countries – has "television" been so transformed by the expansion in channels, especially global and narrow-cast ones, by the crisis in public service – especially in Europe – and by the advent of new technologies such as the VCR and now digital television, that it has become obvious that specifically new questions are arising for the audience as much as for the medium (Becker & Schoenbach, 1989; Neuman, 1991). What will these changes mean for audience theory? And could it lead to a new sensitivity towards interpreting audience findings in relation to the specific period within which research studies are, or were, conducted?

Making audiences visible in media theory

Media theory has always been committed to the integrated analysis of production, texts, and audiences. While traditional approaches to mass communication analyze each as separate but interlinked elements in the linear flow of mediated meanings, cultural and critical approaches stress the interrelations of these elements in the (re)production of cultural meanings (Hall, 1980). But in practice it has too often been the case that the analysis of production and texts has been primary, while the interpretative activities of audiences has been neglected (Livingstone, 1998a). Audience research rectifies this tendency by fore-grounding the cultural contexts within which meanings are both encoded and decoded and acknowledging the importance of the socially shared (or diversified) aspects of those contexts. As Klaus Bruhn Jensen (1993: 26) argues:

> Reception analysis offers insights into the interpretive processes and everyday contexts of media use, where audiences rearticulate and enact the meanings of mass communication. The life of signs within modern society is in large measure an accomplishment of the audience.

Thus, audience research asks, how do the media (through institutional policy, genre conventions, modes of address, etc.) frame relations among people as one of "audience"? Indeed, do certain kinds of texts or technologies produce certain kinds of audience? Or, to put the opposite question, how do the social relations among people, at home, in the neighborhood or the nation, shape the communicative possibilities (electronic or otherwise) of those locales, enabling some and inhibiting others?

During the 1980s and 1990s, empirical audience research became prominent in media studies. I have argued that this success was due to the productive convergence of several traditions, within each of which compelling arguments led inexorably towards empirical research on audiences and, especially, their interpretive activities (Livingstone, 1998b). Indeed, for a while, the perception was that "the concept of audience is more importantly the underpinning prop for the analysis of the social impact of mass communication in general" (Allor, 1988: 217), and that the audience is "a potentially crucial pivot for the understanding of a whole range of social and cultural processes that bear on the central questions of public communication . . . [which are] essentially questions of culture" (Silverstone, 1990: 173).

Things move fast in audience studies, and one may now observe with some disquiet various attempts to retell this convergence as a linear, indeed canonical narrative in which audience reception studies provide a stepping stone in the rise of cultural studies (Alasuutari, 1999; Nightingale, 1996). As Vincent Mosco (1996: 251) observes, "cultural studies reminds political economy that the substance of its work, the analysis of communication, is rooted in the needs, goals, conflicts, failures and accomplishments of ordinary people aiming to make sense of their lives, even as they confront an institutional and symbolic world that is not entirely of their own making." Important though this claim is, by subordinating audience research to the heroic narrative of cultural studies, audience research has in turn become separated from some of the diverse interdisciplinary traditions that stimulated its development, and whose potential contributions have yet to be explored fully. So, let us review briefly the central arguments of these diverse traditions.

Multiple traditions of audience research

We may begin by noting the crucial influence of literary and semiotic theory for the understanding of popular culture. Particularly, in developing the concepts of *the implied reader* or *model reader*, reception–aesthetics theorized how texts anticipated, invited, and so were fitted for, readers with a specific interpretive repertoire of codes, presuppositions, and interpretive frames. Thus Umberto Eco (1979) stressed how readers must strive to realize the necessarily virtual meaning of a text by drawing on their own cultural resources during the process of interpretation. Or, as Wolfgang Iser (1980: 106) put it, "the work itself cannot be identical with the text or with its actualization but must be situated somewhere between the two . . . As the reader passes through the various perspectives offered by the text, and relates the different views and patterns to one another, he sets the work in motion, and so sets himself in motion too."

A parallel argument, encapsulated by Stuart Hall's (1980) *encoding/decoding* paper, began by rejecting the linearity of the mainstream, social–psychological model of mass communication in order to stress the intersections but also the disjunction between processes of encoding and decoding, contextualising both within a complex cultural framework. Influenced by Eco, Hall (1980: 131) incorporated elements of reception-aesthetics into his neo–Marxist account of popular culture, proposing that "the degrees of 'understanding' and 'misunderstanding' in the communicative exchange – depend on the degrees of symmetry/asymmetry (relations of equivalence) established between the positions of the 'personifications', encoder-producer and decoder/receiver." On this view, mass communication is understood as a circuit of articulated practices – production, circulation, reception, reproduction – each of which represents a site of meaning-making (see also Morley, 1992).

Crucially, this cyclic process contrasts with the widespread metaphor of communication transmission (Carey, 1989) that assumes that communication merely requires the more-or-less efficient transport of fixed and already-meaningful messages in a linear manner from sender to receiver. However, the social–psychological tradition attacked by Hall and others relaunched itself through the promotion of the *active* or *selective audience*, making choices about media use. Thus uses and gratifications researchers saw audience reception research as setting the scene for building "the bridge we have been hoping might arise between gratifications studies and cultural studies" (Katz, 1979: 75; see also Blumler et al., 1985), while the social constructivist paradigm in social psychology applied itself to understanding mediated, rather than just face-to-face sources of social influence, thereby uncovering the "*sense-making*" activities of audiences in negotiating the conventions and rhetorics of media texts. Through such concepts as the interpretive "frame," social constructionist researchers sought to understand how people's tacit or local knowledge variously "filled the gaps" or re-framed the meaning of media texts, resulting in divergent interpretations of the very same texts (Gamson, 1992; Hoijer & Werner, 1998; Iyengar, 1991; Livingstone, 1998a and b).

Research on these sense-making activities was appropriated by critical communications research in its advocacy of the *resistant audience* as part of the theoretical shift from dominant ideology theory to the hegemonic struggle between attempts to incorporate audiences into the dominant ideology and sources of resistance to such incorporation, even if this resistance remains tacit or implicit. Although for some, the evidence for resistance or divergence has been overplayed (Curran, 1990; Schiller, 1989), this argument was partly fueled by a desire to uncover the limits of cultural imperialism through an exploration of the sources of local resistance to imported meanings (e.g. Liebes & Katz, 1995). As David Morley (1993: 17) concludes, "local meanings are so often made within and against the symbolic resources provided by global media networks." Also influential among critical theories, particularly in identifying resistant audiences engaged in the construction of alternative cultural rituals and practices, feminist approaches to popular culture promoted a reconsideration of the often vilified popular culture audience within cultural theory, developing a revaluation of, and the giving of a voice to, hitherto *marginalized audiences* (Ang, 1985; Radway, 1984).

Making sense of television

Having argued that media texts are polysemic, that meanings emerge from a context-dependent process of interpretation and so will be mutually divergent (Fiske, 1987), it became obvious that research should investigate the activities of actual audiences in order to know how they interpret programs in everyday contexts. Hence, the stimulating convergence – or at least intersection – of these arguments in favor of empirical audience research produced something of a research "boom" in the 1980s and 1990s. Yet the generation of a sound basis for understanding the activities of audiences was accompanied, theoretically, by a move away from a careful consideration of particular reception theories such as those of Iser, Eco or Hall to a looser grounding in the blanket notion of "reception theory" or "audience reception analysis." This project quickly justified itself through findings showing that audiences indeed do differ from researchers in their reception of media content, and that audiences are themselves heterogeneous in their interpretations – even, at times, resistant to the dominant meanings encoded into a text (in the form of a "preferred reading"; Hall, 1980). This further undermined any claims to presume audience response from a knowledge of media content alone, or of arguing for a direct link between the meanings supposedly inherent in the text and the consequent effects of those meanings on the audience.

As a result of these arguments, attention was redirected to studying the interpretive contexts which frame and inform viewers' understandings of television. Hence, empirical reception studies have variously explored the relationships between media texts – typically the television genres of soap opera, news, among others (Hagen & Wasko, 2000; Hodge & Tripp, 1986; Livingstone, 1998c; Tulloch, 2000; Wilson, 1993) – and their audiences. Audience interpretations or decodings have been found to diverge depending on viewers' socioeconomic position, gender, ethnicity, and so forth, while the possibilities for critical or oppositional readings are anticipated, enabled or restricted by the degree of closure semiotically encoded into the text and by audiences' variable access to symbolic resources. The point is not that audiences are "wrong" but that they construct their interpretations according to diverse discursive contexts which are themselves socially determined. As a result of this now considerable body of work, audiences are no longer thought of according to the popular image which always threatens to recur, as homogenous, passive and uncritical or vulnerable to the direct influence of meanings transmitted, and perhaps manipulated by, the mass media.

Media-centric research?

Critiques of audience research have grown in tandem with its success, centering on the supposed untenability of the central concept of the audience itself: how can we define it, measure it, place boundaries around it, and in whose interest is it if we do so anyway (Ang, 1990; Erni, 1989; Seaman, 1992)? One outcome has been a charge of media-centrism (Schroeder, 1994), attacking audience research for defining its object of study purely in terms of a technological artifact (the television audience, the movie-goer, etc.). This critique has force partly because an increasingly ad hoc collection of objects is included in the category of "media," and partly because if audiences are defined in relation to technology, researchers are drawn into tracking how audiences change as technologies change rather than as society changes. Hence, one may ask whether anything, apart from the label "audience research," integrates such diverse projects as identifying the pleasures of video games, investigating the agenda setting role of the press, incorporating the Internet into schools, or exploring the role of music in peer culture?

The defense from reception studies, I suggest, is that there is indeed a consistent focus underlying these questions, one centered on *communication*. Each is concerned with the conditions, contexts and consequences of the technological mediation of symbolic communication among people (Thompson, 1995). It is charting the possibilities and problems for communication (i.e. for relations among people rather than relations between people and technology), insofar as these are undermined or facilitated, managed or reconstituted by the media, that offers a challenging agenda, and one which puts audiences at the center of media and communication research, rather than locating them – or worse, deferring their study – as the last stage in a long chain of more interesting processes.

The ethnographic turn

> The qualities and experiences of being a member of an audience have begun to leak out from specific performance events which previously contained them, into the wider realms of everyday life.
>
> (Abercrombie & Longhurst, 1998: 36–7)

An influential response to doubts over media-centrism has resulted in a further strand of audience research, namely a more systematic exploration of the *contexts* of media use, thereby moving ever further away from the medium itself in search of the local sites of cultural meaning-making which shape people's orientation to the media. Several arguments led to this focus on context. As Robert Allen (1987) argued, once textual and literary theorists had made the crucial transition to a reader-oriented approach, context flooded in for two reasons: first, the shift from asking about meaning of the text in and of itself, to asking about the meaning of the text as achieved by a particular, contextualised reader (i.e. the shift, in Eco's terms, from the *virtual* to the *realized* text); second, the shift from asking about the meaning of the text to asking about the intelligibility of the text (i.e. about the diversity of sociocultural conditions which determine how a text *can* make sense). Thus the crucial transition was made, from text to context, from literary/semiotic analysis to social analysis (Morley, 1992).

Of course, these should not be posed as either/or options, for the moment of reception is precisely at the interface between textual and social determinations and so requires a dual focus on media content and audience response. But in practice, the demands of more fully contextualising reception in order to understand how audience activities carry the meanings communicated far beyond the moment of reception into many other spheres of everyday life, as well as the converse process of the shaping of reception by the symbolic practices of everyday life, has led to calls for what Janice Radway (1988) called "radical contextualism" in audience research. By this she means the analytic *displacement* of the moment of text–reader reception by ethnographic studies of the everyday, a focus on "the kaleidoscope of daily life" (Radway, 1988: 366) or, for Paul Willis, an analysis of "the whole way of life" (1990). Like Radway, Ien Ang (1996: 250–1) also sees the ethnographic approach displacing reception studies. Thus, she observes that:

> Television's meanings for audiences – textual, technological, psychological, social – cannot be decided upon outside of the multidimensional intersubjective networks in which the object is inserted and made to mean in concrete contextual settings . . . this epistemological move toward radical contextualism in culturalist audience studies has been accompanied by a growing interest in *ethnography* as a mode of empirical inquiry.

Following these arguments, the "ethnographic turn" in audience research shifts the focus away from the moment of textual interpretation and towards the contextualisation of that moment in the *culture of the everyday*. Thus ethnographic audience studies have explored the ways in which media goods become meaningful insofar as they are found a particular kind of place within the home, the domestic timetable, the family's communication ecology. Simultaneously, it is becoming clear that this process of appropriation also shapes, enabling or restricting, the uses and meanings of the medium for its audience or users. Studies of the radio (Moores, 1988), telephone (Moyal, 1995), television (Spigel, 1992), satellite television (Moores, 1996), and diverse other media (e.g. Flichy, 1995; Mackay, 1997), trace the specific contextualization of the media in today's media-rich home.

Media-as-object, media-as-text

Where does the ethnographic turn leave reception studies? Through the concept of double articulation, Roger Silverstone (1994) contrasts the media *qua* material objects such as the television or walkman, namely as technological objects located in particular spatiotemporal settings, with the media *qua* texts such as the news or the soap opera, namely as symbolic messages located within particular sociocultural discourses. Broadly, to focus on the *media-as-object* is to invite an analysis of media *use* in terms of consumption in the context of domestic practices. On the other hand, to focus on the *media-as-text* is to invite an analysis of the textuality or representational character of media contents in relation to the interpretive activities of particular audiences. By implication, then, the audience is also, necessarily, doubly articulated as the *consumer–viewer*.

Frustratingly, researching audiences simultaneously in terms of reception and contexts of use seems hard to sustain. In the classic figure-ground illustration of the Gestalt theorists, we see two heads facing each other with a gap in between, or we see the vase in what was the space while the surrounding objects become unnoticed. Understanding audiences in terms of either what's *surrounding*, or what's *on*, the screen has something of this character: the further one stands back from the television set to focus on the context of the living room, the smaller the screen appears and the harder it is to see what's showing. And vice versa. Yet clearly, the box-in-the-corner is the occasion for social interaction – or isolated pleasures – precisely because of its symbolic content.

In short, people are always both *interpreters* of the media-as-text and *users* of the media-as-object, and the activities associated with these symbolic and material uses of media are mutually defining. And clearly, ethnographic studies of audiences draw on the same insights as reception studies – the stress on active audiences making contingent and context-dependent choices, on fragmentation and plurality within the population rather than the normative mass audience, on audiences as joint producers rather than merely consumers of the meanings of media – in order to develop the study of the local, typically domestic contexts within which media-as-objects are appropriated as part and parcel of everyday life. Hence, it should not be so hard as it seems to be to keep both these activities, reception and use, in the frame simultaneously.

Historicizing audience research

Understanding why a focus on either use or reception seem to be unnecessarily bifurcating audience research requires a historical lens. Consider the early days of television, and indeed the following thirty or forty years, when households were proud to acquire a television and place it in the living room, albeit sometimes frustrated with each other regarding how they were going to use it (Morley, 1986). In Europe, America and other Western countries at that time one could view just a few channels, each addressed to "the nation" according to a predictable schedule (Scannell, 1988). Given these circumstances, the interesting questions for researchers concerned texts more than contexts of use. While the dynamics of family life seemed relatively homogenous and deeply familiar, it was the texts which seemed most innovative, as national cultures transferred, and transformed, their traditions of news, drama, comedy, etc., into audiovisual content.

By contrast, as today's households acquire multiple television sets along with the capacity for multiple channels, multiple video recorders, personal computers, mobile phones and, most recently, the Internet, the proliferation of new media technologies at home has something of the character of old wine in new bottles. For in the main, these intriguing new media objects have carried old media messages, recycling the broadcasters' archives, proliferating new shows using old formats, uploading existing print media onto the World Wide Web. As yet, the promised transformation in content or text is not much in evidence. Hence the figure-ground image in the research literature is shifting, and now it seems to be the ethnographic contextualisation of the changing media environment that poses the most interesting challenge to audience researchers. Judging from recent historical work on past "new" media, this challenge of the new is stimulating some to reevaluate our understanding of the arrival of these past media (e.g. Corner, 1991; Hansen, 1991; Marvin, 1988; Schudson, 1991). This historical perspective serves to reveal the historical specificity of the terms of today's debate over audiences.

From live to mass audiences

The crucial shift – away from the live audience for theatre, spectacles, political meetings, etc., to the distributed audience for mass communication occurred in relation to books and the press, less because of the technological innovation of printing, for that came much earlier, than because of the cultural and institutional innovation of mass education and hence mass literacy. While that earlier model of the audience, which we now distinguish as "live," was characterized by face-to-face communication among people gathered together in public meeting places, the "reading public" of the seventeenth and eighteenth centuries was primarily receptive rather than participatory, dispersed rather than co-located, privatized rather than public (Luke, 1989; McQuail, 1997); and it is this which characterizes audiences for subsequent (mass) media.

Historically, this is not a story of discrete phases, in which one medium displaces another (Fischer, 1994), but rather one of the accumulation of modes of "*audiencing*", as John Fiske puts it (1992), each coexisting in our complex media environment. Nonetheless, at any one time one medium is on the ascendant, discursively positioned as the "new" medium that epitomizes the popular hopes and anxieties of a society. As Kirsten Drotner (1992) has shown, these not-always laudable hopes and fears – for the "proper" development of children's imagination, for the dis/orderly behavior of the working class audience, for the normative reproduction of moral and cultural knowledge across the generations – tend to be repeated as each "new" medium becomes widely available.

Reception leaves no record

In researching past media, it is noteworthy that the history of audiences is particularly problematic. The institutional production of media and the actual media texts are comparatively well recorded – there are memos, letters, policy statements, economic statistics and so forth documenting media production, and there are archives of past films, newspapers, television and radio programs.

While these are never as complete as one would like, they exist. By contrast, beyond the limited records of circulation, box office sales, television ratings, etc., audience history encounters a serious problem of sources. In their routine daily activities audience leave no physical record (although see Richards & Sheridan, 1987). Given the importance to research on contemporary audiences that research makes visible the otherwise taken-for-granted, neglected or misunderstood experiences of ordinary people, one can understand Jensen's (1993: 20–1) anxiety when he notes that:

> Reception does not exist in the historical record; it can only be reconstructed through the intervention of research . . . Whereas ratings and readership figures presumably will survive, the social and cultural aspects of mass media reception are literally disappearing before our eyes and ears.

Historicizing audience reception faces multiple problems. With the shift away from visible and audible participation by live audiences, the activities of the new, mass mediated audiences became highly interiorized and hence inaccessible to the researcher. Methodologically, one is trying to capture experiences which are private rather than public, experiences concerned with understandings rather than practices, experiences of all society not just the elite, experiences which are past rather than present, experiences commonly regarded as trivial and forgettable rather than important.

The surprising history of the active audience

Such evidence as can be discovered is proving intriguing, not only for our understanding of the past, but also for our understanding of the present. Richard Butsch (2000: 2) observes that:

> While the underlying issues were always power and social order, at different times the causes of the problems of audiences had different sources. In the nineteenth century, the problem lay in the degenerate or unruly people who came to the theater, and what they might do. In the twentieth century, worries focused on the dangers of reception, how media messages might degenerate audiences. In the nineteenth century, critics feared *active* audiences; in the twentieth, their *passivity*.

This nineteenth-century audience has a longer history. In Elizabethan England, theater audiences were highly active, asserting their right to participate, vocally critical or appreciative, or even ignoring the action by loudly engaging in conversation, walking about or playing cards during the performance. Indeed, the more noisy they were, the more privileged they were seen to be, actors having the status of servants. As Butsch comments, "aristocratic audience sovereignty affirmed the social order" (2000: 5), a provocative reversal of the present day argument that consumer sovereignty asserts the power of the people against the control of the property-owning elite.

How did things come to change? Butsch shows how, as the plebeian audience followed the example of their betters, incorporating elements of carnival into their own performance as an audience, by the nineteenth century the privileged classes had came to fear, and so to critique and attempt to control, this rowdy, "over-active" lower-class audience. The importance of manners – together with the introduction of such physical constraints as bolting chairs to the floor and dimming the lights – came to dictate attentiveness and deference to the performers on the part of a "respectable" audience in the theatre and the early days of cinema. Meanwhile, "active" engagement with the performance marked the lower classes, with the consequence that "audiences at these entertainments let slip their sovereignty and were contained if not tamed" (2000: 6).

Reception becomes interiorized

One may speculate that it was the contrast with the visible activities of the live audience which preceded it that contributed to twentieth-century worries about the television audience. How much do these worries center on the fundamental ambiguity, to the observer, of physically inactive audiences? Is the person sitting quietly on the sofa watching television part of a respectable audience, paying careful attention and concentrating on understanding and benefiting from the entertainment offered, or are they passive couch potatoes, dependent on media for their pleasures, uncritical in their acceptance of messages, vulnerable to influence? And, if they do not sit quietly, are the active audiences participating in their social world or disruptive audiences, unable to concentrate? Such uncertainties invite prejudiced interpretations inflected by class and gender: a middle-class man attentively watching the news is assumed to be alert and thoughtful; a working-class woman attentively watching a soap opera is assumed to be mindless and uncritical. Other people's children are mindless, your own can concentrate properly (Davison, 1983).

Interestingly, in the days when audiences participated vociferously, marking their pleasure and displeasure, their critical response or their incomprehension, there was, arguably, less of a distinction between media use and media reception – how people acted materially, in time and space, could be taken to reveal their symbolic or cognitive engagement with performances. Undoubtedly, documented accounts of the "reception" of the first production of a Shakespeare play, for example, would feel free to assume what the audience thought from how they acted. Butsch argues that the change came partly because of a transformation in *literary form*, although the introduction of the cinema further sedimented these new conventions. Thus, he suggests that:

> As realism replaced rhetorical styles of dramatic acting in the nineteenth century, the separation of audience from performer became paramount. Realism also required silencing audiences, making them passive. The "well-behaved" audience became

preferred among the middle and upper classes to audiences exercising sovereignty, which became a mark of lower class. (Butsch, 2000: 9)

Such passivity not only describes the social conventions which govern polite behavior but also, as genre studies have argued, audience passivity is assumed by a narrative form dedicated to the construction of an impermeable, closed text in which the audience is firmly required to identify with the hero, no other position being available (McCabe, 1974). Yet, as audience reception studies have shown, audiences increasingly will not have it thus, their rapt and adoring gaze at the Hollywood film being ever less the norm for television (Ellis, 1992). Rather, audiences today read against the grain, finding the opportunities for engaging more creatively, or resistantly, with whatever openness they find within the text or, as television genres blur further one into the other, they delight in contesting the genre itself, questioning the shifting conventions of realism, joining in noisily albeit in the privacy of their living room (Livingstone & Lunt, 1994).

An oral history of the television audience?

Both media use and media reception have continued to change during the twentieth century. In terms of use, it seems that, as each new medium enters the home, it undergoes a gradual transition from pride of place at the center of family life to a variable status pitched somewhere between focal and casual, communal and individualized uses, where these are spread spatially throughout the household and temporally round-the-clock (Flichy, 1995; Livingstone, 2002). Reception, however, remains more difficult. Since that century falls within living memory, I have argued (Livingstone et al., 2001) that the method of oral history could be used, although the difficulties in interpreting such data should not be underestimated (Samuel & Thompson, 1990). Again, we find the familiar problem, for conventional wisdom among oral historians suggests practices are more reliably recalled than meanings (O'Brien & Eyles, 1993). We may therefore have more confidence in asking people to recall going to the cinema in the 1940s than in asking them what they then thought of a particular film and how they interpreted it.

Consider Jackie Stacey's (1994) survey of women fans of Hollywood stars during the 1940s and 50s. Although she acknowledges the problems of oral history – "these histories of spectatorship are retrospective reconstructions of a past in the light of the present and will have been shaped by the popular versions of the 1940s and 1950s which have become cultural currency during the intervening years" (1994: 63) – what comes over clearly is the fascination with glamour and escapism conveyed by her informants. As one comments, "I think in those eras, we were more inclined to put stars on a pedestal. They were so far removed from everyday life, they were magical." Must we conclude only that this viewer has reconstructed the past from the vantage point of the present, now seeing herself as a more knowing and critical viewer? Or can we agree with

Stacey when she also argues that modes of perception, or relations of looking and seeing, are not universal but are historically contingent. As she puts it, the postwar period saw a shift from a spectator/star relationship based upon distance to one based on proximity.

Relevance, realism, relativism

In some recent research, my colleagues and I attempted to extend the oral history of leisure practices to the domain of media reception (Livingstone et al., 2001). The project interviewed different generations, from people in their teens to those in their eighties, about the crime-related media they had seen throughout the postwar period (or such of it as they had lived through). Crime, and its representation in the media, proved a provocative subject, stimulating lively discussion of the media, society and its morals. From listening to what these different generations remembered or found interesting, the ways they talked about the different periods, the different media and, indeed, their lives today, we tentatively identified three changes.

First, and consistent with Stacey's argument, above, it seemed that while in the early postwar period, people found pleasure in crime media primarily for their escapist irrelevance, today's audience is strongly concerned with *relevance* – for them, the point of engaging with the media is that connections are made with one's own life. This stress on relevance motivates not only the gratifications sought from watching crime dramas but also the process of reception, so that where before, the characters and action were interpreted primarily in terms of the internal coherence of the – preferably glamorous – narrative, now interpretation draws more strongly on frameworks or situations from daily life while the narrative is, in turn, made to "speak to" the audience's everyday experiences. That the importance of escapism was once greater is confirmed by Sally Alexander (1994) in her account of becoming a woman in London in the 1920s and 1930s. She argues that the cinema played a crucial role in making it possible for young women to conceive of other ways of living, particularly ways different from those of their mothers – glamour, freedom from drudgery and housework, romance, new conceptions of femininity. In other words, for them at that time, escapism was vital, and as Alexander sees it, positive in value.

Second, and connected with the desire for connection to one's own life, is a change in judgements of realism. The current, young audience preferred representations which they considered realistic (including the appeal of "just like us" soap opera characters dealing with crimes) and able to offer them useful information about crime risks etc. Realism for them means fuzzy moral boundaries, complex situations, seeing both sides of an issue, unresolved endings, seeing for oneself the physical consequences of violence. For the older audience, by contrast, realism was little talked about for past media, but has now been adopted as an evaluative criterion for present-day media. However, for them it is more likely to mean representations with recognizable characters, everyday settings, an absence of glamour or melodrama, a concern with minor crimes, and a lack of gratuitous or gory violence. Using these different criteria, then, we saw younger audiences criticize past media for their lack of realism by comparison with the present, while older audiences make the opposite judgement.

Third, we identified a change in the moral framework for interpreting media crime, from a frame of moral absolutism to one of contextualised relativism. A series of symbolic reversals were enumerated by the older generations: ever since the 1960s, they argued, the world is upside down – the police get sued by the criminals, the criminals get financial compensation or a comfortable life in prison while their victims are shown to suffer, the police are themselves corrupt, and so forth. Yet for younger people, these same observations are interpreted as far from distressing, as a legitimate relativism, realistic in a world where good and bad are a matter of contextualised judgements rather than abstract principles. All this has interesting implications for the reception process for what makes a "good story" has been redefined; with audiences shifting from an interest in working out *who* is the baddie and *how* s/he will be caught to an interest in working out what it *means* to be the baddie and *whether* they will be caught.

From the past to the future

Although we have still little historical knowledge of reception – of people's understandings, interpretations, and critical awareness of media contents – we can hardly suppose these historically invariant. Nor, of course, are these likely to remain constant given the continuing changes in both the media environment and the social contexts of media use. Beyond arguing for the importance of taking a longer-term perspective on audiences' engagement with the media than just the immediate lens of today's concerns, I have also suggested here that the very separation which is currently bedeviling audience research, that between the analysis of the use of media-as-objects and the reception of media-as-texts, is itself historically contingent. For the invisibility, or privatization, of what audience members are thinking, or learning, or feeling is a new (i.e. twentieth/twenty-first century) problem, and one which marks a new degree of separation – in theory, methodology, and practice – between the use of media-as-goods and the reception of media-as-texts.

I will end this chapter by sketching how this look back at the past may illuminate the future, drawing out implications of the above arguments for our understanding of how people engage with new media as objects and as texts. But first, one must address the semantic difficulty that one can hardly begin to analyze the new media without realizing that, in both ordinary and academic language, we currently face an uncertainty over how to discuss people in terms of their relationship with media. The term *audience* was, and to some extent still is, satisfactory for mass media research, but it clearly fits poorly within the domain of new media for, arguably, audiences are becoming "users."

The End of "the Audience"?

The term "audience" only satisfactorily covers the activities of listening and watching (though even this has been expanded to include the activities which contextualize listening and viewing). The term "user" seems to allow for a greater variety of modes of engagement, although it tends to be overly individualistic and instrumental, losing the sense of a collectivity which is central to "the audience," and with no necessary relation to *communication* at all, leading one to wonder whether users of media technologies differ from users of washing machines or cars. Analytically, audiences are being relocated away from the screen, their activities contextualized into the everyday lifeworld. They are also users insofar as they are grappling with the meaning of new and unfamiliar technologies in their homes, schools and workplaces. These media and information technologies open up new, more active modes of engagement with media – *playing* computer games, *surfing* the Web, *searching* databases, *writing* and *responding* to email, *visiting* a chat room, *shopping* online, and so on. We don't even have a verb to capture that increasingly important way in which people are engaging with media, namely fandom: one may be part of an audience for soap opera, but one's relation to Harry Potter, or Barbie, or even Manchester United[1] is precisely intertextual, spanning multiple media and hence multiple modes of engagement.

Rather than offering a new term here, I suggest that no one term can continue to cover the variety of ways in which technologies mediate relations among people. Hence, instead of asking what audiences – conceived as an artificial reification of a particular technological interface – are really like, we should rather conceptualize "the audience" as a relational or interactional construct, a shorthand way of focusing on the diverse relationships among people – who are first and foremost workers, neighbors, parents, teachers, or friends – as mediated by historically and culturally specific social contexts as well as by historically and culturally specific technological forms. For 'audience' researchers, then, the interesting questions are less and less, when and why do people watch television or read a newspaper, if this question means, implicitly, why do they do this instead of doing something else? Rather, as social spaces, and social relations, which are untouched by mediated forms of communication become fewer and fewer, we must instead ask questions about how, and with what consequences, it has come about that all social situations (whether at home or work, in public or in private, at school or out shopping) are now, simultaneously, mediated spaces, thereby constituting their participants inevitably as *both* family, workers, public or communities *and* as audiences, consumers or users?

Reception and use converge

It was argued above that, while in earlier centuries, use and reception were intimately connected, so that reception could be "read off" from the participatory activities of audiences in particular social contexts of media engagement or use, in the age of mass television use and reception became disconnected. In a curious reversal of this trend, I now wish to suggest that in the new media environment, reception may be once again gleaned – at least to some extent – from an analysis of use. For audiences are increasingly required to participate audibly and physically, albeit that their activities require a subtle eye on the part of the observer. Users are, necessarily, clicking on hypertext links in order to create a sequential flow of images on the World Wide Web, typing in order to co-construct the messages of the chat room, externalizing their conception of interface design and genre when producing their website, and manipulating their game character in order to keep the game going. They are also accumulating auditable references to their content preferences through "favorites" folders, inboxes, history files, software downloads, and so on. Although it will remain a methodological challenge to discover what participants are thinking or feeling when they engage with such media, it is intriguing that, increasingly, without physical and hence visible participation in the process of reception, there will be neither text nor reception in the first place. However, most of this remains to be researched, as thus far, perhaps because new media technologies have arrived in our homes in advance of radical new notions of content, more audience (or user) research on new media has focused on media-as-objects rather than media-as-texts.

Undoubtedly, then, the new media pose some interesting challenges to audience research in relation to both reception and use (Livingstone, 1999). First, they facilitate the multiplication of personally-owned media (from mobile phones to the television set), thereby encouraging the privatization of media use, including the media-rich bedroom culture of young people (Livingstone, 2002) and the sound bubble of the Walkman commuter. Further, the diversification of media and media contents is facilitating wider trends towards individualization, in which media goods and contents are used to construct lifestyles no longer grounded in sociodemographically-defined traditions. More recently, the convergence of traditionally distinct media is resulting in a blurring of traditionally distinct social boundaries ("edutainment," "infotainment," tele-working, e-learning), potentially undermining traditional hierarchies of expertise and authority.

Most significantly, however, new media technologies hold the possibility of expansion of interactive forms of media and the resulting potential for transforming a once-mass audience into engaged and participatory users of information and communication technologies. From the literature now emerging, it seems that these first three challenges are already being researched, particularly insofar as these concern changing discourses and practices of media use. But as for the fourth, we have barely begun to investigate the intellectual, symbolic and social contexts for and consequences of engaging with the particular forms and contents of the new media. Some preliminary observations may be offered, however.

From mass to interactive audiences

While the argument for the active audience of traditional media has probably been taken as far as it can go, interactive technologies now coming onto the market increasingly put such interpretative activities at the very center of media design and use. Thus, the new media environment extends arguments in "active audience" theory by transforming hitherto marginal or marginalized tendencies into the mainstream of media use. Audiences – as users – are increasingly active (i.e. selective, self-directed, producers as well as consumers of texts) and therefore plural (i.e. multiple, diverse, fragmented), although Neuman (1991: 166) is among many who question "whether or not the proliferation of new communications channels will lead to fragmentation of the mass audience." At the same time, the once-accessible and supposedly powerful media text is becoming as elusive as were audiences before: because hypertext, characteristic of Internet content, is "a structure composed of blocks of text connected by electronic links, it offers different pathways to users . . . the extent of hypertext is unknowable because it lacks clear boundaries and is often multi-authored" (Snyder, 1998: 126–7). To use Eco's (1979) terms, the distinction between "virtual" and "realized" text is greater for interactive media, particularly for the flexible, impermanent, non-linear, hypertextual data structures of the Internet.

Potentially, the text-reader metaphor of reception studies may prove particularly apt for the new focus on the *interface*. Whether for the Internet, or digital television, or mobile technologies, analyzing the interface is proving demanding, for both designers and users (Star & Bowker, 2002), bringing questions of literacy increasingly to the fore (Tyner, 1998). Literacy has, of course, underpinned all previous phases of "audiencing," from the conventions of participating in public performances, to the emergence of print literacy, the more recent conceptions of audiovisual or media literacy required to decode the genres and conventions of cinema and television, to the new questions posed especially by interactive media, especially the Internet. And, as Luke (1989) points out, literacy – in encapsulating the cognitive and cultural competencies that underpin effective communication, and hence effective social functioning – has always been intimately related to questions of power and inequality. Here we return to a familiar debate within audience studies, now apparently to be replayed in the new media environment. For optimists celebrate the liberating potential of such an escape from the confines of the dominant text:

> In general, then, hypertext seems to *add* dimensions of writing, and to that extent may encourage new practices of reading as well: ones that might prove more hospitable to alternative, non-traditional points of view and more inclusive of cultural difference. (Burbules, 1997: 107)

And others are more pessimistic, identifying ways in which the World Wide Web remains more hierarchical than hypertextual, more commercial than public, more closed than open.

Conclusion

But all this is to anticipate the future. What should now be clear is that, throughout the latter half of the last century, in most industrialized countries, television has been a medium which has dominated and still does, for the moment at least, dominate our leisure hours, our national cultures, our domestic living rooms, and our modes of family life, all with a consistency and durability of reach and scale with which the media both preceding and following have not been able, and are unlikely, to compete (though interestingly, in non-industrialized countries, it remains radio which has the greatest reach). I have argued in this chapter that if research adopts a longer historical lens, we may begin to position our present theories of audiences in relation to actual audiences past and future.

We may then appreciate that to review contemporary audience research is to review a phenomenon unique to twentieth-century industrialized nations, namely the dominance of mass broadcast television and, hence, the heyday of the mass television audience. Such an appreciation makes the case for comparative research, both historical and cultural, ever more compelling. As I have begun to indicate, the history of audiences is now beginning to be told, and it already shows clearly that audiences were not the same before and will not be the same again. Interestingly, both in looking back and in looking forward, it is already proving easier to investigate the contexts within which people use media-as-objects than it is to identify the interpretive "work" with which audiences engage with media-as-texts. In this sense, then, it is in understanding audience reception past and future that the greater challenge remains if we are to keep in focus both audiences as consumers of media goods and audiences as interpreters of symbolic mediations.

Notes

I wish to thank Jay Blumler, Elihu Katz, Peter Lunt, and Angharad Valdivia for their constructive comments on an earlier version of this chapter.

1 Objects of fandom change, of course, but at present Harry Potter, by J. K. Rowling, is the UK's and US's top selling children's book (and, now, movie, game, website, merchandising theme, etc.), and Manchester United is the top UK and possibly European football (soccer) team. Barbie, however, is timeless.

References

Abercrombie, N. and Longhurst, B. (1998). *Audiences: A sociological theory of performance and imagination*. London: Sage.

Alasuutari, P. (ed.) (1999). *Rethinking the Media Audience*. London: Sage.

Alexander, S. (1994). *Becoming a Woman: and other essays in 19th and 20th century feminism*. Virago: London.

Allen, R. C. (ed.) (1987). *Channels of Discourse*. Chapel Hill: University of North Carolina Press.

Allor, M. (1988). Relocating the site of the audience. *Critical Studies in Mass Communication*, 5, 217–33.

Ang, I. (1985). *Watching DALLAS: Soap opera and the melodramatic imagination*. New York: Methuen.

Ang, I. (1990). *Desperately Seeking the Audience*. London: Routledge.

Ang, I. (1996). Ethnography and radical contextualism in audience studies. In J. Hay, L. Grossberg, and E. Wartella (eds.), *The Audience and Its Landscape*. Boulder, CO: Westview, pp. 247–69.

Becker, L. B. and Schoenbach, K. (eds.) (1989). *Audience Responses to Media Diversification: Coping with plenty*. Hillsdale, NJ: Lawrence Erlbaum.

Blumler, J. G., Gurevitch, M., and Katz, E. (1985). REACHING OUT: A future for gratifications research. In K. E. Rosengren, L. A. Wenner, and P. Palmgreen (eds.), *Media Gratifications Research: Current perspectives* . Beverly Hills, CA: Sage, pp. 255–73.

Burbules, N. C. (1997). Rhetorics of the web: Hyperreading and critical literacy. In I. Snyder (ed.), *Page to Screen: Taking literacy into the electronic era*. New South Wales: Allen and Unwin, pp. 102–22.

Butsch, R. (2000). *The Making of American Audiences: From stage to television, 1750–1990*. Cambridge: Cambridge University Press.

Carey, J. W. (1989). *Communication as Culture: Essays on media and society*. New York: Routledge.

Corner, J. (ed.) (1991). *Popular Television in Britain: Studies in cultural history*. London: British Film Institute.

Curran, J. (1990). The new revisionism in mass communication research. *European Journal of Communication*, 5(2–3), 135–64.

Davison, W. P. (1983). The third-person effect in communication. *Public Opinion Quarterly*, 47(1), 1–15.

Drotner, K. (1992). Modernity and media panics. In M. Skovmand and K. C. Schroeder (eds.), *Media Cultures: Reappraising transnational media*. London: Routledge, pp. 42–62.

Eco, U. (1979). *The Role of the Reader: Explorations in the semiotics of texts*. Bloomington: Indiana University Press.

Ellis, J. (1992). *Visible Fictions* (revised edn.). London: Routledge.

Erni, J. (1989). Where is the audience. *Journal of Communication Enquiry*, 13(2), 30–42.

Fischer, C. S. (1994). Changes in leisure activities, 1890–1940. *Journal of Social History*, Spring, 453–75.

Fischetti, M. (2001). The future of TV. *Technology Review*, November, 35–40.

Fiske, J. (1987). *Television Culture*. London: Methuen.

Fiske, J. (1992). Audiencing: a cultural studies approach to watching television. *Poetics*, 21, 345–59.

Flichy, P. (1995). *Dynamics of Modern Communication: The shaping and impact of new communication technologies*. London: Sage.

Gamson, W. A. (1992). *Talking Politics*. Cambridge: Cambridge University Press.

Hagen, I. and Wasko, J. (eds.) (2000). *Consuming Audiences? Production and reception in media research*. Cresskill, NJ: Hampton Press.

Hall, S. (1980). Encoding/Decoding. In S. Hall, D. Hobson, A. Lowe, and P. Willis (eds.), *Culture, Media, Language*. London: Hutchinson, pp. 128–38.

Hansen, M. (1991). *Babel and Babylon: Spectatorship in American silent film*. Cambridge, MA: Harvard University Press.

Hodge, R. and Tripp, D. (1986). *Children and Television: A semiotic approach*. Cambridge: Polity Press.

Hoijer, B. and Werner, A. (eds.) (1998). *Cultural Cognition: New perspectives in audience theory*. Gothenburg: Nordicom.

Iser, W. (1980). Interaction between text and reader. In S. R. Suleiman and I. Crosman (eds.), *The Reader in the Text: Essays on audience and interpretation*. Princeton: Princeton University Press, pp. 237–55.

Iyengar, S. (1991). *Is Anyone Responsible? How television frames political issues*. Chicago: University of Chicago Press.

Jensen, K. (1993). The past in the future: problems and potentials of historical reception studies. *Journal of Communication*, 43(4), 20–8.

Katz, E. (1979). The uses of Becker, Blumler and Swanson. *Communication Research*, 6(1), 74–83.

Liebes, T. and Katz, E. (1995). *The Export of Meaning: Cross-Cultural readings of DALLAS*. Cambridge: Polity Press.

Livingstone, S. (1998a). Audience research at the crossroads: the "implied audience" in media theory. *European Journal of Cultural Studies*, 1(2), 193–217.

Livingstone, S. (1998b). Relationships between media and audiences: prospects for future research. In T. Liebes and J. Curran (eds.), *Media, Culture, Identity: Essays in honour of Elihu Katz*. London: Routledge.

Livingstone, S. (1998c). *Making Sense of Television: The psychology of audience interpretation* (2nd edn.). London: Routledge.

Livingstone, S. (1999). New media, new audiences. *New Media and Society*, 1(1), 59–66.

Livingstone, S. (2002). *Young People and New Media: Childhood and the changing media environment*. London: Sage.

Livingstone, S., Allen, J., and Reiner, R. (2001). The audience for crime media 1946–91: A historical approach to reception studies. *Communication Review*, 4(2), 165–92.

Livingstone, S. M. and Lunt, P. K. (1994). *Talk on Television: Audience discussion and public debate*. London: Routledge.

Luke, C. (1989). *Pedagogy, Printing and Protestantism: The discourse on childhood*. Albany, NY: State University of New York Press.

MacCabe, C. (1974). Realism and the cinema. *Screen*, 15(2), 7–27.

Mackay, H. (ed.) (1997). *Consumption and Everyday Life*. London: Sage.

Marvin, C. (1988). *When Old Technologies Were New: Thinking about electric communication in the late nineteenth century*. Oxford: Oxford University Press.

McQuail, D. (1997). *Audience Analysis*. London: Sage.

Moores, S. (1988). The box on the dresser: memories of early radio and everyday life. *Media, Culture and Society*, 10, 23–40.

Moores, S. (1996). *Satellite Television and Everyday Life: Articulating technology*. Luton: John Libbey Media.

Morley, D. (1986). *Family Television: Cultural power and domestic leisure*. London: Comedia.

Morley, D. (1992). *Television, Audiences and Cultural Studies*. London: Routledge.

Morley, D. (1993). Active audience theory: Pendulums and pitfalls. *Journal of Communication*, 43(4), 13–19.

Mosco, V. (1996). *The Political Economy of Communication*. Thousand Oaks, CA: Sage.

Moyal, A. (1995). The feminine culture of the telephone: People, patterns and policy. In N. Heap, R. Thomas, G. Einon, R. Mason, and H. Mackay (eds.), *Information Technology and Society: A reader*. London: Sage, pp. 284–310.

Neuman, W. R. (1991). *The Future of the Mass Audience*. Cambridge: Cambridge University Press.

Nightingale, V. (1996). *Studying the Television Audience*. London: Routledge.

O'Brien, M. and Eyles, A. (1993) (eds.) *Enter the Dream-House: Memories of cinema in south London from the twenties to the sixties*. London: Museum of the Moving Image.

Radway, J. (1984). *Reading the Romance: Women, patriarchy and popular literature*. Chapel Hill: University of North Carolina Press.

Radway, J. (1988). Reception study: ethnography and the problems of dispersed audiences and nomadic subjects. *Cultural Studies*, 2(3), 359–76.

Richards, J. and Sheridan, D. (eds.) (1987). *Mass-Observation at the Movies*. London: Routledge & Kegan Paul.

Samuel, R. and Thompson, E. P. (eds.) (1990). *Myths We Live By*. London: Routledge.

Scannell, P. (1988). Radio times: The temporal arrangements of broadcasting in the modern world. In P. Drummond and R. Paterson (eds.), *Television and its Audience: International research perspectives*. London: British Film Institute, pp. 15–31.

Schiller, H. I. (1989). *Culture Inc.: The corporate takeover of public expression*. New York: Oxford University Press.

Schroeder, K. C. (1994). Audience semiotics, interpretive communities and the "ethnographic turn" in media research. *Media, Culture and Society*, 16, 337–47.

Schudson, M. (1991). Historical approaches to communication studies. In K. B. Jensen and N. W. Jankowski (eds.), *A Handbook of Qualitative Methodologies for Mass Communication Research*. London: Routledge, pp. 151–62.

Seaman, W. R. (1992). Active audience theory: pointless populism. *Media, Culture and Society*, 14, 301–11.

Silverstone, R. (1990). Television and everyday life: towards an anthropology of the television audience. In M. Ferguson (ed.), *Public Communication: The new imperatives*. London: Sage, pp. 173–89.

Silverstone, R. (1994). *Television and Everyday Life*. London: Routledge.

Slater, D. (2002) Social relationships and identity online and offline. In L. Lievrouw and S. Livingstone (eds.), *Handbook of New Media: Social shaping and consequences of ICTs*. London: Sage.

Snyder, I. (1998). Beyond the hype: reassessing hypertext. In I. Snyder (ed.), *Page to Screen: Taking literacy into the electronic era*. London and New York: Routledge, pp. 125–43.

Spigel, L. (1992). *Make room for TV: Television and the family ideal in postwar America*. Chicago: University of Chicago Press.

Stacey, J. (1994). *Star Gazing: Hollywood cinema and female spectatorship*. London: Routledge.

Star, L. and Bowker, G. (2002). How to infrastructure. In L. Lievrouw and S. Livingstone (eds.), *Handbook of New Media: Social shaping and consequences of ICTs*. London: Sage.

Thompson, J. B. (1995). *The Media and Modernity: A social theory of the media*. Cambridge: Polity.

Tulloch, J. (2000). *Watching Television Audiences: Cultural theories and methods*. London: Arnold.

Tyner, K. (1998). *Literacy in a Digital World*. Mahwah, NJ: Lawrence Erlbaum.

Willis, P. (1990). *Common Culture*. Buckingham, UK: Open University Press.

Wilson, T. (1993). *Watching Television: Hermeneutics, reception and popular culture*. Cambridge: Polity Press.

CHAPTER SEVENTEEN

The Cultural Revolution in Audience Research

Virginia Nightingale

In the late 1960s and 1970s, as a result of cultural revolution in the western world, the university underwent a major change in its cultural and political self-understanding. Indeed, the university was a major contributor to political and cultural unrest.

(Gerard Delanty, 2001, p. 60)

Perhaps because of their relative newness as cultural phenomena, the audiences of broadcast media have been the focus of considerable public concern and academic research since the introduction of radio broadcasting in the 1920s. In the 1960s and 1970s, debates among academic audience researchers focused on method and whether it was better to use quantitative or qualitative, experimental or interpretative approaches. Effects research was stereotyped as quantitative and empiricist, and qualitative research as unscientific, unreliable and interpretative. By the 1970s, the nature of the debate on method had become more sophisticated, and theoretical, and evidence of this shift can be seen in the competing claims made by "uses and gratifications" researchers (Katz, Blumler, & Gurevitch, 1974), and those who believed that a "cultural" approach to audience research was necessary (Carey & Kreiling, 1974; Elliott, 1974). The publication of the "encoding/decoding" model by Stuart Hall in the 1970s was a challenge to "empiricist" researchers, and a vehicle for the presentation of an alternative manifesto. This model outlined a project for what a cultural approach to audiences should encompass. It formed part of the "cultural revolution" in the universities to which Delanty (2001) refers.

In his recent book, Gerard Delanty (2001) has typified this knowledge contest as one between "science" and "culture," and claims that science and culture[1] compete for dominance in the hierarchies of university knowledge cultures. He has suggested that, for the latter half of the twentieth century, Western universities have been required to adapt to increasing demands for instrumentalism in both the academic and the managerial spheres of their activity. At the same time, Delanty claims, divisions within the academy have been exacerbated by a process he described as the democratization of knowledge that has resulted in culture wars over ownership and authorship of knowledge. This process was initiated by the post-World War II expansion of access to higher education, which enabled people previously excluded from the academy through poverty, gender, race or disability, to bring about changes in university curricula and research agendas. These new recruits to university life often pursued a revisionist agenda, which resulted in previously excluded sources of knowledge and ways of knowing being recognized within academic circles as legitimate subjects for rigorous investigation.

Delanty asks us to imagine university knowledge as a pendulum, swinging between culture and science. In the Humanities during the 1960s and 1970s, the knowledge pendulum began to swing away from "science," then often represented by behaviorism, positivism and empiricism, and in the direction of "culture." The swing gathered momentum not only because of the political convictions of younger academics in the mid-1960s, but also because cultural criticism and theory were generating new ideas about the ways culture works. The nexus between psychoanalysis, structuralism, and the analysis of the visual image (see, for example Metz, 1982 [1981]; Berger, 1976) was particularly attractive to media researchers, especially when later linked to social semiotics (see Kress & van Leeuwen, 1990).

Some time during the late 1980s and early 1990s, the pendulum reached its cultural peak and began a trajectory back into "scientific" territory. The return is evident in the ways traditional disciplines have begun to secure their contested boundaries against the interdisciplinary studies that characterized the height of the "cultural" season. "Scientific" advances, particularly in neurobiology, genetics, and neuropsychology, are encouraging researchers to consider re-theorizing "cultural" problems to take the new knowledge generated by science into consideration. Added to this, the achievement of the technical capacity to process large and complex data fields, a feature of the computerized knowledge environment, now suggests that alternative methods and approaches for the study of cultural phenomena may be possible. In other words, some research problems that we previously believed could be solved only by cultural approaches may be recast as questions for "science," and scientific enquiry.

From Science to Culture – the 1970s Revisited

In the audience research context of the 1970s and 1980s, the encoding/decoding approach played a key role in turning the tide against science, and towards culture. It encouraged the recognition of cross-disciplinary and inter-disciplinary studies as a means to explore problems of audience in new ways. Encoding/decoding challenged the instrumental and functionalist approaches to the study of communication that had flourished during the 1950s. That functionalist position had been motivated by political concerns about propaganda and persuasion (Mattelart, 2000; Merton, 1968 [1949]) and about the relationship between control of information and the maintenance of social control. This agenda was turned upside down by the cultural revolution of the 1960s and replaced by a politics of knowledge that sought to empower marginal and excluded voices. In this context, encoding/decoding presented itself as an alternative research practice. In stark contrast to the instrumentalism of the "uses and gratifications" approach, encoding/decoding sought to win over "instrumentalists" by borrowing research methods from other recognized disciplines – most notably ethnography and cultural anthropology, but also from literary theory and linguistics – and by daring to address research problems that were considered "too hard" or "inaccessible" for existing social science methods. The pretensions of encoding/decoding, as scientific practice lay in the complex combination of semiotics, European structuralist anthropology (Lévi-Strauss, 1978), the British culturalist traditions (ethnography and documentarism), cultural history (Raymond Williams and Richard Hoggart), and in the appropriation of Darwin's theory of evolution and its application to culture, as pioneered by George Herbert Mead (1977, pp. 1–18). This multi-disciplinary hotchpotch of science and culture was revolutionary at the time, particularly for its attempt to combine empirical audience research with criticism and cultural activism.

The Encoding/Decoding Model

The encoding/decoding model was first outlined by Stuart Hall in the early 1970s.[2] After the publication of his innovative research into the *Panorama* program, Hall had ventured the opinion that "there seems some ground for thinking that a new and exciting phase in so-called audience research, of a quite new kind, may be opening up" (Hall, 1980 [1973], p. 131). The encoding/decoding model proposed a framework for the study of mass communication that encompassed audiences, production teams and the broader culture, as active players in its process (see Hall, 1980 [1973], p. 130).

The approach included three levels of analysis. At the level of the infrastructure of everyday life, it proposed that the researcher should take account of at least three aspects of social structures: the frameworks of knowledge, the relations of production, and the technical infrastructure that supports these. This is the social context that creates both production teams and audiences, and that generates a need for the continuous remaking of society's ideas about itself (its legitimating discourses), and about the people (historically and culturally situated persons) who endorse and so refresh those discourses in the process of living in that world. Those familiar with Arjun Appadurai's framework for exploring the disjunctures in contemporary society may recognize here, in embryonic form, premonitions of the "*technoscape*," and "*financescape*" (Appadurai, 1996, chapter 2). The social infrastructure was understood as the source of the materials for the production of material culture. In the particular instance addressed by encoding/decoding, material culture takes the form of mass media programmes, which both document and typify the ideas and interests competing for recognition and dominance in society. The second level of analysis focused on the meaning structures that were in operation in the processes of both encoding and decoding. Again, the similarity to Appadurai's notion of the "ideascape" should be noted. The model assumed that the discernment of a "message" in the media programme is subject to the interested/motivated deployment of discourse. Two "moments" exercise a determinative impact on the message: the moment of encoding and the moment of decoding. At the moment of "encoding," message production is subject to the meaning structures in play within the production teams.[3] At the moment of decoding, message production is subject to the meaning structures at play in the life worlds of audience members.[4] The message "decoded" may bear little, if any, relation to the meanings the production teams thought they were creating, but is nevertheless far from random.[5] The third level of analysis concentrated on the programme as "meaningful discourse." It can be likened to an embryonic version of Appadurai's "mediascape." Both encoding and decoding contribute to the socially "meaningful discourse" produced by a programme.[6]

The encoding/decoding model was more successful than other cultural approaches in promoting audience research as a cultural process, but it failed to establish itself as scientific practice. It was, in my view, insufficiently responsive to the methodological difficulties it created and to the requirement, inherent in the model, for a radical re-evaluation of the role of the researcher. I have discussed these issues elsewhere (Nightingale, 1989; Nightingale, 1996), but specifically the model called into question the role of the researcher as a self-appointed spokesperson for an audience.[7] It legitimated a different role: that of advocate and committed group member taking on the role of apologist, translator and interpreter of the interests and ideals of the group.[8] Secondly, the model failed to advocate a sufficiently sophisticated analysis of texts. Once the question of the audience's views of the text is raised, the nature of the audience member's experience of the text must be addressed, and the relation of that knowledge to the researcher's knowledge of the text questioned.[9] The television programme, for example, does not, and cannot, exist as an analyzable entity before interpretation. Interpretation by both the researcher and the audience informs all research discussion of the text. Furthermore, the complexity of television series and serials as cultural forms was underestimated. And lastly, given the pretensions of the model to the contrary, it unnecessarily limited the activity of audiences to a reactive or responsive role.

"Uses and Gratifications" – the 1970s "Instrumental" Alternative

"Uses and gratifications" was the "instrumental" Other to the cultural approach proposed by encoding/decoding. By briefly returning to the debates that surrounded "uses and gratifications" in the 1970s, it is possible to recapture some of the reasons why a "cultural" approach was preferred. When Katz, Blumler, and

Gurevitch (1974) summarized the "uses and gratifications" approach, they presented its five principal assumptions:

1 That audience members are engaged in goal directed activity.
2 The initiative for linking need gratification with media choice lies with the audience member.
3 The media compete with other sources of need satisfaction and therefore should be understood in this context.
4 People are sufficiently self-aware to be able to report their interests and motives.
5 Audience orientations should be explored on their own terms in order to be able to differentiate the findings of "uses and gratifications" research from "much speculative writing about popular culture." (précis based on Katz, Blumler, & Gurevitch, 1974, pp. 21–2)

At first glance these assumptions may not appear particularly "instrumental." Four of the assumptions concern the manner in which people are judged to be "active" in their media choice: they are driven by needs, they take the initiative, they select among the various media available, and they possess the capacity for self-reporting. The fifth "assumption" is more an injunction: the researcher is advised to avoid engaging in speculation about popular culture when interpreting findings, and instead remain true to the terminology chosen by the research participants.

Since most of the researchers who worked on "uses and gratifications" projects were functionalist sociologists or social psychologists, researchers who are less inclined than many to engage in speculative hypothesis, one cannot help wondering what led Katz, Blumler, and Gurevitch to speak so strongly against "speculative writing about popular culture," and to feel the need to distance themselves from it. An answer is available, at least in part, from James Carey and Albert Kreiling (1974) who contributed a useful deconstruction of "uses and gratifications" to the Blumler and Katz reader (1974). Carey and Kreiling contended that even though the assumptions put forward as the ground rules for "uses and gratifications" sound like common sense, they are in fact value-based theoretical positions. They argued that the approach was functionalist, and actively promoted a systems model of the social order; that it was informed by a naïve and undeveloped aesthetic theory, and by an implicit utilitarianism. They were pessimistic about the chances that "uses and gratifications" could adjust to the changes that would be required to provide an adequate critical evaluation of mass communication. They argued that "uses and gratifications" would need to develop, at the very least, a conception of man as a cultural being. This would entail recognizing that the multiple realities[10] in which people participate in the process of everyday living invest a media message with complicated and competing significances. For example, a father may also be a politician, a member of a minority group, a musician and a worker, and therefore, depending on the nature of a news report, respond to it with very mixed emotions and thoughts. They argued that "uses and gratifications" does not make sense as a model of mass communication because it assumes a means/ends relation between people and the media. It proposes that motives must be instrumental, rather than recognizing that they may also be "non-purposive" (Carey & Kreiling, 1974, pp. 242–5).

Carey and Kreiling responded to the "speculative writing" statement by linking it to a popular culture debate which had polarised the US academic community in the late 1950s. The protagonists in the 1950s debate had been Dwight MacDonald, Edward Shils, and C. Wright Mills. Somewhat predictably, according to Carey and Kreiling, MacDonald and Mills had condemned popular culture: MacDonald because he claimed it undermined both folk culture and elite culture; Mills because he saw in popular culture a threat to "authentic democratic community" through the control and manipulation of popular culture by political, economic and academic elites. Shils preferred the "no effects" view, that "taste was neither debased nor exploited" (Carey & Kreiling, 1974, p. 225). The debate lacked protagonists prepared to wholeheartedly defend popular culture, and eventually disappeared from the radar screens of US cultural debate, until, in a strange return of the repressed, it reappeared as a warning light in the "uses and gratifications" manifesto. Carey and Kreiling believed that the study of mass communication and popular culture depended on an appropriate theory of cultural forms. In evidence they cited Katz's own study of the Yom Kippur War in Israel (Peled & Katz, 1974), unarguably one of the best examples of "uses and gratifications" research, and suggested that the strength of the study was dependent in no small measure on the personal experiences and cultural knowledge of the authors, but that this cultural dependence was not acknowledged by "uses and gratifications" researchers. Carey and Kreiling argued that "uses and gratifications" research "fails to link the functions of mass media consumption with the symbolic content of the mass-communicated materials or with the actual experience of consuming them" (Carey & Kreiling, 1974, p. 232).

At the heart of Carey and Kreiling's critique is a dismissal of the ways functionalism had become an exercise in empiricism, and, in this respect, ceased to be "science." Carey and Kreiling criticised the tendency of "uses and gratifications" researchers to regard "psychological and sociological variables as real and primary, and culture as a derivative agent and manifestation of them" (1974, p. 233). In the 1970s it was widely accepted, contrary to the characterization of cultural knowledge advanced by Delanty (Delanty, 2001), that the type of cultural knowledge advocated in encoding/decoding, was "scientific." Encoding/decoding proposed that mass communication be studied in terms of a theory of culture, and for them this meant structuralism.

The criticisms of "uses and gratifications" among British researchers mirrored those expressed by Carey and Kreiling. Morley, for example, identified two major flaws in "uses and gratifications": first, that it was insufficiently cultural, in that it demonstrated little understanding of how popular cultural forms create meaning, and secondly that it was too "psychologistic" and insufficiently "socio-logical" (Morley, 1980, p. 13). Taking a psychological and individualist perspective indicated that the positivist approaches to psychology and social psychology, popular with many US researchers at the time, acted to cover up incipient relativism. The impoverishment of the sociology used in such studies was evident in the unquestioning acceptance of individualism, which meant that the social could take only one form, that of aggregates of individuals. Morley quoted Graham Murdock's argument that:

> To provide anything like a satisfactory account of the relationship between people's mass media involvements and their overall social situation and meaning system, it is necessary to start from the social setting rather than the individual: to replace the idea of personal "needs" with the notion of structural contradiction; and to introduce the notion of subculture. . . . (Graham Murdock, quoted in Morley, 1980, p. 14)

Murdock proposed a contextual approach, whereby social theory would provide an account of social location, and therefore of the structural limitations on the interpretative options open to particular viewers. This is an important understanding, because the statistical methods that are used to explore aggregates of individuals systematically obscure the structural differences that social theory counts as the source of cultural difference. In addition, Murdock drew attention to the British subcultures tradition (see for examples, Halloran, Elliott, & Murdock, 1970; Jock Young, 1971; Willis, 1977; Hebdige, 1975), a tradition which appreciated that media activities occur in localized networks of social relationships, everyday interactions, and class and/or religious affiliations. The subcultures tradition acknowledged that people live their lives, including their media activities, constrained and counseled by those with whom they interact on a daily basis. This is the central concept in a cultural orientation to audience research, and it differentiates the cultural perspective from individualism, which holds that a person is motivated by internally (personal, psychological) driven needs, wants and cognitions. It is the reason why "uses and gratifications" appears to remain an acceptable approach for some psychologists (see, for example Cantor, 1998), but not for culture theorists.

The key differences that separate instrumental approaches like "uses and gratifications" from cultural approaches like "encoding/decoding" include a) a theory of cultural forms, b) a cultural definition of "man," and c) a theory of cultural participation that is rooted in cultural investment in the reproduction of particular ideas, knowledge and imagery. Instrumental approaches, by contrast, focus on expedience and people management; on the choices made by individuals and the ways these can be managed. Delanty (Delanty, 2001) has described this distinction as a difference between cultural democracy and scientific management. In each approach quite a different importance is attached to the role of the researcher and to the rights of research participants to shape the nature of the writing about them.

Culture and Audiences

At the heart of the cultural approach lay recognition of the difference between researching audiences as people and researching audience as an event or happening. The naïve approach to audience imagines audiences as people. This is why the first coherent and complex studies of broadcast audiences in the 1920s were exercises in people counting (e.g. telephone surveys) that led to the establishment of the ratings system (Beville, 1988). But audience measurement does not answer questions about why people tune in and whether they are satisfied with the information and entertainment provided. So, by the 1940s, functionalist researchers had begun to argue for the development of "middle range" theorization (Merton, 1968 [1949], chapter 2) where interest in the media was "instrumental," and cultural variables were represented as "intervening" variables. Intervening variables were seen as interfering with the smooth operation of communication, and ways of systematically grouping them and managing their impact were sought (see De Fleur & Ball-Rokeach, 1977 [1966], for early examples).

In the academic cultural revolution of the 1960s, the control mentality informing this "administrative" way of knowing was strongly questioned and the piecemeal fragmentation of culture into measurable bits was considered unacceptable. The type of "cultural" analysis proposed offered a holistic approach to understanding mass communication by recognizing both the agency and cultural power available to audiences. In doing so, however, it shifted the emphasis away from the *people* researched and onto the *contextual relations* in which they were located, as David Morley (1986) explained in his study of family television viewing patterns (Morley, 1986, chapter 3). This emphasis marks the difference between researching audiences as people and researching audiences as spaces. Ien Ang (1991) has described this distinction in the following way:

> From the institutional point of view, watching television is the decontextualized measurable viewing behaviour that is taken to be the indicator for the existence of a clear-cut "television audience" out there; from the virtual standpoint of actual audiences, watching television is the ill-defined shorthand term for the multiplicity of situated practices and experiences in which television audiencehood is embedded. (Ang, 1991, p. 165)

The idea of audience as a sociocultural space provides a key to explaining the changes cultural approaches have made to the audience research repertoire. Its presence in the assumptions of cultural approaches has made it possible for insights from various humanities disciplines to experiment with interdisciplinary initiatives and multi-genre methods, and particularly for theories of cultural forms and the nature of human engagement with them to be brought to bear on the audience research agenda. Recognition of the difference between audiences (people) and audience (space) is important because it clarifies an ontological distinction masked by the common use of the one word, audience.

Since it is sometimes difficult to come to terms with the fact that the word "audience" does not always refer to a group of people, it is useful is to consider the meanings listed for the word *audience* in a good dictionary. My dictionary, for example, provides four meanings, though this is by no means an exhaustive list of the *signifieds* the word can evoke. Two meanings refer to audiences as people; and two to *happenings* where audience occurs. The meanings cited are:

1 The people assembled at an event or performance.
2 The people addressed by a film, book or play.
3 The unfolding interaction that occurs when one or several person(s) questions or interrogates one or several others (a *happening*).
4 The hearing that occurs when people are permitted to express their views, or present their case, in their own words. (Adapted from the *Concise Oxford Dictionary*, 1995, Oxford: Clarendon Press)

Four discrete phenomena, all described by the term "audience," are expressed in this list: a group of people; an image of a group of people; a happening; and a hearing. The word "*audience*" is used in conjunction with all four meanings. Most research about the "people assembled" and the "people addressed" falls into the category of research about people, but the focus of the cultural approach to audience research has been on the *happening* and *hearing* meanings. *Happening* and *hearing* suggest that the audience may be understood as a space where meanings are created, challenged, negotiated, reassessed, resisted or accepted.

The People Assembled

The practice of researching the people who assemble to witness a performance, or to view/listen to broadcasting, changed very little with the "cultural turn," in spite of a vigorous denunciation of the ratings system by advocates of a cultural approach in the 1980s and 1990s.[11] Audience measurement is cushioned from cultural criticism by its inherent usefulness to key economic and political interests. Audience ratings are a commodity provided to broadcasters and advertisers for the limited and highly specific purpose of providing audience measurement data. Ratings also support a simplistic, but nevertheless appealing myth that broadcasters provide what viewers want. Ratings do contribute to social and cultural change, as Joseph Turow (1997) has shown, because they provide the data on which advertising strategies and production planning and scheduling are based. And advertising strategies fragment the audience, which in turn facilitates cultural change. The emphasis on audience demographics makes it easier to divide the mass audience into segments that are useful for advertising's purposes.[12]

As the critics of "uses and gratifications" pointed out so long ago, seeing audiences as aggregations assumes that allegiance to pre-existing social and cultural formations is irrelevant, and for the TV channel and marketing executives who commission ratings services this is the case. The larger social and cultural groupings to which people belong are ignored while the individual differences that divide people are exaggerated. This has also been the case in much psychological and social-psychological[13] research about audiences. Yet cultural researchers have also failed to take up the challenge of investigating the consequences of the impact of ratings based decision-making on mass broadcasting, and with few exceptions, psychologists, sociologists and market researchers still map and measure audiences, monitor their choices, their spending power and their interests against every conceivable individual difference: demographic, geographic or psychographic.

The "People Addressed"

The second meaning, the "people addressed," refers to a group of people imagined by a person or persons who have created a communication of some kind. It draws attention to the fact that the creators of messages develop ideas and preconceptions about the people who will eventually engage with their communication, and that these ideas are actively deployed during the writing process. Authors, writers and production professionals actively imagine the ways audiences will respond to their works. They try to second-guess this imaginary audience in much the same way that we create imaginary others to comment on our actions in the process of constructing a self. This "image audience" has generated two types of audience research: research about the audience imagined (found in various types of literary criticism, such as reader-in-the-text criticism and reader–response criticism); and research about the real people the message-makers would like to interest in their product (found in audience development research, some marketing research, and taste cultures research).

If we accept that the audience addressed reflects or mirrors a real or potential audience which, given careful marketing and promotion, may materialize as box office sales, then the more that is known about real audiences and their cultural interests, the more successfully products that directly address that audience should be developed, packaged, or marketed. It is assumed that such products will offer greater pleasure and satisfaction to audiences.[14] Audience development is informed by a belief that the more carefully the cultural tastes of the audience are reflected in a cultural form, the more successfully that form will attract users.

Because audience development addresses the conjuncture between the cultural work and its use, it has effectively combined a theory of cultural forms with the study of the use of those forms. This approach has been particularly valued in the arts policy context (see Bennett, Emmison, & Frow, 1999) where the audience research doubles as justification for the allocation of public funding to institutions that cater to small subsets of the general public. Bennett, Emmison, and Frow anchor their research in the early work on taste cultures by Herbert Gans (1974), and on research into the links between social class and cultural taste by the late Pierre Bourdieu (1984 [1979]). Bourdieu's research, in particular, contributed an understanding of the ways preferences for particular genres and forms become ingrained in the ongoing pattern of daily life, and therefore contribute to the structural continuity of such works.

But "audience development" as currently practiced has discarded the more complex argumentation about the nature of publics and taste cultures. The idea that audiences can be actively developed for particular works, and that works should address the tastes of the audience can be seen in the provision of children's culture, where a reception climate is routinely planned as a component of television or film production (Seiter, 1993; Pecora, 1998). Spin-offs are preplanned, merchandizing is licensed, and the ways audiences will incorporate the particular product in their lives is carefully fostered – at least up to the point of sale.

The final site where the concept of the audience as image has begun to make its mark is in the field of Internet marketing, where it is known by the name of customer relationship marketing (CRM). CRM is an approach to data management that proposes to tailor the options offered to a customer to the customer's history of preferences and past choices (Gronroos, 1994). It is a marketing tool, where the emphasis has shifted to the creation and maintenance of a comfortable and ongoing relationship between product development, marketing and customer lifestyle. The emphasis in CRM is on the establishment of an ongoing relationship between businesses and their customers by making the customer's experience of the relationship so comfortable and satisfying that the customer never feels a need to look at a competitor's products.

It is possible then to demonstrate an evolution in audience research, from a cultural approach developed in literary criticism, to an instrumental approach based on the definition of audience as the "audience addressed." This transition has been accelerated by technological developments that make it possible to process very large amounts of data instantaneously, and to translate these into customized options. The combination of a functionalist needs–based model with a theoretical understanding of cultural forms based in taste cultures and the study of media use (Lunt & Livingstone, 1992; Singh, 2001) is again gaining ground.

Audience as "Happening" – an "Interview with the Media" Approach

[The room] has the atmosphere of a showdown. Though there are only four of them, the people in the room seem to make more noise now than in any other game. The din of the kick-off is echoed in this room. Big tackles and skilled play are applauded whole-heartedly by the "team" that makes the movement, and ignored or abused by the two supporters of the team being hit, who blame the referee for inaction with comments such as, "C'mon ref., did you see what he did to us then?" (From the notes of a student participant observer, quoted in Nightingale, 1992, p. 164)

In the incident described above, the "happening" under observation was the domestic viewing of the broadcast of the final match of a football season, and the analysis focused on the repercussions within the household of this particular viewing. Three young men, and the father of one, were all engaged in a boisterous viewing: those present insulted, pushed, wrestled, paced up and down, ran their fingers through their hair, and shouted at each other and at the television set. Even though the dictionary defines the third meaning of audience as a "formal interview with someone in authority," audience researchers have taken up the "interview" model and used it in less strictly formal ways, substituting the media for the authority figure.

There are two reasons why this meaning proved popular with audience researchers, particularly those who pursue cultural approaches. First, it emphasized audience activity, especially physical rather than cognitive activity and secondly it identified the spaces where people engage with media as worthy of study in their own right. In audience, activity is an exercise not just in cognition, but also in physical action. And it takes place "somewhere." Audience demands action from various components of a person's body in addition to their brain: hands, arms, skeletal structure to hold a book or newspaper; eyes to read; ears to listen to radio; fingers/touch to respond to the Internet; voices to provide talk for a talk show. The interview model expanded the scope of activity recognized as relevant to audience. It now includes not just culture and cultural form, but also body and place. Yet the promise of "incorporated" studies of audience has still not been realized.

The reasons for the neglect of embodiment and space in the study of audience lie in the links between the cultural approach and the subcultures model. In the interpretation of audience happenings, researchers sought inspiration from the subcultures research tradition, which had spawned encoding/decoding and which also identified situated practices as its core research data. In definitional terms too, "subcultures" research had sought to differentiate itself from the same generic human groups as audiences: namely, publics, masses, crowds, communities and cultures. It was assumed that methodological approaches that worked for subcultures would also work for audiences. In some cases, particularly in Dick Hebdige's research on popular music, the interchangeability of audience and subculture was almost complete: punks listen to punk music; rastas listen to reggae; in such conjunctures, the origins and meaning of the music are explained by the actions and experiences of the group – except that this neat formula does not explain the popularity of punk music in Japan; or of reggae in Australia. Because its point of departure from a norm was national rather than global, the subcultures approach overlooked the broader "world culture" implications of the intertextual borrowing that was going on (not to mention the considerable mainstream audience for both reggae and punk music). By assuming that the research approaches that explained subcultures would achieve the same results for audiences, cultural research lost touch with mainstream media studies. Clearly, audiences and subcultures cannot be equated, even as analogues of each other, without losing the specificity of audience studies.

Stanley Cohen (1997 [1980]) levelled another criticism against some subcultures researchers. He argued that they were fixated on an unnecessarily limited range of concepts, and complained in 1980, for example, that embodiment had been reduced to style, and performance to symbolic or magical resistance, and that the overuse of these concepts could be held responsible for the stereotypical analyses the subcultures approach produced:

> Whether the objects for decoding are Teddy Boys, Mods and Rockers, Skinheads or Punks, two dominant themes are suggested: first that style – whatever else it is – is essentially a type of *resistance* to subordination; secondly, that the form taken by this resistance is somehow *symbolic* or *magical*, in the sense of not being an actual, successful solution to whatever is the problem. The phrase "resistance through ritual" clearly announces these two themes. (1997 [1980], p. 154)

Cohen believed that the symbolic resistance mindset had the potential to blindfold researchers to the complex and nuanced operations of culture, including the diverse reactions to situations and contexts within a culture or subculture.

Other characteristics of the cultural approach to audience research can also be traced to the subcultures tradition. In 1989, I (Nightingale, 1989) commented on the practice among "cultural" audience researchers of describing their work as "ethnography." The dependence on the subcultures tradition, and on ethnography, was a way of tying research practices and conventions to the broader, Anglo-American history of cultural studies. In audience research, this development offered a release from the empiricist practices of the past. As Sarah Thornton has noted, the subcultures tradition drew on important sociological studies by the Chicago School of Sociology, starting with studies from the 1930s. It had, in her words, created "a productive tension between sociological/anthropological approaches and textual/semiotic approaches to subcultures" (Thornton, 1997, p. 6). Rather than proving a "productive tension" however, the discomfort of the relation created between sociological/anthropological approaches and textual/semiotic approaches, was met with denial. The response to denial was to conflate audience and text, so that both the people and the artefacts of the subculture were treated as texts in their own right. As a result, audiences and audience practices were exoticised. This tendency can be seen in its early stages in Hebdige's study of punk (Hebdige, 1979).

In the 1980s, the passive stereotypes for audiences (couch potatoes; boob tube suckers; drug addicts) were replaced by a Rabelaisian cast of "active" and exotic audience characterizations: nomads, poachers, fanatics, queers. The researcher's chosen terminology usually singled out, and exaggerated, some characteristic of the subculture which was then taken as a "sign" of the inherent nature of its engagement with the media. And the choice of a group to justify the research meant that researchers stopped looking for "audience problems" to investigate.

The exotic nature of the group was sufficient justification for its selection. The exoticization of audience groups encouraged an intensification of the existing identification within cultural approaches to audience research with ethnography, and an escalation of interdisciplinary borrowing.

Interdisciplinary borrowing is a double-edged sword, and it has proved to be so in the case of cultural audience research, where it precipitated the recuperation of the cultural approach back into the traditional discipline, ethnography. Now ethnographic projects displace media problematics. This has left a void where a significant critique of contemporary media should have developed, and it has left the specificity of audience and its contribution to the contemporary mediascape unexamined.

Other cultural approaches have, however, remained focused on audience as "happening." This has been the case with cultural histories that have explored changes in reading, listening and viewing through the ages. For example Richard Leppert (1995), in *The Sight of Sound*, explored the ways visual representation of people laboring to both produce and listen to musical performance reminds us of the variety of body sensations (in addition to listening) that are required to make music; that its visual representation speaks of the ephemerality of music by its silence; that gender and class relations make listening an intensely political activity, and much more. While his research is instructive about people and customs associated with the experience of music from the seventeenth through the nineteenth centuries, his exploration never wavers from its exploration of the experience of the music, even though the musical works cannot be represented in such a study. Similarly, Christopher Small (1998), who has used a very different approach to the history of music in his book, *Musicking*, draws a distinction between the study of music and that of musical works. Small makes the point that, "Music is not a thing at all but an activity, something that people do" (p. 20), and goes on to explain that, "to pay attention in any way to a musical performance, including a recorded performance, even to Muzak in an elevator, is to music" (p. 9). In this context, listening becomes part of the broader context of the phenomenology of music. Again, with the medium of the book, Alberto Manguel (*A History of Reading*, 1997) has explored the experience of reading, from the process of learning to read to the indulgence of guilty reading passions. Every aspect of engagement with the written word is explored with the commonality of reader experiences in mind, and with attention to the technological development and socio-cultural meaning of the medium. Ancient and more recent historical documentation is brought to bear on the task of explaining what the act of reading has meant in the past and what it means today. Finally, Marina Warner's *From the Beast to the Blonde* (1994) noted the manner in which fairy tales are told and the impact of the relationships established between storyteller and listener on the nature and meaning of the tales.

These works explore audience spaces in past and present cultures, and engage in an excavation of the evolution of media experiences. Cultural works feature in these histories, but in their performance, embodiment and contextual relations rather than as cultural representation. Cultural histories such as these provide background knowledge essential for understanding the media today, and demonstrate how cultural approaches to the study of audience have been able to take advantage of opportunities offered by an understanding of audience as a happening, in a specific cultural space, in ways that instrumental approaches could not. Such studies have moved a long way from the early encoding/decoding approach in audience research, and in doing so they produced unexpected outcomes, some promising and some not. Perhaps the most disappointing outcome has been the abrogation of the initial purpose of so-called ethnographic audience research: to explain the media and their sociocultural operations.

Hearing (Audition)

The fourth, and final, meaning of the word audience is as a "hearing" or "audition." The meaning suggested is that a person will be offered an opportunity to have their say, and to be listened to. Good examples of this type of "audience" are available in talkback radio and in some popular television talk shows, like *Oprah*, *Judge Judy*, and *The Jerry Springer Show*, among others, where audience/hearing has become a performance in its own right. These programmes offer "an audience" to the audience. Participants are given an opportunity to put their point of view to a studio audience, or to explain their troubles in a direct way. Programs like these reverse the normal power relations of mass communication, so that, for their few moments on camera, the audience member writes the script and enacts their own show. In *The Jerry Springer Show*, for example, Jerry reverses the role of the studio host. He vacates the podium and stands or sits among the studio audience. He appears restrained in the use of his production power, leaving that to the security staff, and chooses mostly to allow the presenters to perform their personal dramas to a noisy, abusive and judgmental studio audience. Springer encourages the studio audience in its questioning of the "performer" and in its usurpation of his own role as host. Studio security polices both the participants and the studio audience if tempers become overheated, as they usually do. Finally Springer finishes with a homily, stresses particular virtues, and encourages the broadcast audience to emulate his own genial and accepting pose. For such programs, "audience" as "a hearing" has been packaged as a commodity. It takes on a double existence, as both audience and spectacle, and is perhaps a metaphor for a type of noisy, participatory democracy. Such programs are far from benign in their impact on participants, and their capacity to offer a safe environment for the expression of personal grievances is limited, as the assaults and at least one homicide linked to the show demonstrate (Sheehan, *Sydney Morning Herald*, 2 Aug, 2000, p. 20).

There are strong parallels, however, between the *Jerry Springer* "participant observation" model and that of many audience researchers, like myself (see Nightingale, Dickenson, & Griff, 2002), who have justified our research practice on the basis of its capacity to speak for the participating audience members. This is particularly the case with audience research that uses focus groups that are in some senses marginalized in terms of their cultural power, and in their capacity to safeguard their own interests – for example children, the aged, refugees, ethnic minorities The vulnerability of such audiences increases the need for awareness of the ethical responsibilities incurred by offering research participants an "audience." The widespread publication of personal stories, first-hand accounts, and other spontaneous disclosures has placed a burden of responsibility on the researcher to actively guarantee the rights of the research participants. Audience research of this type is now required, by law, to consider in detail the ways the rights of research participants are safeguarded during and after the research, with issues of consent, confidentiality, privacy and protection from harassment, re-use of data, and more, having to be brought to the attention of the research participant during the recruitment process. This care for the participant reflects changing community attitudes and a better understanding of the value of the service the participant is providing for the researcher and for the academic community.

Within media research, the measures required for "participant protection" also reflect the increasing access to mass media enjoyed by even culturally marginal groups. Increasingly ethnic communities, fans, self-help groups and others with sufficient cultural capital prefer to lobby for their own media interests. They are therefore less likely to welcome the patronage of an academic researcher, unless that researcher is also a member of the group. The growing sensitivity to the question of the power and vested interests of the researcher means that the freedom of researchers to adopt a problem, and to unilaterally decide how it will be researched, has changed dramatically. Audience research initiatives are now expected to involve participants more directly in the research process. For example, potential participants may ask for reassurance from the researcher that their participation will "make a difference," and the researcher is therefore called on to promise more than academic outcomes for the participant's investment in the research.

The changing nature of the relationship between the researcher and the research participants has resulted in a trend towards media research doubling as media activism, which tends to compromise the authority of the research as independent or unmotivated knowledge. Activist research seeks to document a particular situation that adversely affects the group involved, and also to argue for changes that will rectify the disadvantage or discriminatory treatment. It is apologist, in that it sets out to "explain" the group, its activities and its interests in order to ensure that it is better understood in terms that make sense both to group members and to the general public (Jenkins, 1992; Baym, 1998). A component of the activism is almost always an attempt to take control of the media's representation of the group, as a first step perhaps to securing better representation of the group's members on decision-making bodies that affect the welfare of the group. Just as with research about audience "happenings," however, the power sharing between researcher and research participants in the "hearing" approach shifts the centrality of the interrogation away from the media and onto the participating group. Audience researchers swap the generation of new knowledge about the media for the role of audience protector, pursuing the group's interests and protecting its members, and policing the group's margins.

All audience research faces the problem of how audiences can be researched with any sort of rigor, given the complexity of the communication processes it involves. Audience experiences have to be put into words, and the words have to be interpreted. We can know about people's media experiences only by observation or direct questioning, but that questioning is about information that has already been interpreted, and the answers will be interpreted yet again by the researcher. A media program (itself a representation of an event or a story) is experienced by a viewer/listener/reader, then reported to a researcher who generates an account of what he or she is told, which is subsequently published and read by other readers/researchers. While we base our argumentation in theory and philosophy, we cannot eradicate the inherent relativism of our project. The study of audience is implicated in the contemporary crisis of knowledge.

Audience Research and Information

> Consumers make their presence felt at most in quantitative terms: through sales figures, through listener or viewer ratings, but not as a counteractive influence. The quantum of their presence can be described and interpreted, but it is not fed back via communication. Of course, oral communication is still possible as a reaction to things which are printed or broadcast. *But the success of scheduled communication no longer depends upon it.* (Niklas Luhmann, 2000, p. 16)

In this paper I have drawn attention to four widely accepted meanings that contribute to the complexity of the phenomena we understand, and research, as "audience." In audience research in the first half of the twentieth century researchers like R. K. Merton, Paul Lazarsfeld and many others sought to understand the media with functionalist theories that reinforced widely held beliefs about individualism and personal choice. In the second half of the twentieth century audience researchers changed direction and followed the leads offered by theories of culture. The use of structuralism, poststructuralism, modernity and postmodernity shifted the focus of our research from individualism to identity and from the social functions to the cultural meaning of the media. Where the functionalist phase had sought to generate theories about the ways media work, the cultural phase assumed culture to be the source of information, about both people and the media. The functionalist researchers used their functionalism to build "middle level" theories that addressed the ways the media work and can be managed. The cultural researchers situated the audience discourses about the meaning of their media experiences back into the general pattern of everyday life, and the search for meaningful cultural identities.

The shift in research practice examined in this paper demonstrates something interesting about the positioning of the researcher and what audience research can realistically achieve. Some forms of audience research clearly are part of the mass communication system: ratings, audience development, market research (Luhmann, 2000). This type of research provides essential components of the "abstract information processing" (Castells, 1998, p. 67) the mass media need in order to continue operating successfully in the Information Age. Apart from some critical analysis of ratings in the 1990s, academic audience research has mostly ignored ratings, even though they actively shape audience and are responsible for the media content available to mass audiences.

On the other hand, cultural approaches to audience situate themselves outside the media system, as commentary on or criticism of the system of mass communication. The knowledge produced by research on audience spaces, however, contributes in a different way to contemporary culture. Kellerman (2000), for example, has suggested that the information society has exhibited at least three phases in its development: (1) the information-rich society of the 1950s and 1960s gradually gave way to (2) the information-based society of the 1980s and 1990s, before emerging as (3) an information-dominated society by the end of the millennium. Cultural approaches to audience research developed in the context of the information-rich phase of this social transformation. They answered the then contemporary demands for information by approaching culture as the source of information. By contrast, Kellerman claims that information *is* the culture, and increasingly also the primary product of the information-dominated society. This bifurcation of information (as culture vs. product) is evident in the approaches to audience described above: researching audience as people generates information commodities, and researching audience as spaces (happenings and hearings) can help us to explore information as culture. So while cultural approaches to researching audiences may not directly affect the mass media system, they nevertheless facilitate the contribution of particular groups to that battle by providing intellectual amplification of their views.

Nevertheless, what is at stake for cultural approaches is changing. Since, as Castells has argued, "cultural battles are the power battles of the Information Age" (quoted in Kellerman, 2000, p. 541) we are again confronted by the manipulation and exploitation of information on both societal and global levels in ways not contemplated since the early twentieth century (Mattelart, 2000). Documentation and advocacy remain important components of the audience research tradition, but something more is required. It is time to return to the challenge of "middle range theorisation" (Merton, 1968 [1949]), to look again at the body/media interface, and to integrate the strengths of cultural research with the almost-forgotten techniques and processes through which particular information effects are generated.

Notes

1 Delanty's proposition of a dialectic between science and culture is deeply flawed. It fails to recognize the scientific nature of cultural research, and shows no insight into the limits to relativism that are part of critical enquiry. It also assumes that so-called scientific approaches are free from wild speculation, which is far from the case. However, Delanty's distinction can help us understand why, during the 1960s, '70s and '80s, social science debates about the relative merits of quantitative and qualitative methods took so long to be resolved.

2 I have found reference to a working paper circulated at the Centre for Contemporary Cultural Studies at the University of Birmingham in 1973.

3 John Tulloch and Albert Moran (1986) provided an excellent example of the ways the production teams for the Australian TV series, *A Country Practice*, devised the meanings encoded in the program.

4 Dorothy Hobson's early study of housewives watching TV provided a good description of a viewing context (Hobson, 1980).

5 An excellent example of the process of decoding, evaluating information in terms of personal life experiences in order to reach a judgement about a broadcast program is available in Livingstone and Lunt (1994, pp. 125–8), and in Nightingale (1992).

6 This is the level of analysis that Ien Ang focused on in her study of Dallas (Ang, 1985), drawing on oppositions between a "melodramatic imagination" learned from years of viewing such programmes and activated at the moment of decoding, and a "tragic structure of feeling" which informs the production team's and the programme's encoding; and between the culturally based ideologies of "mass culture" and "popular culture" that framed the evaluation of the programme as good or bad by her correspondents.

7 Some researchers improvised new solutions to the problems the model created. For example, in her 1986 account of a family watching a video of the film *Rocky 2*, Valerie Walkerdine eloquently and intelligently described the unenviable position of the researcher on a cultural mission (Walkerdine, 1986). Walkerdine acknowledged the anxiety that the role of the researcher produced in her, recognized the difficulty she faced in reading *Rocky 2* in terms that in any way resembled the family's version of the text, and drew attention to her decision to use her personal experiences and academic insights to explain the significance she saw for the family in the video viewing. Her research practice asked questions that were not accessible to instrumental researchers and developed interpretative strategies to overcome the difficulties inherent in the research design.

8 Jenkins 1992 is a good example.

9 Sonia Livingstone and Peter Lunt (1994) have contributed to the understanding of the role of the audience in the construction of public discourse based on TV talk programmes, as has John Corner (1995).

10 The reader is referred to the writings of George Herbert Mead for a thorough explanation (Mead: 1977).

11 See for example: Hartley, 1987; Ang, 1991; Nightingale, 1993; Meehan, 1993.

12 Turow (1997) claims that such advertising practice widens social and cultural divisions and increases segmentation on lines of gender, race and class. Advertising to specific demographics, rather than to the mass audience, has divided the audience into niche markets that become increasingly segregated in terms of interests and tastes. Far from promoting understanding between segments, targeted advertising increases intolerance of differing views.

13 Critical psychology (Blackman and Walkerdine, 2001) is now attempting to revise traditional psychological perspectives on the nature of the individual, the self and identity.

14 There is an echo of "uses and gratifications" in audience development which also focuses on uses and needs, though in a more pre-emptive way than the "uses and gratifications" formulations of the 1970s.

References

Ang, I. (1985). *Watching Dallas: Soap opera and the melodramatic imagination*. London and New York: Methuen.

Ang, I. (1991). *Desperately Seeking the Audience*. London and New York: Routledge.

Appadurai, A. (1996). *Modernity at Large: Cultural dimensions of globalization*. Minneapolis and London: University of Minnesota Press.

Australian Broadcasting Authority and University of Western Sydney (2000). *Children's Views About Media Harm*. Monograph 10. Sydney: Australian Broadcasting Authority.

Baym, N. (1998). Talking about soaps: Communicative practices in a computer-mediated fan culture. In *Tune In, Log On: Soaps, fandom and online community*. Thousand Oaks, CA and London: Sage, pp. 111–30.

Bennett, T., Emmison, M., and Frow, J. (1999). *Accounting for Tastes: Australian everyday cultures*. Cambridge: Cambridge University Press.

Berger, J. (1976). *Ways of Seeing*. Harmondsworth: Penguin.

Beville, H. M., Jr. (1988). *Audience Ratings: Radio, television, and cable*. Hillsdale, NJ: Lawrence Erlbaum.

Blackman, L. and Walkerdine, V. (2001). *Mass Hysteria: Critical psychology and media studies*. Houndmills and New York: Palgrave.

Bourdieu, P. (1984 [1979]). *Distinction: A social critique of the judgement of taste* (trans. Richard Nice). Cambridge, MA: Harvard University Press.

Cantor, J. (1998). Children's attraction to violent television programming. In J. Goldstein (ed.), *Why We Watch: The attractions of violent entertainment*. New York and Oxford: Oxford University Press, pp. 88–115.

Carey, J. and Kreiling, A. (1974). Popular culture and uses and gratifications: Notes towards an accommodation. In J. Blumler and E. Katz (eds.), *The Uses of Mass Communications: Current perspectives on gratifications research*. London and Berverly Hills: Sage, pp. 225–48.

Castells, M. (1998). *End of Millennium*. Malden, MA and Oxford: Blackwell.

Cohen, S. (1997 [1980]). Symbols of trouble. In K. Gelder and S. Thornton (eds.), *The Subcultures Reader*. London and New York: Routledge, pp. 149–62.

Corner, J. (1995). *Television Form and Public Address*. London: Edward Arnold.

De Fleur, M. and Ball-Rokeach, S. (1977 [1966]). *Theories of Mass Communication*. New York: Longman.

Delanty, G. (2001). *Challenging Knowledge: The university in the knowledge society*. Buckingham, UK and Philadelphia: Open University Press.

Elliott, P. (1974). Uses and gratifications research: a critique and a sociological alternative. In J. Blumler and E. Katz (eds.), *The Uses of Mass Communications: Current perspectives on gratifications research*. London and Beverly Hills: Sage, pp. 249–68.

Gans, H. (1974). *Popular Culture and High Culture: An analysis and evaluation of taste*. New York: Basic Books.

Gronroos, C. (1994). Quo vadis, marketing? Towards a relationship marketing paradigm. *Journal of Marketing Management*, 10, 347–60.

Hall, S. (1980 [1973]). Encoding/decoding. In S. Hall, D. Hobson, A. Lowe, and P. Willis (eds.), *Culture, Media, Language: Working papers in cultural studies, 1972–1979*. London: Hutchinson, pp. 128–38.

Halloran, J. D., Elliott, P., and Murdock, G. (1970). *Demonstrations and Communication: A case study*. Harmondsworth: Penguin.

Hartley, J. (1987). Invisible fictions: television, audiences, paedocracy and pleasure. *Textual Practice*, 1(2), 121–38.

Hebdige, D. (1975). Reggae, rastas and rudies. In S. Hall and T. Jefferson (eds.), *Resistance Through Rituals*. London: Hutchinson.

Hebdige, D. (1979). *Subculture: The meaning of style*. London and New York: Methuen.

Hobson, D. (1980). *Crossroads: The drama of a soap opera*. London: Methuen.

Jenkins, H. (1992). *Textual Poachers: Television fans and participatory culture*. London and New York: Routledge.

Katz, E., Blumler, J. G., and Gurevitch, M. (1974). Utilization of mass communication by the individual. In J. G. Blumler and E. Katz (eds.), *The Uses of Mass Communications: Current perspectives on gratifications research*. Beverly Hills and London: Sage, pp. 19–32.

Katz, E. and Lazarsfeld, P. (1955). *Personal Influence*. New York: The Free Press.

Kellerman, A. (2000). Phases in the rise of the information society. *Info*, 2(6), 537–41.

Kress, G. (1985). *Linguistic Processes in Sociocultural Practice*. Geelong: Deakin University Press.

Kress, G. and Hodge, B. (1979). *Language as Ideology*. London: Routledge and Kegan Paul.

Kress, G. and van Leeuwen, T. (1990). *Reading Images*. Geelong, Australia: Deakin University Press.

Leppert, R. (1995). *The Sight of Sound: Music, representation and the history of the body*. Berkeley, Los Angeles, London: University of California Press.

Lévi-Strauss, C. (1978). *Myth and Meaning*. London: Routledge & Kegan Paul.

Livingstone, S. and Lunt, P. (1994). *Talk on Television: Audience participation and public debate*. London and New York: Routledge.

Luhmann, N. (2000). *The Reality of the Mass Media* (trans. Kathleen Cross). Cambridge: Polity Press.

Lunt, P. and Livingstone, S. (1992). *Mass Consumption and Personal Identity*. Buckingham, UK and Philadelphia: Open University Press.

Manguel, A. (1997). *A History of Reading*. London: Flamingo.

Mattelart, A. (2000). *Networking the World, 1794–2000* (trans. Liz Carey-Libbrecht and James A. Cohen). Minneapolis and London: University of Minnesota Press.

Mead, G. H. (1977). *On Social Psychology: Selected papers*. Chicago and London: University of Chicago Press.

Meehan, E. (1993). Heads of household and ladies of the house: Gender, genre and broadcast ratings 1929–1990. In R. McChesney and W. Solomon (eds.), *Ruthless Criticism*. Minneapolis: University of Minnesota Press, pp. 204–21.

Merton, R. K. (1968 [1949]). *Social Theory and Social Structure*. New York: The Free Press.

Metz, C. (1982 [1981]). *The Imaginary Signifier: Psychoanalysis and the cinema*. Bloomington: Indiana University Press.

Morley, D. (1980). *The "Nationwide" Audience: Structure and decoding*. London: British Film Institute.

Morley, D. (1986). *Family Television: Cultural power and domestic pleasure*. London: Comedia.

Nightingale, V. (1989). What's "ethnographic" about ethnographic audience research? *Australian Journal of Communication*, 16, 50–63.

Nightingale, V. (1992). Contesting domestic territory: watching Rugby League on television. In A. Moran (ed.), *Stay Tuned: An Australian broadcasting reader*. North Sydney: Allen & Unwin, pp. 156–66.

Nightingale, V. (1993). Industry measurement of audiences. In S. Cunningham and G. Turner (eds.), *The Media in Australia: Industries, texts, audiences*. Sydney: Allen & Unwin, pp. 271–80.

Nightingale, V. (1996). *Studying Audiences: The shock of the real*. London and New York: Routledge.

Nightingale, V., Dickenson, D., and Griff, C. (2002). Children's views on media harm. *Metro*, 131/132, 212–24.

Pecora, N. (1998). *The Business of Children's Entertainment*. New York and London: The Guilford Press.

Peled, T. and Katz, E. (1974). Media functions in wartime: The Israeli home front in October 1973. In J. Blumler and E. Katz (eds.), *The Uses of Mass Communications: Current perspectives on gratifications research*. London and Berverly Hills: Sage, pp. 49–69.

Seiter, E. (1993). *Sold Separately: Parents and children in consumer culture*. New Brunswick: Rutgers University Press.

Sheehan, P. (2000). Death by television as journalism loses itself in the real world. *Sydney Morning Herald*, News and Features, 2 August, p. 20.

Singh, S. (2001). Gender and the use of the internet at home. *New Media and Society*, 3(4): 395–415.

Small, C. (1998). *Musicking: The meanings of performing and listening*. Hanover and London: Wesleyan University Press.

Thornton, S. (1997). General Introduction. In K. Gelder and S. Thornton (eds.), *The Subcultures Reader*. London and New York: Routledge, pp. 1–7.

Tulloch, J. and Moran, A. (1986). *A Country Practice: "Quality" soap*. Sydney: Currency Press.

Turow, J. (1997). *Breaking Up America: Advertisers and the new media world*. Chicago and London: University of Chicago Press.

Walkerdine, V. (1986). Video replay: Families, films and fantasy. In V. Burgin et al. (eds.), *Formations of Fantasy*. London: Methuen, pp. 167–99.

Walkerdine, V. (1999). *Daddy's girl: Young girls and popular culture*. Houndmills and London: Macmillan.

Warner, M. (1994). *From the Beast to the Blonde: On fairy tales and their tellers*. London: Chatto and Windus.

Willis, P. E. (1977). *Learning to Labour: How working class kids get working class jobs*. Farnborough: Saxon House.

Young, J. (1971). *The Drugtakers: The social meaning of drug use*. London: MacGibbon and Kee.

CHAPTER EIGHTEEN

Practicing Embodiment
Reality, Respect, and Issues of Gender in Media Reception

Joke Hermes

A strong tradition of feminist reception analysis and media ethnography has been established over the last 25 years. Its value for feminism has been to provide an empirical means to question established notions of femininity and masculinity, and to provide new theorizations of gender. Its value for media and cultural studies is perhaps usefully understood in contrast to what could be called its academic adversary, textual analysis. Reception research stands out for its engagement with actual, lived practices of media use and the intricate forms our attachments and identifications as viewers may take. Rather than identify mere theoretical possibilities or reading positions (the implied reader), reception research has opened our eyes to the vast range of possibilities offered by texts that are actualized in audience practice and thus to how social subjectivity is produced. It has taken us beyond the notion that texts control their own meanings, or that identity constructions are governed one-dimensionally by either gender, class, ethnicity, sexual preference and so on. Usually more than one of these dimensions of social power relations are part of the process of making media texts meaningful and deriving pleasure from them. Related to that pleasure is to reinscribe the many identifications they offer and thus to give depth to the meaning of being a specific kind of human being. In practice that means to take up some invitations to identify while leaving others alone, to feel included in some ways and to be excluded in others. Last but not least, reception research has taken us beyond any self-congratulatory position as academics: empirical audience research tends to humble most of us. To do justice to the vast complexity of everyday audience practice requires patience, a wide cultural literacy, intelligent associative thinking, writing skill and above all respect for those whose help we have been given in uncovering how media texts become meaningful.

In this chapter, I will argue that the strength and political engagement of reception analysis can be traced back to its feminist roots. Most of my examples will come from feminist reception analysis, some my own, some by others. This is not to suggest that there is no other research than feminist research, or that the feminist scholars have had an easy or undisputed march to glory. Although authors such as Charlotte Brunsdon (1997), Ann Gray (1999) and Kirsten Drotner (1994) have pointed to the importance of feminist scholarship for the development of reception analysis in media and cultural studies, this legacy tends to be overlooked and can certainly do with being asked for renewed attention (as e.g. by Lotz, 2000). Taking the feminist legacy seriously means we will have to look at how feminism has been both an asset and a restraining factor for the development of reception studies. Christine Geraghty (1998) suggests that the feminist wish to focus on women, on small groups and on working with fans has limited the possibilities of what is fundamentally one of the most exciting methods in media and cultural studies research. After all, its very pragmatics make audience studies attractive: "If we want to find out about audiences, why not ask them?" (1998, p. 143) In the course of her discussion of television audience research, the irony of the question becomes clear. We have not asked audiences plural about their viewing practices, but have focused on specific audience groups and even members. We have given little attention to the methodological pitfalls inherent in self-description and how it is virtually impossible to verify any account given (cf. Alasuutari, 1995). At the same time Geraghty's question echoes a comment by David Morley: "(S)hould you wish to understand what I am doing, it would probably be best to ask me. I may well, of course, lie to you or otherwise misrepresent my thoughts or feelings, for any number of purposes, but at least, through my verbal responses, you will begin to get some access to the kind of language, criteria of distinction and types of characterizations, through which I construct my (conscious) world" (1989, p. 25). Between them Geraghty and Morley suggest how spectacularly easy to do and accessible to all audience studies are – we simply start asking people about what they watch or read, or how they use their video recorders, dvds and computers at home – and they make clear what remains most difficult to grasp about this area of research: as audience researchers we work with and within language. This means we are always one step removed from what really happened or even happens, while we have to deal with the recalcitrance of that very reality.

A Modernist Tale

Generally, reception studies as an area of academic research has set itself the goal to understand and explain (by theorizing empirical audience material) how media texts become meaningful and are relevant to audiences, rather than to predict audience preference or media effects or generalize findings to large populations.

As such it has preferred the micro- and meso-level to the macro level of much mass communications research. Since the first part of the last century there has been a strong interest in the effects and meanings of the media for its audiences, mostly explored within the tradition of mass communication research. It is not unusual for an account of reception studies to be told as a modernist tale in which it is the logical conclusion or end station of this research tradition. Such tales suggest a developmental logic that progresses from a past beset with problems and unsound thinking, to a future of enlightenment. The past in the case of reception studies would be early mass communications research. Although there is much of interest in early mass communications research (e.g. Herzog's early research amongst radio soap audiences, Herzog, 1944), it has been written up as the period of the hypodermic needle or the magic bullet. The media according to this metaphor have a direct effect on their audiences. The model does not allow much room for questioning how media texts become meaningful or how differences between audience groups, or even audience members should be understood. It is succeeded by such models as the two-step flow (media influence is relegated via central informants) and the spiral of silence (McQuail, 2000; Noelle-Neumann, 1974). Again there is no question of problematizing either the range of meanings possibly contained with the media text, or that audiences might do different things with these texts. Enlightenment in this tale follows upon the introduction of uses and gratifications research. Uses and gratifications, or gratificationist research, turned around the question of what the media do with the people, to ask: what do people do with the media? Much criticized for its lack of theoretical underpinning and its circular logic (do the uses lead to gratifications, or does expected gratification lead to use?), as well as its devotion to modeling and quantifying its results, uses and gratifications research (such as McQuail et al., 1972) does deserve credit for breaking the hegemonic consensus over the power of the media.

Media and cultural studies reception research, also called the New Audience Research (Corner, 1991), would then be understood as the last step, the end of this particular history. Reception research proved capable of building on theoretical work, and of theorizing empirical material. It has questioned that media texts have singular or monolithic meanings; it has even questioned the wisdom of looking only at the audience side for how media texts become meaningful. It has in that sense transcended both of the traditions it is thought as stemming from and being in dialectical opposition to: studies associated with textual analysis (and often with psychoanalysis) such as published in the 1970s in the film journal *Screen*; and mass communication research which has tended to be overly interested in media effects and in sociological (often functionalist) questions in relation to the media audience. In much reception research the context of use, the text itself, and how media texts are made meaningful are all three integral components of the research. There is usually an underlying notion that the meanings of media texts are constructed in or by interpretive communities. Such communities should be understood as discursive practices rather than as (always) materially existing social groups. That is to say that they stand for the shared discourses or cultural resources upon which we, the media audience draw in according meaning to a television show, a book or a record, as do media producers and critics. Such discourses also suggest to us who we are and how we are placed in society in relation to others.

Although the last bit of this story is as precise a rendition of what reception analysis is about as I could give, I am not very comfortable with the tale of origins that precedes it here. Such a tale goes against the very logic that reception analysts have tried to deconstruct. The media and cultural studies lineage in reception research is built on a strong political motivation to break open the naturalizing effects of mainstream or hegemonic ideology. There is no self-evident or natural history to this particular historical moment in academic history. It is as much a product of its past as of its context. It could be a moment of rupture. Its significance is, moreover, not to be found in how it is connected with what came before or the traditions it legitimizes, but by what new work, ideas and cultural criticism it enabled. A new page should be turned then, and it could well start with how new audience researchers questioned a modernist sense of academics as avant-garde, as a group that has better or higher knowledge and insight in the workings of power, in what is and is not true. Against such a paternalist view, reception analysts have presented themselves in a more Gramscian sense as "organic intellectuals" (Gramsci, 1971). Gramsci distinguished between traditional and organic intellectuals on the basis of their allegiance to the powers that be. Moreover he understood organic intellectuals to have a specific role or task in translating common sense knowledges and to bring out their critical potential. After all, suggests Gramsci, power works best via hegemony: a balancing act in which the powerful allow some room for the dominated in order to seduce them to think of the power structure as just, and as their own. This makes power systems fundamentally unstable, and organic intellectuals agents of change. Of course, this is also in a way a self-gratifying definition that may give undue importance to us, intellectuals. Even so, this self-conception has worked well within a postmodern understanding of identity and agency, key terms in much of the work done on media reception.

The New Audience Research: A Key Example

A famous example of early reception research is Ien Ang's *Dallas* study, *Watching Dallas* (1985). Ang had placed an ad in a national young women's magazine. It said that she often got odd reactions when people heard she liked watching *Dallas*. If readers liked watching it too, or disliked it, they could write (1985, p. 10). The material was to be used for what would be her MA thesis. Ang received 42 letters. On the basis of this material she identified two main ideologies that governed the reception of the American television show. The one ideology she called the ideology of mass culture, the other populism. By opposing the two, Ang could make clear that the prime-time television program (about an extraordinarily rich American oil family and its relational problems) was the subject of an (ideological) struggle. On the one hand there is derision of *Dallas* as a form of typically American (and hence worthless, capitalist trash) culture – which was likened to fast food: no nutritious value. *Dallas* as low culture is found to be wanting when contrasted to "high" culture. Taste is a matter of cultivation. Those who hated *Dallas* had an easy time deriding the show, using the terms of this ideology. Those who love to watch *Dallas* had a much more difficult feat to accomplish. They have to fend with the mass-culture ideological slant on popular culture for instance by adopting an ironical viewing attitude. A form of this would be to focus on the fun made of the show while watching it. Those who simply loved the program, have to defend what, within this ideology, is a weird preference. The populist ideology on the other hand, has no axe to grind with the distinction between high and low culture, it is based upon a notion of use value. Taste cannot be a matter of dispute. Ang illustrates this via the letters of writers who clearly feel there is nothing to defend: there is, within populism, no accounting for tastes, after all.

These ideologies obviously align with class difference. But Ang is not interested in such instrumental linking. After referencing Bourdieu's notion of cultural capital and his notion that cultural capital is based on how one distinguishes oneself using the cultural knowledge one has (a somewhat more nuanced understanding of how class difference works and is certainly not only dependent on economic capital), she goes on to explore how a feminist (such as herself) could be posed in between these two ideologies. She uses the insights derived from the audience study to suggest that *Dallas* as text should be understood via its tragic structure of feeling. Related to melodrama (or the melodramatic imagination which savors sentiment, sensation and moral reassurance) the tragic structure of feeling has strong emotional veracity, and makes audiences understand and value the text for what Ang calls its emotional realism. For instance in one of the letters she quotes, the writer speaks of knowing someone just like the show's bad guy (JR). He is not as rich, nor is he an oil baron – he is just a builder – but has the same kind of manipulative character.

Although Ang is very careful not to write *Watching Dallas* in overly autobiographic mode, her authorial voice is personal and the project at all levels bespeaks her personal quest to understand the attractions of this particular show. *Watching Dallas* thus brings together a number of traits that will come to define reception studies, or the new audience research. There is the ethnographic intention of the author to understand the media text from the point of view of its actual audience, that is, as part of a community of viewers. Of course this is not ethnography as it has been understood by anthropologists, but then neither is it a research practice that reinscribes colonialist relations between the Western observer and the exotic Other. However we want to label this new kind of work on media reception, the fact remains that Ang did not just use her own experience or address the text in isolation, even though she could have, given that a tradition of critical feminist writing about popular cultural texts had been established in the 1970s and early 80s, from Friedan (1974 [1963]) and Greer (1970) in the 60s and early 70s, to Brownmiller (1984), that extends to today (Kaplan, 1986; Bordo, 1990, 1993).

The ethnographic intentions of the author are understood as a political moment. It is a move away from an implicit paternalism in which the intellectual knows best and may speak on behalf of the audience which she does not have to consult about this. But the political engagement of Ang's study (and of later audience studies) goes further: it is also aimed against earlier communications research and the implicit and decontextualising politics of model building, as well as a feminist project. The same type of characteristics can be found in another early and important new audience research study: Janice Radway's *Reading the Romance* (1984). Radway worked within the context of American studies but wished to explore the little-researched and undervalued area of popular literature. The strength of Radway's work is especially in her use of interview material gathered via a bookseller, named Dot in the book, who provided her customers with a newsletter about new romances. Radway, like Ang, addressed both the audience and the text. What sets these studies apart is that they look at the popular cultural text through the eyes of its audience, its fans even, rather than via the preconceived notions that are part of the academic community and that tend to value high culture and literature implicitly (see also Radway's later work with the Book of the Month Club, 1999).

Towards A Postmodern Understanding of Reception Analysis

Rather than understand these two studies as the logical or natural outcome of a tradition of mass communication research or as a protest against the textual determinism of 1970s *Screen* studies, I would prefer to take what has been dubbed the "postmodernism" of this type of research more seriously and apply it self-reflexively and politically to what came after. This means I need to trace back today's work to these studies, and understand Ang and Radway's work (as well as David Morley's groundbreaking studies, *Nationwide* and *Family Television*, 1980, 1986) as a critical moment rather than as an inevitable result. After all, the mass communications tradition of audience research has also spawned a number of other types of traditions and methods. There is the closely related work of Liebes and Katz (1986) with *Dallas* audiences, which tries to be true to a descriptive and non-intrusive ideal of ethnographic research, rather than commit to a self-reflexive version as do Ang and Radway (Liebes & Katz, 1986). But there is also a resurgent tradition of mass psychological research into media entertainment which is cast in terms of a modernist logic of concern over vulnerable audiences, fright reactions in children and so on, which is more easily read in terms of the natural outcome of the mass communications tradition of audience research.

Postmodernism in the field of audience studies and reception theory can be characterized by its self-reflexivity and by its combination of a commitment to theorization, to politics and to popular culture. Many authors draw up much and much longer lists (cf. Hebdige on this phenomenon in *Hiding in the light*, 1988) but these are the central elements, and this is precisely what a postmodern position has been most criticized for. James Curran (1990) famously and unjustly criticised Radway for writing more about the relationship of her readers to patriarchy (the theoretical notion as well as the underlying political project) than to their flesh and blood husbands (presumably everyday reality is transparent and should be understood as the undisputable bedrock of empirical truth, which it is questionable could ever be attained no matter what). Others besides Curran have also found fault with the identification of popular pleasures with a political agenda. Although Ien Ang and I (Ang and Hermes, 1991) presented a hardly radical view in an overview article of the research and theory on gender and media consumption, the article has been much quoted and criticized for the postmodern feminist position it argues. Rather than understand gender as given, and as transparently understandable from social reality, we suggest it is constructed and perhaps not always or in all situations the most relevant identity aspect. Gender neutrality may be open to women as well as to men. Reception analysis, or ethnography in our view was the best route to further the then somewhat meager theorization of the subject.

If gender is not given but constructed, we need to understand how this happens. Three elements present themselves for consideration: the media text, the contexts of using, reading or viewing these texts and individual biography. They can be used, as we put it in 1991, to explore gender definitions, positions and identifications. Both sets come together in what can actually be researched in a reception study: that is the shared cultural knowledges that we draw upon in interpreting the media texts we use. We need to accept as a matter of fact that as media and cultural studies scholars we have no direct access to what goes on in someone's head when or after they have seen a television show, read a book, or been to a movie. I am not all that interested in what is the realm of psychology and psychiatry either. As a cultural studies scholar positioned in between the social sciences and the humanities, I wish to develop grounded media criticism, based on a social and cultural understanding of the importance of specific texts or media for its audiences or culture in a broader sense. Therefore, what I need to do is delve beneath the surface of interviews or observation material to find out what are the connecting elements in what is said about either a group of programmes or by a specific group of media users.

The beneath-the-surface connecting elements I allude to here are not a deeper truth, or a higher insight. Rather they should be understood as a reconstructed knowledge based on the jigsaw puzzle bits that everyday conversation and the ethnographic (or lengthy open) interview provide us with. Such a reconstruction is exactly what is suggested by the notion of what an organic intellectual might do: translate and while doing so, structure popular understanding or common sense. What one finds when doing so is a mixture of highly conservative and progressive elements that cannot usually be understood as describing a person (or a position). In fact, many times, I have observed in interviews and in every-day conversation that all of us use the cultural knowledges at our disposal loosely and inconsistently, but that there is only a limited overall variety to that cultural knowledge. In analysis, cultural knowledge is often reconstructed into reper-toires, discourses or vocabularies (cf. Whetherell & Potter, 1988). It depends on the style and ability of the author to label these discourses as evocatively (or soberly) as possible, in order for others to gain an understanding of how a specific text or texts become meaningful, and what place they hold in the com-plex fabric of everyday life. The range here is wide: it extends from fan texts (Lewis, 1992; Douglas, 1994) to such highly insignificant, interchangeable genres as women's magazines or everyday television (cf. Hermes, 1995; some of the examples in Morley, 1986).

Recent Audience Studies: Establishing A Tradition

Over the last decade, debates over reception analysis and media and cultural studies in general have become more incidental. Although much criticism is still, and often somewhat unreflectedly given (Ferguson & Golding, 1997, reply by Morley, 1998), a tradition of research has been established. I would like to look at some of this newer work to see how we can trace it back to that key moment of the coming into being of the New Audience Research in the first half of the 1980s. In doing so, I want to tag on to Christine Geraghty's discussion of ethnographic research in television studies (Geragthy 1998). Geraghty outlines a number of faultlines. She starts by questioning the self-evidence of the label "audience studies." As a closer look will reveal, important audience studies have actually focused on texts (such as Jenkins's work with *Star Trek* fans, 1991), on specific groups of viewers, such as adult women (female viewers of soap opera in Mary Ellen Brown, 1994), the context of viewing or on household technology (Gray, 1992: on women's use of the video recorder). Audiencehood in itself is clearly a theme we need to look at more closely. Geraghty continues her discussion by looking at how audiences were approached, how fieldwork was set up and how the material gathered was analyzed. Again, she makes a clear point. Although the label "ethnography" is often used to describe the new audience research (and it should be noted that this is usually a "second-hand" label, not used by its practitioners, cf. Seiter, 1999, p. 10), it is actually a loosely bundled collection of studies that draw upon (more or less) spontaneously offered descriptions and observations by audience members. Methods used include: letters, open, semi-structured interviews and participant-observation. What holds these modes of research together is that they are based on the establishment of trust and a high degree of empathy of the researcher. They depend, as Geraghty points out, on feminine skills (1998, pp. 152–3), rehabilitated in the 1970s and 80s by women's studies and the general acceptance of feminism as appropriate to academic theory and method (see also Drotner, 1994). They mask in many ways the power that the researcher has on grounds of her or his institutional affiliation and her or his discursive control over the reproduction of the conversations held.

Although she would claim herself to be a somewhat old-fashioned feminist doing old-fashioned audience research among television and new media audiences, it has to be doubted that Seiter describes herself well. Her work is a strong example of what good reception analysis may look like. In her recent book *Television and New Media Audiences* (Seiter, 1999) she both reports on three research projects and on the methodological issues involved. One of the studies is based on participation in and interviews held with a parent support group Seiter herself was a member of. It deals with television viewing and draws the portraits of four couples. The women were also interviewed separately. Although Seiter interprets her material using the work of Joan Acker, written in the early 1970s "at odds with postmodern conceptions of gender" (1999, p. 52) to highlight the ways in which raising children tends to lock down gender roles, I felt that she was able to draw out subtle differences in how motherhood, that most traditional of feminine constructions affected, the women she portrayed. This underlines the point I made in the beginning of this chapter: actual audience experience may explode any simple notion of how gender is constructed. At the very least it becomes obvious here that gender is defined in relation to social roles, and that these roles change over time and changes in personal history (having one child, or more and so on). Even before the television text (in this case) enters the stage, most definitions, expectations and identifications are firmly in place. Amongst these are the "the leisure gap." The home for many mothers is a place of work and not a place of leisure. They therefore tend to feel guilty for taking time for themselves for instance by watching a favourite television programme, even if they also work outside the home (see also Ann Gray, 1992). Of special interest for reception studies is how the leisure gap, and the guilt over television viewing, both by the women themselves and by their children, reinforces the ideological given that television is bad for you.

Seiter's project is of the unreconstructed feminist kind. She wishes to give a voice to the mothers she spent time with in the parent-support group and whom she interviewed (1999, p. 55). Although several commentators have suggested that more men be included, or more diverse audience groups are studied in reception research, Seiter feels there is enough work left to do with (groups of) women, to not simply follow such a fashionable complaint. Moreover, there is an experiential difference from the perspective of the woman researcher to interviewing men and women that suggests that it would be easier for men to interview men than for women to do both. In her work generally (as in this book), Seiter understands herself in terms of a Gramscian organic intellectualism, that is both meant to correct what in a later chapter is called the "hype against computers" (1999, p. 129) prevalent in common talk and to bring out ideals for television or computer programming (1999, p. 133), to counter the fact that audiences are so much used to making do with what they get. Although it is not her central concern, Seiter's work does bring out many of the characteristics of audiencehood and how being an audience is inscribed in a multitude of contextual identities. These may of course all converge in producing what is easily recognized as a traditional feminine identity, such as motherhood. Upon a closer look, these traditional identities are, as a rule, far less straightforward or simple than the ideological force with which they are (re)produced suggests. In fact, we tend to lump together an enormous diversity of identities, views and feelings under labels such as masculinity and femininity. Like race or ethnicity, these tend to work like magnetic force fields, attracting whatever contains a mere scrap of metal, or in this case gender definition. Work such as Seiter's is important for the close look it takes at these force fields of gender identity. By giving it depth and definition, she loosens the bounds of ideological naturalization and problematizes the automatic reinscription of such identities again and again (cf. Butler, 1990).

In a useful overview of how feminism has related to the category of women (or denied the existence of that category altogether), Charlotte Brunsdon (1997) has suggested there are three phases in feminist work on the media: transparency, a recruitionist or hegemonic mode, and a fragmented mode. Seiter's wording lets us know that as an intellectual she belongs in the category of the "hegemonic relationship": we should open the eyes of audiences to the price they pay, not so much, ironically, for their pleasures but for their anxieties about these pleasures, whether as television viewers or as caretakers temporarily relieved of their duty by television in the role of electronic nanny. Contrary to the earlier feminist authors Brunsdon describes who do not give a second thought to how they may be different from women in other social positions (woman is after all an undeniable and inseparable category), she is aware of the differential positions she and the audience occupy. She remarks for instance that her own middle-class background may make her more relaxed about television as a medium, whereas for those with less economic and cultural capital, it is much more important to keep up the distinction by disavowing popular culture. "Among members of the middle class – those with education but not much economic capital – anxieties about media effects are most acute. I suspect that this group cannot afford the luxury of indulging a love for popular culture; for fear that they will appear uneducated in interviews. In interviews, I have found that those with the largest stake in appearing educated make the 'worst' informants about television viewing" (Seiter, 1999, p. 131).

This makes Seiter's work both the perfect and too easy a choice to illustrate how important its feminist heritage is for audience studies. By presenting it here nonetheless, I hope to shed light on how for all reception studies, the relationship between researcher and informants is fraught with dangers of over- or under-identification, of not recognizing what binds the researcher to her informants, or of not recognizing this enough. After all, the underlying discourses I am personally interested in and see as that which reception analysis can most usefully uncover, tie all of us into its discursive folds as well as into the social mechanism of distinguishing oneself to belong in as culturally "high" an echelon as possible: one way or another we are defined by our audiencehood and, in turn, we ourselves help define what it may mean that we are. The difficulties Seiter's respondents have in deciding how much television their children can watch, at the very least suggests that I should have a story, a tale to tell about why I let mine watch as much as they want. In all honesty I should probably also add that my partner, like the husbands in the parental support group, holds much stricter views of how much television is good for a child. Whereas Seiter wants reception analysis to break up restricting definitions in terms of gender, I would also like researchers to tackle the force of such monumental ideological "truths" as the one according to which television is addictive for each and all of us if given half a chance. A humanistic versus a discourse analytic choice: both, however, may be faced with the dangers of not recognizing our own embodiment radically enough.

Implicit Paternalism: The Continuing Story of the Feminist Roots of Reception Research

I recently had a chance to write about a group interview that did not sit well with me. It was a group interview about crime fiction, with two women and a man. Apart from me there was a second interviewer, a young woman who was my research assistant. I used an earlier publication by Ellen Seiter (1990) also about a group interview, with two men, conducted by Seiter and a male colleague, that had not gone well either, partly for comparable reasons. In both cases we had been confronted by a certain arrogance, and by not being taken very seriously. Although I differ from Seiter in how important I think it is to give a voice to women as a category (I would rather break open gender as a category in its entirety), I share with her a hegemonic intention in my work, which in the case of the troubling interview was directed against what I thought was the low status of detective novels. My informants were clearly upset about this and firmly disagreed that their favourite reading fell short of the category of literature. The interview was something of a fight. It forced me to rethink what I would expect the relationship between researcher and researched to be. In the subsequent publication (Hermes, 2000) I argue that it is my own paternalist feminism that was most problematic here. As a feminist I have learnt to, and indeed teach others to, understand informants to have less power and to be, in many ways at your mercy. However true this may be, such a way of thinking closes off further work in one of the directions suggested by Geraghty: namely with other groups than especially women, and with powerful informants, rather than like-minded fans, readers, viewers, users of popular genres or media.

In the crime fiction interview I worried unduly about having offended my interviewees with my characterization of crime fiction which they had reacted against so fiercely. My (implicit) goal had been to function in a role of subservience to a group process of self-expression. Such self-expression, again following my earliest feminist training, can be seen to score high on "naturalism" and on "truth." I was out to get "the real story" and the real story turned out not to exist. There was above all a firm difference of opinion. The bottom line is that it does not matter whether or not there are other stories to tell about reading detective novels, which might have been elicited by a different opening of the interview by me. Reminded by the Morley quotation offered above, I did in the end decide to focus on what was said, on what means of expression were used, in short how the interview had functioned discursively in building forms of agency and identity for the three readers present. To have as one's intellectual goal to give voice to others can backfire. After all, how do we know what that voice is? Powerful informants tend to have their own voice and may not share a camp intellectual attitude to popular culture, which allows for the possibility to know-ingly enjoy forms of trash and to not mind categorizing an entire genre with its lesser examples or according to dismissive forms of cultural knowledge. It is important that we not generalize interview and analytic strategies developed for working with socially less-powerful groups to working with other groups of informants or interviewees. In all cases, one is well-advised to adhere to dis-cursive analysis rather than to naturalistic approaches in reception studies, and to continuously reflect on one's own position as a researcher and as a critic of reception analysis (see also Lotz, 2000, p. 464). Any problems we have with finding our own position and voice, in dealing with our informants, or our material, are epistemological and stem from too little reflection on who we are and what we do. I suspect they are seldom based in ontology. Any left-over paternalism from that very first feminist phase described by Brunsdon, which suggests that the relationship between the woman intellectual and the category of women is unproblematic, is bound to be a time bomb in any research project. Turning back to Geraghty and her criticism of the state of the art in audience studies, we need to see how we come full circle if our political engagement leads to naturalistic assumptions about the audience we study. This may both blind us to the inherent power difference there is between us and our informants, or worse still, to us not wishing to recognize that some power differences go the other way: in the eyes of our informants we may not always hold all wisdom but actually have disputable ideas or views. This suggests at the very least one task that needs to be undertaken in the audience studies of the near future: work with powerful informants, learn from debate and disagreement, and be modest, explicit and polemical. Learn to fight our corner in debates about the media with honorable and verifiable means.

Possibilities for Future Research

I have tried to draw a picture of reception analysis by following a trail back to a key moment in the history of the New Audience Research. Feminism was an integral force in how this now established field of research was developed. The formative influence of the feminist legacy in reception research becomes clear in the attention paid to (small) groups of women as audience members (I discussed Seiter's research as an example), in the preoccupation with popular culture and the private sphere (Ang's work on *Dallas* illustrates this well). But the small numbers of informants deemed sufficient to generalize on, is certainly also related. In fact, if as a researcher you belong to the group you have studied, you are in a privileged position to guarantee the veracity of what informants say. You will be able to relate the material to your own experience and base your conclusions on recognition rather than on a more analytic process of interpretation. Even the feminist call for self-reflexivity can thus become an obstacle, a hindrance rather than an asset. Getting locked into an implicit naturalist mode of research, which is based on an intuitive understanding of the truth of what informants say, will nullify the critical importance of bringing counter-knowledges to bear on your material and your own reflection. On these grounds, I suggest that our political commitment is best allied to a post-structuralist approach and understanding of audience research. Such an approach, to me, would seem the best guarantee for the strengths of the feminist project that also forged this area of research to remain a resource rather than a possible pitfall.

Recent studies in fact show that feminist post-structuralism, or a cultural studies approach to media and media reception, is in fact a productive starting-point. Anna McCarthy's highly original *Ambient Television* (2001) is a case in point. McCarthy is interested in television outside the boundaries we usually draw around this medium in research. Rather than look at television reception in the context of the home, she is interested in tracing the site-specific meanings of televisions in public spaces: taverns, department stores, shopping malls, waiting areas. These are, as McCarthy points out, obviously gendered spaces. In drawing out the social and institutional tasks television is asked to carry out in these spaces, she can also offer a new understanding of how gender is (pre)structured in public space, and especially how this happens in unobtrusive, everyday settings that we hardly notice but experience as simply and naturally there (2001, p. 9). To do so, she uses an amalgam of historical, ethnographic and feminist-post-structuralist research tools. Her ultimate goal is to counter pervasive and very arrogant notions of television. "Television, in different ways, is frequently characterized by journalists and academics alike in singular terms: as the privatization of public space, as a contaminant polluting the polis, bombarding us with images, destroying the pristine space of the public sphere" (2001, p. 4). These notions or typifications of the public and the private sphere are – again – highly gendered in their own right: the one as a rational masculine sphere, the other, invading it, as a sphere of sensation, irrationality and emotion, which in the modernist logic connecting the feminine with all of these, ultimately will lead to passivity and weakness (cf. Huyssen, 1986; Hermes, 1998). Although McCarthy's work in some ways moves in the outer regions of reception analysis (in looking at professional journals for retailers, for examples), it covers highly central concerns in other ways.

While McCarthy's work is clearly linked to the feminist project underlying the New Audience Research, as illustrated by her interest in the public versus the private sphere, the gendering of spaces and the power dynamics structured within them, it also poses questions that have more generally been taken up by cultural studies recently. One of these questions is how communities are produced. McCarthy suggests we ask how localized TV practices help designate forms of spatial belonging that can be understood in terms of community construction (2001, p. 20 and see chapter 7). No naive idealist, McCarthy discusses a no-less-than disastrously failed Atlanta video wall project in her last chapter. Nonetheless in her discussion she makes clear how different constituencies for a mall, for any public space for that matter, have their (historical) roots in both material and in interpretive communities. In this regard her discussion echoes recent work on cultural citizenship (Hartley, 1999; Gripsrud, 1999) which seeks to understand the same type of located interrelationships between audiences, media texts, the reputations of media and media genres and wider communities.

Another type of work, in which the concern with community is also echoed, is work that relies on researcher involvement in Internet chat groups or sites. Soukup (1999) participated in a sports-related (masculine-dominated) chatroom and a female-based and feminine-dominated chatroom. He labels his work "a critical ethnographic study." Earlier research has suggested that computer-mediated communication is certainly no utopian space when it comes to gender codes. Soukup's short article suggests that much more could be published exactly on the question of how gender is in many ways a question of style, rather than of concrete embodiment. The male chatroom characteristically has jokes and personal attacks (1999, p. 172), while the women's chatroom shows at first sight innocuous but nonetheless important strategies for establishing rapport (Soukup, 1999, p. 173). In both chatrooms men and women participated, often following socially established gender-appropriate codes. Most interesting from my perspective was the importance given to age by the chatters. Age clearly signifies mature behavior. This suggests that categories such as gender could perhaps be turned upside down by investigating them from the vantage point of the attractions of either or not being grown up.

The obvious example here is the work of David Buckingham (1993, 2000) who published a number of articles and books on children and the media. In a recent study, Buckingham and associates (Davies, Buckingham, & Kelley, 2000), discussed just this theme of the many attractions (for children) of not being a grown-up in enjoying media texts. Buckingham's work in general suggests to me that reception analysis will develop strongest and most heuristically if we are wary of how concerned we are about our research subjects. As feminists and as media and cultural studies scholars we owe the people who so generously share their time with us, or allow us to participate in their everyday lives, respect more than concern. Respect is the bottom line of any feminist venture and it should be of any study involving media audiences. Too easily set notions of the low value or even dangers of popular media such as television rub of on those we select as subjects of our research. They are in most cases not that different from other people nor from us academics and critics. It is more than anything the mechanics of academic research that can turn living, breathing, thinking people into mindless guinea pigs. The media are an integral part of how power is exercised in this society. No need for critical academic research to play that game on the side of the powerful. By analyzing how media use and the meanings of media texts are discursively structured, rather than by turning to individuals and the positions they have taken up, we avoid that thorny problem of generalizing from samples that are really far too small to do so and we may instead usefully theorize as well as criticize media texts, media use and media institutions while trying to keep up with its ever-changing forms and attractions. As Ellen Seiter notes discussing how a group of school children use *The Flintstones* to subtly rebel against school mores by quoting cartoon culture: today's world is a hall of (media) mirrors, with media texts embedded in a myriad of ways in everyday interaction (Seiter, 1999, p. 2). We might as well try and achieve a similar deftness in addressing power relations. This is not a plea to revere television culture as such or to celebrate "couch potatoism." As Buckingham notes, it is such terms that obstruct the possibility of making valid distinctions between different kinds of experience bound up with cultural production and consumption (cf. Buckingam, 1993, p. 211). Ultimately to understand these different experiences and to validate serious discussion of all of them is what reception analysis should be about.

References

Alasuutari, P. (1995). *Researching Culture*. London: Sage.

Ang, I. (1985). *Watching Dallas: Soap opera and the melodramatic imagination*. London: Methuen.

Ang, I. and Hermes, J. (1991). Gender and media consumption. In J. Curran and M. Gurevitch (eds.), *Mass Media and Society* (2nd edn.). London: Arnold, pp. 325–47.

Bordo, S. (1990). Feminism, postmodernism and gender-scepticism. In L. Nicholson (ed.), *Feminism/Postmodernism*. London: Routledge, pp. 133–56.

Bordo, S. (1993). *Unbearable Weight. Feminism, western culture and the body*. New York: Farrar, Straus and Giroux.

Brown, M. E. (1994). *Soap Opera and Women's Talk. The pleasure of resistance*. London: Sage.

Brownmiller, S. (1984). *Femininity*. New York: Fawcett Columbine.

Brunsdon, C. (1997). Identity in feminist television criticism. In C. Brunsdon, J. D'Acci, and L. Spigel (eds.), *Feminist Television Criticism: A reader*. Oxford: Oxford University Press, pp. 114–25. (Originally published in 1993.)

Buckingham, D. (1993). Conclusion: Re-reading audiences. In *Reading Audiences. Young people and the media*. Manchester: Manchester University Press.

Buckingham, D. (2000). *After the Death of Childhood. Growing up in the age of electronic media*. Cambridge: Polity Press.

Butler, J. (1990). *Gender Trouble. Feminism and the subversion of identity*. New York: Routledge.

Corner, J. (1991). Reappraising reception. Aims, concepts and methods. In J. Curran and M. Gurevitch (eds.), *Mass Media and Society* (2nd edn.). London: Arnold, pp. 280–304.

Curran, J. (1990). The new revisionism in mass-communication research: A reappraisal. *European Journal of Communication*, 5(2–3), 135–64.

Davies, H., Buckingham, D., and Kelley, P. (2000). In the worst possible taste. Children, television and cultural value. *European Journal of Cultural Studies*, 3(1), 5–26.

Douglas, S. J. (1994). *Where the Girls Are: Growing up female with the mass media*. New York: Time Books.

Drotner, Kirsten (1994). Ethnographic enigmas: "The everyday" in recent media studies. *Cultural Studies*, 8(2), 341–57.

Ferguson, M. and Golding, R. (eds.) (1997). *Cultural Studies in Question*. London: Sage.

Friedan, B. (1974 [1963]). *The Feminine Mystique*. New York: Dell.

Geraghty, C. (1998). Audience and ethnography: Questions of practice. In D. Lusted and C. Geraghty (eds.), *The Television Studies Book*. London: Arnold, pp. 141–57.

Gillespie, M. (1995). *Television, Ethnicity and Cultural Change*. London: Routledge.

Gramsci, A. (1971). *Prison Notebooks*. New York: International Publishers.

Gray, A. (1992). *Video Playtime. The gendering of a leisure technology*. London: Routledge.

Gray, A. (1999). Audience and reception research. The trouble with audiences. In P. Alasuutari (ed.), *Rethinking the Media Audience*. London: Sage, pp. 22–37.

Greer, G. (1970). *The Female Eunuch*. London: Paladin.

Gripsrud, J. (ed.) (1999). *Television and Common Knowledge*. London: Routledge.

Hammersley, M. and Atkinson, P. (1995). *Ethnography: Principles in practice* (2nd edn.). London: Routledge.

Hartley, J. (1999). *Uses of Television*. London: Routledge.

Hebdige, D. (1988). *Hiding in the Light: On images and things*. London: Routledge (Comedia).

Hermes, J. (1995). *Reading Women's Magazines. An analysis of everyday media use*. Cambridge: Polity Press.

Hermes, J. (1998). Gender and media studies: No woman, no cry. In J. Corner, P. Schlesinger, and R. Silverstone (eds.), *International Media Research. A critical survey*. London: Routledge, pp. 65–95.

Hermes, J. (2000). Of irritation, texts and men. *International Journal of Cultural Studies*, 3(3): 351–68.

Herzog, H. (1944). What do we really know about day-time serial listeners? In P. Lazarsfeld and F. N. Stanton (eds.), *Radio Research 1942–3*. New York: Duell, Sloan and Pearce, pp. 2–23.

Huyssen, A. (1986). Mass culture as woman: Modernism's other. In T. Modleski (ed.), *Studies in Entertainment: Critical approaches to mass culture*. Bloomington: Indiana University Press.

Jenkins, H. (1991). *Textual Poachers: Television fans and participatory culture*. New York: Routledge.

Kaplan, C. (1986). *Sea Changes: Culture and Feminism*. London: Verso.

Lewis, L. (ed.) (1992). *The Adoring Audience. Fan culture and popular media*. London: Routledge.

Liebes, T. and Katz, E. (1986). Patterns of involvement in television audiences. A comparative analysis. *European Journal of Communication*, 1(2), 151–72.

Lotz, A. D. (2000). Assessing qualitative television audience research: Incorporating feminist and anthropological theoretical innovation. *Communication Theory*, 10(4), 447–67.

McCarthy, A. (2001). *Ambient Television. Visual culture and public space*. Durham, NC and London: Duke University Press.

McQuail, D. (2000). *McQuail's Mass Communication Theory*. London: Sage.

McQuail, D., Blumler, J., and Brown, J. (1972). The television audience: A revised perspective. In D. McQuail (ed.), *Sociology of Mass Communication*. Harmondsworth: Penguin, pp. 172–94.

Morley, D. (1980). *The Nationwide Audience*. London: British Film Institute.

Morley, D. (1986). *Family Television: Cultural power and domestic leisure*. London: Methuen.

Morley, D. (1989). Changing paradigms in audience studies. In E. Seiter, H. Borchers, E. Warth, and G. Kreutzner (eds.), *Remote Control*. London: Routledge, pp. 16–43.

Morley, D. (1998). So-called cultural studies: Dead ends and reinvented wheels. *Cultural Studies*, 12(4), 476–512.

Noelle-Neumann, E. (1974). The spiral of silence: A theory of public opinion. *Journal of Communication*, 24, 24–51.

Potter, J. and Whetherell, M. (1987). *Discourse and Social Psychology*. London: Sage.

Radway, J. (1984). *Reading the Romance: Women, patriarchy and popular literature*. Chapel Hill: The University of North Carolina Press.

Radway, J. (1999). *A Feeling for Books. The Book-of-the-Month Club, literary taste, and middle-class desire*. Chapel Hill: University of North Carolina Press.

Seiter, E. (1990). Making distinctions in TV audience research: Case study of a troubling interview. *Cultural Studies*, 4(1), 61–84.

Seiter, E. (1999). *Television and New Media Audiences*. Oxford: Oxford University Press.

Soukup, C. (1999). The gendered interactional patterns of computer-mediated chatrooms: A critical ethnographic study. *The Information Society*, 15(3), 169–76.

Whetherell, M. and Potter, J. (1988). Discourse analysis and the identification of interpretive repertoires. In C. Antaki (ed.), *Analysing Everyday Explanation: A casebook of methods*. London: Sage, pp. 168–83.

CHAPTER NINETEEN

Salsa as Popular Culture
Ethnic Audiences Constructing an Identity

Angharad N. Valdivia

As the fields of media studies and popular culture continue to expand into both the dedicated study of audiences as a terrain for active creation of both cultural texts and individual and group identities (Ang, 1991; Hermes, 1995, this volume; Nightingale, 1993, 1996, this volume) and to the inclusion of ethnicity as a diverse, dynamic, and shifting social construct (Aparicio & Chávez Silverman, 1997; Flores and McPhail, 1997; García Canclini, 1995; Gilroy, 1993; Parameswaran, 1999, this volume), it behooves us to focus on the active construction of identity and culture by ethnic groups (Flores, 1993, 2000; Grossberg, 1996; Hall, 1996). In particular in the United States Latina/os compose the largest single minority and are projected to become the majority by the middle of the century (Gutiérrez, 1999; Darder & Torres, 1998; Davis, 1999; Oboler, 1995). Coupled with this demographic trend, which of course inspires marketing strategies (Dávila, 2000, 2001; Halter, 2000), we have the resurgence of Latin music and Latin pop in the US, so much so that in the past few years musical indicators such as the top 40 list and music awards have been consistently populated by Latina/o artists ranging from Ricky Martin, to Jennifer Lopez, Carlos Santana, Gloria Estefan, Los Van Van, the Buena Vista Social Club, Shakira, Marc Anthony, Enrique Iglesias, etc. Iconic Latinas such as Jennifer Lopez and Rosie Perez began their careers as dancers and, along with Salma Hayek, are often portrayed dancing in film and video so as to underscore their own Latinidad and to foreground the current popularity of Latin music and dance. As an accompanying practice, dance is seldom discussed although it is often the interface through which certain audiences and communities publicly represent their identity in relation to music and ethnicity. Through the study of salsa as a community building musical and dance practice, we have an opportunity to engage in a project that allows the combination of the focus on ethnicity, popular culture/media studies, and active audiences.

This essay is based on a multi-pronged study of a Midwestern, US community referred to as Cornsoya. In particular, I have sought to understand how it is that disconnected and heterogeneous "minority" groups and individuals as well as dominant culture peoples construct a community of affinity along ethnic lines through music and dance as forms of expressive popular culture. Through participant observation in a number of settings including dance instruction, band rehearsals, salsa parties, and dance nights at local bars as well as extensive interviews with different members of this community ranging from immigrant field workers and local residents to graduate students, faculty, and university administrators in the local university, I investigate (Denzin, 1997) the conscious process of identity formation which goes on in a community with little or no history of Latina/o populations.

This Cornsoya community exhibits a very active model of audience participation and creation which challenges us to revise our understanding of active audiences beyond the present preoccupation with resistance, too often limited to merely individualist audience-reported responses to popular culture texts (Valdivia, 2000). Instead I direct attention to the production of self, group, and media through the engagement with and extension of a particular form of cultural expressivity. This is in part informed by a new context of the dynamics related to globalization and hybridity. My arguments here are partly informed by how these new audience practices are linked to an understanding of globalization in which the phenomenon of migration and mobility deeply inform cultural practices and the composition of audiences. Furthermore like Lipsitz (1999b) reminds us, we must not over romanticize this migration which for many is an involuntary flight from a "scorched" homeland, where international capital ran roughshod over human and natural resources. These migrants co-exist with the more voluntary mobile populations of interstate and international students as well as with more rooted groups whose mobility might be yet to come.

What audiences are is not what audience research was built on anymore (Nightingale, 1993, 1996), and this is clearly supported by other contributors to the audience section of this volume. We now have a diasporic audience informed by different ethnic traces and migratory flows (Brathwaite, 1977; McCarthy, 1998; Sarup, 1996). It is a different context which leads to different types of audiences which engage with different types of texts. This creative practice challenges the previous model of ethnic-based subcultures who interpret certain texts in non-dominant or non-intended ways and proposes instead ethnically inspired hybrid populations who create their own communities and identities at the margins of mainstream culture. This active creation, coupled with the growing influence of Latinidad – that is, the dynamic process of constructing a Latina/o identity both from within and without – as a particularly central or important instance of this diasporic dynamic that is changing the relationship of audience to text and to popular culture makes a different claim of audience relationship to text – one that exceeds the notion of individual consumption or resistance to text to one that involves the active practice of identity work and community formation. Cultural expressivity is informed by communities that are coming from all over because of different contexts and different needs and desires with respect to cultural form. In turn the global affects the local so that the salsa scene includes diasporic and local groups and individuals (Wilson & Dissanayake, 1996). This type of study moves active audiences from the area of reception into the area of production and thus challenges that long standing binary opposition within media studies.

In terms of the emerging interdiscipline of US Latina/o Studies (Darder & Torres, 1998; garcia, Leger and Valdivia, forthcoming), this research project also urges us to look at ethnic hybridity in the US, beyond the still dominant black and white formulation and beyond the bi-coastal geographic tendencies. Much of the work in the Latina/o Studies interdiscipline has up to now focused on Mexican-Americans in the Southwest, Puerto Ricans in the East, and, to a lesser extent, Cubans in Miami. However a growing number of Latina/os live throughout the US in very heterogeneous communities composed of different Latina/o people as well as of a combination of other ethnicities, including Anglos. The creativity at this juncture is bound to be far more active as there are no pre-existing relationships, communities, histories, or groups on which to build a Latinidad. Finally, this study alerts us to the porosity of ethnic groups and popular culture forms, as the salsa community is not totally Latina/o and includes many post-colonial groups whose predilection for dance and music are not met by the mainstream as well as many US Anglos, especially males, who love to dance yet cannot totally indulge in that activity given that the US mainstream codes dancing both as a "color" and/or "gay" thing.[1] As such this study extends theory and method both of active audience and of gender and ethnic studies.

Latin Music and Dance

There are many forms of "Latin" music and dance. In fact, the apparent simplicity of the concept "Latin" is hard to sustain as it can be applied to anything coming from the many Latin countries, which would include the complete range of musical and dance possibilities, as well as to US notions of what Latin music and dance are, which is a much more reductive category (Storm Roberts, 1999). It is this latter approach which concerns me in this study of Latina/o American popular culture because this is the context in which salsa communities in the US construct an identity and a space for affinity. There is a nearly irresistible tendency, at least within US popular culture, and in many other cultures partly influenced by the successful exportation of US popular film and television, to associate Latin and now Latina/o populations with dance[2] and conversely to associate dance with Latina/os. If movies are any reliable indicators[3] an easy way to code a festive tone, at the very least, or a sensual-leading-into-sexual moment, in a more intense deployment of Latin signification, is to background the scene with Latin music, whether it be bossa nova, cha cha cha, samba, tango, or salsa. Latin music has come to signify not just Latina/o populations but also festivity, sensuality, and sexuality. Latin music and dance are crucial components of the tropicalizing tropes that Aparicio and Chávez-Silverman (1997) have identified in US mainstream popular culture as a way to signify Latinos and Latinidad.

Salsa is one of these forms of Latina/o music and dance. The study and popularity of salsa seems to have taken off lately with entire books devoted to the topic such as Frances Aparicio's *Listening to Salsa* (1998) and even articles in two consecutive issues of the journal *Cultural Studies* (Aparicio, 1999; Hosokawa, 1999; Sánchez González, 1999) about salsa, one of them about Orquesta de la Luz, the Japanese salsa group which, before disbanding in 1997, produced a number of hits crossing all sorts of borders. However, the majority of essays and books about salsa focus on the music, its roots, its influences, its popularity, and its changing characteristics but not on the dance itself (Bergman, 1985; Leymarie, 1985; Calvo Ospina, 1995; Storm Roberts, 1999; Waxer, 1999). In fact there are numerous books and essays about popular Latin music of all sorts (for example, in addition to the above, Best, 1995; Manuel, 1995; Rohler, 1990) and yet a small but burgeoning scholarship about popular Latin dance (Delgado & Muñoz, 1997; garcia, 1997; Lipsitz, 1999b; Roman Velazquez, 1999; Valdivia, 1999). Desmond (1997) urges us to approach the study of music and the study of dance together. This is all the more important, she suggests, given that dance is a much bracketed form of expressive culture. First, at least in the United States, dance "mark[s] clearly the continuing rhetorical association of bodily expressivity with non-dominant groups" (Desmond, 1997, p. 35) and is often linked to African-American and Latina/o populations. This, of course, is yet another instance of the nature/culture divide wherein peoples of color's dances are seen as part of our "nature" in opposition to, for example, the dance of ballet which is a cultural form to be studied and written about in the academy – one can major in ballet but not in salsa as a Fine Arts student. Not surprisingly, there are plenty of studies on ballet, the "classical" dance. Dance also serves to mark others in terms of sexuality and masculinity. If real white men don't dance, then male dancers must either be coded as gay or move to alternative, non-mainstream dance spaces. Second, dance remains to be seriously studied as a text, based on a semiotics of dancing. Desmond (1997) also challenges us to unmask the supposed transparency of dance expressivity. While there are many possible Latin dances to study, such as cumbia, merengue, tango, samba, quebradita, vallenato, etc., the focus of my study is on salsa partly because one of its origins is traced to the United States. Thus Hernando Calvo Ospina (1995) entitles his book, *!Salsa! Havana Heat, Bronx Beat*, explicitly dating the roots back to Cuba but the active creation to the Bronx in New York City.[4] Although there is quite a bit of disagreement as to the roots of salsa, there is nonetheless a nod to the possibility that salsa is a music and dance created by Latina/o populations living in the US as a result of an active, resistant, and dynamic, combination and extension of previous musical and dance forms in a minority and hostile cultural situation.

As such the creation of both the music and the dance is linked to previous cultural forms available in popular culture, albeit the popular culture of an ethnic group, and to the enlisting or "hailing" in Althusserian terms of the target audience, that is Latina/os in the US and those wanting to partake in Latina/o culture. However, as we know from the study of a broad range of cultural forms, it is difficult to police the boundaries of cultural expression (Benítez-Rojo, 1992; Flores, 2000; Rodríguez, 1997; Saldívar, 1997; Shohat, 1998; Shohat and Stam, 1994). So salsa as a form of cultural expressivity spreads internationally throughout the Americas but particularly in the Spanish/Hispanic Caribbean nexus – Cuba, Puerto Rico, Cali in Caribbean Colombia, Veracruz in Caribbean Mexico, Venezuela, Miami, and New York, both of the latter sites of much Caribbean migration. This is all to be expected, the proximitous spread of a cultural form. However, and undoubtedly building on the historically grounded coding of Latin music as dance music, salsa also spreads much more broadly both throughout the rest of the Americas, though not with as much intensity as in the previously mentioned areas, and through the world. Of course Spain is a logical place but Japan and Turkey also participate in this global movement of salsa so that Orquesta de La Luz, a Japanese salsa band whose lyrics are in Spanish, achieves global popularity until its disbanding in 1997 (Hosokawa, 1999). There are salsa bands in different countries of Africa (Fusco, 1999). Finally once can usually find a salsa club or a Latin music night that foregrounds salsa almost anywhere in the world. This has to do both with the spread of the musical form and with the diasporic population of Latina/os.

In terms of the United States the presence of Latina/os throughout the country means that, of course, one should expect to find salsa in New York and Miami. However, perhaps unexpectedly to many, one can also find salsa in many other places such as Detroit, Chicago, Champaign, Saint Louis, Seattle, New Orleans, San Diego, Austin, and San Antonio. In these and many other locations one can find some or all of the following: salsa bars, salsa nights, salsa lessons and/or Latin nights where salsa is a popular form of dance and music. Furthermore, just as the national boundaries cannot be policed, neither can the human ones so that one finds a diversity of people dancing salsa, especially in locations where there isn't a large homogeneous Latina/o community. This is the "noctural map" (Garcia Canclini, 1995) of salsa.

The Setting

Cornsoya is a small Midwestern community rich in corn and soya fields lying somewhere between two major US cities. It is the location for one of the major "Big Ten" universities, a consortium of institutions of higher education which reside on land grant locations and exchange resources as well as battle each other on collegiate sports, most notably US football and basketball. This community ranges from 100,000 people during the university terms to about 65,000 people when the university is on break. As such it is a classic university small town. There is really nothing nearby except hundreds of miles of agricultural fields which in the US employ large numbers of seasonal, mostly Latina/o labor. The community has a range of residents, both permanent and temporary, ranging from highly paid professionals to the poverty ridden agricultural and fast food workers. This is the human mix. Whenever possible I will give the ethnicity, profession or student status, and residency status of the participants in this community as it is important to show the broad diversity of origins as well as of occupations of those who are active in the formation of a community of expressive culture.

The cultural scene in this Midwestern town is somewhat predictable. Given the predominance of the university, the bulk of the bars cater to undergraduate students. Away from the university there are a couple of bars which occasionally host live entertainment, some bars with juke boxes, others with a "Country Western" theme, and the obligatory topless bar (which is constantly under attack by the police and the community). This is not a racially or ethnically progressive scene. Recently an African doctoral student celebrating his successful dissertation defense and job acquisition was denied entrance to one of the bars and beaten to death by the bouncers as his friends and fiancée were unable to secure help before it was too late. If a person wants to go to a bar or performance out of town, they have to drive for hours, if they have a car.

The Salsa Story

Within this somehow isolated yet unexpectedly heterogeneous context many groups and individuals host parties in their homes or in some type of hall. It was in one such occasion that Rodrigo, a Colombian computer science student, decided to teach a couple of girls at a party to dance salsa. The reaction was swift – all the girls wanted to learn. Rodrigo decided to begin hosting lessons in his living room, but even these small, word-of-mouth occasions proved to be challenging to handle inside a student's quarter. Another local resident, Scott, an Anglo young man and former violin university student who was born and raised in this community happened to be walking home drunk after another party when he came upon one of Rodrigo's lessons/parties (inevitably all of these lessons would turn into a festive occasion) and could not walk by without stopping. Scott was hooked and returned for more week after week. From Suriname, Margarita had traveled to Louisiana to pursue graduate computer studies. While there she organized an international, Latin American student group which would also celebrate with dances. When she moved to this community, she gravitated to the Rodrigo group and by the time Scott's drunken trip home took him by the lesson she was there, as Rodrigo's girlfriend, to help Scott learn to dance. These are some of the principals in this Midwestern story of community formation through cultural expressivity. I mention them in the same way that Rigoberta Menchú begins her book *Me Llamo Rigoberta Menchú y Así me Nació mi Conciencia*, not to single out these individuals but rather to show the arbitrariness of the forces that came together to begin a thriving salsa community in the middle of corn fields and thus to underscore the potential for creativity and community formation in even the most unlikeliest of places.

Of course Rodrigo was not the only person who could salsa and regular parties with other Colombians, Latina/os, Spanish, etc., students and local residents began to spring up. Rodrigo had to get an assistant, a fellow Colombian, to help him teach the classes and had to secure a larger place, which he did through the School of Music, to teach an ever growing number of people who wanted to take the classes. As well, as with any rapidly growing and evolving social organism, he had to begin to differentiate between the salsa students and offer beginner, advanced beginner, intermediate, and advanced classes. He claims he used all of the proceeds from the nominal instruction fee to pay for new music and for the huge parties he'd throw so that those taking classes could practice their lessons in a more "natural" setting.

At this time the university Latina/o cultural center and the university dance club, both official university groups, began to offer salsa and, to a lesser extent, merengue lessons to the community at large. The former were taught by a Peruvian community resident and the latter by Anglo students at the university. The fees were either nonexistent or very minimal so that it truly cannot be said that instruction costs were a barrier to entry to anyone. Simultaneously Chloe, a Chinese Canadian graduate student in ethnomusicology began her own salsa band. By nearly all accounts this early version of this band was "uneven" yet it galvanized many and served notice to the larger community as well as to local bars that there was both desire and audience for this type of music. All of this coalesced into the creation of a salsa community with several main players, different levels of "authenticity" of groups and players, and different locations for the learning and performance of salsa, the music and the dance.

This would be a modernist tale of progress were it not for the fact that a university community has a shifting and unstable population and that since many of the salseros of note, like Rodrigo, Margarita, and Chloe, were students, there were bound to be breaks and mobility. Nearly simultaneously Rodrigo left to study computer science abroad, and Chloe went to Cali, Colombia to conduct her ethnographic research on the salsa scene there. The lessons had to be taught by someone else. The band folded, albeit temporarily. Yet, this was not a moment of death but rather a moment of expansion and change. Margarita took over the lessons and sought help from her Colombian friend Helena. They approached dance instruction in a very different manner than Rodrigo had. They made out instruction plans, dissected salsa moves, and enlisted a drummer to incessantly beat the *clave*[5] to those rhythm-impaired souls taking the classes. They were very democratic in the assistance they provided to class participants, and, in all frankness, were aided by their gender as they could dance with the women whereas neither the male teachers nor the male students would dance with each other.[6] Margarita and Helena were very punctual in their approach to instruction, and, in addition to plastering community boards with announcements, began to develop an email list serve through which they would notify class takers, at least those who were online, of location changes, parties, radio shows, etc. The inclusionary and exclusionary potential of this electronic device would become more explicit as the salsa scene developed. They also enlisted Scott, who by this time resided in a perfectly suited large wooden floored loft, and had traded in his Birkenstocks for dancing shoes to host the parties. Furthermore they established a dress code for these parties so they would be even more like salsa dancing in the big cities. This dress code was widely advertised. Parties drew hundreds of people so that Margarita and Scott had to sit at the door and turn people away. Also, and as an amusing aside which reveals the policing tendencies of the larger community, party goers had to leave at 2 a.m., when the police would ticket anyone parked in a city spot, and move their cars to a private parking lot. Many salseros experienced police inspection[7] either at the point of moving their vehicles or at the point of leaving the party.

Despite these inspections (see Lugo, forthcoming), not surprisingly within one term of Margarita and Helena's dedicated approach, the number of students showing up for the beginner class jumped from roughly 20–30 in the early Rodrigo days to over 150! The class had to be divided into two, and Margarita co-taught one of these with Scott who by then had become a highly proficient dancer. Helena co-taught with Kevin, a Filipino medical student. Both classes had an ethnically diverse teaching couple, one of them without a Latina/o component. To aid and augment this process, Margarita began to pursue other venues. She approached the local community radio station for airtime. They would only grant her a half hour weekly show of "world music." She also began to approach local bars and dance halls for the opportunity to DJ a regular salsa night. She successfully gained access to one bar only to be summarily replaced by a male DJ. She then moved to another bar and later to a large dance hall which has the best and largest dance floor in town. Margarita, with the help of Helena and Manuel, a Cuban medical student, became the salsa impresario in this community.

At this time Eliseo, an undergraduate Mexican–American music education undergraduate student began to form his own band. Putting together a combination of local musicians and students proved to be quite a challenge in this isolated university community. To begin with, nearly all salsa musicians are self-trained as the university does not offer anything near salsa music instruction – a manner of policing "music" from whatever falls beyond, i.e. ethnic popular music. This made it very difficult to find a vocalist for nearly all Spanish-speaking singers had no vocal training and none of the local vocal students had any training in salsa singing. After an initial effort at importing band members from Chicago, two-and-a-half hours away, this proved economically unfeasible, and Eliseo had to try finding people locally. The results were rather disastrous at times – with a classically trained woman vocalist totally undermining the band's efforts and a totally untrained male Latino singer doing pretty much the same. This band eventually found the perfect female lead vocalist but only at the farewell performance of the band, shortly before its founder and many of its members were about to graduate and move out of town. Prior to that the band had a rather hunky looking trio of male singers, none of whom stood out as singers yet all of whom looked good in front of the band, a Milli Vanilli approach to salsa. The vocalist dilemma applied to instrumentalists as well, especially to the pianist. In fact, once a good pianist was found he ended up playing for both Eliseo's band and the new version of Chloe's band, which by all accounts was much better than the original. Thus, for a while this community actually had two competing homegrown salsa bands.

The return of Chloe and Rodrigo to the community coincided with Margarita's and later Helena's departure, the former to Holland and the latter to Colombia. Chloe assiduously set about reforming the band, and enlisted Manuel, the DJ and drum player previously employed by Margarita and Helena to beat the *clave* during lessons. Upon Margarita's departure Manuel took over DJ duties though he had already began to host a radio show which he later canceled because of its ungodly hour, two to four a.m., and resulting low audience. Other enlisted members included a university professor and a university cultural center director. Both bands were composed of a heterogeneous group of students, faculty, and local residents however Chloe/Manuel's band was able to enlist a more steady line-up of very attractive and charismatic Puerto Rican female singers. This band was also able to get gigs as far as Chicago and in the surrounding communities. Manuel proved to be a consummate businessman as well as a drum player and salsa dancer.

Many members of the now fully developed and growing salsa community noted that neither band was headed by a "real" salsero. Chloe's Chinese-Canadian features coupled with her attire, hair style, and make up could have easily "passed" as Latina, yet to most of those interviewed she remained, until her departure, a "Latina wannabe." Eliseo, a Mexican-American trumpeter and an excellent dancer himself was questioned because he was Mexican, and Mexico is not seen as a source of salsa or of dancing music, especially by the other Latina/os and Latin Americans of the community. In contrast, some of the Anglo musicians in this developing scene really appreciated Eliseo's musical sense, both as band director and as occasional DJ, as well as his "suave" dancing style. In short, the community had grown to a size and level of specialization that its members had began to police their own borders and to differentiate between each other. The active audience in constructing a community and an identity started in a Nietszchean manner to define itself in opposition to an other (McCarthy, 1998). Whereas previously the community rose partly in response to being policed by and out of the mainstream, by then it was developing its own set of inclusions and exclusions. There were now a mainstream and margins within the salsa scene.

At this point in time the salsa scene was in full bloom. In addition to two local bands, there were at least three different sets of non-university teachers who taught different levels of salsa five times a year (twice each semester and once during the summer term); one dance hall which also offered salsa classes; the university's Latina/o students' cultural house whose own director played in one of the bands also offered classes which offered free lessons; and the university students' dance club offered classes and sponsored Big Ten dance competitions which included some Latin dances, and of course one of them was salsa. Members of the salsa community regularly offered salsa parties, and university organizations such as the French House offered them as well. Even local activist groups, such as El Centro de los Trabajadores, a migrants' rights organization, held salsa fund raisers with the bands donating the proceeds. On the radio there was a regular salsa show, whereas before the "world music" slot had to cover any and all "Third World" music. Some of the salsa instructors began to, and to this day, keep e-mail list-serves informing its members of lessons, movies, parties, performances, and related events such as tango lessons and visiting master teachers. Performances of Chloe's band at the local dance hall would draw hundreds of dancers. As well the most popular bar outside of campus town began to host a regular salsa night on Sundays which would entirely fill up the place. Other bars, ranging from five to one at any given time, began offering salsa nights, often hosted by the instructors or band members and also offering salsa lessons prior to the beginning of the DJ music. For example Rodrigo, who before leaving taught his classes with Patricio, an Argentine graduate biology student, hosted a bar night as did Manuel and also Eliseo. Different bars attempted the Salsa Night thing – though none during the prime bar time of Friday and Saturdays because salsa dancers just do not drink as much as other types of music or dance audiences. Nonetheless, all of a sudden you could salsa four or five nights a week, quite usually to live music.

Authenticity and Belonging

From the beginning of the scene, certain characteristics of the founders influenced the way salsa was seen and to whom it "belonged" in this particular community. Certain national origins were more legitimate than others. Rodrigo's initial and now legendary status – he has since left the community as he finished his degrees – coded salsa dancing as something Colombians did extremely well. In fact, Colombians possess great authenticity points for a number of other reasons. The New Year's Salsa Festival in Cali, Colombia, which hosts and has hosted most of the worlds' major salsa bands and singers, holds the imagination of many, including many in this community. In fact not only did one prominent member, Chloe, write her entire dissertation about salsa in Cali, but many of the people, Colombian or not, have traveled to Cali in a sort of salsa pilgrimage. One particular graduate French student, who chose to study at this university, as opposed to many others, because of the salsa community, actually arranged to teach French in Colombia so she could experience salsa in its "natural" setting. Unfortunately she was stationed in northern Colombia where vallenato reigns supreme, and could only get to Bogotá once. She never made it to her mecca,

Cali. As well, Helena, an excellent dancer, teacher, and story teller, would regale listeners with her tales of trips to Cali – "overnight from Colombia; once I almost got killed in a car accident . . ." In fact the type of hard-driving salsa that Cali and Colombians produce, or at least are known for producing for undoubtedly there is a variety of Colombian salsa, remains popular in this community with the new DJ Pancho in a new dancing spot playing almost exclusively that type of music. The combination of Colombian teachers, Cali, and musical style all influenced the high status of authenticity of Colombians within this community which meant that Colombians who could not dance salsa were and continue to be seen as an anomaly. At least one such male student stopped attending salsa nights because of the incessant incredulity of others when they found out he was a Colombian who could not salsa. In this community being Colombian equaled being a salsero.

The two other nationalities claiming a direct and authentic connection to salsa were Cubans and Puerto Ricans, whether recent immigrants, temporary students, or second- or third-generation citizens of the US. These two nationalities signed as such authentic components of the salsa scene that not only did people not question their right to belong and rule, but they also attributed to them particular characteristics about dancing. For example, "Cubans are *caballeros*," and "Puerto Ricans look away when they dance with you." There is really no overwhelming agreement as to the attributes, but their dancing was complex and authentic enough to deserve differentiation. As well, very good dancers were often assumed to be either Cuban or Puerto Rican though they actually came from any number of places.

Lagging behind the Colombians, Cubans, and Puerto Ricans were a polyglot mix of other nationalities who somehow acquired salsa skills, sometimes in local lessons or sometimes in other communities, but seldom in their land of origin. By and large this third group learned to salsa in the United States, though many of them were attracted to the music and the dance in their country of origin. This group included many of the other Latina/os and Latin Americans. Whereas Rodrigo claimed to have learned salsa "in the womb" and Rodolfo, a Venezuelan graduate student, learned it at home dancing with his mother, this third group had to seek some type of formal or informal instruction. As an Argentinean sociology student tells it, "When I moved to Texas I found I was no longer Argentinean but Latina. Then I found that to be really Latina I had to dance salsa. So I took lessons from a Chilean teacher who had gone through the same process a few years earlier." When I asked Patricio, the Argentine co-instructor with Rodrigo how he came to be such a proficient salsero, he answered "Pero ché, es que soy Latino" demonstrating that he had already internalized both the Latino identity and the notion that Latinos are "naturals" at dance. In this third group we also had a lovely Chilean dancer whom everyone thought was Puerto Rican, precisely because she danced so well.

Beyond the Latin Americans who learned to dance salsa, this third group, included Black Diaspora peoples, whether African American, Caribbean, South

American, or European, for example Afro-Portuguese. By virtue of skin color, many in the salsa community assigned these participants high legitimate status despite their wide variety of origins and salsa competencies. For example, whereas a Costa Rican medical student was quite proficient in salsa, a recent Ghanaian immigrant was encountering it for the first time. It is important to note that the Costa Rican student learned the dance here in the US as the Ghanaian student would soon be able to claim. Nonetheless, they were both treated as insiders within this third group category which extended to those considered Latin and/or of color enough to be included as insiders partly because they would be the same ones coded as outsiders within the mainstream of US popular culture.

A fourth group was a little bit more heterogeneous and, arguably, the most dedicated to salsa as they consciously sought to refashion their identity within this Latina/o coded community. This group included an Anglo art student who learned to salsa while traveling through Mexico; a Turkish molecular biology doctoral student who taught classes with Scott and was sometimes confused as a Latina because she was little, cute, had curly dark hair, and was an excellent dancer; a Moroccan woman with "Latina" features and superior dancing skills; an assortment of Spanish students, many of whom learned to dance salsa in Spain and others who took classes in this community; and French, Indian, and Russian – to name a few of the many nationalities – students and community residents who had gravitated to the salsa scene as a place of belonging and where they could dance or watch others dance. Some of these people told me they could not separate social from dancing occasions. As one Vietnamese graduate student said, "In White parties people drink, smoke and talk but whenever you get people of color there is also dance." This third group was very heterogeneous yet composed of people accepted as salseros, albeit not the "truly authentic" ones.

The fifth group, and possibly the most numerous of all of them, was a heterogeneous combination of Mexicans and Mexican-Americans. While there are many commonalities among them, there are also strong identity differences between them. Many of the Mexican-Americans were first-generation, working-class college students, both undergraduate and graduate. The Mexicans however were composed of two distinct groups; some of them came from upper-middle or upper classes in Mexico and attended the university as students whereas the bulk of them were seasonal agricultural and low-wage migrant workers. As is the case with most Latin American countries (see Lugo, forthcoming) skin color roughly maps out over class in Mexico. This resulted in the Mexican university students being lighter, by and large, than the workers. Of course, members of the community who spoke Spanish could differentiate among these three Mexican-American groups by their different language competencies and accents. Among those who could or cared to tell a difference among the members of this group, there was also a tendency to lump this group into one undifferentiated category in relation to the other groups. In sum there was a barely subterranean anti-Mexicanness in this community among many other Latina/os and Latin Americans. This hostility was lost on non Latina/os and non Latin Americans.

Unexpectedly, many Mexicans and Mexican-Americans also seemed unaware of this prejudice.

Attitudinal as it was, this prejudice nonetheless presented itself both in the dance floor as well as in access to the dance floor. Thus when Manuel attempted to play some Mexican ranchera music at a Sunday salsa night at one of the most popular and crowded bars, prominent salseros, including many of the ones foregrounded in this study, loudly proclaimed "This is not music!" or "This is against my religion" and conspicuously walked out of the bar till either merengue or salsa was played. Manuel himself tried to play a wider range of music than just salsa and merengue but noticing some of these reactions reverted to the two musics with an occasional Latin rock intervention. Interviews with other salseros suggested that non-Mexican Latina/os and Latin Americans shared a prevailing anti-Mexican perspective in general that in the salsa community translated into the view that Mexico has neither contributed music nor dance to "Latin" culture. Some of those interviewed, especially those who had recently migrated to the United States from Latin America, reported being mildly confused when referred to as Latina/os in the US but highly insulted when called "Mexican." This resulted in a number of exclusionary patterns. At the very least some of the reservation towards Eliseo's band was due to his Mexican-American-ness. Some members of the community who learned to dance from Eliseo were chided by more "authentic" participants of the first two groups for learning from a Mexican-American. Similarly, Miriam, a Mexican-American salsera in Chloe's band was often incredulously questioned about her salsa singing and dancing ability given that she was Mexican-American. This was all beyond the radar of many of those in groups four through six. In fact, some of the most proficient non Latina/o American dancers loved to dance with Eliseo and never questioned Miriam's place in the band and the dance floor.

However, even more specific measures, other than verbal policing, were developed to minimize Mexican and Mexican-American participation. After the local dance hall canceled salsa nights because of smoking in the dance floor and outdoor "disturbances," there was disagreement over who caused this ruckus. Many suggested it was a "bunch of rich Colombians" who would occasionally show up drunk and/or under the influence of other controlled substances. However, it was also argued that it was Mexicans and Mexican-Americans who lacked the manners to participate in this social space. This was all the easier to sustain given the general class difference and therefore access to decision making within the salsa community between the bulk of Latina/os and Latin Americans not of Mexican descent, who were either students or middle-class members of the community, and many of the Mexicans who were either farm or fast food workers. A plan was worked out to reopen the dance hall but with a revised dress code – as if the dress code itself could take care of class differences, which in a cosmetic way it did. However, this decision was accompanied by also stopping the posting of notices about salsa nights and classes in local Mexican grocery stores and Mexican food restaurants so as "to not attract that undesirable group."

This had the effect of reducing the participation of working class Mexicans as few of them are online. Of the few who managed to find out about the dances and show up, some were turned away at the door because of violation of dress code.[8] I have been taking notes at the door when a group of cleanly dressed, well behaved, non English speaking Mexicans showed up and were denied entry. Despite the fact that their jeans were washed and ironed and their T-shirts or flannel shirts were equally prepared, they did not meet the dress code. Often they did not understand why they were being turned away as they had neither access to the information nor to the codes – the English language, the dress code, or the consumption patterns which differentiate between sneakers and "dance" shoes. Of course hegemony is leaky, and several Mexican salseros became part of the in-group. One of them became the DJ in the most popular salsa night and another, who entered the community as a recent farm worker immigrant, even placed in local salsa competitions. However it is important to note that there is this undercurrent of discrimination, which is invisible to the non Latina/o or Latin American members of the community.

The sixth group consists of an ever growing group of mostly Anglos in process of learning to dance, or more fundamentally, learning to tell the difference between merengue and salsa and to recognize the beat within each of these musics. Some of them, mostly gringos, doggedly participate in this scene, and, as Margarita noted, "Sadly cannot get the beat." This group of beat-impaired souls sometimes included members of all the groups, but more numerous among them were Anglo students like George, who got dragged into his first salsa class by a friend who wanted "to pick up chicks" and he stayed though his friend left. He continued to take salsa lessons, always struggling with the beat, and always marked as an outsider, albeit a well-liked one. After getting his doctorate George included in his relocation criteria the availability of a salsa scene in a city before he'll accept a job. Not surprisingly, George decided to take his first postdoctoral position in the same community where he'd been dancing for years.

Among this sixth group were participants who had taken part in this community since its very inception. Like George, Scott fell into this default group. Thus while he became a consummate dancer, dated and hung out with the best female dancers, many of them of high legitimacy status, he was never quite considered an insider. The following comment could often be heard as he danced: "He sure dances well, for a gringo!" Perhaps due to the fact that he is tall, blue eyed, and has long blonde hair, his appearance deviated too much from the "Latino" look to fit in, despite the fact that he often danced with US or Euro-Anglo women whose status in the community was not nearly as policed. Certainly there were both gender and phenotypic markers which rendered Scott a permanent outsider, especially among Latino men, many of whom have very Anglo features though perhaps not as overly performed as Scott's. Undoubtedly, resistance to Scott among many of the legitimate and authentic dancers also included a healthy bit of envy. After all women like to dance with a good dancer, mostly regardless of appearance. In fact one of the female dancers proudly confessed, "There is a lot I forgive from a man, if he is a good dancer." One could plainly see this dynamic in the dance floor as proficient short male dancers deftly guided statuesque women around the floor. This is no small feat given both the tendency in heterosexual couplings for women to choose a taller male and the fact that in salsa the male turns the woman *under* his arm, quite a difficult move for a man six or more inches shorter than his female dancing partner. There were many in this community for whom salsa became part of their lives and their identity and for whom salsa became a requisite part of their community, wherever it may be. Whether George stayed or Scott left, they both continue to regularly dance salsa. In fact, Scott credits salsa with saving him from depression and aimless wondering after he was forced to give up violin performance following a sports accident. For Scott salsa was a saving grace.

All of the participants in this dance scene sought an alternative place for music, dance, community, and cultural affinity. Whether Latina/os and Latin Americans sought to reconstruct a dance hall/party feel in contradistinction to the hard rock beer hall predominance in a university town, or whether all sorts of other people, from all over the country and the world, gravitated toward a more porous space of ethnicity, music, and dance, all of the participants in this salsa scene actively moved and contributed to the salsa scene in Cornsoya. These participants were both reacting to mainstream popular culture tendencies and creating a new space for leisure and desire. More than taking a particular text and interpreting it differently, they were looking at the fabric of this university life and seeking and building an alternative space. As such, their role as active audience crossed over into agency and labor into the production of an alternative space. These participants were also being lured by bars who recognized an opportunity for profit, albeit one whose numbers did not translate into huge alcoholic consumption. Accordingly, the most enduring salsa space remains the dance hall, where drinking is a reduced and limited side activity and entry fees pay for the use of the space.

Within this burgeoning heterogeneous and dynamic community in Cornsoya composed of hybrid individuals and groups who found themselves in proximity to others from a diverse set of origins for a diverse set of reasons, there were no easy demarcations between belonging and outsider status. In a sense everyone was simultaneously an insider, in the salsa community by choice, and an outsider, in the mainstream music and dance community, both by choice and design. Therefore the borders around authenticity were extremely difficult to police though that did not stop people from trying. Because of the particular, and partly random, origins of this salsa community, Colombians achieved hyperauthentic status. Yet, it would be difficult for most in the larger community – that is, beyond the salseros – to tell the difference between a Colombian and a Turk. In fact, as mentioned above, it was often difficult for members of the salsa community to determine origin and therefore authenticy for many of the participants in the salsa scene. Many could, and did become, ethnic cross-dressers. In fact, studies of heterogeneous communities, such as this one, force us to acknowledge the difficulty of determining ethnicity as well as of drawing boundaries around ethnic populations and ethnic cultural forms. Once dislocated from their origins, both populations and forms take on other meanings in a radically contingent manner. Often, as Dávila (2001) and Halter (2000) have documented, cultural forms lend themselves quite easily to mainstream commodification. Fusco (1995) reminds us that in the mainstream this commodification extends only to acceptance of products and cultural forms and not necessarily to the people who produced or originated those products and cultural forms. The creation of this salsa scene provided for some the opportunity to engage in a cultural form of choice with a broad range of people. Still, this was not a community without internal prejudice.

This whole area of scholarship is made more complex by the radical hybridity of Latina/o populations both in the US and throughout the world (see Haney López, 1996). The US Census, for example, separates white Hispanics from other Whites – thus the category "white, not hispanic" – while not making the same distinction for Blacks. There is no equivalent "Black, not Hispanic." In the US one can be Hispanic if from Spain, Portugal, or anywhere in Latin America and the Caribbean. This includes at least two major languages, Spanish and Portuguese, as well as a number of others including English, Dutch, and French, and many indigenous languages present in the Americas prior to the Spanish landing. Even if one decided to trace Latina/o origins to Spain, that does not solve the problem of racial purity as, unlike most popular and academic efforts suggest, Spain is not a site for Whiteness. The Moorish occupation of the Andalusian region for centuries guarantees, at the very least, a hybrid Spanish population of Arab and African descent. In fact, as Lipsitz (1999a) reminds us, a turn to Latina/o Studies forces us to explore the radical hybridity that composes every population, especially in the US.

The scholarship on active audiences is a welcome addition to the fields of popular culture and media studies. We certainly needed to move beyond the formulation of media and culture as determinant of meaning. Whereas there undoubtedly exist numerous instances of individual responses, often based on gender and ethnic background, which differ from the intended ones, we must envision the potential of active audiences beyond mere responses or textual readings, even if negotiated or oppositional. A theoretical framework guided by the study of identity as practice and community formation as labor in an age of globalization, leads us into a far more active conceptualization of active audience from the realm of reception into the realm of production. Audiences can produce communities and as such they can adopt cultural forms to signify their identity as a community. Community formation does not map easily over single ethnicity lines. Furthermore ethnicities themselves are highly complex and diverse. In particular, it is difficult to sustain a pure Latina/o ethnicity when the roots of Latinidad are so diverse and complex.

This case study of salsa in a Midwest community highlights that the process of diasporic flows results in the creation of communities in unlikely places. Furthermore, these communities can be thriving and alter the cultural scene of any given location – the global changes the local. The process of creation is quite dynamic. It involves an approach which includes teaching classes, forming bands, securing radio programs, sustaining websites, and gaining bar access. All the while the community kept itself informed of developments within and without. Different media are used to reach different populations. The decision to stop using printed announcements in Mexican restaurants, for example, can mean the exclusion of a whole range of people. The net is a wonderful way to communicate if you have access to computers updated enough to sustain today's web servers. As well, while the main players and their status contain both arbitrary and predictable elements, there is nothing natural about this constructed community based on hybrid identities. There is, for example, no natural reason why Colombians sign in as the most authentic salseros. This aura of authenticity had to be created and maintained, albeit not in a necessarily conscious effort. Furthermore, the salsa scene cannot and ought not to be reduced to Latina/os as it is impossible in this global age to keep populations and cultural affinities separate. Thus we must move toward a study of Latinidad, the process whereby that which is seen as Latina/o, enters different cultural spaces rather than a study of what Latina/o individuals and groups do on their own and *vis-à-vis* popular culture.

Moreover, we must be cautioned not to romanticize this creation beyond critical inquiry. As this study suggests, this community exhibits, indeed creates, exclusionary tendencies along gender, class, and ethnic lines as well as in terms of national origin, which should cause us to pause both in terms of homogenizing ethnic groups such as Latina/os (among ourselves, it turns out, we are not without prejudice) and of romanticizing the unity and conviviality at the margins. Latina/os discriminate against other Latina/os. Some Latina/os internalize essentialist notions that Latina/os, for example, are natural dancers. Nearly everyone in the community, including Latina/os and non Latina/os, immediately assumed that African Diaspora participants also had an innate dancing ability. This automatic inclusion was achieved through uncritical acceptance of narratives of racial difference. Some women achieved high authenticity status both through performing Latinidad in appearance and achieving dance skills while other crossers were found to be "trying too hard" and were labeled "wannabes." The fissures and attempts to differentiate within the community were deployed both through behavior and access practices. Thus it was quite possible for the most numerous component of US Latinidad, Mexican-Americans, to find themselves at the margins of this salsa community. Human beings as well as prejudices cross borders. Some of these exclusionary tendencies were more evident to some than others but nonetheless structured some groups' participation and saliency in the community.

Finally we cannot assume that ethnicity and its forms of cultural expressions function as puddles of oil in a pool of water. Salsa is a metaphor for Latinidad but not only Latina/os salsa. In the salsa halls of this community new identities were being constructed and relationships between and among ethnic groups flourished. Differential migratory patterns influenced the power of individual and group players – still migration, of both people and cultural form, enabled this new space for the performance of identity. Salsa, rather than any particular ethnicity, functioned as the loose ingredient which drew people together in this amorphous community. Salsa thus is a way for Latinidad to police its borders as well as, in the more traditional sense, for Anglo mainstream communities to engage in a desire of the other, or in a more enduring sense for the larger community, the global one that is, to include a pleasurable and internally conflictual form of expressive culture in its mix of dynamic and hybrid local and global identities.

Notes

1 While also beyond the scope of this essay, one of the components of the "marked" status of dance in the US is the gendered aspect. Women are seen as the "natural dancers" and therefore any man, especially a white dominant culture man, who likes to and engages in dance, is coded as "abnormal" or homosexual. Notice the moment of realization in the recent movie *In and Out* comes when the protagonist realized he is indeed gay because he cannot keep himself from dancing.

2 While out of the focus of this book, the recently coined identity marker of Latina/o proposes, among other components, a pan-Latina/o and pan-ethnic diverse identity whose boundaries are still quite unclear. For example, some exclude Brazilian origin populations despite that country's immense contribution to musical and dance trends while others include Spanish origin people, such as Antonio Banderas and Penélope Cruz.

3 For example, in the *Battle of Algiers*, the colonial French teenagers in a soon to be bombed discotheque are dancing to some cha-cha-cha, and I have interviewed people from places as diverse as Ghana and Turkey who associate dancing music with Latin music. I choose the *Battle of Algiers* as an example precisely because it is not a Hollywood film yet it is still subject to particularly US proclivities.

4 This book is also a testament to the global spread of salsa and of salseros, as the book was originally published, in Dutch, in Antwerp.

5 The *clave* is the basic 2–3 beat of salsa. It is what distinguishes salsa from merengue or cha cha cha or from other forms of music and dance.

6 This was a real problem when Rodrigo and another man taught the class and male students had to learn by watching whereas female students could practice dancing with the teachers.

7 I myself was stopped by a policeman on the way home after a salsa night at a downtown bar. The policeman let me go with a warning once I showed my university faculty identification card. Not everyone was so lucky. Others received tickets.

8 A sample e-mail dress code warning goes as follows: "The X is a smoke free environment and strictly enforces the dress code so don't forget about it specially if you bring new friends to the dance. Dress code: No hats, No jeans or baggie pants, No tennis shoes or boots. Shirts tucked in please."

References

Ang, I. (1991). *Desperately Seeking the Audience*. New York: Routledge.

Aparicio, F. R. (1998). *Listening to Salsa: Gender, Latin popular music, and Puerto Rican cultures*. Hanover, NH: Wesleyan University Press.

Aparicio, F. R. (1999). The blackness of sugar: Celia Cruz and the performance of (trans)nationalism. *Cultural Studies*, 13(2), 223–6.

Aparicio, F. R. and Chávez-Silverman, S. (eds.) (1997). *Tropicalizations: Transcultural representations of latinidad.* Hanover: University Press of New England.

Benítez-Rojo, A. (1992). *The Repeating Island: The Caribbean and the postmodern perspective.* Durham, NC: Duke University Press.

Bergman, B. (1985). *Hot Sauces: Latin and Caribbean pop.* New York: Quill.

Best, C. (ed.) (1995). *Barbadian Popular Music and the Politics of Caribbean Culture.* New York: Alterations Consultants Inc.

Brathwaite, E. (1977). *Contradictory Omens: Cultural diversity and integration in the Caribbean.* Kingston, Jamaica: Savacou Publications Ltd.

Calvo Ospina, H. (1995). *!Salsa!: Havana heat, Bronx beat.* New York: Monthly Review Press.

Darder, A. and Torres, R. D. (eds.) (1998). *The Latino Studies Reader: Culture, economy and society.* London: Blackwell.

Dávila, A. (2000). Mapping Latinidad: Language and culture in the Spanish TV battlefront. *Television and New Media,* 1(1), 75–94.

Dávila, A. (2001). *Latinos Inc.: The marketing and making of a people.* Berkeley: University of California Press.

Davis, M. (1999). Magical urbanism: Latinos reinvent the US big city. *New Left Review,* 234 (March/April): 3–43.

Delgado, C. F. and Muñoz, J. E. (eds.) (1997). *Everynight Life: Culture and dance in Latin/o America.* Durham, NC: Duke University Press.

Denzin, N. K. (1997). *Interpretive Ethnography: Ethnographic practices for the 21st century.* Thousand Oaks, CA: Sage.

Desmond, J. C. (ed.) (1997). *Meaning in Motion: New cultural studies of dance.* Durham, NC: Duke University Press.

Flores, J. (1993). *Divided Borders: Essays on Puerto Rican identity.* Houston: Arte Público Press.

Flores, J. (2000). *From Bomba to Hip-Hop: Puerto Rican culture and Latino identity.* New York: Columbia.

Flores, L. and McPhail, M. (1997). From Black and White to *Living Color*: A dialogic exposition into the social (re)construction of race, gender, and crime. *Critical Studies in Mass Communication,* 14(1), 106–122.

Fusco, C. (1995). *English is Broken Here: Notes on cultural fusion in the Americas.* New York: The New Press.

Fusco, C. (1999). Personal conversation.

garcia, m. (1997). "Memories of El Monte": Intercultural dance halls in post-World War II greater Los Angeles. In J. Austin and M. Nevin Willard (eds.), *Generations of Youth: Youth cultures and history in twentieth-century America.* New York: New York University Press.

garcia, m. Leger, M., and Valdivia, A. (forthcoming). *Geographies of Latinidad: Mapping Latina/o studies into the twenty-first century.* Durham, NC: Duke.

García Canclini, N. (1995). *Hybrid Cultures: Strategies for entering and leaving modernity.* Minneapolis: University of Minnesota Press.

Gilroy, P. (1993). *The Black Atlantic: Modernity and double consciousness.* Cambridge, MA: Harvard University Press.

Grossberg, L. (1996). Identity and cultural studies – Is that all there is? In S. Hall and P. du Gay (eds.). *Questions of Cultural Identity.* London: Sage.

Gutiérrez, D. (1999). Migration, emergent ethnicity, and the "third space": The shifting politics of nationalism in Greater Mexico. *The Journal of American History,* 86(2), 481–517.

Hall, S. (1996). Introduction: Who needs "identity"? In S. Hall and P. du Gay (eds.), *Questions of Cultural Identity.* London: Sage.

Halter, M. (2000). *Shopping for Identity: The marketing of ethnicity.* New York: Shocken Books.

Haney López, I. F. (1996). White lines. In *White By Law: The legal construction of race.* New York: New York University Press, pp. 1–35.

Hermes, J. (1995). *Reading Women's Magazines. An analysis of everyday media use.* Cambridge: Polity Press.

Hosokawa, S. (1999). "Salsa no tiene frontera": Orquesta de la Luz and the globalization of popular music. *Cultural Studies*, 13(3), 509–34.

Leymarie, I. (1985). Salsa and Latin jazz. In B. Bergman (ed.), *Hot Sauces: Latin and Caribbean pop*. New York: Quill.

Lipsitz, G. (1999a). Remarks made to the "Territories and Boundaries: Interdisciplinary Perspectives on Theory, Methodology, and Curriculum in Latina/o Studies" at the Center for Advanced Study, University of Illinois, Champaign-Urbana, March 24.

Lipsitz, G. (1999b). "Home is where the hatred is": Work, music, and the transnational economy." In H. Naficy (ed.), *Home, Exile, Homeland: Film, media and the politics of place*. New York: Routledge.

Lugo, A. (forthcoming). Border Inspections: The case of the El Paso-Juarez area. In m. garcia, M. Leger, and A. Valdivia (eds.), *Geographies of Latinidad: Latina/o studies into the twenty-first century*. Durham, NC: Duke University Press.

Manuel, P. (1995). *Caribbean Currents: Caribbean music from rumba to reggae*. Philadelphia: Temple University Press.

McCarthy, C. (1998). *The Uses of Culture: Education and the limit of ethnic affiliation*. New York: Routledge.

Nightingale, V. (1993). What's "ethnographic" about ethnographic audience research? In J. Frow and M. Morris (eds.), *Australian Cultural Studies: A reader*. Urbana: University of Illinois Press.

Nightingale, V. (1996). *Studying Audiences: The shock of the real*. London: Routledge.

Oboler, S. (1995). *Ethnic Labels, Latino Lives: Identity and the politics of (re)presentation in the United States*. Minneapolis: University of Minnesota Press.

Parameswaran, R. (1999). Western romance fiction as English-language media in postcolonial India. *Journal of Communication*, 49(2), 84–105.

Rodríguez, C. E. (1997). *Latin Looks: Images of Latinas and Latinos in the U.S. media*. Boulder, CO: Westview Press.

Rohler, G. (1990). *Calypso and Society in Pre-Independence Trinidad*. Port of Spain, Trinidad: Gordon Rohler.

Roman Velazquez, P. (1999). *Making of Latin London*. London: Ashgate.

Saldívar, J. D. (1997). *Border Matters: Remapping American cultural studies*. Berkeley: University of California Press.

Sánchez González, L. (1999). Reclaiming Salsa. *Cultural Studies*, 13(2), 237–50.

Sarup, M. (1996). *Identity, Culture and the Postmodern World*. Athens, GA: The University of Georgia Press.

Shohat, E. (1998). *Talking Visions: Multicultural feminism in a transnational Age*. New York: MIT Press.

Shohat, E. and Stam, B. (1994). *Unthinking Eurocentrism: Multiculturalism and the media*. New York: Routledge.

Storm Roberts, J. (1999). *The Latin Tinge: The impact of Latin American music on the United States*. New York: Oxford.

Valdivia, A. N. (1999). Reconstructing Latinidad through salsa: Cultural struggle and formation in the prairie. Paper presented to the "Culture, Place, and the Cultures of Displacement" First Annual Spring Conference of the Illinois Program for Research in the Humanities at the University of Illinois, April.

Valdivia, A. N. (2000). *A Latina in the Land of Hollywood and Other Essays on Media Culture*. Tucson: University of Arizona Press.

Waxer, L. (1999). Consuming memories: The record centered salsa scene in Cali. In C. McCarthy et al., *Sound Identities: Popular music and the cultural politics of education*. New York: Peter Lang.

Wilson, R. and Dissanayake, W. (eds.) (1996). *Global/Local: Cultural production and the transnational imaginary*. Durham, NC: Duke University Press.

PART FIVE

Effects

CHAPTER TWENTY

Race and Crime in the Media
Research from a Media Effects Perspective

Mary Beth Oliver

Fear of crime and support for harsh forms of criminal punishment seem out of step with decreasing crime rates. Despite the fact that murder rates are lower now than they have been in the last eight years (Butterfield, 2001; Uniform Crime Reports, 1999), concern about criminal victimization is apparent in a variety of contexts, including neighborhood watches, house- and car-alarm systems, and the purchase of handguns for personal protection. In many respects, the pervasiveness of crime apprehension means that *anyone* may be perceived as a potential threat or danger. But research on racial stereotyping and perceptions of crime suggest that, in the United States at least, individuals express particular fear of and perceived danger of minorities, and particularly African Americans. For example, numerous studies show that Whites report greater fear of crime when in the actual or perceived presence of Blacks than Whites, and that perceived guilt is more likely to be assumed for Blacks accused of crimes than for Whites accused of the same crimes (Bodenhausen, 1990; Gordon, Michels & Nelson, 1996; St. John & Heald-Moore, 1995).

Naturally, stereotyping of African Americans and other minorities as "dangerous criminals" reflects hundreds of variables and is entrenched in a long history of discrimination and oppression. Consequently, attempts to isolate any single factor are both unproductive and naive. Nevertheless, the extent to which individuals report relying on television for information about crime (Russell, 1995) suggests that greater research attention needs to be given to explorations of the role that media may play in creating and sustaining these harmful stereotypes.

The purpose of this chapter is to provide a broad overview of research on race and crime in the media, and the ways that scholarship from a media effects tradition has contributed to our understanding in this area. However, the use of the phrase "media effects" to describe the quantitative, social scientific studies of the psychology of media may be misleading to many people outside of this particular approach. On the one hand, a great deal of research that can be subsumed under the overarching term "media effects" pertains to media portrayals themselves – aside from how these portrayals may have influence on their audiences. More importantly, however, most scholars from a media effects tradition enthusiastically embrace the notion that viewers' selection, interpretation, and memory of media content play central roles in the influence that media portrayals may have on attitudes, beliefs, and behaviors. Consequently, the label "media effects" captures only a small slice of the types of scholarship and methodologies that are routinely employed by researchers in this area.

With an eye toward recognizing the breadth of research that falls within the purview of media effects scholarship, the first section of this chapter will focus on content analytic research, the second section will examine studies of viewers' responses to media portrayals of race and crime, and the final section will consider research that has examined the ways that media portrayals are thought to influence beliefs and attitudes.

Content Analyses of Race and Crime

Crime is a staple of media content – not only in the more obvious form of news depictions, but also in terms of entertainment and news-entertainment hybrids (i.e. reality-based programming). Numerous content analyses that have explored the extent of crime and violence on television have shown that the world of television news and entertainment is a much more dangerous and hostile place than actual crime statistics suggest (e.g. Gerbner, Gross, Morgan, & Signorielli, 1994; News of the Nineties, 1998). Given the preponderance of crime, and particularly violent crime, that permeates the media landscape, how is criminal involvement characterized in terms of race? Overall, research suggests that the answer to this question may largely depend on whether the media content is fictional entertainment, or whether the content is news related or "reality" based.

Fictional crime entertainment

Examples of Black and Latino criminal suspects in fictional entertainment programming are easy to imagine. In fact, minorities being arrested, questioned, and harassed by police officers seems to be a staple of much fictional programming. Nevertheless, more systematic content analyses of both criminal activity and of aggression per se in fictional television programming suggest that White criminality and aggression is most typical. For example, Potter and Ware (1987) content analyzed anti- and prosocial behaviors contained on fictional, network, prime-time programming, and reported that among all characters shown committing any type of anti-social act, 10.4 percent were Black, and among all characters shown committing major felonies (i.e. murder, rape, kidnapping, and robbery), only 4.5 percent were Black (see also Potter et al., 1995). Tamborini, Mastro, Chory-Assad, and Huang (2000) reported similar findings in their content analysis of character portrayals in network, prime-time programming. In their study, Blacks and Latinos accounted for 13 percent and 4 percent of all law-enforcement/court officers respectively, and 11 percent and 4 percent of all criminals respectively. These results are partially consistent with Gunther's (1998) analysis of portrayals of violence in television dramas shown in the UK. Specifically, Gunther (1998) reported that the majority of aggressors and victims of violence were White, with Blacks representing a small percentage of both (5.1 percent aggressors; 4 percent victims). However, Gunther (1998) also found that portrayals of aggressors varied as a function of where the drama originated, with Black perpetrators more likely to be featured in law-enforcement roles in UK dramas, but in criminal roles in US dramas.

Reality-based programming and news

In contrast to research on fictional programming, studies that have explored more "realistic" depictions of violence and criminal activity tend to report much more negative portrayals of minorities. Here, content analyses have shown that television tends to not only overrepresent minority involvement in crime and underrepresent White involvement, but that media portrayals also tend to feature different *types* of portrayals that may suggest to viewers that people of color are particularly dangerous and threatening. Although reality-based crime programs are clearly billed as "entertainment" rather than as news per se, most programs in this genre employ video footage or reenactments of crimes, and they stress to the viewing audience that the content is "actual" or "real" (e.g. "The *real* men and women of law enforcement . . ."). Consequently, reality-based crime programs represent a hybrid of entertainment and news, but unlike fictional entertainment, encourage a news-like interpretation of the events that are depicted. Given that reality-based programs presumably heighten viewers' perceptions of authenticity, analyses of this genre's portrayals of violence and race are particularly troubling. For example, Danielson et al.'s (1996) content analysis of reality-based programming found that not only were police programs more violent than any other reality genres also examined, but that *every* police program included in their sample featured visual displays of violence. How is violence depicted in terms of race in these types of programs? Potter et al.'s (1997) content analysis of a broad variety of reality-programming (e.g. news, talk shows, crime shows, etc.) reported that Blacks accounted for 18.5 percent of all perpetrators of anti-social acts portrayed and for 25 percent of all perpetrators of violent criminal acts specifically. Similarly, Oliver's (1994) content analysis of four months of reality-based cop shows reported that while the majority of White characters featured in these programs (61.6 percent) were police officers rather than criminal suspects, the vast majority of Black (77 percent) and Latino

(85.9 percent) characters were criminal suspects rather than police officers. Oliver (1994) also reported that police officers were more likely to be shown using aggression than were criminal suspects, but aggression toward criminal suspects varied as a function of the suspects' race. Specifically, Black and Latino characters were significantly more likely to suffer police aggression (e.g. shoving, restraining) than were White suspects, even after controlling for numerous other variables including the type of crime under investigation and the suspects' use of aggression.

The association of people of color with crime and danger is, of course, not isolated to the realm of media entertainment. Both earlier and more recent content analyses of news programming show a great deal of consistency in terms of the overrepresentation of African Americans as criminal suspects – and particularly suspects associated with violent crime. For example, Sheley and Ashkins (1981) analyzed news content in New Orleans, and reported that 93 percent of all robbery suspects in local newspapers and 80 percent on local television were African American. Similarly, Entman's analysis of local television news coverage in Chicago (Entman, 1990, 1992; Entman & Rojecki, 2000) revealed strong associations between African Americans and criminal activity. In one study, Entman (1990) reported that 41 percent of all the news stories that prominently featured Blacks during a week's worth of programming focused on violent crime. Furthermore, during the week studied, violent crime was the most frequent lead story on the newscasts, meaning that news featuring violent, Black criminals was particularly prominent. In a later analysis of local news programs over a six-month time period, Entman (1992) reported that 84 percent of all crime stories about Black suspects pertained to violent rather than nonviolent crime, compared to 71 percent of crime stories about White suspects. In addition, he demonstrated that the *manner* in which criminal suspects were shown differed considerably as a function of race. Specifically, Black criminal suspects were significantly more likely than White criminal suspects to be shown as poorly dressed and as physically held by police officers, and significantly less likely to be associated with pro-defense sound bites. In addition, images of Black criminal suspects were less likely than images of White criminal suspects to feature the name of the accused; a practice that Entman suggested likely contributes to the homogenization of Blacks as criminal or dangerous.

Certainly the disparity in the way that Black and White crime is reported in the news is cause for alarm. However, skeptics of the argument that these portrayals are problematic typically suggest that these types of portrayals merely "reflect reality." Nevertheless, more recent research comparing media crime with law enforcement records suggests that media portrayals are inconsistent with actual crime statistics. Dixon and Linz's (2000a) content analysis of crime stories on local television newscasts in the Los Angeles area showed that compared to police and employment records for the local area, these news portrayals significantly overrepresented Whites as police officers and overrepresented Blacks as perpetrators of crime. In a later study, Dixon and Linz (2000b) reported similar results in terms of news portrayals of victimization. In general, African Americans were almost twice as likely to be portrayed as perpetrators than as victims of crime, whereas Caucasians were more likely to be portrayed as victims than as perpetrators. In addition, comparisons with actual, local crime statistics recorded during the same time period revealed that African Americans were significantly overrepresented as crime perpetrators in the news, whereas Caucasians were overrepresented as victims. Latinos were generally underrepresented as both victims and as perpetuators, suggesting a general underreporting of events within the Latino community (see also Romer, Jamieson, & deCoteau, 1998).

To summarize, media effects researchers who have employed content analytic procedures to examine media portrayals of race and crime tend to report divergent findings that vary as a function of the nature of the genre. While fictional programs do not appear to paint an overly biased picture, at least in terms of head counts, more realistic content including reality-based programming and news appears much more problematic, both in terms of strongly associating people of color with crime, and also in terms of featuring more subtle images that imply that minority criminals are particularly threatening or dangerous.

Before turning to research pertaining to viewers' responses, two points about content analyses should be highlighted. First, any reader of content analyses needs to keep in mind that numerical results can be understood in a multitude of ways, and the manner in which the author chooses to report the data can have a profound impact on encouraging one sort of interpretation over another. For example, a given researcher may report that among all criminal suspects shown during a given period, only 5 percent were Black. At the same time, what might be hidden from the reader is the fact that among all Black characters shown, 80 percent were criminal suspects! The lesson here is that data can be presented in a variety of ways, and readers would be well advised to consider various possible interpretations when examining tables of results. The second issue that should be acknowledged is that while content analyses provide a particularly useful way of quantifying the prevalence of certain types of portrayals and are therefore useful in making comparative claims, they can also suffer from missing the subtleties of context and from oversimplifying the complexities of meanings that viewers can derive from the manner in which portrayals are framed. In this regard, both readers and scholars should be open to using a variety of methodologies in ways that enjoy the strengths allowed by a diversity of research approaches.

Viewers' Responses to Race and Crime

While content analyses and other interpretations of media texts provide a useful way of describing media content, one temptation for scholars in this area is to make leaps to claims concerning how viewers interact with such content. That is, describing media portrayals is distinct from discussions of how viewers actually interpret, remember, and react to portrayals. Consequently, media effects scholars typically regard content analyses as useful starting points for later studies that more directly examine viewers' responses. This section overviews research that has explored viewers' reactions to media portrayals of crime and race, including enjoyment, interpretations, and memory.

Enjoyment of media crime

One possible way to interpret the prevalence of violent crime in news portrayals may be, at least in part, in terms of informational utility. That is, viewers may be willing to tolerate threatening and frightful news stories because such stories provide viewers with a way of monitoring their environments in order to avoid danger. This line of reasoning, however, falls short in explaining why viewers would *choose* to view, and presumably enjoy, crime and victimization in entertainment programming, or why news programs would adopt policies reflecting the rule of thumb that "if it bleeds, it leads."

If portrayals of violence and criminality lead to greater feelings of fear and insecurity as suggested by some researchers (e.g. Gerbner et al., 1994), what could explain the apparent popularity of such images in both news and entertainment? One possible explanation that has implications in terms of both racial portrayals and viewers' racial attitudes is disposition theory (Zillmann, 1991, Zillmann & Cantor, 1977). In essence, disposition theory suggests that enjoyment of entertainment is largely a reflection of viewers' dispositions toward media characters and the outcomes that the characters experience during the course of the entertainment. When liked or beloved characters experience positive outcomes and/or when hated or despised characters suffer negative outcomes, enjoyment is thought to be greatest. Furthermore, disposition theory also acknowledges that perceptions of "good" and "bad" can vary between individuals, implying that some people may harbor stronger affective dispositions than others, thereby leading to differential levels of enjoyment, depending on the outcome experienced by the character portrayed.

How might disposition theory apply to viewers' responses to crime portrayals? In terms of crime entertainment per se, Zillmann and Wakshlag (1985) noted that while television presents a particularly dangerous and threatening view of crime, it simultaneously "conveys the message that good forces (i.e. police, private investigators, vigilantes) are out there mopping up the scum of society . . . This kind of message should be music to the ears of troubled citizens, allowing them to relax and put their worries about crime and personal safety to rest" (p. 148). In this regard, Zillmann and other researchers have argued that crime drama may be especially appealing to individuals who are fearful or who harbor a particularly strong distaste for criminal suspects because crime drama typically features the ultimate punishment of those individuals who are seen as threatening, harmful, or hated (see also Raney & Bryant, 2002; Wakshlag, Vial, & Tamborini, 1983).

Although the application of disposition theory to crime entertainment has generally assumed that viewers hold negative dispositions toward criminals, Oliver and Armstrong (1995) noted the importance that race may play in viewers' dispositions toward the criminal suspects in reality-based programs. Specifically, these authors reasoned that because reality-based police shows routinely feature portrayals of Black and Latino criminal suspects being aggressively punished by police, these programs should be particularly appealing to viewers who not only harbor punitive dispositions, but who also harbor negative racial attitudes. Consistent with predictions, these authors reported that among the White respondents in their telephone survey, higher levels of punitiveness and higher levels of racial prejudice were associated with greater viewing and reported enjoyment of reality-based police shows (e.g. *Cops, America's Most Wanted*), but these same attitudes were unrelated to viewing and enjoyment of fictional police programs that presumably do not feature racial portrayals that are as consistently negative.

In a later experiment, Oliver (1996) employed similar reasoning to examine White viewers' responses to portrayals of police aggression in reality programming. In this study, assessments of authoritarian attitudes were first collected as indicators of both punitiveness and racial prejudice. At a later time, participants were shown brief episodes from *Cops* that featured police aggression toward either White or Black criminal suspects. The results of this experiment showed that authoritarianism predicted greater enjoyment of the portrayals of police aggression, but only if the criminal suspects were Black rather than White.

Interpretations of race and crime

Although enjoyment of media content and interpretations of media content are conceptually distinct responses, viewers' interpretations of media content likely play important roles in their enjoyment. In this regard, studies that have examined viewers' interpretations of media content illustrate many of the same patterns as have studies that have assessed gratifications, with research generally indicating that viewers tend to interpret or understand portrayals in a way that is consistent with or affirming of existing attitudes or beliefs (e.g. Vidmar & Rokeach, 1974).

The most straightforward illustration of the importance of viewer interpretation of media portrayals of race and crime is in terms of viewers' evaluations of the characters portrayed. As with similar research that has examined individuals' assessment of guilt in non-media contexts (e.g. courtroom trials), studies of viewers' perceptions of news and entertainment crime suggest that viewers tend to perceive Black criminal suspects more negatively than White criminal suspects. For example, in the aforementioned study on viewers' enjoyment of reality-based scenes of police aggression, Oliver (1996) also reported that authoritarianism was associated with more favorable evaluations of police officers (e.g. ethical, professional, responsible) and more negative evaluations of the criminal suspects (e.g. threatening, violent, dangerous, and aggressive), but only when the criminal suspects were Black rather than White.

Peffley, Shields, and Williams (1996) also obtained a similar pattern of viewer interpretation in their experiment concerning White viewers' responses to a violent-crime news story. In their study, participants viewed a television news story concerning the murder of a prostitute, with half of the stories showing a White suspect being led away in handcuffs, and the other half featuring a Black suspect. Reponses to the news story showed that among the participants who endorsed negative stereotypes of African Americans, perceived guilt was high for the Black suspect, but was low for the White suspect. Similarly, negative racial attitudes were associated with more harsh recommendations of punishment (i.e. years in prison) for the Black suspect, but more lenient recommendations for the White suspect. These results are consistent with the idea that existing attitudes and beliefs can have a strong impact on how media content is understood, and in the case of race and crime portrayals, imply that even equitable portrayals of Blacks and Whites can encourage confirmation of stereotypes of African Americans as threatening, dangerous, and punishable.

Memory of crime news

The idea that viewers tend to interpret media content in a way that is consistent with existing attitudes has also been explored in the context of memory for crime news. Here, again, research generally suggests that what viewers take away from the screen may reflect viewers' stereotypes as much, if not more, than what is actually portrayed. For example, in several studies, Oliver (1999; Oliver & Fonash, 2002) has reported that White viewers are more likely to misidentify Black than White individuals as criminal suspects who were supposedly seen in crime news stories (but who were actually never pictured), but particularly so when the crime news stories feature violent as opposed to non-violent crime. Similarly, Dixon and Azocar's (2000) research found that viewers are likely to misremember having seen a Black criminal suspect in news stories, even when the actual criminal suspect was White or when no racial information was provided at all. Dixon and Azocar interpreted their findings as suggesting that crime news, even in the absence of racial portrayals, may serve to prime existing stereotypes of Black, male criminals.

To summarize, research that has explored viewers' enjoyment, interpretation, and memory of media portrayals of race and crime suggest a clear pattern in which viewers' existing attitudes, beliefs, and stereotypes play a large role in the way that media content is received. Overall, this literature supports the notion that a great deal of variability in viewers' responses reflects tendencies to respond to media content in ways that affirm existing stereotypes. However, it is important that this summary not be misunderstood as suggesting that the media images themselves play an inconsequential role in contributing to stereotypes of persons of color as dangerous or criminal. In contrast, it is important for the reader to note that while most studies examining viewers' perceptions of media content typically take great pains to equate the way that Whites and minorities are portrayed for purposes of experimental control, in actuality, media portrayals of race and crime are far from equitable. Consequently, additional research within the area of media effects has explored not only how viewers respond to media images, but also how media images may affect viewers' attitudes and beliefs concerning race and crime.

Effects of Race and Crime

The idea that media may play *any* role, much less a substantial role, in contributing to stereotypes of race and crime may seem ludicrous in light of the countless social and interpersonal factors involved in attitude and impression formation. Obviously, stereotypes about any phenomena reflect thousands of variables, and media effects scholars are generally more than ready to acknowledge that media exposure accounts for only one portion of the universe of possible factors that are important predictors of attitudes and beliefs.

With this said, however, there are several important characteristics about crime attitudes specifically and about the ways in which media present crime information that suggest that media portrayals have the opportunity to serve as important contributors to stereotypes associating persons of color with criminality and danger. First, as mentioned at the beginning of this chapter, most individuals in the United States report that the media serve as their primary source of news information (Russell, 1995). Given the reliance on media rather than on less attractive options such as first-hand experiences with crime, individuals may not be as readily able to critically evaluate or discount biased or distorted portrayals that are routinely featured. Second, much of the mostly negative portrayals of race and crime are contained within content such as reality-based programming or news that encourage greater perceived reality. Given a long history of research suggesting more pronounced effects of realistic than fictional content on viewers' attitudes and beliefs (see Potter, 1988), the framing of stereotypical portrayals of race and crime as "realistic" implies that these portrayals may be particularly influential. Finally, as discussed earlier, once stereotypes are in place, they are likely to play important roles in how new information is understood or interpreted. In terms of media effects, this not only means that media portrayals may serve to create negative stereotypes, but that they may also serve to activate stereotypes once the stereotypes are in place.

Cultivation of attitudes and beliefs

In the most general terms, cultivation approaches can be understood broadly as focusing on how long-term and cumulative exposure to repeated patterns in media messages shapes viewers' perceptions of their environment. In this regard, Gerbner and his colleagues (e.g. Gerbner et al., 1994) have typically focused on media violence, suggesting that heavy viewers of television content are, by definition, heavy viewers of violent content. Consequently, heavy viewers are more likely than are light viewers to overestimate the amount of violence and crime in the real world, to support more harsh criminal penalties, and to take steps to protect themselves from the world that they perceive as "mean and scary."

Although cultivation theory has generated considerable debate and criticism among a multitude of scholars, more recent research has shifted the focus from criticisms per se to explorations of the mechanisms that may help explain how media portrayals may influence viewers' judgments of reality under some circumstances. For example, Shrum's (1996) heuristic model explains cultivation effects in terms of attitude accessibility and heuristic processing of information. Specifically, this model points out that when making judgments about the prevalence of a given phenomenon, individuals often mentally search for examples of the phenomenon. When examples come to mind easily and quickly, estimates of prevalence tend to be inflated. Applied to television, this means that phenomena that are frequently shown (e.g. crime) provide viewers with numerous examples that can later serve to inflate estimates. Similarly, Zillmann and his colleagues' work in exemplification theory points out that when individuals process information about a given phenomenon, the examples that are featured in the information can exert a profound influence on perceptions, above and beyond any base rate information that may also be presented (see Zillmann & Brosius, 2000). For example, a news story may state that people generally have a 10 percent chance of dying when diagnosed with a given illness, but may then go on to provide 10 examples of individuals who died. In this instance, research on exemplification would predict that readers of the news story would be likely to attend to the examples rather than the statistics, thereby inflating their estimates of the risk of the illness in question.

In terms of individuals' perceptions of race and crime, the aforementioned perspectives would suggest that long-term exposure to television that features a preponderance of examples of minorities as criminal suspects should lead to inflated estimates of the extent to which minorities are involved in crime. Oliver and Armstrong (1998) employed this reasoning in their telephone survey concerning media viewing and perceptions of crime. Their results showed that greater viewing of reality-based police shows (unlike fictional police shows) was associated with higher estimates of crime prevalence, and particularly with higher estimates of Blacks' rather than Whites' crime involvement. Although the results of this study are consistent with the idea that media portrayals associating crime with persons of color lead to inflated estimates of minority involvement in crime, correlational survey methods are not in the position of definitively establishing causal relationships between variables. That is, one rival interpretation of these results may be that heightened perceptions of Black involvement in crime led to greater viewing of reality-based police shows. Within media effects research, as in most social sciences, the most trusted method of establishing causal relationships is through experimental design in which the predicted causal agent is manipulated systematically by the researcher and participants are randomly assigned to experimental conditions. However, experimental studies typically assess reactions to a stimulus at one given point in time, and are therefore questionable in terms of exploring theories such as cultivation that assume effects resulting from cumulative viewing.

Clearly, different types of research designs offer unique strengths and weakness in exploring any phenomenon. Often, though, similar patterns of results are obtained across different methodological approaches. For example, Gilliam and Iyengar (2000) conducted both a survey and an experiment to examine the influence of news exposure on viewers' perceptions of crime and racial attitudes. In the survey, participants were asked to report the frequency of their local television news viewing, and in the experiment, viewers were exposed to a television crime story in which the criminal was portrayed as Black, as White, or racially-unidentified. In both studies, participants reported their attitudes about crime, punitiveness, and racial stereotypes. The survey showed that news viewing was associated with greater punitiveness toward criminal suspects and with higher levels of racism. The experiment revealed similar findings, but only if the participants had previously viewed a Black or racially unidentified criminal suspect rather than a White suspect. Gilliam and Iyengar (2000) interpreted these studies as suggesting that news broadcasts of crime present viewers with a script associating Blacks with criminality, and that even brief exposure to this script is sufficient to influence crime- and race-related attitudes. While these authors did not refer specifically to cultivation in the interpretation of their results, the findings obtained from the survey are consistent within a general cultivation framework. In contrast, the effects observed in the experiment were obviously caused by something other than long-term exposure, and are therefore more consistent with other studies that have explored the ways in which media images can prime or activate racial stereotypes.

Priming of racial stereotypes

Associative priming theories of media effects rest on a large body of research in cognitive psychology showing that individuals organize their thoughts and feelings such that semantically-related thoughts are connected (Jo & Berkowitz, 1994). These connections imply that when one thought or feeling is activated or "primed," the activation radiates out and primes related thoughts and feelings, and thereby increases the likelihood that the activated cognitions will be employed in subsequent behaviors and interpretations of new stimuli. For example, if a person associates thunderstorms with thoughts of monsters, an approaching storm may prime thoughts of ghosts and goblins, and a benign stimulus such as a knock at the door may be interpreted with great shock or fear in a way that would not normally be the case under other circumstances. In the context of media effects, one implication of associate priming is that media content may act as a prime for a host of related cognitions. Insofar as these cognitions associate minorities with danger or criminality, these primed cognitions should influence perceptions and judgments of additional stimuli, even if the stimuli may be seemingly unrelated to the media content at hand.

Johnson, Adams, Hall, and Ashburn (1997) employed the idea of priming in their research exploring how exposure to violent-crime news stories affected perceptions of a subsequently described crime. In their study, participants first read a series of newspaper stories that described either violent crimes or that described issues unrelated to crime. In a second, ostensibly unrelated study, participants read a vignette of a crime that featured a defendant who was either Black, White, or race-unidentified. The results showed that participants' judgments of the Black defendant in the vignette reflected greater dispositional attributions for his behavior (i.e. violent personality) among participants who had previously read the crime-related rather than non-crime stories. Judgments of the White or racially unidentified defendant were unaffected. These authors interpreted their findings as suggesting that the violence contained within the news stories was sufficient to prime existing stereotypes of the "violent Black male," thereby increasing dispositional attributions of the defendant in the subsequently encountered vignette (see also Johnson, Trawalter, & Dovidio, 1999).

In Johnson et al.'s (1997) research, the connection between the violence in the news stories and the violence in the vignettes is readily apparent. However, associative priming theory would also suggest that any type of media content that primes related stereotypes could have a similar influence on judgments. For example, if a person's stereotypes of Blacks include both violence and buffoonish humor, then humor alone could be sufficient to prime related stereotypes such as those associating Blacks with criminality. Ford (1997) demonstrated this type of effect in his experiment in which White participants viewed comedic television skits featuring either stereotypical portrayals of African Americans or neutral portrayals. Afterward, participants read a vignette describing a criminal incident, and then rated their perceptions of the guilt of the alleged offender. The results showed that when the alleged offender in the vignette was described as White, guilt ratings did not differ as a function of the previously viewed type of comedy. In contrast, when the alleged offender was described as Black, guilt ratings were significantly higher among the participants who had previously viewed the stereotypical rather than the neutral comedy skits. These findings suggest that once stereotypes are in place, the priming of any element of the stereotypes can serve to prime associated characteristics, which then, in turn, have the potential to play important roles in subsequent judgments and interactions.

Before leaving this discussion of priming theory and of media effects research in general, it is important to recognize some additional implications of this line of scholarship that imply several directions for future study. First, for priming effects to occur, it is necessary that the viewer have the mental associations in place that connect cognitions, attributes, and feelings. In other words, for media to prime racial stereotypes, racial stereotypes must exist – otherwise they cannot be primed. This does not mean, of course, that media have no role in contributing to stereotyping. In fact, research from cultivation and related perspectives would suggest that the media's pairing of minorities and crime may contribute to the formation of the cognitive associations, which can then, in turn, be primed or activated by subsequent exposure.

Second, though, the importance of the existence of cognitive associations should not be understood as suggesting that viewers must endorse or approve of stereotypes associating minorities with crime and danger. In contrast, a growing body of literature suggests that the common exposure to stereotypes that are transmitted through a host of socially and culturally shared experiences means that most individuals, regardless of racial prejudice, are likely familiar with stereotypes, and are therefore likely to automatically activate stereotypes when encountering individuals who are stigmatized (Bargh, 1999). As a result, even people who do not endorse or identify with stereotypes may have stereotypes primed or activated nevertheless, with this activation having the potential to affect subsequent behaviors and thoughts. In essence, this line of research suggests that everyone, regardless of explicit prejudice, may be influenced by the stereotypes contained in media content, with this influence not necessarily within conscious awareness. The idea that negative stereotypes may be primed without either our consent or necessarily our awareness is a troubling state of affairs, but the importance that stereotype activation can play in our judgments and behaviors makes this line of research particularly worthy of future investigation.

Concluding Comments

Content analyses demonstrate that media portrayals associate persons of color with criminality, danger, and aggression. Studies of media influence suggest that these portrayals have the potential to contribute to viewers' stereotyping, and research on viewer enjoyment suggests that viewers who endorse these stereotypes are particularly likely to find these types of images gratifying. How might research from a media effects tradition summarize these patterns? At the beginning of this chapter, I argued that the phrase "media effects" captures only one portion of the work done in this area of scholarship. Research on race and crime in the media illustrates not only the breadth of scholarship in this area, but also the idea that content, responses, and effects must *all* be explored together to understand how media operate in the lives of most people. In terms of race and crime specifically, it is likely that portrayals influence attitudes and beliefs; beliefs, in turn, influence exposure; and exposure encourages media outlets to provide viewers with greater examples of the problematic media content. Obviously this is a vicious cycle, and one that may seem overly pessimistic. However, it is imperative that scholars recognize the importance of their work in helping to break vicious cycles like this one. Media effects scholarship, along with research from a diversity of disciplines, stands to make important contributions by exposing and critically evaluating media images, by encouraging greater media responsibility, and by exploring ways to empower individuals to be critical and literate viewers. By applying our theories and research to issues of social good, we all stand to move beyond merely academic discussions, and toward scholarship that works toward the betterment of us all.

References

Bargh, J. A. (1999). The cognitive monster: A case against the controllability of automatic stereotype effects. In S. Chaiken and Y. Trope (eds.), *Dual-Process Theories in Social Psychology*. New York: Guilford Press, pp. 361–82.

Bodenhausen, G. V. (1990). Second-guessing the jury: Stereotypic and hindsight biases in perceptions of court cases. *Journal of Applied Social Psychology*, 20, 1112–21.

Butterfield, F. (2001). U.S. crime figures were stable in '00 after 8-year drop: Homicide down slightly. *The New York Times*, May 31, A1, A14.

Danielson, W., Lasorsa, D., Wartella, E., Whitney, C., Campbell, S., Saam Haddad, S., Klijn, M., Lopez, R., and Olivarez, A. (1996). Television violence in "reality" programming: University of Texas, Austin study. In *National Television Violence Study: Scientific papers, 1994–1995*. Studio City, CA: Mediascope, Inc., pp. II-1–II-55.

Dixon, T. L. and Azocar, C. (2000). Psychological Reactions to Portrayals of Black Criminality on Television News. Paper presented at the annual meeting of the International Communication Association, Acapulco, Mexico.

Dixon, T. L. and Linz, D. (2000a). Overrepresentation and underrepresentation of African Americans and Latinos as lawbreakers on television news. *Journal of Communication*, 50(2), 131–54.

Dixon, T. L. and Linz, D. (2000b). Race and the misrepresentation of victimization on local television news. *Communication Research*, 27, 547–73.

Entman, R. M. (1990). Modern racism and the images of Blacks in local television news. *Critical Studies in Mass Communication*, 7, 332–45.

Entman, R. M. (1992). Blacks in the news: Television, modern racism and cultural change. *Journalism Quarterly*, 69, 341–61.

Entman, R. M. and Rojecki, A. (2000). *The Black Image in the White Mind: Media and race in America*. Chicago; University of Chicago Press.

Ford, T. (1997). Effects of stereotypical television portrayals of African Americans on person perception. *Social Psychology Quarterly*, 60, 266–75.

Gerbner, G., Gross, L., Morgan, M., and Signorielli, N. (1994). Growing up with television: The cultivation perspective. In J. Bryant and D. Zillmann (eds.), *Media Effects: Advances in theory and research*. Hillsdale, NJ: Lawrence Erlbaum, pp. 17–41.

Gilliam, F. D., Jr. and Iyengar, S. (2000). Prime suspects: The influence of local television news on the viewing public. *American Journal of Political Science*, 44, 560–73.

Gordon, R. A., Michels, J. L., and Nelson, C. L. (1996). Majority group perceptions of criminal behavior: The accuracy of race-related crime stereotypes. *Journal of Applied Social Psychology*, 26, 148–59.

Guntter, B. (1998). Ethnicity and involvement of crime on television: Nature and context of on-screen portrayals. *Journal of Black Studies*, 28, 683–703.

Jo, E. and Berkowitz, L. (1994). A priming effect analysis of media influences: An update. In J. Bryant, and D. Zillmann (eds.), *Media Effects: Advances in theory and research*. Hillsdale, NJ: Lawrence Erlbaum, pp. 43–60.

Johnson, J. D., Adams, M. S., Hall, W., and Ashburn, L. (1997). Race, media, and violence: Differential racial effects of exposure to violent news stories. *Basic and Applied Social Psychology*, 19, 81–90.

Johnson, J. D., Trawalter, S., and Dovidio, J. F. (1999). Converging interracial consequences of exposure to violent rap music on stereotypical attributions of Blacks. *Journal of Experimental and Social Psychology*, 36, 233–51.

News of the Nineties: The top topics and trends of the decade. (1998). *Media Monitor*, 11(3), July/ August. Retrieved January 20, 2000, from http://www.cmpa.com/Mediamon/mm0708.htm.

Oliver, M. B. (1994). Portrayals of crime, race, and aggression in "reality-based" police shows: A content analysis. *Journal of Broadcasting and Electronic Media*, 38, 179–92.

Oliver, M. B. (1996). Influences of authoritarianism and portrayals of race on Caucasian viewers' responses to reality-based crime dramas. *Communication Reports*, 9, 141–50.

Oliver, M. B. (1999). Caucasian viewers' memory of Black and White criminal suspects in the news. *Journal of Communication*, 49(3), 46–60.

Oliver, M. B., and Armstrong, G. B. (1995). Predictors of viewing and enjoyment of reality-based and fictional crime shows. *Journalism Quarterly*, 72, 559–70.

Oliver, M. B., and Armstrong, G. B. (1998). The color of crime: Perceptions of Caucasians' and African Americans' involvement in crime. In. M. Fishman and G. Cavender (eds.), *Entertaining Crime: Television reality programs*. New York: Aldine de Gruyter, pp. 19–35.

Oliver, M. B., and Fonash, D. (2002). Race and crime in the news: Whites' identification and misidentification of criminal suspects. *Media Psychology*, 4, 137–56.

Peffley, M., Shields, T., and Williams, B. (1996). The intersection of race and crime in television news stories: An experimental study. *Political Communication*, 13, 309–27.

Potter, W. J. (1988). Perceived reality in television effects research. *Journal of Broadcasting and Electronic Media*, 32, 23–41.

Potter, W. J., Vaughan, M. W., Warren, R., Howley, K., Land, A., and Hagemeyer, J. C. (1995). How real is the portrayal of aggression in television entertainment programming? *Journal of Broadcasting and Electronic Media*, 39, 496–516.

Potter, W. J. and Ware, W. (1987). Traits of perpetrators and receivers of antisocial and prosocial acts on TV. *Journalism Quarterly*, 64, 382–91.

Potter, W. J., Warren, R., Vaughan, M. W., Howley, K., Land, A., and Hagemeyer, J. C. (1997). Antisocial acts in reality programming on television. *Journal of Broadcasting and Electronic Media*, 41, 69–75.

Raney, A. A. and Bryant, J. (2002). Moral judgment and crime drama: An integrated theory of enjoyment. *Journal of Communication*, 52(2), 402–15.

Romer, D., Jamieson, K. H., and deCoteau, N. J. (1998). The treatment of persons of color in local news: Ethnic blame discourse, or realistic group conflict? *Communication Research*, 25, 286–305.

Russell, C. (1995). True crime. *American Demographics*, 17, 22–31.

Sheley, J. F. and Ashkins, C. D. (1981). Crime, crime news, and crime views. *Public Opinion Quarterly*, 45, 492–506.

Shrum, L. J. (1996). Psychological processes underlying cultivation effects: Further tests of construct accessibility. *Human Communication Research*, 22, 482–509.

St. John, C. and Heald-Moore, T. (1995). Fear of Black strangers. *Social Science Research*, 24, 262–80.

Tamborini, R., Mastro, D. E., Chory-Assad, R. M., and Huang, R. H. (2000). The color of crime and the court: A content analysis of minority representation on television. *Journalism and Mass Communication Quarterly*, 3, 639–53.

Uniform Crime Reports. (1999). *The Federal Bureau of Investigation*. Retrieved May 17, 2001, from http:www.fbi.gov.

Vidmar, N. and Rokeach, M. (1974). Archie Bunker's bigotry: A study in selective perception and exposure. *Journal of Communication*, 24(1), 36–47.

Wakshlag, J., Vial, V., and Tamborini, R. (1983). Selecting crime drama and apprehension about crime. *Human Communication Research*, 10, 227–42.

Zillmann, D. (1991). Empathy: Affect from bearing witness to the emotions of others. In J. Bryant and D. Zillmann (eds.), *Responding to the Screen: Reception and reaction processes*. Hillsdale, NJ: Lawrence Erlbaum, pp. 135–67.

Zillmann, D. and Brosius, H. B. (2000). *Exemplification in Communication: The influence of case reports on the perception of issues*. Mahwah, NJ: Lawrence Erlbaum.

Zillmann, D. and Cantor, J. R. (1977). Affective responses to the emotions of a protagonist. *Journal of Experimental Social Psychology*, 13, 155–65.

Zillmann, D. and Wakshlag, J. (1985). Fear of victimization and the appeal of crime drama. In D. Zillmann and J. Bryant (eds.), *Selective Exposure to Communication*. Hillsdale, NJ: Lawrence Erlbaum, pp. 141–56.

CHAPTER TWENTY-ONE

The Appeal and Impact of Media Sex and Violence

Jennings Bryant and Dorina Miron

Representations of sex and violence may well count among the achievements that distinguished our species from primates as they demonstrate the emergence of human consciousness. Primitive people struggling to survive in the wilderness rendered in various media (paintings on cave walls, clay and stone engravings and statuary) large animals that threatened them and other hominids that attacked them. Sexuality was the second most important theme represented in primitive art. In those times when human life was constantly in danger, if intensive reproduction had not compensated for the high mortality, our species would not have survived. The imagery created by our ancestors generally indicates that their minds were occupied by strong negative emotions (fear of animals and con-specific hostility) and strong positive emotions (desire related to sexual activity) that energized and directed their actions. How enjoyable that highly emotional primitive life was remains a matter of speculation. Now that human civilization has more or less solved the problems of individual safety and species dominance on the planet, it is rather surprising that violence and sex are still at the top of our minds, and we make extensive use of communication media to simulate life-threatening dangers that most of us no longer encounter in reality or utilize to arouse us sexually.

The attraction of media sex and violence probably would have received limited attention, only from curious scientists, if it had not been for certain developments that forced these issues onto the public agenda: children's increasingly easy access to pornographic and violent media contents (e.g. Alloway & Gilbert, 1998; Finkelhor, Mitchell & Wolak, 2000; Grossman, 2001; Hill, 1997; Jipping, 2001; Raschke, 1990; Zillmann & Bryant, 1989; Zillmann, Bryant & Huston, 1994), the proliferation of sex–violence mixtures (e.g. Barron & Kimmel, 2000), the enhanced telepresence afforded by technological progress (Sheridan, 1992; Tamborini, 2000), and the school-shooting phenomenon in the United States

(Torr, 2001). There is growing consensus that these developments are related and need to be addressed as a systemic problem. This chapter examines the effects of sexual and violent media fare on our lives.

Conceptual Clarifications

Before we can embark on any discussion of reasons, roles, or effects, we need to define the objects of our interest – sexual and violent media content, and enjoyment (pleasure). Terms such as sexually explicit, erotic, and pornographic may have very different meanings for different people. For example, the Final Report of the Surgeon General's Commission on Pornography (1986) classified pornographic materials as follows: (1) sexually violent materials that portray rape and other instances of physical harm to persons in a sexual context; (2) nonviolent materials that depict degradation, domination, subordination, or humiliation of women, and present women as masochistic, subservient, and overresponsive to the male interest; (3) nonviolent and nondegrading materials that typically depict a couple having vaginal or oral intercourse with no indication of violence or coercion; (4) nudity that displays the naked human body with no obvious sexual behavior or intent; and (5) child pornography that involves minors. For purposes of this chapter, we more typically rely on less "loaded" terms, such as "sexually oriented materials," which fits Harris's (1999) notion that "sex in media is not limited to explicit portrayals of intercourse or nudity, but rather may include any representation that portrays or implies sexual behavior, interest, or motivation" (p. 212).

Violent media content is not always associated with sex. Therefore, it deserves attention as a separate issue. Harris (1994) defined violence as "intentional physical harm to another individual" (p. 186). This definition is operationally convenient for diagnosing violence based on observable behavior.

Gerbner's research group, who examined the cultivation effect of media on the audience, provided a definition of media violence as "overt expression of physical force (with or without a weapon, against self or other) compelling action against one's will on pain of being hurt and/or killed or threatened to be so victimized as part of the plot" (Gerbner, Gross, Morgan, & Signorielli, 1980, p. 11). The notion of unwilling engagement of victims in the actions initiated by their aggressors points to a psychological component of physical harm. Moreover, Gerbner and his associates classified as violence mere threats with physical harm. Their more inclusive definition proposes violence as a continuum rather than a dichotomous (violent/nonviolent) category. This allows for escalation of violence from threat to action, and from smaller harm to greater harm, and even from nonviolent to violent behavior.

As noted by Zillmann (1979), the problem of defining violence is aggravated by the growing inventory of harms and damages that humans can project in their minds and effect in reality. We often see indirect forms of aggression such as communicated threats, aggression against target surrogates (e.g. destruction of photographs, records, and property), and fantasizing about retaliations against frustrators. More often than physical aggression, we witness, maybe even practice, nonphysical assaults such as "disadvantaging, embarrassing, humiliating, or scorning someone" (p. 28). On the other hand, the meaning of harm/injury has been stretched to accommodate expression of annoyance such as swearing after striking one's own thumb with a hammer. Such developments have blurred the notion of violence, but we believe this is not an insuperable problem.

If we define violence as infliction of physical harm by humans on other humans, either as an end in itself or as a means to achieve other purposes, then we are faced with additional issues such as goals and justifications. These expand the discussion of violence to include psychological processes and ethical (cultural) criteria. Such a multi-level approach to violence retains the advantage of Harris's definition, allowing for easy identification based on observable physical activity, but adds psychological depth that enables us to explain rather than label violence.

The theoretical debate over possible deleterious effects of sexual and/or violent media content is inextricably associated with the enjoyment of such content, especially when presented to the public as entertainment fare. The way we derive pleasure from real life, "artificial realities" such as theater or games, and media content (representations of reality or fantasy) is basically the same in the sense that we process all available stimulations – and we are basically very similar to one another in terms of processing mechanism. On the other hand, the environment that stimulates us is a continuum between naturalness and artificiality rather than a discrete world of separable natural and artificial things. Man-made objects are closely related to human needs experienced during interaction with nature and they may be isomorphic with natural objects in various degrees.

Classic views of pleasure

Aristotle (384–322 BC), in his *Poetics* (1999), distinguished between bodily pleasures and pleasures of the soul (e.g. righteousness or justice). The former were associated with sense perceptions (sight, hearing, and smell in the sphere of temperance; smell and touch, associated with food, drink, and sex, in the sphere of intemperance); the latter were associated with the exercise of moral judgment. Aristotle believed that an activity was promoted by its enjoyment, which also inhibited alternative activities (Urmson, 1968). This observation is a precursor of the modern displacement concept, popular especially in the literature of media effects on children. Displacement is actually a hard to test hypothesis that tempting entertainment activities take up time traditionally devoted to educational activities and thus jeopardize children's learning processes. On the other hand, Aristotle's description of bodily pleasures as self-promoting may also be considered a precursor of the modern concept of addiction, or irrepressible consumption of pleasurable things. One striking thing in Aristotle's classification is the diversity of sensorial pleasures as compared to a single soul/intellectual pleasure, which seems to indicate that in terms of pleasure, he expected more from the senses than from intelligence. The criterion of temperance points to the critical issue of pleasure control. Within the Aristotelian framework, two-way control was theoretically possible, either inhibiting or enhancing pleasure, but inhibition was problematic for the intemperate senses.

Epicurus (341?–270 BC) defined pleasure as the opposite or complete absence of pain or discomfort, as an end-state towards which we can work by removing troubles or sources of pain (e.g. hunger, thirst, sexual pressure) (Epicurus, 1993). Epicurus warned that if pursuits (eating, drinking, sexual activities) were confounded with the end-state (pleasure/happiness), anxieties and addictions would develop (Anderson, 2001). Although Epicurus' concept of end-state was rendered obsolete by psychological science, which demonstrated the simultaneity of sensorial stimulation and pleasure, the pain–pleasure dichotomy persisted in modern hedonic science.

Modern views of pleasure

Thinkers' interest in the issue of pleasure continued for two millennia but was confined to speculations until experimental psychology developed and started to clarify how pleasure really "works." Campbell (1973) redefined pleasure in neurophysiological terms as "activation of the limbic areas" (p. 70). "In normal animals, including man, the pleasure areas deep inside the brain are activated when the sense organs on the periphery of the body are stimulated" (pp. 40–1). It is no coincidence that we speak of "feeling pleasure" (p. 65). Neurophysiological science thus confirmed Aristotle's bodily pleasures.

Bousfield (1926[1999]) refined the Epicurean model. He proposed that pain is not a true antithesis of pleasure. "Pleasure appears to be in some measure proportional to the rate of fall of tension" (p. 28) and is therefore "a factor of time, as well as of tension" (p. 29) – which supports Freud's (1920[1989]) theory that pain and pleasure depend on the quantity of excitation present in the psychic life and the amount of diminution or increase of tension in a given time. Bousfield (1926[1999]) concurred that "the degree of unpleasant affect is relatively proportional to the degree of tension present" (p. 26) and further observed that "there is no loss of tension without tension having first being produced, and so there can be no pleasure without pain or potential pain having first being present, so finally, it may be there can be no love unless hate or potential hate has first existed" (pp. 88–9).

Such modern elaborations do not essentially contradict Epicurus' belief that pleasure is the elimination of pain, although they support Aristotle's intuition that pleasure is not a result but a process. The Freud-Bousfield line of argument would justify us to make peace with art and entertainments in general, admitting that they have to include pain and build up tension in order to provide pleasure.

Other contemporary theorists question the concept of pleasure as tension reduction based on findings that pleasure and pain appear to be mediated by different neurotransmitters, and approach and avoidance tendencies can occur simultaneously or in rapid alternation, generating internal conflict (Kahneman, Diener, & Schwarz, 1999). The model proposed as an alternative posits that affective evaluation is bivalent rather than bipolar (Cacioppo & Berntson, 1994; Ito & Cacioppo, 1999). Davidson (1992) suggested that the brain may compute both the sum and the difference of the levels of activity in the separate systems that mediate positive and negative affect, and proposed that the good/bad (GB) value corresponds to the difference, and the emotional arousal corresponds to the summed activity in the two systems – which would account for forms of entertainment that are felt to be exciting without being perceived as "good."

The concomitance of pain and pleasure is particularly important in the discussion of media-related pleasure, because media content can simultaneously effect bottom-up sensorial stimulation – a capacity greatly enhanced by technological progress in the area of telepresence (Tamborini, 2000) – and trigger top-down cortical activity that reaches the pleasure areas (for bottom-up and top-down processes, see Hobson, 1994). This possibility of activating neural networks that may include various pains and pleasures poses an acute problem of hedonic management – and this is the theoretical problem at the top of hedonic research agenda.

Media Effects

The effects of media violence and pornography have traditionally been addressed separately, recognizing, nevertheless, an overlap in the area of violent sexual content. From a theoretical perspective, both types of materials enhance autonomic activity, which results in feelings of pleasure. The major difference in terms of effect size in real life (also applicable to media exposure) is that "relatively few sexual encounters with the same partner are required to reduce drastically autonomic sensation" (Campbell, 1973, p. 203) through habituation, but "a large number of repetitions of violence and crime are needed to dull the autonomic input, because danger is ever present in these pursuits" (p. 202). In a way, conflict and violence "save" sex from boredom and pleasure decay. The inconvenience is that violence also creates habituation, which is compensated through escalation of aggressive behaviors, with an inherent risk that fear and panic reverse sexual attraction into aversion and flight response (for reversal theory, see Apter, 1982, 1989, 1992, 1994).

From a "technical" media perspective, the close relationship between sexual and violent content is facilitated by their common action framework that is easy to translate into stories and series of stories that perpetually feed the entertainment industry. Mourlet (1991) pointed out that "cinema is the art most attuned to violence, given that violence springs from man's actions" (p. 233). James Cameron, the director of the *Terminator* films, explained that "basically action and violence are the same thing. The question is a matter of style, a matter of degree, a matter of the kind of moral stance taken by the film, the contextualization of the violence" (cited by Plagens, Miller, Foote, & Yoffee, 1991, p. 52). Campbell (1973) cynically noted, "the fun only really starts when the girl begins to object and the scene is set for an ugly rape" (p. 203). According to Plagens, Miller, Foote, and Yoffee (1991), "the very manner in which sexual scenes are shot causes rape to look like an activity that is energizing" (p. 51). On the other hand, "sadism demands a story, depends on making something happen, forcing a change in another person, a battle of will and strength, victory/defeat, all occurring in a linear time with a beginning and an end" (Segal, 1993, p. 260, citing Mulvey, 1975). Creating a story of sex and violence is a "seduction," and "invitation" extended to the audience to participate in the generation of pleasure by anticipating events, and the reading or watching of the story becomes "a mutually-generating cycle of representation and action . . . a complicity" between story-writer and media consumers (Turner, 1995, p. 299). The role of anticipation in viewing violence is to increase excitement through suspense (for the suspense theory, see Zillmann, 1980, 1991a, 1996). A viewer is "playing a game with individual expectation and the director's imagination" (Hill, 1997, p. 34), guessing "how far the director will go in utilizing the visual effects of violence" (p. 27). "With the new sort of violent cinema . . . it's more difficult to anticipate the violence and that makes it more challenging. It is much more interesting and imaginative" (p. 34). Cowie (1993) explained the role of anticipation during exposure to pornography as follows: Fantasy "is a place in which the subject 'remodels' reality to his own liking" (p. 147). "The pleasure of sexual fantasy and pornography is desired for itself, not as a simple means to physical sexual gratification. It is the continuing imagining of a possible sexual satisfaction which drives desire" (p. 137).

Considering the similar and mutually enhancing psychological mechanisms underlying the effects of media sex and violence, as well as the similar and usually combined recipes used by the media for these "spicy" ingredients, we will discuss sex and violence jointly as sources for each particular effect.

Arousal Effects

Because autonomic arousal in response to media depictions is largely nonspecific to particular emotions, it may have some unwanted behavioral consequences. The excitation transfer theory predicts that "residues of excitation from a preceding affective reaction will combine with excitation produced by subsequent affective stimulation and thereby cause an overly intense affective reaction to the subsequent stimulus" (Zillmann, 1991b, p. 116). It should be noted, though, that excitation does not favor hostile, aggressive, or violent reactions; if prosocial responses are motivated, these responses are likely to be energized.

The most arousing media messages are those including sex and violence, followed by violence–only and sex–only materials. Residual arousal from media violence has been found to intensify subsequent asocial feelings and destructive actions (e.g. Zillmann, 1971; Zillmann, 1991b). The effects of sexual nonviolent media content are controversial. Several studies have demonstrated that prolonged use of nonviolent sexual materials is capable of facilitating aggression (e.g. Baron, 1979; Zillmann, Bryant, Comisky, & Medoff, 1981). Other researchers provided support for the thesis that aggression increases only when material featuring sexual violence (e.g. rape scenes, or slasher films) is consumed (e.g. Linz, Donnerstein, & Adams, 1989; Linz, Donnerstein, & Penrod, 1984). Probably the closest to reality is the compromise position that exposure to sexual violence is more arousing than exposure to nonviolent sexually explicit fare and consequently favors to a larger extent subsequent aggression (e.g. Final Report of the Surgeon General's Commission on Pornography, 1986; Lyons, Anderson, & Larson, 1994). Certain scholars emphasized the mediating effect of individual differences in users, which determine whether a viewer becomes disgusted or sexually excited (e.g. Bancroft & Mathews, 1971; Malamuth, Check, & Briere, 1986; Sapolsky & Zillmann, 1981; White, 1979). The problem with all these studies is that arousal effects could not be separated from schema priming and learning effects. The participants who received experimental treatments consisting of sexual and/or violent media materials may have experienced responses to those materials as well as an activation of memories of more or less similar situations and associated responses in real life or presented by the media. Memory activation makes prior life experience with sex and violence a serious confound variable that is hard to control because memory cannot be simply turned off for experimental purposes, and each person has an overall unique life experience, combined with broader experience patterns that are typical for the culture and subculture(s) the person belongs to.

According to hedonic theory, pleasure-seekers tend to escalate arousal (Greenfield, 2000), which makes them respond more and more strongly to any stimulation. In general, we may expect a slight rise in the base level of arousal at the individual level (as a person grows older and a wider range of experiences allows for more diverse and intense stimulation), but that rise should be kept in check through mood management (Bryant & Zillmann, 1984; Zillmann, 1988). Solomon's (1980) opponent-process theory of addiction proposed that any behavioral excess could lead to dependence on that particular excessive behavior to feel normal. Carnes (1991) found that "one of the most destructive parts of sex addiction [including pornography addiction] is that you literally carry your own source of supply . . . being able to get high on your own brain chemicals" (p. 30). Aggravating the danger of excessive exposure to pornography is the convenience of modern technology. "Today, the keywords for access to pornography appear to be 'no effort, no fear.' Pornography of almost any ilk is readily available in the privacy of one's home via premium cable, video-cassettes, the telephone, the Internet, and many other media sources" (Bryant & Zillmann, 2001, p. 241).

Another general expectation is that the base level of arousal for society as a whole will rise as culture progresses toward more and stronger means of stimulation. That rise can be kept in check through public policies and regulation. Theoretically, arousal alone is not bad; it should increase pleasure. Whatever harm sexual and violent media content cause to the audience comes from the excessive consumption of arousing materials and the meanings associated with sexual and violent situations. States of high arousal coupled with negative meanings are experienced as displeasure.

Emotional Disturbances

How does such displeasure typically occur? Failures of pleasure-seeking strategies typically plunge people – especially inexperienced children and youth – into strong negative emotions. We will limit our discussion to two types of disturbances: fright reactions and depression.

Fright reactions

Cantor (1994) and associates have conducted programmatic research on children's fright reaction to media violence. They investigated what type of media violence frightens children, examined developmental differences in fright reactions, and assessed strategies for preventing or reducing unwanted fear reactions. Their emphasis has been on "immediate emotional response that is typically of relatively short duration, but that may endure, on occasion, for several hours or days, or even longer" (Cantor, 1994, p. 214). This area of research takes on added importance because of recent trends in media programming for children that incorporate scary and horrific depictions, and because of the increased access of children to what has traditionally been considered programming for adults. Cantor's team examined developmental differences in children's fear and found that preschool children "are more likely to be frightened by something that looks scary but is actually harmless than by something that looks attractive but is actually harmful," whereas for elementary schoolchildren "appearance carries much less weight relative to the behavior or destructive potential of a character, animal, or object" (Cantor, 1994, pp. 231–2). "As children mature, they become more responsive to realistic, and less responsive to fantastic dangers depicted in the media" and "become frightened by media depictions involving increasingly abstract concepts" (p. 233).

Obviously, age brings about repetition of experiences and learning, that is, development and corrections of schemata. The fact that younger children experience higher arousal from exposure to media violence and are easier to scare can be accounted for through novelty. Children orient more intensely than adults do because very many things are still unknown to them. On the other hand, schemata of novel things are small, involving limited neural activation (few neural links). This characteristic allows for high neural turnover, which creates the possibility of fast stimulus change resulting in intense pleasure, but carries the risk of too fast succession of new stimuli, which triggers panic and fear

(Greenfield, 2000). As novelty decreases with age and neural turnover slows down, this kind of emotional disturbance should disappear.

Depression

Another symptom that worries parents is teenagers' depression, paradoxically caused by indulgence in their favorite leisure activities, such as listening to music. Jipping (2001), citing research reports, observed that "the average teenager listens to 100,500 hours of rock music during the years between the seventh and twelfth grades, and music surpasses television as an influence in teenagers' lives" (p. 63). For example, in the early 1990s, teenagers' favorite music used to be heavy metal. In a study of Australian adolescents, Martin, Clarke, and Pearce (1993) found statistically significant relationships between a preference for heavy metal rock music and suicidal thoughts, deliberate self-injury, depression, delinquent behavior, drug use and family dysfunction, particularly among girls. They also found that the most disturbed teens reported feeling sadder after listening to their preferred music. Stack, Gundlach, and Reeves (1994) found that youth suicide rates were highest in states that also had the highest penetration of heavy metal magazine subscriptions. They suggested that the heavy metal subculture nurtures pre-existing suicidal tendencies. K. R. Roberts, Dimsdale, East, and Friedman (1998) found significant positive associations between strong emotional responses to music and engaging in risk-taking behaviors (e.g. physical fights and use of weapons, fire setting, stealing, alcohol and drug use, unprotected sexual activities, multiple sexual partners).

If we analyze the music-driven depression and suicide of teenagers in hedonic theory terms, we must consider Greenfield's (2000) definition of depression as anhedonia or "lack of a whole spectrum of emotions" (p. 119). According to her, "depressives lock themselves away in a highly personalized inner world" (p. 120). Their problem is "a tilted balance in favor of inner resources over the sensuality of the outside world" materialized in "abnormally large constellations" of neurons (p. 123). Depressives develop a too coherent and stable system of sensorial stimulation and too widespread, coherent, and stable networks of associated thoughts. Neural turnover is minimal and so is pleasure. Because they are "stuck," they feel tempted to blow off their brains and "evade" from the life that makes them prisoners. The natural cure for depression is exposure to new and fast changing sensorial stimulation that creates new small neural constellations and beaks the overly large ones.

Learning Effects

Desensitization

The desensitization hypothesis argues that repeated exposure to media sex and violence causes a reduction in emotional responsiveness and increased callousness (e.g. Zillmann & Weaver, 1989). Desensitization is, in fact, habituation to stimuli that initially appeared to signal either danger or opportunities for enjoyment, but when the same stimuli were repeated, the harm/pain or pleasure proved small and negligible in comparison with other (competing) stimulations. A person gets desensitized by learning about effects through repeated experiences.

Consumers of sexual and violent media content become desensitized to such media stimuli and, more importantly, to similar real-life stimuli. This notion has been widely touted to explain, for example, why onlookers failed to come to the aid of mugging victims – not even making an anonymous phone call to the police from the privacy of their homes. Desensitization effects of pornography were documented especially for male consumers (e.g. Linz, 1985; Linz, Donnerstein, & Adams, 1989; Linz, Donnerstein, & Penrod, 1984; Zillmann & Bryant, 1982a, 1982b, 1984; Zillmann & Weaver, 1989).

Such findings are consistent with the general rule of habituation in hedonic theory. Habituation is not intrinsically bad. It has been put to therapeutical use for the treatment of phobias (e.g. Bandura & Barab, 1973; Bandura & Menlove, 1968; Sparks & Sparks, 2000). The serious danger associated with habituation to media sex and violence comes from the fact that humans will not resign to the naturally decreasing stimulation from the same stimuli (Miron, in press). They will seek increasingly sexual and violent sources of stimulation (entertainments), which will drive up sexuality and violence in media content.

Disinhibition

The idea of disinhibition is that watching, reading, or listening to media violence may serve to undermine learned social sanctions against using violence that usually inhibit aggressive behavior. This reduced inhibition from watching media violence enables people to legitimize using violence in real life, so they become more aggressive. The number of experimental investigations that have explored disinhibition effects of media violence is not very large (e.g. Berkowitz, 1964, 1965; Check & Guloien, 1989; Donnerstein, 1980a, 1980b; Malamuth, 1984) but their findings consistently support the disinhibition hypothesis (Gunter, 1994). In general, disinhibition effects were more pronounced when viewers of violence were already angry while they viewed or read violent media fare (Berkowitz, 1974). The explanation may be that the initial anger effected selective perception and retention from the media, which systematically minimize negative effects of violence anyway. Thus the media pro-risk bias was amplified through the challenge(risk)-biased selectivity caused by anger.

A cultural-ethnographic study of homeless males living in a church-supported shelter (Fiske & Dawson, 1996) examined the enjoyment of violent movies and the meanings derived by those viewers. The researchers did not specifically address disinhibition, but their findings are very helpful for understanding the disinhibition mechanism. Fiske and Dawson reported that "movies like *Die Hard* mattered immensely to the men. We observed more vitality, enthusiasm, and pleasure in their watching of representational violence than in any other aspect of their daily lives" (p. 306). The explanation of the findings revolved around people's sense of identity, self-esteem, and feeling of being in control, which the social order severely limits through education, regulation, and enforcement geared toward the "inhibition" of spontaneous aggressiveness.

An interesting case of disinhibition is that of shock rocker Marilyn Manson, whose songs have some of the most violent lyrics in the US market. Manson explained in an interview that when he attended a public school "they would always kick my ass . . . So I didn't end up having a lot of friends and music was the only thing I had to enjoy" (Jipping, 2001, p. 62). On CNN's "The American Edge" program, Manson accounted for the violence of his music in the following terms: "You are your own god. It's a lot about self-preservation . . . It's the part of you that no longer has hope in mankind. And you realize that you are the only thing you believe in" (Jipping, 2001, p. 62). Manson was ordained in the Church of Satan. The history of Manson's life shows that he suffered from social oppression and found relief in music, which enabled him to regain his self-esteem and feeling of power and control. His extreme and destructive expression of individualism provided an arena for liberation/disinhibition for large numbers of teenagers that felt repressed. As long as music is considered pure fantasy and entertainment activity, Manson and his fans are happy and "safe" in their world of hatred and imagined aggression. When violence starts spilling over into real life – as it happened with his fans Eric Harris and Dylan Klebold, the killers in the Columbine High School shooting – the music haven for violence comes under legislative scrutiny and the Manson brand of pleasure-seekers may suffer some more "inhibition" of their activities.

The desensitization and disinhibition processes spiral between entertainment and real life aggravating violent behavior. What drives the vortex is the spillover phenomenon: Scripts of violent behaviors depicted by the media in realistic settings can easily be enacted in real life by audience members who believe such scripts to have high potential for pleasure, as suggested by much of the current entertainment fare that play down or omit negative effects and overemphasize positive effects of violent actions. On the other hand, in a general context of inhibition, violent media content that pictures the breaking of inhibitory rules by others occasion highly enjoyable vicarious experiences because of the perceived justice and the lack of physical harm for viewers. From a hedonic theory perspective, the intense pleasure temporarily tilts the hedonic balance in the viewer's consciousness: The danger is perceived as insignificant and the fear is minimized. So, disinhibition is emotion-caused misjudgment. Much reduced, the "social-order threats" can be temporarily habituated: The fear-aversion links of the currently activated neural networks are disconnected so that pleasure can be fully enjoyed. Consequently, the immediately following actions taken by the viewer will be "disinhibited," that is, will lack the self-protection (law-observance) limitations. If the viewer engages in violent actions as primed by the media content, he/she will have a drastically reduced sense of risk and may cause serious harm to self and others.

Imitation

Discussions of imitation of media violence usually refer to Bandura's (e.g. 1971, 1973, 1978) social learning theory. According to Bandura (1994), humans "have evolved an advanced capacity for observational learning that enables them to expand their knowledge and skills on the basis of information conveyed by modeling influences" (p. 66). Because fictional characters in novels, television, motion pictures, and video games so often use violence to solve their problems, young viewers may learn that violent behavior is a useful and appropriate way of handling tough situations. The best-known early empirical examination of the modeling of violence were Bandura's Bobo doll studies (e.g. Bandura, 1965; Bandura, Ross, & Ross, 1963; Bandura & Walters, 1963), in which young children watched someone (either live or on film) behave aggressively toward a large inflatable doll designed to serve as a punching bag. The children were later placed in a playroom with a Bobo doll, and their behavior was observed. It was found that children frequently imitated violent behaviors, whether the aggressive model was live or on film.

Evidence of imitation of media sex and violence is mostly anecdotal because ethical government and university research regulations tend to prohibit experiments that involve risks to participants, especially to children. Events cited to illustrate the copycat effect range from the imitation of the autoerotic asphyxiation in Hustler to the report of forced bondage, rape, murder, and mutilation of an eight-year-old girl after her perpetrators read about and viewed photographs of bondage in Penthouse (see Harris, 1994). Felson (1996) mentioned the possibility of contagion effects for "highly publicized violence, such as airline hijacking, civil disorders, bombings, and political kidnapping" (p. 118).

Hedonic theory predicts that scripts (acquired through direct or vicarious experience) are selected from memory based on their potential for pleasure versus pain. The media are notorious for trivializing the unpleasant effects of violence. But even if the pain associated with a script were correctly (completely and proportionally) represented, the viewer would suffer no physical harm and his/her pain would be milder than real-life pain. Consequently, his/her pleasure/pain balance for any vicarious sexual or violent experience will be biased toward pleasure, and the scripts provided by the media will be assessed as more pleasurable than they are in real life. This makes imitation more tempting/likely and puts a pro-violence spin on media consumers' behavior. On the other hand, imitative behaviors will generally be experienced as more painful than expected, and real life will turn out disappointing by comparison with entertainment fiction.

Priming

Priming "essentially holds that when people witness, read, or hear of an event via the mass media, ideas having a similar meaning are activated in them for a short time afterwards, and these thoughts in turn can activate other semantically related ideas and action tendencies" (Jo & Berkowitz, 1994, p. 45). Primed schemata can alter the way people interpret and respond to incoming stimuli. As media fare has a higher frequency of sexual and violent schemata than real life has, extensive media consumption can be expected to bias heavy consumers' perception and behavior toward eroticism and aggressiveness.

Survey research demonstrates that the correlation between the amount of exposure to television violence and frequency of aggressive behavior generally varies between 0.10 and 0.20 (Freedman, 1984; also see Paik & Comstock, 1994, for slightly higher estimates). An early meta-analysis of 31 laboratory experiments with media violence concluded that, overall, viewing violence led to greater aggression than viewing control materials (Andison, 1977). Another meta-analysis of 28 experiments in which the participants were free to display "natural aggression" found that "the mean effect of exposure to violent media on unconstrained aggression is in the small to moderate range, typical of social psychological predictors" (Wood, Wong, & Chachere, 1991, p. 379). Comstock and Paik (1991) macroanalyzed more than 185 different media violence investigations and concluded that the association between exposure to television violence and aggression is quite robust: "The data of the past decade and a half strengthens rather than weakens the case that television violence increases aggressive and anti-social behavior" (p. 54). Centerwall (1989, 1992) conducted epidemiological studies comparing homicide rates over a 30-year period (1945–1975) in the United States, Canada, and South Africa. They found that television set ownership significantly increased homicide rates. Centerwall (1992) speculated that "if, hypothetically, television technology had never been developed, there would be 10,000 fewer homicides each year in the United States, 70,000 fewer rapes, and 700,000 fewer injurious assaults" (p. 3059).

Epidemiological findings about sexual crimes appear to be less consistent and suggest the mediation of culture. According to the Final Report of the Surgeon General's Commission on Pornography (1986), in Denmark and Japan, increases in the availability of sexually explicit materials were associated with decreases in the reporting of sex crimes (a possible habituation/desensitization effect may have affected the perception of sexual crimes and thus confounded the reporting of such crimes); but in Australia, the United States, and many other Western nations, the opposite pattern of association was found (which suggests stronger priming than habituation).

Greenfield (2000) showed that a person's memory tends to individualize her pleasure-directed behavior, progressively differentiating her from other people. But constant priming by the media with routine sex and violence scripts keeps at the top of many people's minds a common set of such behaviors and thus undermines the individualization of their memory and pleasure-seeking behaviors. From a cultural-critical perspective, this may be considered a form of manipulation and homogenization of the public.

Cultivation

Gerbner and associates' cultivation theory (e.g. Gerbner, Gross, Morgan, & Signorielli, 1986, 1994) held that the world of television provided an inescapable environment that shaped people's knowledge of the real world. This phenomenon was conducive to convergence of outlooks or mainstreaming (e.g. Gerbner, Gross, Morgan, & Signorielli, 1980, 1982). Gerbner and his colleagues were also concerned that television did not accurately represent realities, and the knowledge people derived from it was dysfunctional. For example, the disproportionate representation of criminality on television was found to cause a "mean world syndrome" (e.g. Signorielli, 1990). Both mainstreaming and dysfunctionalities were found to be more severe with heavy viewers of television.

Nowadays, television is no longer the reigning medium and we need to consider a mix of media as sources of beliefs, values, and attitudes. But the focus of most media on sex and violence is likely to continue to foster convergence of outlooks at least in these two areas of human behavior. Research results support this expectation. For example, prolonged exposure to sexually explicit messages was found to produce changes in sexual callousness, rape proclivity, moral values, family values, perception of normalcy in sexual behavior, attitudes toward censorship, general attitudes toward women, and many other cognitive effects (e.g. Zillmann, Bryant, & Huston, 1994). Exposure to stereotypical images of gender and sexuality in music videos was found to increase older adolescents' acceptance of non-marital sexual behaviors and interpersonal violence (Kalof, 1999).

The perennial concern expressed by anti-porn feminist critics of media content has been "fueled by the gender skew" (Harris & Scott, 2001), that is, an asymmetrical gender relationship in which women are commodified and used for men's pleasure. Jacob (2000) noted the word pornography comes from the Greek root porne, meaning prostitute or female captive/slave, so "the very root of the word means female sexual slavery" (Jacob, 2000, p. 110). Considering the pervasiveness and economic power of pornography – an estimated 11–16-billion dollar a year industry (Jacob, 2000, p. 116) – its influence appears to be extensive and long-term.

Media effects analysts are increasingly worried about the development of a video game culture, strongly male-focused, aggressive, and violent (Braun & Giroux, 1989), using "hegemonic discourses of masculinity" (Alloway & Gilbert, 1998, p. 97). This culture aligns masculinity with power, violence, "competitiveness at any cost, disregard for others and the environment, and self-aggrandizement through conquest" (p. 113). The acculturation process is enhanced by the coordination of discourse across various media. Interactive CD versions of "sexploits" are now available (p. 105). Specialized magazines make "intertextual connections with cinematic versions of the games" (p. 103) and give game-players a voice through editorials. Such synergistic practices of the entertainment industries increase involvement and give game-players multiple opportunities and forms in which to practice the new gender politics of male hegemony that is "intrinsically homophobic" (p. 100) and "borders on misogyny" (p. 105). Alloway and Gilbert (1998) have cautioned that, "while such texts may be naively driven by the simplest market strategies, . . . they may produce more complex social outcomes than are perhaps intended" (p. 103).

The dangerous "outcomes" can already be discerned in the freest pornography market, which is the Internet. Newsgroups make it possible for participants to cheaply produce and obtain the pleasure-giving materials they want. The Internet seems to be the most massive and democratic pornography source and outlet currently available. Barron and Kimmel (2000) compared Usenet alt.sex.stories with magazine and video pornography and found an alarming evolution associated with direct production of pornography by consumers on the Web: the frequency of nonconsensual sex soared from 7.7 percent in magazines and 3.1 percent in videos to 47.5 percent on Usenet; the frequency of male as perpetrators of sexual violence rose from 38.5 percent in magazines to 60.2 percent in videos and 62.7 percent on Usenet; the frequency of females as victims of sexual violence jumped from 61.5 percent in magazines to 79.6 percent in videos and 84.7 percent on Usenet. These findings appear to support the notion of an increasingly masculine hegemonic culture. The threat posed by the Internet pornography is high on researchers' agenda. A US national survey of 10–17-year-olds who regularly use the Internet found that one out of four encountered unwanted pornography and one out of five was exposed to unwanted sexual solicitations or approaches (Finkelhor, Mitchell, & Wolak, 2000).

Hedonic theory is consistent with Gerbner and associates' cultivation theory and Zillmann's (1999) exemplification theory in relating the consumption of sexual–violent media content with the convergence of sex-and-violence beliefs, values, attitudes, and behaviors at both the individual and the social levels. Repeated activation of sex–violence–pleasure links leads to chronic accessibility. Cross-media variations serve to defeat habituation. The dense sex–violence–pleasure constellations of neurons that are ready to fire ensure wide spreading of activation (i.e. deep/strong/rich conscious experience). The fads pattern similar chronically accessible neural constellations across cohorts, cultivating relatively homogeneous and stable appetites and "tastes" for (aesthetics of) sex and violence. Pleasure as the common denominator for the default hedonic choice at the individual level is thus projected into social life. Sex-and-violence pleasure turns out to be the lowest common denominator of entertainment in our society.

Cultural spillover

We are witnessing synergistic effects of the current hedonistic practices of pleasure seeking. These effects have started to cross the traditional divide between the individual and the social levels of effects. Moreover, according to the cultural spillover theory, violence in one sphere of life leads to violence in other spheres (Felson, 1996). At the violent end of the behavioral spectrum, a possible scenario could be the following: Teenagers visit some porn sites on the Net, listen to

Marilyn Manson singing "no time to discriminate, hate every motherf***er that's in your way" (Jipping, 2001, p. 62), possibly consume drugs, then play Mortal Kombat, then go out in the street and shoot others. "People consume rage as entertainment; they plunk their money down, turn up the volume, and shout themselves hoarse. They shout Public Enemy's black nationalism, Slayer's ambivalent Satanism, Living Colour's warnings of environmental disaster, Nine Inch Nails' self-laceration, Anthrax's moral dialectics, Skid Row's triumphal Machismo. For a while, it feels like actual power – until – the music stops. Or until the killing starts" (Jipping, 2001, p. 66). The school shootings in the US have shown that the danger of violence spillover from media content to actual life is real. In order to better understand the phenomenon, we need to put it into historical perspective.

Violence spillover is not new

The spreading of violence from entertainment to social life has been a problem since the emergence of mass entertainment. Here are two historic examples: "After a victory by Porphyrius in 507 in the circus at Antioch, the jubilant Greens ran wild and, in the course of the riot, burned the local synagogue (Guttmann, 1998, p. 14). In 532, in Constantinople, "supporters of the Blues and Greens joined forces. Prisoners about to be executed were rescued by the mob," which also "proclaimed a new emperor [to replace Justinian], to whom a number of senators paid hasty homage. . . . General Belisarius arrived in time to save the day – at the cost of an estimated thirty thousand lives" (Guttmann, 1998, p. 14). More recently, high-stake games occasionally ended up in massive violence and destruction. For example, in 1964 in Lima, a Uruguayan referee disallowed an equalizing goal toward the end of a Peruvian soccer match against Argentina. The crowd set fire to the stadium and almost 300 spectators were killed (Guttmann, 1998; C. Roberts, 1980). Despite the use of these "classic" examples, it should be noted that this problem has not disappeared in modern times. Many fiercely contested high school, college, and professional sports events today continue long after the final whistle has blown, with fisticuffs between aggrieved fans in parking lots, bars, and a wide variety of other pugilistic venues.

Accounting for spillover

Theoretically speaking, when the arousal buildup reaches very high levels, an extensive activation of aggression-linked neural networks occurs. The first opportunity sets off violent activities. In a public context, such activities escalate because of the fight-or-flight reaction. Police intervention further aggravates the situation by adding to the mix the ethical component (outrage caused by perceived injustice). Media presence pours gas on fire by hugely expanding the arena for the justice show.

The media's preference for sexual and violent content is the outcome of free market logic taking advantage of people's natural orienting response. In addition, violence and sex are the strongest natural sources of excitement. If the public wants excitement, the media want sales (ratings), and consequently they compete in terms of sex and violence, no matter what content (news, sports, music, fiction). On the other hand, "violence embodies conflict, and conflict is the heart and soul of drama" (Bryant & Zillmann, 1996, p. 196). Dramatic stories have the power to hold people's attention. They can be serialized, which increases their commercial potential. Violence is also a quick and easy way to solve problems, a convenient shortcut to more complex forms of conflict resolution.

Media's response to spillover complaints
In response to the increasing tendency of public opinion to blame the media for the spillover of violence from entertainment to real life, the media claim that they supply what the market demands. "The most common response by the television industry is that programming merely reflects what people already wish to consume, that the medium is entirely reactive and does not cause anything" (Jipping, 2001, p. 63).

Both professional education and market socialization of media writers, editors, producers, and directors foster an obsession with competitiveness and, associated with it, an apprehension that absence of the sexual and violent ingredients condemns a media product to failure. Time after time, media message creators and providers rationalize heavy doses of gratuitous violence by saying, "we're only giving people what they want," or "they'll go elsewhere for entertainment if we don't stick in some violence" (e.g. Easton, 1993).

The "what bleeds, leads" rationale is arguable, though. Under the mood management theory (Bryant & Zillmann, 1984; Zillmann, 1988), only a bored population would exhibit a massive preference for violent and pornographic media stimulation. Otherwise, a balanced distribution of over- and under-stimulated people would result in mixed preferences for exciting and relaxing media content. The balanced-needs hypothesis seems to be supported by the very inconclusiveness of empirical evidence about preference for sex and violence in the media. For example, Diener and colleagues (Diener & DeFour, 1978; Diener & Woody, 1981) found that viewers either exhibit no preferences or slight preferences for violent content when choosing media fare. Cantor (1998) argued that "there are other types of offerings that are even more popular [than violence] with children" (p. 96), and Goldstein (1998) claimed that "violent entertainment is the preferred form of entertainment only for a minority of the general audience. Most viewers appear to prefer comedies and sitcoms" (p. 225). On the other hand, Bryant and Musburger (1989) reported that child viewers rated a violent version of an animated television program significantly higher in enjoyment than humorous, action-packed, or control versions of the same program. Moreover, the prospect theory (Kahneman & Tversky, 1979, 1984) cautions about "a general priority of negative over positive affect in hedonic experience" (Kahneman, 1999, p. 18), which manifests itself as loss aversion, risk aversion, and scanning the environment for danger rather than opportunities.

In this context of ongoing theoretical debate, a legitimate question is: What danger/opportunity ratio do we experience in real life, and what is the danger/opportunity ratio in the media fare? As observed by Gerbner and Gross (1976), "fear is a universal emotion and easy to exploit" (p. 193). The cultural indicators analysis conducted by Gerbner and associates showed an inflated violence rate in television entertainment. "If a disproportionate number of available movies are violent and people want to watch something, then high quantities of violence will be consumed" (Sparks & Sparks, 2000). According to Gerbner's cultivation theory, the audience is "mainstreamed" (homogeneized) by the media and persuaded that real life is more violent than it currently is, which causes behavioral responses that are disproportionately violent and thus escalates violence in the real world. From this perspective, media critics seem justified to suspect media strategies of manipulativeness.

Freedom or Censorship? – The Lid on the Pressure Cooker

Freud (1927) proposed that humans have an inherent drive toward destruction and death that needs to be recognized and accommodated in order to avoid an increase in the malaise of our civilization. Frau-Meigs and Jehel (1997) contended that the extreme social liberalism (i.e. Social Darwinism) "constitutes a major risk of disaggregation for the social structure and for the subject himself" (p. 19). If so, the problem is how to accommodate violence, what kind of place we design for it in society.

Arrow's (1967) socially conditioned theory of value posited that "all nontrivial actions are essentially the property of society as a whole and not of individuals" and they involve joint participation (pp. 7–8). The widespread consumption of sexual and violent media entertainment indeed qualifies as nontrivial action, therefore societal "ownership" and management of such entertainment activities is warranted. DeCarolis' (1975) socially conditioned theory of value and pleasure suggested that critics should be in charge of making and directing cultural choices and stewarding public consumption based on their expert knowledge and the knowledge of what can maintain the society and what cannot. Historically, governments also got involved in issuing censorship legislation that barred obscenity and/or violence from the public speech and entertainment. The main reason for legislative action is that "purely sensuous pleasure, a pleasure of the extreme and autonomous physicality, is always political, even and especially in its apparent refusal or liquidation of the political realm" (Connor, 1992, p. 216). Grossmann (2001) argued during US Congress hearings about media violence, "not everybody who ingests media violence is a killer, but they are all sickened by it . . . and our society is subsequently influenced by them" (p. 70). Feminist critic Jacob (2000) warned that the current "paradigm of male–female sexuality reinforces a dangerous power imbalance" and results in "a cultural climate that is inherently hostile to women" (p. 110).

The problem that Western societies are currently facing is how to accommodate people's pursuit of sexual and violent entertainment and what kind of place to make for it in the social order. Censorship has been criticized on grounds that it is "an effect-oriented solution" that "works with power" in order to "silence the culture of the oppressed" and thus contributes to their oppression" (Fiske & Dawson, 1996, p. 306). As remarked by Bok (1998), we are facing a dilemma between rights and needs, and resolving this dilemma involves the will to ban and censor. It is an exercise of social responsibility that requires not only strength, but especially knowledge of actual and possible short- and long-term effects of exposure to the media.

References

Alloway, N. and Gilbert, P. (1998). Video game culture: Playing with masculinity, violence and pleasure. In S. Howard (ed.), *Wired-Up: Young people and the electronic media*. London: UCL Press, pp. 95–114.

Anderson, E. (2001). Hedonism and the happy life: The Epicurean theory of pleasure. Retrieved March 13 from http://www.epicureans.org/intro.htm.

Andison, F. (1977). TV violence and viewer aggression: A cumulation of study results, 1956–1976. *Public Opinion Quarterly*, 41, 314–31.

Apter, M. J. (1982). *The Experience of Motivation: The theory of psychological reversals*. London: Academic.

Apter, M. J. (1989). *Reversal Theory: Motivation, emotion and personality*. London: Routledge.

Apter, M. J. (1992). *The Dangerous Edge: The psychology of excitement*. New York: The Free Press.

Apter, M. J. (1994). Why we enjoy media violence: A reversal theory approach. Paper presented at the International Conference on Violence in the Media, St. John's University, New York, October.

Aristotle (1999). *Poetics*. Cambridge, MA: Harvard University Press.

Arrow, K. (1967). Public and private values. In S. Hook (ed.), *Human Values and Economic Policy: A symposium*. New York: New York University Press, pp. 3–21.

Bancroft, L. and Mathews, A. (1971). Autonomic correlates of penile erection. *Journal of Psychosomatic Research*, 15, 159–67.

Bandura, A. (1965). Influence of models' reinforcement contingencies on the acquisition of imitative responses. *Journal of Personality and Social Psychology*, 1, 585–95.

Bandura, A. (1971). *Social Learning Theory*. New York: General Learning Press.

Bandura, A. (1973). *Aggression: A social learning analysis*. Englewood Cliffs, NJ: Prentice-Hall.

Bandura, A. (1978). A social learning theory of aggression. *Journal of Communication*, 28(3), 12–29.

Bandura, A. (1994). Social cognitive theory of mass communication. In J. Bryant and D. Zillmann (eds.), *Media Effects: Advances in theory and research*. Hillsdale, NJ: Lawrence Erlbaum, pp. 61–90.

Bandura, A. and Barab, P. G. (1973). Processes governing disinhibitory effects through symbolic modeling. *Journal of Abnormal Psychology*, 82, 1–9.

Bandura, A. and Menlove, F. L. (1968). Factors determining vicarious extinction of avoidance behavior through symbolic modeling. *Journal of Personality and Social Psychology*, 8, 99–108.

Bandura, A. and Walters, R. H. (1963). *Social Learning and Personality Development*. New York: Holt, Rinehart & Winston.

Bandura, A., Ross, D., and Ross, S. A. (1963). Imitation of film-mediated aggressive models. *Journal of Abnormal and Social Psychology*, 66, 3–11.

Baron, R. A. (1979). Heightened sexual arousal and physical aggression. *Journal of Research in Personality*, 13, 91–102.

Barron, M. and Kimmel, M. (2000). Sexual violence in three pornographic media: Toward a sociological explanation. *Journal of Sex Research*, 37, 161–8.

Berkowitz, L. (1964). The effects of observing violence. *Scientific American*, 210(2), 35–41.

Berkowitz, L. (1965). Some aspects of observed aggression. *Journal of Personality and Social Psychology*, 2, 359–69.

Berkowitz, L. (1974). Some determinants of impulsive aggression: The role of mediated associations with reinforcements for aggression. *Psychological Review*, 81, 165–76.

Bok, S. (1998). *Mayhem: Violence as public entertainment*. Reading, MA: Merloyd Lawrence and Addison-Wesley.

Bousfield, P. (1999). *Pleasure and Pain: A theory of the energic foundation of feeling*. London: Routledge. (Original work published 1926.)

Braun, C. and Giroux, J. (1989). Arcade video games: Proxemic, cognitive and content analyses. *Journal of Leisure Research*, 21, 92–105.

Bryant, J. and Musburger, R. (1989). Children's enjoyment of action, violence, and humor in animated television programs. Paper presented at the Annual Convention of the Broadcast Education Association, Las Vegas, April.

Bryant, J. and Zillmann, D. (1984). Using television to alleviate boredom and stress: Selective exposure as a function of induced excitational states. *Journal of Broadcasting*, 28, 1–20.

Bryant, J. and Zillmann, D. (1996). Violence and sex in the media. In M. B. Salwen and D. W. Stacks (eds.), *An Integrated Approach to Communication Theory and Research*. Mahwah, NJ: Lawrence Erlbaum, pp. 195–209.

Bryant, J. and Zillmann, D. (2001). Pornography, models of (effects on sexual deviancy). In C. D. Bryant (ed.), *Encyclopedia of Criminology and Deviant Behavior*, vol. 3. Oxford: Brunner/Routledge, pp. 241–4.

Cacioppo, J. T. and Berntson, G. G. (1994). Relationships between attitudes and evaluative space: A critical review with emphasis on the separability of positive and negative substrates. *Psychological Bulletin*, 115, 401–23.

Campbell, H. J. (1973). *The Pleasure Areas: A new theory of behavior*. New York: Delacorte.

Cantor, J. R. (1994). Fright reactions to mass media. In J. Bryant and D. Zillmann (eds.), *Media Effects: Advances in theory and research*. Hillsdale, NJ: Lawrence Erlbaum, pp. 213–45.

Cantor, J. R. (1998). Children's attraction to television programing. In J. H. Goldstein (ed.), *Why We Watch: The attractions of violent entertainment*. New York: Oxford University Press, pp. 88–115.

Carnes, P. J. (1991). *Don't Call It Love*. New York: Bantam.

Centerwall, B. S. (1989). Exposure to television as a cause of violence. In G. A. Comstock (ed.), *Public Communication and Behavior*, vol. 2. Orlando: Academic, pp. 1–53.

Centerwall, B. S. (1992). Television and violence: The scale of the problem and where to go from here. *Journal of the American Medical Association*, 267, 3059–63.

Check, J. V. P. and Guloien, T. H. (1989). Reported proclivity for coercive sex following repeated exposure to sexually violent pornography, nonviolent dehumanizing pornography, and erotica. In D. Zillmann and J. Bryant (eds.), *Pornography: Research advances and policy considerations*. Hillsdale, NJ: Lawrence Erlbaum, pp. 159–84.

Comstock, G. A. and Paik, H. (1991). The effects of television violence on aggressive behavior: A meta-analysis. In A. J. Reiss and J. A. Roth (eds.), *A Preliminary Report to the National Research Council on The Understanding and Control of Violent Behavior*. Washington, DC: National Research Council, pp. 41–54.

Connor, S. (1992). Aesthetics, pleasure and value. In S. Reagan (ed.), *The Politics of Pleasure: Aesthetics and cultural theory*. Buckingham, UK: Open University Press, pp. 203–20.

Cowie, E. (1993). Pornography and fantasy: Psychoanalytic perspectives. In L. Segal and M. McIntosh (eds.), *Sex Exposed: Sexuality and the pornography debate*. New Brunswick, NJ: Rutgers University Press, pp. 132–52.

Davidson, R. J. (1992). Anterior cerebral asymmetry and the nature of emotion. *Brain and Cognition*, 6, 245–68.

DeCarolis, A. (1975). The Role of the Expert in a Theory of Pleasure. Unpublished master's thesis, Bowling Green State University, Bowling Green.

Diener, E. and DeFour, D. (1978). Does television violence enhance program popularity? *Journal of Research in Social Psychology*, 36, 334–41.

Diener, E. and Woody, W. (1981). TV violence and viewer liking. *Communication Research*, 8, 281–306.

Donnerstein, E. (1980a). Aggressive erotica and violence against women. *Journal of Personality and Social Psychology*, 39, 269–77.

Donnerstein, E. (1980b). Pornography and violence against women: Experimental studies. *Annals of the New York Academy of Sciences*, 347, 277–88.

Easton, N. J. (1993). America's mean streak: It's cool to be cool. *Los Angeles Times Magazine*, February 7, 16–20, 43–4.

Epicurus (1993). *The Essential Epicurus: Letters, principal doctrines, Vatican sayings, and fragments* (trans. E. O'Connor). Buffalo, NY: Prometheus.

Felson, R. B. (1996). Mass media effects on violent behavior. *Annual Review of Sociology*, 22, 103–28.

Final Report of the Surgeon General's Commission on Pornography (1986). Nashville: Rutledge Hill.

Finkelhor, D., Mitchell, K., and Wolak, J. (2000). *Online Victimization: A report on the nation's youth*. Washington, DC: National Center for Missing and Exploited Children.

Fiske, J. and Dawson, R. (1996). Audiencing violence: Watching homeless men watch *Die Hard*. In J. Hay, L. Grossberg, and E. Wartella (eds.), *The Audience and Its Landscape*. Boulder, CO: Westview, pp. 297–316.

Frau-Meigs, D. and Jehel, S. (1997). *Les ecrans de la violence: Enjeux economiques et responsabilites sociales* [The screens of violence: Economic interests and social responsibilities]. Paris: Economica.

Freedman, J. L. (1984). Effects of television violence on aggressiveness. *Psychological Bulletin*, 96, 227–46.

Freud, S. (1927). *Essays de psychoanalyse*. Paris: Payot.

Freud, S. (1989). *Beyond the Pleasure Principle*. New York: Norton. (Original work published 1920.)

Gerbner, G. and Gross, L. (1976). Living with television: The violence profile. *Journal of Communication*, 26, 173–99.

Gerbner, G., Gross, L., Morgan, M., and Signorielli, N. (1980). The "mainstreaming" of America: Violence profile no. 11. *Journal of Communication*, 30(3), 10–29.

Gerbner, G., Gross, L., Morgan, M., and Signorielli, N. (1982). Charting the mainstream: Television's contributions to political orientations. *Journal of Communication* 32(2), 100–27.

Gerbner, G., Gross, L., Morgan, M., and Signorielli, N. (1986). Living with television: The dynamics of the cultivation process. In J. Bryant and D. Zillmann (eds.), *Perspectives on Media Effects*. Hillsdale, NJ: Lawrence Erlbaum, pp. 17–48.

Gerbner, G., Gross, L., Morgan, M., and Signorielli, N. (1994). Growing up with television: The cultivation perspective. In J. Bryant and D. Zillmann (eds.), *Media Effects: Advances in theory and research*. Hillsdale, NJ: Lawrence Erlbaum, pp. 17–41.

Goldstein, J. H. (1998). Why we watch. In J. H. Goldstein (ed.), *Why We Watch: The attractions of violent entertainment*. New York: Oxford University Press pp. 212–26.

Greenfield, S. (2000). *The Private Life of the Brain: Emotions, consciousness, and the secret of the self*. New York: Wiley.

Grossman, D. (2001). Violent video games teach children to enjoy killing. In J. D. Torr (ed.), *Violence in the Media* (Current Controversies Series). San Diego, CA: Greenhaven, pp. 67–71.

Gunter, B. (1994). The question of media violence. In J. Bryant and D. Zillmann (eds.), *Media Effects: Advances in theory and research*. Hillsdale, NJ: Lawrence Erlbaum, pp. 163–211.

Guttmann, A. (1998). The appeal of violent sports. In J. Goldstein (ed.), *Why We Watch: The attractions of violent entertainment*. New York: Oxford University Press, pp. 179–211.

Harris, R. J. (1994). The impact of sexually explicit media. In J. Bryant and D. Zillmann (eds.), *Media Effects: Advances in theory and research*. Hillsdale, NJ: Lawrence Erlbaum, pp. 247–72.

Harris, R. J. (1999). A cognitive psychology of mass communication (3rd edn.). Mahwah, NJ: Lawrence Erlbaum.

Harris, R. J. and Scott, C. L. (2001). Effects of sex in the media. In J. Bryant and D. Zillmann (eds.), *Media Effects: Advances in theory and research* (2nd edn.). Hillsdale, NJ: Lawrence Erlbaum, pp. 307–31.

Hill, A. (1997). *Shocking Entertainment: Viewer response to violent movies*. Luton, UK: University of Luton Press.

Hobson, J. A. (1994). *The Chemistry of Conscious States: How the brain changes its mind*. New York: Little, Brown & Co.

Ito, T. A. and Cacioppo, J. T. (1999). The psychophysiology of utility appraisals. In D. Kahneman, E. Diener, and H. Schwarz (eds.), *Well-Being: The foundations of hedonic psychology*. New York: Russell Sage Foundation, pp. 470–88.

Jacob, K. K. (2000). Crime without punishment: Pornography in a rape culture. In J. Gold and S. Villari (eds.), *Just Sex: Students rewrite the rules on sex, violence, activism, and equality*. Lanham, MD: Rowman & Littlefield, pp. 105–20.

Jipping, T. L. (2001). Popular music contributes to teenage violence. In J. D. Torr (ed.), *Violence in the Media* (Current Controversies Series). San Diego, CA: Greenhaven, pp. 61–6.

Jo, E. and Berkowitz, L. (1994). A priming effect analysis of media influences: An update. In J. Bryant and D. Zillmann (eds.), *Media Effects: Advances in theory and research*. Hillsdale, NJ: Lawrence Erlbaum, pp. 43–60.

Kahneman, D. (1999). Objective happiness. In D. Kahneman, E. Diener, and H. Schwarz (eds.), *Well-Being: The foundations of hedonic psychology*. New York: Russell Sage Foundation, pp. 3–25.

Kahneman, D. and Tversky, A. (1979). Prospect theory: An analysis of decision under risk. *Econometrica*, 47, 313–27.

Kahneman, D. and Tversky, A. (1984). Choices, values, and frames. *American Psychologist*, 39, 341–50.

Kahneman, D., Diener, E., and Schwarz, H. (eds.). (1999). *Well-Being: The foundations of hedonic psychology*. New York: Russell Sage Foundation.

Kalof, L. (1999). The effects of gender and music video imagery on sexual attitudes. *Journal of Social Psychology*, 139, 378–86.

Linz, D. (1985). Sexual violence in the media: Effects on male viewers and implications for society. (Doctoral dissertation, University of Wisconsin, Madison.) *Dissertation Abstracts International*, 46, 1382B.

Linz, D., Donnerstein, E., and Adams, S. M. (1989). Physiological desensitization and judgments about female victims of violence. *Human Communication Research*, 15, 509–22.

Linz, D., Donnerstein, E., and Penrod, S. (1984). The effects of multiple exposures to filmed violence against women. *Journal of Communication*, 34, 130–47.

Lyons, J. S., Anderson, R. L., and Larson, D. B. (1994). A systematic review of the effects of aggressive and nonaggressive pornography. In D. Zillmann, J. Bryant, and A. C. Huston (eds.), *Media, Children, and the Family: Social scientific, psychodynamic, and clinical perspectives*. Hillsdale, NJ: Lawrence Erlbaum, pp. 271–310.

Malamuth, N. M. (1984). Aggression against women: Cultural and individual causes. In N. M. Malamuth and E. Donnerstein (eds.), *Pornography and Sexual Aggression*. Orlando, FL: Academic Press, pp. 19–52.

Malamuth, N. M., Check. J. V. P., and Briere, J. (1986). Sexual arousal in response to aggression: Ideological, aggressive, and sexual correlates. *Journal of Personality and Social Psychology*, 50, 330–40.

Martin, G., Clarke, M., and Pearce, C. (1993). Adolescent suicide: Music preference as an indicator of vulnerability. *Journal of the American Academy of Child and Adolescent Psychiatry*, 32, 530–5.

Miron, D. (in press). Enjoyment of violence. In J. Bryant, D. Roskos-Ewoldsen, and J. Cantor (eds.), *Communication and Emotion: Essays in honor of Dolf Zillmann*. Hillsdale, NJ: Lawrence Erlbaum.

Mourlet, M. (1991). In defense of violence. In C. Gledhill (ed.), *Stardom: Industry of desire*. London: Routledge, pp. 233–6.

Paik, H. and Comstock, G. (1994). The effects of television violence on antisocial behavior: A meta-analysis. *Communication Research*, 21, 516–46.

Plagens, P., Miller, M., Foote, D., and Yoffee, E. (1991). Violence in our culture: As America binges on make-believe gore, you have to ask: What are we doing to ourselves? *Newsweek*, April 1, 46–9, 51–2.

Raschke, C. A. (1990). *Painted Black: From drug killings to heavy metal: The alarming true story of how Satanism is terrorizing our communities*. San Francisco: Harper & Row.

Roberts, C. (1980). Violence in sports. In H. S. Nelli (ed.), *Sports in Society: past and present*. Lexington, KY: University of Kentucky.

Roberts, K. R., Dimsdale, J., East, P., and Friedman, L. (1998). Adolescent emotional response to music and its relationship to risk-taking behaviors. *Journal of Adolescent Health*, 23, 49–54.

Sapolsky, B. S. and Zillmann, D. (1981). The effect of soft-core and hard-core erotica on provoked and unprovoked hostile behavior. *Journal of Sex Research*, 17, 319–43.

Segal, C. (1993). Philomela's web and the pleasures of the text: Reader and violence in the *Metamorphoses* of Ovid. In I. J. F. DeJong and J. P. Sullivan (eds.), *Modern Critical Theory and Classical Literature*. Leiden, The Netherlands: Brill, pp. 257–80.

Sheridan, T. B. (1992). Musings on telepresence and virtual presence. *Presence: Teleoperators and Virtual Environments*, 1, 120–6.

Signorielli, N. (1990). Television's mean and dangerous world: A continuation of the cultural indicators perspective. In N. Signorielli and M. Morgan (eds.), *Cultivation Analysis: New directions in media effects research*. Newbury Park, CA: Sage, pp. 85–106.

Solomon, R. L. (1980). The opponent process theory of acquired motivation: The costs and benefits of pain. *American Psychologist*, 35, 691–712.

Sparks, G. G. and Sparks, C. W. (2000). Violence, mayhem, and horror. In D. Zillmann and P. Vorderer (eds.), *Media Entertainment: The psychology of its appeal*. Mahwah, NJ: Lawrence Erlbaum, pp. 73–91.

Stack, S., Gundlach, J., and Reeves, J. L. (1994). The heavy metal subculture and suicide. *Suicide and Life Threatening Behavior*, 24, 15–23.

Tamborini, R. (2000). The experience of telepresence in violent video games. Paper presented at the 8th annual convention of the National Communication Association. Seattle, WA, November.

Torr, J. D. (2001). Introduction. In J. D. Torr (ed.), *Violence in the Media* (Current Controversies Series). San Diego, CA: Greenhaven, pp. 13–15.

Turner, J. G. (1995). The whores rhetoric: Narrative, pornography, and the origins of the novel. In C. H. Hay and S. M. Conger (eds.), *Studies in Eighteenth-Century Culture*, vol. 24. Baltimore, MD: Johns Hopkins University Press, pp. 297–306.

Urmson, J. O. (1968). Aristotle on pleasure. In J. M. E. Moravcsik (ed.), *Aristotle: A collection of critical essays*. Notre Dame, IN: University of Notre Dame Press, pp. 323–33.

White, L. A. (1979). Erotica and aggression: The influence of sexual arousal, positive affect, and negative affect on aggressive behavior. *Journal of Personality and Social Psychology*, 37, 591–601.

Wood, W., Wong. F. Y., and Chachere, G. (1991). Effects of media violence on viewers' aggression in unconstrained social interaction. *Psychological Bulletin*, 109, 371–83.

Zillmann, D. (1971). Excitation transfer in communication-mediated aggressive behavior. *Journal of Experimental Social Psychology*, 7, 419–34.

Zillmann, D. (1979). *Hostility and Aggression*. Hillsdale, NJ: Lawrence Erlbaum.

Zillmann, D. (1980). Anatomy of suspense. In P. Tannenbaum (ed.), *The Entertainment Functions of Television*. Hillsdale, NJ: Lawrence Erlbaum, pp. 133–63.

Zillmann, D. (1988). Mood management: Using entertainment to full advantage. In L. Donohew, H. E. Sypher, and E. T. Higgins (eds.), *Communication, Social Cognition, and Affect*. Hillsdale, NJ: Lawrence Erlbaum, pp. 147–71.

Zillmann, D. (1991a). The logic of suspense and mystery. In J. Bryant and D. Zillmann (eds.), *Responding to the Screen: Reception and reaction processes*. Hillsdale, NJ: Lawrence Erlbaum, pp. 281–303.

Zillmann, D. (1991b). Television viewing and physiological arousal. In J. Bryant and D. Zillmann (eds.), *Responding to the Screen: Reception and reaction processes*. Hillsdale, NJ: Lawrence Erlbaum, pp. 103–33.

Zillmann, D. (1996). The psychology of suspense in dramatic exposition. In P. Vorderer, H. J. Wulff, and M. Friedrichsen (eds.), *Suspense: Conceptualizations, theoretical analyses, and empirical explorations*. Hillsdale, NJ: Lawrence Erlbaum, pp. 199–231.

Zillmann, D. (1999). Exemplification theory: Judging the whole by some of its parts. *Media Psychology*, 1, 69–94.

Zillmann, D. and Bryant, J. (1982a). Effects of massive exposure to pornography. In N. M. Malamuth and E. Donnerstein (eds.), *Pornography and Sexual Aggression*. New York: Academic.

Zillmann, D. and Bryant, J. (1982b). Pornography, sexual callousness, and the trivialization of rape. *Journal of Communication*, 32(4), 10–21.

Zillmann, D. and Bryant, J. (1984). Effects of massive exposure to pornography. In N. M. Malamuth and E. Donnerstein (eds.), *Pornography and Sexual Aggression*. Orlando, FL: Academic, pp. 115–38.

Zillmann, D. and Bryant, J. (eds.) (1989). *Pornography: Research advances and policy considerations*. Hillsdale, NJ: Lawrence Erlbaum.

Zillmann, D. and Weaver, J. B. (1989). Pornography and men's sexual callousness toward women. In D. Zillmann and J. Bryant (eds.), *Pornography: Research advances and policy considerations*. Hillsdale, NJ: Lawrence Erlbaum, pp. 95–125.

Zillmann, D., Bryant, J., and Huston, A. C. (1994). *Media, Children, and the Family: Social scientific, psychodynamic, and clinical perspectives*. Hillsdale, NJ: Lawrence Erlbaum.

Zillmann, D., Bryant, J., Comisky, P. W., and Medoff, N. J. (1981). Excitation and hedonic valence in the effect of erotica on motivated intermale aggression. *European Journal of Social Psychology*, 11, 233–52.

CHAPTER TWENTY-TWO

The Role of Interactive Media in Children's Cognitive Development

Ellen A. Wartella, Barbara J. O'Keefe, and Ronda M. Scantlin

Since the early days of radio in the 1930s, mass media have been a part of the home environment. In recent years, a wide variety of media sources have been adopted by American families, creating a generation of children growing up in multimedia households. Two recent nationally representative surveys from the Kaiser Family Foundation (Roberts, Foehr, Rideout, & Brodie, 1999) and the Annenberg Public Policy Center (Woodard, 2000) illustrate just how prevalent media are in the home. Using averages to summarize the results of a recent national study of children's media use and access, Roberts and his colleagues indicate that "the typical American child enters the twenty-first century living in a household with three television sets, two VCRs, three radios, three tape players, two CD players, a video game player, and a computer" (Roberts et al., 1999, p. 9). Indeed, results of Annenberg's annual study of media in the home confirm that American families live in multimedia households. Nearly half of the 1,235 families in the study with children between the ages of two and seventeen (48 percent) had a television set, a VCR, video game equipment, and a personal computer (Woodard, 2000). Of course, family financial resources have an impact on the amount of media present in the household. Only 28 percent of lower income households (family annual income of $30,000 or less) had all four media technologies whereas 62 percent of higher income households (family annual income of $75,000 or more) have all four media sources (Woodard, 2000).

Consumption of mass media is clearly the dominant activity of childhood. Children spend more time with media than they do with any other activity besides school and sleeping (Stanger & Gridina, 1999; Roberts et al., 1999). Both the Kaiser Family Foundation (Roberts et al., 1999) as well as the Annenberg study (Woodard, 2000) indicate that children between the ages of two and eighteen spend about six hours per day with some form of mediated communication device. Furthermore, both studies report that on average children spend about four hours per day in front of screens, that is watching television or videotapes, playing video games, using the computer, or browsing the Internet (Roberts et al., 1999; Woodard, 2000). It should be noted, however, that children often engage in more than one mediated communication technology at once. For example, children often read while watching television or use the computer while talking on the phone or listening to music. Therefore, children's media *exposure* is likely to be higher than actual time measurement of media use. For example, although the Kaiser report indicates that children's actual person hours devoted to media per day is about five and a half hours, their actual daily media exposure is about six and a half hours because of simultaneous use of different media (Roberts et al., 1999).

With the exception of television viewing, media use evolves as children grow older. According to findings of the Annenberg study, preschool aged children (ages 2–5) spend the largest amount of time watching video tapes (80 average daily minutes) while school-age children (ages 6–11) spend the most time reading books (58 average daily minutes) and adolescents (ages 12–17) spend the most time using the Internet (46 average daily minutes), playing video games (55 average daily minutes), and generally using the computer (63 average daily minutes) (Woodard, 2000). The Kaiser report indicates that television viewing starts early with 2–4 year-olds viewing two hours daily, rises throughout childhood peaking at the end of grade school at three and a half hours per day by the ages of 8–13, then declines to about two hours and forty-five minutes per day in late adolescence (ages 14–18) (Roberts et al., 1999). These findings are consistent with other research regarding television viewing (Comstock & Paik, 1991; Wright et al., 2001). According to the Kaiser report (Roberts et al., 1999) and the Annenberg study (Woodard, 2000), as children mature, they spend more time playing video games and using the computer. Regarding content choices of video games, younger children (ages 0–5) play more educational games than older children and older school-age children (ages 9–12) play more sports games than younger children (ages 6–8) (Wright et al., 2001). Regardless of age, according to both the Kaiser and Annenberg studies, boys spend more time watching television and playing video games than do girls. In short, children today live in a media-saturated world and like earlier generations of children, they are quickly adopting the newer interactive media into their lives.

Much of this pertinent research on children's use of media and its role in their lives has focused on the uses of *particular* media (e.g. books, television, computers, Internet) and not on the whole media environment. The literature on print literacy has virtually no overlap with the literature on children and television, and these in turn have little connection with literature on children and computers. While this may have been a useful simplifying strategy in the past, it appears increasingly less viable in an age of media convergence.

Media convergence refers to a process in which formerly distinct methods of communication merge to create new media. We can understand this process at a technical level, in terms of the hardware, software, and standards that make such convergence possible. We can understand it at a social and cognitive level, in terms of the ways in which previously distinct information sources and new capabilities such as interactivity or telepresence alter the flow of information and influence. Or we can understand it at an institutional level, in terms of the ways in which communication policies and industries are realigned in response to new social challenges and business opportunities. But however we choose to look at these processes of convergence, it is clear that they are going to change the media environment into a more seamless presentation system, in which discourses – packages of communication content – interact with audiences across multiple media.

Moreover, the impact of such convergence will be felt even more strongly in light of the increasing pervasiveness of digital media. "Pervasive computing" refers to the incorporation of computational and representational capabilities into the spaces, objects, and tools with which we surround ourselves. To the extent that such pervasive computing is networked, as everyone now expects it to be, we will see the emergence of a highly interconnected, constantly available digital media environment. Of course, we should not forget that the prospect of pervasive and convergent media is not equally available to all. To the extent that educational or socioeconomic barriers limit access, the ideal of pervasive communication will not be a reality, as was noted in the previous section.

Nonetheless, media products increasingly involve coordinated presentation of content in multiple media. As an example, consider the phenomenon of "Pokemania." *Pokemon*, released originally as a Nintendo game in 1996, was instantly popular with elementary school students, first in Japan and then in the US as well. The game was followed by a cartoon series on television, trading cards, toys, and comics. A very successful *Pokemon* motion picture was released in late 1999, coordinated with a community-building program sponsored by Burger King in which children met on a specific night at their restaurants to trade *Pokemon* cards. *Pokemon* moved across multiple media, evolved, and was incorporated into children's culture via its repeated manifestation in their lives. Understanding the impact and influence of *Pokemon* requires understanding its presence in an increasingly more seamless communications environment and its integration into children's culture and relationships.

In this review, we offer a view of the special role of interactive media – including interactive television, video games, CD-ROMS, interactive toys, wireless devices, the Internet and other interactive software in children's cognitive development. We draw from varied theoretical backgrounds to examine the potential and actual evidence of how interactive media influence children's learning and cognition. Unlike much of the literature on children's learning from television which is rooted in a model of how children use and are affected by television content, the literature on interactive media's impact on cognitive development relies on the media socialization literature.

The concept of media socialization, which examines specifically how different kinds of media influence children's cognitive growth, is a perspective which has emerged over the last fifteen years as a key framework for understanding how and what children take from their experiences with communication. It is grounded in classic thinking about the nature of language socialization (Schieffelin & Ochs, 1986), the nature of education and learning (Hickman, 1990; McDermott, 1981; Pea, 1994), mind, self, and society (Mead, 1934), cognitive development (Piaget, 1964), social cognitive development (Vygotsky, 1962) and dialogue (Bahktin, 1990). Following Scribner and Cole (1981) we believe that such a framework can be generalized to understand the role of any communications medium in learning.

Socialization is the process of acquiring roles and the knowledge and skills needed to enact them. We all encounter situations first as novices, unpracticed and untutored. We meet the challenges of a new situation with the resources we bring (situated knowledge), the assistance of our fellow actors (scaffolding), the process of discovery through which we acquire new resources (inquiry), the process of communication through which we involve others in our learning (dialogue), and a point of view within which to make sense of new activities and determine how to use what we are learning (framing). We can consider each of these processes.

Situated Knowledge

Within one influential theory of human development, cognitive growth is simply the acquisition of situated knowledge and skills. This view, commonly identified with Vygotsky (Vygotsky, 1962; for an overview and commentary, see Wertsch, 1991) but also reflected in the work of contemporary activity theorists (Cole, 1985; Engstrom, 1992; Lave, 1988), treats cognitive structures and skills as the outcomes of learning how to enact roles in particular activities. That is, learning and development reflect the accumulation of learned performances, each specific to a particular activity. From this standpoint, one would expect learning to be highly situation-specific, and indeed, there is a strong case that cognitive skills are situated and not easily generalized from one setting to the next (for an overview, see Lave, 1988). For example, tool use is not generalizable from one tool (sewing machine) to another (drill). Powerful and widely-cited examples of this principle have been offered in studies of navigation in Puluwat (Hutchins, 1995), weaving in Zinacanteco (Childs & Greenfield, 1980), reading and writing among the Vai (Scribner & Cole, 1981), and tailoring in Liberia (Lave, 1977; Reed & Lave, 1979).

As a consequence of the situated character of knowledge and skills, it is often difficult to demonstrate the impact of media experiences on general cognitive growth. However, where researchers have conducted assessments of learning or impact that are closely tied to the kinds of media activities children have participated in, they have been able to show significant effects, at least in the short term. For example, in research on what children learn from playing video games, skill gained in learning to play a video game generalized to very closely related visual and spatial reasoning tasks (Subrahmanyam & Greenfield, 1996; Okagaki & Frensch, 1996) but not to less closely related tasks (Greenfield, Brannon, & Lohr, 1996). Indeed, Greenfield (1996) has argued that different media, which rely on different representational systems, promote the acquisition of distinctive types of cognitive skills. Moreover, as we have learned from prior media research, the medium itself is not the single entity that facilitates change in our perceptions, affect, or cognition. As Salomon wisely noted, "Children's cognitions are not affected by 'Television' or by 'the Computer;' they are affected by specific kinds of *programs* with which they carry out specific kinds of *activities*, under specific kinds of external or internal *conditions* for specific kinds of *goals*" (Salomon, 1990, p. 27).

The primary vehicles through which we acquire situated knowledge are performance and dialogue, which in turn are produced and understood in relationship to specific social activities. Communication plays a key role in the acquisition of situated knowledge. It is through communication that socializing agents such as parents, teachers, siblings, or peers teach children about new activities, and in particular, how they should enact their roles (including those involving communication) in those activities.

At the same time, communication itself depends on shared, situated knowledge. It is a well-established fact within contemporary language and communication theory that understanding involves not only decoding messages but also making additional inferences about meaning based on knowledge of the context (e.g. Bateson, 1972; Bransford & McCarrell, 1974; Schank & Abelson, 1977). Contextual knowledge includes knowledge of roles, purposes, objects, behaviors, and other elements of an event. So there is a reflexive relationship between messages and activities – messages teach us about activities, and knowledge of activities helps us understand messages (Greeno, 1989; Brown, Collins, & Duguid, 1989).

Scaffolding

The foregoing arguments point to two seemingly contradictory conclusions: First, participation in activities requires substantial situated knowledge and skill; and second, the only way to gain situated knowledge and skills is through participation. This apparent contradiction is resolved in practice, where novices seldom encounter situations alone, but rather are supported by more experienced partners and social structures that are tailored to help the learner. Using these supports and their ability to engage in practical reasoning, learners are able to participate in activities and thereby learn their structure and content. This is an "apprenticeship" model of learning, in which knowledge is acquired in the process of performing.

We already know a great deal about the ways in which parents and other partners support children in learning about how to use verbal communication.

It has been observed consistently, across cultures, that parents provide explicit instruction in what to say and how to say it. Parents prompt children to speak, including modeling utterances for children to repeat. They also label current activities by name, ask leading questions, simplify messages to make them easier to understand, repeat utterances or actions with the child as a direct participant or observer, or expand the child's utterance to make it an appropriate contribution (Ochs, 1986).

For example, in her groundbreaking study of the role of family dialogue in children's literacy activities, Shirley Brice Heath (1983) examined children's literacy events both in and out of schools. "Literacy events" are activities that involve reading and writing. Common literacy events for preschoolers are bedtime stories; reading labels, advertisements and signs; and interpreting instructions for games and toys. She studied preschoolers and their families to learn how they used reading – when they read, how they read, and most important, what they took from their reading. She observed that as parents and teachers read to children and discuss books with them, they provide a framework for understanding the material and abstracting it for use in other settings.

Similarly, prompts, hints, pointers, and dialogues can be built into the social environment and used to support unskilled performance. This sort of support is a cornerstone of good human–computer interface design, in which even very unskilled users can often be successful when navigating an interface because their behavior is guided by visual pointers, dialogue boxes, hints, and help systems. Such assistance for the learner is also pervasive in the designed environments in which we live and work, where it enables easier movement into unfamiliar situations (Brown, Collins, & Duguid, 1989).

With visual materials (e.g. film and television), formal features of the presentation provide analogous guidance to the viewer. Formal features are the result of production and editing. They include visual techniques (e.g. zooms, pans, and special effects), auditory features (e.g. sound effects and music), and more global dimensions of program pace, action, and variability of scenes (Huston & Wright, 1994). Formal features attract a child's attention, provide information about program content, and help children process the information presented.

For example, perceptually salient features are important in drawing young children's attention to a television program when they are not looking at the set (Wright et al., 1984). As children grow older, their developing cognitive skills and increased experience with television enable children to use the formal features to select programs that will be meaningful and interesting to them (Anderson & Lorch, 1983; Huston & Wright, 1994). For example, animation, children's voices, and visual special effects signal that the content is intended for a child audience, and such formal features are associated with increased attention to the screen for older children.

Children use formal features of media presentations to guide their sense of relevance and aid in information processing. For instance, formal features can highlight particularly important aspects of a message (Huston & Wright, 1994).

Rice (1984) found that "Sesame Street" and "Mister Roger's Neighborhood" contained single words, repetitions, literal meanings, and pictures of words being referred to in the program. Such formal features have been called the "syntax of television," and are important in understanding how children learn from television (Neuman, 1991). Media literacy depends in part on a child's understanding of the production conventions that make such formal features informative. Calvert (1994) examined the impact of computer presentational features (i.e. action and verbal labels) on children's production and recall of objects presented in a list versus a story format. Kindergarteners relied more upon both types of features for production and recall of objects than did second graders. The research suggests that features including action and labels play an important role in information processing activities for very young children; furthermore, educational software designed for young children should use these features to target important informative content (Calvert, 1994), thereby facilitating learning of that content.

Bruner (1977) called these and other supports for children's performance "scaffolding." Structures such as these make it possible for children to participate in activities well before they are capable of doing so independently, and in that sense provide a scaffold or platform to support or enable performance. Scaffolding is what allows novices to enter a situation sufficiently to learn not only how to reproduce the activity but also the content that is embedded in the activity.

To summarize, the core model for situated learning is apprenticeship (Collins, Brown, & Newman, 1989). The young child, as with any novice, enters a situation unable to perform competently, but performances are organized in a way to include him/her nonetheless – perhaps first through observation, then by performing increasingly more complex and responsible tasks, with less and less support from others. The setting and the tools it contains also provide scaffolding for the learner. Even when a novice participates "peripherally" in an activity (say, when a pre-linguistic child is included as a participant in a mock dialogue, see Stern, 1987), he or she gains knowledge and skill. With increasing knowledge and skill, the learner is able to take on a greater scope of activity, participate more "centrally" in the activity, and function as a more independent learner (Lave & Wenger, 1991). Hence, where learning is viewed as apprenticeship, the primary dimension of growth is dependence–autonomy.

Inquiry

The key process in apprentice-learning is inquiry. Concepts of learning as inquiry are traced back to classic theories in education and child development, particularly the pragmatist philosophy of John Dewey (Hickman, 1990; McDermott, 1981; Pea, 1994), and the cognitive developmental theories of Piaget and Vygotsky. All contemporary learning theories recognize that children are active learners, and an emphasis on the "active child" dates back to Jean Piaget's theory of intellectual development. Piaget's *constructivist* view asserted that children develop an understanding of the world through active engagement, not passive observation (Ginsburg & Opper, 1988). A related view, known as *constructionism*, asserts that knowledge is not simply transmitted from teacher to student, but is actively constructed by the mind of the learner; furthermore, children are more likely to create ideas when they are engaged in a particular project or making of an artifact – a computer program, a robot, a poem (Kafai & Resnick, 1996). Finally, *social constructivist* views of learning emphasize the role of dialogue in structuring and supporting apprenticeship.

This understanding of children's learning underlies a broad array of current efforts at designing computer-based tools to help children learn. This includes work at the MIT Media Lab, from the early work of Seymour Papert and colleagues with the creation of the programming language *Logo* (Papert, 1980) to recent work with the *Programmable Brick* (Sargent, Resnick, Martin, & Silverman, 1996); work being done in the context of large-scale projects in schools (for example, those conducted by TERC, the Center for Innovative Learning Technologies at SRI, and the Center for Learning Technology in Urban Schools at Northwestern University); and a host of interesting projects that use collaborative inquiry environments to promote learning (e.g. Lajoie & Derry, 1993; O'Neill & Gomez, 1994; Scardamalia, Bereiter, McLean, Swallow, & Woodruff, 1989). These and other projects have documented the many benefits to children of learning in an inquiry framework, which include motivation to learn, authentic learning, and active engagement in learning.

Dialogue

Increasingly, researchers have focused on the role of dialogue in guiding the process of inquiry. Dialogue – interchange with a human or mediated interlocutor – creates not only a structure through which scaffolding can be provided but also an opportunity for child learners to articulate and organize their emerging understandings. Dialogue refers to the ways in which attention and mental activity are engaged and structured by the presence and presentations of others. Theories of dialogue (Bahktin, 1990; Goffman, 1981; Wertsch, 1991) provide a framework within which to understand the role of interpersonal communication and social interaction in learning. There are three critical topics for a theory of dialogue: Identity, interaction, and collaboration.

Identity refers to the social self – the person one is taken to be in a social situation. It is the performance of one's character in context. Communicating and negotiating identities is an implicit process in every activity, since the identity one attempts to enact might or might not be supported by others with whom one interacts (Goffman, 1967). When one's identity is not supported, then it must be revised. Therefore, identity is always understood to be socially situated and fluid or changing.

Mead (1934) was early to point out that games provide a critical opportunity for children to acquire the distinctive perspectives associated with social identities and voices. As Denzin (1973) has shown, an important function of children's fantasy play is to provide opportunities to practice enacting an identity. In research on children's use of online interaction – chat rooms, role-playing games, and the like – a key focus has been their use of such opportunities to take on and rehearse identities that are unfamiliar to them but which they wish to explore. Sherry Turkle's (1984) work on the way adolescents and young adults "try on" identities in multi-player game environments (MUDs and MOOs) and Bruckman's (1997) related work on social interaction in collaborative learning environments have documented the critical role of identity-related play in online communication systems.

Interestingly, it appears that many of the most critical communication processes related to identity management are evoked equally well by computers and humans. Reeves and Nass (1996) have shown in a series of experiments that people respond to computers as though they are human, including showing politeness, deference to feelings, and other identity related message behaviors.

The second key topic for a theory of dialogue is interaction. Media, including interactive media, and genres of content within them are characterized by different types and degrees of interactivity. Media differ along a number of dimensions, but one key differentiator is the type of participation structure it provides for interaction. Participation structures (Levinson, 1993) govern what can occur on the message space or "floor" in a communicative event. This shared message space is the place in which the contributions of the various parties can be encountered and responded to. A medium is not interactive if there is no floor, and interactive media differ quite substantially from each other in terms of what can be placed on the floor and how contributions on the floor can be taken up. So, for example, broadcast television is in general not an interactive medium: While messages are offered in a public space, there is no opportunity for viewers to contribute to that space. Computer-based communication, whether it involves interaction with a program or with other humans via a network, almost always involves a shared message space to which multiple communicating agents contribute. This quality of interactivity, distributed and shared participation, is very important for learning, since active engagement in interaction is a determinant of learning outcomes (for example, people learn more from participating in a conversation than overhearing the same conversation, Clark, 1992).

While in some media the floor is relatively simple, in most interactive media this shared message space is quite complex. Many different kinds of displays can be put on the floor in computer-mediated communication: text, sound/voice, still pictures/video, animations and visualizations, or representations of the interaction setting (both realistic and imaginative). Telepresence refers to the degree to which these different types of displays contribute to a sense of sharing a setting or world with another. In general, the more fully the floor or shared message space supports displays for the human senses – by introducing sound, motion, three-dimensional visualization, touch, smell – the greater the sense of telepresence, of shared reality, embodied in the floor and the more complex the interactivity.

Additionally, media differ in the way they link together the contributions of different participants. A critical issue is whether a particular medium uses temporal placement to link contributions ("synchronous" communication) versus some other mechanism ("asynchronous" communication). In synchronous media, adjacent temporal spaces ("turns") are used to link contributions. By contrast, asynchronous media use other mechanisms to link displays and responses. One common mechanism is spatial proximity: responses are placed in a space near to the display. A good example of this is asynchronous text conferencing, which is now generally organized as a set of themes called "threads." The original message is shown, and messages that respond to it are tagged as responses and displayed near to the original message in a message list.

Finally, media differ in the degree to which they can sustain participation. Can the response provided by a participant be responded to, in turn, by other agents? Many interactive software programs and websites provide the opportunity to respond to a display, but do not in turn respond to the response. The ability to sustain a dialogue, and moreover to sustain a chain of relevant contributions to a common activity, varies dramatically across media. Sustained participation is a quality of human–human dialogue (whether computer-mediated or not) that is quite difficult to emulate in human–computer interactions, and currently can only be achieved in cases where the contributions of the human are restricted to a predictable range of responses.

A medium is interactive when it creates the possibility of such dialogue – of display and response. But the quality of interactivity is a function of the richness of the display possibilities, the nature of the response options (in particular, the degree to which synchronous responding is possible), and the ability to sustain a chain of interaction. This is important because a key hypothesis for children's development is that interactivity itself may be a critical determinant of cognitive outcomes. For instance, it might be noted that some of the best children's programming on television (such as *Sesame Street* or *Blue's Clues*) has found ways to use dialogue to elicit active processing and problem solving by child viewers. In this way, television, a passive medium, can elicit active responses.

The final key topic for a theory of dialogue is collaboration. Dialogue takes place in the context of shared effort – people cooperate to achieve some goal, whether it is as simple as having a pleasant conversation or as complex as designing a new airplane. Collaboration provides not only scaffolding, in Bruner's sense, but also a context that evokes more mature performance. So for example, children's communication with peers about how to solve a science problem can improve science learning (Roschelle, 1991). Cassell and Ryokai (2001) illustrate the potential of collaboration in an interesting project called *StoryMat*, a type of interactive toy. They observed that storytelling, particularly in collaboration with peers, is a critical arena for children's cognitive development. Based on this observation, they designed *StoryMat*, a system that supports and records children's story-telling play. *StoryMat* is a quilt-like play mat that is appliquéd with familiar objects. It was designed to provide a play space that would stimulate children to tell stories, and it incorporates recording technology to capture and play back the stories. When a child tells a story, it is compared to similar stories recorded by the mat, and those similar stories are played back. Past stories then become a stimulus for further telling by the child. Cassell and Ryokai (2001) found that use of *StoryMat* promoted developmentally advanced forms of performance in children, of the kind that provides a bridge to written literacy.

In another study examining collaborative learning effects, Strommen (1993) observed 28 pairs of fourth grade children using an educational software program under two conditions: (1) A cooperative condition in which two children played against the computer, and (2) a competitive condition in which two children played against one another. Results indicated that the cooperative condition elicited more correct answers from the children than did the competitive condition. The findings suggest that with little or no encouragement, children spontaneously develop cooperative strategies, which can increase their learning (Strommen, 1993).

The findings of Mayer, Schustack, and Blanton (1999) provide encouraging evidence that informal, collaborative experiences with quality educational software can facilitate the development of content-specific cognitive skills. The authors studied children's computing experiences in informal settings (e.g. boys and girls clubs and after-school programs) over a one-year period. The children often worked with peers or adult mentors on computer activities. The children demonstrated improvement in (1) content knowledge about computing (computer literacy), (2) comprehension of written instructions, (3) strategies for problem solving, and (4) basic academic skills. Mayer, Quilici, and Moreno (1999) and Mayer, Schustack, and Blanton (1999) suggest that part of what is learned by playing an educational interactive game is the ability to more easily learn features and strategies of playing novel educational games and activities. This suggests that skills developed in a particular activity may transfer to new situations. Educational researchers are particularly interested in the use of cooperative learning strategies and methods in the classroom environment. Studies such as the above illustrate the potential of interactive technologies to facilitate cooperative behaviors and facilitate learning.

Framing

The frame for a message includes knowledge of its point, topic, and relevant background information; it provides the context for interpreting communication. As Goffman (1974) and others have pointed out, the impact of experience is a function of how that experience is interpreted, or framed. A classic demonstration of this phenomenon was provided by Bransford and McCarrell (1974), who showed that what people learned from narratives depended on the frame they were given. The general rule for communication theory, then, is that the effects of communication content are mediated by the frames people use in processing that content.

Oddly, while there has been great concern about the content of children's interactive media (particularly violent "first person shooter" video games), there has been relatively little attention to the ways that children frame the material they encounter (Gailey, 1996). Kinder (1996) provides an interesting counterpoint to this reaction; she looked at the way episodes of violent action in computer games can be understood in relationship to broader cultural conventions and practices relating to the use of violence in entertainment media, and specifically to gender depictions. Kafai (1996) allowed 16 boys and girls to build their own games, and found that the narratives and types of action used in the games were framed differently as a function of gender, with boys building games that more fully reflected that conventions of commercial video games; she attributed this to the boys' greater experience with video games. As Greenfield (1996) has argued, many of the gender differences observed in this area may be accountable in terms of the ways that culture frames both the activity of game playing for boys and girls and the specific kinds of content (such as violence) children encounter in interactive games.

Effects on Children's Cognitive Development

The final issue, then, is the question of whether media experiences and media socialization play a significant role in determining the cognitive developmental outcomes of greatest significance to parents and others who care about children. In this final section, we draw some overall conclusions about critical cognitive outcomes.

Communications media rely on different kinds of symbol systems and so provide children with different kinds of situated learning opportunities. Media can be described by their technology, symbol systems, and processing capabilities (Kozma, 1991; Salomon, 1979). Knowledge of the unique characteristics and symbol systems of media determine how each medium can best be used by children and how the information presented is differentially processed. For example, books are characterized by the symbol systems of text and static pictures. The stability of text allows the reader to slow down, pause, or re-read in order to comprehend difficult passages; reflect on the meanings of unfamiliar words, expressions, or ideas; or read selectively in search of particular categories of information. By contrast, television delivers content via the symbol systems of verbal language and visual images, particularly images in motion. Computers are distinguished by what they can do with information: their capability to process symbols. For example, print, equations, and numbers can be transformed into visually depicted graphs. Combinations of information technology often called "multimedia" present the prospect that the various advantages of the individual medium (i.e. print or television) can be brought together in a single instructional environment and used strategically to facilitate learning (Kozma, 1991).

Increasingly, research on children's learning shows that (as would be expected within media socialization theory), the skills children acquire from using media reflect the specific kind of symbolic experience a particular medium offers. For example, in the research cited earlier by Greenfield and others (Greenfield, 1996), experience with interactive video games has effects on children's growth, but the effects tend to be specific to the kind of spatial–visual representational medium that is used for such games. In general, experience with these games does not have effects on other cognitive skills.

There is an assumption that children's access to and use of computers at home does influence their experiences with computers in the school setting, and vice versa. The influence of home computer use on academic achievement or performance in various contexts, however, is not clear. This relationship appears to be influenced by several complex factors. In an early study of ethnic differences in home computer use and its effects on in-school achievement, Attewell and Battle (1999) found that forms of social inequality beyond access (gender, SES, and ethnicity) may modify the frequency of home computer use, the ways in which computers are used, and subsequently influence the educational benefits derived from home computing. The authors examined the relationship between home computing and school performance using the data from the National Educational Longitudinal Study (NELS) of 1988. They found that having a home computer was associated with higher test scores in math and reading for eighth graders, even after controlling for family income and social capital. It was also found, however, that children from higher SES homes achieved larger educational gains than did children from lower SES homes. One possible explanation for these findings is level of parental involvement in the children's computing activities (Giacquinta, Bauer, & Levin, 1993; Giaquinta & Lane, 1990; Rocheleau, 1995). In general, children who engage in beneficial computing activities have parents who interact with them or communicate about those computing activities. Given the fact that the primary reason cited by parents for purchasing a home computer and connecting to the Internet is education (NSBF, 2000), it is surprising that we have very little research to document whether and what types of at-home interactive media use contributes to school achievement.

Summary

What can we say about the influence of new technologies on cognitive development? Do children benefit from using interactive media? It seems that educators also struggle to answer this urgent question, as significant financial resources are committed to integrating technologies in classrooms. Asking general questions about this phenomenon we call "cognitive development" may not be a useful way of addressing the issue. "Effectiveness statements are of little use unless they elaborate the children's ages, the subject, the software used, the kinds of outcomes that were sought, and how the study was done" (Kirkpatrick & Cuban, 1998). Researchers need to consider matching software claims with assessment of those particular cognitive outcomes. Interactive media have the potential to benefit children in many important and life-altering ways. To determine the "effectiveness" of using various technologies, researchers will need to (1) adopt a developmental perspective, (2) consider diverse populations, (3) use varied methodologies to address similar questions, and (4) target specific outcomes of interest.

Research on the influence of interactive media on children's cognitive development should first provide conceptual descriptions and analyses of these media and their content. All too often, people see one example of a violent video game or disturbing chat room conversation and assume that is what all games or chats are like. But are they? What is needed is a "road map" to these interactive media: a classification of the different types of interactive experiences children might have and the kinds of content they might encounter. For example, we might establish a consortium of media laboratories to examine, review, and evaluate each new computer game. Parents, teachers, and others could use this information to find great on-line experiences for youth and protect them from doubtful ones.

Furthermore this road map should consider elements of these media, which may influence both their usability for children of different ages and their learning with them. Critical elements of interactive media such as interactivity and its influence on cognitive engagement and learning outcomes should be studied further. Similarly, how various modalities of messaging such as the presentation of visualizations, data or agents using images and or sound, and their impact on learning outcomes should be studied.

One common assumption is the idea that "interactivity" itself, regardless of content, may have an effect on the way children create and process information. Does active involvement with a computer activity influence processing of the information, such as increased comprehension and retention, or does it influence perceptions of the task, such as increased motivation for sustained engagement? Can we assume that "interactivity" facilitates learning? What are the cognitive consequences of interactive materials, which encourage children to build, design, and create narratives, objects, virtual worlds, and other things?

Before addressing questions regarding effects on cognitive, social, or health-related outcomes, the concept of interactivity itself needs to be further conceptualized and empirically demonstrated. It should be pointed out that different types of interactive experiences may be elicited by different types of interactive media. For instance, interactive pets probably engage children differently than interactive computer games. Research examining Salomon's four characteristics of successful educational software (i.e. interactivity, guidance and informative feedback, multiple symbol systems, and supplanting users' memories allowing them to engage in higher order thinking) would be a useful first step in thinking about interactive media (Salomon, 1990; Salomon & Almog, 1998). Much richer conceptual development of this concept of "interactivity" or a cognitive psychological experience is clearly needed. In spite of broad claims about the likely positive impact of interactive media on children's cognitive development and educational achievement, the research evidence is less compelling than the theoretical arguments. Much more systematic, developmental research evidence is needed to bolster the popular claims that interactive media will change the way children think.

The public discourse around the promise of interactive technologies to improve children's learning is often juxtaposed to the public discourse around the perils of interactive media content for children's social development. Healthy social relationships, violence, safety, and privacy are all issues raised in the next section as we consider the roles of interactive technologies in children's social lives.

For children and adolescents, the promise of interactive technologies and networked environments is their potential to influence learning and social growth in positive ways. We can achieve this by developing exciting educational and entertaining materials that young people can use out of school, and that can traverse the home to school environment. The first step, however, to understand how these interactive media affect children – their cognitions, emotions, social relationships, and even their health. Our review of the literature has found numerous effects of interactive media on these domains of development. Clearly, however, there is a need for coordinated and systematic research to tackle what we do not yet know. This research will provide useful findings for academics engaged in research on interactive technologies, for parents and others concerned with children's care-taking, for educators who want to teach about and teach with interactive media, for the production community interested in developing quality interactive entertainment and educational materials for children, and for policymakers interested in ensuring that media exert a positive influence. Thoughtful, programmatic research can help all these constituencies advance the promise and limit the potential perils of interactive media in the lives of our children.

References

Anderson, D. R. and Lorch, E. P. (1983). Looking at television: Action or Reaction? In J. Bryant and D. R. Anderson (eds.), *Children's Understanding of Television: Research on attention and comprehension*. New York: Academic Press, pp. 1–33.

Attewell, P. and Battle, J. (1999). Home computers and school performance. *The Information Society*, 15, 1–10.

Bahktin, M. (1990). *Speech Genres and Other Late Essays*. Austin, TX: University of Texas Press.

Bateson, G. (1972). *Steps to an Ecology of Mind*. New York: Ballantine.

Bransford, J. D. and McCarrell, N. S. (1974). A sketch of cognitive approach to comprehension. In W. B. Weimer and D. S. Palermo (eds.), *Cognition and the Symbolic Processes*. Hillsdale, NJ: Lawrence Erlbaum, pp. 299–303.

Brown, J. S., Collins, A., and Duguid, P. (1989). Situated cognition and the culture of learning. *Educational Researcher*, 18, 32–42.

Bruckman, A. (1997). MOOSE Crossing: Construction, community, and learning in a networked virtual world for kids. MIT: Unpublished doctoral dissertation.

Bruner, J. (1977). *The Process of Education*. Cambridge, MA: Harvard University Press.

Calvert, S. L. (1994). Developmental differences in children's production and recall of information as a function of computer presentational features. *Journal of Educational Computing Research*, 10, 139–51.

Cassell, J. and Ryokai, K. (2001). Making space for voice technologies to support children's fantasy and storytelling. *Personal Technologies* 5,(3), 203–24.

Childs, C. P. and Greenfield, P. M. (1980). Informal modes of learning and teaching: The case of Zinacanteco weaving. In N. Warren (ed.), *Advances in Cross-Cultural Psychology*, vol. 2. New York: Academic Press.

Clark, H. (1992). *Arenas of Language Use*. Chicago: University of Chicago Press.

Cole, M. (1985). The zone of proximal development: Where culture and cognition create each other. In J. Wertsch (ed.), *Culture, Communication, and Cognition: Vygotskian perspectives*. Cambridge: Cambridge University Press.

Collins, A., Brown, J. S., and Newman, S. (1989). Cognitive apprenticeship: Teaching the craft of reading, writing, and mathematics. In L. B. Resnick (ed.), *Knowing, Learning, and Instruction: Essays in honor of Robert Glaser*. Hillsdale, NJ: Lawrence Erlbaum.

Comstock, G. and Paik, H. (1991). *Television and the American Child*. San Diego, CA: Academic Press.

Denzin, N. (1973). The work of little children. In N. Denzin (ed.), *Children and Their Caretakers*. Transaction Publishers.

Engstrom, Y. (1992). *Learning, Working, and Imagining: Twelve studies in activity theory*. Helsinki: Orienta-Konsultit Oy.

Gailey, C. W. (1996). Mediated messages: Gender, class, and cosmos in home video games. In P. M. Greenfield and R. R. Cocking (eds.), *Interacting with Video: Vol. 11. Advances in applied developmental psychology*. Norwood, NJ: Ablex, pp. 9–23.

Giacquinta, J. B., Bauer, J., and Levin, J. (1993). *Beyond Technology's Promise*. New York: Cambridge University Press.

Giacquinta, J. B. and Lane, P. A. (1990). Fifty-one families with computers: A study of children's academic uses of microcomputers at home. *Educational Technology Research and Development*, 38, 27–37.

Ginsburg, H. P. and Opper, S. (1988). *Piaget's Theory of Intellectual Development*. Englewood Cliffs, NJ: Prentice-Hall.

Goffman, E. (1967). *Interaction Ritual: Essays on face-to-face behavior*. Garden City, NY: Anchor Books.

Goffman, E. (1974). *Frame Analysis: An essay on the organization of experience*. New York: Harper & Row.

Goffman, E. (1981). *Forms of Talk*. Philadelphia: The University of Pennsylvania Press.

Greenfield, P. M. (1994, 1996). Video games as cultural artifacts. *Journal of Applied Developmental Psychology*, 15, 3–12. Reprinted in In P. M. Greenfield and R. R. Cocking (eds.), *Interacting with Video: Vol. 11. Advances in applied developmental psychology*. Norwood, NJ: Ablex, pp. 85–94.

Greenfield, P. M., Brannon, C., and Lohr, D. (1996). Two-dimensional representation of movement through three-dimensional space: The role of video game expertise. In P. M. Greefield and R. R. Cocking (eds.), *Interacting with Video: Vol. 11: Advances in applied developmental psychology*. Norwood, NJ: Ablex, pp. 169–86.

Greeno, J. G. (1989). Situations, mental models, and generative knowledge. In D. Klahr and K. Kotovsky (eds.), *Complex Information Processing*. Hillsdale, NJ: Lawrence Erlbaum.

Heath, S. B. (1983). *Ways with Words: Language, life and work in communities and classrooms*. Cambridge: Cambridge University Press.

Hickman, L. A. (1990). *John Dewey's Pragmatic Technology*. Indianapolis: Indiana University Press.

Huston, A. C. and Wright, J. C. (1994). Educating children with television: The forms of the medium. In D. Zillmann, J. Bryant, and A. C. Huston (eds.), *Media, Children, and the Family: Social scientific, psychodynamic, and clinical perspectives*. Hillsdale, NJ: Lawrence Erlbaum.

Hutchins, E. (1995). *Cognition in the Wild*. Cambridge, MA: MIT Press.

Kafai, Y. B. (1996). Gender differences in children's constructions of video games. In P. M. Greenfield and R. R. Cocking (eds.), *Interacting with Video: Vol. 11. Advances in applied developmental psychology*. Norwood, NJ: Ablex, pp. 39–66.

Kafai, Y. B. and Resnick, M. (eds.) (1996). *Constructionism in Practice: Designing, thinking, and learning in a digital world*. Mahwah, NJ: Lawrence Erlbaum.

Kinder, M. (1996). Contextualizing video game violence: From *Teenage Mutant Ninja Turtles 1* to *Mortal Kombat 2*. In P. M. Greenfield and R. R. Cocking (eds.), *Interacting with Video: Vol. 11. Advances in applied developmental psychology*. Norwood, NJ: Ablex, pp. 25–37.

Kirkpatrick, H. and Cuban, L. (1998). Computers make kids smarter – Right? *TECHNOS Quarterly*, 7(2). http://www.technos.net.

Kozma, R. B. (1991). Learning with media. *Review of Educational Research*, 61, 179–211.

Lajoie, S. P. and Derry, S. J. (eds.) (1993). *Computers as Cognitive Tools*. Hillsdale, NJ: Lawrence Erlbaum.

Lave, J. (1977). Cognitive consequences of traditional apprenticeship training in West Africa. *Anthropology and Education Quarterly*, 8, 177–80.

Lave, J. (1988). *Cognition in Practice*. Cambridge: Cambridge University Press.

Lave, J. and Wenger, E. (1991). *Situated Learning: Legitimate peripheral participation*. New York: Cambridge University Press.

Levinson, S. (1993). Activity types and language. In P. Drew and J. Heritage (eds.), *Talk at Work*. Cambridge: Cambridge University Press.

Mayer, R. E., Quilici, J. L., and Moreno, R. (1999). What is learned in an after-school computer club? *Journal of Educational Computing Research*, 20, 223–35.

Mayer, R. E., Schustack, M. W., and Blanton, W. E. (1999). What do children learn from using computers in an informal, collaborative setting? *Educational Technology*, 39, 27–31.

McDermott, J. J. (1981). *The Philosophy of John Dewey*. Chicago: University of Chicago Press.

Mead, G. H. (1934). *Mind, Self, and Society from the Perspective of a Social Behaviorist*. Chicago: University of Chicago Press.

National School Boards Foundation (NSBF) (2000). *Safe and Smart: Research and guidelines for children's use of the Internet*. Alexandria, VA: National School Boards Foundation. http://www.nsbf.org/safe-smart/br-overview.htm.

Neuman, S. B. (1991). *Literacy in the Television Age: The myth of the TV effect* (2nd edn.). Norwood, NJ: Ablex.

Ochs, E. (1986). Introduction. In B. B. Schieffelin and E. Ochs (eds.), *Language Socialization Across Cultures*. Cambridge: Cambridge University Press, pp. 1–13.

Okagaki, L. and Frensch, P. (1996). Effects of video game playing on measures of spatial performance: Gender effects in late adolescence. In P. M. Greenfield and R. R. Cocking (eds.), *Interacting with Video: Vol. 11. Advances in applied developmental psychology*. Norwood, NJ: Ablex, pp. 115–40.

O'Neill, D. K. and Gomez, L. (1994). The collaboratory notebook: A distributed knowledge-building environment for project-enhanced learning. In T. Ottmann and I. Tomek (eds.), *Educational Multimedia and Hypermedia, 1994: Proceedings of Ed-Media '94*. Charlottesville, VA: AACE, pp. 416–23.

Papert, S. (1980). *Mindstorms: Children, computers, and powerful ideas*. New York: Basic Books.

Pea, R. (1994). Seeing what we build together: Distributed multimedia learning environments for transformative communications. *The Journal of the Learning Sciences*, 3, 285–99.

Piaget, J. (1964). Development and learning. In R. E. Ripple and V. N. Rockcastle (eds.), *Piaget Rediscovered*. Ithaca, NY: Cornell University Press.

Reed, H. and Lave, J. (1979). Arithmetic as a tool for investigating relations between culture and cognition. *American Ethnologist*, 6, 568–82.

Reeves, B. and Nass, C. (1996). *The Media Equation: How people treat computers, television, and new media like real people and places.* New York: Cambridge University Press.

Rice, M. L. (1984). Television language and child language. In J. P. Murray and G. Salomon (eds.), *The Future of Children's Television.* Boys' Town, NE: Father Flanagan's Boys Home, pp. 53–8.

Roberts, D. F., Foehr, U. G., Rideout, V. J., and Brodie, M. (1999). *Kids and Media @ the New Millennium.* Menlo Park, CA: Kaiser Family Foundation. http://www.kff.org.

Rocheleau, B. (1995). Computer use by school-age children: Trends, patterns, and predictors. *Journal of Educational Computing Research,* 12, 1–17.

Roschelle, J. (1991). Students' construction of qualitative physics knowledge: Learning about velocity and acceleration in a computer microworld. Unpublished doctoral dissertation. Berkeley, CA: University of California.

Salomon, G. (1979). *Interaction of Media, Cognition, and Learning.* San Francisco: Jossey-Bass.

Salomon, G. (1990). Cognitive effects with and of computer technology. *Communication Research,* 17, 26–44.

Salomon, G. and Almog, T. (1998). Educational psychology and technology: A matter of reciprocal relations. *Teachers College Record,* 100, 222–41.

Sargent, R., Resnick, M., Martin, F., and Silverman, B. (1996). Building and learning with programmable bricks. In Y. B. Kafai, and M. Resnick (eds.), *Constructionism in Practice: Designing, thinking, and learning in a digital world.* Mahwah, NJ: Lawrence Erlbaum.

Scardamalia, M., Bereiter, C., McLean, R. S., Swallow, J., and Woodruff, E. (1989). Computer-supported intentional learning environments. *Journal of Educational Computing Research,* 5, 51–68.

Schank, R. and Abelson, R. (1977). *Scripts, Plans, Goals, and Understanding.* Hillsdale, NJ: Lawrence Erlbaum.

Schieffelin, B. B. and Ochs, E. (eds.) (1986). *Language Socialization Across Cultures.* Cambridge, MA: Cambridge University Press.

Scribner, S. and Cole, M. (1981). *The Psychology of Literacy.* Cambridge, MA: Harvard University Press.

Stanger, J. D., and Gridina, N. (1999). *Media in the Home: The fourth annual survey of parents and children.* Washington, DC: Annenberg Public Policy Center.

Stern, D. (1987). *The Interpersonal World of the Infant.* New York: Basic Books.

Strommen, E. F. (1993). "Does yours eat leaves?" Cooperative learning in an educational software task. *Journal of Computing of Childhood Education,* 4, 45–56.

Subrahmanyam, K. and Greenfield, P. M. (1996). Effect of video game practice on spatial skills in girls and boys. In P. M. Greenfield and R. R. Cocking (eds.), *Interacting with Video: Vol. 11. Advances in applied developmental psychology.* Norwood, NJ: Ablex, pp. 94–114.

Turkle, S. (1984). *The Second Self: Computers and the human spirit.* New York: Simon & Schuster.

Vygotsky, L. (1962). *Thought and Language.* Cambridge, MA: MIT Press.

Wertsch, J. V. (1991). *Voices of the Mind: A sociocultural approach to mediated action.* Cambridge, MA: Harvard University Press.

Woodard, E. H. (2000). *Media in the Home: The fifth annual survey of parents and children.* Washington, DC: Annenberg Public Policy Center.

Wright, J. C., Huston, A. C., Ross, R. P., Calvert, S. L., Rolandelli, D., Weeks, L. A., Raeissi, P., and Potts, R. (1984). Pace and continuity of television programs: Effects on children's attention and comprehension. *Developmental Psychology,* 20, 653–66.

Wright, J. C., Huston, A. C., Vandewater, E. A., Bickham, D. S., Scantlin, R. M., Kotler, J. A., Caplovitz, A. G., Lee, J. H., Hofferth, S., and Finkelstein, J. (2001). American children's use of electronic media in 1997: A national survey. *Journal of Applied Developmental Psychology,* 22,(1), 31–47.

Further reading

Behrman, R. E. (ed.) (2000). *The Future of Children*. Special Issue: Children and Computer Technology, 10(2). http://www.futureofchildren.org/pubs-info2825/pubs-info.htm?doc_id=69787).

Livingstone, S. and Bovill, M. (eds.) (2001). *Children and their Changing Media Environment: A European comparative study*. Mahwah, NJ: Lawrence Erlbaum.

Singer, D. G. and Singer, J. L. (2001). *Handbook of Children and the Media*. Thousand Oaks, CA: Sage.

Wartella, E., O'Keefe, B., and Scantlin, R. (2000). *Children and Interactive Media: A compendium of current research and directions for the future*. New York: Markle Foundation. http://www.markle.org/programs/_programs_children_utexas.stm.

CHAPTER TWENTY-THREE

The Impact of Stereotypical and Counter-Stereotypical News on Viewer Perceptions of Blacks and Latinos
An Exploratory Study

Michael C. Casas and Travis L. Dixon

Over the past several decades, academic researchers in the area of news media portrayals have uncovered an alarming trend. People of color are more likely to be associated with criminal activities in the news media compared to Whites (Dixon & Linz, 2000a; Entman, 1992; Gilliam, Iyengar, Simon, & Wright, 1996). In particular, Blacks and Latinos are more likely to be linked with issues of crime, drugs, and unemployment. Exposure to these types of portrayals may lead viewers to develop negative perceptions of Blacks and Latinos as dangerous and irresponsible members of society (Gilliam et al., 1996; Johnson, Adams, Hall, & Ashburn, 1997; Peffley, Shields, & Williams, 1996; Power, Murphy, & Coover, 1996). The purpose of this study is to examine the impact of stereotypical and counter-stereotypical representations of Blacks and Latinos in the news media. Our goal is to uncover how ethnic criminal stereotypes (e.g. Black bank robber) compare to positive counter-stereotypical portrayals (e.g. successful Black businessman) in shaping Whites' perceptions of people of color. This study is an experiment in which White participants were exposed to stereotypical or counter-stereotypical portrayals and then asked about their social reality perceptions regarding crime and the extent to which they believed people of color were irresponsible. The experiment is informed by a number of prior content studies that suggest that people of color are associated with criminality in the news. These studies are reviewed below. Subsequently, we examine some of the research which suggests that these images might affect viewer perceptions of Blacks and Latinos. Lastly, we discuss three theoretical perspectives that might explain the outcome of exposure to either stereotypical or counter-stereotypical portrayals of people of color in the news.

The News and Ethnic Portrayals

Over the years, content analyses examining race and ethnicity in the news have revealed that people of color are consistently associated with criminal activity in the news media (Entman, 1990, 1992, 1994). Whether in newspapers or television news programs, stories about drugs and shootings often times involve poor Blacks or Latinos (Dixon & Linz, 2000a; Turk, Richstad, Bryson, & Johnson, 1989). For example, Martindale (1987) conducted a longitudinal study of several newspapers and found that Blacks were often central figures in crime stories. In a different content analysis of six southwestern newspapers, Greenberg, Heeter, Burgoon, Burgoon, and Korzenny (1983) found that a significant percentage of the content in those newspapers dealt with Latino involvement with crime.

Similar patterns of representation were also found in television news programming. For example, Entman (1992) conducted a content analysis of several local TV news programs in Chicago. He found that Blacks were more likely than Whites to be portrayed as physically threatening perpetrators in television news stories dealing with crime. In a separate content analysis of Los Angeles television news, Dixon and Linz (2000a) found that Blacks and Latinos were more likely than Whites to appear as perpetrators. In contrast to stories about people of color, Whites are seldom portrayed as the perpetrators of crime in news stories. In fact, Whites are much more likely to appear as victims or police officers in crime news than as perpetrators (Dixon & Linz, 2000a, 2000b; Oliver, 1994).

The above studies suggest a clear pattern with regards to representations of crime and race. People of color are often times relegated to stereotypical criminal roles such as that of perpetrators in the news. Two things, however, that have not been explicitly addressed by these studies are: (1) the effect of these stereotypical portrayals on viewers' perceptions of ethnic groups and crime, and (2) the presence and impact of counter-stereotypical portrayals on viewers. Below we review some of the empirical studies which have attempted to assess the impact of stereotypical crime portrayals. Afterwards, we offer three theoretical perspectives which may inform us about the impact of both stereotypical and counter-stereotypical portrayals on viewers.

Psychological Impact of Stereotypical Portrayals

Only recently have investigators begun to assess how portrayals of Blacks and Latinos as criminals on television news impact perceptions of people of color and crime policy. Many studies suggest that for some people, exposure to one news story featuring a Black perpetrator is enough to prime stereotypes of Blacks as criminals. For example, Gilliam et al. (1996) exposed White participants to a crime story in which either a Black male or White male was the perpetrator. Their study indicated that participants who endorsed negative stereotypes about Blacks were more likely to blame Blacks for crime and to favor punitive policies when exposed to a Black male perpetrator, than those who did not endorse negative stereotypes. Peffley, Shields, and Williams (1996) also found that after exposure to a news story featuring either a Black or White suspect, those exposed to a Black suspect and who held negative stereotypes of African Americans, judged a Black target more harshly than a White target. Some researchers have now concluded that Blacks and crime are so well linked in the minds of news audiences, that simply exposing viewers to examples of race-unspecified violence in the news can prime stereotypes of African American criminality (Johnson et al., 1997).

Although these studies give us an indication of the impact of stereotypical portrayals on White viewers, they do not explicitly address the two issues previously mentioned. First, none of the prior work specifically studies portrayals of Latinos. As reviewed earlier, there is some similarity between the depiction of Latino and Black stereotypes on television news. Second, none of the prior effects studies explicitly investigates counter-stereotypical portrayals and their effects on ethnic group perceptions. Is it possible that counter-stereotypical imagery could offset the impact of the stereotypical news depictions of Latinos and Blacks? Below, we introduce three theoretical perspectives that make predictions about the impact of stereotypical and counter-stereotypical images.

Theoretical foundation

This study draws from several scholars in the area of racial stereotypes in order to establish a theoretical framework for our experiment. These scholars have advanced three theoretical perspectives which we believe may explain how stereotypical and counter-stereotypical images influence ethnic perceptions. The first perspective we examine is priming, followed by generalized appraisals, and lastly, enlightened racism.

Priming stereotypes

According to Gray (1989), the continuous association of poor Blacks with crime in news programs ultimately leads people to assign personal blame for social problems on ethnic groups. He claims stereotypical representations lead Whites to overlook racial discrimination as a possible explanation for crime committed by people of color, and focus more on personal irresponsibility as the reason. As a result, Blacks and Latino suspects are generally seen as more dangerous and ultimately responsible for crime. Gray's ideas are echoed by social psychologists and communication scholars who study stereotypes and priming.

According to priming research, the activation of a stereotype increases the likelihood that this knowledge will be used in subsequent judgments. For example, a crime story featuring images of a Black suspect in handcuffs may lead to the priming of Black criminal stereotypes. This in turn then results in attributing blame to African Americans even in crime stories where the race of a sought suspect is unspecified (Gilliam et al., 1996; Oliver, 1999; Peffley et al., 1996; Power et al., 1996). According to social cognition theorists who have advanced this paradigm, stereotypes are cognitive structures or categories that affect the encoding and processing of information, particularly information pertaining to groups to which the perceiver does not belong (i.e. out-groups) (Hamilton & Trolier, 1986; von Hippel, Sekaquaptewa, & Vargas, 1995). These structures or schemas direct attention to some stimuli and away from others, influence categorization of information, help us "fill-in" missing information, and influence memory (Fiske & Taylor, 1991; Oliver, 1999). As a result, exposure to Black or Latino criminals in the news may lead the news viewer to evaluate them as dangerous because these images are consistent with the stereotypes of African Americans and Latinos.

Generalized appraisals

If stereotypical portrayals do in fact lead to what Gray claims, could counter-stereotypical portrayals be the solution to counter these negative effects? According to Bodenhausen, Schwartz, Blass, and Wanke (1995), counter-stereotypical representations may increase people's awareness of the racial discrimination that Blacks and Latinos still face today. They believe that successful and "well-liked" representations of middle and upper class people of color can remind Whites that these people are not well represented in these social levels and that racial discrimination needs to be eliminated in order for more of them to join those ranks. This theory, known as "generalized appraisals," would thus predict that counter-stereotypical portrayals can reduce the negative effect of criminal ethnic stereotypes by increasing awareness of discrimination against people of color.

Enlightened racism

Jhally and Lewis (1992) would not concur that counter-stereotypical representations of people of color could counteract the negative effects of stereotypical portrayals. According to their theory of "enlightened racism," counter-stereotypical portrayals may actually enhance the negative effect of stereotypical criminal representations. By providing examples of successful Blacks, for example, counter-stereotypical representations may actually evoke utopian notions of achieved racial equality in Whites' minds. Counter-stereotypical examples would be taken as proof that anyone can succeed in life if they only work hard enough. Racial inequalities and social discriminatory barriers thus become void as valid excuses for people of color who may not have been able to succeed and had to turn to a life of crime. According to the enlightened racism perspective, counter-stereotypical representations would not be the solution to combating the effect of stereotypical portrayals of ethnic groups.

Research Questions

In the current study, we test whether priming, generalized appraisals, or enlightened racism best explain the effect of exposure to stereotypical or counter-stereotypical portrayals in the news media. We expose White participants to three news story conditions: (1) stereotypical, (2) counter-stereotypical, or (3) a combination of stereotypical and counter-stereotypical. Afterwards, we assess whether their fear of crime and feelings towards acceptance of responsibility are affected. Two research questions are addressed by this study.

Research Question 1: Do stereotypical news portrayals increase the perception of danger and irresponsibility by Blacks and Latinos?

According to priming, stereotypical portrayals would lead to higher perceptions of danger and irresponsibility. Black and Latino linkage with crime in the media would lead to the development of stereotypical categories. These categories would then be used to make social judgments of irresponsibility and danger after exposure to the stereotypically congruent stimuli.

Research question 2: Do counter-stereotypical news portrayals decrease the perception of danger and irresponsibility by Blacks and Latinos?

If the generalized appraisal perspective is operating, counter-stereotypical representations would increase awareness regarding racial discrimination. As a result of this awareness, Whites should not necessarily perceive Blacks and Latinos as criminally dangerous and irresponsible. If on the other hand, enlightened racism is operating, counter-stereotypical portrayals should enhance negative perceptions of Latinos and Blacks. Whites will see counter-stereotypical portrayals as proof to the lack of racial barriers, reinforcing the notion that people of color are just predisposed to criminal activity and irresponsibility.

Methodology

Participants and design

In order to test for stereotypical and counter-stereotypical news effects, we conducted an experiment in which we exposed participants to different variations of news coverage about Blacks and Latinos. One hundred and thirty White undergraduate students (F = 98) from a large mid-western university were assigned to read news stories in one of the following conditions: (1) stereotypical news, (2) counter-stereotypical news, (3) a combination of stereotypical and counter-stereotypical news. A fourth group was not exposed to either stereotypical or counter-stereotypical news stories. This last group served as a baseline comparison for the other three conditions. In each of the above conditions, with the exception of the no exposure group, participants were required to read a packet of nine newspaper stories. Six of the stories were either completely stereotypical, counter-stereotypical, or a combination of three stereotypical and three counter-stereotypical stories. The remaining three stories were "neutral" in content or had nothing to do with race or ethnic stereotypes. These stories were placed in the packet to serve as distracters so as not to raise participant suspicions regarding our interest in criminal stereotypes.

Stimulus materials

All of the stories used in this experiment were drawn from a large cosmopolitan newspaper. One counter-stereotypical story, for example, dealt with a Black businessman who helped organize a business convention for other African American business owners in Los Angeles. Another stereotypical story featured a Black suspect accused of committing an armed robbery. We also manipulated these stereotypical and counter-stereotypical stories in two ways. First, we inserted pictures of either Black or Latino persons into the body of the story. The pictures were headshots obtained from image searches on the Internet. All of these pictures were configured to be the exact same size. Second, we added Spanish names and surnames to all of the Latino characters in the stories to reaffirm the ethnicity of the persons. We did not want there to be any doubts in participants' minds as to whether the people pictured were Latino, Black, or any other ethnicity.

Pre-test of stimulus materials

In order to ensure participants were perceiving our stimulus materials according to our notions of stereotypical and counter-stereotypical content, we pre-tested all of our materials prior to conducting our experiment. All of the photos used were pre-tested to determine whether respondents would categorize the ethnicity of the characters in the story as either Black or Latino. In addition, news story content was pre-tested to confirm that respondents perceived the themes as either stereotypical (i.e. typical crime story featuring either a Black or Latino as the perpetrator) or counter-stereotypical (i.e. atypical story dealing with a Black or Latinos in a positive, non-criminal manner).

Photo pre-test

A total of 10 participants were given black and white photos of persons and asked to rate on a Likert scale of one (not very likely) to seven (very likely) the extent to which the character was either Black, Latino, or White. Each picture response was subjected to a statistical analysis of a paired sample t-test. All tests were conducted at a significance level of $p < 0.05$. As we anticipated, these tests were statistically significant in indicating that subjects correctly identified the ethnicity

Table 23.1 Mean ethnic ratings of Black photos

	Ethnic Rating		
Black Photos	*Black*	*Latino*	*White*
Photo 1	6.8 (0.63)	3.0 (1.3)	1.2 (0.63)
Photo 2	6.5 (0.71)	3.0 (1.6)	1.6 (0.97)
Photo 3	6.7 (0.67)	2.0 (1.4)	1.4 (0.70)
Photo 4	6.3 (1.06)	3.5 (1.7)	1.4 (0.70)
Photo 5	6.6 (0.70)	2.3 (1.3)	1.3 (0.67)
Photo 6	6.5 (0.71)	2.7 (1.3)	1.5 (1.08)

Note: Higher means indicate the degree to which the rater was confident that the photo depicted a member of a particular ethnicity. Numbers in parentheses are standard deviations. T-tests revealed that the Black means versus the Latino and White means were all significant at $p < 0.001$.

Table 23.2 Mean ethnic ratings of Latino photos

	Ethnic Rating		
Latino Photos	*Black*	*Latino*	*White*
Photo 1	2.1 (0.88)	5.9 (0.74)	2.9 (1.45)
Photo 2	2.3 (1.42)	5.9 (1.20)	2.6 (1.84)
Photo 3	1.8 (1.32)	6.1 (0.87)	3.3 (1.94)
Photo 4	2.1 (1.30)	6.2 (0.92)	2.3 (1.64)
Photo 5	2.2 (1.62)	5.8 (1.03)	3.3 (1.77)
Photo 6	1.5 (0.71)	5.9 (0.88)	3.6 (1.71)

Note: Higher means indicate the degree to which the rater was confident that the photo depicted a member of a particular ethnicity. Numbers in parentheses are standard deviations. T-tests revealed that the Latino means versus the Black and White means were all significant at $p < 0.01$.

of the African American in the photo as African American, compared to either White or Latino (see table 23.1). The same was also found to be true of the Latino photos which were also correctly perceived as Latino compared to either White or African American (see table 23.2).

News story pre-test

The stereotypical and counter-stereotypical news stories we chose for our study were also pre-tested. A total of 50 participants rated them with regards to whether or not the stories were "typical" of the types of news narratives they routinely read regarding African Americans and Latinos. Participants rated these stories on a Likert scale of one (strongly disagree) to seven (strongly agree). A statistical analysis using a paired sample t-test was undertaken to determine whether or not readers found the stories stereotypical or counter-stereotypical. Each test was conducted at the $p < 0.05$ significance level. All of our stereotypical

Table 23.3 Stereotype ratings of news stories

Stereotypical Stories M (SD)	Counter-stereotypical Stories M (SD)
4.66 (0.92)	3.61 (0.93)

Note: Higher means indicate the degree to which the rater was confident that the story was stereotypical. Numbers in parentheses are standard deviations. T-tests revealed that the stereotypical news story means were significantly different than the counter-stereotypical means at $p < 0.001$.

stories were interpreted as significantly stereotypical. All of our counter-stereotypical stories were also interpreted as significantly counter-stereotypical (see table 23.3).

Procedure

Participants were initially told that they were to take part in a memory study of news, even though our real interests revolved around race and ethnic perceptions. We did this to maximize the possibility that participants might be more candid about these topics. Once in the laboratory, participants were given a consent form to fill out as well as a packet of news stories to read carefully. Once participants were done reading the packet, they were given a short questionnaire testing their memory about the content of the stories they had just read. After finishing with that questionnaire, participants were asked to take part in a second study in which they were administered the dependent measures. Only after participants had finished the second questionnaire, were they debriefed and told about the true nature of the study.

Dependent measures

We developed 27 Likert-type items with a one (strongly disagree) to seven (strongly agree) range in order to tap a spectrum of beliefs about irresponsibility and crime. These items were then submitted to a factor analysis with varimax rotation. We set a minimum factor loading criteria of 0.70 for included items. From this, we were able to develop two measures of interest. The items for each of these scales were then summed and averaged. The scales were later dubbed the "irresponsibility scale" (e.g. "People today are quick to blame others for their failures"; two items, alpha = 0.74) and the "danger scale" (e.g. "The world is simply becoming too dangerous to feel comfortable and safe"; five items, alpha = 0.70). The "irresponsibility" scale assesses the belief that people generally fail to take responsibility for their negative actions and are too quick to blame others for their failures. The "danger" scale, on the other hand, assesses the extent to which people feel society has become too dangerous.

Covariate measure

We also included one covariate measure in the study. Covariate measures improve the estimates of the relationship between the independent variables and the dependent variables by controlling for a factor that may help explain the relationship between the predictor and outcome measures. In addition, covariates also may help explain the variation in the dependent measure. In the present study, prior news exposure was assessed as a covariate in order to determine what impact, if any, prior news exposure had on perceptions of danger and irresponsibility. We assessed this by recording the extent to which participants read newspapers and watched television news each week. They were asked the amount of hours engaged with these two news media per day and their responses were summed into a weekly total. If heavy patterns of news consumption were evident in participants, we wanted to be able to account for its effect in our analysis via our covariate.

Results

An analysis of covariance (ANCOVA) was conducted with exposure condition (i.e. stereotypical, counter-stereotypical, or a combination of both kinds of news stories) as the independent variable and irresponsibility and danger as the dependent variables. Total news consumption served as the covariate. All statistical tests were conducted at the $p < 0.05$ significance level. Each condition contained a minimum of at least 29 participants.

Irresponsibility scale

The ANCOVA test on the measure of irresponsibility was significant, $F(3, 129) = 2.64$, $p < 0.05$. Exposure to news was not a significant covariate. Means and standard deviations for the irresponsibility scale are contained in table 23.4. Pairwise comparisons revealed that Whites exposed to stereotypical, counter-stereotypical or a combination of both, were more likely to indicate that Blacks and Latinos are less responsible for their actions compared to Whites not exposed to any type of news programming.

Danger scale

The ANCOVA test on the measure of danger was also significant, $F(3, 129) = 2.71$, $p < 0.05$. Prior exposure to news was a significant covariate. Means and standard deviations for the danger scale are also contained in table 23.4. Pairwise comparisons reveal that Whites exposed to the stereotypical condition were more likely to indicate a sense of danger compared to Whites exposed to counter-stereotypical, a combination, or those not exposed to news.

Table 23.4 Means and standard deviations for irresponsibility and danger ratings

News Conditions

Dependent Measures (range)	Stereotypical M (SD)	Counter-stereotypical M (SD)	Combination M (SD)	No Exposure M (SD)
Irresponsibility (1–7)	5.14 (0.89)[a]	5.29 (0.87)[a]	5.31 (1.02)[a]	4.75 (0.79)[b]
Danger Scale (1–7)	3.46 (0.85)[a]	2.92 (0.94)[b]	3.00 (0.97)[b]	3.00 (0.92)[b]

Note: [a], [b]: Means that do not share a superscript differ at $p < 0.05$.

Discussion

Our study set out to answer the following questions: (1) Do stereotypical news portrayals increase the perception of danger and irresponsibility of Blacks and Latinos? (2) Do counter-stereotypical news portrayals decrease the perception of danger and irresponsibility of Blacks and Latinos? We used an experimental approach to address these questions. Our results indicated that Whites experience a heightened sense of danger after encountering stereotypical news exposure. Prior news viewing and reading as measured by our covariate also appeared to be related to perceptions of danger. The current study did not reveal, however, that counter-stereotypical portrayals decreased perceptions of irresponsibility. Instead, we found that any news portrayal (i.e. stereotypical, counter-stereotypical, or a combination of both) led White participants to perceive Blacks and Latinos as more irresponsible than those not exposed to news. Below, we discuss the implications of these findings as well as some of the limitations of this study.

Stereotype activation and stereotypical/counter-stereotypical portrayals

Our data indicated that Whites who encountered stereotypical portrayals of Blacks and Latinos associated with crime were significantly more likely to perceive the world as unsafe and dangerous. This effect may be due to stereotype activation. Whites may perceive Blacks and Latinos as predisposed to criminal behavior (Johnson et al., 1997; Power et al., 1996). When they encounter Latino and Black perpetrators in the news media, it reminds them of this propensity for these groups to commit crime. This in turn conjures notions of crime as a largely Black and Latino phenomena that cannot be easily controlled because these groups are innately more violent and criminal than Whites (Hewstone, 1990;

Pettigrew, 1979). These portrayals, therefore, evoke fear because of the strong association between people of color and criminality in the news.

Our data also indicated that whether Whites encountered counter-stereotypical, stereotypical, or a combination of both news depictions, they perceived Blacks and Latinos as generally failing to take responsibility for their actions. This sense of irresponsibility evoked in White participants by all three conditions, may also be linked to stereotype activation. Because Blacks and Latinos are associated with laziness (Gilens, 1999; Gray, 1989), White participants who encountered Blacks and Latinos in any form expressed their feelings that these groups generally fail to take responsibility for their actions.

Enlightened racism and stereotyping

Based on these findings, Gray's theoretical perspective and Jhally and Lewis' theory of enlightened racism seem to best account for our results. When participants in our study encountered stereotypical depictions of Blacks and Latinos, they were more likely to perceive them as dangerous. Gray suggests that the news media links people of color with crime, and this in turn provides a basis for stereotype creation.

Jhally and Lewis' theory of enlightened racism predicts that counter-stereotypical portrayals add to the negative sentiment towards Blacks and Latinos by providing evidence that people of color could succeed if they only tried hard enough. Their theory appears to have received some support in our study as well. Participants exposed to counter-stereotypical, stereotypical, or a combination were more likely to believe that Blacks and Latinos were irresponsible compared to those not exposed to news. We believe that when confronted with the counter-stereotypical portrayals this only increased the perception of these groups as less hard working and irresponsible because it reminded them that most Blacks and Latinos do not fit this mode. Stereotypical news portrayals provided actual evidence that Latinos and Blacks were not taking responsibility for their actions.

Limitations and future studies

One of the primary criticisms of this study might revolve around the need to better differentiate between the psychological impact of crime and the impact of the persons committing that crime. In other words, one might ask if Whites develop a fear of crime because they witnessed a murder or because they witnessed a person of color committing the murder. For present purposes, we do not believe that this differentiation is extremely important. As discussed above, crime and race/ethnicity are very often linked in news coverage. Therefore, when a person encounters crime, they are most often also encountering a person of color as the perpetrator.

Future studies in this area may address the above concern by creating stimulus stories in which no race or ethnicity of the suspect is mentioned. Measures of sentiment towards social groups such as Blacks and Latinos can then be taken. This would allow for a comparison between exposure to crime alone and exposure to crime committed by a Latino or African American. As a result, two possibilities could then emerge. First, participants exposed to the race of the perpetrators and the crime might have a higher sense of fear and irresponsibility than participants exposed to crime alone. Second, there might be no difference between those exposed to crime alone and those exposed to crime featuring Black and Latino perpetrators because crime and race are so linked in the minds of the viewers. Future research could also assess the reaction to White perpetrators. If sentiments of danger and irresponsibility are just as high for Whites as people of color, then this fear can be attributed theoretically to crime and not to race.

Finally, future studies in this area may also want to consider the use of television news clips as their primary stimulus when testing for media effects. While stereotypes may be visible in any form of news media, we believe audiovisual presentations may provide more effective stimuli for future researchers than print. The impact of moving images and sounds may serve to evoke more realistic images of ethnic groups and their stereotypes.

References

Bodenhausen, G., Schwartz, N., Blass, H., and Wanke, M. (1995). Effects of atypical exemplars on racial beliefs: Enlightened racism or generalized appraisals? *Journal of Experimental Psychology*, 31, 48–53.

Dixon, T. L. and Linz, D. (2000a). Overrepresentation and underrepresentation of African Americans and Latinos as lawbreakers on television news. *Journal of Communication*, 50(2), 131–54.

Dixon, T. L. and Linz, D. (2000b). Race and the misrepresentation of victimization on local television news. *Communication Research*, 27(5), 547–73.

Entman, R. (1990). Modern racism and the images of blacks in local television news. *Critical Studies in Mass Communication*, 7, 332–45.

Entman, R. (1992). Blacks in the news: Television, modern racism, and cultural change. *Journalism Quarterly*, 69, 341–61.

Entman, R. (1994). Representation and reality in the portrayal of blacks on network television news. *Journalism Quarterly*, 71, 509–20.

Fiske, S. T. and Taylor, S. E. (1991). *Social Cognition* (2nd edn.). New York: McGraw-Hill, Inc.

Gilens, M. (1999). *Why Americans Hate Welfare: Race, media, and the politics of antipoverty politics.* Chicago: University of Chicago Press.

Gilliam, F. D., Iyengar, S., Simon, A., and Wright, O. (1996). Crime in Black and White: The violent, scary world of local news. *Harvard International Journal of Press/Politics*, 1, 6–23.

Gray, H. (1989). Television, Black Americans, and the American dream. *Critical Studies in Mass Communication*, 6, 376–86.

Greenberg, B., Heeter, C., Burgoon, M., Burgoon, J., and Korzenny, F. (1983). Local newspaper coverage of Mexican Americans. *Journalism Quarterly*, 60, 671–6.

Hamilton, D. L. and Trolier, T. K. (1986). Stereotypes and stereotyping: An overview of the cognitive approach. In J. Dovidio and S. Gaertner (eds.), *Prejudice, Discrimination, and Racism.* Orlando, FL: Academic Press, pp. 127–63.

Hewstone, M. (1990). The "ultimate attribution error"? A review of the literature on intergroup causal attribution. *European Journal of Social Psychology*, 20(4), 311–35.

Jhally, S. and Lewis, J. (1992). *Enlightened Racism: The Cosby Show, audiences, and the myth of the American dream.* Boulder, CO: Westview Press.

Johnson, J. D., Adams, M. S., Hall, W., and Ashburn, L. (1997). Race, media and violence: Differential racial effects of exposure to violent news stories. *Basic and Applied Social Psychology*, 19(1), 81–90.

Martindale, C. (1987). Changes in newspaper images of Black Americans. Paper presented at the 70th annual meeting of the Association for Education in Journalism and Mass Communication, San Antonio, Texas.

Oliver, M. B. (1994). Portrayals of crime, race, and aggression in "reality-based" police shows: A content analysis. *Journal of Broadcasting and Electronic Media*, 38(2), 179–92.

Oliver, M. B. (1999). Caucasian viewers' memory of Black and White criminal suspects. *Journal of Communication*, 49(3), 46–60.

Peffley, M., Shields, T., and Williams, B. (1996). The intersection of race and crime in television news stories: An experimental study. *Political Communication*, 13, 309–27.

Pettigrew, T. F. (1979). The ultimate attribution error: Extending Allport's cognitive analysis of prejudice. *Personality and Social Psychology Bulletin*, 5(4), 461–76.

Power, J. G., Murphy, S. T., and Coover, G. (1996). Priming prejudice: How stereotypes and counter-stereotypes influence attribution of responsibility and credibility among ingroups and outgroups. *Human Communication Research*, 23(1), 36–58.

Turk, J. V., Richstad, J., Bryson, R. L., and Johnson, S. M. (1989). Hispanic Americans in the news in two southwestern cities. *Journalism Quarterly*, 66, 107–13.

von Hippel, W., Sekaquaptewa, D., and Vargas, P. (1995). On the role of encoding processes in stereotype maintenance. *Advances in Experimental Social Psychology*, 27, 177–254.

PART SIX

Futures

CHAPTER TWENTY-FOUR

Where We Should Go Next and Why We Probably Won't

An Entirely Idiosyncratic, Utopian, and Unashamedly Peppery Map for the Future

John D. H. Downing

I should make it clear from the outset that my principal target of attack here is established US communication media research, which still constitutes the bulk of what is published across the world, and enjoys considerable hegemony both conceptually and in terms of research priorities. I attack it because I consider media research to be a critically important project in order to understand the contemporary world's dynamics, and media technologies themselves as capable of being used for very constructive purposes – even if the reverse is often the case in practice. So it matters how we research them, and how they are quite frequently researched in the US at the time of writing.[1]

In view of this I will proceed to discuss the topic under eight headings, commencing with two issues I frame as ground-clearing observations and then proceeding to six specific topics. The headings are (1) the urgent need to junk what I call concept-fetishism; (2) the importance of comparative research beyond purely Anglo-American settings; (3) the importance of social movements and their media; (4) the urgency of rescuing interpersonal and group communication research from scientism; (5) the priority we need to give to research targeted to progressive policy-formulation; (6) the crucial significance of a human rights focus in research; (7) the neglected significance of religion; and (8) the tabu topic of social class.

I do not suppose I am alone in considering the topics I select here as significant, nor do they exhaust the issues that need addressing.[2] At the same time, if many more media researchers would engage with one or more of them, it would certainly be refreshing. At the very least it would serve to establish this field of study as a trailblazer rather than as the perpetual parvenu the longer established fields of study take us as being. Those of us who attend annual communication research conferences know only too well how hard it can be to find a panel that addresses original issues or old issues in an original manner. Replication and temporary fads are all too frequently the leathery and tasteless diet on the conference menu.[3]

Even the advent of the Internet illustrates the problem, for an all-too-frequent research response has been a plethora of papers that never address what we actually mean by fundamental issues of interactivity, interface, performance, code, surveillance, intellectual property and cultural capital. Some might respond that what I am objecting to would be more fairly characterized as an inevitable period of mapping of a new phenomenon, but nonetheless this period has given rein to interminable conference papers seemingly content with unconceptualized replicative description, and the mania shows little sign of ending any time soon.

1 Concept-Fetishism

Over the final 20 years of the last century, US media and communication research was greatly invigorated by the infusion of fresh perspectives mostly derived from European sources, notably British, French, German, Italian and Spanish (though because of the dominance of English, quite often filtered through British texts). Sources of such perspectives include Stuart Hall, Michel Foucault, Jürgen Habermas, Antonio Gramsci, Deleuze and Guattari, and Manuel Castells. However, with this positive hybridization has also come an entirely negative feature of the European intellectual scene, namely a sequential fetishization of particular concepts. The list is a long one. Beginning in the 1970s, these concepts included at one time or another deep structure, ideology, the public sphere, globalization, identity, cultural studies, the state, discourse, space/place, deconstruction, modernity, postmodernism, the information society, technologies of power, hegemony, feminism, postcolonialism, multiculturalism, hybridity, civil society, governmentality, panopticon, rhizomes, heteroglossia, dialogism.

Each one of these terms has something to offer, some more than others, depending on one's intellectual focus and personal taste. The proposal here is not to junk them, but to ladle steaming heaps of derision on their all-too-frequent abuse, which typically takes the form of holding on to one of them as a master-idea, almost a religious mantra, that supposedly offers a uniquely privileged hermeneutic vantage-point. They have come and gone of course: ideology and the state were big in the 1970s, hegemony and discourse in the 1980s, the information society and public sphere in the 1990s, identity and globalization and civil society in the 2000s.

The persistence of this fetishizing is no doubt due in part to the fact that these terms and others akin to them enable certain things to happen that academics like to do, such as to meet together in seminars, and to debate vigorously and even interminably by using the terms in different senses that are not identified as such. This permits the debate to be energetic because people think they are standing on the same ground. Journal articles and conference papers jet themselves out like sausages from a well-oiled machine. The success of all these terms, if success is the appropriate term for what happens, is partly due to their very vagueness, which ought to make the business of their definition extremely pressing, but all too rarely does so.[4]

The question of translation also intervenes in this process. Two examples will suffice, one of a shift in meaning that has occurred in translation, the other of a pedantry in translation derived from adulation of a Great Thinker which rendered the Great Thinker's thought much more mysterious – perhaps numinous! – than it actually was.

The shift in meaning to the *spatially* oriented notion of "public sphere" or "public realm" from the *communicatively* oriented sense of the German word *Öffentlichkeit* (which it customarily translates in Habermas's work), tends to pull attention in Anglophone circles toward the notion of a particular place and/or physically defined area within which debate takes place. This twists and narrows the concept's sense. The German term has nothing necessarily to do with location or site at all, and is simply focused on the dynamics of public opinion formation and publicity. In Habermas's discussion of eighteenth-century London coffee-houses and Paris salons, places and spaces were indeed involved, but as enabling factors for the kinesis of face-to-face exchange. They did not constitute the debate itself or its consequences.

The other example, of translation pedantry contributing to the aura of a Great Mind was a repetitive misplaced literalism in translation of Louis Althusser's prose.[5] In French, the verb "to think" (*penser*) may be transitive ("to conceptualize") as well as intransitive ("s/he is thinking . . ."), whereas in English to write or say "to think capitalism" sounds distinctly odd.[6] Althusser's translators, seemingly anxious not to misinterpret the Oracle and seemingly also a little less fluent in French than they needed to be, repeatedly transliterated rather than translated *penser*, as in the frequent phrase "to think the relations of production," which sounded either weird or – since it couldn't possibly *be* weird given that a Great Thinker was involved – meant something so deep that extensive meditation was required to become aware of the awesome dimension of the issue that Althusser was communicating.

These two examples serve to illustrate some extra potential consequences of taking a concept and working it to death. To a certain degree, the "cultural cringe" factor[7] that ennobles all continental European discourse is also to blame. At such and similar points the genuine enrichment these conceptual debates have enabled in communication research indeed passes into fetishism, pure and simple, and consequently into fog. But fog also has its academic pleasures. . . .

2 Comparative Research

Whether in the shape of Marx's attempt to decipher global capitalism, Weber's to pin down the cultural dynamics of major world religions and their relation to capitalist development, Gramsci's to unpick Fordism as a new phase in international capitalist labor-organization, Barrington Moore's to disentangle the strands in political revolutions, Wallerstein's world system theory or Castells' *The Information Age* trilogy, comparative research is hardly a novel project. But it has to be said that at least until very recently in communication and media research, global and comparative approaches have been honored much more in the breach than in the observance. The boring and irretrievably ideological *Four Theories Of The Press* (Siebert et al., 1956) and the deeply flawed *Diffusion Of Innovations* (Rogers, 1962) or Daniel Lerner's *The Passing Of Traditional Society* (1958) were prominent exceptions to this rule, but not ones on which in our field we should pride ourselves (Simpson, 1994).[8]

Thus until recently the predominance of US and British communication and media research has been mirrored very closely by the overwhelming empirical focus of their journals and monographs alike on media issues thought important there, in those two nations. While it may seem unkind to carp at this – probably in most countries the bulk of social research is national, for evident logistical and funding reasons – what is unnerving is the readiness of so many researchers to extrapolate by silent implication from their findings about a single country or part of it, to the nature of media and communication processes universally. Perhaps too the imperial histories of the two nations in question make this extrapolative tendency appear something even more than tiresome but actually objectionable, as though it were an implicit assertion that what is significant has still to be American or British.

But the issues, of course, go far beyond mere irritation at ethnocentric follies. How, in the name of rigorous research, is it conceivable to generalize across the planet about communication and media on the basis of two nations with such a great deal in common with each other culturally and politically, and correspondingly less in common with most of the other nations of the world? I have made the point more extensively elsewhere (Downing, 1996) but on the basis of language, political stability, economic affluence levels, cultural traditions, the USA and Britain are particularly close to each other, and rather close to almost all the other OECD nations as well. This, of course, is not meant to erase the fact that even within the similarities between the USA and Britain there are also differences. For example, of particular relevance to media studies, the public service development of broadcasting in the UK differs markedly from the US's unabashedly commercial and corporate deployment of the same technology and cultural form.

On the other hand, the economic crises, levels of extreme poverty, endemic political instability, top-heavy states, violent ethnic and analogous confrontations, which are quite frequent either together or in part over large tracts of the rest of the planet, represent a different landscape and therefore mediascape. Only the most unrepentant media-centricity or nationally blinkered pseudo-scientific "communicationism"[9] could dismiss these differences as intellectually marginal to our research agenda.

Thus it is either meaningless or brashly reductive to describe any national study as one that *tout court* explains "media." If weighed by the sheer frequency of their unqualified academic use, the words "the media" often appear effectively to come to denote the media system of the United States or perhaps that of Britain. The confusion caused is intensified by the frequent use of "the media" as a singular collective noun, as in the phrase "the media is . . ." This is not the archaizing complaint of a Latinist. It is an additional habit which constitutes a strong push in the same direction of homogenizing and essentializing media, most probably – under current conditions – in an implicitly Anglo-American frame.

Partly, to return to ethnocentric follies for a brief moment, these warty distortions are also a product of English language hegemony and arrogant monolingualism. Not everyone, admittedly, is good at learning other languages, but in many parts of the world even entirely illiterate people are accustomed to being able to converse on a daily basis in three or four languages, even in tongues with little or no linguistic kinship. How can serious Communication scholars presume to defend their lack of even a *reading* knowledge of another language, given that to date the non-Anglo-American-Australian-Canadian research literature has overwhelmingly been in closely cognate languages, Romance or Teutonic? The research literature with a direct bearing on media and communication research is beginning to grow now in other tongues, some of them notably difficult to learn such as Chinese, Korean, Japanese. Maybe in those cases there will be some continuing excuse . . .

For the English, time is running out on this front. The combination of the European Union, which some English folk fantasize will fade by morning, and of the ongoing dissolution of England's "internal" empire over Scotland, Wales and Ireland, mean that those 43 kilometres (yes, kilometres!) of water between them and continental Europe are increasingly, indeed, not the English Channel but rather just a channel. For US Americans, NAFTA has pulled us a little closer to Québec and México, and if the FTAA continues to take shape, to the Americas in general (this is not an endorsement of either trade regime in its present form, I should add). At least one or more of three very closely cognate languages (French, Portuguese, Spanish) could be made part of our academic armory in the USA, and we could conduct comparative research in the hemisphere. Life will continue, even on this front, to deal researchers in the Americas an easier deal than most, unless we get into Guaraní, Quechua, Aymara, Maya, Mapuche, Navajo or other indigenous tongues. But our insularity becomes more and more comic . . . except perhaps to ourselves . . .[10]

There are welcome signs of change. The volumes *Trajectories: Inter-Asia cultural studies* (Kuan Hsing Chen et al., 1998) and *De-Westernizing Media Studies* (Curran

& Park, 2000) are both indices in point, as is the 2001 special issue of *Javnost – The Public* edited by Colin Sparks on media and democracy in Asia. The London-based journal *Media, Culture & Society* has been a consistent forum for global media studies, and *Gazette: the international journal for communication studies*, under Cees Hamelink's editorship, has particularly taken this tack since the mid-1990s.[11] The International Association for Media and Communication Research has foregrounded this emphasis throughout its nearly 50 years, and the International Communication Association has begun moving increasingly in this direction since the early 1990s. But contented ruminant monolingualism will likely prove the primary obstacle to further progress.

3 Social Movements and their Media

Marx suffered dreadfully from boils on his butt, a product of poor diet and poverty, and of far too many hours at a time perched on the self-same posterior in the British Museum Library. He sourly forecast that the bourgeoisie would come to regret those boils. Media research suffers dreadfully too, but not with boils, rather from galloping gigantism, the instinctive obsession with large audiences, mega-corporations, long-running series, newspapers of record, global Internet portals. Yet it is doubtful in the extreme that as a result of this obsession anyone will regret anything much at all. I am not saying these should not be researched or don't matter. The problem is in the uninspected interstices of that research priority, namely the core assumption that the local, the small-scale, the evanescent, the ephemeral, the underfunded, the misspelt, the low-production-values, the Arbitron- and Nielsen-inaccessible, the wacky, represent pure flotsam and jetsam bobbing about uninvitingly on the water's surface, waiting to sink beneath the waves and meet their due and deserved oblivion.

PIFFLE!

Communication and media research is, it seems, perpetually in danger of self-imprisonment in these gigantist assumptions. Is this a peculiar residue of the days of Joseph Klapper and the early Elihu Katz, when media were effectively defined as epiphenomenal, barely worthy of research? So that only *monumentally massive* media matter?

On the contrary. Social movements have always been significant in human history, but visibly more and more so in the twentieth century. With the very common current decline of parliamentary parties' prestige and political function in liberal democracies, social and political movements are likely to play, not a substitute role, but increasingly important functions on the political stage. Their relation with mainstream media is one very rich vein for research, but richer still, even more so today with the possibilities enabled by digital media, are the movements' own media. I have argued this extensively elsewhere (Downing, 2001), there is a rapidly growing body of research in this area (e.g. Rodríguez, 2001; Atton, 2001; Gumucio Dagron, 2001; Soley, 1999; and Fairchild, 2001), and it is to be hoped that substantial size alone will not continue forever to be thought to correlate particularly or even always significantly with substance. It is distinctly odd in the era of digital micro-circuitry, the genome project and subatomic particle research, that gigantism should have had such unique and unquestioned play in media research, but let us hope it will soon stop being allowed to sprawl out over the entire settee.

So let us acknowledge that *samizdat* and *glasnost*, the Democracy Wall and Tiananmen Square processes of 1978–9 and 1989, the Quit India movement of the 1920s–40s, the national and international antiapartheid movement of the 1950s–90s, the US Civil Rights movements of the 1950s and 1960s, the international antiwar movement of the 1960s and 1970s, the vast anti-Shah movement of the 1970s in Iran, the feminist and gay/lesbian movements of the last three decades, the environmental movement, represent some of the most significant forces for social change in the previous century. Let us, if we will, look further back to the Reformation, the American Revolution, the French Revolution, the Haitian Revolution, the Taiping Rebellion of 1850–64, as some among the most significant of such happenings in earlier centuries. Let us acknowledge that communicating, with and without media technologies, was essential to their operation, from the *Flugschrift*[12] to the Internet. Let us acknowledge that much of this communication was molecular and capillary, invisible to the survey researcher and the parachute-journalist alike, even on occasion to the secret police as well.

And let us, in the name of common sense if nothing more, focus serious research on this so far seemingly submerged continent and develop sensitive and acute methods for that research. One of the most intriguing media developments at the present time is that of the Independent Media Centers, the grandmother of which is the Seattle Indymedia Center (www.indymedia.org) which began its life shortly before and during the anti-WTO confrontations in that city at the end of 1999. By 2002 some 70 such centers had mushroomed, more in the USA and Canada than elsewhere, but representing a very interesting model of non-hierarchical multiple-media facilitation around specific locations of contestation where global agencies such as the IMF, the World Bank, the G8 governments had their meetings. After the specific confrontation, most often the new IMC would continue, linked to all the others (Downing, 2002a; Downing, 2002b).

Now the examples I have cited are of movements and media that mostly hewed to a broadly progressive agenda, but the media of fascist, white supremacist, anti-Semitic, anti-immigrant and fundamentalist movements are also very important to study. So too are what might be called banal alternative media, whether those of sport enthusiasts, TV-show fans, or cooking and gardening aficionados, for these less attention-getting examples help us understand many of the popular cultural skeins that occupy our and our fellow-citizens' lives.

The one note of caution to sound is that students in search of a topic for their special projects, theses and dissertations might descend upon this submerged continent of the micro and produce the kind of endless replication studies that we see so often in the sciences and in history, anthropology and sociology dissertations. Replication is not an ill in itself, but in academic hands it can easily become a comfortable end in itself and thus divert energy from more challenging intellectual and/or ethical research priorities.

4 Interpersonal and Group Communication Research and the Great Gobi Desert

In 1961 Newton Minow famously described US commercial television as a vast wasteland (Barnouw, 1990). Whether that was fair or not I will not explore here, but if anyone is hunting for an intellectual desert they could conserve their energy by stepping straight into the world of interpersonal and group communication research. There they will find the purest scientism blossoming exuberantly, the trivial enthroned on a seat of sheer splendor, and banalities bubbling away brilliantly. Count it and it counts, two-tail-test it and it's true. The quarterly *Human Communication Research* is a magnificent example of the genus.

This is a profound shame. The small scale *is* significant, fetishizing media technologies in the study of communication *is* crazy, all the emailing, chatrooms and videoconferencing in the world *cannot* come near dislodging the importance of FtF communication, media communication *is* impossible to understand without the interpersonal communication of media producers and audiences/readers. This much is common sense.

But why is it thought productive, even permissible, to filter this firm reality through the peculiar and sludgy mesh of an empiricist social psychology? Not that somehow some interesting insights have not accidentally emerged as a result, not least in the field of nonverbal communication. But it feels almost as though they have emerged in spite of, rather than in any way because of, the methods applied to their study. However, if the empiricist desert dwellers are happy in their habitat, let us not disturb them there. But please let *us* go where there is water and wine and where vegetation may be found.

So this is an urgent call for the reinvention of interpersonal communication research, using sources such as feminist research, Freud, Goffman, elements of cultural and social anthropology and of descriptive sociolinguistics, the accumulated experience of focus group research, the novel, the short story, theater, popular music lyrics and poetry, clinical psychotherapy, humanistic psychology, and what used to be called environmental psychology. The upsurge in qualitative audience and readership research over the past couple of decades has been a pointer in this same direction, and in a sense gives a clue to appropriate ways of proceeding in that it is one way to dovetail media and interpersonal communication research, whose virtual apartheid has everything to do with different research methodologies and nothing to do with common sense.

I would cite four instances to illustrate my point, the first a study of media producers, the others of media audiences.

The first is Mark Pedelty's (1995) fascinating anthropological study of the national and international press corps in El Salvador in the period leading up to the close of the country's bloody 1979–92 US-sanctioned military repression, in which 50,000 or more were killed, mostly civilians at the hands of the armed forces, and maybe 20 percent of the population fled the country. Not only does this fit the bill I urged above of research conducted outside the Anglo-American dyad, but it also illustrates the advantages of weaving together media and non-media communication. Pedelty's ethnographic perspective and method enabled him to move beyond listing the journalists' sociological attributes in analyzing their professional roles, and to pierce through to the core of their collective – and contrasting, as regards the difference between nationals and foreigners – newsgathering operations. The dynamics of their mutual interactions and the sub-culture that emerged in the main hotel that US journalists lived in, represented a crucial element in their professional performance, as did their interactions with the US embassy in San Salvador, the capital. Only this interpersonal and group communication focus can make full sense of the news frame generated by the foreign press corps in El Salvador, year after year of the repression.

The second example is drawn from an essay in a recent book by the editor of this volume, written with her daughter (Valdivia with Bettivia, 2000). It is conceptually based, but drawn empirically from their conversations about girl culture in a US high school. The centrality of gossip in that culture, of intensive telephone use between classmates in the evenings,* is absorbing in itself and cannot but be centrally articulated with media uses. Whereas much audience research would take that level of analysis as indicating foreign ground that need not be trodden, and much interpersonal and group communication analysis would endeavor to identify constants and variables ripped out of their context, this study acknowledges both its importance and its accessibility by means of focused conversation.

The third example consists of research by Susana Kaiser (2002) on the sources of young people's memories of the bloody 1976–83 Argentinean dictatorship, almost a generation after it finally collapsed. Focusing on schooling, news media, family communication, public monuments and *escraches*,[13] as interrelated sources, actual and potential, of memories of how the military had behaved, she found a continuing culture of public fear combined with a gradually expanding combativeness in the face of continued cover-ups and denials. But only by engaging with *all* these interpersonal communication circuits and linking them with media processes – for example, by taking into account some feature films exposing the dictatorship that were used as discussion material by a significant number of high

---

* Rhiannon, the daughter, says (p. 31) "When I am absent from school, I don't worry about missing math, because it's easy. It's like $y = mx + b$. I worry about missing gossip because it's much more complicated, and you don't get a formula for that!"

school teachers in their classes – was it possible to capture the full dynamics of the political culture.

The fourth example is Kwamena Kwansah-Aidoo's (2001) examination of the roles of anecdotes as both a mode of interpersonal communication and as a key source of audience data. His specific focus is on the reception of environmental news among urban Ghanaians with a university education, and he makes much of the culture of diffidence in expressing personal views to strangers in Ghana that constitutes a major roadblock to conventional survey research. For him, the interpersonal communication of telling anecdotes offers a methodological solution appropriate to that context. Although he is careful to limit his assertions to Ghana, suggesting only in passing that they might be applicable in other African nations, we might go further and consider that it might be very productive to explore how far media use research in non-African contexts would also be enhanced by similar strategies.

5 Policy-Research

Calling for communication policy research is hardly a challenge to orthodoxy. There is a mass of it out there, and by this time next year there will be a whole lot more. Telecommunications studies are a huge chunk of the communication policy research pie at present, most of them highly descriptive and not only a-conceptual but also dominated by corporate funding priorities.[14] Some communication researchers may lament how little impact all this seems to make. Some others may look enviously at economists and psychologists who appear to be respected in "the real world." Or at least to be paid.

But it is the nature of that "real world" that I wish to concentrate on here. The "real world" often lies way out beyond the horizon of policy researchers, and this is sadly true in any discipline or area you care to mention, not just ours. Effectively, policy research today is normally what it always has been, research by the crafty courtier – or team of courtiers – for the monarch or monarch-substitute. "Successful" policy research means policy research that is adopted by the power structure and turned into something that actually happens. The narcissistic excitement of thus "transcending" the "limitations" of the classroom is palpable among academics who manage this feat.

Yet all too often this, to my mind, has much more to do with egotism than with any desire to contribute to constructive policy-making. The Beltway phenomenon is one familiar from many other nations, where a body of self-congratulatory mutually back-stabbing intellectuals compete "to make a dent" – but for most, a dent is the sole and quite abstract currency, not what it is or how it is made. Successfully advising politicians on how to hone their televisual skills makes a dent. What does it do for the public?

The communication policy research that really needs to be accomplished is research that begins from a listening position, a habit of having ears alert to the public – not in the flamboyant populist exploitation accomplished by the world's Rush Limbaughs, not in the "over-their-heads-and-for-their-good" mode of liberal policy wonks – but in a Freirian dialogic sense (Husband, 1996). Communication policy research which, beginning from this position, makes a dent in the normal disempowerment of the public, which enhances the public's agency, if only in one place at one time, is the kind of research the field most urgently needs. In a famous and blistering address to an alternative caucus at the 1968 annual conference in Boston of the American Sociological Association, and in the midst of the tumults of that decade, Martin Nicolaus (1972) called for "eyes-up" research, focusing on the doings and arrangements of the powerful, as opposed to the "eyes-down" research on the general public that is often all that is countenanced (or funded).[15]

Within the US, the zone above all where policy research is required continues to be what W. E. B. DuBois (1997 [1903]) presaged back in 1903 as *the* problem of the twentieth century, the problem of the color line, now set to be *the* problem of the twenty-first as well. In a nation where the wealthy lock themselves into gated communities and staggering numbers of minority-ethnic citizens into prisons, the pollyanna prediction that the open wound of racial injustice has been salved ever since the Civil Rights movements is one that communication policy-researchers should take as their symbolic emblem of willful idiocy. They should proceed not simply to demolish it – which does not take long or much effort – but much more to engage in research that promotes practical steps of all kinds, in all spheres, private and public, to close up this chasm in communication, economics and politics that otherwise shows no sign of abating.

There is in fact quite a lot of research emerging now on ethnic identities, including a whole spate of studies of the meaning of "whiteness." Both developments are fine in principle. As a result of global labor migration, former ethnic dualities (Québécois/Anglo-Canadian, Black/White, Maori/Pakeha) are being broken up, and the recognition of White status as constructed rather than as a natural given was long overdue. Yet the multiplication of ethnicities can quickly lead in the hands of academic researchers to the exoticization of the human zoo, and the interest in whiteness to a narcissistic self-absorption. The key research issue is, and should remain for the foreseeable future, that of racism and communication.

6 Human Rights

In a number of ways this issue overlaps the one just addressed, but it is nonetheless important to flag it independently. It is a topic with multiple dimensions, from the individual to the collective, from the national to the international (it is certainly not a uniquely "Third World" issue), and from the political to the economic to the cultural to the legal. It is a problem that for official government spokespeople only ever exists in nations not their own, so that when Human

Rights Watch or Amnesty International or any of the other human rights bodies draw attention to abuses in one country, the same government that will seize on such reports to belabor that nation will also evince a magnificently brazen refusal to consider its own record as anything other than unblemished. This continuing contradiction alone should draw the interest of communication researchers.

However, there are many more reasons than official hypocrisy that warrant a human rights priority for communication researchers. The principal one, perhaps all too obviously, is the necessity for finding *effective* channels to publicize human rights abuses in a *sustained* manner. Communicating these abuses nationally and internationally does not instantaneously or automatically bring redress, but there can be little to no doubt that their non-communication or miscommunication will definitely not bring redress. Here indeed is a prime area for policy research.

Secondly, over and above a frequent ethnic dimension to human rights issues there is an equally powerful, often starkly etched, gender dimension which, given women's widespread role in bringing up children, most often overflows on to children as well. To communication researchers concerned with gender, which one would hope would be true in some measure of all researchers, human rights situations and histories should be very pressing candidates for systematic attention. To communication researchers concerned with global topics and/or with social movements, human rights will equally prove a highly productive focus.

For example, the essay collection *Human Rights and the Internet* (2000) is based upon a Canadian government-sponsored conference on the subject in 1998. Its mostly descriptive essays are on regions and nations (e.g. Africa, Latin America, Europe, East Timor, women's cross-national Internet use in post-Yugoslavia), on specific issues (e.g. racist hate sites, child porn sites, Canadian free speech and privacy law under the Charter of Rights and Freedoms, commercial and political surveillance), and on activist projects (e.g. Derechos Human Rights/Equipo Nizkor and the Web's potential for human rights education). The book is a very useful compendium on a critically important topic, here and there inevitably a little dated by now, occasionally repetitive (some extra editing would have been useful), but a project that would serve as a valuable course text in this understudied zone in Communication research.

7 The Neglected Role of Religion

There is something almost comic in the disinclination of media researchers to examine the religious dimensions of media, communication and culture. I do not mean from the perspective of a believer, though that is a perfectly legitimate vantage point, but simply in acknowledgement of the tremendous continuing force of religious beliefs of many kinds in the contemporary world. Indeed I suggested above that the fetishization of particular concepts or writers represents a facet of the religious impulse, albeit in secular garb. Many media researchers, like myself, are secular in orientation and have little truck personally with religion.

But to allow our own habits of heart and mind to deflect us from such a major cultural and mediatic phenomenon is impermissible.[16]

Religious formations of all kinds, from the dynamic role of many Jesuits in Latin America to the protestant mega-churches of the US South, from Sufi mysticism to American Jewish converts to Buddhism, from *santería* and *candomblé* in Cuba and Brazil to global televangelism, from the quasi-theocratic state structures of Iran, Israel and Pakistan to the political uses of Shinto by the Japanese right, are all part of the cultural tapestry of the world we inhabit.

Excellent examples are provided by Linda Kintz's and Julia Lesage's edited volume surveying the media strategies of the US religious right, and by Annabelle Sreberny-Mohammadi's and Ali Mohammadi's study of media in the 1978–9 Iranian revolution that brought Ayatollah Khomeini to power (Kintz & Lesage, 1998; Sreberny-Mohammadi & Mohammadi, 1994). The overall problem with the research literature, aside from its pitiful size, is that it tends implicitly to focus only upon Marx's attacking aphorism that religion is a social narcotic, and not on his observations a sentence earlier, which I would suggest are much more perceptive, that often religion is "the *expression* of real distress and also the *protest* against real distress . . . the heart of a heartless world . . . the spirit of spiritless conditions" (Marx, 1975, emphases in original).

8 The Tabu Topic of Social Class

Tendentially here I am writing as an American researcher for American researchers. Class is not nearly so tabu, or not at all so, outside the USA (DeMott, 1992). Nonetheless, given the enormous volume and international influence of published media research coming out of the USA, the problems this tabu generates concern more than just US debates. One could search far and wide for the contextual sources of the tabu, since it is nowhere written down as such. Maybe the honeyed seduction of the American Dream, maybe the lingering effects of the Cold War and McCarthyism, maybe the long decline of labor unionism, maybe the dominance of "race" in the national imaginary, maybe the thin success of bourgeois versions of feminism,[17] maybe the comforts of economic empire, maybe in the academy the pervasive culture of faculty arrogance toward staff that helps to normalize class attitudes, and maybe a combination of such factors, have served to displace social class from the research agenda of US media studies as of other social research disciplines.

When class does turn up it is often under the heading of "inequality," "poverty," "inner city," or – at the other end – particular affluent neighborhoods (Beverly Hills, the Upper East Side, the Loop, Beacon Hill, Georgetown, "the Hamptons"), both of them emphases which effectively focus attention on the income, consumption and lifestyle aspects of social class. While these are not insignificant, they fall terribly short of a thoroughly defined approach to the question. In particular they are kinetically challenged. That is to say they entirely fail to suggest any connection between class and the dynamics of social change. They are like a geological or anatomical sectioning of society conceived as a static and thus inevitable naturalized reality: shale, schist, granite or muscle, synapse, artery or poor, middle class, wealthy. These approaches also stunningly gloss over the relation between class and political power.

If instead social class is conceived as an economic power relationship among classes, and if then the corporate class, notwithstanding the evident clefts and battles for advantage within its ranks, is perceived as the leading power sector,[18] and if consequently wage-earners of a variety of stripes are acknowledged as one of the highly complex vectors of this relational system: then the notion of class becomes a great deal richer, its bearing on questions of economic, political and cultural change and power much more salient.

It does not make the concept into an explain-all, but heuristically speaking it points toward questions worth asking, questions that transcend the epi-phenomena of income distribution and collective lifestyle. It does not mean the epiphenomenal is analytically irrelevant, it does not mean we should "do" political economy rather than cultural studies, nor does it mean that monitoring and warning against the global intensification of media monopoly trends con-cludes the task of socially responsive media researchers. It does mean that we are working with a research model that prompts us to look for the interconnections of inequality at every plane. Not in a functionalist mode which sees intercon-nections as nearly always effective (and implicitly benign), but in a mode that is tuned to explore conflictual *and* conformative relations between the macro and the micro, the kinetic and the stable, the processual and the institutional, *simul-taneously* (e.g. Miller, Govil, McMurria, & Maxwell, 2001; Maxwell, 2001).[19]

Concluding Observations

So why did I describe these directions in the heading of this chapter as utopian? Why will we probably *not* set out along the paths I have been suggesting in this short exercise in diplomatic restraint?

Aside from perfectly proper debate over their relevance, and maybe the resulting emergence of much stronger proposals, a major influence would be that of simple inertia, an inertia like quite no other, as the professoriate knows all too well. Learning other languages, becoming well-informed about other nations, digging into untidy and unpredictable social movements, sacrificing the comfortable prop of concept-fetishism, engaging with the painful realities of "race" and learn-ing to *listen* on that subject as well as communicate about it, sustaining a focus on human rights, grappling with religious issues that many of us think little about in the first place, tussling with entrenched scientism in interpersonal communication research, dealing imaginatively with the complexities and realit-ies of social class: it all sounds like hard work. And what is the tenure and promotion pay-off?

Perhaps not all that much, maybe in given instances none. Nothing to compare with the cozy glow of inertia.

Yet it could also be argued and to my mind with great force within the profession of communication research, that it is precisely the task of such researchers to connect up the dots. In other words, to dissect and expose the communicative mediations (Martín Barbero, 1993)[20] between the global and the personal, between human rights and "race," between religion and social class, indeed between all of these, and furthermore between them and a whole complex of other processes. The cross-cutting research agenda I have sketched out here would help realize the promise contained in the very focus of our field and would preserve us from being just another academic specialty carving out its little niche. Not everyone will enthuse over the challenge, but the intellectual excitement and the policy-formulation potential for those who do are substantial.

Notes

1 An earlier version of this chapter was presented in the panel "Where should communication research go?" at the International Communication Association conference in May 2001 in Washington, DC.

2 I have consciously, for example, not addressed two very key topics, namely feminist research and Internet research. In my judgment at the present time, both have a sufficient head of steam behind them within the USA and a number of other nations where media research is established, for it not to be necessary for me to flag them as new directions. If I am incorrect in this assessment, then I accept the appropriate blame.

3 To be fair, the same may be said of most annual conferences. But do communication researchers have to go with the flow?

4 An American sociologist of my acquaintance was present in the late seventies at a London University seminar on Foucault, newly enthroned as the latest conceptual demiurge in British academia. After listening to a paper of 30 minutes' duration in which the term "discourse" was incessantly invoked, he politely requested a clarification of the term, explaining that the new guru's fame had not yet penetrated to his native Oregon. The speaker was totally flummoxed and found himself incapable of defining the word as he (or Foucault) employed it. It was a symptomatic collapse of the stout party . . .

5 Notably in the book Althusser wrote with Rancière et al. (1970). In media research circles he is best known for his 1971 essay "Ideology and ideological state apparatuses," written in the aftermath of the French student revolts and labor strikes of May–June 1968.

6 It is possible to say that someone "thinks dollars" or "thinks sport" but that is an idiomatic sense of the verb, signifying "is 100 percent focused upon," and actually depends upon the normal intransitive generalizing sense for its impact. The ironic expression "s/he thinks great thoughts" functions similarly.

7 This term has been much used in Australia to lampoon the foolishly subservient posture of some Australians toward European and US artists, thinkers and cultural commentators.

8 Christopher Simpson has taken this argument a step further, based on his study of declassified research papers written over the period 1945–60 for the Pentagon and other agencies by Lerner, Schramm, and many more media researchers, and argues that "international communication research" was in actuality largely psychological warfare research His argumentation at times relies too much on correlatives, and also does not sufficiently engage with the differences between Stalinism in the Soviet bloc and endogenous political upsurges in other parts of the

world (any more than the Cold Warriors did), thereby understating the appeal of combating Stalinism. Nonetheless, his research clarifies some very significant dimensions of the major postwar era of funded US media research.

9 This deliberately ugly neologism is constructed on the model of reductive intellectual approaches such as "economism," "psychologism" and "sociologism."

10 Institutionally speaking, developing extended undergraduate Communication major programs combined with modern language departments would be a forward-looking move.

11 Especially see special issues 59.4–5 (October 1997) on media in Africa, 62.3–4 (July 2000) on Canadian media, and 63.2–3 (May 2001) on mediated culture in the Middle East.

12 The term for pamphlets produced in great number as part of the Reformation movement in Germany.

13 *Escraches* was the Argentinean term coined to refer to mid-90s demonstrations in which the protestors would identify a house or apartment block in which former military torturers were living comfortably, and at peace with their neighbors and community, and hold a noisy mass denunciation outside, pointing out to all within earshot the monster they had living in their midst. The point was to try to condemn them to public repudiation, since successive post-dictatorship regimes had cravenly accorded them amnesty and thus impunity for their extreme crimes.

14 For an example of telecommunications research that bucks the trend, see R. G. Lentz (2000).

15 Specifically he said: "The professional eyes of the sociologists are on the down people, and the professional palm of the sociologist is stretched toward the up people . . . So far, sociologists have been schlepping this knowledge that confers power along a one-way chain, taking know-ledge from the people, giving knowledge to the rulers" (pp. 40–1). Today, telecommunications policy researchers are mostly obsessed with network architecture, pricing, regulation sub-clauses, and quite often do not even trouble to research the down people. What, after all, would they know that is worth recording? Such is progress.

16 For a careful historical dissection of the paradox that coverage of religion is minimal in US media too, despite the religiosity of the American public, see Hoover & Wagner (1997).

17 See the acutely perceptive study of US class and gender discourses in *Cosmopolitan* magazine by Ouellette (1999).

18 A paradox of Anglo-American research discourse is the reluctance to use the term bourgeoisie, as if its abuse by Soviet and Maoist hacks had somehow deprived it of legitimate meaning. There is no need to subscribe to a tidy quasi-Hegelian schema that defines the bourgeoisie as automatically digging its own grave, as Marx once put it, in order to use the concept. Its merit is that it suggests the multiple historical, cultural, economic and political dimensions of those in significant control of society's economic levers, much more than the terminology I have just deployed in obeisance to the Anglo-American distaste for the word.

19 Some good recent examples of what I have in mind here are Miller, Govil, McMurria, and Maxwell (2001) and Maxwell (2001).

20 An absorbing study that is sadly currently out of print.

References

Althusser, L. (1971). Ideology and ideological state apparatuses. In *Lenin and Philosophy and Other Essays*. London: New Left Books, pp. 123–73.

Althusser, L., Rancière, J., Macherey, P., Balibar, E., and Establet, R. (1970). *Reading Capital*. London: New Left Books.

Atton, C. (2001). *Alternative Media*. London: Sage.

Barnouw, E. (1990). *The Tube of Plenty: The evolution of American television* (2nd revised edn.). New York: Oxford University Press.

Curran, J. and Park, M. (eds.) (2000). *De-Westernizing Media Studies*. London: Routledge.

DeMott, B. (1992). *The Imperial Middle: Why Americans can't think straight about class*. New Haven, CT: Yale University Press.

Downing, J. (1996). *Internationalizing Media Theory: Transition, power, culture: reflections on media in Russia, Poland and Hungary, 1980–1995*. London: Sage.

Downing, J. (2001). *Radical Media: Rebellious communication and social movements*. Thousand Oaks, CA: Sage.

Downing, J. (2002a). Independent media centers: A multi-local, multi-media challenge to global neoliberalism. In M. Raboy (ed.), *Global Media Policy in the New Millennium*. Luton, UK: Luton University Press, pp. 215–32.

Downing, J. (2002b) Radical media projects and the crisis of public media. In R. Mansell, R. Samarajiva, and A. Maham (eds.), *Networking Knowledge for Information Societies: Institutions and interventions*. Delft, The Netherlands: Delft University Press, pp. 320–7.

DuBois, W. E. B. (1997) *The Souls of Black Folk*. Boston: Bedford Books. (Originally published 1903.)

Fairchild, C. (2001). *Community Radio and Public Culture*. Cresskill, NJ: Hampton Press.

Gumucio Dagron, A. (2001). *Making Waves*. New York: Rockefeller Foundation.

Hoover, S. M. and Wagner, D. K. (1997). History and policy in American broadcast treatment of religion. *Media, Culture and Society*, 19(1), 7–27.

Husband, C. (1996). The right to be understood: Conceiving the multi-ethnic public sphere. *Innovation*, 9(2), 205–11.

Kaiser, S. (2002). *Escraches*: Demonstrations, communication and political memory in post-dictatorial Argentina. *Media, Culture and Society*, 24(4), June, 499–516.

Kintz, L. and Lesage, J. (eds.) (1998). *Media, Culture and the Religious Right*. Minneapolis: University of Minnesota Press.

Kuan-Hsing Chen, K., with Kuo, H., Hang, H., and Ming-Chu, H. (eds.) (1998). *Trajectories: Inter-Asia cultural studies*. London: Routledge.

Kwansah-Aidoo, K. (2001). Telling stories: The epistemological value of anecdotes in Ghanaian communication research. *Media, Culture and Society*, 23(3), 359–80.

Lentz, R. G. (2000). The e-volution of the digital divide in the US: A mayhem of competing metrics. *Info*, 2(4). Online at www.camfordpublishing.com.

Lerner, D. (1958). *The Passing of Traditional Society: Modernizing the Middle East*. Glencoe, IL: The Free Press.

Martín Barbero, J. (1993). *Communication, Culture and Hegemony: From the media to mediations*. Thousand Oaks, CA: Sage.

Marx, K. (1975). Contribution to the critique of Hegel's *Philosophy of Law*. In Karl Marx and Frederick Engels, *Collected Works*, vol. 3. London: Lawrence & Wishart, p. 175.

Maxwell, R. (ed.) (2001). *Culture Works: The political economy of culture*. Minneapolis: University of Minnesota Press.

Miller, T., Govil, N., McMurria, J., and Maxwell, R. (2001). *Global Hollywood*. London: British Film Institute.

Nicolaus, M. (1972). Sociology liberation movement. In T. Pateman (ed.), *Counter Course*. Harmondsworth: Penguin.

Ouellette, L. (1999). Inventing the Cosmo Girl: Class identity and girl-style American dreams. *Media, Culture and Society*, 21(3), 359–83.

Pedelty, M. (1995). *War Stories: The culture of foreign correspondents*. New York: Routledge.

Robinson, Mary (2002). *Human Rights and the Internet*. New York: Palgrave.

Rodríguez, C. (2001). *Fissures in the Mediascape*, Cresskill, NJ: Hampton Press.

Rogers, E. (1962). *Diffusion of Innovations*. Glencoe, IL: The Free Press.

Siebert, F., Peterson, T., and Schramm, W. (1956). *Four Theories of the Press*. Urbana, IL: University of Illinois Press.

Simpson, C. (1994). *Science of Coercion: Communication research and psychological warfare, 1945–1960*. New York: Oxford University Press.

Soley, L. (1999). *Free Radio*. Boulder, CO: Westview Press.

Sreberny-Mohammadi, A. and Mohammadi, A. (1994). *Small Media, Big Revolution: Communication, culture and the Iranian revolution*. Minneapolis: University of Minnesota Press.

Valdivia, A. N. with Bettivia, R. S. (2000). Girl culture: We must continue to revisit it. In A. N. Valdivia, *A Latina in the Land of Hollywood*. Tucson: The University of Arizona Press.

CHAPTER TWENTY-FIVE

All Consuming Identities
Race, Mass Media, and the Pedagogy of Resentment in the Age of Difference

Cameron McCarthy

Over the years, I have come to see multiculturalism – as a set of propositions about identity, knowledge, power and change – as a kind of normal science – as a form of disciplinarity of difference in which the matter of alterity has been effectively displaced as a supplement. On the terms of its present trajectory, multiculturalism can be properly diagnosed as a discourse of power that attempts to manage the extraordinary tensions and contradictions existing in modern life that have invaded social institutions including the university and the school. At the heart of its achievement, multiculturalism has succeeded in freezing to the point of petrification its central object: "culture" and its main, but not only, vehicle, the mass media. Within the managerial language of the university, for example, culture has become a useful discourse of containment, a narrow discourse of ascriptive property in which particular groups are granted their nationalist histories, their knowledges and alas, their experts. Cultural competence then becomes powerfully deployed to blunt the pain of resource scarcity and to inoculate the hegemonic knowledge paradigms in the university from the day-light of subjugated knowledges and practices.

It is a wish fulfillment on the part of university bureaucrats, however, to attempt to hold still or at bay the extraordinary social currents unleashed in pop-ular life now bearing down upon the modern subjects that inhabit contemporary industrial societies. These currents can be located, in part, in the destabilizing political economy and cultural imperatives produced in the push and pull of globalization and localization. On the one hand, the tensions and contradictions of economic reorganization, downsizing, and instability in the labor market have spawned paranoia and uncertainty among the working and professional classes. On the other, culture and ideology ignite the false clarity of essential place, essential home, and the attendant practices of moral and social exclusionism. These dynamic forces have taken hold in the "body politic" so to speak. They reveal themselves at the level of the subject in terms of an excess of desires, unfulfilled appetites, incompleteness, and general insecurity, anger and violent passions, frustrations and resentment. At the level of social institutions these tensions of unfulfillment must be understood as a problem of social integration of difference in a time of scarcity. As a compensatory response, cultural transactions of every kind – from education to family birthday celebrations – have become the reinvigorated sites of unbridled consumerism and shopping for futures in the context of what C. L. R. James calls "the struggle for happiness" (James, 1993, p. 166).

For cultural and media critics like myself, a key place to read these dynamics is at the level of the popular, especially, but not solely, as exemplified in mainstream mass media. As much as educators may derive significant benefits from taking on a wider purview of issues and in the process examining the implications of mass media for schooling, media critics might do well to look at education as a site suffused with tensions and contradictions that are in part deeply informed by the pivotal role that media culture plays in the lives of the young (Kenway & Bullen, 2001). Like Jane Kenway and Elizabeth Bullen, I am very interested in thinking about the nexus between education and the media. I therefore want to take the topic of multicultural education that is normally considered outside the circuit of the field of popular culture and the mass media and its diversity, knowledge and power to a place where the terrain of popular culture and its pedagogies of wish fulfillment and desire meet and contribute to the formation of educated subjects and global citizens. Desire is understood here as a productive agency of lack: the excess rising below and above needs, the latent wish for totality and completeness in a context of containment, limits and constraints – power disguised and raw.

In so doing, I want to shift attention from the multiculturalist complaint over current modes of teaching and curriculum, per se, to the broader issue of the cultural reproduction of difference and the coordination of racial identities, what Larry Grossberg (1992) calls "the organization of affect." I want to look at the problem of diversity and difference in our time as a problem of social integration of modern individuals and groups into an increasingly bureaucratic, commodified, and deeply colonized and stratified life world. All of this raises the stakes for the practices of cultural reproduction and their role in identity formation, foregrounding the connections between the production and reproduction of popular cultural form and the operation of power in daily life. Power is understood, here, as a modern force in the Foucauldian sense, inciting and producing certain possibilities, subject positions, relations, limits and constraints. Power in this sense does not simply prohibit or repress. It is a force that is dispersed. It circulates. It is not outside relations. It produces relations. It is not simply a question of who or what exercises power but how power is exercised in the concrete (Hall, 1980).

Power is above all discursive – technologies and practices of "truth" which deeply inform how social individuals conduct themselves in relation to each other in the domain of the popular. This is the whole area that Michel Foucault calls "governmentality": the site at which state, industry/economy and education meet the massive technologies of textual production and meaning construction associated with media and the popular arts. The locus of power struggles in the modern society is not now to be found pure and simple in the classic sites of state politics, labor-capital arm wrestling, or bulldozing actions of civil rights and union-based political actors and their detractors. Modern power struggles are quintessentially to be located in the deeply contested arena of the popular, the domain of struggles over social conduct, popular commitments, anxieties and desires, and ultimately the disciplining of populations (Miller, 1998).

The cultural Marxist, C. L. R. James, similarly maintains that understanding popular culture is critical to understanding the play of power in modern life. In critical ways, as James insists in books such as *American Civilization* (1993), one can get a better insight into the tensions and contradictions of contemporary society by observing and interpreting popular culture than by analyzing canonical literary or social science texts. James makes this argument in a radical way, in his essay, "The Popular Arts and Modern Society":

> It is in the serious study of, above all, Charles Chaplin, Dick Tracy, Gasoline Alley, James Cagney, Edward G. Robinson, Rita Hayworth, Humphrey Bogart, genuinely popular novels like those of Frank Yerby (*Foxes of Harrow, The Golden Hawk, The Vixen, Pride's Castle*) . . . that you find the clearest ideological expression of the sentiments and deepest feelings of the American people and a great window into the future of America and the modern world. This insight is not to be found in the works of T. S. Eliot, of Hemingway, of Joyce, of famous directors like John Ford or René Clair. (p. 119)

What James is pointing toward through this revisionary strategy is the fact that what we call popular culture is our modern art; a modern art deeply informed by and informative of the crises and tensions of cultural integration and reproduction in our time.

One of the principal crises of social integration in modern life is the crisis of race relations. I am defining racial antagonism, in this essay, as an effect of the competition for scarce material and symbolic resources in which strategies of group affiliation and group exclusion play a critical role. This crisis of racial antagonism must be seen within the historical context of the contradictions of modern society and the rapid changes taking place in the material reality and fortunes of people, their environments, the institutional apparatuses that govern and affect their lives, their relations with each other, and their sense of location in the present and in the future. Rapid changes of this kind have meant rapid movement and collision of peoples. And above all, as Arjun Appadurai (1996) has argued, they have necessitated a diremption of the central site of the work of the imagination from the ecclesiastic arena of high art and aesthetics to the banality of everyday practices and the wish fulfillment of the great masses of the people.

These tensions, as I have argued elsewhere, must be foregrounded in any discussion of the resurgence of racial antagonism and the accompanying rest-lessness among the working and professional white middle classes (McCarthy, 1998; Dimitriadis & McCarthy, 2001). In what follows, I try to understand these developments by reading patterns of re-coding and re-narration in public life as foregrounded in popular culture and public policy discourses. I direct attention in this area to the twin processes of racial simulation or the constant fabrication of racial identity through the production of the pure space of racial origins and resentment (the process of defining one's identity through the negation of the other). I look at the operation of these two processes in popular culture and education. I argue that these two processes operate in tandem in the prosecution of the politics of racial exclusion in our times, informing key debates over popular culture and public policy.

The Public Court of Racial Simulation

In his book, *Simulations*, Jean Baudrillard (1983, p. 1) recounts a story told by the Latin American writer, Jorge Luis Borges. It is the story of some special map makers, the Cartographers of the Empire, who draw up a map so detailed that it ends up covering the entire territory that was the object of the Cartographers' map making. Baudrillard uses the fable to announce the ushering in of the epoch of simulation, our age, the age in which the real is often replaced by the hyperreal and the line between reality and fiction is forever deferred. The photo opportun-ity is our only contact with the president. The Patriarch only/never blooms in autumn. The copy has in this case completely usurped the original. There is no place like home any more in this new world order of constantly collapsing global space.

I would like to take up the Borges story as a point of departure in my explora-tion of the articulation of race relations and racial identities in popular culture and in education at the beginning of the twenty-first century. In doing so, I will draw directly on Baudrillard's ostensible theme in the above passage that re-counts the trials and tribulation of the Emperor's Cartographers – the theme of the centrality of simulation in our contemporary age. For the idea of the copy that constantly recodes, usurps and appropriates the original is a very precise insight on the way in which racial difference operates in popular culture and intellectual life today. And, it is this theme of simulation that I will want to return to in a moment. But let me say that I believe that the Borges' allegory is a fable about identity which I understand to be a drama of social crisis and recuperation, of exclusion and affiliation, of exile and return. Racially dominant identities do depend on the constant ideological appropriation of the other. Racial identity, racial affiliation, and racial exclusion are the products of human work, human effort (Said, 1993). The field of race relations in popular culture, but also in education, is a field of simulation. The story of map making is also a story ultimately of the excess of language that is involved in racial discourse. There is always something left over in language that never allows us to gather up our racial identities in one place and to fix them in invariant or neatly bounded racial slots. The Emperor needs the Empire. The Emperor exists for the fact of Empire. Without it, he does not exist. Worst yet, as Baudrillard might suggest, without the Empire, he does not know himself to exist. He is like the Devil/ Landlord in Derek Walcott's *Ti Jean and His Brothers* (1970) who wants to drink at the pool of mortality. He wants to be human. But the peasants will burn down his Great House. The Landlord is a homeless Devil.

Understanding the operation of racial logics in education, paradoxically, requires an understanding of their constant simulation in literature, popular culture, and the mass media – in the imaginary. It is this blend of the educational and the popular that I want to explore briefly here. For one of the current diffi- culties in the educational literature on race relations is its refusal of the popular. Yet paradoxically, it is in popular culture, especially through the mass media, that issues of race are constructed and reworked and then infused into the expressive and instrumental orders of school life.

Highlighting the centrality of simulation and resentment foregrounds the fact that US American middle-class youth and suburban adults "know" more about inner-city Black and Latino youth through electronic mediation, particularly film and television (e.g. the US Fox Network show, *Cops*), than through personal or classroom interaction or even through textbooks. Yet, these processes are co-constitutive, as school textbooks, like academic books, generally, have become part of a prurient culture industry with their HD (high-definition) illustrations, their eclectic treatment of subject matter, and their touristic, normalizing dis- courses of surveillance of marginalized groups. In this sense, education (and multicultural education in particular) is articulated to popular culture in ways that implicate broader cultural imperatives.

The logics here are multiple and complex. Hence, critical pedagogues like Shirley Steinberg and Joe Kincheloe (1997) are correct to note the ways popular cultural texts and their complex pleasures and pedagogies are elided from domin- ant classroom culture today, an insight underscored by an important body of work in cultural studies and education (see e.g. Dimitriadis & McCarthy, in press; Giroux, 1996). In this sense, school life is often formally divorced from the realities of the popular and ignores the myriad ways that the mass media penetrate the classroom and school yard. However, in another and equally im- portant sense, schools are, in fact, entirely imbricated in the kinds of market logics and imperatives so intrinsic to popular culture and mass media. As Andy Green (1997) notes, for example, movements for "school choice" index the ways schools are accommodating, not contesting, dominant discourses of consumer capitalism. These discourses are implicated at all levels of the educational pro- cess – from decisions about policy and administration to the situated realities of the classroom. As such, Ruth Vinz notes the "shopping mall" approach to multi-cultural education so prevalent today, giving a most compelling (hypothetical) example:

> On Monday of a given week, students begin their unit on Native Americans. They learn that Native Americans lived in teepees, used tomahawks to scalp white folks, wore headdresses, and danced together around a fire before eating their meal of blue corn and buffalo meat. By Wednesday of the same week, literature is added as an important cultural artifact; therefore, one or two poems (sometimes including Longfellow's "Hiawatha") represent tribal life of the past and present. By Friday, students take a trip to The Museum of the American Indian with its unsurpassed collection of artifacts and carry home their own renditions of teepees, tomahawks, or headdresses that they made during their art period. (Vinz, 1999, pp. 398–9)

The following week, she notes, students might continue their virtual tour of the globe, moving to, for example, Latin American cultures – i.e. "During the second week, students study Latinos." As Vinz makes clear, dominant approaches to multicultural education evidence a kind of market logic, putting multiple and fabricated cultural products at the fingertips of students to consume in very superficial ways.

In this sense, educational institutions are always in sync with popular culture in terms of strategies of incorporation and mobilization of racial identities. Indeed, we live in a time when "pseudo-events" fomented in media-driven representations have usurped any relic of reality beyond that which is staged or performed, driving incredibly deep and perhaps permanent wedges of difference, between the world of the suburban dweller and his or her inner-city counterpart. Daniel Boorstin writes, "We have used our wealth, our literacy, our technology, and our progress, to create a thicket of unreality which stands between us and the facts of life" (1975, p. 3). These Durkheimian "facts of life" – notions of what, for example, Black people are like, what Latinos are like – are invented and reinvented in the media, in popular magazines, in the newspaper, and in television, music, and popular film. As critics such as Len Masterman (1990), Henry Giroux (1996), and Greg Dimitriadis point out (2001) point out, by the end of his or her teenage years, the average student will have spent more time watching television than he or she would have spent in school. In the United States, it is increasingly television and film that educates youth about race. Again, popular culture and mass media and dominant educational imperatives are mutually articulated in complex ways.

Resentment, Identity-Formation, and Popular Culture

In his *On the Genealogy of Morals* (1967), Friedrich Nietzsche insisted that a new ethical framework had come into being in the industrial age that informed all patterns of human exchange in the bureaucratic arrangements of social institutions. He called this moral framework "ressentiment" (resentment) or the practice in which one defines one's identity through the negation of the other. Nietzsche conceptualized resentment as the specific practice of identity displacement in which the social actor consolidates his identity by a complete disavowal of the merits and existence of his social other. A sense of self, thus, is only possible through annihilation or emptying out of the other, whether discursively or materially. This is a process governed by the strategic alienation of the other in forms of knowledge building, genres of representation, and the deployment of moral, emotional and affective evaluation and investments. One sees this in operation in the whole contemporary stance in educational institutions towards the topics of difference, multiplicity, and heterogeneity. One sees this especially now in the fratricidal wars taking place on campuses across the country over the question of the canon versus multiculturalism and the traditional disciplines versus alternative forms of knowledge such as cultural studies and postcolonial theory. But, we also see this antipathy to difference in popular culture and public policy in the United States – a country in which the professional middle-class dwellers of the suburbs have appropriated the radical space of difference on to themselves, occupying the space of social injury, the space of social victim and plaintiff. In so doing, this suburban professional middle class denies avenues of complaint to its other: the inner-city poor. It projects its suburban world view out into the social world as the barometer of public policy displacing issues of inequality and poverty and replacing these with demands for balanced budgets, tax cuts, and greater surveillance and incarceration of minority youth. All of this is accompanied by a deep-bodied nostalgic investment in Anglo-American cultural form and its European connections. These practices of ethnocentric consolidation and cultural exceptionalism now characterize much of the tug-of-war over educational reform and multiculturalism – and the stakes could not be any higher, for all parties involved.

Indeed, resentment has become perhaps the preeminent trope in and through which "whiteness" is lived in the US today. Whiteness is an unspoken norm, made pure and real only in relation to that which it is not. "Its fullness," as Michelle Fine and Lois Weis note, "inscribes, at one and the same time, its emptiness and presumed innocence" (Fine & Weis, 1998, pp. 156–7). Offering a key example, Fine and Weis explore, in telling ethnographic detail, the saliency of resentment for the white, working-class men of Jersey City, New Jersey and Buffalo, New York – two cities ravaged by deindustrialization. As they note, these men, men who have lost the economic and cultural stability of the past, blame "ethnic others" for their condition. While the marginalized Black men Fine and Weis interviewed (as part of the same research project), are more apt to offer critiques of "the system," White men ignore such considerations. Personal resentment reigns supreme. Larger structures, the structures that have traditionally supported and served them, are left uninterrogated and naturalized. Fine and Weis write:

> Assuming deserved dominance, [White working-class men] sense that their "rightful place" is being unraveled, by an economy which they argue privileges people of color over white men in the form of affirmative action, and by pressure from blacks and Latinos in their neighborhoods wherein they feel that their physical place is being compromised. (p. 133)

Hence, resentment has become a key way to buck a growing and, for these men, painful tide of difference.

These feelings of resentment have been realized, as well, in the most brutal and vicious kinds of physical violence. Howard Pinderhughes, in a key example, documents the feelings, attitudes, and worldviews of White working-class teens in Bensonhurst and Gravesend, two neighborhoods in Brooklyn, New York. Bensonhurst, in particular, is forever marked by the highly publicized 1989 murder of Yusef Hawkins, a Black teen assaulted by a mob of twenty-something White youths. The White teens Pinderhughes interviews share much with the older men in Fine and Weis's study. As Pinderhughes (1993) argues, these teens feel a persistent "sense of victimization," one "heightened by their fear that blacks were taking over the city" (p. 79). African Americans, they feel, "are taking jobs away from whites," "are responsible for crime in the city," and "are not sufficiently punished for their criminal activity" (p. 80). This kind of resentment, Pinderhughes suggests, can fuel the most horrific acts of violence, including the murder of Hawkins, who made the deadly mistake of shopping for a used car on "the wrong side of town." As one teen put it, "What is a 16 year old kid without a driver's license [Yusef Hawkins] doing walking into an all-white neighborhood at 9:30 at night looking for a used car? He was out looking for trouble and he found it. Those guys did what they had to do" (p. 82).

This sense of resentment, it is important to note, is reinforced and undergirded by several key discourses made available in popular culture and academic circles today, discourses which seek to manage the extraordinary complexities and tension which so mark contemporary cultural life. These discourses have become most salient for white men, but they cannot and have not been so-contained. Rather, they proliferate in complex and contradictory ways, offering and enabling multiple effects for differently situated groups and individuals.

I will limit my discussion to four such discourses. First, I would like to call attention to the discourse of origins as revealed, for example, in the Eurocentric/ Afrocentric debate over curriculum reform. Discourses of racial origins rely on the simulation of a pastoral sense of the past in which Europe and Africa are available to US American racial combatants without the noise of their modern tensions, contradictions, and conflicts. For Eurocentric combatants such as William Bennett (1994) or George Will (1989), relationship and kinship between Europe and the USA are of a self-evident and transcendent cultural unity. For Afrocentric combatants, Africa and the African Diaspora are one "solid identity," to use the language of Molefi Asante (1993). Proponents of Eurocentrism and Afrocentrism are themselves proxies for larger impulses and desires for stability among the middle classes in US American society in a time of constantly changing demographic and economic realities. The immigrants are coming! Jobs are slipping overseas into the Third World! Discourses of Eurocentrism and Afrocentrism travel in a time warp to an age when the gods stalked the earth.

These discourses of racial origins provide imaginary solutions to groups and individuals who refuse the radical hybridity that is the historically evolved reality of the United States and other major Western metropolitan societies. The dreaded line of difference is drawn around glittering objects of heritage and secured with the knot of ideological closure. The university itself has become a playground of the war of simulation. Contending paradigms of knowledge are embattled as combatants release the levers of atavism holding their faces in their hands as the latest volley of absolutism circles in the air.

For example, Michael Steinberg (1996) tells the story of his first job (he was hired during the 1980s) as "the new European intellectual and cultural historian at a semi-small, semi-elite, semi-liberal arts college" in the northeast region of the United States. As Steinberg notes, during a departmental meeting, he unwittingly contradicted the hegemonic hiring practices of his new institution by "voting for the appointment to the history department of an African Americanist whose teaching load would include the standard course on the Civil War and Reconstruction." Several minutes after the meeting, one of the White academic elders of this northeastern college informed Steinberg that: a) his function as a European intellectual was "to serve as the guardian of the intellectual and curricular tradition;" b) that he should "resist at all costs the insidious slide from the party of scholarship to the party of ideology;" and c) that if he "persisted in tipping the scales of the department from tradition to experimentation and from scholarship to ideology," he would be digging his own grave insofar as his own, "traditionally defined academic position would be the most likely to face elimination by a newly politicized institution" (p. 105). Unwittingly, Steinberg had been thrown directly into the war of position over origins in which the resources of the history department he had just entered were under the strain of the imperatives of difference.

A second resentment discourse at work in contemporary life and popular culture is the discourse of nation. This discourse is foregrounded in a spate of recent ads by multinational corporations such as IBM, United, American Airlines, MCI and General Electric (GE). These ads both feed on and provide fictive solutions to the racial anxieties of the age. They effectively appropriate multicultural symbols and redeploy them in a broad project of coordination and consolidation of corporate citizenship and consumer affiliation.

The marriage of art and economy, as Stuart Ewen (1988) defines advertising in his *All Consuming Images*, is now commingled with the exigencies of ethnic identity and nation. One moment, the semiotic subject of advertising is a free US American citizen abroad in the open seas sailing up and down the Atlantic or the translucent, aquamarine waters of the Caribbean Sea. In another, the same citizen is transported to the pastoral life of the unspoiled, undulating landscape of medieval Europe. Both implicate a burgeoning consumer culture undergirded by the triumph of consumer capitalism on a global scale.

Hence, the GE "We Bring Good Things to Life" ad (which is shown quite regularly on US channels CNN and ABC as well as in some of their international versions) in which GE is portrayed as a latter day Joan of Arc fighting the good fight of US American entrepreneurship overseas, bringing electricity to one Japanese town. In the ad, GE breaks through the cabalism of foreign language, bureaucracy, and unethical rules in Japan to procure the goal of the big sell. The US as a nation can rest in peace as the Japanese nation succumbs to superior US technology.

Third, there is the discourse of popular memory and popular history. This discourse suffuses the nostalgic films of the last decade and a half or so. Films such as *Dances with Wolves* (1990), *Bonfire of the Vanities* (1990), *Grand Canyon* (1993), *Falling Down* (1993), *Forrest Gump* (1994), *A Time to Kill* (1996), *The Fan* (1997), *Armageddon* (1998), *Saving Private Ryan* (1998), and *American Beauty* (1999) foreground a White middle-class protagonist who appropriates the subject position of the persecuted social victim at the mercy of myriad forces – from "wild" Black youth in Los Angeles (in *Grand Canyon*), to Asian store owners who do not speak English well (in *Falling Down*), to a Black baseball player, living the too-good life in a moment of corporate downsizing (in *The Fan*). All hearken back to the "good old days" when the rules were few and exceedingly simple for now-persecuted White men.

Joel Schumaker's *A Time to Kill* is a particularly good example here, offering interesting pedagogical insight about social problems concerning difference from the perspective of the embattled white suburban dweller. The problem with difference is, in Schumaker's world, symptomatic of a crisis of feeling for white suburban middle classes – a crisis of feeling represented in perceived blocked opportunity and wish fulfillment, overcrowding, loss of jobs, general insecurity, crime, and so forth. The contemporary world has spun out of order, and violence and resentment are the coping strategies of such actors.

In *A Time to Kill*, Schumacher presents us with the world of the "New South," Canton Mississippi, in which social divides are extreme. Blacks and Whites live such different lives they might as well have been on separate planets. But this backwater of the South serves as a social laboratory to explore a burning concern of suburban America: retributive justice. When individuals break the law and commit acts of violent anti-social behavior then the upstanding folks in civil society, the film argues, are justified in seeking their expulsion or elimination. The film thus poses the rather provocative question: when is it respectable society's "Time to Kill"? Are there circumstances in which retribution and revenge and resentment are warranted? The makers of *A Time to Kill* say resoundingly "yes!" This answer is impervious to class or race or gender. As a technology of truth the film works to piece together a plurality of publics.

In order to make the case for retributive justice, Schumaker puts a Black man at the epicenter of this White normative discourse – what Charles Murray (1984) calls "white popular wisdom." What would you do if your 10-year-old daughter is brutally raped and battered, defecated on, and left for dead? You would want revenge. This is a role-play that has been naturalized to mean White victim, black assailant – the Willy Horton shuffle. In *A Time to Kill*, however, the discourse is strategically inverted: The righteously angry are a Black worker and his family, as two redneck assailants brutally raped and almost killed his daughter. Carl Lee, the Black lumberyard worker, gets back at these two callous criminals by shooting them down on the day of their arraignment. One brutal act is answered by another. One is a crime; the other is righteous justice. Crime will not pay. In this revenge drama, the message of retributive justice is intended to override race and class lines. We are living in the time of an eye for an eye. The racial enemy is in our private garden. In the face of bureaucratic incompetence we have to take the law into our own hands.

These films are seeped in a nostalgia of the present, enmeshed in the project of rewriting history from the perspective of bourgeois anxieties and the feelings of resentment, which often drive them. This project is realized perhaps most forcefully in the wildly successful *Forrest Gump* (1994). A special-effects masterwork, this film literally interpolates actor Tom Hanks into actual and recreated historical footage of key events in US history, re-narrating the later part of the twentieth-century in ways that blur the line between fact and fiction. Here, the peripatetic Gump steals the spotlight from the civil rights movement, the Vietnam War protesters, the feminist movement, and so forth. Public history is overwhelmed by personal consumerism and wish fulfillment. "Life," after all, "is like a box of chocolates. You never know what you're gonna get." You might get another Newt Gingrich. But who cares? History will absolve the US consumer.

Finally, I wish to call attention to the conversationalizing discourses of media culture. From the television and radio talk shows of Oprah Winfrey and Jenny Jones to the rap music of P. Diddy, Biggie Smalls and Tupac Shakur to the pseudo-academic books like *The Bell Curve*, *The Hot Zone* and *The Coming Plague*, to self-improvement texts like *Don't Sweat the Small Stuff . . . and It's All Small Stuff*, these examples from popular culture all psychologize, individualize, and seemingly internalize complex social problems, managing the intense feelings of anxiety so much a part of contemporary cultural life. Television talk shows, for example, reduce complex social phenomena to mere personality conflicts between guests, encouraging them to air their differences before staging some kind of denouement or resolution. Histories of oppression are thus put aside as guests argue in and through the details of their private lives, mediated, as they often are, by so-called experts. Racial harmony becomes a relative's acceptance of a "bi-racial" child. Sexual parity is reduced to a spouse publicly rejecting an adulterous partner. Psychologistic explanations for social phenomena reign supreme, and are supported by a burgeoning literature of self-improvement texts, texts that posit poor self-esteem as the preeminent societal ill today. These popular texts and media programs are pivotal in what Deborah

Tannen calls *The Argument Culture* (1998) in which the private is the political, and politics is war by other means.

Identities are thus being formed and re-formed ("produced," following Edward Said [1993]) in this complex social moment, where the "tide of difference" is being met by profound re-narrations of history. It is precisely this kind of rearticulation and recoding that I have called elsewhere "nonsynchrony" (McCarthy, 1998). Here, I have tried to draw attention to how these complicated dynamics operate in debates over identity and curriculum reform, hegemonic cultural assertions in advertising, popular film, and in the conversationalizing discourses of contemporary popular culture as articulated through the mass media. Further, as I have tried to show, these discourses are imbricated in an emergent popular culture industry, one that has radically appropriated the new to consolidate the past. This is the triumph of a nostalgia of the present as "difference" comes under the normalizing logics and disciplinary imperatives of hegemonic power. Diversity, as such, can sell visits to theme parks as well as textbooks. Diversity can sell AT&T and MCI long distance calling cards as well as the new ethnic stalls in the ethereal hearths of the shopping mall. And sometimes, in the most earnest of ways, diversity lights up the whole world and makes it available to capitalism (Klein, 2000).

Popular Culture, Policy and the Pedagogy of Resentment

Importantly and most disturbingly, I wish to note, this kind of disciplined diversity is also increasingly informing – indeed, producing in the Foucauldian sense – social policy, particularly in the area of education, on both the right and left, as evidenced by several key debates now circulating in the refeudalized public sphere in the United States. These debates have had very real material effects on the dispossessed, those quickly losing the (albeit meager) benefits of affirmative action (e.g. California's Proposition 209), bilingual education (e.g. California's Proposition 227 – the so-called "English for the Children" initiative), and the need-based financial aid (e.g. the steady whittling away of Pell Grants). The idea of high-quality (public) education as the great potential equalizer – a good in and of itself – is now being lost to the bitter resents at the heart of contemporary culture, lost to petty market logics and the free-standing subject-positions so enabled by them. This weak kind of diversity, as noted, is encouraged by a consumer capitalism that is entirely linked to the imperatives of resentment explored throughout. In a particularly stark example of this process, Martin Luther King, Jr.'s revolutionary dream of the day when his "four little children will . . . live in a nation where they will not be judged by the color of their skin, but by the content of their character," has been appropriated by right-wing commentators like Shelby Steele and Dinesh D'Souza to contest the advances of affirmative action.

How the discourse of resentment has (explicitly) propelled the conservative agenda here is fairly obvious. A new and seemingly beleaguered middle class is looking to recapture its once unquestioned privilege by advocating "color blind" hiring and acceptance policies (in the case of affirmative action) while forging a seemingly unified – and, of course, White Anglo – cultural identity through restrictive language policies (in the case of bilingual education). Indeed, the consolidation of seamless and coherent subjects so at the heart of contemporary cultural media flows (as explored above) has enabled and encouraged the overwhelming public support and passage of bills like California's Propositions 209 and 227 (in the case of the latter, by a two to one margin of the popular California vote). These evidence the popular feelings of resentment that Fine and Weis so powerfully document among white working-class men in *The Unknown City* (1998).

Yet, these resentments run deep and operate on numerous levels here – hence, the tensions now erupting between and within African Americans and Latinos *vis-à-vis* many such bills. A recent *Time* magazine article entitled "The Next Big Divide?" explores burgeoning conflicts between African Americans and Latinos in Palo Alto over bilingual education, noting that these disputes

> arise in part from frustration over how to spend the dwindling pot of cash in low-income districts. But they also reflect a jostling for power, as blacks who labored hard to earn a place in central offices, on school boards and in classrooms confront a Latino population eager to grab a share of these positions. (Ratnesar, 1997, p. 1)

It has been suggested, in fact, that efforts to institute "Ebonics" as a second language in Oakland, California were prompted by competition for shrinking funds traditionally allotted to bilingual (Spanish) programs. Resentment, spawned by increasing competition for decreasing resources, is key to unraveling the complexities of these struggles, for, as Joel Schumaker tells us, its power transcends racial lines of affiliation pure and simple. Indeed, as Black neoconservative intellectuals and activists like Shelby Steele and Justice Clarence Thomas have shown, resentment cuts at right angles to race as middle-class needs, interests and desires operate to block common affiliation within racially marginalized groups themselves.

Just as importantly the discourse of resentment is also informing more seemingly neoliberal responses to these issues and bills as well. The importance of public education in equalizing the profound injustices of contemporary US American society is increasingly downplayed in favor of discourses that foreground self-interest and possessive individualism. Within neoliberal policy logic, affirmative action, thus, is a good because education will keep dangerous minorities off of "our streets" by subjecting them to a life-time of "civilizing" education, crafting them into good subjects for global cultural capitalism.

These discourses inform the debate on bilingual education, as well, a debate that has similarly collapsed liberal and conservative voices and opinions. Indeed, bilingual education, many argue, should be supported (only) because it will prepare young people for an increasingly polyglot global cultural economy, hence keeping immigrants and minorities off of public assistance, allowing them to compete in an increasingly diverse (in the sense developed above) global community. Cultural arguments are also elided from and within these positions, for, as many so eagerly stress, bilingual education really helps immigrants learn English and become assimilated faster – a bottom-line supported by an ever-present spate of quantitative studies.

Market logics are all-pervasive here and are deeply informed by self-interest and resentment. These forces have shown themselves most clearly in recent decisions to provide less need-based financial aid for higher education to the poor, apportioning the savings to attract more so-called qualified middle-class students (Bronner, 1998). Competition for the "best" students – seemingly without regard for race, class, and gender – has become a mantra for those insensitive to the issue of educational access for the dispossessed. Indeed, why, many argue, should poor minorities take precious slots away from the more qualified wealthy? The resentment of the elite has now come full circle, especially and most ironically, in this moment of unmatched economic wealth for that icy elite of American society. As Jerome Karabel, professor of sociology at UC Berkeley (the site of key roll-backs in affirmative action) comments, "College endowments are at historically unprecedented heights, so the number of need-blind institutions should be increasing rather than decreasing" (p. 16). These are not lean, mean times for all of us. We live in era of unbridled wealth, won in large measure, for the elite through the triumph of resentment and its ability to dictate public policy.

Conclusion

Resentment, in sum, is produced at the level of the popular mass media, at the level of the textual, and the material practices of everyday life. Its implications run deep, across myriad contexts, including public policy that is increasingly defined by the logics of resentment. Thus, those of us on the left, those wishing to help keep, for example, the promise of public education a real one, must question the terms on which we fight these battles. We must question if our responses will further reproduce a discourse with such devastating and wholly regressive implications. As Foucault reminds us, we must choose what discourses we want to engage in, the "games of truth" we want to play. Indeed, what will be our responses to the burgeoning trend of eliminating need-based financial aid policies? What game will we play? And towards what end?

Such questions are crucial and pressing, as this moment is replete with both possibility as well as danger. This period of multinational capital is witness to the ushering in of the multicultural age – an age in which the empire has struck back, and first world exploitation of the third world has so depressed these areas that there has been a steady stream of immigrants from the periphery seeking better futures in the metropolitan centers. Waves of recent migration promise/threaten to radically hybridize the population of the United States. With the rapid growth of the indigenous minority population in the US, there is now a formidable cultural presence of diversity in every sphere of cultural life and in every region of the country. If this is an era of the post, it is also an era of difference – and the challenge of this era of difference is the challenge of living in a world of incompleteness, discontinuity and multiplicity. It requires generating a mythology of social interaction that goes beyond the model of resentment that seems so securely in place in these times. It means that we must take seriously the implications of the best intuition in the Nietzschean critique of resentment as the process of identity formation that thrives on the negation of the other. The challenge is to embrace a politics that calls on the moral resources of all who are opposed to the power block.

This age of difference thus poses new, though difficult, tactical and strategic challenges to critical and subaltern intellectuals as well as activists. A strategy that seeks to address these new challenges and openings must involve as a first condition a recognition that our differences of race, gender, and nation are merely the starting points for new solidarities and new alliances, not the terminal stations for depositing our agency and identities or the extinguishing of hope and possibility. Such a strategy might help us to better understand why in media studies attention to the issue of diversity in schooling and its linkages to the problems of social integration and public policy in modern life is absolutely crucial. Such a strategy might allow us to "produce" new discourses as well, especially and most importantly in this highly fraught and exceedingly fragile moment of historical complexity.

References

Appadurai, A. (1996). *Modernity at Large: Cultural dimensions of globalization*. Minneapolis: University of Minnesota Press.

Asante, M. (1993). *Malcolm X as Cultural Hero and Other Afrocentric Essays*. Trenton: Africa World Press.

Baudrillard, J. (1983). *Simulations*. New York: Semiotext(e).

Bennett, W. (1994). *The Book of Virtues*. New York: Simon & Schuster.

Boorstin, D. (1975). *The Image: A guide to pseudo-events in America*. New York: Atheneum.

Bronner, E. (1998). Universities giving less financial aid on basis of need. *The New York Times*, June 21, A1+.

Dimitriadis, G. (2001). *Performing Identity/Performing Culture: Hip Hop as text, pedagogy and lived practice*. New York: Peter Lang.

Dimitriadis, G. and McCarthy, C. (2001). *Reading and Teaching the Postcolonial: From Baldwin to Basquiat*. New York: Teacher's College Press.

Dimitriadis, G. and McCarthy, C. (in press). Creating a new panopticon: Columbine, cultural studies, and the uses of Foucault. In J. Bratich, J. Parker, and C. McCarthy (eds.), *Governing the Present: Foucault and cultural studies*. New York: SUNY Press.

Ewen, S. (1988). *All Consuming Images: The politics of style in contemporary culture*. New York: Basic Books.

Fine, M. and Weis, L. (1998). *The Unknown City: Lives of poor and working-class young adults.* Boston: Beacon Press.

Giroux, H. (1996). *Fugitive Cultures: Race, violence, and youth.* London: Routledge.

Green, A. (1997). *Education, Globalization and the Nation State.* London: Macmillan.

Grossberg, L. (1992). *We Gotta Get Out of this Place: Popular conservatism and postmodern culture.* New York: Routledge.

Hall, S. (1980). Cultural studies: Two paradigms. *Media, Culture, and Society,* 2, 57–72.

James, C. L. R. (1993). *American Civilization.* Oxford: Blackwell.

Kellner, D. (1993). *Media Culture.* New York: Routledge.

Kenway, J. and Bullen, E. (2001). *Consuming Children: Education–entertainment–advertising.* Philadelphia: Open University Press.

Klein, N. (2000). *No Logo.* London: Flamingo.

Masterman, L. (1990). *Teaching the Media.* New York: Routledge.

McCarthy, C. (1998). *The Uses of Culture: Education and the limits of ethnic affiliation.* New York: Routledge.

Miller, T. (1998). *Technologies of Truth: Cultural citizenship and the popular media.* Minneapolis: University of Minnesota Press.

Murray, C. (1984). *Losing Ground: American social policy, 1950–1980.* New York: Basic Books.

Nietzsche, F. (1967). *On the Genealogy of Morals* (trans. W. Kaufman). New York: Vintage.

Pinderhughes, H. (1993). Down with the program: Racial attitudes and group violence among youth in Bensonhurst and Gravesend. In S. Cummings and D. Monti (eds.), *Gangs: The origins and impact of contemporary youth gangs in the United States.* New York: SUNY Press, pp. 75–94.

Ratnesar, R. (1997). The next big divide? *Time,* December 1, 52.

Said, E. (1993). The politics of knowledge. In C. McCarthy and W. Crichlow (eds.), *Race, Identity and Representation in Education.* New York: Routledge, pp. 306–14.

Steele, S. (1990). *Content of Our Character: A new vision of race in America.* New York: St. Martin's Press.

Steinberg, M. (1996). Cultural history and cultural studies. In C. Nelson and D. P. Gaonkar (eds.), *Disciplinarity and Dissent in Cultural Studies.* New York: Routledge, pp. 103–29.

Steinberg, S. and Kincheloe, J. (eds.) (1997). *Kinderculture: The corporate construction of youth.* Boulder, CO: Westview Press.

Tannen, D. (1998). *The Argument Culture: Moving from debate to dialogue.* New York: Random House.

Vinz, R. (1999). Learning from the blues: Beyond essentialist readings of cultural texts. In C. McCarthy, G. Hudak, S. Miklaucic, and P. Saukko (eds.), *Sound Identities.* New York: Peter Lang, pp. 391–427.

Walcott, D. (1970). *"Dream on Monkey Mountain" and Other Plays.* New York: Noonday Press.

Will, G. (1989). Eurocentricity and the school curriculum. *Baton Rouge Morning Advocate,* December 18, 3.

CHAPTER TWENTY-SIX

Expanding the Definition of Media Activism

Carrie A. Rentschler

"[M]edia attention is itself a political resource."
Edie Goldenberg, from *Making the Papers* (1975)

Political activism around the mass media is on the rise. Some community organizers suggest that an increase in media activism over the past decade is due to the growing frustration of politically progressive organizations who lack consistent and good mainstream news media coverage of their activities, if they receive any at all (Wallack, et al. 1999; Center for Community Change, 1999). Social movement and advocacy organizations are figuring out how to communicate to mass media audiences, how they are institutionalizing strategic media and communications plans; and how to make media work part of their mission. Others – many, in fact – turn to media activism for fundraising. Still others, like victim advocacy organizations and domestic violence coalitions, use the media to publicize services they offer, or to aid people who appear in the news media often, but not from their own choosing, such as victims of violence and disaster.

Media work has become central to advocacy work because of the economic conditions and ideological constraints corporate media conglomerates and their cohorts in corporate public relations create for public action. Social movement advocacy in many ways has to function as a kind of advertising or public relations to compete for media attention. Activists have to draw the media spotlight to important social and political issues through media stunts, visual demonstrations, and very organized media-friendly messages. According to Thomas Streeter (2000), advocacy groups grow in the wedge between corporate and government public relations, where the "regulations, procedures, and venues are in place to allow the Time-Warners, RCAs, and Microsofts of the world to solicit positive press coverage, file petitions with the FCC, and lobby congressional subcommittees" (p. 78). Advocacy groups use these same avenues to lobby, produce press releases and otherwise garner media attention; in essence, they have to compete with corporate advertising in the production and distribution of politicized, media-friendly messages. As Streeter argues, advocates must operate within an arena "circumscribed by the broader goal of corporate organization for which the arena was originally created" (p. 81). Those advocates whose messages *do* appear in mainstream corporate media outlets usually do not push anticorporate agendas or any other agendas which are too system-oppositional. This means that advocates are put into the position of having to dismantle the master's house with the master's tools.

The mass media are tools, but they are also the necessary means for communicating with policy-makers and establishing public debate. For our purposes here, we will define media advocacy in two ways. It is the strategic use of the mass media, and sometimes paid advertising, in support of community organizing to push public policy initiatives (Wallack et al., 1999, p. ix). This kind of advocacy seeks to make some social change through the use of the mass media. But it can also be advocacy directed at the mass media in order to create a more democratic media system (McChesney, 1999; McChesney & Nichols, 2001). In this case, media advocacy doesn't use the tools of the mass media as much as it challenges them. Sometimes these two forms of advocacy intersect. The alternative press offers an example of this. Publications like *The Nation* and Fairness and Accuracy in Reporting's *Extra!* provide a space for thinking outside of the mainstream. These well-established alternative magazines, particularly *The Nation*, are major fora for people calling for media reform. They also provide outlets for social movements to get their messages out to interested, like-minded people. At other times, these two forms of advocacy do not intersect. Many social movements from the political Right to the political left make strategic use of the media without also seeking to change the corporate, profit-oriented structure of the media. They train people in how to draw media attention to their work and how to become regular news sources. Some, as I discuss later, even intervene into journalism education, transforming the professional practices of journalists from the inside. This latter strategy identifies another target for media activism – journalism schools – which most social movements have probably never considered.

As media scholars and citizens working toward more democratic, public-run media systems, we have a lot to learn about the possibilities of using strategic media techniques. We also must recognize the limitations with which media activists are faced. There are few financial resources available to people interested in anticorporate advocacy. The political right has far more access to resources because they are, save for a few, corporate friendly. As a result, they have far more access to the mainstream corporate media. While David Trend (1993) suggests in his article "Rethinking Media Activism" that attitudinal problems account for the left's lack of success with media activism, we should look to the very real constraints facing anyone engaged in anti-corporate activism instead of engaging in more left-bashing. In the meantime, we should not cede the use of these techniques to everyone else.

To this end, this chapter will examine four broad typologies of media activism to expand its definitions and increase the number of possible practices that are available to social movement actors. The four typologies are: media reform movements, the alternative press, flak, and the strategic use of public relations and news writing techniques. The first three have been extensively researched within the field of Media Studies, while the fourth has mostly been developed and researched by nonprofit organizations that train community groups in how to use the media in their organizing. This chapter particularly attends to the fourth typology because of this relative lack of scholarly attention. As I suggest, we often have to look in hard-to-find places to see successful media activism at work, such as in small publications, localized print campaigns, hyper-targeted media outlets, and in emergent new media. After briefly discussing the movement context from which most of the chapter's examples come, the chapter proceeds by covering each of typology in turn. Within each section, I address what the particular type of media activist practice is designed to do, what kinds of effects it can have, and some current examples of each.

I will draw on my own research into the media activist practices of the national crime victim movement and related antiviolence social movement organizations to provide examples within these typologies. The crime victim movement in the US is an unusual social movement. It represents an uneasy confluence of feminists, law-and-order advocates, and the criminal justice system. Like the antipornography movement before it, the crime victim movement defies "left–right" categorization. Despite their contrasting politics, feminist and law-and-order identified victim advocates have the same publicity priorities: they want access to media outlets; they want to provide sources for news; and they want to encourage news stories that promote their specific policy agendas. The movement's relative de-centralization and its marked contentiousness have produced a wide range of media practices that can provide some sense of the breadth and practical processes of media activism in general. As such, the movement provides a number of examples of media activism that do not fall into any neat categories of "Right" and "Left." As media scholars, we can look to the media activism within this movement for examples of techniques that work because of, and sometimes in spite of, political orientation.

Typologies I and II: Media reform movements and the alternative press

Media Studies scholarship on media activism tends to study media reform movements and the alternative press. Some of the most well known work on media activism comes from political economy scholars. Robert McChesney's scholarship, for instance, focuses on the history and current status of broadcast reform movements. His 1994 book *Telecommunications, Mass Media and Democracy* tells the history of the vibrant and contentious 1930s Broadcast Reform Movement around the passage of the 1934 Communications Act. His book *Rich Media, Poor Democracy* pays particular attention to current media reform movements around the future of the Internet, information privacy, micro-power radio, and corporate media conglomeration. McChesney, and other scholars such as Herbert Schiller, George Gerbner, Vincent Mosco, Janet Wasko, and Eileen Meehan, argue that political progressives must make reform of the corporate control of the mass media a central priority in political organizing and policy initiatives. The mass media are a public utility, a set of public spaces that have been "donated" to corporations in the name of the public. As Schiller (1989) argued, culture industries are now the main centers of public symbolic production. They separate the "elemental expressions of human creativity from their group and community origins for the purposes of selling them to those who can pay for them" (p. 31). The culture industries' commodities are our "social glue." The result has been to force cultural producers to think and act like marketers if they want to support themselves.

McChesney (1999; McChesney & Nichols, 2001) and Schiller (1989) both argue that corporate control of the media must be reformed through a broad-based movement of public citizens and cultural producers. Many organizations and emergent Independent Media Centers currently engage in battles over media reform, including Fairness and Accuracy in Reporting, the Media Alliance, MediaChannel, the Center for Digital Democracy, and Citizens for Independent Public Broadcasting, among others. But for the most part, these and other local media watch groups are resource-poor organizations. And because they specifically advocate against corporate media fare, they not surprisingly receive little mainstream media coverage.

In a recent issue of *The Nation*, McChesney and John Nichols present a plan for a coalitional media reform movement. Such a movement requires a broad coalition of diverse political and social movement organizations who can direct their combined forces against the continued corporate consolidation and centralization of the mass media. Such a movement requires three things: they must combine resources and carefully direct their use; they need to launch a massive outreach effort to popularize the issue of media reform; and they need media reform proposals at which to direct advocacy (2001, p. 16). The protests against corporate consolidation of the mass media at the September 2000 meeting of the National Association of Broadcasters (NAB) in San Francisco provide a recent visible example of this kind of activism. With very little mainstream media coverage of this event, and a similar lack of coverage of the protests over the Pacifica radio reorganization in Berkeley, for the majority of the population it is easy to believe that a media reform movement does not even exist (see FAIR, 2000a and 2000b). When anticorporate activism does appear in the mainstream media, it is often drastically misrepresented. Media coverage of the WTO protests in Seattle and Washington, DC, for instance, dismissed activists as unwashed, freakish youth who misunderstand international trade politics (Ackerman, 2000; Coen, 2000).

Activist messages don't appear in the mainstream media very often, and when they do, it is usually after people working behind-the-scenes have put in considerable work advocating for their story. Activist forms of media can appear in unlikely places, like on cable networks or even the nightly news. Some corporate media, like the cable networks Bravo, IFC, Sundance, HBO and Showtime, will broadcast independent documentaries and TV specials co-produced with advocate organizations that otherwise would not see the light of day.[1] Capitalist media like cable networks seek out specialized audiences, and some of those audiences are politically engaged and interested in progressive, independent media productions. Besides these few limited resources for a very small number of independent media productions, most activists must look to alternative press outlets for their media advocacy.

McChesney and Nichol's (2001) article is in fact a good example of the relationship between media reform movements and the alternative press. *The Nation* provides an important forum for the discussion of media reform. It presents politically mobilizing information to a group of readers already predisposed to agree with the need for media reform and other progressive platforms. Some public health and youth advocates make alternative and politically progressive coverage of youth crime and race available to youth groups, high schools, and public health advocacy organizations in the form of magazines, newsletters and websites. Groups such as We Interrupt This Message, Building Blocks for Youth, and the Berkeley Media Studies Group, for instance, have all produced critical and activist-oriented analyses of news media crime coverage. Not only do they critique news media coverage of race and youth crime, they also provide advice to readers for how to create one's own alternative news coverage. As examples of the alternative press, these publications continually mobilize and re-educate the same groups of people, a necessary step in moving people toward social action (see Klandermans and Oegema, 1987). In some ways, this is also the limitation of the alternative press – it reaches those people who are already in the position to be mobilized toward such ways of thinking and acting.

A number of other alternative media practices work on the same basic premise as *The Nation* and other alternative press publications. They provide forums for discussing ideas outside of the mainstream, but in non-news formats such as video, pop art, popular independent music recording and 'zines. Cultural activists have used the Situationist strategy of juxtaposition and other avant-gardist artistic conventions to provide critical commentary on the mainstream media. *AdBusters* magazine, for example, publishes artists' own appropriations of commercial advertising campaigns in the creation of critical non-commercial artistic messages. These artists take the tools of mainstream advertising and put them to different, often dissonant uses. In one issue, an artist used an image of a shrunken Joe Camel, the Camel cigarette mascot, sitting in a hospital bed with an IV in his arm. The accompanying text tells us that Joe Camel is dying from lung cancer from smoking. The ad's use of images that are not normally juxtaposed with each other provides a way of commenting on Camel's corporate and advertising practices that is immediate and visually alluring. Another example is RTmark.com, a website that provides directions for re-programming corporate websites and products. The Barbie Liberation organization used this website to show people how to re-program Mattel's talking Barbie and Ken dolls, so that Barbie spoke in Ken's voice and Ken in Barbie's. They challenged the stereotypical gender norms of these dolls by creating gender-bending Barbies and Kens, using Mattel's own tools.

These and other "culture jamming," independent media practices provide critical commentary on corporate media through the use of existing corporate media tools. Many of these practices operate in the independent media sector, which the corporate media depends on for new ideas and new audiences (Schiller, 1989). One down side is that the mainstream media can point to alternative media outlets to demonstrate that the corporate media system "works" – because it hasn't totally wiped out independent producers. But the corporate media can insure that these independent producers remain relatively cash-poor. And should any independent publication or music label get big enough to even approach competitiveness with the major media, the corporate media will buy them out. Thus, there are real limitations to the alternative media. They have limited reach and they mostly circulate among small groups of like-minded people.

Overall, the media reform movement supports the alternative press, like *The Nation* and FAIR's *Extra!*, but until these alternatives have a distribution base closer to that of major newspapers and magazines, they will tend to circulate mostly within the movement itself. Some alternative media do receive wide circulation; the political Right, however, funds most of them. Funding for the right-wing press greatly outweighs foundation funding for liberal and progressive news sources. Beth Schulman, editor of *In These Times*, found that between 1990 and 1992, five foundations (the John Olin Foundation, the Sarah Mellon Scaife Foundation, the Carthage Foundation, the Lynde and Harry Bradley Foundation, and the Smith-Richardson Fund) provided $2.7 million in grants to four magazines: *American Spectator, The National Interest, The Public Interest* and *The New Criterion*. Unlike the political right, the political left's alternative press is severely underfunded. In Shulman's study, a mere $269,500 in foundation grants went to support four progressive publications: *The Nation, Mother Jones, The Progressive*, and *In These Times*. The foundations that support progressive publications also earmark their money for special uses rather than for general operating costs, which means that this funding does not support the basic costs that go into maintaining the press itself. The right's funding, on the other hand, covers infrastructural costs to insure the longevity of their publications.

The right also has corporate money to work with, unlike the media reform movement and most of the alternative press. Anyone can use the media for strategic ends, but those with money and power have more direct access to mass media corporations than resource-poor organizations. In the US, right-wing movements have made some of the most effective activist uses of the media, in large part due to their ability to mobilize economic and technical resources into communication infrastructures. With the financial support of ultraconservative business elites, like beer magnate Joseph Coors (who funded the Heritage Foundation) and Paul Weyrich (who funded the Free Congress Foundation), and thousands of small donations through direct mail and televangelism, the political right built communication and organizational infrastructures that enabled a right-wing movement to flourish (see Diamond, 1995; Herbst, 1994).

In essence, the right developed a set of alternative communication networks through which everyday people could connect with movement leaders. These networks enable political organizers to tap into potential constituencies' often loosely defined emotions and political sentiments and direct them toward specific political action, electoral campaigns and fundraising goals. Susan Herbst (1994) refers to these networks as back channels. Back channels are "alternative discursive spaces" where political communities come together through interaction with books, periodicals, correspondence and conversation that happen outside of mainstream communication channels. They can tap into constituencies and their social and political sentiments in ways mass mediated communication channels miss, or fail to directly mobilize. As Herbst argues, "within marginal publics, community building is critical." Marginalized political groups (whether marginalization is chosen, forced or imagined, as in the case of the right) create parallel public spaces, where they develop behind-the-scenes communication back channels to develop political community and mobilize political resources (Herbst, 1994, pp. 2–4).

These back channels create alternative discursive spaces that are primarily linguistic rather than geographic. They "circumvent the structures and rules in political communities of various sorts – neighborhoods, cities and nations" (Herbst, 1994, pp. 128–30). As a kind of public sphere, communication back channels have their own "infrastructure of public opinion" (Herbst, 1994, p. 19). They provide the means through which people form public opinions and express them through both mass and interpersonal channels. Communication networks enable people to politically organize outside of, parallel to, against and through mass mediated public debates.

The right has been particularly adept at developing back channels because of how they used their economic resources. Unlike liberal and progressive political donations from the 1970s, which largely went to advocacy groups and social service agencies, right-wing foundations and elite donors' investments readily translated into movement building and political organizing (Bleifuss, 1995; Covington, 1997; Hardisty, 1999, pp. 15–19, 61; Schulman, 1995). The right invested in what Sara Diamond (1995) calls "mobilizing structures": research centers, think tanks, publications, academic fellowships and organization building – in other words, institutions whose sole purpose has been to create publicity.[2]

Typology III: Flak

The right's publicity organizations also enable them to pressure the mainstream media to cover their issues from their sources. This is called flak. In Edward Herman and Noam Chomsky's (1988) propaganda model of the media, flak institutions function as one of five news filters. Flak institutions essentially discipline the mass media through complaint. Thus, flak refers to negative responses directed at the media (p. 26). It can come in the form of letters, phone calls, telegrams, petitions, lawsuits, public speeches, and Congressional hearings among other punitive, threatening actions. Powerful institutions with significant monetary resources can coerce media outlets to change their content, their ideological bent, and/or their personnel. Flak can also be directed at the media's own constituencies, such as advertisers, stockholders, and major sources. As Herman and Chomsky (1988) argue, flak machines "receive respectful attention, and their propagandistic role and links to a larger corporate program are rarely mentioned or analyzed" by the news media (p. 28). Flak institutions can become trusted news sources, because they provide free and regular media commentary and content to news media organizations who favor and rely on consistent and professional input.

Institutions without significant resources, however, can also work as flak institutions, especially if they have the ability to embarrass or morally sanction the media and its corporate advertisers. Resource poor organizations can also make use of current news stories on their respective issues as points of entry into the news media. Parents of Murdered Children (POMC) launched such a flak campaign in 2000, when the Italian clothing company Benetton ran a special "We, On Death Row" magazine insert in *Talk* magazine's February 2000 issue, and a related death penalty advertising campaign in the *New Yorker*, *Vanity Fair* and *Rolling Stone* magazines. POMC is a national murder victim support organization. While they do not take a stand on the death penalty, they do assist parents of murdered children who have an investment in the death penalty. We could not call POMC a progressive political organization but their techniques can nonetheless be put to progressive uses.

Benetton's campaign raised controversy for several reasons. For one, Benetton hired the Milanese photographer Oliviero Toscani (he also photographed their United Colors campaigns) to run their campaign, giving him full artistic control. He took that control and posed as an Italian reporter to gain unlimited access to a high security Missouri state prison. Toscani wrote in a letter to Missouri state officials that the project was being conducted by the National Association of Criminal Defense Lawyers, and that Benetton was simply underwriting the campaign, which was untrue. On February 9, 2000, Missouri's Attorney General sued Benetton for trespass and fraudulent misrepresentation. Another part of the controversy was that Benetton paid the death row inmates they used in the photo essay $1,000 each (Chen, 2000b). Additionally, because of the controversy over the campaign's subject matter, major news media covered Benetton's campaign. Benetton certainly succeeded in getting their provocative campaign covered in spaces other than those bought for them (Lloyd, 2001).

In the campaign, death row inmates are photographed alongside their name, birth date, sentence and execution date. Benetton prevented inmates from expressing remorse or talking about their crimes (Chen, 2000a). Instead, the campaign's content includes elements that humanize the inmates' lives while on death row, which has raised the ire of some surviving family members of homicide victims. Inmates are asked what their life is like, what they would be doing if they were free, how they were treated as children, what death row smells and sounds like, and so on.

Parents of Murdered Children launched a major letter writing and phone campaign in response to the Benetton campaign, after surviving family members of some of the victims killed by inmates serving time on death and that appeared in the Benetton campaign saw billboards of the inmates. For instance, one couple in Kentucky saw a billboard of the man convicted for torturing and killing their teenage son. POMC also launched their own billboard campaign, a photo collage of murder victims with the caption "Behind Every Murderer is the Face of an Innocent Victim." Parents of Murdered Children succeeded in convincing *Rolling Stone* magazine not to run the ad campaign, and they convinced Sears, Roebuck, and Co. to pull their Benetton clothing line. This was a huge blow to Benetton because Sears had agreed to incorporate their clothing line into 800 of their superstores. Benetton had less than 200 outlets in total prior to the Sears deal. POMC could also succeed in their campaign because they hold the moral high ground; they represent victims' plight, and in the political context of the United States, it is difficult to publicly challenge victims. They also made use of the mainstream news coverage of the controversy around the campaign as well as Missouri's lawsuit against the company. In this way, a relatively resource poor organization could make use of several openings in the media to launch their own related flak campaign.

POMC also runs a public relations campaign called Murder is Not Entertainment, which functions as another flak mechanism. They directed one of their campaigns at Ebay, the large Internet auction site, for its agreement to host auction sites for serial killer memorabilia, crime scene and autopsy photos and other artifacts associated with murder. The campaign encouraged people to boycott Ebay, bring petitions to local churches and schools, and to write Rosie O'Donnell of the "Rosie O'Donnell Show" (she is a supporter of Ebay), John Walsh of Fox TV's "America's Most Wanted," and talk show hosts Montel Williams and Sally Jesse Rafael.

Clearly there are drawbacks and limitations to flak. POMC could succeed because they hold the moral high ground around issues of victimization and innocence. They also create media-friendly stories of victims of violence and their suffering and had a clear platform already prepared for them in the news. Anticorporate media reformers, on the other hand, do not have media-friendly messages, and they do not have good heroes and villains with which to provide desirable news stories. There are also very few news stories on corporate owner-ship of the media onto which media reformers can piggyback. For some move-ments, these elements can be developed. Partly this is a matter of learning how to tell stories in a way that does not compromise one's activist goals and yet will still garner news media attention. Such stories require drama, good visuals, and a clear story line about individuals fighting the odds (see Ryan, 1991, pp. 75–94). But in other ways, this is a matter best left to the exploration of other strategic media options.

Typology IV: Techniques of strategic media advocacy

For a lot of us, we do not have ready access to corporate resources and our issues are not regularly covered in the news media. In these cases, we have to look to the power of organized people and their abilities to draw attention to and advo-cate for important political and social issues in other ways. Many resource-poor organizations discover that they have the ability to attract media attention to their causes under the right conditions, like Parents of Murdered Children did (Goldenberg, 1975). According to Charlotte Ryan (1991), the first goal of media activism is to turn the news into contested terrain (p. 4). This means telling a different story about public issues that speaks from the perspective of everyday people in order to change how issues are politicized (see Bennett & Edelman, 1985). By and large, this goal aims to turn social movement organizations into long-term sources for the news media – or at least making sure one's foot is in the door so that you can offer the news alternative narratives on social problems than the ones they typically offer.

For social movement organizations, doing media work means directing the news spotlight onto their issues and how they frame them. As Walter Lippman (1922) argued, "[The press] is like the beam of a searchlight that moves restlessly about, bringing one episode and then another out of darkness and into vision" (excerpted from *Public Opinion* in Davis, 1994, p. 302). Social movement organ-izations can garner the news spotlight, but they first need to know how to do so, and how to do so repeatedly. Additionally, organizations must figure out what they want to communicate to the news media before drawing their attention. Many organizations fail to sustain media activism because they fail to plan out their activist strategies and how those strategies fit into their overall mission (Ryan, 1991). Others fail because they have a message that does not resonate with other like-minded people (Advocacy Institute, 1992; Center for Com-munity Change, 1998, 1999). With these limitations in mind, let's turn to some strategies that work. This section will address three sets of strategies: becoming news sources, training journalists, and synthetic techniques that cut across categories.

Becoming news sources

To become successful at media activism, social movement organizations must institutionalize media strategies into their day-to-day work. In other words, they must begin to function as credible information and news sources. Rather than treating media activism as something that gets added on to other work, it has to become central to the overall mission of the movement. Doing so will not change the episodic and disconnected nature of news stories, but it will help social movement organizations establish themselves as viable news sources. To appear more regularly in the news, especially in response to individual cases of larger social problems, is to start to change the way those social problems are discussed and alleviated (Klein et al., 1997).

A majority of the media work in the national crime victim movement trains advocacy organizations to become reliable news sources. News and entertainment media organizations have for a long time tapped visible victim advocacy organizations for stories on crime and crime victims. Mark Fishman (1980) refers to this as "bureaucratic affinity" where media institutions tap other officially recognized, credible institutions to go to for information, and more importantly, for the ideological frames they provide for constructing viable media narratives. News workers go to government and private agencies to produce news stories out of practical necessity: bureaucracies produce regular and generally reliable information because they are organized to do so, especially government agencies. Private institutions, on the other hand, must organize themselves to function like bureaucracies: to produce dependable and credible information and, most importantly, establish long-term relationships with news reporters.

Victim advocacy organizations constitute part of a whole network of institutions that share and exchange information and resources in the production and distribution of media representations on crime and crime victims. Many of these organizations are just now reorganizing themselves to work more proactively with the news media in particular – they are learning how to bring their stories directly to the news media rather than waiting for the news media to come to them. They can provide information, position statements and research to interested news media. As an example, Karen Jeffreys, Communications Director for the Rhode Island Coalition Against Domestic Violence (RICADV) has created perhaps the most well-organized and efficient communications strategy in the field of domestic violence advocacy. RICADV has fully incorporated communications and media work into their overall mission, establishing themselves as a reliable news source on domestic violence in Rhode Island. They develop yearly media calendars, as well as successful cross-media publicity campaigns. They provide an extensive media training manual to their advocates and sister organizations. Additionally, they produced a manual for journalists, which provides data on domestic violence, advice on how to cover domestic violence murders, lists of who to go to in the field of domestic violence advocacy as sources, and a list of suggested language and story approaches. The manual for journalists followed a study RICADV commissioned on news coverage of domestic violence murders demonstrated that Rhode Island newspapers were uneducated in the issue of domestic violence. Through these measures, RICADV has become a trustworthy news source. They have received extensive news coverage from across the state of Rhode Island, in print and TV news, all as a direct result of their media campaign strategies and planning.

For the domestic violence movement, *not* doing media activism has not been an option because of the concerted right-wing backlash against feminist anti-violence organizing and research. In 1996, around the O. J. Simpson trial, five national domestic violence organizations formed a media advocacy project to address the misconceptions of domestic violence that were publicized through the trial. The result of this project has been a nation-wide media campaign, backed by public opinion studies that demonstrate the campaign's successes (see Klein et al., 1997). The Family Violence Prevention Fund (FVPF) and the National Coalition Against Domestic Violence (NCADV) worked with a social justice-identified public relations firm in Washington, DC, called PR Solutions and directed by Lisa Lederer, to develop this media advocacy campaign. Lederer explained the project to me in a phone interview.

> The media advocacy project started around O.J., around race, and things that were just wrong. Correcting these wrong impressions [of domestic violence, and this case in particular] was an opportunity to get our own messages out there, to correct false impressions. There's also a real backlash against the movement, especially by women, which you may already be aware of. They are out there whenever Congress is debating legislation having to do with domestic violence. They misread the data on domestic violence. Being quiet and doing your work at a program or shelter is not enough. You have to be an advocate as well. That's difficult because the movement is consumed by providing services, and when you're turning people away [from over-crowded shelters], you don't have time to think about the media. . . . There's a siege mentality in the movement; the feeling that everyone is against us. It's hard. There's a different culture between media and service providers. Advocates are trained in services not sound bites. (phone interview, January 31, 2001)

As part of this work, the Family Violence Prevention Fund published "The Backlash Book: A Media and Political Guide for Battered Women's Advocates," a training manual that teaches advocates about the tactics of the new right, their media resources and the practical techniques battered women's advocates can use to counter the right's backlash against domestic violence organizing. The manual emphasizes that advocates should build a presence in the media, and it provides the following to help them do that: practical talking points for spokespeople, information on how to use reliable data on domestic violence to counter the right, and tactics for controlling interview situations and developing local allies. This manual is unusual in that it trains advocates in how to criticize the media and the right's tactics at the same time as it trains them in practical strategies. Most training materials focus on the latter to the exclusion of the former. The fact that FVPF's manual includes this extra training speaks to the position domestic violence advocacy occupies *vis-à-vis* the resources of the right.

Organizations within the crime victim movement use other strategies as well to bolster their status as news sources. Some provide interested news media with access to survivors of violence and victim advocates who are willing to talk with the media. Over the past few years, some national victim advocacy organizations, like the National Center for Victims of Crime, provide less and less news media and talk show access to victims and victim advocates because of reports of their insensitive treatment. They are also learning how to negotiate with the media when victims want to be interviewed with the help of an advocate.

National organizations within the crime victim movement also function as information and news sources. They produce and distribute media training manuals, videos and seminars. They show advocates and survivors of violence how to be media spokespeople, how to write press releases and produce public service announcements. They train not only themselves and emergency workers (like police, paramedics, hospital staff, legal advocates) in these media strategies, they also direct these training materials to journalists. All of these materials teach advocates about how the news production process works so that they can assist victims who are being approached by the news media, learn how to place news stories and learn how to speak to the media. Most of these training aids teach advocates about news basics such as: deadlines, how stories are developed, news pegs and leads, and the jobs and functions of different news personnel.

All of these techniques demystify how the news media function and what the typical news production process is like. They can succeed in training activists in how to make themselves and their materials media-ready, but there is no guarantee that taking these steps will result in news coverage. This is one of the limitations of becoming a news source – there is no guarantee that the news will use you and your perspective, or if they do, it may not be in the way you had intended or preferred. Ultimately, advocates have little control over the final news product, even when they do work as news sources. The crime victim movement has proven that it can function as a reliable news source, and since some of their messages support the criminal justice system and seek to improve its efficiency, they have pretty reliable access to mainstream news media because they also have close relationships with the criminal justice system.

Training journalists

Another set of practical media training techniques are directed at working journalists and journalism schools. Most of this training teaches journalists how to alter their professional practices and their demeanor on the job. In regards to crime coverage, this training challenges journalists to take a different approach to covering crime than the typical slash-and-burn treatment, where on-the-scene video images capture victim's blood stains and crying people have cameras and microphones shoved in their faces. Intervening at the level of journalism education can actually prevent or at least directly challenge typical journalistic practices. Most of this intervention, however, does not directly challenge the topics the news media covers, or the overall narratives the news media tend to tell.

Victim advocates have pushed the field of journalism to become more reflexive about its coverage of crime and disaster, especially towards those supposedly most affected by the coverage: the victims. For journalism, this is also partially a practical concern. Many news and entertainment media organizations use victim advocacy organizations for access to victims as sources, and for official spokespeople on criminal justice legislation. As a field long concerned with the appearance of objectivity and the meaning of its own professionalism, journalism education began to develop victim-centered training protocols for journalism students in concert with victim advocacy organizations in the early 1990s. There are two educational goals of victim-centered journalism education: (1) training journalists in how to be more empathic in their interactions with victims and their subsequent news writing; and (2) studying journalists as victims of the process of covering violence. This kind of education in journalism teaches students how to sensitively interact with victims while also psychologically preparing them for the experience of repeatedly witnessing scenes of violence. Each victim-centered journalism program combines these two training goals.

Trauma curricula are integrated into existing news writing and media ethics courses. These curricula frame violence and trauma as issues of professional ethics: how one conducts oneself on the job depends upon journalists' abilities to recognize signs of trauma in victims and to learn how to speak with them in an empathic manner. Students learn how to speak with victims and survivors in a way that encourages their participation in news interviews and grants them some level of control over the interaction. They learn how to encourage victim participation through the manipulation of minute details in interpersonal communication. Students are also encouraged to recognize victims' rights to control the interview. They learn how to ask victims if they want to be interviewed at all, how to ask general questions first, and how to let victims speak for as long as they want. Trauma training teaches journalism students how to interpret victim behavior and how to ostensibly give some control over to victims in the interview process. Working journalists have begun to receive similar training. Professional organizations, such as the National Press Photographers Association, and news media, such as Oklahoma City's *Daily Oklahoman* and Denver's *Rocky Mountain News*, have respectively produced booklets and tip sheets for news workers and news media organizations in how to cover disaster and crime in ways less emotionally injurious to victims and journalists.

For victims and victim advocates, victim-centered journalism education represents an intervention into victims and survivors' roles in the news making process. It also represents the institutionalization of a victim perspective on crime and violence reporting within journalism schools. The crime victim movement's success in helping to develop these curricula suggests that other advocacy movements could also intervene into journalism education in some way. They could also teach journalists different ways of covering public issues and why doing so would benefit many people. But journalists need to know how to do this through practical techniques. They need to know that there are alternative ways of covering issues like crime and violence, including the use of alternative news sources. Imagine if journalists first called up the flak groups We Interrupt This Message or the Berkeley Media Studies Group when they covered stories on race and youth crime. If journalism students could learn to look for altern- ative news sources, and could learn to ask questions that help mobilize broad- based social action, journalism might begin to look very different. Of course, this would also depend on their editors' willingness to accept alternative news sources.

Strategic techniques that cut across categories

Another set of strategies utilizes newer entertainment media forms and com- bines them with more steadfast forms of media action, such as public service announcements. Some social activists are beginning to explore the possibilities of creating synthetic media campaigns that will reach audiences that most media activism misses. Additionally, these techniques are being used to produce media content that seeks to change people's norms, beliefs and practices – in other words, mobilizing information that does not readily appear as such. Some advocacy organizations have produced completely new media advocacy campaigns through the use of popular media styles and formats, like soap operas and popular music. These campaigns offer unique messages in styles that appeal to audiences on more levels than just that of information gathering. These cam- paigns can also more readily target social action messages to particular audiences, based on cultural differences, ethnic differences, gender-specific needs, neigh- borhood and city differences, and so on.

The Family Violence Prevention Fund has blazed the trail in the use of these synthetic and popular media strategies. In 1998, they developed a 12-part radio serial campaign called "It's Your Business" directed at African-American com- munities around the US. Unlike most one-time radio public service announce- ments, the series contained twelve 90-second story parts, narrated by the main character, a talk show host by the name of "Ma Bea" played by actress Lynne Thigpen (who plays a character on the TV drama "The District") and with music by Stevie Wonder and Babyface. The campaign used popular entertain- ment media forms – soap opera narrative style, popular music, and recognizable and respected entertainers – to deliver antiviolence prevention information par- ticularly directed at young African-American men. According to Richard Wray's (2000) dissertation on the campaign, freelance writers experienced in writing dramatic materials for African-American audiences wrote the scripts. UniWorld Group, Inc., the world's largest African-American marketing agency, recorded and produced the series. And the American Urban Radio Network, a national chain of African-American-owned radio stations distributed the series, with the Ad Council, to radio stations (p. 9).

For all practical purposes, this was a well-designed and well-distributed radio campaign. The goal of the campaign was to encourage young men to speak to each other about domestic violence and to challenge abusive behaviors they see in other men. The campaign's focus on prevention also sets it apart from other media advocacy work. Most victim-oriented media advocacy still tends to publicize the problem of domestic violence and offer hotline numbers without offering direct prevention information. The "It's Your Business" social drama campaign sought to change norms, beliefs and practices related to domestic violence in individuals who interact with those directly involved in abuse, in a culturally-specific format (see Wray, 2000, pp. 7–9). It combined mobilizing information and cultural messages in more popular entertainment media forms.

Evaluations of the radio serial, however, found that overall it failed to have a substantial impact, but not because of any apparent limitations of the serial drama itself (Wray, 2000). Radio stations were unwilling to play the spots because of their length, and because of their need to sell those spots to commercial advertisers. Many stations that had agreed to run the spots didn't, and those that did ran them sporadically and in undesirable late-night spots (interview with Kelly Mitchell-Clark, Acting Communications Director, Family Violence Prevention Fund, January 17, 2001). As the first national dramatic series dedicated to the delivery of a specific health message, the "It's Your Business" campaign established the next direction in public service announcements. But without commercial backing – or, more importantly, the combined efforts of media reform and new prevention information – these campaigns won't get off the ground. The resources to do this work still need to be mobilized. But the thinking behind this campaign offers important guidance to advocates who are looking to explore alternative media formats and who want to appeal to media audiences on many different levels. This campaign suggests that news media formats may reach mass audiences, but they do not necessarily move people.

Conclusion

The mass media are a contested terrain, and as such, they can be utilized to different ends than those imagined by their corporate owners. As media studies scholars, we can look to the media activist practices of existing social movements, like the national crime victim movement and related anti-violence social movements, for models to shape the future of media activism. Many of these techniques aim to turn the news into more contested terrain, where social movements can serve as powerful news sources and steer public debate on important public issues. Others combine techniques from a host of entertainment media conventions, such as soap opera drama formats and popular music, to speak to populations particularly at risk about violence and oppression in ways news media formats simply fail to address. Still others seek to intervene in the training of young journalism students in hopes that they will learn to produce different kinds of news stories before they are inundated with corporate news imperatives. And still others train young people how to analyze news coverage of youth violence and their biases against youth of color, in addition to training them how to create their own news coverage of issues important them.

As media studies scholars, we can provide examples of these media activist practices and distill their basic techniques in order to direct more attention to more democratic and public-spirited visions of the world. We can point to resources and critical practices that can be used by coalition-based social movements to link up media reform practices with other social justice practices. Charlotte Ryan argues in her book *Prime Time Activism*, that

> To be useful to social movement organizers, theoretical models must embody a tension between constraints and possibilities; they must acknowledge the power of the social forces lined up against social movements, and yet allow – not the certainty, but the possibility of – change. In relation to media, specifically, the models must recognize that modern mass media permit little input from *the masses*, i.e. mass media opportunities are very limited for those of us not representing powerful political, social, and economic groups or institutions. Yet the models must allow that the collective efforts of social movements (as opposed to individual of isolated efforts) could move the mass media in more democratic directions. Without denying the power lined up against us, are there aspects of media organizations which we can use to push for fuller and more diverse coverage? Are there ways we can mobilize journalists who share our criticisms of mass media? Are there better ways to think about the interplay between mass media and public opinion? Can single victories in gaining access accumulate to create pressure for broader structural change? Can social movements achieve any control of these largely monopolized media? (p. 11)

The media activist practices discussed in this chapter suggest that the means and abilities exist for us to answer "Yes!" to each of Ryan's questions. There is much work to do. There are many resources yet to be mobilized. There are connections that must be made between democratic media reforms and other social justice movements. But the human resources and capacities currently exist for us to undertake this work. And it is our job to remind others that it is possible.

Notes

1 For example, Barbara Trent's documentary film "The Panama Deception" on the US invasion of Panama was broadcast on the cable network Bravo after PBS refused to air it. As another example, HBO co-produced four TV specials on victim issues with the National Center for Victims of Crime, including one on new victim–offender mediation programs.

2 The right wing's power and efficacy comes from the tangible investments they make in funding their institutions' infrastructural needs. According to one report, right-wing fundraising continues

to be invested into research institutions, policy, and activist training. Between 1992 and 1994, right-wing foundations spent $210 million to support policy and institutional reforms, out of the $300 million available to them through grants. $16.3 million of the $210 million financed alternative media outlets, flak institutions and right-wing public affairs programming (Covington, 1997, p. 5).

References

Ackerman, S. (2000). Prattle in Seattle: WTO coverage misrepresented issues, protests. *Extra! Newsletter of Fairness and Accuracy in Reporting*, January/February. Online at www.fair.org/extra/0001/wto-prattle.html.

Advocacy Institute (1992). *Telling Your Story: A guide to preparing advocacy case studies*. Washington, DC: Advocacy Institute.

Bennett, W. L. and Edelman, M. (1985). Towards a new political narrative. *Journal of Communication*, August, 156–71.

Bleifuss, J. (1995). Building plans. *In These Times*, July 10, 12–13.

Center for Community Change (1998). *How to Tell and Sell The Story of Your Work Part II: A guide to developing effective messages and good stories about your work*. Washington, DC: Center for Community Change.

Center for Community Change (1999). *How to Tell and Sell Your Story: A guide to media for community groups and other nonprofits* (2nd edn.). Washington, DC: Center for Community Change.

Chen, H. H. (2000a). Death row fashion ads spark outrage. *APBnews.com*, January 10.

Chen, H. H. (2000b). Victims' parents blast Benetton death row ads. *APBnews.com*, February 16.

Coen, R. (2000). For press, magenta hair and nose rings defined protests. *Extra! Newsletter of Fairness and Accuracy in Reporting*, July/August. Online at www.fair.org/extra/0007/imf-magenta.html.

Covington, S. (1997). *Moving a Public Policy Agenda: The strategic philanthropy of conservative foundations*. Washington, DC: National Committee for Responsive Philanthropy.

Davis, R. (1994). *Politics and the Media*. Englewood Cliffs, NJ: Prentice-Hall.

Diamond, S. (1995). *Roads to Dominion: Right-wing movements and political power in the United States*. New York: Guilford Press.

Diamond, S. (1998). *Not by Politics Alone: The enduring influence of the Christian right*. New York: Guilford Press.

Fairness and Accuracy in Reporting (FAIR) (2000a). Activism update: Over 1,000 march against NAB: Corporate media ignore demonstrations against corporate media, September 26. Online at www.fair.org/activism/nab-update.html.

Fairness and Accuracy in Reporting (FAIR) (2000b). Action alert: San Francisco Chronicle gives short shrift to NAB protests, October 2. Online at www.fair.org/activism/nab-chronicle.html.

Fishman, M. (1980). *Manufacturing the News*. Austin: University of Texas Press.

Goldenberg, E. (1975). *Making the Papers*. Lexington, MA: Lexington Books.

Hardisty, J. (1999). *Mobilizing Resentment: Conservative resurgence from the John Birch Society to the Promise Keepers*. Boston: Beacon Press.

Herbst, S. (1994). *Politics at the Margin: Historical studies of public expression outside the mainstream*. Cambridge: Cambridge University Press.

Herman, E. and Chomsky, N. (1988). *Manufacturing Consent: The political economy of the mass media*. New York: Pantheon Books.

Klandermans, B. and Oegema, D. (1987). Potentials, networks, motivations, and barriers: Steps towards participation in social movements. *American Sociological Review*, 52 (August), 519–31.

Klein, E., Campbell, J., Soler, E., and Ghez, M. (1997). *Ending Domestic Violence: Changing public perceptions/halting the epidemic*. Thousand Oaks, CA: Sage.

Lloyd, J. (2001). Come one: Look at me! *New Statesman*, January 29, 130(4,522), 13–16.

McChesney, R. (1994). *Telecommunications, Mass Media, and Democracy: The battle for control of US broadcasting, 1928–1935*. New York: Oxford University Press.

McChesney, R. (1999). *Rich Media, Poor Democracy*. Urbana, IL: University of Illinois Press.

McChesney, R. and Nichols, J. (2001). The making of a movement: Getting serious about media reform. *The Nation*, January 7/14, 11–17.

Ryan, C. (1991). *Prime Time Activism: Media strategies for grassroots organizing*. Boston: South End Press.

Schiller, H. (1989). *Culture, Inc.* New York: Oxford University Press.

Schulman, B. (1995). Foundations for a movement: How the right wing subsidizes its press. *Extra! Newsletter of Fairness and Accuracy in Reporting*, March/April. Available online at www.fair.org/extra/9503/right-press-subsidy.html.

Streeter, T. (2000). What is an advocacy group, anyway? In M. Sussman and G. Rossman (eds.), *Advocacy Groups and the Entertainment Industry*. Westport, CT: Praeger.

Trend, D. (1993). Rethinking media activism: Why the left is losing the culture war. *Socialist Review*, Summer, 5–33.

Wallack, L., Woodruff, K., Dorfman, L., and Diaz, I. (1999). *News for a Change: An advocate's guide to working with the media*. Thousand Oaks, CA: Sage.

Wray, R. J. (2000). Alternative explanations: Examining exposure recall, selective perception, and response bias in the evaluation of a domestic violence prevention campaign. Dissertation, University of Pennsylvania.

Further reading

Summan, M. S. and Rossman, G. (eds.) (2000). *Advocacy Groups and the Entertainment Industry*. Westport, CT: Praeger.

Wallack, L., Dorfman, L., Jernigan, D., and Themba, M. (1993). *Media Advocacy and Public Health: Power for prevention*. Newbury Park, CA: Sage.

CHAPTER TWENTY-SEVEN

Realpolitik and Utopias of Universal Bonds
For a Critique of Technoglobalism

Armand Mattelart
Translated by Samira Hassa

For a long time, the project of international space as an exclusive construction of nation-states blurred the role of the project of a "single workshop" and a "universal mercantile Republic" formulated in 1776 by Adam Smith. Various factors favored a vision of movement towards worldwide unification as the result of an interstate dialogue. These included the development of modern nationalism which defined territory as the foundation of the sovereignty and the imaginary community and the forms adopted by the imperial domination of the European powers, then of the United States, and finally the Cold War. The end of bipolar tension, together with the reinforcement of trade links in the configuration of the world-space, modified the topology of its actors. The generalized interconnection of societies, of their economies and cultures, through information and communication networks, meant a qualitative jump in the multi-age-old trajectory of the ante-Babel idea of a "universal community" (Mattelart, 2000a, 2000b).

The concept of globalization appeared in order to understand this moment in the history of the worldwide integration process. Borrowed from the English language by most of the other languages, this term aspires to cover the unification process of the economic field and, by excessive extrapolation, to report on the general situation of the planet and its future. Indeed nobody can deny that the term "globalization" embraces a set of new realities destined to deeply change the forms of universal social bonds. But it also refers to an ideological scheme, or a particular concept of the world. It is one of these loaded terms that contribute to confusing the understanding of the complexity of new ways of interaction and transaction between the societies composing the planet. Rebuilding the genealogy of this terminology is important if one does not want to see an increase in the difficulties of distinguishing the fanciful from the realistic in a field already widely open to mythology.

The Symbol of the Global Community: The "Twilight" Thesis

The compound nouns formed with the adjective "global" made their timid appearance in the sixties. Until then, they had been the domain of the Pentagon military strategists who applied them to the Soviet superpower, the "global enemy." During the space race Marshall McLuhan launched the expression "Global Village" (McLuhan & Fiore 1968) and then applied the notion to draw some conclusions about the Vietnam War. This first live-on-TV war demonstrated, according to him, the ability of the electronic image to make history. The power of TV set up a "veritable global Communism," much more authentic than the one claimed by the so-called Communist regimes. The electronic link would propel the backward countries towards development. The war impulse would give way to a pacified world (McLuhan & Fiore, 1968). This techno-determinism ignored the complexity of the cultures and societies in which the messages landed.

Parallel to this, geopolitics forged the notion of "Global Society." Zbigniew Brzezinski speculated on the evolution of the confrontation between blocs under the effects of the "technotronic revolution," resulting from the convergence of computer, telecommunications and TV (Brzezinski, 1969). His central argument: the expansion of information and communication networks would speed up the movement toward world unity; mastery of information and cultural resources would play an ever greater strategic role in defining world power; "network diplomacy" would take the place of "gunboat diplomacy"; the planet would therefore become a "Global Society." But up to now, the only country which, thanks to its ubiquitous power, deserved the name of "Global Society" was the United States, because it communicated more than any other society. US American society would become the lighthouse which would light the way for other nations. In political terms, it meant that from now on, one could no longer speak of the cultural imperialism of the United States *vis-à-vis* the rest of the world – a theme that would however, mobilize numerous theories and movements critical of American hegemony, during the 1970s. American cultural industries and fashions were in fact naturally universal, and offered models of life, behavior and organization to imitate. The "global society" which took shape on the world level would not be anything but the extrapolation of this archetype born and achieved in the United States. In fact, Brzezinski expounded the "twilights" or "ends" thesis that US American political science had been peddling for about 10 years, notably in Seymour Martin Lipset's "Political Man" (1959) and Daniel Bell's *The End of Ideology* (1960): the end of politics, the end of the ideology, the end of class distinctions, the end of confrontations, the end of the commitment of the intellectuals, and therefore, the end of intellectuals and of critical theory.

On the trade community side, the US management theoretician, Peter Drucker, hastened to designate the new era as the Global Shopping Center era, represented, according to him, by IBM's production and distribution networks (Drucker, 1971). The nation-state became the main enemy starting in the early seventies: accused of being too big for the small problems of existence. It was also accused of becoming too small for the big problems (Bell, 1979). These following three earlier hypotheses on the world evolution remain essential to understand the stock of underlying beliefs in the contemporary uses of the "global" semantic.

The Network Enterprise: A cybernetic vision of the world

The introduction of the notion of globalization occurred in the eighties, under the auspices of geo-economy and trade pragmatism, rather than those of geo-politics and the speculations of sociologists and political scientists. It arose from an evolution in the management of some transnational firms and the globalization of the financial sphere, the only field of the international economy to realize in real time the generalized interconnection of its activities and its information and communication networks. Before the end of the decade, this comprehensive vision, born in the heart of geo-finance, had impregnated the whole economic field and greatly increased its audiences. The global scale inspired a doctrine of company organization of networking extrapolated into the foundation of the reorganization of the planet, and presented as being in the interest of all. Since then, it has been relayed by a vast transnational network of management sciences education, bestsellers on re-engineering workshops, lobbying and trade associations. The global business class or community has not stopped naturalizing notions that are used by all of them for naming the world. The age of networks follows the hierarchical model of Fordism and opens the way to the "network company." The global and "relational" firm is an answer to an organic structure in which each part is supposed to serve the whole. Guaranteeing the fluidity, internal as well as externally oriented communication has to be omnipresent. Any "inter-operational" default between the parts, any failure in the free flow of exchange, involves the risk of seizing up the system. Communication has been thus ennobled in meeting the theories of organization. A watchword rules over this new logic of the company: "integration." This word expresses the cybernetic managers' vision of the world in terms of integration of geographical scales, but also of conception, production and consumption, and even between separate spheres of activities. One can think, for instance, of the unrestrained race toward synergy between the container and contained industries, hardware and the software. Local, national and international scales are not compartmentalized levels anymore, but in interaction. The consumer loses his passive agent status and is now promoted to the rank of "co-producer" or "pro-consumer," according to this revealing semantic marriage.

Global Lifestyle

The big multimedia groups and the networks of the global advertising agencies contributed greatly to the construction of techno-globalism throughout the eighties, the blessed period of the growth of the communicational myth. Through their instrumental vision of culture, there began to be talk of "cultural convergence and the end of the cultural heterogeneity" – extending the "ends" speeches (end of the social, of politics, of history and of ideology). Let us cite, as illustrative, this extract from promotional literature which accompanied the mega-mergers of these companies and their sagas of conquest of the world market, often with major failures, for instance, the one of the emblematic Maxwell group: "We are experiencing an era of global communications. Scientists and technologists have achieved what statesmen and the military tried unsuccessfully for a long time to achieve: the global empire. Capital markets, products and services, management and manufacturing/production techniques all became naturally global. As a result, companies are increasingly thinking that they have to compete in the global marketplace all over the world. This new development emerges at the same time when global technologies are transforming information and communication" (Saatchi & Saatchi, 1986). Aside from the megalomania of this assertion, it is over this corporate notion of globalization that the fate of a battle for the interpretation of history is being decided. The presupposed notions of this prose, which creates the image of a firm, have been explained by a marketing and management theorist: "The time of regional or national differences is far behind us. Differences due to culture, norms, and structures are remains of the past. Convergence – the trend of anything to become like any other – is pushing the market towards a global community." Even more clearly: "Individual desires and behaviors tend more and more and everywhere to evolve the same way. The subject can be Coca Cola, microprocessors, jeans, movies, pizzas, beauty products or drills" (Levitt, 1983a, 1983b). InfoTech, the foundation of the "Republic of technology" allows the coming of the "converging commonality," this homogeneous space of trade exchange. One does not deny the existence of segmented markets. One postulates, however, that these segments obey more of a global logic than a national one. Groups of similar persons who reside in different countries can have the same needs and demands for the same products. There are more similarities between groups living in certain neighborhoods of Milan, Paris, Stockholm, São Paulo and New York than between a Manhattan and a Bronx inhabitant. Hence the decision of elaborating transfrontier typologies of lifestyles or "sociocultural mentalities" that gather and classify individuals in *consumption communities* according to their life conditions, value systems, priorities, tastes and norms. Thus, segmentation and globalization appear to be the two facets of the same process that lead the world towards this above-mentioned community. Brought by the Internet, the segmentation of the consumption field – which I call tailoring of consumption – progresses as fast as the improvement of computerized data bases and other *mapping* technologies or cartographies of socio–eco–cultural targets (Mattelart, 1991). This so-called global culture searches for universals. Talk about the "unique market of images" bases itself on the "capitalization of universally recognized references and cultural symbols." If there is a "cultural convergence of consumers" or a confluence of attitudes and behaviors towards a "global lifestyle," it is because of previous consumer education investments that have been distilled with the passing of years by commercials, movies and programs, particularly the ones from the USA, considered as "natural supports/media of universality." This media-alphabetization to the common global denominator laid down the premises of McLuhan's "Global Village." This phenomenon was perfected by the multiplication of flows driven by business trips, tourism, cuisine, fashion, or interior decoration. But the most important factor in the acceleration of the development of a single global lifestyle "remains the English language – homogenizing agent above all else – that asserted itself as the universal language" (Naisbitt and Aburdene, 1990, p. 140). The logo of such firms or global brands as Marlboro, Levi-Strauss, Pepsi, IBM, McDonald's, and Nike as well as non-US companies such as Adidas or Nestlé – became the big story of the ubiquity of a lifestyle (Klein, 2001). Other theorists of the field turn out to be more insightful. Most of the failures of global strategies – as they notice – come precisely from a lack of cultural sensitivity, recognition of values or attitudes that make a successful strategy in one country appear to be harmful in an other one. This has reinforced the necessity of taking into account the different levels of marketing – local, national, and international – and to think of them simultaneously. It is this requirement which gave birth to the neologism *globalization*, launched originally by the specialists in Japanese management, fruit of a contraction between the local and the global. But in this quarrel causality is not the heart of the problem. After all what separates the one from the other are only divergences about the rhythm of the construction of this global space and the methods to follow to reach it. And it is a strong bet that the oscillation between macro and the micro, the logic of the great sets and logic of proximity will long remain a constitutive feature of the process of construction of the integrated world market. "Massification" alternates with "de-massification," the latter contributing to move back the bounds of the former, to overcome resistance to "universal standardization." CNN-type television realized this very quickly in "decentralizing" their global broadcasting (in Spanish or even in Turkish, for example), not to mention drawing on the global advertising networks, previous masters of the micro/macro combination. The unified approach at the strategic level joins with the tactical methods of autonomy able to marry the variety of territories and particular contexts.

The most relevant objection to techno-globalism comes from the critical economists. "The global company (and consequently the global economy that it intends to control) are more a project than a reality," affirms Robert Boyer, who precisely entitles his article "Words and realities," in which he reviews the illusions of managerial thought overlaid on the world totality (Boyer, 2000). Let us add for our part that this incompleteness (and inevitably the uncertainties resulting from it on the future outcome of the process) makes talking about globalization a central part in the device of symbolic management of the economic and social model related to the new phase of the commercial deterritorialization. Everything takes place as if "communication" (and it is now recognized as a "managerial function" by the company) made reality occur, as if the announcement hastened the event. The managerial imaginary event serves to some extent as drawing the project upwards by giving coherence to an order said to be global to particular realities.

The freedom of commercial expression

The hegemonic place which the company actor has acquired in the life of society confers strategic importance on these corporate visions of the future of the world. The managerial doctrine is a political war machine serving the interests of the global business community which aims to reduce the "global communality" to its own definition. The strategic vision of the total actors of the market is not beneath modifying the rules of the game as regards regulation of the communication networks. For proof, the standpoints and the lobbying actions of its corporate organizations act in order to influence in their direction the strategies of regulation of cultural flows by the public authorities. The shift of the debate about the GATT (General Agreement on Tariffs and Trade, renamed WTO, or World Trade Organization, in 1995) as the principal institutional place of the controversy is revealing. The fact that culture has been reduced, in this technical organization, to the non-material and invisible flows of cataloged "services," expresses the centrality acquired by the economic conception of cultural exchanges in symbiosis with techno-globalism.

The clashing positions during negotiations between the European Union and the United States concerning the flows of information and communication are a political lesson. I am not only speaking here about the debates on flows of audio–visual products (films and television programs) but also of those relating to the increase of advertising space and the constitution of data banks composed of individual sociocultural profiles, essential for the marketing of segmentation of the targets. World expansion collides with the principle of respect for personal data. The protection of the latter was indeed in 1998 the subject of a "Directive" on the protection of the privacy enacted by the European Union that the Washington government considered to be inadmissible.

A major lesson of these controversies is provided by the tension which came to light between a conception of the freedom of expression, brought back to the "freedom of commercial speech," and the one that has been defined by the UN Declaration of Human Rights and by political constitutions. The former assumes that the market acts responsibly in determining the susceptible areas being exploited through advertising, through mechanisms of self-discipline and auto-regulation. The latter foregrounds the concept of freedom of expression and of the democratic control authorities as the condition of the existence of a public sphere. It was in this context that the neopopulist concept of a global democratic marketplace emerged, the centerpiece of the legitimating of neoliberal free trade. Only the free will of the consumer in the market of the free supply should govern the circulation of cultural flows. In the debates within GATT – and then WTO – on the need for a regulation of flows of programs, this axiom of the "absolute sovereignty of the consumer" was thus presented by Jack Valenti, president of the MPEAA (Motion Picture Export Association of America): "Let them at what they want. Let them be free to appreciate. Let us trust their common sense. The only sanction applied to a cultural product must be its failure or its success on the market." Or: "Let them determine what they want to see, just as they determine for whom they vote" (Valenti, 1993). The identification and equivalency between the language of marketing and that of the public sphere is complete. The objections which one has the right to make to this mercantile conception of freedom are immediately labeled by the lobbies of being attempts to establish censorship. Such arguments make null and void the many debates on the need for formulating public policies in the field and give a new life to the old doctrine of the free flow of information. Taking advantage of these arguments, the entrepreneurial organizations became essential partners in the preparation of cases and decision-making concerning the forms of establishment of the information and communication macro-systems. The historical decision made in February 1995 by the countries of the group of the most industrialized countries (G7) – assembled in Brussels for the first time for the question of "a global society of information" – of relying on market forces to build this computerized "road" infrastructure, is more than a serious warning (Schlesinger & Doyle, 1995; Raboy, 1997; Mattelart, 1998). The public is not invited to these meetings, where it has only the right of a folding seat. Consequently, it invites itself, while protesting from the street, as can once again be observed, in Genoa in 2001.

Reedeeming Technology

We ask technology to redeem the world. Celebrated as a creator of a "new agora," a new democracy, it announces the end of the big social and economical imbalances of the planet. A point of convergence of the geopolitics and the managerial discourse of the geo-economy, this redeeming conception of the network impregnates the project of the "super highway of information" named by Al Gore while vice-president of the United States in his *Global Information Infrastructure* (GII). In his speech to the delegates of the International Union of Telecommunication (UIT) gathering in Buenos Aires, of which the main topic of the conference was "development and telecommunication," he said in 1994,

"I believe that an essential prerequisite to sustainable development, for all members of the human family, is the creation of this network of networks. . . . The GII will not only be a metaphor for a functioning democracy, it will in fact promote the functioning of democracy by greatly enhancing the participation of citizens in decision-making. And it will greatly promote the ability of nations to cooperate with each other. I see a new Athenian Age of Democracy forged in the fora the GII will create" (Gore, 1994). The necessary condition to this vision is the adhesion to the neoliberal doctrine of deregulation. Gore cited as examples for his project Chile and Mexico. He also saluted the willingness of the Argentine government to follow this path. A few months later, Mexico fell into crisis. Seven years later, Buenos Aires was the scene of violent demonstrations against the model of the structural readjustment imposed by the IMF!

The mythical link between network communication and direct democracy is not new. For each technical generation, ever since the optic telegraph (1794), this belief has been recycled with a frankly religious connotation. Communication has always shared with religion the same function of "religare," set forth by the Saint-Simoniens in the nineteenth century, disciples of the precursor of the social sciences Claude Henri de Saint Simon (Mattelart, 1996, 2000a; Robins & Webster, 1999), and did not the invocation of the "great human family" take its first steps under the sign of the Roman church? But on the brink of the third millennium, we are far from the time when prophecy could still appear as a monopoly of reformers or social snipers. Techno-utopia has become a major ideological weapon in the campaign of influence aimed at naturalizing the vision of "free trade" as the world's order. The elaboration of the futurist script has become a lucrative profession. As an expert said, we should cultivate the "art of propagandizing" the future. All the big gurus of computer science have their own *think tanks* that sell that kind of professional services. The one in which Nicholas Negroponte, MIT professor and stockholder of the magazine *Wired*, the Bible of the connected people, participated is simply called *Global Business Network*. But the fall of evangelism will be a hard one. The discourse of the Department of Commerce in the United States quickly exchanged the idea of the El Dorados of the numeric democracy for that digitalized area of free exchange of merchandise. The image of the planet divided into virtual communities segments is linked to global *consumption communities*, beloved by marketing specialists.

This naturalization of the economic model of neoliberalism brings inevitably amnesia. We blot out the fact that the first laboratories of the market economy, countries which aspired to join the First World, such as Chile, were certainly not models of democracy. Rather they were pushed to an ultraliberalism by ferocious authoritarian regimes. We forget that, because its cost is infinite, the global model of reorganization of societies has as part of its price the reinforcement of "security" (at a class, national and international level) and the heavy logic of the security ghetto participates as well in the creation of new uses of information technology and communication.

The obvious example is the legislation against terrorism adopted or expanded in the large industrial countries after September 11, 2001, which extensively reinforced the techno-monitoring of the activity of the citizens. By virtue of hearing it said that the nation-state is moribund, one believes it. One no longer attaches any importance to the role the state plays in restructuring, particularly the defense communications industries of the major industrial nations, nor to the evolution of military doctrine of national security in the context of commercial competition. The rule in these areas is opacity, not transparency.

The Fissure of History: World communication

"Globalization means never having to say you're sorry," noted the writer and theoretician of Mexican popular culture, Carlos Monsivais. As a symbol of the general process of depersonalization and denationalization, the global bond drains the world of its social actors. At the end of the fifties Roland Barthes (1957) talked about the "bourgeoisie as an anonymous society." Today, it is to the *world's business class* that this label best applies. Wide interdependency between nations, the multiplicity of actors, the high stakes and the so-called weakened hierarchies in the world space give rise at this point to the notion of "complex, volatile and interactive" power, which thus becomes inconsistent and defies analysis (Nye, 1988). The responsibilities at the heart of the global system become diluted to the point where there is no way to identify its actors, and so, it is not possible, and not necessary, to consider a response against the globalization project. We are going back to the old schema of the "invisible hand" of Adam Smith. The individual emancipates himself by pursuing his personal goals. The realization of the general interest does not arise from will and intelligence expressed through human actions, but from the market established as a "providential" space. So the regulated order transcends understanding. Sovereign in his function of "consumer," the individual is reduced to experience his historical demise, since he participates in it only in an unconscious and involuntary manner. Thus we complete the blurring of the stakes of power which the reorganization of the world order implies, which started under the sign of the "global village," as a way of denying the differences between societies and the continuation of relations of force and of the collective interest.

Out of the globalist belief comes a vision from the said society of communication as a transparent and an equal society. In reality, technical mastery and its networks have not stopped, since the beginning of the nineteenth century, digging the moat between the "developed" world and the rest of the planet. This is what Fernand Braudel and Immanuel Wallerstein demonstrated in their analysis on the formation of the world economy (Braudel, 1981–4). That law of unequal exchange remains an essential basis for analyzing relations between economies, societies, and cultures. The logics of exclusion are those which today try to propound the notion of "world communication," a notion that brings history to the front of the stage (Mattelart, 1994). Everywhere new forms of competition oppose territories to each other and produce different conflicts within them. The project of globalization produces a two-speed social geography. The so-called impassable horizon is "techno–global–apartheid" or "the archipelago economy" with its mega-poles of technological excellence, nodal market places and the world network. This is the reality that the sub-comandante Marcos painted with lucidity, referring to the generalized war against the "deshechables" (dis-posables) of the neoliberal planet as beginning the "fourth world war." "The suppression of the commercial boundaries," he wrote, "the explosion of tele-communications, the information highways, the power of the financial markets, the international free trade agreements, all that contributes to the destruction of the nation-state. Paradoxically, globalization produces a fragmented world, made of tight compartments barely linked by economic footbridges; a world of broken mirrors that reflect the futile worldwide unity of the neoliberal puzzle." And he continues, "It is one of the paradoxes that I call the fourth world war: destined to eliminate boundaries and to unite nations, it provokes a multiplica-tion of boundaries and a pulverization of nations. But neo-liberalism is not only fragmenting the world that it would like to unite, it is also producing the political-economical center which conducts the war. It is urgent to speak of the *megapolitic*" (Marcos, 1997, p. 5).

It is on this chaotic map of fragmentations that the new mode of opposition to the neoliberal *realpolitik* is being written, what Marcos calls the "pockets of resistance." If there is a domain in which, since the second half of the 1990s, the media representations of this resistance have been associated with the image of democratic agora on the planetary level, it is that of the areas of protest created and taken over by the social movements mobilized against the model of ultraliberal globalization. This new political basis of global protest burst into view in Seattle, both in the heart of the United States as well as in the midst of the technological Bill Gates revolution, at the end of November early December 1999, during the mobilization of nongovernmental organizations, unions and associations of con-sumers against the drift and the dangers of a "total market" world symbolized by the WTO. Since then, none of the financial and commercial institution summits occur without having resistance network hold parallel counter-summits sup-ported by the logistics of the new digital technology.

It is on this map of fragmentation as well where what I called the "parasitic networks" and what the geo-politicians baptized "the new planetary fronts of disorder," the "spaces of shadow," and the "anti-worlds" appear: transnational flows of the clandestine diasporas of the underground economy, mafia networks, and illicit traffic (from narcotics to pedophilia passing through electronic smug-gling), fronts of sects, and fronts of fundamentalist terrorism. The apocalyptic attacks of September 11, 2001 and the multiple reactions which they evoked all over the world threw a rude light on the sources of violence generated by an exclusive and unidimensional model of the development of humanity. They also revealed the false premises of the techno–global rhetoric.

In the face of the crisis, the return to nationalism and Keynesianism has disproved the myth of the end of the nation-state so touted since the onset of the era of deregulation. In the aftermath of the call for security, the idea of censorship or self-censorship of the media has resurfaced. And for the first time, al-Jazira, a television channel in Qatar, has presented an Arab vision of events. The United States has thus discovered how much the world television landscape has changed since the Gulf War and how much their image has deteriorated to the point of having to officially envision resorting to commercials on the Arab station to sell the brand "the United States." We are definitely far from the diplomatic and military doctrines that have explicitly set up, ever since the fall of the Berlin Wall, the "cultural universals" propagated by the American audio-visual products as the natural base of a new form of world hegemony, soft power.

A baroque system

The techno–globalist notion is built around a notion of history that recycles the old ideology of progress. "The meaning of history is always threatening to change and needs to be always reinterpreted" wrote Maurice Merleau-Ponty half a century ago, refuting the scheme of the historical maturation of history-modernity-progress, or the concept of history in slices, as proposed by Fernand Braudel. "The principal stream is never without counter currents nor whirl-pools. It is not given as a fact. It is revealed through asymmetry, survivals, and diversions. It is comparable to things, perceived to be shapes that do not have any form except from a certain point of view and which never absolutely exclude other modes of perception" (Merleau-Ponty, 1955, pp. 61–2)

To a compact and abstracted vision of the economical system, the pioneer philosopher of social phenomenology responded with the notion of "a baroque system" to account for the complexity of the concrete economic system. Globalism denies these fissures in a shifting history. Peter Drucker (1993) wrote: "The educated man of tomorrow will have to expect to live in a globalized world, which will be a Westernized world." Reviewed and corrected by the new neo-liberal Darwinism, we see the resurfacing of the old diffusion theories of linear progress formulated by the classic ethnology of the nineteenth century and updated by the sociologies of modernization/Westernization of the following century in the battle against "underdevelopment" of the sixties and the seventies. The cultural models of modernity can only radiate from the middle to the periphery. The modernity of the first one plays the role of anticipating of the future of the second on the condition that it follows the canonical phases of the evolution through which the adult nations passed.

The new critical methods for apprehending the formation of modernity which emerged in the eighties take precisely the counter-view of this theory of a one-way culture, which legitimizes the hegemony exerted on the total economy by the "triadic power" (North America, European Union, Japan), another expression of the segregationist concept of the world espoused by the Japanese theorist of management Kenichi Ohmae, (1985, 1995). The idea of "necessary" progress exclusively defined starting from the Euro-American experience of modernity created a crisis, precipitating questions about the processes of appropriation of global flux by cultures and particular territories. The new questions around the alchemy of the intersections between the "modern" and the "traditional" break this image of an archetype of modernity produced by western logocentrism (Ortiz, 1988). From Rio to Bombay, from Tokyo to Singapore, from Seoul to Mexico City, cultural anthropology discovers the expressions of cross-breed modernities, forcing the old centers of modernity to take another look at their own history (Appadurai, 1996). In counterpoint to the new hybrid landscapes, but related inextricably to the same reconstruction of the process of identity in the age of global flows, there are insurrections of cultural singularity which respond by rejecting the "otherness" which they interpret as the threat of homogenization.

It can never be said too often, on the one hand; only desire is universal, and not the goods and the lifestyle which ubiquitous merchants daily shine in the shop windows of the media. On the other hand, it is illusory to think that there is a direct relation between transmission and reception. The time when sociologies of modernization, copied from the mathematical theory of information formulated by a telecommunications engineer, were exalted by the media as agents of the "revolution of increasing expectations" has long passed. On the horizon, we see the specter of the "revolution of increasing frustrations," product of the distance which separates the promises of integration to a global lifestyle and the situations of exclusion in concrete life.

The return to the logic of re-territorialization of total flow is obviously ambivalent. The danger is to seize upon it to recommend a cultural relativism which can co-exist with the pamphleteers of the free choice of the individual–consumer. Allergic to any idea of social determination in the name of the principle of self-regulation, the cultural relativism displayed by new liberalism denies the need for regulating intervention by public authorities or governments into the businesses of the actors of the geo-economy.

The Semiotic War

In its protean form, the concept of globalization is used as panacea. If it undoubtedly shelters internal criticisms, which nag at it and make one forget the connotations of its managerial origin, it is also the door through which have disappeared numerous discourses marked by capitulation *vis-à-vis* structuring logics of the total order. One understands Pierre Bourdieu criticizing the deep ambiguities of the vulgar globalizer (Bourdieu, 2001). One can understand Alain Touraine who, in a colloquium on "Globalization and democracy," organized in São Paulo by the Latin American Association of Sociology (ALAS) said, by way of provocation, "Globalization is imperialism with another name, purged of an ideological tension that the concept expressed at the time of the Cold War" (Touraine, 1997). One understands even better the reaction of this sociologist if one does not focus on the use of the word "imperialism," which at a time was a buzzword which, since the second half of the eighties, had been heard over and over, reiterating like a liberating refrain, "Imperialism is dead. Long live globalization!" (Tomlinson, 1991; Robertson, 1992). In response to this new form of conformism, nothing is better than the corrosive irony of Carlos Monsivais, whom I cited above. By rallying to an uncritical concept of globalization, many writers forget the main question of the reformulation of the forms of control of the affects and impulses of the great multitudes which require the expansion of the integrated world capitalism. Instead of wanting to change the world, one is satisfied to describe it. Integration is also on the agenda. The new economic and social model requires collecting the breeding grounds of gray matter, which until now have been on the margin of capital intensive valorization. What Antonio Gramsci named the process of formation of organic intellectuals is the category that seems to greatly interest Peter Drucker. Against boredom and drabness: Managers and Intellectuals, the same battle! How to interpret otherwise the vigorous plea launched in 1993 by this theorist of management in favor of a vast alliance toward the construction of the "post-capitalist society" or, as Bill Gates used to say, "Capitalism free of frictions"? "The intellectual, if he is not supplemented by the manager, creates a world where each one does what he wants but where no one does anything. The world of the manager, if it is not supplemented by the intellectual, becomes a bureaucracy, the brutish drabness which dominates the global organization man" (Drucker, 1993). Instrumentally, the concept of culture in the global era relates to an equally utilitarian definition of the intellectual, displaying in passing his complicity with the cliché of an antiintellectualism characteristic of commercial populism.

"To name things badly is to add to the misfortune of the world," said the novelist Albert Camus. It is more than probable that we will long be condemned to communicate with each other by using and abusing the globalist terminology. But, as Marcos said, the "fourth world war" has only started, and, he adds, this war is also a "semiotic war," a war against all the Orwellian "new speaks". To fight against the impoverishment of the words which indicate the future of the planet is also to fight against the lack of memory. In addition to the vocabulary of globalization, I will add to the number of words which appear to me to belong in the ranks of the targets of a war declared for the reconquest of meaning. I will enumerate three concepts which lately have been abused by the meta-discourse on globalization: complexity, the whole, and resistance, three essential concepts in order to restart "talking about megapolitic." Here are some working notes on this subject and these concepts which have become part of my research project.

Complexity: Do not use it as an alibi. It is necessary to re-invest the idea with all its heuristic force. That makes it possible to exceed linear causality, to integrate fluidity and uncertainty by substituting for the paradigm disjunction/reduction the paradigm disjunction/conjunction (Morin, 1990) – to make war with "funnel-speeches" which speculate profusely on the increasing complexity of our societies but are confined in practice to a reductive equation. The techno–globalist thesis is an exemplary perversion of the concept. While insisting that "human societies are more and more complex," the discourse of its operators remains classifying and one-dimensional. "I am optimistic," claims Nicholas Negroponte, friend of complexity, in a chapter entitled "The Age of Optimism" in his *Being Digital* (Negroponte, 1995). The optimistic positivism of prophets of cyberspace, who suppose that any critical attitude can only be "pessimistic" (and thus "technophobic"), betrays Manichean thought. The contradictory process of construction of the social uses of digital technologies disappears, giving way to a rudimentary evolutionism.

The Whole: Don't leave the job of interpreting world history to the grid of mercantile totality. Try to assemble, to establish "networks of social significance," to use Michel de Certeau's expression. Try to return from the private, the local, and the fragmentary to the whole. The problem is obviously not to rejoin the schemes of abstract totalities defined by the macro-subjects (Power/State/Society) which marked the all-inclusive explanations of the era before the fundamental rupture with the monolithic conceptions of the power which took place starting at the end of the seventies. This work is inextricably linked with a return to the history of long duration. This return implies taking one's distance from this race toward the contemporary current in which social sciences have been engaged.

Resistance: To rip out the concept of resistance from the universe of theoretical inconsistency and the neo-Darwinist metabolism of the necessary adaptation, both of them signs of the capitulation of intellect, appears to us to be one of the priority duties of critical intellectual work. To lift the ambiguity generated by these heavy tendencies which push a number of researchers, sometimes without their knowledge, to the legitimating role of a total system of "domination" (because it is necessary to stop being pusillanimous about the term, as Michel de Certeau was, who spoke of the consumer as "dominated," de Certeau, 1980). One needs a certain courage to question the tendency to lodge "resistance" exclusively in the interface of the individual/program, which many ethnographic studies on the audiences have revealed. If one can only celebrate the significant rupture that meant, starting at the end of the seventies, the paradigm of reception compared to the functionalism of the fatal reproduction of the relations of being subject to a social and productive order, it is also necessary to dare to closely examine its drifts towards empiricism. Otherwise, we are likely to see further watering down of the issues of communication. Pioneers of the studies of audiences, such as David Morley in one of his last works, where he joins the geographer Kevin Robins, invites us to such a reevaluation (Morley & Robins, 1995). To resist is to take into account the fact that, in addition to the difference from that which wants to make us admit the commercial doctrines about the freedom of the individual atom, a broad part of the subjective reality of the person is external to him, as embedded as it is with social and historical relations.

In 1986, in the book *Penser les Medias*, translated six years later into English under the title *Rethinking Media Theory*, Michele Mattelart and myself indicated the possible sources of ambivalence in the new "paradigm of post linearity" and the return to the basic subject, in particular through the use which it made of the media: "All these developments can be understood and experienced only with reference to the reconciliation between the pragmatic humankind spoken of by Kant, and which signifies, no doubt, the recognition of the needs of concrete individuals, but also the beginning of infinite negotiations – that is, not only endless but without finality, because they are born just at the point where Utopias end" (Mattelart & Mattelart, 1992, p. 54).

However, democracy is not possible without hope. The freedom of the consumer or the user is not a given thing, as neo-Darwinist naturalism claims; it is constructed. Better yet, it is acquired. It is what Philippe Breton, who made a life's work of studying epistemology, reminds us: "The construction of norms which would guarantee freedom of reception (of mediated communications) raises a living reflection, which can take place only within culture, i.e. systems of education, teaching and research" (Breton, 2000). It is this challenge which was raised in particular research which began focusing its attention on audiences and the types of television genres used in the development of active teaching methodologies (Orozco Gomez, 1996).

Never forget the series of the 3 Rs. The word resist (*resister*) covers only a few things if it is not combined with the verbs to think (*reflechir*) and to realize (*realiser*). To reflect is to try to think of a "culture of responsibility," the only one which can help to repopulate society with its multiple actors, in all their contradictions. It is a culture which combines the two ends of the chain: on the one hand, being aware of the global dimension of the problems arising from a communicational framework, which underlies the project of a new order for the planet, to think in terms of networks of solidarity and transborder associations; on the other hand, to continue to anchor itself in a concretely located territory, because, until proven wrong, this territory remains the place of the first exercise of citizenship and the social contract. Do not play with the concept of national or international civil society by making it the ideal place of liberation of all spontaneity and perfect communication, as contrasted with the leviathan of the state, but think of it in its conflict relationship with the state. To achieve this we must try to fill the gap between the producers of knowledge and the actors of the social world. In response to the discourse of commercial expertise and the siren songs of the gurus of management, we need to propose a new type of relationship with the actors who move society. In order to resist, to think, and to realize, it is necessary to accept the challenge of the rupture with ambient conformism.

To fight the impoverishment of the words which define the world, and also to counter the lapse of memory, for my part, I would like to exhume from the long history of the social networks which were opposed to the industrialist's and technocratic doctrines ever since the beginning of the twentieth century, the expression, "democratic Cosmopolitanism." It appeared in 1842 from the pen of

Flora Tristan, five years before Marx and Engels's Manifesto launched the idea of the necessary internationality of the oppressed. A feminist pioneer and at the crossing of two cultures, living in Paris with a French mother and Peruvian father, she struggled throughout her life exploring and experiencing the tensions between solidarity and interculturality, what she termed "Democratic Cosmopolitanism." Here is an idea and an ideal for which it seems possible to fight more than 150 years later.

References

Appadurai, A. (1996). *Modernity at Large: Cultural dimensions of globalization*. Minneapolis: University of Minnesota Press.

Barthes, R. (1957). *Mythologies*. Paris: Seuil.

Bell, D. (1960) *The End of Ideology*. New York: The Free Press.

Bell, D. (1979) Communications technology. For better or for worse. *Harvard Business Review*, May–June, 20–42.

Bourdieu, P. (2001). *Contre-feux*. Paris: Raison d'agir.

Boyer, R. (2000). Les mots et les réalités. In S. Cordellier (ed.), *Mondialisation au-delà des mythes*. Paris: La Découverte.

Braudel, F. (1981–4). *Civilization and Capitalism: 15th–18th Century*, 3-vol. translation, revised by S. Reynolds. London: Collins.

Breton, P. (2000). *La parole manipulée*. Paris: La Découverte.

Brzezinski, Z. (1969). *Between Two Ages. America's role in the technetronic era*. New York: Viking.

(de) Certeau, M. (1980). *Arts de faire. L'invention du quotidien*. Paris: Editions 10/18.

Drucker, P. (1971). *The Age of Discontent*. London: Pan Books.

Drucker, P. (1993). *Post-capitalist Society*. London: Butterworth-Heinemann.

Gore, A. (1994). Remarks prepared for Delivery by vice-president Al Gore to the IUT Development Conference, March 21. Washington, DC: United States Information Agency.

Klein, N. (2001). *No Logo: No space, no choice, no jobs*. London: Flamingo Press.

Levitt, T. (1983a). *The Marketing Imagination*. New York: The Free Press.

Levitt, T. (1983b). The globalization of markets. *Harvard Business Review*, May–June, 92–102.

Lipset, S. M. (1959). *Political Man*. London: Mercury Books.

McLuhan, M. and Fiore, Q. (1968). *War and Peace in the Global Village: An inventory of some of the current spastic situations that could be eliminated by more feedforward*. New York: Bantam; San Francisco: Hardwired.

Marcos (sub-commandante) (1997). La quatrième guerre mondiale a commencé. *Le Monde Diplomatique*, August, p. 5.

Mattelart, A. (1991) *Advertising International. The privatization of public space* (trans. M. Chanan). London: Routledge.

Mattelart, A. (1994). *Mapping World Communication: War, progress and culture* (trans. S. Emanuel and J. Cohen). Minneapolis: University of Minnesota Press.

Mattelart A. (1996). *The Invention of Communication* (trans. S. Emanuel). Minneapolis: University of Minnesota Press.

Mattelart, A. (1998). European film policy and the response of Hollywood. In J. Hill and P. Church Gibson (eds.), *The Oxford Guide to Film Studies*. Oxford: Oxford University Press, pp. 478–85.

Mattelart, A. (2000a). *Histoire de l'utopie planétaire. De la cité prophétique à la société globale*. Paris: La Découverte.

Mattelart, A. (2000b). *Networking the World 1794–2000* (trans. L. Libbrecht and J. Cohen). Minneapolis, University of Minnesota Press.

Mattelart A. and Mattelart, M. (1992). *Rethinking Media Theory. Signposts and new directions* (trans. M. Urquidi and J. Cohen). Minneapolis: University of Minnesota Press.

Merleau-Ponty, M. (1955). *Les aventures de la dialectique*. Paris: Gallimard.

Morin, E. (1990). *Introduction à la pensée complexe*. Paris: ESF.

Morley, D. and Robins, K. (1995). *Spaces of Identity: Global media, electronic landscapes and cultural boundaries*. London: Routledge.

Naisbitt, J. and Aburdene, P. (1990). *Megatrends 2000: Ten directions for the 1990's*. New York: Avon Books.

Negroponte, N. (1995). *Being Digital*. New York: Vintage.

Nye, J. S., Jr. (1988–9). Understanding US strength. *Foreign Policy*, 73, Winter.

Ohmae, K. (1985). *The Triad Power*. New York: The Free Press.

Ohmae, K. (1995). *The End of the Nation State*. London: Harper-Collins.

Orozco Gomez, G. (ed.) (1996). *Miradas latinoamericanas a la televisión*. Mexico: Universidad Iberoamericana.

Ortiz, R. (1988). *A moderna tradiçao brasileira*. São Paulo: Brasiliense.

Raboy, M. (1977). La global information infrastructure (GII): Un projet impérial pour l'ère de la mondialisation. *Communications et Stratégies*, 25.

Robertson, R. (1992). *Globalization: Social theory and global culture*. London: Sage.

Robins, K. and Webster, F. (1999). *Times of Technoculture: From the information society to the virtual life*. London: Routledge.

Saatchi and Saatchi (1986) *Annual Report*, London.

Schlesinger, P. and Doyle, G. (1995). Contradictions of economy and culture: The European Union and the information society. *Cultural Policy*, 2(1).

Tomlinson, J. (1991). *Cultural Imperialism: A critical introduction*. London: Pinter.

Touraine, A. (1997). Un diagnostico do Brasil. *Jornal do Brasil*, September 10, B1.

Valenti, J. (1993). Interview in *Le Monde*, March 11 and 24.

CHAPTER TWENTY-EIGHT

Intellectual Property, Cultural Production, and the Location of Africa

Boatema Boateng

The international regulatory arena of intellectual property has changed considerably since the 1970s. Increasingly intellectual property rights have tended to promote the economic interests of corporations – particularly within the media, pharmaceutical and computer software industries – even as individual creators and artists have experienced diminished protection of their rights. Intellectual property regulations have also been harnessed to the exploitation of knowledge from the South without equally protecting such knowledge in its places of origin. In the mainstream discourse on intellectual property, the South is portrayed almost exclusively as pirating the knowledge of the North, while the latter's appropriation of knowledge from the South receives little if no attention. Some of these trends have been studied by communication scholars such as Cees Hamelink (1994), Mark Alleyne (1995), Ronald Bettig (1996) and Shalini Venturelli (2000). On the whole, however, there has been relatively little attention within media studies to issues of power within intellectual property, particularly as they pertain to the global South generally and Africa in particular.

The work of James Carey is helpful in discussing the unequal relationships of power in the regulation of intellectual property. Carey, proposing a ritual approach to understanding communication, defines the latter as "a symbolic process whereby reality is produced, maintained, repaired and transformed" (1989, p. 23). Following this definition, the "media" of communication come to include the cultural artifacts through and around which reality is produced – from policies through newspapers to clothing. This broadened approach to communication and the ways in which it occurs makes it possible to examine intellectual property policymaking as a communicative arena within which certain kinds of reality are produced and maintained. Such policy-making, in turn, shapes other communicative spheres.

Typically, intellectual property regulates the circulation of knowledge and information – elements that are basic to communication. As diverse forms of cultural production have been drawn into the global economy in ways that raise issues of ownership and protection, intellectual property regulation has become crucial as a potential means for protecting the rights of groups that have hitherto remained outside this regulatory framework. However the ways in which intellectual property is conceptualized and regulated places cultural production in a hierarchy that excludes certain forms of knowledge from protection. Through this exclusion intellectual property regulation has facilitated the exploitation rather than the protection of the knowledge of certain groups. Even where inventions, scientific formulae, musical compositions and other kinds of knowledge that are generally considered to be subject to intellectual property protection are concerned, intellectual property regulation operates unevenly and protects the interests of owners of such knowledge over those of its producers.

The goal of this chapter is twofold: first, it critically examines some of the basic premises and categories of intellectual property in order to reveal the ways in which the exclusions described above occur. Secondly, it suggests ways in which the regulation of cultural production can be undertaken such that it does not merely "produce, repair and maintain" an unequal status quo but transforms it in order that the circulation of knowledge can occur more equitably and democratically. The chapter is organized in two main parts. The first describes the prevailing order of intellectual property regulation, including basic assumptions underpinning intellectual property protection and the ways in which those assumptions have operated to limit the rights of producers and increase the rights of owners, as the international regulatory framework has changed over the last three decades.

The second section draws upon Ghana's copyright protection of folklore to extend the arguments that have been made against the current conceptualization of intellectual property and its consequences for the policy treatment of different kinds of knowledge. It examines the challenges in protecting forms of cultural production that fall outside the usual framework of intellectual property regulation. In the case of Ghana, those challenges are both international and local and include an international regulatory context that is not conducive to the protection of folklore and other kinds of "indigenous" knowledge, as well as the pitfalls of making the state, rather than artisans, the owner of the rights to folklore. The chapter concludes by using the Ghanaian case to illustrate the ways in which attention to the protection of forms of culture originating in Africa (and other parts of the South) contributes to media studies by highlighting the need to challenge the taken-for-granted perception of the South as a consumer rather than producer of knowledge, and of intellectual property as relating to some forms of cultural production and not others. Based upon these challenges, it considers ways in which the regulation of intellectual property might be transformed.

The terms "South" and "North" are used here in place of "Third World" and "First World" or "developing" and "developed" nations as the latter suggest a ranking that locks the South in a subordinate relationship to the North. As this chapter will argue, that subordination is not borne out by the increasing importance of the South as a source of knowledge. North–South have been suggested by Claude Ake (1992) as a useful means of expressing the polarized relationship between world regions – especially since the disappearance of the East–West pole following the end of the Cold War. These terms are used while recognizing, as Ake does, that they do not "accurately describe these polarized formations for (they are) only a short-hand for a plurality of highly asymmetrical relations of power, especially economic, technological, political and military" (1992, p. 14).

The Prevailing Order

Intellectual property and its main component parts of patents, trademarks and copyright have come to assume such a taken-for-granted status that the larger concept is often defined in terms of those parts. Some basic legal texts (for example, Miller & Davis, 1983) do not even offer a definition of intellectual property but proceed straight to a discussion of its three main areas. This is partly due to the fact that patents, copyrights and trademarks existed for centuries before the term "intellectual property" emerged as a summary description of these forms of protected knowledge. Nonetheless, such a commonsense understanding of intellectual property is one way in which the concept operates as a "discourse of dominance" (van Dijk, 1993). Discourses of dominance operate by making particular explanations of reality seem natural and apparent to the extent that they are left unquestioned even when they function oppressively. In this case, the nature of and justification for intellectual property are treated as self-evident, leaving little space for challenging the status quo.

The varying definitions that go beyond component parts to describe intellectual property in terms of its own inner logic not only reflect its complexity but also suggest that it is a contested concept, since different definitions stress different properties. Thus it is defined by the *New Shorter Oxford English Dictionary* (1993) as "property that is the product of creativity and does not exist in tangible form." Posey and Dutfield (1996) define intellectual property *rights* as "legal rights (that) can attach to information emanating from the mind of a person if it can be applied to making a product that is made distinctive and useful by that information," while Drahos (1996) defines those rights as "rule-governed privileges that regulate the ownership and exploitation of abstract objects in many fields of human activity."

By not tying intellectual property to any particular kind of knowledge, these definitions make it possible to conceive of intellectual property law as regulating the ways in which different forms of knowledge circulate. Drahos's definition points to the fact that such circulation often occurs through a process of exploitation – frequently *economic* exploitation. Further, the lack of any reference to the individual, in that definition, makes it possible to conceive of intellectual property rights as applicable to both individually and collectively produced knowledge. Similarly, Posey and Dutfield – by not specifying the criteria by which information-based products are made "distinctive and useful" – provide scope for applying criteria other than the economic ones that predominantly govern intellectual property protection. The "abstract objects" and "information" that are defined, above, to be the object of intellectual property protection are referred to interchangeably in this chapter as "knowledge" and "cultural production." Cultural production, as used here, refers to the outcomes of the communicative activity described by Carey, above, whether those outcomes are scientific formulae or textiles.

The conceptualization of knowledge as not only individual but also collective, and its usefulness as derived from criteria other than economic ones, flies in the face of established practice in the regulation of intellectual property. A basic assumption underpinning intellectual property is that it is individually generated and therefore individually owned. Further, intellectual property rights are conceived of as fostering creativity by giving inventors and artists an economic incentive for their work in the form of monopolies that enable them to profit exclusively from their work for a limited period of time. The incentive function, in particular, has been the impetus behind the changes that have occurred in the regulatory framework of intellectual property over the last thirty years, even though it has been challenged by communications scholars (Bettig, 1996) and economists (Primo Braga et al., 2000). Although intellectual property regulation has undergone several transformations since the granting of the first patents and copyrights in the fifteenth century, the changes of the last 30 years have been especially significant in their consequences for producers of knowledge.

The foundations for the current international framework for the regulation of intellectual property were established when various European states came together in the late nineteenth century to establish three major agreements. These were the Paris Convention for the Protection of Industrial Property (1883), the Berne Convention for the Protection of Literary and Artistic Works (1886) and the Madrid Agreement Concerning the International Registration of Trademarks (1891). The three treaties were joined as one secretariat in 1893, and in 1967 the World Intellectual Property Organization (WIPO) was created to administer them. WIPO became a United Nations agency in 1974. The 1970s witnessed intense activism in the international arena on the part of the nations of the South, many of which had gained independence from colonial empires in the 1950s and 1960s. These nations formed a significant lobby within the United Nations system and were in the forefront of calls for a New World Information and Communication Order within the framework of the United Nations Educational Scientific and Cultural Organization (UNESCO). These efforts were underpinned by the view that there must be equitable distribution of global resources, including information and communication. In the area of intellectual property regulation, the demands of the South were for policies that would provide them with access to knowledge originating in the North – knowledge that would enable them to reduce the technological disparities between the two regions.

Such calls for equity were regarded by the North as "political" demands that had no place in the discussion of "technical" issues (Alleyne, 1995). In the 1970s and 1980s industries in the North – particularly in the United States – began to lobby for greater copyright and patent protection of information of importance to them. These lobbying efforts were anchored in the view that without such protection, the incentive to generate new products would be eroded, since they would be easily accessible to all without payment of due compensation to all. Indeed, the "piracy" of competitors in other countries was part of the evidence used by this lobby to support its demands. With WIPO dominated by the nations of the South, the industrialized nations sought to make intellectual property regulation an area of international trade policy, not in a United Nations forum but in the General Agreement on Tariffs and Trade (GATT) and its successor, the World Trade Organization (WTO). These efforts culminated in the WTO's 1994 Agreement on Trade Related Aspects of Intellectual Property Rights (TRIPS). While WIPO continues to be an important forum of intellectual property regulation, it has effectively been relegated to the background of intellectual property policymaking by TRIPS.

The TRIPS Agreement provides the stronger protections sought by the United States and other lobbies of the North. However it does so at the expense of the nations of the South and issues of concern to them in the regulation of intellectual property. These issues include TRIPS' inclusion of forms of plant and animal life among products that can be patented – a measure that has been opposed by African nations (Dawkins, 1997). Another way in which TRIPS undermines the interests of the South is in the reduced scope for democratic policy-making in the WTO as compared to the one-nation-one-vote arena of WIPO. The erosion of democratic principles in international intellectual property policymaking means that it has become much harder for the countries of the South to press for their concerns and interests within the new order. Although WIPO continues to provide them with a forum within which they can express those concerns, translating those concerns into internationally recognized and binding regulations is much harder since enforcement lies within the purview of TRIPS, where they lack a strong voice.

The stronger protections accorded intellectual property and the increasing centrality of economic factors in its regulation have been cause for concern on the part of some observers. Scholars like Bettig (1996) and Drahos (1996) have noted that intellectual property rights protect the rights of owners of knowledge at the expense of the rights of producers of knowledge. Thus in the case of music, for example, those who profit most are not individual musicians but the production companies that acquire the rights to, and exploit the work of, the former. Others, like Venturelli (2000), have noted not only the diminished rights of authors under the prevailing order but also the increased restrictions on public access to information. Such restriction is considered inimical to the vitality of liberal democracies that depend for their proper functioning on an informed populace.

An important way in which the TRIPS Agreement upholds the rights of owners of creative work at the expense of producers is by relieving its members of the obligation, included in the Berne Convention on Copyright since 1928, to uphold the moral rights of creators of literary and artistic works. While the moral rights principle has problematic aspects, such as its assumption of individual creativity, it is nonetheless important in giving authors and other creative workers some degree of control over their work even after they have transferred the economic rights. Those moral rights include the right to have a say in how and whether the work may be changed, and the right to be recognized as the creator of the particular work. The moral rights principle goes against the increasingly dominant regulatory view, upheld by TRIPS, that the protection of creative work is not a right but a privilege, and a temporary one at that. More significantly, it favors stronger players over weaker ones in the regulation of intellectual property.

The tendency to favor stronger players is a longstanding feature of intellectual property protection that has been intensified by the TRIPS Agreement. It is also in large part due to the increasing concentration in the ownership of media and other industries in a few hands. This is a trend that has been discussed by scholars like Schiller (1989), Bettig (1996), and Herman and McChesney (1997). Such concentration in ownership works to the disadvantage of producers of intellectual property in two ways. First, with industries such as publishing and recording dominated by a few corporations, it is extremely difficult for individual writers and musicians to produce and effectively market their own work. Second, intellectual property law protects corporate and individual owners of copyright equally in giving the former the status of legal persons, as discussed further below. Corporate owners are better able to profit from intellectual property protection than individual owners since the former can claim ownership of not only the initial creative work but also of products derived from it. Producing such derivations is much harder for individual copyright owners.

The concentration of ownership does not only affect individual creators but also the industries of the South. In Africa the development of indigenous music production and publishing industries has been impeded by the stranglehold of a few large corporations. John Collins (2000) argues that under the guise of preventing piracy, the large major recording companies of the North acted to stamp out the fledgling music recording industry in Ghana and Nigeria in the mid-1980s. Similarly, the Kenyan publisher, Henry Chakava (1996) notes the reluctance of publishers in the North to grant publishing licenses to their African counterparts. He states that whether European publishers are granting or buying publishing rights, they do so on terms that are unfavorable to their African counterparts. He adds,

> (t)he international watchdog agencies that police copyright infringement are not geared toward protecting copyright in works originating from Africa. They are

concerned more with guarding the interests of the North, whose publishers produce the majority of copyrightable materials. African publishers, themselves, with
or without assistance from their own governments, do not have the capacity,
know-how, experience or even the will to defend the little that they have. (Chakava,
1996, p. 85)

Apart from the advantages provided to large corporations, there are other
problems that arise with the principles of individual authorship and ownership.
Individual authorship has been challenged by scholars like Bettig (1996), Boyle
(1996) and Lessig (2001) who question whether any single artist or inventor can
claim to be the sole creator of a work. These scholars point out that creative work
occurs within the context of a tradition and builds upon that tradition. The
assumption of individual ownership also works against the interests of groups
that claim collective rather than individual ownership of creative work. The
law's response to group ownership has been to treat groups as "legal persons."
This is the principle applied when a corporation seeks copyright protection of
knowledge that has been generated by its employees. Apart from this option of
treating groups as individuals, there is no established means of legally protecting
group ownership. Thus the claims by groups in the South to collective ownership of various forms of knowledge are resisted because such ownership cannot
be accommodated within the prevailing framework.

Two assumptions within intellectual property that also have implications for
the regulation of some forms of knowledge produced by the South are the view,
within copyright, that folklore belongs in the public domain and the requirement
of non-obviousness in the granting of patent protection. In intellectual property
law, knowledge passes into the public domain after the term of protection has
expired. Knowledge in the public domain may be freely accessed and used by all.
Folklore is an area of knowledge that is typically assumed to belong in the public
domain. However this assumption erodes the rights of people, like Ghanaian
artisans, who produce knowledge in traditions that are regarded as folkloric. A
further impediment to the protection of some forms of knowledge can be found
in the requirement that knowledge that is the subject of patent protection must
be novel and "non-obvious." The fact of being communally known disqualifies
much indigenous knowledge from patent protection since such knowledge is
deemed to be obvious.

The protection of knowledge from the South has become a contentious issue
in intellectual property regulation because of the increasing appropriation of
such knowledge without the consent or compensation of its producers. The
general perception of the South, in discussions of intellectual property, is that of
a region that "pirates" knowledge originating in the North. For example, in their
study on the differing interests of the "developed" and "developing" worlds
around intellectual property regulation, Gadbaw and Richards (1988) evaluate
the policies of the South on the basis of their effectiveness in preventing the
pirating of the intellectual property of the North. A number of scholars have

pointed out, however, that casting the South as a vector of piracy is not only inaccurate but a means of justifying increased control. One such scholar is Debora Halbert, who describes this use of the term piracy as follows:

> Pirates serve a function in the narrative the United States is constructing on intellectual property and the way it should be protected internationally. Conceptual fences are being built around intangible property and pirates serve as justification for tough laws and harsh penalties . . . Pirates are used to articulate the boundary between ownership and exchange internationally. Identifying pirates for punishment helps average citizens understand the difference between legitimate and illegitimate uses of new technology. In the process, the pirate becomes a scapegoat for economic insecurity and is elevated to the level of a national "threat." In the 1990s, pirates have become threatening criminals. (1999, p. 93)

Halbert further points to the United States' own piracy, stating, "the United States has gone from being one of the world's most prolific pirates to copyright's most dedicated defender" (1999, p. xiv). Frances Boyle asserts that contrary to the popular perception of the South as a consumer of knowledge, it is in fact a producer of knowledge although not recognized as such by the regulatory establishment. He states,

> Cultural forms, dances, patterns, traditional medical knowledge, genetic information from the plants of the rain forest, or from peasant-cultivated seed varieties, all flow out of the developing world unprotected by property rights. In return, the developed countries send their cultural forms – Mickey Mouse, the X-Men, Pearl Jam, Benetton, Marlboro, and Levis. The developed world also sends in its wonderful medicines – Prozac and Tagamet – its computer programs – WordPerfect and Lotus 1-2-3 – its novels and its industrial designs. Almost all of *these* things, of course, are well protected by intellectual property rights. (1996, pp. 141–2, emphasis in original)

The unprotected flow described by Boyle has, in some instances been facilitated by intellectual property protection. Exploiting the principle of non-obviousness in patent protection, corporations have modified healing substances known to communities in the South. Through such modification, they have claimed to introduce a non-obvious element that gives them the right to patent the substance concerned without any recognition of or compensation for the communities in which the knowledge originates. Further, the perception of folklore as existing in the public domain has led to the economic exploitation of several forms of folklore. Increasingly such exploitation is being challenged by groups and nations in the South at a number of levels. Some groups have called for a radical rethinking of the conceptualization and policy treatment of knowledge in order that different forms are accorded protection. As pointed out by Posey and Dutfield (1996), indigenous knowledge is valued in its places of origin not just for its marketability but also because of its religious, social, and cultural aspects. Further, such knowledge does not readily fit into the established categories of intellectual property protection. These observations undermine the increasing centrality of the market in determining the value of knowledge as well as the fixed categories of intellectual property. Other challenges have been less radical and have used the existing framework of intellectual property protection to protect indigenous knowledge and folklore. Ghana's copyright protection of folklore is an example of this strategy and represents a pragmatic compromise with the prevailing order.

The Ghanaian Case

It is within the above context of international policy-making that Ghana's copyright protection of folklore must be placed. In 1985 Ghana passed a new copyright law that, *inter alia*, protected folklore. This was in response to the appropriation of different forms of Ghanaian folklore for international markets. As documented by Ross (1998), Ghanaian kente cloth is extremely popular among African Americans as a means of expressing a distinctive African identity. This cloth has been mass-produced by factories outside Ghana for both the African and United States markets. The protection of folklore was retained when Ghana undertook the wholesale revision of its intellectual property laws in 2000 in order to make them TRIPS-compliant. The revised copyright law defines folklore as *the literary, artistic and scientific works belonging to the cultural heritage of Ghana which are created, preserved and developed by ethnic communities of Ghana or by unidentified Ghanaian authors, and includes kente and adinkra designs and any similar work designated under this Act to be works of Ghanaian folklore*. The rights to folklore are vested in the Ghanaian State as embodied in the President of the Republic and continue in perpetuity. Despite the existence of this law, the de facto protection of Ghanaian folklore to the extent that its foreign appropriation is curtailed is an uphill task in the international arena described in the previous section.

Apart from the South's limited influence in the WTO, folklore is not universally recognized as a form of knowledge that is deserving of intellectual property protection and, as previously mentioned, is usually placed in the public domain and therefore accessible to all. Countries like Ghana have argued, however, that such folklore is still being produced and is therefore a living tradition of creativity analogous to other creative forms like novel writing or music composition. As the law states, folklore is also considered to be part of the national cultural heritage and its unauthorized exploitation therefore contravenes not only the rights of artisans but the sovereignty and integrity of the nation. Another challenge faced by Ghana in using copyright to protect folklore is the assumption of an individual inventor or creator of knowledge. In the Ghanaian situation, authorship of folklore is in fact often simultaneously communal and individual, as noted by Tsikata and Anyidoho (1988), and this further complicates its regulation within the dominant framework of intellectual property.

The assumption of individual authorship is so deeply held that knowledge that is communal in its origins is considered to fall outside the purview of intellectual property protection even though, as pointed out earlier, corporations are routinely granted the status of legal persons and in that capacity are granted intellectual property protection for knowledge generated by their employees. It is here that the consequences of the underlying assumptions of intellectual property protection for the regulatory treatment of different kinds of knowledge are most obvious. Different kinds of knowledge are effectively ranked by the principles of intellectual property in a hierarchy that places "scientific," "artistic" and "literary" knowledge in a superior position to "indigenous" and "folkloric" knowledge. In this situation, the forms of knowledge at the lower end of the hierarchy are not recognized as worthy of protection in their own right. It is only when they are converted into science and art that they become subject to protection. Frequently that conversion involves the removal of ownership from the producers of that knowledge to the appropriating corporations and individuals. In this way, intellectual property protection serves to produce and maintain a particular form of regulatory reality in the "communicative" process described by Carey.

Ghana's response to the public domain status of most folklore has been to protect its own folklore in perpetuity so that it never enters the public domain. The issue of simultaneously recognizing communal and individual ownership is avoided by vesting the rights to folklore in the state rather than individuals or communities of artisans. In this way the regulatory assumptions of individual creativity and ownership are in fact upheld. The state claims to hold the rights to folklore "on behalf of and in trust for the people of Ghana" (Government of Ghana, 2000, p. 2). While these measures are understandable and even justifiable, in the light of the ways in which intellectual property tends to be conceptualized, they represent an imperfect solution. Of particular concern is the vesting of the rights to folklore in the state. By this means, the supposedly protective Ghanaian state assumes ownership of the rights to folklore in a move that pits it against the producers of folklore. This is reinforced by the state's control of royalties from the copyright protection of folklore. That control undermines the state's claim to hold the ownership rights to folklore "on behalf" of folklore producers. Further, although the state claims to hold these rights in trust for the people of Ghana, the latter do not benefit from the copyright protection of folklore. On the contrary, Ghanaians seeking to use the copyright that is ostensibly theirs must nonetheless pay royalties like any other user.

In protecting folklore, then, the Ghanaian state replicates the owner–producer power disparities that arise from the regulation of intellectual property and further restricts access to a creative resource even for the Ghanaian people in whose name the state claims to protect folklore. A more equitable solution, in this case would be to make provision for folklore producers in allocating the royalties that accrue from the protection of their work. The latter's views of what does and does not constitute appropriation, discussed below, also suggest that the state must reconsider its definitions of "fair use" for different kinds of knowledge.

The Ghanaian case illuminates other problems with the regulation of folklore within the standard conceptualization of intellectual property. One such problem arises from the existence of separate categories such as copyright, patents, trademarks and geographical indicators. As stated in the Ghanaian law, protected folklore includes the designs used in the production of adinkra and kente textiles. The concern of some of the craftsmen who produce these textiles, is not only with the appropriation of their designs, however, but also with the media in which they are copied, with imitations in textile form considered as more threatening than imitations in other forms. Once one takes the medium of appropriation into account, copyright law becomes inadequate to the protection of these textiles, and ensuring their adequate protection using the established framework of intellectual property necessitates the use of multiple categories of intellectual property law, including industrial designs and geographical indicators. Effecting such multiple protection, however, cannot be done without radically transforming the way in which intellectual property is currently understood and regulated.

Probably the most important challenge faced by Ghana in protecting folklore is in gaining international recognition and enforcement of that protection. While nations of the South have been discussing the need to protect their knowledge from appropriation since the 1970s, this has not translated into international recognition of that need. The scope for doing so within the TRIPS era is even more limited than it was thirty years ago when nations like Ghana could form an effective lobby in the international regulatory arena. This contrasts with the success of the North in lobbying for a 1996 amendment that brought two additional treaties into being. The first of these, on copyright, was significant in defining computer programs and databases as creations similar to the literary and artistic works protected under the Berne Convention and therefore worthy of the same protection. It is also telling that although Ghanaian copyright protection of folklore has existed since 1985, there have been few instances of would-be users of folklore respecting that law and paying royalties to the Ghana government. This inability to enforce its copyright law stands in sharp contrast to the enforcing power of the TRIPS regime.

While Ghana's attempts to protect its folklore are laudable, the ways in which it has chosen to do so conform with the established conceptualizations and boundaries of intellectual property more than they challenge the latter. However the Ghanaian example is important in signaling that folklore comprises forms of knowledge that deserve the same recognition as those typically protected by intellectual property regulation. Demands for the protection of folklore and other forms of knowledge that have hitherto been outside the established framework of intellectual property are not only justifiable on the basis of the sovereignty of the nations and peoples of the South, important though that sovereignty is. They are justified by the fact that such knowledge is being exploited for profit in the same way as knowledge that is conventionally protected by intellectual property. That exploitation undermines any claims that such knowledge does not meet the conditions of copyright and patent protection; if it can be commercially exploited then it can be protected.

Conclusion

The people and nations of the South have been involved in a growing movement since the 1970s for the value of the knowledge that they produce to be recognized by according it protection similar to that provided by intellectual property regulation to "scientific and literary works." This protection has become particularly crucial as that knowledge has been widely exploited by the North. While there have been a number of successful challenges to such appropriation, these are the exception rather than the rule. Africa has been largely absent from the debates on the issue, especially within media studies, and yet the Ghanaian case shows that the cultural production of African people is being exploited along with that from other regions. It also shows how the production and maintenance of a particular conceptualization of intellectual property has worked against the interests of Ghana and of other African nations seeking to protect their knowledge from exploitation. The way in which the Ghanaian state has chosen to protect folklore further demonstrates the difficulty of challenging the dominant framework from within.

The location of Africa within intellectual property regulation, then, is one that undermines the assumptions underlying that regulation. However it is also a location within the South, where the "asymmetric relations of power" with the North, as described by Ake (1992), typically work against its interests. From this second location the task of transforming, rather than merely maintaining the current reality of intellectual property regulation is an immense one. This task cannot be construed solely as an African one, however, for the African situation simply highlights features of intellectual property regulation that work universally against principles of fairness and democracy. Rather, the location of Africa in intellectual property regulation is one that points scholars and activists within and outside media studies to ways in which they can play a role in radically transforming the prevailing regulatory framework.

References

Ake, C. (1992). *The New World Order: A view from the south*. Lagos: Malthouse Press.
Alleyne, Mark A. (1995). *International Power and International Communication*. New York: St. Martin's Press.
Bettig, R. V. (1996). *Copyrighting Culture: The political economy of intellectual property*. Boulder, CO: Westview Press.
Boyle, J. (1996). *Of Shamans and Spleens: Law and the construction of the information society*. Cambridge, MA: Harvard University Press.

Carey, J. W. (1989). *Communication as Culture*. Boston: Unwin Hyman.

Chakava, H. (1996). International copyright and Africa: The unequal exchange. In *Publishing in Africa: One man's perspective*. Place: Bellagio Publishing Network and East African Educational Publishers.

Collins, J. (2000). Trans-National Culture and Ghanaian Music: Copyright conundrums in a developing nation. Paper presented at the Center for African Studies Fall Colloquium on Transnational Culture Industries in Africa and Local Sites of Production. Urbana-Champaign.

Dawkins, K. (1997). *Gene Wars: The politics of biotechnology*. New York: Seven Stories Press.

Drahos, P. (1996). *A Philosophy of Intellectual Property*. Aldershot: Dartmouth Publishing Company.

Gadbaw, R. M. and Richards, T. J. (1988). *Intellectual Property Rights: Global consensus, global conflict?* Boulder, CO: Westview Press.

Government of Ghana (2000). *Copyright Bill*. Accra: Government Printer, Assembly Press.

Halbert, D. J. (1999). *Intellectual Property in the Information Age: The politics of expanding ownership rights*. Westport, CT: Quorum Books.

Hamelink, Cees J. (1994). *The Politics of World Communication: A human rights perspective*. London: Sage.

Herman, E. S. and McChesney, R. W. (1997). *The Global Media: The new missionaries of corporate capitalism*. London, UK and Washington, DC: Cassell.

Lessig, L. (2001). *The Future of Ideas: The fate of the commons in a connected world*. New York: Random House.

Miller, A. R. and Davis, M. H. (1983). *Intellectual Property: Patents, trademarks and copyright in a nutshell*. St. Paul, MN: West Publishing Co.

Posey, D. A. and Dutfield, G. (1996). *Beyond Intellectual Property: Toward traditional resource rights for indigenous peoples and local communities*. Ottawa: IDRC.

Primo Braga, C. A., Fink, C., and Paz Sepuvelda, C. (2000). Intellectual property rights and economic development. *World Bank Discussion Paper* no. 412. Washington DC: World Bank.

Ross, D. (1998). *Wrapped in Pride: Ghanaian kente and African-American identity*. Place: UCLA Fowler Museum of Cultural History.

Schiller, H. I. (1989). *Culture Inc.: The corporate takeover of public expression*. New York and Oxford: Oxford University Press.

Tsikata, Fui S. and Anyidoho, K. (1988). Copyright and oral literature. *Power of Their Word: Selected papers from proceedings of the 1st National Conference on Oral Literature in Ghana*. University of Ghana-Legon.

van Dijk, T. (1993). Principles of critical discourse analysis. *Discourse and Society*, 4(2).

Venturelli, S. (2000). Ownership of cultural expression: Speech and culture in the new intellectual property rights regime of the European Union. *Telematics and Informatics*, 17.

Index